2012
THE BEST TEN-MINUTE PLAYS

2012
THE BEST TEN-MINUTE PLAYS

Edited and with a Foreword
by Lawrence Harbison

Smith and Kraus Publishers

ISSN 2164-2435
ISBN 1575257939
ISBN 9781575257938

Typesetting and layout: Elizabeth E. Monteleone
Cover design: Borderlands Press

Smith and Kraus book
177 Lyme Road, Hanover, NH 03755
editorial 603.643.6431 To Order 1-877-668-8680
www.smithandkraus.com

Printed in the United States of America

CONTENTS

PLAYS FOR THREE OR MORE ACTORS

FOREWORD

In this volume, you will find fifty terrific new ten-minute plays, culled from the several hundred I read last year, all successfully produced during the 2011-2012 theatrical season. They are written in a variety of styles. Some are realistic plays; some are not. Some are comic (laughs); some are dramatic (no laughs). The ten-minute play form lends itself well to experimentation in style. A playwright can have fun with a device which couldn't be sustained as well in a longer play. Many of the plays employ such devices.

I have also included, for the first time in this series, a comprehensive list of theatres which do ten-minute plays.

In years past, playwrights who were just starting out wrote one-act plays of thirty to forty minutes in duration. One thinks of writers such as A. R. Gurney, Lanford Wilson, John Guare and several others. Now, new playwrights tend to work in the ten-minute play genre, largely because there are so many production opportunities. Fifteen or so years ago, there were none. I was Senior Editor for Samuel French at that time, and it occurred to me that there might be a market for these very short plays. Actors Theatre of Louisville had been commissioning them for several years, for use by their Apprentice Company, and they assisted me in compiling an anthology of their plays, which did so well that Samuel French has published several more anthologies of ten-minute plays from ATL. For the first time, ten-minute plays were now published and widely available, and they started getting produced. There are now many ten-minute play festivals every year, not only in the U.S. but all over the world.

What makes a good ten-minute play? Well, first and foremost I have to like it. Isn't that what we mean when we call a play, a film, a novel "good?" We mean that it effectively portrays the world *as I see it*. Aside from this obvious fact, a good ten-minute play has to have the same elements that *any* good play must have: a strong conflict, interesting, well-drawn characters and compelling subject matter. It also has to have a clear beginning, middle and end. In other words, it's a full length play which runs about ten minutes. Many of the plays which are submitted to me are scenes, not complete plays; well-written scenes in many case, but scenes nonetheless. They leave me wanting more. I chose plays which are complete in and of themselves, which I believe will excite those of you who produce ten-minute plays; because if a play isn't produced, it's the proverbial sound of a tree falling in the forest far away. In the back of this book you will find information on whom to contact when you decide which plays you want to produce, in order to acquire performance rights.

There are a few plays in this book by playwrights who are fairly well-known, but most are by terrific playwrights you've probably never heard of who I have no doubt will become far better known when their full-length plays start getting produced by major theatres. And you read their work first here!

Lawrence Harbison
Brooklyn, New York

PLAYS FOR TWO ACTORS

BEDTIME STORY

Christopher Lockheardt

PRODUCTION NOTES:

Heartland Theatre Company
10th Annual 10-Minute Play Festival
June 16, 2011
1110 Douglas St
Normal, IL 61761
(309) 452-8709
Directed by John W. Kirk

Cast:
JESS, Cristan Embree
BILLY, Nick McBurney

CHARACTERS:
JESS, early thirties
BILLY, early thirties

At Rise: (It is a cold September night. Jess, in her early 30s, stands stage right on the front step of her home. She is wearing a football jersey, boxer shorts, and wool socks. Billy, about the same age, stands closer to center. He is wearing a hooded sweatshirt, jeans, and work boots. He stands in the frame of light from a window above.)

JESS: Hey.
BILLY: Hey.
    (pause)
JESS: Why are you here?
BILLY: Your light was on.
JESS: It's late.
BILLY: I know. Sorry.
JESS: It's 1:30.
BILLY: I know. I'm sorry.
    (pause)
  Trouble sleeping?
    (pause)
JESS: Yeah.
BILLY: Sorry.
JESS: I'm used to it.
    (pause)
  So why are you here?
    (pause)
BILLY: You know, when I was here, you slept fine.
JESS: When you were here?
BILLY: Yeah. When I stayed over.
JESS: You never stayed over.
BILLY: That one time I did. Remember? I told you that story? "Once upon a time . . ."?
JESS: You never stayed over. You left before I woke up.
BILLY: Yeah, but you slept, Jess. That's what I'm saying.
    (pause)
JESS: Billy, why are you here?

BILLY: Can you believe it's getting cold at night already? I had to go back into the house to grab this. You cold?

JESS: No.

BILLY: You're not wearing anything. You want my sweatshirt?

JESS: No.

BILLY: We can go in.

JESS: No.

BILLY: I can't believe it's getting cold already. It was just summer yesterday. Don't it feel like that?

(pause)

JESS: Why are you here?

BILLY: I don't know. Trouble sleeping.

JESS: Yeah? Why don't you have your wife make you a glass of warm milk then?

(pause)

BILLY: Right.

(He turns around and exits. She watches him go, then slumps down on the door step. She rubs her face with her hands. She looks up.)

JESS: Billy!

(She jumps to her feet and runs across the stage.)

BILLY!

(She turns around and walks back to the door step. She sits down. Billy walks back on stage.)

BILLY: Yeah?

JESS: Why are you here, Billy?

BILLY: I told you. I couldn't sleep.

JESS: Where does she think you are?

BILLY: Downstairs watching TV, I guess. She's fast asleep, probably doesn't even know even know I'm gone. She's a helluva good sleeper.

(pause)

I wonder what that's like, to be a good sleeper. To be here, awake, one second, and then gone the next. Not even knowing you're asleep until you wake up. Hardly even knowing you were trying to fall asleep in the first place.

JESS: Must be nice.

Lawrence Harbison   15

BILLY: Must be.

>*(pause)*

I saw myself falling asleep once. It was a dream, I guess. Or maybe I really did see it. I was lying there, waiting, you know? And my eyes must have been open, because I saw everything starting to pull away from me, down this tunnel. The whole room started shrinking down this tunnel, until it was a dot, so small, so far away, just an eye blink away from disappearing altogether.

JESS: Like dying.

BILLY: Yeah. Exactly. I saw everything just an eye blink away from being taken from me, taken away forever, so I yanked myself awake, yanked myself back out of sleep and back into life, terrified out of my skull. I didn't go back to bed for three days. I finally fell asleep in a booth at Denny's, my finger still hooked in the handle of my coffee mug.

>*(pause)*

JESS: I think about that night a lot.

BILLY: Yeah? The night I stayed?

JESS: You didn't stay.

BILLY: I couldn't stay.

JESS: You told me that story.

BILLY: Yeah. "Once upon a time . . ." I got, like, 30 seconds into it and you were out. Snoring almost. Completely dead. I almost laughed, it was so quick. I had to bite my lip.

JESS: It was the story.

BILLY: Yeah?

JESS: Yeah. It helped somehow. What made you think of it?

BILLY: The story?

JESS: Telling it.

BILLY: I don't know.

JESS: My daddy told me stories. To put me to sleep.

BILLY: Yeah?

JESS: He liked to tell me stories from the movies. My favorite was Babes in Toyland.

BILLY: That a movie?

JESS: It was a movie he used to like. One of those old movies. He said he'd seen it a hundred times. He used to tell me the story of it. With Stannie and Ollie and Silas Barnaby and the Toymaker. He used to put me in the story. I was Little Bo Peep and I had to marry Silas Barnaby so he wouldn't take our shoe away, but Stannie tricked him by dressing up like me at the wedding.

BILLY: That's the craziest-ass story I ever heard. That would have given me nightmares.

JESS: My daddy's stories never gave me nightmares. He'd always start them by telling me, "Now this is one of those happy ever after stories, so don't you get worried."

(pause)

BILLY: Mine was a happy ending story.

JESS: Was it?

BILLY: It was going to be. I didn't get very far in it. But I kept going after you fell asleep, thinking maybe you could hear it in your dreams. Like when you fall asleep with the TV on and your dreams take over from the show you were watching.

JESS: Did you finish it?

BILLY: No. You were pretty out. I figured you didn't need it anymore. I figured your dreams would do a better job of finishing it than I would.

(pause)

JESS: What was it about?

BILLY: The story?

JESS: Yeah.

BILLY: You.

JESS: Me?

BILLY: Yeah, you. "Once upon a time there was a beautiful princess who lived in the Kingdom of Summer."

JESS: I like that. "The Kingdom of Summer." It sounds pretty.

BILLY: Yeah. Lonely though.

JESS: Yeah?

BILLY: Very lonely. The princess lived all by herself in a big castle.

JESS: Not very big.

BILLY: No, but not bad for a princess on her own if you think about it.

JESS: Lonely though.

BILLY: Very lonely. Until one day the woodcutter's son showed up at the castle gate, lost and hungry and far from home.

Lawrence Harbison 17

JESS: Poor guy.

BILLY: He didn't have any other place to go. So he shouted up at the castle for someone to let him in. But the princess didn't answer.

JESS: Why didn't she answer?

BILLY: Because you were asleep.

JESS: Already?

BILLY: I told you!

JESS: So how's it end?

BILLY: The story?

JESS: Yeah.

BILLY: I don't know. The wood cutter's son breaks the curse or kills the troll or finds the ruby songbird or some story-thing like that and he and the princess live together for the rest of their lives in the Kingdom of Summer.

JESS: A happy ever after story.

BILLY: A happy ever after story.

    (pause)

JESS: Why are you here, Billy?

BILLY: I thought you might be having trouble sleeping.

    (pause)

I thought maybe I could finish the story.

    (pause)

JESS: We finished our story.

BILLY: No, Jess. No, we didn't. We just—

JESS: We finished it.

BILLY: No, we—

JESS: It's finished.

    (pause)

BILLY: Okay. But we could start a new one.

JESS: Summer's over, Billy.

BILLY: Yeah?

JESS: Yeah.

BILLY: It goes quick, don't it?

    (pause)

JESS: I'm going back in, Billy.

BILLY: Back to bed?

JESS: Yeah.

BILLY: Think you'll be able to sleep?

JESS: I hope so.

BILLY: What if you can't?
JESS: I'll do my best.
BILLY: But what if you can't?
JESS: Then I won't.
> *(pause)*
BILLY: You know, with me, you slept.
JESS: Yeah. I did.
> *(pause)*
BILLY: I could tell you a story.
JESS: About what?
BILLY: About a beautiful princess. About a wood cutter's son.
> About the Kingdom of Summer.
JESS: Is it a happy ever after story?
> *(pause)*
> Is it?
BILLY: Maybe this time.
> *(pause)*
JESS: It's late, Billy.
BILLY: I know.
JESS: I have to get up.
BILLY: I know.
JESS: Good night, Billy.
BILLY: Good night, Jess.
> *(She turns to the door.)*
BILLY: Jess?
> *(She turns back.)*
> Sweet dreams.
JESS: You too, Billy. You too.
> *(She exits. Billy watches her, then looks up. He stands for a few moments in the light of her bedroom window. The lights go out.)*

The End

Beyond a Reasonable Doubt

Bara Swain

Production Notes:

Aching Dogs Theatre
Pam Scott, Artistic Director
Hudson Guild Theatre, NYC
November 3-7, 2011
Directed by Bara Swain

Cast:
OLIVIA, Lisa Peart
LLOYD, Timothy J. Cox

Women at Work Festival at Stage Left Studio, NYC
Cheryl King Productions
September 25 & October 3, 2011
Directed by Bara Swain

Cast:
OLIVIA, Elly Berke
LLOYD, Nick DeSimone

CHARACTERS:
OLIVIA, early-late twenties
LLOYD, her fiancé mid twenties-early thirties

TIME: Present, 3am
PLACE: The Sun Bright Hotel, Chinatown

At rise: Lights to half. Lloyd and Olivia are in bed. Lloyd, wearing pajama bottoms, is asleep on the SR side of the bed. Olivia, wearing Lloyd's pajama top and a wedding veil, is asleep at his left. In the black, we hear Lloyd's heavy snoring. Olivia, mouth wide open, snores gently. Lights up. Suddenly, Olivia bolts upright, eyes wide open.

OLIVIA: *Do you think there was a reason that the killer sodomized your husband with a banana?*
> *(Olivia closes her eyes and lies back down. She's in a dead sleep again, mouth hanging open. Suddenly, She bolts upright again. Olivia rotates her neck for the role playing.)*

Olivia Benson: *Did you tell her that her grandson is also her stepson?*

Woman: *What?*

Olivia Benson: *Your husband's been cheating on you. With his own daughter.*
> *(Olivia lies down again. After a moment, SHE bolts upright.)*

Olivia Benson: *What's your name?*

Perp: *Screw you!*

Olivia Benson: *Screw You, you are under arrest, you have the right to remain silent. Anything you say can and will be used against you in the court of law.*
> *(Lloyd has awakened. He reaches out for Olivia and taps her back.)*

LLOYD: Olivia?

OLIVIA: Don't do it!
> *(Olivia jumps out of bed, and draws her finger at Lloyd.)*

Drop your weapon. DROP YOUR WEAPON!

(Lloyd swings his legs over the bed.)
LLOYD: Jesus Christ, Liv! What're you . . . what's going on!?
OLIVIA: Put your hands where I can see them.
 (Confused, Lloyd extends his hands towards Olivia. Then, He rises and moves towards her.)
LLOYD: Honey, you're having a bad dream—
OLIVIA: RAISE YOUR HANDS ABOVE YOUR HEAD!
 (Lloyd stops short, and thrusts his arms into the air.)
LLOYD: I'd be more comfortable—I think we'd both be more comfortable—if you stopped waving your . . . your gun! . . . at me.
 (Olivia looks at Lloyd warily. She speaks in an aside to an invisible Munch.)
OLIVIA: Olivia Benson: *Munch, we're positive it's him?*
 Munch: Unless there's a white-van-driving, dentally-challenged, pedophile convention in town, I'd say yes.
 (to Lloyd)
WHERE WERE YOU BETWEEN 6PM and 10PM?
LLOYD: With you! Olivia . . . don't you remember? We had dinner at Bacaros. I ordered risotto with asparagus, and you had Linguini con le Vongole. You love steamed clams in wine sauce, Liv. And . . .
 (Lloyd lowers his arms. He steps towards Olivia.)
. . . and I love you.
OLIVIA: GET DOWN ON THE FLOOR.
LLOYD: What!?
OLIVIA: You heard me, Pervert. ON YOUR HANDS AND KNEES.
 (Lloyd lowers himself to the floor.)
LLOYD: Honey, I think you're—
OLIVIA: Keep your mouth shut, Dirtbag. Unless you want someone to do it for you.
 (Olivia swivels her neck.)
Lawyer: *You're badgering my client, miss.*
Olivia Benson: *It's Detective. And save your legal mumbo jumbo for the courtroom where someone gives a damn. We're in MY house now.*
LLOYD: Olivia, look at me. We're at the Sun Bright Hotel on Hester Street. It's three o'clock in the morning. And tomorrow . . . we're getting married.

OLIVIA: Is that the best you can come up with, Romeo?

LLOYD: It's Lloyd! Lloyd, your fiancé!

> *(Olivia retreats. She makes an aside to her invisible partner.)*

OLIVIA:

> Olivia Benson: *You buying this, Elliot?*
>
> Elliot Stabler: *My gut says he's lying.*
>
> Olivia Benson: *Your gut's a genius.*
>
> *(to Lloyd)*
>
> You're lucky I don't knock your teeth down your throat . . . Lloyd.

LLOYD: *(frantically)* WAKE UP, OLIVIA! PLEASE WAKE UP!

OLIVIA: Olivia Benson: *What's wrong, Tutuola.*

> Tutuola: *Somebody tried to bust my eardrums.*
>
> Olivia Benson: *You mean this scumbag in front of me?*
>
> Tutuola: *I'm gonna bust they ass.*
>
> Olivia Benson: *Not if I get to him first.*
>
> *(Olivia strides towards Lloyd, who is cowering on his hands and knees. Suddenly, she stops short)*
>
> Lawyer: *DETECTIVE! My client has no previous history. You have no probable cause.*
>
> Olivia Benson: *Oh, yeah?*
>
> *(Olivia hovers over Lloyd menacingly.)*
>
> COME ON, YOU PIECE OF FILTH. GIVE ME PROBABLE CAUSE.
>
> *(Olivia circles behind Lloyd. Lloyd, terrified, begins to cry. As He whimpers, Olivia continues to circle him, and then—unnoticed—quietly returns to a chair. She sits, closes her eyes, her mouth drops open, and She falls asleep. Olivia snores gently. Lloyd leans forward to muffle his sobs with his hands, preparing for a beating . . . that doesn't occur. As his crying quiets down, Lloyd hears something. It is Olivia's snoring. Tentatively, He raises his face and sees Olivia asleep in the chair. Still weak with fear, Lloyd crawls over to her and sits at her feet.)*

LLOYD: Olivia?

> *(He shakes her.)*
>
> Honey, wake up.

OLIVIA: *(startled)* What happened?

LLOYD: You had a bad dream. Can you stand up?

OLIVIA: I think so.

LLOYD: *(gently)* Then what do you say we get some Zs, huh? Look at me, Liv.

> *(He holds her face in his hands.)*

I love you. Everything's going to be fine. You know that, right?

> *(Olivia nods)*

Then let's go back to bed.

> *(Lloyd holds her hand and slowly guides her towards the bed as He cajoles.)*

Tomorrow's a big day. First stop, City Hall. Then we'll swing back to the hotel to get dressed for the reception. I called Jing Fong's with the final number of guests.

OLIVIA: One hundred eighty-eighty.

LLOYD: One-hundred eighty-seven. Uncle Trevor's flight was delayed.

> *(Olivia stops short at the oriental curtains. Pause. Suddenly, She jerks her hand loose. She touches the curtain, then looks at Lloyd wide-eyed.)*

OLIVIA: Lloyd!?

LLOYD: What's the matter?

> *(Olivia, agitated, starts walking in circles. She shakes her head and her hands and makes general gibberish. Sometimes she jumps up and down.)*

OLIVIA:	LLOYD:
I can't . . . No no no. This can't be happening. Why me? Why now? That's it! That's what the dream was—was . . . Oh, my God, no. Oh, Lloyd! It's an omen. It's an omen. And then . . . This isn't right. This can't be right. Am I wrong?	Stop . . . Look at me. What can't be happening . . . You're scaring me, Liv. Olivia! . . . Stand still. You're not making sense. A nomen? Why're jabbering on what? What the hell's a Nomen?

LLOYD: Talk to me, Olivia!

OLIVIA: I can't marry you, Lloyd!

LLOYD:	OLIVIA:
Because there's heavy fog at San Francisco Airport	No no no no no no no no no no no no no no no.

OLIVIA: BECAUSE DR. HUANG APPEARED IN LAW & ORDER—ONE-HUNDRED AND EIGHTY-SEVEN TIMES!

LLOYD: So?

> (*Olivia stares at the Oriental patterns on the shades. Then She swings back towards LLoyd.*)

OLIVIA: I can't marry you, Lloyd, because . . . I THINK I'M IN LOVE WITH B.D. WONG!

LLOYD: What!?

OLIVIA: (*flourishing*) The vase.

> (*flourishing*)

The DREAM.

> (*running over to the bed*)

THIS SHORT LITTLE BED! And now 187 guests? . . . We weren't meant to be, Lloyd. It's a sign.

> (*Olivia is exhausted. She flops onto the bed. Lloyd crosses to her.*)

GO AWAY!

> (*She curls into a ball.*)

LLOYD: (*quietly*) No.

> (*Olivia rolls away from him.*)

OLIVIA: GO AWAY!

LLOYD: (*firmly*) No.

> (*Silence. Then Lloyd begins to talk.*)

When I was 8 years old, I went to school on Cabrini Boulevard . . . at P.S. 187. When I was 12 years old, I had 187 Tiger Eyes in my marble collection. When I was 17, I fell asleep at my S.A.T.s . . . and I scored a 187 . . . in math.

> (*Olivia is paying attention.*)

When I was 25, I met a girl ... who took my breath away.

> (*Lloyd reaches for Olivia. She doesn't resist.*)

There are 187 reasons that I love you, Olivia. Please . . . be my wife.

> (*Olivia's lips quiver. She looks bashfully at Lloyd.*)

OLIVIA: You can still love me . . . after what I put you through tonight?

LLOYD: Beyond a reasonable doubt.

(Olivia wraps her arms around Lloyd's neck. They embrace. Long pause. The silence is broken by Olivia's snores. Her mouth remains open while Lloyd gently tucks her into bed. He climbs in, too, and the lights fade to half. Within moments, Lloyd and Olivia are both snoring. Then, suddenly, Lloyd bolts upright. He rotates his neck for the role-playing.)

Ari Gold: *In this envelope, Lloyd, there are the names of eight agents. If anyone catches you, eat it. Nod if you understand me.*

Lloyd: *I understand.*

Ari Gold: *You can't just fucking nod? Lloyd, I want you to . . . to swear your undying loyalty to me.*

Lloyd: *Ari . . .*

(Lights to black.)

Ari Gold: *Silence is fucking golden, Lloyd.*

The End

A COUPLE OF METAL GODS SITTING

AROUND TALKING

Trace Crawford

PRODUCTION NOTES:

Sundog Theatre Company
Staten Island, NY
April 2-17, 2011
Directed by Jake Turner

Cast:
STEVE, Jon Kakaley
JOE, Jai Brandon

Produced as part of the Artists
Exchange/Black Box Theatre's
Sixth Annual One Act Play Festival
Cranston, RI
August 5-28, 2011
Directed by Rich Morra

Cast:
STEVE, Chris Ferreira
JOE, Mark Carter

CHARACTERS:

STEVE: In his early-mid twenties. The singer in a heavy metal band on the cusp of something big. This isn't some lame-o hair band—these guys are in it for real.

JOE: Also in his early-mid twenties. The guitarist in the same band. Apparently going through a crisis of heavy metal faith.

SETTING: The back porch of a run down row house apartment.

TIME: 1989. Summer.

> *Scene: The back porch of a run down row house apartment.)*
> *(AT RISE: Steve and Joe are seated, enjoying a pair of hotdogs—their breakfast. It is 3pm. A guitar, as always, is within arms length.)*

STEVE: Damn, this is a good dog.

JOE: I know right?

STEVE: I mean . . . damn! You weren't kidding.

JOE: It's the natural casing. Adds a pop.

STEVE: No shit it does. But the flavor, too. This is just . . . I mean . . . Damn!

JOE: Well, you're welcome.

STEVE: Hey, when you're right, you're right. When it comes to lips and assholes, your wisdom knows no bounds. Your humble servant, forever.
> *(He bows, elaborately, and kneels in genuflection.)*

JOE: Ok, ok, I get it. Get up, already.

STEVE: *(Rising.)* Dude, I'm just saying. *(Beat.)* Damn!
> *(A pause as they both savor the conclusion of their feast. Then, with a sigh of total contentment . . .)*
> There's a reason "dog" spelled backwards is "God." Perfect way to start the day.
> *(A pause.)*

JOE: You know, there *was* something I wanted to talk to you about.

STEVE: Sounds serious. You're not coming out are you?

JOE: What? No! I—Ass! What's wrong with you?

STEVE: I don't know, man. You've been looking at me

funny.

JOE: *(laughs.)* Shut up. *(beat)* I've been doing some thinking.

STEVE: Better late than never. So?

JOE: I've been thinking about . . .

STEVE: What?

JOE: Well, I've been thinking . . . we've been doing really well.

STEVE: Yeah.

JOE: The band. We're . . . we've been doing really well.

STEVE: Hell, yeah!

JOE: *Really* well . . . We're getting a good Following . . . the bars . . .

STEVE: The girls!

JOE: A good Following, that . . . well . . . follows us . . .

STEVE: Damn straight they do. We're Men on a Mission! What the hell are you trying to stammer out?

JOE: I'm just saying . . . we've got fans.

STEVE: Yes. You are correct. Fans are the thing that we have. You got *another* Muppet News Flash in there or are you done?

JOE: No, no . . . Look . . . I'm just saying . . . we've got fans . . .

STEVE: You said that.

JOE: A sound . . .

STEVE: Yeah . . . ?

JOE: Expectations.

STEVE: And?

JOE: Expectations that we can either continue to meet . . . or . . .

STEVE: Or . . . ?

JOE: *(Beat.)* Why do so many of the great ones fade away?

STEVE: Why do . . . What?

JOE: They fade away because they got stale. They kept doing the same thing over and over—they didn't change with the audience—and the audience got bored with them . . .

STEVE: Yeah . . . ?

JOE: So, I was thinking—instead of just fading away . . . being forgotten . . . maybe it was time we switched it up?

STEVE: Switched it up?

JOE: Yeah. Added a song here or there that *wasn't* the same . . . stylistically . . . we . . . switch it up.

STEVE: You want to change our sound.

Lawrence Harbison

JOE: No! No. No, not *change* our sound . . . just add a little variety.—Look—all the greats changed—*evolved*—over time. Bad Brains—they go back and forth between hardcore and reggae, right? What about The Kinks? Hell, look at how much The damn Beatles grew before Yoko ruined it.

> *(BOTH cross themselves and spit, Gypsy-Curse-style.)*

Come on, man, even a group of posers like Poison's got "Every Rose Has It's Thorn."

STEVE: *(Beat. Smiles. Taunting Joe.)* Ahhhhh. I get it. You want to do a love song.

JOE: No! No. You—I don't . . . I—

STEVE: You do, you little wuss. You want to add a love song.

JOE: *(Overlapping.)* No, I don't—It's—DAVE *(Overlapping.)* Alright, who is she?

JOE: No. It's not like—It's not a love song . . . Not a love song, per se.

STEVE: Then what is it?

JOE: I don't know, I just thought . . . adding a ballad to the set might mix things up a bit . . . add variety.

STEVE: *(Suspicious.)* A ballad?

JOE: Yeah, a ballad. What's wrong with a ballad?

STEVE: You don't think that might confuse people a bit?

JOE: How so?

STEVE: How so? How *not* so? You really think a ballad will fit well sandwiched in between "Your Skull on a Stick" and "Die, Pigfucker, Die?"

JOE: I really don't think you're giving the audience enough credit.

STEVE: Enough credit? Dude, that just isn't the sort of thing we do. I mean, come on! Look at us! The only unicorns people want to hear us singing about are decapitated ones.

JOE: *(Stung.)* Fine. Fine. Forget it. If you're gonna bird-shit all over it, just forget I even—

STEVE: *(Overlapping.)* I didn't bird-shit all over anything. Don't start getting all sensitive artist on me.

JOE: I'm sorry. I just thought it would be a good idea.

STEVE: I really don't see *how* it could be a . . .

JOE: I even wrote a song and everything.

STEVE: *(beat)* A ballad. *(laughs.)* You wrote a ballad?

JOE: *(beat)* Yeah.

STEVE: You actually *wrote* a ballad? Musical masturbation? You know that's a sin, right?

JOE: I thought it might . . . I don't know . . . but you're right, it's . . .

STEVE: Well, this I gotta hear.

JOE: *(Beat)* Seriously?

STEVE: Yeah. If you already wrote it, come on, out with it. Let's hear this brand new hymn for humanity.

JOE: You sure?

> *(Steve raises his "two for flinching" fist in response. Joe flinches.)*

OK!

> *(Getting His guitar and notebook.)*

It's called "Sleeping Together in Separate Beds."

> *(He flips through the notebook as He prepares to sing.)*

STEVE: *(laughs.)* It's called what?!

JOE: "Sleeping Together in Separate Beds." What?

STEVE: *(laughs.)* Jesus, you couldn't come up with something a little more cheesy?

JOE: What . . . ?

STEVE: Dude, I mean, the seventies are over. There isn't exactly an AM radio market anymore . . .

JOE: I knew you wouldn't—

STEVE: What, you expect us to play to the Barry Manilow crowd now?

JOE: Hey, listen—

STEVE: Planning for us to do a guest spot on the Andy Williams Christmas Special?

JOE: Will you just let me . . . ?

STEVE: Working on a theme song for a spin off of *Rhoda*?

JOE: Why are you being such a . . .

STEVE: I'm sorry, I'm sorry. I'll stop. *(beat.)* An ABC After School Special?

> *(Laughs. Joe is pissed.)*

Look, I'm sorry, alright? It's just the title really caught me off guard.

> *(Beat. Grabs Joe's notebook and pretends to look at his reflection in it. Then a Spinal Tap impression.)*

"It's like how much more lame could it be and the answer is none. None more lame."
>   *(laughs.)*
JOE: Stop it! This is serious.
STEVE: OK, OK. I'm done. I'm done. *(Beat.)* So what's it about?
JOE: *(Beat. Should He tell him?)*
>   My parents.
STEVE: What?
JOE: My parents. It's about my parents.
STEVE: Your parents?
JOE: Well, it's not just them. It's like how distant we were as a family. Like we just didn't connect.
STEVE: Dude, I am *not* gonna sing a song about your parents.
JOE: I knew you'd be a dick about it.
>   *(Joe gets up to leave.)*
STEVE: *(Still laughing.)* I'm not!
JOE: So, are you going to listen?
STEVE: *(Overly serious.)* Oh, yes.
JOE: Really?
STEVE: I swear.
>   *(He puts his hand on his heart and raises His middle finger— the Metal version of the Boy Scout salute.)*
>   Scout's honor.
>   *(Joe is rightly skeptical.)*
>   Come on. Let me hear it. I'm riveted. I'm dying to hear this magnum opus you've written about your disconnected family. Just sing the damn song!
JOE: *(Beat. Should he?)*
>   Ok. *(Beat)* Ok.
>   *(Readies himself and sings. Unfortunately, it is not the power ballad Joe wants to think it is.)*
WE'VE BEEN TOGETHER ALL THESE YEARS
WE'VE HAD OUR SHARE OF JOY AND TEARS
BUT AS THE TIME TO LEAVE HERE NEARS
WHY DON'T YOU CARE ABOUT MY FEARS?
>   *(Steve, who has been struggling to maintain His composure throughout, bursts out laughing on this last line.)*
Aww, come on, Man! You're not even giving it a chance!

STEVE: I know, I know. But, "care about my fears?" Dude! Seriously? We're supposed to create fears, not care about them. Seriously, Dude . . . totally not metal.

JOE: Just hear me out.

STEVE: This is really the direction you want to move in?

JOE: I just . . .

STEVE: You start singing crap like that and it's like two steps from playing alongside Iron Maiden to

STEVE: *(continued)* being backup dancers for Cher.
> *(Again, BOTH cross themselves and spit, Gypsy-Curse-style.)*

JOE: You're not even—

STEVE: I mean, I though you and I were the same. I thought we were the real deal.

JOE: We are, man . . .

STEVE: No, no. See, I thought you had the Spirit.

JOE: Dude, I am all about the Spirit—

STEVE: I thought you had the Calling. I thought you were a Man on a Mission.

JOE: What do you want me to say?

STEVE: I thought you said you and I were the Prophets . . . the Messengers . . . the Goddamn *Messiahs* of Rock and Roll!

JOE: Hey, I never said we were gods.

STEVE: Gods?! Gods?! We're *not* gods. You and I'll never *be* Gods! *Lemmy* is God! We are simply His messengers, sent to do His will and disseminate His message to the unwashed, un-Metal masses.

JOE: Don't you think I know that?

STEVE:	JOE:
I thought we came here with a purpose . . .	
	We did!
A plan . . .	Why are you doing this?
A plan to preach the Gospel . . .	
	Don't you question my Faith!
STEVE: *(continued)*	JOE: *(continued)*
To convert the unbelievers . . .	My Faith is unwaivering!

To make them Disciples . . .
To join our Mission . . .
Our Brother Apostles . . .
Testifying . . .
For the one and only true Savior . . .
The Spirit . . .
of Rock and Roll!

My Faith is a Rock!
I will never stop Rocking!
Bring them to the fold!
Light the way!

Blaze a path for the Word!
Let me hear it!
Halle—fucking—lujah!!!

> *(Steve and Joe have struck wild religious poses—arms outstretched unto the Lord!)*

JOE: *(Slowly recovering from his epiphany. Then, almost to tears . . .)*
Man, I'm . . . I'm so sorry. I don't know what I was thinking. It just—I was weak.
> *(Joe kneels at Steve's feet.)*
I feel so ashamed. Please . . . please forgive me.

STEVE: Fear not, little lamb. Our spiritual journey may be fraught with doubt, but it is when we *answer* the questions encountered upon the Path, that our commitment to the Calling becomes steadfast.
> *(Puts his hand on Joe's shoulder)*
You'd do the same for me . . . Brother.

JOE: *(Looks up at Steve. Clasps his hand. Beat.)* Brother!
> *(Beat.)*
In Metal . . .

BOTH: We . . . are . . . One! ONE, TWO, THREE, FOUR!
> *(Something loud and fast in the spirit of Motorhead plays us out as Joe and Steve air guitar and slamdance with gleeful religious abandon.)*

The End

DOS CORAZONES

Richard Hellesen

PRODUCTION NOTES:

City Theatre
Miami, Florida
June 2, 2011

Cast:
CHERYL, Finnerty Steeves
ANA, Ceci Fernandez

Directed by Gail Garrisan
Scenic Design by Sean McClelland
Costume Design by Leslye Menshouse
Lighting Design by Ron Burns
Sound Design by Matt Corey
Properties Design by Jodi Dellaventura
Production Stage Manager: Michael John Carroll

Theatre 40
Beverly Hills, California
January 12, 1994,
directed by Peter Ellenstein.

Cast:
CHERYL, Suzanne Goddard
ANA, Jill Remez

CHARACTERS:
CHERYL, early to mid-thirties
ANA, early to mid-twenties

SCENE: A semi-private room on the maternity ward of an urban hospital.
TIME: The present. Around 11:30 at night.

A note on the Spanish: as written, *Dos Corazones* primarily uses the Mexican-influenced idiom of Southern California. However, subsequent productions have discovered that it's desirable to reflect the language as actually spoken in the locality where the play is performed—e.g., Cuban Spanish in Miami, the Puerto Rican or Dominican Spanish of New York, etc. So the actor playing Ana should feel free to find the version of her dialogue (words, tenses, etc.) which is most accurate and appropriate to her specific theatre and audience.

Muchisimas gracias a Cristina Guerrero y José Cruz González . . . and of course to Suzanne Goddard, Jill Remez, and Peter Ellenstein.
—R.H.

In the dark, a woman humming a lullaby.
The lights fade slowly up. We see a darkened hospital room, with bright moonlight filtering in through a window. A rocking chair is set downstage left. Two standard hospital beds are visible, flanked by standard hospital dressers. Both dressers have the basic supplies you'd find in any maternity ward—plastic tray with water pitcher and cup, various medications, Kleenex. Beyond that, the dresser next to the stage right bed is packed with personal items: stuffed animals, congratulatory cards, a new copy of a parenting magazine, a small jewelry box with torn gift-wrapping—and this is all virtually buried under a mass of flowers. A bundle of helium-filled balloons are tied to the back of the bed; one, with a far-too-jolly stork, lets us know that "It's A Girl!" Also next to the bed, within reach, is a sleeping baby in a plastic tray from the nursery, wheeled in on a metal cart and parked. The baby is not visible—it appears to be merely a

*bundle of blankets with a white stocking cap—and in any case
our view of is blocked by the pink card on the end of the tray
which identifies her. Another tray is to the left of the stage left
bed; this one has a blue card on it. The dresser behind this cart
also has a few hospital necessities, but otherwise it contains
only two items. One is a solitary red rose which has been placed
in some piece of medical glassware borrowed for the purpose.
The other is a small portrait of Our Lady of Guadaloupe, who
smiles beatifically in the direction of the baby tray. The child
is not in the tray; he is being rocked slowly by a woman in the
rocking chair, who is quietly humming the lullaby.*

*The reclining part of the stage right bed is up, and CHERYL
lays there, asleep. She may well be gorgeous, but we'll never
know; the only attractive thing about her is the frilly maternity
nightgown which she wears, and even that is a mess. CHERYL
herself is pretty much a disaster—no makeup, exhausted eyes,
hair which has long since been given up on. In fact, given
her appearance—and the profusion of flowers—were she not
moving, we might mistake this for a viewing at a funeral home
rather than a very late night on the maternity ward. But she is
moving—in the throes of an increasingly intense dream. ANA—
the other mother—stops rocking and returns her baby to his
tray. She settles the baby, then turns her attention to CHERYL,
who thrashes and ultimately cries out. The cry wakes her; she
seems to be gasping for air, then is startled by ANA's presence.
She turns on the light next to her bed, exhales deeply, and sinks
back into her pillow. A moment, as she appears to be holding
back tears; then she turns to ANA, who simply watches.*

CHERYL: I, um . . . . I'm sorry. I was just . . . . listening to the
   rain, and . . . . . Dreams, you know? . . . . Water . . . .
      *(Sighs; shakes her head. Then she looks at ANA for
      a moment, who is still silent. Tired and somewhat
      mystified:)*
   I was . . . .swimming. In some sort of lake—I was way out
   there. Like I was going to swim across it or something. And
   I got so tired of kicking . . . . my legs just got heavier and
   heavier, and I started to sink. The water just kept . . . rising
   up over me. And I tried to fight it, but the harder I tried the
   faster I went down. And I just . . . went down. *(Slight pause)*

And then I remembered . . . that the human body floats. Right
If you just let it go, it floats. So I just . . . . let everything go.
And sure enough, I went straight up like a cork—and when
I popped out, I just breathed and breathed, and . . . . looked
up at the sky, and breathed . . . . *(Pause)* Finally I decided
that I would just drift back to the shore. Only there wasn't
any shore. I looked around, and there wasn't any land at all.
I thought, My God, I'm going to be floating here forever.
And nobody knows where I am.
>   *(Tears up.)*

CHERYL: *(cont.)* Nobody knows.
>   *(She deals with the tears, but there is a long pause.
>   ANA continues to look at her; CHERYL responds with
>   a half-smile.)*

Well. At least the rain stopped. *(Long pause)* Good night.
>   *(She lays down and turns her back to ANA. A pause,
>   then:)*

ANA: ¿Tu bebé está bien? [Is your baby alright?]
>   *(CHERYL and ANA look at each other. More delib-
>   erately:)*

Tu bebé . . . [Your baby . . .]

CHERYL: Oh boy . . .

ANA: ¿Está bien? [Is she alright?]

CHERYL: *(Slight pause; nods a bit too much.)* Um . . . .Yes,
she's mine . . . .Definitely mine . . .
>   *(Smiles at ANA, who smiles back and nods. Indicates
>   ANA's baby.)*

Yours?

ANA: Era un poco malo al principio—pero, es mejor ahora. [He
was a little sick at first—but he's better now.]

CHERYL: *(Who hasn't understood a word, nods.)* Ah. *(pause)*
Listen, um . . .
>   *(Louder, as though that would help.)*

I'm sorry I woke you up. Uh . . . usted . . . were, um . . . . .Oh
God, what is it . . . I used to know this . . . .Bailar.
>   *(ANA offers a puzzled laugh.)*

No, that's not it . . . . Dormir? Dormiendo?
>   *(ANA nods.)*

Usted were dormiendo and I—you know . . . I'm sorry. That
you're not dormiendo anymore.

ANA: Casi despertí. [I was sort of awake.]
CHERYL: No, really, I'm . . . I'm sorry, OK?
    (More to herself:)
    I'm sorry about everything.
ANA: No hablo mucho Inglés— [I don't speak much English—]
CHERYL: Oh. Um, whatever . . .
ANA: —pero, algunas veces puedo entender. ¿Sabes? [—but I
    can understand it sometimes. You know?]
    (Gestures to her ear and her head.)
    ¿Inglés? [English?]
CHERYL: You . . . .hear it OK?
ANA: Más o menos. ¿Hablas Español? ¿Un poco? [Sort of. You
    speak Spanish? A little?]
CHERYL: Um, yeah, un poco. El Español de High School,
    but . . .
    (Gestures as of language flying out of her head.)
    Ffftt. Adios.
ANA: Otra lengua—es muy difícil. [Another language—it's
    very hard.]
    (With great effort:)
    "Have a nice day."
CHERYL: Oh, the basics, huh? Um . . . "Dos margaritas, por
    favor."
ANA: Eso no estuviera mal . . . .. [That wouldn't be so bad . . .]
    "Big Mac with fries."
CHERYL: "Hola, Paco! Qué tal?"
ANA: "Call 9-1-1."
CHERYL: "Lave los manos."
ANA: "I am having a baby."
CHERYL: I am having a baby . . .
    (Her smile fades.)
ANA: ¿Está bien? [Is that O.K.?]
CHERYL: Sure. Perfecto.
        *(She sniffles again and reaches for Kleenex. ANA
        watches her for a moment.)*
ANA: Tu hija es muy bonita. [Your daughter is very beautiful.]
    (Slight pause.)
CHERYL: Oh. A girl. You have a little boy?
ANA: Sí. [Yes.]
CHERYL: Your first? Primero?

Lawrence Harbison   41

ANA: *(Pause; nods slowly.)* Sí. Nuestro primero. ¿Tú también?
   [Yes. Our first. You too?]
CHERYL: Mmm-hmm.
ANA: ¿Como se llama? [What's her name?]
CHERYL: Um . . . Me llamo Cheryl.
ANA: Mucho gusto. Me llamo Ana. (Slight pause) ¿Y la bebé?
   [And your baby?]
CHERYL: (as though she's just discovered the name herself)
   Clare. It's Clare.
ANA: Clare. Bonito. [Clare. Pretty.]
CHERYL: How about yours? Como se llama?
ANA: Martín.
CHERYL: Marteen. That's a nice name . . . . . You must be
   happy to have a son. Very proud.
      (Does "proud".)
ANA: Sí. [Yes.]
CHERYL: I think Nate wanted a boy. He didn't say anything,
   but . . .
      (Begins absently fingering necklace she wears.)
ANA: *(after a moment)* Tu collar es muy bonito. [Your necklace
   is very pretty.]
CHERYL: *(in her own thoughts)* Hmmm?
ANA: *(pointing)* Tu collar—[Your necklace—]
CHERYL: This?
ANA: Sí. Es tan bonito. ¿Tu esposo te lo regaló? [Yes. It's so
   pretty. Your husband gave it to you?]
CHERYL: Yeah. It's from my esposo.
ANA: Dos corazones. [Two hearts.]
CHERYL: Dos . . .
ANA: Corazones. [Hearts.]
      (Does the "heart" beating in her chest.)
CHERYL: Hearts. Yes.
ANA: ¿Con diamantes? [With diamonds?]
CHERYL: Um, yeah . . . . There's a little diamond there, be-
   tween the aquamarines.
ANA: Ah . . . . que bueno. [Ah . . . . Nice.]
CHERYL: (flatly) Yes it is. (Pause; begins to cry again.) This
   is so stupid . . .
ANA: ¿Que te pasa? [What's the matter?]
CHERYL: I just . . . . never mind.

ANA: *(after a pause)* ¿Por qué estás tan triste? [Why are you
    so sad?]
CHERYL: Sorry, I don't . . .
ANA: ¿Triste? Estás muy triste. [Sad. You're very sad.]
CHERYL: Sad?
ANA: Sí. ¿Por qué? [Yes. Why?]
    (Slight pause; CHERYL looks away.)
    Tienes un bebé bonita—es un tiempo feliz—pero estás
    triste. ¿Por qué? [You have a beautiful baby——it's a happy
    time—but you're so sad. Why?]
CHERYL: Porque . . . . .It's all such a lie! Everything they tell
    you, everything they say is going to happen to you . . . .no
    es verdad, you know?
ANA: *(puzzled)* ¿"No es verdad"? ["It's not true?"]
CHERYL: It's just—this is the answer to the question, right?
    One of the questions. "How much weight have you gained?"
    Four hundred pounds—go away. "Was it planned?" None
    of your damn business. And "When are you due?" When
    when when. My God, there it is, just staring at you! . . .
    And then it's next week, and then it's this week, and then
    it's tomorrow . . . and then it's today . . . .And then it's
    yesterday, and then it's last week, and then . . . it happens.
    And it's such a lie.
ANA: No entiendo . . . [I don't understand . . .]
CHERYL: Here. Por ejemplo.
    *(Retrieves magazine from table, opens it to a page,
    shows ANA.)*
    Look at that. Tell me that's the truth. She just had a baby?
    Right. I mean, look at her! She's so . . .
ANA: "Blonde."
CHERYL: No. Well . . . yes.
ANA: *(indicating money with her fingers)* Rica. [Rich.]
CHERYL: Sexy! She looks sexy! Like, "That was fun—wanna
    start on another one?" Look at me! I lost thirty pounds in
    thirty seconds—I feel like some kind of cow.
    (ANA offers the magazine back.)
    It's OK—you can keep it. We got four gift subscriptions.
    (ANA looks through the magazine some more.)
    But that's the way you're supposed to be, right? Glowing—
    like the moon. *(Slight pause)* And nobody cares. Nobody.

Lawrence Harbison

Except the nurses, and all they want to know is "How are your stitches? Have you had a bowel movement yet?" NO, I haven't had a bowel movement, BECAUSE I have stitches AND I'm too stiff to walk to the bathroom AND I'm afraid that if I DO go I will split myself in two, so if you don't mind I'll just lay here and get constipated until I die!

(Shakes her head, sniffling.)

Everything was supposed to stop and wait—and it just kept going. Just kept right on going, like, So what? You thought you were special? (Pause) Yes. I thought I was. Kind of forgot to tell me about the triste, huh?

ANA: *(Nods quietly, almost to herself.)* "En tristeza tendrás hijos." ["In sorrow thou shalt bring forth children."]

CHERYL: Hmmm?

ANA: ¿En el Biblio? ¿Dios? Es . . . su primero castigado. En todas las madres—tristeza. "En tristeza tendrás hijos." [In the Bible? God? It's . . . his first punishment. On all the mothers yet to come—sorrow. "In sorrow thou shalt bring forth children."]

CHERYL: I guess.

ANA: Pues . . . . ¿Por qué tuviste un bebé? [So . . . . why did you have a baby?]

CHERYL: Por qué . . .

ANA: La bebé. ¿Por qué? [The baby. Why?]

(A pause; CHERYL shrugs.)

¿Pero, sí la quieres, no? ¿Sí la querías? [But you wanted her, didn't you? You must have wanted her . . .]

CHERYL: Wanted?

ANA: Sí. [Yes.]

CHERYL: I don't know . . . I don't remember . . .

ANA: No entiendo . . . . ¡Tienes un bebé, y eres tan . . . resentida! [I just don't understand . . . . You have a baby, and you're so . . . resentful!]

CHERYL: Look—

ANA: ¿Por que? ¡Tienes flores, y globos, y tienes una hija saludable—! [Why? You have flowers, and balloons, and a healthy child—]

CHERYL: I DON'T REMEMBER, OK? I DON'T REMEM-BER WHY. Just . . .

(quieter)

I don't remember.

(ANA turns away. CHERYL looks over at her, after a long pause:)

Part of me . . . por mi madre, maybe. So there's one less thing she can hang over me. (Slight pause) And . . . por mi esposo. To have . . . something more between us. Mas . . . .amor . . .

(fingering the necklace again)

And Nate was incredible. He really was—the whole pregnancy. We took those classes—clases? De childbirth? We'd do these pretend delivery room scenes, and he was totally in charge! "No monitors." "We're not gonna have drugs." "Get that I.V. away from her!" I felt so safe. *(Slight pause)* And then this morning . . . He didn't say a word all the way to the hospital. We get here, inside of fifteen minutes they've got me on a monitor and an I.V., they've ordered the drugs—and . . . . And you know what he does? He leaves. Hasta la vista. My labor takes off, and he goes to the bathroom! I couldn't believe it!

(A sniffle or two.)

Oh, and then? When he finally comes back? All this crap from the childbirth books finally kicks in. "Honey! I'm so proud of you! hank you for working so hard!" He's watching the contractions. "Gee, honey, that one wasn't as good as the last one." The hell with you! Any contraction I get through is a good one! "Look, honey! Here it comes! There's the head! Can you feel it?!" CAN I FEEL IT? I can feel this head the way I have NEVER felt a head in my LIFE! *(Pause; quieter)* And then it's over. And I hold out my hand for him . . . . and I look up to see his face. What depth of love that I've never seen before will I see in his eyes? And you know what? I don't know. Because he's across the room looking through the video camera which he's holding about six inches over the baby. "Isn't this great? God, this is so great!"

(tearing up again)

He never even looked at me. *(Slight pause)* I felt like I was laying there for an hour. Until the doctor finally wandered over and said, "Hey, let's stitch you up, huh?" Yes. Let's.

(Lays back, exhausted.)

I swear . . . . I felt closer to the afterbirth. I mean, it held her for nine months—that was her home. And they just . . . throw it away. Just throw it away.

(Pause; playing with the necklace again)
And mi wonderful esposo . . . . went away for a long time,
and then he came back—and he gave me this.
(Tears up again.)
He thought I was crying because I was happy.
ANA: *(referring to the necklace.)* ¿No le gusta? [Don't you
like it?]
CHERYL: I have no idea what it means! You want to know
"por qué"? Well so do I! Por qué this?! It doesn't make
any sense!
ANA: Dos corazones. [Two hearts.]
CHERYL: I know that, but . . . . Which two?!
*(ANA shakes her head slightly, that she doesn't com-
pletely understand.)*
Una familia? But that's three hearts, not two! Or, it's him
and me? Like when you get married, it's two hearts with
an arrow through them or something? Only it's not him and
me anymore! That's over.
(Sniffles a bit.)
Or maybe it's something about what he loves—the baby and
me. But he should be wearing that, not me! I don't know
what it means! He's hanging it around my neck, and I don't
know what it means!
ANA: ¿Y tú? [And you?]
CHERYL: What . . .
ANA: Y tú . . . [And you . . .]
CHERYL: What about me.
ANA: Tuviste el bebé por tu mamá . . . y por tu esposo . . . .¿No
la tuviste por tí? [You had a child for your mother, and for
your husband. What about for yourself?]
CHERYL: I told you, I don't remember! No recuerdo.
ANA: Pero . . . cuando la abrazas . . . ¿No te acuerdas por qué
la tuviste? [But . . . . when you hold her . . . .You remember
then, don't you? Why you wanted a child?]
(Cradles an imaginary baby.)
Cuando la abrazas . . . [When you hold her . . .]
CHERYL: When I hold her . . . ?
ANA: Sí. Cuando están aquí . . . . ¿Te acuerdas por qué la
querías? [Yes. When they're right here . . . You remember
why you wanted her?]

(ANA looks at CHERYL, who is silently crying.)
¿Cuando la abrazas? [When you hold her?]
(CHERYL shakes her head, trying not to sob.)
¿No?
(CHERYL shakes her head again; very gently:)
¿Por qué? [Why not?]
CHERYL: Because I've never held her.
(ANA looks at her, not quite understanding.)
I've never . . .
(Imitates the action of holding the baby, then throws her hands up.)
ANA: ¿No has abrazado? [You've never held her?]
CHERYL: I can't . . . .I just . . . .
(Lets herself cry.)
I wanted her so much—and then . . . . Everybody else had her. She was stressed, during the delivery—they took her down to the ICU for awhile . . . I never even got to touch her. I was so afraid . . . what if she was dead, or . . . ?
ANA: No, no.
CHERYL: But when they brought her back later . . . .I didn't want to touch her . . . .I wanted them to take her away. Something in me . . . . I wanted her to be dead.
(She continues to weep. ANA climbs into CHERYL's bed and puts her arms around her.)
How can I be her mother? I can't even hold her!
ANA: Ssshhhh . . .
CHERYL: I want her so much . . .
ANA: Allí está. [But she's there.]
CHERYL: Here. I want her here.
(Her womb.)
I want her inside, where she's safe, and . . . .she's mine . . . and I can hold her with my whole body, all the time—not out where they can take her away . . .
ANA: Está bien . . . [It's alright . . .]
CHERYL: I want her on the inside, and Nate and me on the outside . . . and nothing would change. But she's gone . . . . And he's . . . . And I'm . . . .
(Looks at ANA for a moment; then, a tearful laugh.)
And you don't understand a thing I'm saying do you? God . . .

ANA: ¿Yo no—? [I don't—]

CHERYL: Usted . . . no conoces . . . . Never mind.

ANA: Pero sí te entiendo. [But I do understand.]

CHERYL: No, you don't . . . .

ANA: No, no, no—escuchas . . . [No, no, no—now listen . . . .]

CHERYL: You can't—

ANA: Escúchame. [Listen.]

> *(Backs off so that CHERYL can see her full face.)*
> *Nos entendemos aquí. [We understand each other here.]*
> *(Her heart.)*

Es la única cosa que importa. [That's the only thing that matters.]

> *(indicating the babies)*

ANA: *(cont.)* Porque tenemos nuestros niños. Porque somos madres, ahora. Y creo . . . . . Los hombres—¿sí?— [Because we have our children. Because we are mothers, now. And I think . . . . . Men—yes?]

CHERYL: Men.

ANA: Hablan de "corazones rompidos." ¿Sabes? [They talk about "broken hearts." You know?]

> *(Makes a breaking motion with her hands.)*

Corazones rompidos.

CHERYL: Broken hearts?

ANA: Todo el tiempo—los hombres: [All the time—men:]

> *(Doing despairing male voice)*

"¡Ay! Ella se rompió mi corazón. ¡Voy a morir!" ["Oh! She broke my heart. I'm going to die!"]

> *(CHERYL smiles.)*

Los corazones de los hombres nunca se rompen. Rompen sus cabezas——sus abrazos— [Men's hearts never really break. They break their heads—their arms—]

> *(A dismissive gesture. Slight pause.)*

Pero, por nosotros . . . . en eso . . . [But for us . . . .in this . . .]

> *(Gestures around the room, the babies.)*

El corazón de la mujer en verdad se rompe. [The heart of a woman truly breaks.]

> *(The breaking motion again, using her own heart.)*

Rompe a la mitad. [Breaks in half.]

> *(using each fist as a heart)*

Y eso es que sabe solamente las madres: como siente tener dos corazones en un cuerpo. Uno aquí—[That's what only mothers know: how it feels to have two hearts in one body. One here—] (her chest)—y uno aquí. [—and one here.]
(her womb)
Y un corazón siempre pulsa cerca la otra. Aunque cuando se vaya de su cuerpo. [And that heart always beats near your own heart. Even when it goes out of you.]
(Indicates the second heart leaving her body.)
Aunque cuando se pierda . . . .Aunque si se morió su niño, tienes dos corazones. Siempre. [Even when you lose it. Even if your child dies, you have two hearts. Always.]

CHERYL: *(Slight pause; getting sense of the last part.)* Wait—morió . . . ?

ANA: *(touching the necklace)* Creo que tu esposo te quiere mucho— [I think that your husband must love you very much—]

CHERYL: No—something—

ANA: —para te entiende tan bien. [—to understand you so well.]
(She slowly returns to her own bed.)

CHERYL: Morió . . . dies? A child—dies?
(ANA says nothing.)
What—qué niño?
(ANA says nothing.)
Martin . . . . Es your first—your primero . . .

ANA: *(looking at her baby, and nodding)* Sí. El primero. [Yes. The first.]

CHERYL: How many . . . . . Sus niños. How many have . . . morió.
(Pause; ANA holds up three fingers. A long moment, then:)

ANA: Dos . . . [Two . . .]
(Gestures as of something flushing out of her body.)
Eso ya paso. Ellos no viviera—nunca serán bebés. [It happens. They wouldn't have lived—they were never really babies anyway.] *(Slight pause)* La tercera . . . . Su cuerpo nació—pero su espíritu . . . [The third one . . . . Her body was born—but her soul . . .]
(Indicates a soul flying up—gone.)

Ya se fue. *[Was already gone.]*
(Smiles slightly.)
Era muy pequeña, pero . . . . era tan linda. [She was very small, but . . . . she was so pretty.]
(Again, cradles an imaginary baby.)
La abraze por tanto tiempo como pude. Pretendí que ella estaba durmiendo. [I held her as long as they'd let me. I pretended that she was just sleeping . . .]
(She begins to hum the lullaby—first without words, then adding the words quietly. After a moment, ANA sees CHERYL staring at her, and stops singing abruptly.)
Perdóname—es tarde. [I'm sorry—it's late.]
CHERYL: No . . . .It's a beautiful song.
(Looks down, holding the necklace in the palm of her hand.)
ANA: No te preocupe que significa el collar. [Don't worry about what it means.]
(indicating the baby.)
Abrazala. Mientes puedes. [Hold her. While you can.]
(A pause. ANA checks on her own baby; as she does, CHERYL slowly and painfully moves to the edge of her bed. ANA begins humming the tune again. CHERYL walks hesitantly over to her baby, then stands and looks down at her. The room light, and then the moonlight, fade out.)

The End

Extracurricular

Frank Tangredi

Prodcution Notes:

The 17th Annual New York City 15 Minute Play Festival Presented by American Globe Theatre and Turnip Theater Company Festival producer Gloria Falzer, gfalzer@gmail.com
May 6-7, 2011
Directed by Catherine Siracusa

Cast:
JULIA, Dara O'Brien
KIP, Hazen Cuyler

CHARACTERS:

JULIA, A business executive, thirties. Attractive and sophisti-
cated. Beneath her self-assurance, she has been bruised by
life and is fundamentally insecure.

KIP, A college English major, twenty-one. Nice-looking, but
not *too* nice-looking. Though far from inexperienced with
women, he has an appealing air of naiveté.

SETTING: The play is set in a room in a good quality hotel
room in Manhattan. Time is a little after 11 pm on a Friday
night in the fall.

> *AT RISE: LIGHTS UP. JULIA enters. She is astefully dressed
> for an evening on the town. She puts her urse down and waits
> for a beat.*

JULIA: You can come in, Kip.
> *(KIP enters. He is also dressed for an evening out
> and carries it off fairly well. He seems slightly ill-
> at-ease.)*

KIP: Oh, right. Right. I know, I was just . . . .

JULIA: Yes, I understand.

KIP: Wow. I mean, wow. This room is bigger than the whole
lounge at my dorm.

JULIA: It is nice, isn't it?

KIP: That bed is huge! And that view rocks! And that's . . . uh,
that's one huge bed.

JULIA: My company treats me well.

KIP: Your company? They're not—?

JULIA: No. That comes out of my own pocket.

KIP: Right. Right. Whew. . . . Yep. Yep. Sure is one . . . big
. . . bed.
> *(beat)*

JULIA: I had a lovely time. This evening.

KIP: Thank you. I mean, so did I.

JULIA: You're a very gracious escort. And you dance surprisingly well.

KIP: Well, that's one of the things you asked for.

JULIA: Surprising for someone so young, I mean.

KIP: My mom and dad are into ballroom dancing. They taught

us all. Me and my sisters.

JULIA: They taught you well. I'm sure they're very proud of you.

KIP: Maybe. Maybe—not so much . . . . So. Deirdre explained about the . . . you know, the—

JULIA: The payment? Yes, she did.

KIP: That if we're . . . if we're *done* . . . then you give me a . . . certain amount.

JULIA: Yes, that's right.

KIP: And then I'll take off. But if we're *not* . . . done . . . then you give me a . . . *different* amount. So once I see the . . . the amount . . . the I'll know if we're . . . done.

JULIA: You seem nervous, Kip.

KIP: Me? No. No, no, no . . . .

JULIA: Have you ever done this before?

KIP: Who? Me? Are you kidding? Have I ever done this before? Have I—? No.

JULIA: That's what I thought.

(JULIA sits on bed.)

KIP: Don't get me wrong! I've done *it* before. Plenty! I've just never done . . . *this* before.

JULIA: I understand.

KIP: But you don't have to worry. I am totally, totally good at it. I mean, if you decide . . . you know . . . you will absolutely get your money's— . . . I mean, you won't be disappointed.

JULIA: *If* I decide . . . you know . . . I'm sure I won't be.

(KIP takes cell phone out of his pocket.)

KIP: Do you need a reference? There's somebody I can call.

JULIA: No, that's fine.

KIP: Let's see, what was her name?

JULIA: Kip, put the phone away. Now.

KIP: Sorry.

(KIP puts phone away.)

JULIA: And could you please hand me my purse?

KIP: Sure.

(KIP hands JULIA the purse and awkwardly watches her as she thinks it over.)

JULIA: Kip, I know you're anxious, but could you please not hover?

KIP: Oh. Sorry.

JULIA: Thank you.

> *(KIP strolls over to look out window.)*

KIP: Hey, I think I can see the Brooklyn Bridge from here!

JULIA: I hadn't noticed.

KIP: And the Williamsburg, too . . . . Did you ever read "The Bridge"?

JULIA: I don't think so.

KIP: It's a poem. I did a paper on it for 20th Century American Lit.

JULIA: Do you like poetry?

KIP: I love poetry! I'm an English major.

JULIA: Well, that puts you one up on the last man I dated. The only poems he knew were pornographic limericks.

KIP: I know lots of those, too.

JULIA: Here you are.

> *(JULIA hands bills to KIP. He counts them carefully, nods, puts the bills in his wallet, and immediately starts undressing.)*

JULIA: Kip.

KIP: Yes?

JULIA: There's no need to rush.

> *(KIP stops undressing.)*

KIP: Oh. Okay. I figured the sooner we got started . . . .

JULIA: Are you that anxious to get it over with?

KIP: No! That's not what I meant! I meant the sooner we get started on the first time, then the less time I need before I'm ready for the second time. Then, the sooner—

JULIA: I get the idea.

KIP: I figured, that way, you get more bang for your—God, that sounds really bad, doesn't it?

JULIA: I've heard better. Come here.

KIP: Okay.

> *(JULIA pats the bed next to her. KIP smiles and sits next to her. He puts his arm around her. After a slightly uncomfortable pause, he begins kissing her tenderly.)*

JULIA: That's nice.

KIP: Yeah.

JULIA: You're a very good kisser.

KIP: Thank you. You, too.

JULIA: You don't have to say that.

KIP: It's true, though.

(KIP kisses JULIA again, more fervently.)

KIP: Let me know when you want me to undress you. Or if you want to undress yourself . . .

JULIA: KIP—

KIP: Or maybe you'd rather I got undressed first. Whatever you want, you're the boss.

JULIA: Must you act so much like this is a job?

KIP: Well . . . I mean, it kind of is, you know. Don't take that the wrong way! It's a good job. Hell, it's a *great* job. It sure beats operating the merry-go-round at Kiddie Village.

JULIA: I can't tell you how happy I am to hear that.

KIP: I said something stupid again, didn't I?

JULIA: Not at all. Would you like a drink?

(JULIA rises and crosses to minibar. While her back is turned, KIP slaps himself in forehead.)

KIP: Sure. Do they have any beer, or is this place too fancy?

JULIA: I'm sure there's beer. In fact, I'll have one myself.

KIP: You drink beer?

JULIA: Once in a while.

KIP: I would drink beer every day. Actually, I *do* drink beer every day.

JULIA: Please tell me you're old enough to drink.

KIP: I told you, I'm twenty-one. And two months. Do you want to proof me?

JULIA: That won't be necessary.

(JULIA crosses to KIP with two bottles of beer.)

KIP: Thanks. Cheers

JULIA: Cheers.

(JULIA and KIP clink bottles and drink.)

KIP: Man. This stuff is *good!*

JULIA: It's Belgian.

KIP: I think you just spoiled me for my next game of beer pong.

JULIA: Everybody deserves to be spoiled now and then.

KIP: I'm down with that.

(JULIA and KIP drink. The atmosphere starts to get a little more relaxed.)

JULIA: Merry-go-round, you said?

KIP: Yeah. The last two summers . . . . Hey. Guess what the worst thing about operating a merry-go-round is.

JULIA: I have no idea.

KIP: Six straight hours of calliope music.

JULIA: *(laughing)* That never would have occurred to me.

(KIP and JULIA drink. Beat.)

KIP: Julia, can I ask you something?

JULIA: Certainly.

KIP: Have *you* ever done this before?

(JULIA stiffens; this hits a nerve.)

JULIA: *(Trying to maintain a light tone)* That really isn't any of your business, Kip.

KIP: I know. It's just that you seemed a little nervous, too, so I wondered if—

JULIA: *(Snapping)* I said it's none of your damned business!

KIP: Sorry. I mean, you asked me the same—

JULIA: I am not paying you to psychoanalyze me, I'm paying you—

(JULIA stops, suddenly mortified.)

KIP: Oh, wow. Wow.

JULIA: Kip, I'm sorry. I didn't mean that. I don't know what came over me—

KIP: No, it's not that. It's just . . . I don't think it really hit me. Not till then . . . I'm a hooker!

JULIA: No.

KIP: I am. I am. I'm a hooker.

JULIA: Kip, I won't blame you if you don't want to go through with this . . . .

KIP: I *do* want to go through with it. But . . . . When Kevin asked me to fill in for him, it sounded like a great way to make some extra cash. I mean, textbooks are expensive, you know? I didn't think of it as being a hooker. I thought of it as getting paid to do something I like to do anyway. It feels kind of weird. You know?

JULIA: I do know. Exactly . . . . You were right. This is the first time I've done anything like this.

KIP: Why do you even need to? I mean, you're pretty hot.

JULIA: Oh, please.

KIP: You are! You totally, totally are! So I don't get it.

JULIA: What don't you get? You're a 21 year-old male. You

must know what it's like to want something uncomplicated. Clean, and raw, and absolutely uncomplicated.

KIP: Sure I do, but—

JULIA: Maybe I deserve an adventure, all right? A little brush with youth. Somebody who won't grunt, roll over, and start snoring. Maybe I need to be the one in control for a change. And maybe . . . just maybe . . . I'd like something where's there's absolutely no danger of being rejected. No chance of getting hurt. Just one—goddamn—time!

(JULIA is in tears. KIP panics a little, then puts his arm around JULIA. He kisses her. The kiss becomes passionate, then KIP gently pulls away.)

KIP: I don't think I can do this.

JULIA: Oh, God. I can't even get a college student aroused.

KIP: It's not that! Don't you think that!

JULIA: What else do you expect me to think?

KIP: I mean it! If I wasn't . . . I mean, if you were, like, some hot friend of my . . . of my older sister's . . . I would be on you so fast, you wouldn't know what hit you. Trust me on this. Been there, done that.

JULIA: Then what's the problem?

KIP: I'm a hooker is the problem! You're paying me is the problem! Usually, when I'm with a girl, believe me, she's pretty damn satisfied. I mean, that really matters to me! Not like some guys. But still. Sometimes, things happen . . . I mean, sometimes they *don't* happen . . . for her, I mean, not for me, and . . . well, that's the way it goes. But this is different. You're *paying* me. You're paying me to . . . to perform. You're expecting certain things. And I don't think I can handle that kind of pressure!

JULIA: I see . . . . So I guess that's that.

KIP: I guess.

(JULIA hangs her head. KIP thinks a moment. He takes bills from his pocket, counts some off, and puts them on nightstand.)

JULIA: What are you doing?

KIP: *(Indicates money in his hand)* This money . . . this I *have* to take. You know, for the first part of the night. *That* . . .

JULIA: I understand. And I did have a lovely time. When I told you that, I meant it.

KIP: So did I.

(KIP starts to undress.)

JULIA: What are you doing?

KIP: I'm getting ready to have sex with you.

JULIA: But—

KIP: I am not taking money for this. I am not going to bang you because you're paying for it. You're a nice person, and I like you, and I want to bang you because you're hot, period.

JULIA: Kip, in its own peculiar and highly uncomfortable way, that's the sweetest thing anyone has said to me in a long time. I thank you. Now go home.

KIP: But—

JULIA: It's suddenly gotten complicated. Here. I want you to take a little extra.

(JULIA gives KIP an extra bill.)

KIP: I don't know if I can do that.

JULIA: Please. Nobody has to know. I want you to have it because you made me feel good. Buy some books of poetry. Now go home, and don't ever try doing this again.

KIP: Oh, I won't! Don't you ever, either. Okay?

JULIA: I promise. And, Kip, if you ever need a reference . . . please don't call me.

(KIP nods. He turns to go, then looks back at JULIA.)

KIP: She walks in beauty, like the night of cloudless climes and starry skies And all that's best of dark and bright

(KIP waits. JULIA smiles and shakes her head.)

KIP: Hey, I gave it a shot! See ya.

(KIP exits. JULIA starts laughing—and crying. FADE OUT.)

The End

THE FOUR SENSES OF LOVE

Arthur M. Jolly

PRODUCTION NOTES:

    Prop Theatre
    Chicago
    produced by the n.u.f.a.n. Ensemble
    Directed by Tommy Akouris
Cast:
    CALDWELL, David Retseck
    MELITA, Christine O'Keefe

    American Globe Theatre
    New York
    May 2011
    Directed by Stephanie Riggs.
Cast:
    MELITA, Lindsey Carroll
    CALDWELL, Cory D.Shoemaker

    The Westport Community Theatre
    Westport, CT
    July 2011
    Directed by Rob Watts
Cast:
    CALDWELL, Adam Loewenbaum
    MELITA, Rachel Rothman-Cohen

CHARACTERS:
CALDWELL, Late twenties, guarded, scars on his hands.
MELITA, Late twenties, wary.

PLACE: A coffee shop.
TIME: The present.

SETTING: We are in a coffee house, although the fourth wall is flexible—the actors address the audience directly, and can "step out" of the scene to do so.

> *AT RISE: Upstage, a small table, a couple of chairs—a corner in a coffee house. Downstage, CALDWELL addresses the audience.*

CALDWELL: Ya know what bugs me? Blind people. Piss me off. Sometimes, I just tap 'em on the shoulder. They turn around: Who's there? Who did that?! I don't answer. Let them figure it out! Pfff. Blind people.
> *(beat)*
> If I go to a movie, or I'm at a play, you know—with one of the blind guys from this support group I belong to, and I'm describing what's going on for them . . . I make stuff up. A woman walks off stage, and I say: Oh my God, he just stabbed her! Later on, they're all like: wait, I thought she died in the first act, and I say: she's a ghost. They got her in green make—up. Oh wait—you don't know from green. Same color as an orange . . . . What? No, no, they're green. Yeah, it's a confusing name. Makes sense to us—you just don't get colors. We can see them with our eyes closed. 'S true. We can't make out shapes so good, but colors—yeah, we love colors. They feel good . . . they feel like . . . like a . . . like a . . .
> *(pause)*
> I don't feel.
> *(beat)*
> I mean—I don't feel. Born with it—kind of hypothalamic disorder—I never—I feel pressure. Weight. I push down on a bed—and it pushes back—negative weight. I used

to rub my hands on things as a kid—spend ages, trying to. . . . to figure out what everyone was talking about. Feeling . . . it's just different kinds of weight. Silk sheets? Steel wool?

(beat)

A silk sheet has no weight—any direction. Steel wool—a little weight down, a little negative weight if it's dry—but it's got side weight. Pull your hand across it—it tugs—there's an effort to moving across it. If you do it a lot—like, you're six years old, and you're feeling side weight and trying to understand, you drag your hand across some steel wool for five, ten minutes—suddenly there's pain.

(beat)

Oh, yeah. I get pain. That much I got—not on the top. Look at the scars. Underneath pain—that I feel. Got a toothache once—never told my Ma. Just let it fester—it was always there—this blinding, brilliant pain. I never felt so alive. My jaw swelled up—Ma saw, took me to the dentist. He asked if I wanted Novocaine, and I wanted to hit him. Give up this wonderful agony? But then—those vibrations—the buzzing inside my head. I think

CALDWELL: *(cont.)* that's what heaven is—a big dentist office where everything buzzes and grinds and scrapes forever.

(beat)

I don't enjoy pain—I'm not an idiot. It hurts... but hurting's better than nothing, right?

(beat)

They say that people with my condition, we never bond with other people. There was this guy in the sixties—put baby monkeys in cages with two fake mama monkeys. One made out of wire with milk bottles attached, the other was soft fur—like a teddy bear. No milk. The baby monkeys would cling to the fur ones, even if they starved. More important than food—touch. This guy—real nice guy—put some of the baby monkeys with nothing but the wire shapes. The monkeys never developed right. Grew up loners, never accepted other monkeys. It was all—in the touch. We don't bond without it—we never connect in the right way. I'm a wire—mama—monkey boy.

(beat)

Two months ago, this girl joins my support group.

(MELITA enters.)

MELITA: I don't smell.

CALDWELL:She doesn't smell.

(beat)

I don't feel, she doesn't smell—got it? Don't be stupid.

MELITA: If you don't smell, you don't taste either. Ever eat food with a heavy cold? Like that—only more so. I am tasteless.

CALDWELL: I wasn't impressed.

MELITA: To me, chocolate might as well be frozen butter—

CALDWELL:Didn't care a bit. Didn't talk to her.

MELITA: If you could have frozen butter at room temperature.

CALDWELL: I never got temperature. I once started shaking—shaking violently for no reason—I thought I was having a seizure! . . . I was shivering—it was a really cold day. No one told me.

MELITA: When I was a girl, I would eat blueberries, and go into the bathroom and stick out my tongue in the mirror and it would be bright blue—and I would think: That's taste. That's what taste looks like.

CALDWELL: After the group, I always go get coffee. I'm sitting at a table. Someone had spilled sugar, and I was playing with the side weight it. She walked in. I think she followed me.

(CALDWELL sits down at the small round table, running his finger across the table.)

MELITA: When I was nine, I got a blueberry stuck up my nose. I quit trying after that.

(MELITA approaches CALDWELL.)

MELITA: You're making a mess.

CALDWELL: *(as he draws his finger across the different textures)* Slow varnish tabletop—quick rolling sugar—sticky wet—sugar—spilled—coffee tugs!

MELITA: *(to the audience)* I don't have to be noticed... but I

don't want to be ignored. Who the hell is this guy—sits in
my sensory deprived group and never even looks at me?
    (to CALDWELL)
Caldwell, right? Is anyone sitting here?

CALDWELL:Does it look like anyone's sitting there?

MELITA: What's wrong?

CALDWELL:Why does everyone always ask me that?
    (to the audience)
Why does everyone always ask me that?

MELITA: You know, when you tap Steve's shoulder and then
don't answer—he knows it's you. He always has.

CALDWELL: *(to audience)* Then I looked at her, I mean—really
looked. For the first time. Wow.

MELITA: He has nice eyes. Pity they were focused below my
face.

CALDWELL:I kept staring at them.

MELITA: *(to the audience)* I get that a lot.

CALDWELL: Then I looked at her face.

MELITA: Finally.

CALDWELL:I don't know. There was something . . . I'm sure
for you guys, it's no big deal... but for me, I—I don't want
to say "I felt something", cause that's cheap. I didn't. I don't
feel—I just wanted to talk to her.
    (to MELITA)
Could I get you some coffee?

MELITA: No thanks. Maybe some tea.

CALDWELL:How d'you take it?

MELITA: It doesn't matter. Really.
    (CALDWELL gets up, goes to the counter.)

MELITA: *(to the audience)* The group is big on not "passing." If
you're blind, everyone knows it. You can't hide blind. But
taste? Damn right, I try and fit in. Think I wanna go around
telling people I have no taste—no taste at all? If I'm out
with friends, I'll get tea—just to, you know. D'you know
the nutritional value of tea? Exactly the same as hot water.
Two bucks for dirty brown color. But I'll spend it.
    (beat)

MELITA: *(cont.)* Once, this girl Julie—I knew her from the gym,
we saw each other all the time. You know—early friendship,
but real. I mean, I could see being her bridesmaid, down the

road. We coulda been . . . Well, we went out, me and her and her boyfriend Rick. Rick keeps saying: "you gotta try this place, you gotta try this coffee place"—and we all pile in his ratty BMW, and I'm wedged in the back with my knees up under my chin, and we get to this little cafe, and Rick says hi to the guy behind the counter—and it's like this whole show he's putting on for Julie, cause really—it's a coffee place, you meet, you talk. He brings me over this something something something latte. And it was warm water with a faintly slimy foam and a little grit on top—cinnamon. Like very fine sawdust. And he's all: "How is it? It's the best right, what d'I tell ya, the best." Why is he asking if he's already got the answer? So I'm sitting there, and I started playing with the foam. I would put my tongue in it—and then roll the cinnamon between my tongue and the roof of my mouth. Texture—gritty, sandpaper rolling.

(She starts miming it—getting more and more into it. Lots of foam—licking tongue action.)

Foam bubbles bursting, little points of contact, the tip of my tongue delving into the foam, the hot water, the temperature between the hot and the warm foam and the cool of the edge of the cup. . . . Playing with the foam . . . feeling the grit . . .

(She's getting totally carried away. She stops dead, looks up from her imaginary cup.)

Rick was staring at me. Julie got so mad. Screaming at me, said I was a . . . all kinds of things.

(beat)

I was just playing with the foam. Hot water. That's why they use that phrase—getting in to hot water. . . . That was the last time I saw her.

(beat)

Rick called a whole bunch of times.

(CALDWELL returns, carrying two cups of tea.)

CALDWELL: I got you Earl Grey.

MELITA: It's brown.

CALDWELL: Yeah.

MELITA: Not grey.

CALDWELL: Are you stupid?

MELITA: *(to the audience)* Caldwell has difficulty connecting to people. It takes a while to get used to it.

CALDWELL: *(to the audience)* Luckily, she has really low self esteem. I think she usually dates total jerks. Guys who just take advantage of her.

MELITA: There's such a thing as too honest.

CALDWELL: Why else would she have gone out with me?

MELITA: There's a disconnect. He looks at people like he's outside them—like he's examining them all through a microscope. The world is Caldwell's petri dish. But he's . . . he sees things most people... I don't know. He'll . . . he'll never lie to me. Never. Yeah. That's a change . . . Takes a while to get used to that.

CALDWELL: We talked for a couple of hours. The tea got cold.

MELITA: I didn't care. Cold water—ooh.

CALDWELL: I didn't even know.

> *(SHE reaches out—touches his hand. CALDWELL looks down.)*

CALDWELL: She squeezed my hand. I have no idea how long she'd been holding it before she did that.

MELITA: I was worried my palm was sweaty.

CALDWELL: Might've been. Who knows?

MELITA: Who knows?

> *(THEY rise, walk downstage, still holding hands.)*

CALDWELL: The first time we made love—

MELITA: Hey!

CALDWELL: What?

MELITA: You're skipping some stuff.

CALDWELL: Yeah.

MELITA: You went from hand holding to . . . I mean, you make it sound like it was that night. I'm not what Julie said I was.

CALDWELL: I never said it was that night.

MELITA: We went on dates . . .

CALDWELL: Movies.

MELITA: Yeah.

CALDWELL: And the car getting that flat—

MELITA: Not his car—

CALDWELL: I borrowed this car—

Lawrence Harbison

MELITA: —gets a flat—

CALDWELL:—pouring rain—

MELITA: Yeah. You're skipping all that.

CALDWELL:Yup.
> *(to the audience)*
> Our first night together—

MELITA: (to the audience)You know what foreplay is like with a guy who can't feel? It's like . . .
> *(beat)*
> Okay, it's not that different.

CALDWELL:I tried. Touching her. I mean, I'm pushing . . . moving things.

MELITA: Not that different.

CALDWELL: It didn't really do much—

MELITA: Don't I know it.

CALDWELL: I meant for me.
> *(MELITA reacts—it's the first time she's heard that.)*

CALDWELL: (continued) I wish I could say it got better—

MELITA: Okay, stop—

CALDWELL: Bits of her have negative weight—

MELITA: Just shut up—

CALDWELL:It's all—nothing. The weight of a body. The negative weight of the mattress springs.

MELITA: Please—

CALDWELL:So what is there?

MELITA: Stop! For God's sake!
> *(SHE's on the verge of tears.)*
> *(CALDWELL notices. HE reaches for her—but stops. He looks at his hand—his fingertips.)*

CALDWELL: No touch. No connection. What is there?

MELITA: Movies. Flat tires.

CALDWELL: Last night—there was a moment.

MELITA: Don't. Don't tell that.

CALDWELL:She reached with her fingertips—and she ran them down my face. Lightly brushing—feeling. Feeling my skin. Rubbing my face in it.

MELITA: And.

CALDWELL: And I licked her cheek. Tasted her sweat.

MELITA: That was vicious.

CALDWELL: No! . . . No, it wasn't. When . . . when your fingertips dragged across my lips . . . what I tasted . . . I tasted the side weight. The drag of the ridges of your fingerprints across my

CALDWELL: *(cont.)* tongue—the vibrations on my lips. I could taste the vibrations. It was . . . it was touch. I felt it. I felt you.

(A moment.)

MELITA: Your kiss. After you licked my cheek . . . I kissed you and felt the salt on your tongue. I could feel it. Feel the taste.

CALDWELL: For one moment.

MELITA: For one moment.

(Slowly—they kiss.)

(LIGHTS FADE OUT)

The End

GREEN DATING

Chantal Bilodeau

PRODUCTION NOTES:

The Movement Theatre Company's Go Green!
New York City
April 29, 2009
Directed by Barbara Harrison

Cast:
GIRL, Quinn Warren
BOY, Eugene Oh

Manhattan Theatre Source
Estrogenius Festival
October 19-22, 2011
Jen Thatcher, Executive Producer, Estrogenius
177 MacDougal Street
New York, NY 10011
212.260.4698
estrogenius.festival@gmail.com

CHARACTERS:
GIRL, A high school teenage
BOY, A high school teenage

SETTING: A street corner. Now.

A street corner. Two teenagers, their tongues down each other's throat, making out like nobody's business. After a beat, the GIRL: comes up for air.

GIRL: Wow. I mean fuck, it's like, you know?
BOY: Yeah.
GIRL: Like this, I don't know, this, I mean I hope I don't freak you out but I'm like completely like . . . WOW.
BOY: I hear ya. I mean this is like totally fucking awesome. You know, like TOTALLY. And I swear to God I've never said that before. I mean I liked your profile and everything but the real thing is just like, FUCK.
GIRL: Really? I mean like you really mean that like for real?
BOY: Ye-ah! You're just like . . . *(makes the gesture of stabbing himself in the heart)* ahhhhh! And your ass? Your ass is like . . . it's like Iron Man's suit. It's like Batman's batmobile. Your ass is so fucking perfect it's like a piece of ART.
   (Giggles.)
BOY: And it's not just your ass, it's like everything. Swear to God. And I'm not objectifying you 'cause when I say everything, I really mean like EVERYTHING. Including your personality and shit.
GIRL: Well, I'm glad 'cause I'm just like . . . *(pretends to pounce on him)* Roar! I'm just like this guy is like OH MY GOD and I mean I'm sorry but like I totally want to get into your pants.
BOY: Fuck yeah.
   (He pounces on her. They go at it again. This time, he tears himself away.)
BOY: And you know what? You know what? I fucking LOVE the fact that you're GF too. Love it. I mean usually I'm just like the weird guy, you know? The like HIGH MAINTE-NANCE dude. Like, What do you mean you can't have a burger? It's ORGANIC.

GIRL: Yeah and like no matter how many times you tell them, they never remember, right? Sometimes I feel like I should have it tattooed on my forehead: GF. GLUTEN-FREE.

BOY: But they still wouldn't get it 'cause they're like morons or something. The other day, the guy at the restaurant was like, Gluten? Isn't that a muscle in your ASS?

GIRL: TOTALLY.

(Footsteps. They try to act casual. She adjusts her clothes. He examines his shoes. They acknowledge the invisible passerby with a smile or a nod.)

BOY: So anyway . . .

(She checks the time on her cell.)

GIRL: I should probably go.

BOY: Yeah me too.

GIRL: So um . . .

BOY: Well so like do you think— . . . I mean I'm just asking, you know but do you think maybe we can do this again some other night and uh . . . well . . . maybe get to the "get into your pants" part?

GIRL: I was gonna ask you the same thing.

BOY: Cool.

(He's happy. Then confused.)

BOY: So . . . does that mean yes?

GIRL: Yes.

BOY: Sweet!

(A victory dance.)

GIRL: But I have, I mean I hope you don't mind but I need to ask you something before. I mean before we like you know . . .

BOY: Sure. Anything. Shoot.

GIRL: And it's not I mean don't take this the wrong way OK 'cause it's really about me. Like I just need to ask you this thing 'cause well . . . 'cause it's like important to me.

BOY: I don't have another GIRL: on the side if that's what you wanna know.

GIRL: Oh no, that's not— . . . I mean that's great. But like I'm cool with that. Not that you SHOULD have another GIRL but sometimes you gotta check what's in the other store to make sure you're buying the right thing. So like, as long as you tell me 'cause I'm not too good with lying and shit

---

—that just makes me mad and then I get real ugly—but as long as you tell me I'm cool.

BOY: OK. I'm cool too. I mean, you know. You shop, I shop . . . *(Pause.)* But uh . . . Like . . . Are you a big shopper?

GIRL: Depends. Right now I'm kind of digging what I see in this store.

BOY: Oh yeah?

(He struts.)

BOY: Good merchandise, huh? Slick. Fully equipped. *(to someone across the street)* Hey! Don't you agree that this here is some good merchandise?

(She hits him playfully.)

GIRL: Stop!

(He gets an appreciative whistle in response.)

BOY: See? But the thing is you really gotta take it for a test drive if you wanna feel the HORSEPOWER.

GIRL: I AM gonna take it for a test drive. But first—

(She takes out her cell.)

GIRL: Promise you won't get mad?

BOY: Promise.

She turns her back to him and texts something. After a beat, his cell shouts or barks—something obnoxious. He checks it. She looks at him expectantly.

GIRL: So?

BOY: What the fuck?

GIRL: Hey, you promised.

BOY: Are you serious?

GIRL: Well yeah.

BOY: You're asking me this?

GIRL: Yeah.

BOY: Like, you're REALLY asking me this?

GIRL: Yeah. I'm really asking you this.

BOY: You don't know me. You don't know my life. Why are you asking me this?

GIRL: 'Cause.

BOY: 'Cause why?

GIRL: 'Cause if we gonna do this, we should do it right.

BOY: This is not doing it right. This is getting into a guy's BUSINESS. And I don't like people getting into my business. Don't like it one bit.

GIRL: Come on. It's not that big of a deal.

BOY: It IS that big of a deal! It's like a HUGE fucking deal, OK? I mean I don't ask you to like— ... I don't know but like I don't make ASSUMPTIONS about you.

GIRL: I'm not making—... Look, if you want me to ride your HORSEPOWER, the least you can do is put a little effort into it. I mean HELLO-O? I don't know what kind of girl's you've been hanging with but I got STANDARDS.

BOY: Well, actually—

GIRL: And sorry if that's like annoying to you but that's just the way it is.

(Her cell sings.)

GIRL: That's my dad. *(She picks up.)* Hi, dad ... Yeah, I know. I'm almost there. I'll be home in like fifteen minutes, OK? ... OK. Bye.

BOY: Look, I'm clean OK? I'm VERY clean. I'm like cleaner than fucking Mr. Clean.

GIRL: You don't know that.

BOY: I DO know that.

GIRL: No, you don't. Nobody knows. You can't know unless you get tested.

BOY: Maybe you got the tightest hardest most like unbelievably awesome ass in the whole fucking world and maybe I'm just like dying to lick every inch of it like the frosting off a donut but I'm not—you hear me?—NOT getting tested. And I can't believe you even asked. That's just like ... RUDE!

GIRL: Chill, OK? So I asked you to get tested. What? You can't do that for your girl?

BOY: Why 'cause you think I'm just like Mr. Irresponsible? Mr. Testosterone-brain? Mr. like I just think about myself and FUCK THE WORLD?

GIRL: I told you, it's not about YOU.

BOY: Well it sure FEELS like it.

GIRL: It's about ME. 'Cause it took me like TWO YEARS to clean myself up so I don't wanna be with some guy who's gonna MESS ME UP again. I mean, you know? You're probably fine—

BOY: I AM fine!

GIRL:—but if you're not ... well, I don't know but like it doesn't mean that it's your fault or anything. I mean that's

---

Lawrence Harbison   73

how it happened for me. I was just talking with that girl at school, you know Briana, the one with the big boobs. She's always busting my balls and she was like, GIRL . . . just looking at you I can tell your numbers are OFF THE CHART. And I was like, SHUT UP. 'Cause she didn't know, you know? And you can't tell just by LOOKING at someone.

BOY: EXACTLY.

GIRL: But she was like, I'M TELLING YOU and she was pissing me off 'cause she's always like Miss Perfect and everything so I went and got tested just to shut her up. So like the woman at the clinic asked me all these questions and I was doing real well but then she said to me, she said, GIRL you got a PROBLEM. And I was like, NO I DON'T. 'Cause I had already made my dad trade his SUV for a hybrid and change all the light bulbs in the house so I KNEW I was OK. But she was like, I got your numbers right here in front of me and they say you got a carbon footprint the size TEXAS. And I was like, EXCUSE ME? And she was like, Uh-huuuuuuh. And I was like, are you calling me a POLLUTER? 'Cause maybe I've never been to Texas but I know it's BIG so I get your metaphor, LADY. And I was so fucking insulted, I was like, You know what? Fuck this shit. Fuck you, fuck Briana and fuck everything! 'Cause like WHATEVER. I mean, it's not like I was still using PLASTIC BAGS! But then a few weeks later, I went to this place where I used to go with my dad. It's way up North, you know, like WAY THE FUCK. And there's like NOTHING up there, like for real, just mountains and forests and lakes, nothing else. So we're there right and except for the mosquitoes, it's like AWESOME and my uncle comes for a visit 'cause he always comes for a visit, it's like a tradition. And my uncle is this SUPER COOL guy, you know like he SNOWBOARDS and he's been around the world and stuff so he's like AMAZING. And so he has this small plane and he used to fly us around, one by one 'cause it's a two-seater so you can only have one passenger. And I used to go with him a lot and throw up all the time 'cause on top of being GF I got real bad motion sickness but I didn't care I would go anyway 'cause from up there, you can see really far and it's like this GIANT green carpet for like FOREVER, you know? For like AS FAR AS YOU CAN SEE . . . And I know it freaks people out sometimes to be with a big nature like that but me, it makes me feel SAFE. 'Cause I look at those trees and I tell myself, I tell myself as long as there's more of them than of us, nothing can go wrong, you know? And so like, my uncle asks me if I want to go flying again and of course I say yes and we go and I throw up for old time's sake and it's like FUCKING AWESOME all over again with the forests and the mountains and the blue lakes but then we get to one of my favorite spots you know and . . . and . . . *(She tears up.)* Fuck.

(He makes a move toward her. She waves him off.) I'm fine . . . *(She breathes.)* So anyway, I'm on the plane and I look down and . . . and you know all those mountains? . . . They were BALD . . . Just like . . . Nothing. Gone. All the trees had been cut down. And it was like . . . it was like looking at a cancer patient who's just lost all her hair . . . It was so PAINFUL . . . 'Cause you know in your guts that it's WRONG. Nobody has to tell you. You just KNOW. And so I was looking at these BALD mountains with only the stumps left all over like ugly SCARS and I thought . . . I thought about the clinic and it finally clicked, you know, I thought . . . It's ME. I'm that mountain's CANCER . . .

(a beat)

BOY: Here.

(He offers his sleeve. She wipes her eyes and nose with it.)

GIRL: Great. Now you gonna think I'm all girly and shit.

BOY: Girly's cool. I got no problems with girly.

GIRL: Whatever.

BOY: Aw, come on girly's better than a CANCER.

GIRL: Don't make fun.

BOY: I'm not!

GIRL: So anyway . . . After that, I . . . I decided to DO something, you know . . . To make it better for the EARTH. So my dad and I, we stopped using the dryer and started hanging the laundry instead. And me and another girl—that was MY idea—we walk my sister and her classmates to school. That way the parents don't have to drive them. And the next thing I wanna do is get a compost bin—

BOY: I can help you with that.

GIRL: You can?

BOY: I built the one at our place.

GIRL: You got a COMPOST BIN?

BOY: My mom's an Energy Auditor. We got everything.

GIRL: Oh.

> *(A beat. He cups his ear as if he's just heard something.)*

BOY: Did I just hear a thump?

GIRL: What?

BOY: Was that a thump? Did you just like fall off a really HIGH horse?

GIRL: Fuck off.

BOY: 'Cause I mean, I couldn't hear very clearly but that's kind of what it sounded like.

GIRL: OK, so I feel like an HUGE FUCKING ASSHOLE, are you happy? I mean, how the fuck was I supposed to know your mom was an ENERGY AUDITOR?

> *(She turns to leave.)*

BOY: Whoa, whoa, wait a minute . . .

GIRL: What.

> *(He types something on his phone.)*

BOY: Where's that clinic at?

GIRL: Why?

BOY: I wanna know.

> *The GIRLS phone sighs seductively.*

GIRL: Did you just text me?

> *(She checks her cell. Reads the message.)*

GIRL: Shut up.

BOY: It's true.

GIRL: You're just fucking with me.

BOY: No, I swear to God, it's true.

GIRL: What, like you really mean this?

BOY: Yeah. And I'm gonna get tested just to prove it to you. But you better watch out 'cause my carbon footprint is gonna kick your carbon footprint's ASS.

GIRL: Ha! Good luck. 'Cause in case you didn't know, I got MAJORLY AWESOME numbers.

BOY: Then I'm gonna have even MORE majorly awesome numbers.

GIRL: Dude, my numbers are so awesome, I'm almost in the SINGLE DIGITS.

BOY: Girl, I live with the energy efficiency QUEEN. Do you got any idea what that means? That means I'm gonna have NEGATIVE numbers. I'm gonna be so fucking energy efficient that my sole EXISTENCE is gonna reduce carbon emissions.

   (A beat.)

GIRL: OK, that's kind of hot.

BOY: Oh yeah? Like your climate is warming?

GIRL: Maybe like a degree or two.

   (She moves toward him seductively. He jumps back just before she touches him.)

BOY: Then see you tomorrow. AFTER I get tested.

   He takes off. A beat. Her phone sighs. She checks it. A big grin.

GIRL: Fucker.

The End

HATE THE LOSER INSIDE

Jon Kern

PRODUCTION NOTES:

City Theatre's Summer Shorts Festival 2011
June 2 – July 3, 2011, Miami, Florida
Directed by Stephanie Norman

Cast:
COACH DONNY BROADHAUS, Stephen Trovillion
WENDELL, Gregg Weiner

CHARACTERS
COACH DONNY BROADHAUS, forties or fifties
WENDELL, thirties

SETTING: A commercial shoot set.

// indicates an overlap
/ indicates the following comes quick on the heels of the line

[Coach Brodhaus is sitting at a table. On the table is a breakfast plate of eggs, bacon, and pancakes. There is also half a grapefruit in a bowl, a glass of milk, a box of cereal, a bowl of cereal, silverware, and a napkin.]

COACH BRODHAUS: I'm Coach Donny Brodhaus,
Winner of this year's college football national championship.
And when I sit down for a championship breakfast,
I make sure MY KITCHEN
    [gestures to behind him]
Has cabinet fronts and counter tops by Winston's Kitchens and Design.
Take it from a winner like me,
When it comes to home furnishings,
Winston's is the real champion.
They've been providing high-quality kitchen interiors since 1970.
And with their low, low prices,
You won't need to make millions
To look like you do.
    [awkward pause]
So score a touchdown with your neighbors
With the style and class of a Winston's home.
Winston's Kitchens and Design:
It's what completes a real, really complete, real breakfast.
    [blank]
Fuck.

WENDELL: *[offstage]*
>Cut!
>>*[enters, script in hand]*
>That was good.
>That was really good.

COACH BRODHAUS: I keep fucking up that last line.

WENDELL: It's a tongue twister. It's . . .
>>*[slight pause]*
>Are you ready?

COACH BRODHAUS: Yeah, yeah,
>Just give it to me.

WENDELL: It's "It's what really makes a breakfast complete."

COACH BRODHAUS: "It's what really makes a breakfast complete."
>"It's what really makes a breakfast complete."

WENDELL: Good.Good.
>Can I just say, Coach,
>We're really proud to have you for this commercial.
>You're the man who brought the title back to Illinois/

COACH BRODHAUS: You don't need to butter me up.
I'm not a Thanksgiving turkey.

WENDELL: Okay.
>[slight pause]
>So let's just jump back on.

COACH BRODHAUS: "It's what really makes a breakfast complete."

WENDELL: [exits]
>>*[offstage]*
>Okay.
>And rolling.

COACH BRODHAUS: So score a touchdown with your neighbors
>With the style and class of a Winston's home.
>Winston's Kitchens and Design:
>It makes a breakfast what is real.
>Son of a whore!

WENDELL: [offstage]
>Cut!

[enters]

Maybe . . .

COACH BRODHAUS:Is there anyway I can just skip that line?

WENDELL: I'm sorry.

That's been the slogan for Winston's Kitchens and Design for more than twenty years.

Maybe we should back it up.

Start in the middle and work your way to the line.

COACH BRODHAUS:Sure, I'll give that a shot.

You know what might also help . . .

If we could get a real kitchen.

WENDELL: I already explained,

The kitchen will be put in post.

Post-production.

That way, throughout the commercial,

We can change the Winton's design in the background.

[Coach Brodhaus reaches into the box of cereal and starts eating a dry handful.]

What we need from you is to just look at the camera,

And . . .

And don't shift anything on the table.

Everything on the table is placed careful,

So the camera picks it up,

But it doesn't block your face.

[Wendell adjusts the cereal box back in place.]

COACH BRODHAUS: I get that.

I just think it'd be a little easier to focus on talking about a kitchen,

If there was an actual kitchen.

But I don't want to hold this up, so . . .

WENDELL: So let's take it from . . .

COACH BRODHAUS: Can I see the script?

WENDELL: [hands the script to Coach Brodhaus.]

So let's take it from

"They've been providing high quality kitchen interiors since 1970."

COACH BRODHAUS: Huh?

WENDELL: Right . . .

There.

COACH BRODHAUS: Could we start with something shorter?

WENDELL: I'm confident you can get it.

And I want you to add/

COACH BRODHAUS: You want me to add something?

WENDELL: I want you to add,

After the line

"You won't need to make millions

To look like you do."

Add a wink to the camera.

Can you wink?

COACH BRODHAUS: Like this:

can't help but use two eyes.]

WENDELL: No, more like . . .

[Coach Brodhaus winks]

Just one eye.

Like . . .

[Coach Brodhaus winks]

Try to keep the other . . .

[Coach Brodhaus winks]

. . . the other eye open.

[Coach Brodhaus winks]

[Wendell tries to hold Coach Brodhaus's eye open.]

Now try.

[Coach Brodhaus winks. Both eyes close.]

Don't fight it.

Don't fight . . .

Open the other eye!

[Coach Brodhaus winks.]

WENDELL: (con't) Forget . . .

[blank]

Just forget the wink.

COACH BRODHAUS: Alright.

WENDELL: Can you instead . . .

Cross your arms

And smile?

[demonstrates]

Cross you arms,
> *[crosses arms]*

Then smile.
> *[smiles]*

COACH BRODHAUS: Like this?
> *[crosses arms]*
> *[smiles]*

WENDELL: Perfect.
After the line/

COACH BRODHAUS: "You won't need to make millions
To look like you do."

WENDELL: Perfect.
And . . .
And take it from
"Take it from a winner like me."

COACH BRODHAUS: Uh . . .
> *[looking at the script]*

WENDELL: Oo, can't have that in the shot.
> *[snatches script]*
> *[exits]*

WENDELL: (con't)
> *[offstage]*

Places.
> *[slight pause]*

Ready, Coach?

COACH BRODHAUS: I'm ready.

WENDELL: *[offstage]*
And rolling.
> *[Coach Brodhaus takes mark.*
> *Look to camera.*
> *Coughs to clear his throat.]*

WENDELL: *[offstage]*
Still rolling.

COACH BRODHAUS: *[little cough]*
> *[blank]*

Take it from a winner like me,
When it comes to home furnishings,
Winston's is the real champion.
They've been providing high-quality kitchen interiors

since 1970.
And with their low, low prices,
You won't need to make millions
To look like you do.
    [stiffly crosses arms, no smile;
    sudden, bright-ass smile]
So score a touchdown with your neighbors
With the steel and clips of/
Cock and balls!
WENDELL: *[offstage]*
That was good.
Let's go again.
Take it from
"And with their low, low prices."
COACH BRODHAUS: And with their low, low prices,
You won't need to make millions
To look like you do.
    [bright-ass smile;
    then no smile, stiffly crosses arms]
Kick in my scrotum.
I just did that backwards, right?
WENDELL: *[offstage]*
Not a problem.
Take it again.
Still rolling.
COACH BRODHAUS: And with their low, low prices,
You won't need to make millions
To look like you do.
    [crosses arms; smiles]
So score a touchdown with your neighbors
With the style and clams of a Winston's fern.
Finger a dick.
WENDELL: *[offstage]*
Cut!
    [enters]
Coach, you're doing good.
Really.
COACH BRODHAUS: I don't get it.

My whole brain has been—
Plplplpfff—
Has been shat out of my head!
WENDELL: These things happen.
    You're not the first.
COACH BRODHAUS: I won a national football championship,
    And now I can't do some cheap, local commercial.
COACH BRODHAUS: *(con't)*
    [speaks so fast in turns into gibberish]
    I can't speak.
    I can't schpleak.
    I kant schpeak.
    I kant schpeak.
    I kant schpeak.
WENDELL: We're still doing good.
COACH BRODHAUS: It's the damn arm crossing.
    Before I just had problems with the last line.
    Now I can't do shit for any of it.
WENDELL: We can do the arm cross in a close-up.
    Insert it in later.
COACH BRODHAUS: *[grabs a chair and rattles it against the floor]*
WENDELL: Do you need a moment?
COACH BRODHAUS: I'm good.
    I just want to get this done.
    It's my head that's a sack of farts.
        [taps fists on table; restrained anger]
    You know what I told my players before the Tostitos
    Fiesta Bowl,
        [dramatic pause]
    I told them,
    "Give me your 100%,
    And you will forever be the greatest there ever was."
        [slight pause]
    Those kids were gladiators that night,
    Motorized by a passion I inspired.
    And now I can't piss the word kitchen
    Without my brain burning,
    Like I've got a head full of syphilis.

WENDELL: Yeah, it can be hard . . .
>Keeping your mind on track,
>Just so you can get through the day
>Without feeling like an asshole.
>>*[blank]*
>I wanted to go to Hollywood,
>When I was in my twenties,
>Go to Hollywood and become the Midwestern Kurosawa.
>But then . . .
>You fall in love with a girl who wants to settle down,
>And so you settle for whatever will pay.
>Then that girl divorces you,
>And now you're working twice as much 'cause of the alimony,
>And . . .
>And you realize your's is an all too common tale.
>You look around you
>And all you notice is marinara crusting on dishes
>And a whole lot of shit that needs to be Swiffered.
>And you start to think of the kid you were . . .
>As the dumbest fuck . . .
>Who ever once walked this earth.
>As if what you were—
>What you still are—
>Is unforgivable.

COACH BRODHAUS: What's your name again?

WENDELL: Um . . .
>Wendell.
>It's Wendell.

COACH BRODHAUS: Well, Wendell,
>When I hear your story,
>You know what I hear?

WENDELL: No.

COACH BRODHAUS: I hear the whining whimper of a quitter.

WENDELL: *[clapping to the crew]*
>Alright, everybody!

COACH BRODHAUS: I hear a man who didn't fight for what he wanted.

WENDELL: *[to the crew]*
    Can we get ready?
    We're going to roll in a second.
COACH BRODHAUS: You're going to hear no a lot in life,
    Sure.
    But you can't ever say no to yourself.
    In every one of us,
    There lives a loser and winner.
    If you want the winner to succeed,
    You've got to hate the loser inside.
    That's how you become a champion,
    Wendell.
WENDELL: We have to continue on.
    We're going to start from the very top, okay?
    [exits]
COACH BRODHAUS: *[to self]*
    C'mon, Donny.
    You're not a failure!
    You can whup this commercial!
WENDELL: *[offstage]*
    Are you ready, Coach?
COACH BRODHAUS: *[to self]*
    Crush it,
    Donny boy,
    Crush it.
    [to Wendell]
    Yeah, I'm good.
WENDELL: *[offstage]*
    Okay.
    [Coach Brodhaus takes mark]
    And we're rolling.
COACH BRODHAUS: *[to camera]*
    I'm Coach Donny Brodhaus,
    Winner of this year's college football national championship.
    And when I sit down for a chumpionshap brakfust . . .
    [sigh]
    Jesus H. Christ playing hockey.

Let's keep going.
[to camera]
I'm Coach Donny Brodhaus,
Winner of this year's college football national championship.
And when I sit down for a championship breakfast,
I make sure MY KITCHEN
[gestures to behind him]
Has cabinet fronts and counter tops by Winston's Kitchens and Design.
Take it from a whimper like pluh/
We're not going back.
Fuck it.
I'm going to keep marching forward.
WENDELL: *[offstage]*
Still rolling.
COACH BRODHAUS: *[to self]*
You're a champion.
You're a champion with a poophead,
But you're still a champion.
[takes mark]
[to camera]
Take it from a winner like me,
When it comes to horn fumishings/
Staple my anus!
[to camera]
Take it from a winner like me,
When it comes to home furnishings,
It would help to remember your line.
COACH BROADHAUS: (*con't*)
[to camera]
Take it from a winner like me,
When it comes to home furnishings,
Winston's is the crapalapa dong ding.
[picks the apple up off the table and hurls it against the wall]
WENDELL: *[offstage]*
We don't need the apple.

Lawrence Harbison

Apple's not important to the shoot.

We're rooting for you, Coach.

I know you can finish this.

COACH BRODHAUS: Don't cut.

I'm going to slate this fucker.

[stiffly shakes out his body like Frankenstein's monster clearing himself of negativity vibes]

WENDELL: *[offstage]*

C'mon, Coach,

Woo,

You can nail this copy.

COACH BRODHAUS: Don't patronize me.

WENDELL: *[offstage]*

I'm . . .

I'm not/

COACH BRODHAUS: *[to camera]*

I'm Coach Donny Brodhaus,

Winner of this year's college football national championship.

And when I sit down for a championship breakfast,

I make sure MY KITCHEN

[gestures to behind him]

Has cabinet fronts and counter tops by Winston's Kitchens and Design.

Take it from a winner like me,

When it comes to home furnishings,

Winston's is the real champion.

They've been providing high-quality kitchen interiors since 1970.

COACH BROADHAUS: (*con't*)

And with their low, low prices,

You won't need to make millions

To look like you do.

[crosses arms; smiles]

So score a TD with your neighbors

With the style and class of a Winston's home.

Winston's Kitchens and Design:

It breakfasts completely.

AAGH!
[picks up the half grapefruit and crushes the juice
out of it;then he bites the rind]
WENDELL: *[offstage]*
That was great.
Lets go back to/
COACH BRODHAUS: Wendell.
Quiet.
Let me just . . .
[blank]
Let me get this done.
'kay?
So fucking quiet,
Wendell.
[deep cleansing breath;
cracks neck]
[to camera]
So score a TB with your nighborts/
[slams fist in the plate of eggs, bacon, and pan-
cakes]
[to camera]
So score a touchdown with your neighbors
With the style and class of a Winston's home.
Winston's Kitchens and Design:
It's what really makes a breakfast clompete.
[sucks teeth]
[to camera]
So score a touchdown with your neighbors
With the style and class of a Winston's home.
Winston's Kitchens and Design:
Eat bitches and die.
[grabs the box of cereal, shakes it and crushes it
(cereal should come out)]
COACH BROADHAUS: (*con't*)
[to camera]
Winston's Kitchens and Design:
Pleep pop poop.
[to camera]

Winston's Kitchens and Design:
It's a breakfast. Actually, it's a kitchen.
[to camera]
Winston's Kitchens and Design:
Where the fuck is the kitchen!
It's not here!
[to self]
You will not be defeated.
You will not lose.
You are the strongest.
You are the BEST.
[to camera]
So score a touchdown with your neighbors
With the style and class of a Winston's home.
Winston's Kitchens and Design:
It's what a complete breakfast makes.
[blank]
[trembling]
BITCH NIPPLES!
*[Coach Brodhaus starts flipping plates on the table,
slamming food against the floor or walls.]*
[slight pause]
*[Coach Brodhaus stares at the wreckage.
He's trembling.]*
BY THE COCK OF GOD, I AM SICK OF THIS.
*[He starts slamming chairs, tossing them to the floor.
He goes berserk. He flips the table. As extreme as
possible.]*
[Wendell enters.]
[picks up the chair and brandishes it at Wendell]
No. NO!
Stay back!
[Wendell scurries off]
[sets chair down and takes mark]
[to camera, calmly and professionally]
I'm Coach Donny Brodhaus,
Winner of this year's college football national champi-
onship.

And when I sit down for a championship breakfast,
I make sure MY KITCHEN
>   *[gestures to behind him]*
Has cabinet fronts and counter tops by Winston's Kitch-
ens and Design.
Take it from a winner like me,
COACH BROADHAUS: *(con't)*
>   When it comes to home furnishings,
>   Winston's is the real champion.
>   They've been providing high-quality kitchen interiors
>   since 1970.
>   And with their low, low prices,
>   You won't need to make millions
>   To look like you do.
>   *[crosses arms; smiles: NAILS IT!]*
>   So score a touchdown with your neighbors
>   With the style and class of a Winston's home.
>   Winston's Kitchens and Design:
>   It's what really makes a breakfast complete.
>   *[the sound of his heaving breath is now audible]*
>   *[A slow clap offstage.]*
WENDELL:
>   *[enters, slow clapping]*
>   *[slow clapping]*
>   *[still slow clapping]*
>   *[amid the wreckage,*
>   *Coach Brodhaus basks in the glory.]*
>   *[fade]*

>   *[blackout]*

>   The End

ICEBERG TO NOWHERE

Samantha Macher

PRODUCTION NOTES:

Iceberg to Nowhere was produced as part of Just the Tip: Theatre of NOTE's Late Night 10-Minute Plays (Los Angeles, CA)
Directed by Brian Allman

Cast:
   PHIL, Lisa Dring
   LYLE, Crystal Diaz

Produced by John Money and David LM McIntyre

Iceberg to Nowhere was also produced in June of 2011 as a part of Hell-Tro Theatre Collective's "HAPPENING" in Brooklyn, NY.
Directed by Sarah Azzinaro

Cast:
   LYLE, Sarah Azzinaro
   PHIL, Liz Torres

CHARACTERS:
PHIL: A penguin.
LYLE: Another penguin.

SETTING: An iceberg. To nowhere.

NOTE: The penguins have British accents.

Two penguins are on the tip of an iceberg drifting at sea. One penguin, Lyle is reading the paper. The other, Phil, is contemplating the cold.

PHIL: So.
LYLE: So.
> *Pause.*
PHIL: S'cold out here.
LYLE: S'Antarctica.
PHIL: S'warmer home.
LYLE: I reckon.
PHIL: But not much.
LYLE: No. Not much.
> *Plans for the holiday?*
PHIL: Swimmin'.
LYLE: Home?
PHIL: In-laws.
LYLE: Have they—
PHIL: Stopped trying to eat me?
LYLE: I reckon not—
PHIL: No. S'pose that's the risk you run when you marry for love.
LYLE: They warn against it, you know.
PHIL: Marryin' for love?
LYLE: Marryin' a Pole.
PHIL: Now that's just myopic.
LYLE: Co-minglin' with her kind—
PHIL: S'warm at night.
LYLE: She's at least twice your size.
PHIL: And her fur is so soft.
LYLE: But her teeth, bloke. And the fact alone that her family is constantly trying to eat you. Just seems.

PHIL: What?

LYLE: I dunno. 'Gainst nature I reckon. They look at one another.

PHIL: S'that's what you really think, huh?

LYLE: You know what? I take it back. I don't think anything.

PHIL: Sheila is lovely and you would know that if you'd even bother to come for dinner when she invites you.

LYLE: I've met her. I know she's lovely—

PHIL: Then why won't you come?

LYLE: Winter is busy—

PHIL: It's always winter—

LYLE: It's always busy.

> *(Pause.)*

PHIL: The last—

> *He clears his throat.*

The last time—

LYLE: What?

PHIL: —Nothin'

LYLE: What? What is it? What?

PHIL: She cried.

LYLE: Sheila?

PHIL: Sheila.

LYLE: What? Why?

PHIL: She thinks you don't like her.

LYLE: 'Course I like her. Just 'cause I don't think your relationship is—

PHIL: You cancelled last minute. After she spent all that time catching fish. She was very upset.

LYLE: Well you can tell her that I bloody well like her.

PHIL: S'hard to tell.

LYLE: I was the witness at your wedding.

PHIL: So?

LYLE: So?

PHIL: Yes. So.

LYLE: Doesn't that mean anything?

PHIL: Not necessarily. I mean, it's not like you had to rent a tux—

LYLE: What do you want me to do then?

PHIL: Prove you like her. Come for dinner.

LYLE: Fine. I'll come for dinner.

PHIL: Tuesday?

LYLE: Tuesday. Sounds lovely.

PHIL: Well, actually, Tuesday doesn't work. Board meeting. Thursday?

LYLE: Thursday.

PHIL: Ring round 'bout six.

LYLE: I don't get off 'til six.

PHIL: Drinks at six thirty then.

LYLE: Sounds delightful.

(He opens his paper back up and begins to read.)

PHIL: Look, if you're going to be a wank about it, don't bother.

LYLE: What is it you want, Phil?

PHIL: I want you to like Sheila.

LYLE: Fuckin' Christ. I already told you I like her, but if you want me to wax poetic, I think Sheila's a treasure, a bloody wonderful treasure of bounteous joy and beauty.

PHIL: And mirth. Don't forget mirth.

LYLE: A beacon of shinin', glorious mirth.

PHIL: Damn right she is.

LYLE: Splendid then. We agree.

(Pause.)

PHIL: I certainly hope so.

LYLE: Mm.

He goes back to reading.

PHIL: Seein' anyone?

LYLE: Unfortunately.

PHIL: Why don't you bring her round with you on Thursday?

LYLE: No.

PHIL: Why not?

LYLE: I'm not ready for that kind of commitment.

PHIL: Are you embarrassed of Sheila?

LYLE: No—

PHIL: Because if you are, don't bother coming. Don't bother at all—

LYLE: Phil.

PHIL: Because that is my wife! And I love her in spite of her enormous size, hairy body, and bone-crushing mandibles—

LYLE: Phil.

PHIL: And she loves me, all of me. Even down to my tiny beak.

(He points to his beak.)

LYLE: That is quite a tiny beak.

PHIL: I thought of having it enlarged, but Sheila says I'm perfect, just the way I am. Now that's acceptance if ever I've heard of—

LYLE: Hey Phil?

PHIL: What is it?

LYLE: Sod off.

PHIL: What?

LYLE: I'm not embarrassed of Sheila.

PHIL: What then?

LYLE: Can you just—

PHIL: Are you embarrassed of me?

LYLE: Constantly.

PHIL: Because I can't change who I am, and neither can Sheila—

LYLE: I just don't—

PHIL: We are a united front. Standing up against oppression. We are a source of hope for all inter-species couples, yearning to be—

LYLE: Stop talking!

PHIL: I don't think it's physically possible to do that.

LYLE: Just for a moment.

PHIL: What's wrong?

LYLE: My girl.

PHIL: What about her?

LYLE: She's with egg.

PHIL: Well! Congrats old man, that's quite excitin'—

LYLE: No. You don't understand.

PHIL: Sheila will make you something high in omega-three fatty acids for dinner on Tuesday.

LYLE: I thought we were meeting on Thursday?

PHIL: Right. Thursday. Sheila can catch some fish for you. Do you like fish?

LYLE: Don't worry about it.

PHIL: It's her specialty. First she catches it, and then we eat it.

LYLE: I'm sure it's delicious, but it won't be necessary.

Lawrence Harbison

PHIL: Look, if your girl doesn't like fish, I'm afraid she's out of luck. For all her talents, Sheila can really only make one dish. And that dish is fish.

LYLE: Fish is fine it's just that—

PHIL: Although I sometimes wonder what it might be like to eat something else. Something less fishy—

LYLE: Phil!

PHIL: And because she catches it herself, sometimes her hair gets in it, which is unappetizing at best—

LYLE: Phil—

PHIL: Now, don't say anything. But once, I saw Sheila eat a penguin.

LYLE: What?

PHIL: Barbaric, I know, but there was something so sexy about it. Dangerous! Like it could happen to me at any time—

LYLE: That's horrendous.

PHIL: I didn't say it wasn't horrendous, terrifying even, but very sexy, nonetheless. The way she pounced on that little butterball. She's got so much control, but when she loses it, oooh momma. Say, have you ever wondered what it would be like to eat another penguin?

LYLE: I'm leaving her.

PHIL: I bet it would taste like really delicious fish.

LYLE: Did you hear me? I'm leaving her.

PHIL: Who?

LYLE: My girl.

PHIL: The girl with the egg?

LYLE: Yes.

PHIL: But I thought—

LYLE: What?

PHIL: S'common in fact—

LYLE: What is common?

PHIL: That penguins. Well. We mate for life.

LYLE: I know.

PHIL: S'unnatural to—

LYLE: I know.

PHIL: S'against nature even—

LYLE: I know.

PHIL: But what will happen to the—

LYLE: I don't know.

PHIL: Because the father—
LYLE: I know.
PHIL: Have you told her?
  Silence.
 Alright. One fish then.
LYLE: Six-thirty?
PHIL: Six-thirty.
LYLE: This is my stop.
  He jumps into the water.
PHIL: See you Thursday.
  Lights down.

The End

iha df unbut dr ankt oom uch...
(the story of my life)

Craig McNulty & Nicole Pandolfo

PRODUCTION NOTES:

The STICKY Festival at the Bowery Poetry Club
04/01/2011
Directed by Ali Ayala

Cast:
GINA, Abby Lee
PAT, Matt Salmela

CHARACTERS:
PAT (thirty) Irish-American cousin to Gina
GINA (twenty-nine) Italian-American cousin to Pat

TIME: Noon.
PLACE: Church Reception Hall

AT RISE: PAT is dressed in an ill—fitting suit and is self consciously pouring the contents of his flask into a plastic cup. (THEY ARE DRINKING BUT AT NO POINT IS EITHER CHARACTER DRUNK . . . MAYBE A LITTLE BUZZED)

GINA: Can I get some of that?
PAT: Hey.
> *(They give each other a very awkward hug)*
> Gina, didn't see you at the church?
GINA: Couldn't get my goddamn mother out of the fuckin' beauty parlor in time. She woke up and decided she just had to be a blonde again. I guess if you've seen one First Holy Communion you've seen them all, right?
PAT: How you doing?
GINA: I'll be doing better with a . . .
> *(She indicates for him to pour her some booze)*
PAT: Yea, sure.
> *(Pat pours briefly into Gina's plastic cup)*
GINA: A drink Pat.
PAT: What's that?
GINA: A fucking sip.
> *(Grabs Pat's Flask)*
> If one more person asks me when I'm gonna find a husband and get married I'm gonna fucking lose it. I told Big Mike if he asked me again I'd rip his balls off and gouge his eyes out.
PAT: You could just say you don't wanna talk about it . . . that level of violence is very . . . specific.
GINA: Why does everyone give a shit, why don't they just keep getting fat and leave me the fuck alone?
PAT: I guess they need to project their self-loathing onto someone.

GINA: Yea, well I got enough of it from myself that I don't need anymore.

(Gina pous another shot)

PAT: Yo leave me some. This is a long day, come on, I need my medicine.

GINA: There's plenty left. And who are you kidding, you're halfway drunk as it is. You look like shit.

PAT: Thanks.

GINA: Oh Jesus my mom is giving me that 'don't make an asshole of yourself tonight' look. I wanna say 'excuse me are you or are you not the same woman who raised me with a Manhattan in your hand all the fucking time?'

PAT: Manhattan is a good drink. Classy and yet still strong.

GINA: Yea . . . *I'll have a Manhattan, I'll take a Manhattan, gimme a Manhattan . . .*

PAT: What's it been like a year since I saw you?

GINA: 13 months.

PAT: You look good.

GINA: Thanks.

PAT: You gotta boyfriend?

GINA: No. Do you have—

PAT: No. But I did just break up with someone.

GINA: I'm sorry.

PAT: It's ok. She sucked anyway.

GINA: Oh, well then congratulations.

PAT: Thanks.

GINA: You know what I like most about drinking with you?

PAT: My wit and humor only get amplified with each libation?

GINA: No. That no matter how fucked up I get I can look at you and not feel so bad.

PAT: Thanks. I'm self-conscious about this shit as it is, being from the Irish wing of the family.

GINA: Oh, yea, cause it's not like Italians drink.

PAT: But your tribe is known more for, ya know, pizza and mob shit and spaghetti sauce.

GINA: Its gravy.

PAT: Whatever.

GINA: It's not whatever, it's called gravy.

PAT: You go into a store it's called sauce, so everyone else other than fucking Italians are wrong?

GINA: Yes, we invented the shit you asshole!

PAT: Why are you yelling at me?!

GINA: How come you never called me?!

PAT: What?

GINA: How come you never called me after the last time we saw each other?

PAT: I . . . I don't know. I was confused.

GINA: Yea no shit, so was I. And I still called. You fuck!

PAT: Jesus Gina give me a break ok. There's no manual for how to deal with the aftermath of fucking a cousin.

GINA: Asshole! I actually used to think you were cool.

PAT: I still am, maybe not this second but/

GINA: /I'm so pathetic—you couldn't give a shit about that night. You were like, the one fucking person I looked forward to seeing at these family shit bag events.

PAT: You think this is easy for me? I been having panic attacks thinking about seeing you today! I been on a two week bender of Xanex and Scotch cause I didn't know how this would go, ok, so I do give a shit!

(PAT POPS ONE PILL, MAYBE SEVERAL)

GINA: You really went on a run of booze and pills because of me?

(pause)

That is so sweet.

PAT: This is fucking great, I just put my ass out there and you break my balls.

GINA: I'm serious! I'm always the asshole who ends up having Jack and OJ everyday for breakfast to get over some guy.

PAT: When we hooked up you had just broken up with Vinnie.

GINA: Which one?

PAT: Fuck should I know, what, maybe the pool cleaner from Perth Amboy?

GINA: Vinnie number 3—really good looking, really fucking stupid.

PAT: Yea,ok, that's great. You came to the wedding all weepy and emotional and it was an open bar.

GINA: Best fucking thing about weddings.

PAT: And you looked so bummed out and it reminded me of when Bernice broke my heart and—

GINA: Freshman year of high school Bernice? The one who

gave you crabs? You were sad about that?

PAT: Yea. My first broken heart. And I just related and I knew the only thing that would make you feel better would be to get drunk.

GINA: Oh God, remember I pissed all over myself and my handbag in the parking lot?

PAT: Yea. It was really well lit in that parking lot.

GINA: You kept feeding me all those mini—bar drinks in the room.

(GINA STARTS GIVING PAT DIRTY LOOK.)

You know, come to think of it, it sounds like I was really so drunk that us doing it mighta been you taking advantage of me.

PAT: What? I didn't take advantage of you. You were drunk but not that drunk. You were begging me for it.

GINA: Begging you? You fucking wish.

PAT: You wanted me. Said you always had.

GINA: I don't, really remember, saying quite that.

PAT: It's ok. I always wanted to fuck you too.

GINA: Pat!

PAT: Sorry.

GINA: Well we did, so hooray.

PAT: Yea*h,* I mean, you were really into it.

GINA: So were you.

PAT: Yea, but you were like really really into it.

GINA: I don't do shit half assed.

PAT: You kept saying you just wanted somebody to love you. Over and over. Just someone to love you. You were so sad I just wanted to make you feel better.

GINA: So . . . wait, let me get this straight, I was a sympathy fuck!

PAT: No, Jesus, I was, after, I felt, I was worried that you'd think I was some asshole and not someone who like . . .

GINA: What?

PAT: Loves you!

GINA: Pat, what the fuck?! You can't just say something like that! Oh Christ, you're drunk.

PAT: I AM NOT! *(pause)* Significantly buzzed, yes. But that's not what this is about!

GINA: You fucking say you love me, why cause you think it'll get you a repeat of our night at the Ramada?

Lawrence Harbison   107

PAT: No! Well, yea, I mean I wanna be with you but not in a drunken one night stand of having sex on the bed, in the shower, on the bathroom floor, against the wall, in the window and in the closet kinda way, but, like, us, together, in a real way.

GINA: I don't remember us doing it in closet.

PAT: You wanted to hold onto the clothes hanger while I . . .

GINA: Ok Pat, yes, now I'm remembering.

PAT: Yea. You're the only person I've ever been with where there was nothing missing.

> *(pause)*

GINA: Me too . . . with you I just feel good.

PAT: Everyone else there's always something that's just not there—they don't get you, you don't get them, blah blah blah. Same shit that ruins every relationship, but when I was with you I didn't feel that way. It felt right.

GINA: Then why the fuck didn't you call me?

PAT: Because Gina, we're cousins. Ok, how could I let myself fall in love with a cousin? Christ, I can remember you at 11 with pigtails and an overbite.

GINA: Thank god my mom was sober long enough to get me braces.

PAT: And now I've had my dick in you. This kinda shit isn't supposed to happen. And worse, I'm in love with you.
You don't have sex with a cousin and you really don't fall in love with one.

GINA: Please don't say you love me unless you mean it.

PAT: I swear to Christ I do.

GINA: Cause if you're fucking with me I'll rip your balls out with a rusty spoon and shove them up your ass as I watch you die.

> *(pause)*
> Pat?

PAT: Yea, I was just picturing that. Your threats of violence are always so very very . . . specific.

GINA: Ok, so even though you know all my shit and how crazy I can get and all the trouble that I am and all of that you still want to be with me?

PAT: More than anything.

GINA: You never know if a night of crazy drunk sex is going

to be a one niter where you can only hope your first guess at their name the next day is right and you didn't get herpes . . . or if it's gonna be the real thing . . . always hope it's the real thing then I never—

PAT: This is the real thing.

GINA: My mom's gonna be really pissed.

PAT: Probably.

GINA: Definitely. Oh my god, family events are gonna be awkward. Like way more than usual.

PAT: That's why God invented alcohol & Xanex.

GINA: Wait, this isn't illegal or anything, is it?

PAT: Not in New Jersey.

GINA: If we had kids would they have all that assburgers thing?

PAT: Like would they turn out to be like that banjo playing kid in deliverance?

GINA: Yea. Because, that would suck.

PAT: There's only a 4.4% chance. I googled it. I'd really like to give this a try.

GINA: I cried a lot over you after that night. Like, for six months straight. And then another six months with seething bitter anger towards you. I don't know if I can go through that again.

PAT: Let me make it up to you . . .

HE REACHES FOR HER HAND, SHE GIVES IT TO HIM. THEY EMBRACE. LIGHTS DOWN.

The End

ITALY

Steven Schutzman

Alive Theatre
The Lafayette Building
528 East Broadway
Long Beach, CA 90802
August-September, 2010
Directed by Dennis Hoffman

CHARACTERS:
WOMAN, thirties
MAN, thirties

TIME: The present.
SETTING: A bedroom. A bed and a chair at least.

*(WOMAN and MAN in bed after love making. WOMAN, tense
and wide awake, MAN: blissfully asleep. Distantly, a WOM-
AN sings a haunting, wordless melody. Singing fades.)*

WOMAN: *(Prodding him.)* Hey, you better go.
MAN: Huh?
WOMAN: You've got to go.
MAN: What? Huh?
WOMAN: Go. You need to go now.
MAN: Go? I . . . . Go where?
WOMAN: Away.
MAN: You want some space?
WOMAN: Just go.
MAN: If you want some space, Sweetie, just say so?
WOMAN: You've already left so you might as well leave. Go.
    Go. Go to where you've already gone. Far away from here.
    Clean, quick and far.
MAN: But I haven't gone anywhere . . . I was just asleep . . .
    That was so nice. Right? Come here. *(She's rigid)* You
    want to talk?
WOMAN: No.
MAN: Okay. *(beat)* Okay. Where have I gone?
WOMAN: How should I know? A beautiful country, far from
    here.
MAN: Cool.
WOMAN: A country known for its pleasures.
MAN: Like Italy. You know how I love Italian food.
WOMAN: Italy. Italy. I should have known you'd go to Italy.
MAN: I'd love to go to Italy with you.
WOMAN: Go. Get out. Quick, clean and far. So I can't even
    reach you by phone.
MAN: You can always reach someone by phone these days.
    There's no getting away from the phone anymore.

WOMAN: I should be used to it.

MAN: What?

WOMAN: But I'm not used to it.

MAN: What *(beat)* Feeling vulnerable, Sweetie? Come here.

WOMAN: Stay away from me.

MAN: Come here, Sweetheart. I thought you were drifting off too, like we usually do.

WOMAN: I will mourn as if you had died. *(He reaches for her)* Stop it and get out.

MAN: Okay.

> *(He doesn't move. Beat. Beat.)*

WOMAN: Why are you doing this to me?

MAN: What?

WOMAN: This. This.

MAN: What? What is it? Sadness. You're sad. Come here, Baby.

WOMAN: No. Don't touch me.

MAN: I'm sorry I fell asleep.

WOMAN: Too late. Get out.

> *(Long pause.)*

MAN: I think you like being sad.

WOMAN: Now that's helpful.

MAN: Well, it's true.

WOMAN: You're either sad or you're not sad. Liking sadness has nothing to do with it.

MAN: That makes sense.

WOMAN: Someone has to be sad and I know you won't be.

MAN: I've never been happier in my life.

WOMAN: See, I told you.

MAN: I give up. *(Beat)* So you're sad because I'm not sad, is that it? *(beat)* So because I'm not sad you're going to make me sad? *(beat)* That's not fair.

WOMAN: I'll tell you what's not fair: You being in Italy while I'm in the sinking boat of this bed trying to bail the water out all by myself.

MAN: I'll help. I really want to help. Just show me the water. Show me where it's coming in. Give me a bucket. Please, tell me what's going on.

WOMAN: Too late. If you don't know, I'm not telling you.

MAN: People can't always feel the same thing at the same time.

Lawrence Harbison

WOMAN: How's the weather in Italy?

MAN: You want me to be sad with you? Is that it? Because sadness is part of loving. I know that.

WOMAN: Loving is impossible to bear.

MAN: A few minutes ago, we were happy, ecstatic.

WOMAN: That was sex. Loving is impossible to bear.

MAN: And getting more impossible all the time.

WOMAN: Is that a threat?

MAN: I love you. I've never been happier in my life.

WOMAN: Too late. Isn't it great to be in Italy where the women are beautiful and undemanding and never sad? Isn't it great to be in Italy?

MAN: But . . .

WOMAN: Get out. Get out. Get out.

MAN: Oh all right.

(MAN gets out of bed and sits in chair nearby.)

WOMAN: If I feel alone, I might as well be alone.

(MAN starts to get dressed. He gets an idea and pretends to write.)

MAN: My Dearest Darling, I can't tell you how much I regret this stupid trip. Nothing but rain and cold for days on end. I've never been so miserable in my life. I thought Italy was supposed to be warm and sunny.

WOMAN: Finally. Loneliness.

MAN: It's been raining for so long the local vineyards are about to lose their entire crop of grapes; the wheat had to be harvested before it was ready; the roots of the basil plants have rotted from the constant damp; and mushrooms have begun to sprout from the faces of the town's old men.

WOMAN: The loneliness I was made for.

MAN: What a disaster. Cold and damp everywhere, even under these covers. Impossible to get warm. I miss you terribly and can't wait to hold you in my arms again. Signed, your true and everlasting love. So much for Italy.

WOMAN: The local people are used to this period of constant rain. It happens every year and they frolic in it like sleek otters. Local tradition has named it the 'downpour de las bombas' because of how the rain makes the white peasant blouses cling to the ripe breasts of their young women who have nothing else to do in the bad weather but serve the needs of the town's only tourist.

MAN: Thousands of rats have swarmed from the flooded sewers seeking higher ground. They line the rooftops like vicious pigeons and grind their teeth at passers by. There are rumors of plague in the region. I can't stop shivering. I need immediate medical attention but the mountain roads have become impassable and all the phone lines are down.

WOMAN: A fire burns constantly in the stone fireplace in the hotel room of the town's only tourist, the wine of the region flows like wine and the beautiful young women pile their great steaming tits on top of the tourist to keep him warm.

MAN: Pile their great steaming tits. Wow. That's terrific. See, we're terrific together. Can I please come back to bed? I'll do things to you.

(WOMAN throws her hand up like a traffic cop to stop him.)

WOMAN: The isolation of this mountain region has created a Rubenesque female gene pool.

MAN: Jesus Christ, that's good. You don't know how electric you are to me right now. I have never loved you so much. Please don't make me leave.

WOMAN: You've already left. How's Italy?

MAN: I spend every rain-ruined day under the damp covers writing letters to my love back home, letters I can never mail in this one horse town without a horse or a doctor. But still I write as a hopeless act of devotion to the only one who can end my misery. I write of how much I love her, of how I am filled with regret, of how much more of this rain-soaked penance I would endure to be forgiven for the selfish act of falling asleep after lovemaking. My body quakes with fever, my brain swells and my stiffening fingers smear the ink into an indecipherable mess but still I write her these unreadable letters I can never send.

WOMAN: I knew this would happen. I haven't heard from the son of a bitch since he left. I turn my bedroom upside down and scrape it for his skin oils. I play our favorite music so many times it becomes nonsense to me. I sweep the floor of our commingled hair and burn it in exorcism.

MAN: This is the end. I'm burning up, dying. My shivering won't stop, I can't breathe or hold food down and have lost

---

Lawrence Harbison

thirty pounds. Insects dot the ceiling like greedy relatives waiting for me to die, the stone walls of my room glow with cold and no one here speaks a word of English.

WOMAN: Language has always been the greatest obstacle to pure animal pleasure. First, a thought inserts itself into the left brain . . .

MAN: Left brain? Come on, Sweetie. I'm sick and dying in Italy.

WOMAN: Quiet. Don't interrupt. Language has always been the greatest obstacle to pure animal pleasure. First, a thought penetrates your left brain and then that thought lays its eggs like an insect queen, the eggs hatch into words and you can't stop thinking them. It's the signal disorder of modern man, too many words, super self-consciousness. The sexy and free, unthinking and non-verbal, young women of this isolated region have no such problems.

MAN: That's very good, how you made that connection. I really can't keep up with you. Okay. Okay. *(beat)* The young women of the town don't think at all, or bathe. Civilization never really reached this remote place.

WOMAN: Civilizing ideas like marriage and . . .

MAN: You want to get married? Is that it? Let's do it.

WOMAN: Civilizing ideas like marriage and . . .

MAN: . . . toothpaste . . .

WOMAN: Like marriage and sexual taboos have never reached this isolated mountain region where there are no phone lines and cell phones are as useless as watches, umbrellas and . . .

MAN: . . . toothpaste . . .

WOMAN: As watches, umbrellas and brassieres. Uncomplicated creatures serving the town's tourist trade, each young woman lets the foreigner have his way with her.

MAN: These smelly women cling to me like the mold on the hotel walls. I can't get a moment alone.

WOMAN: Finally. Loneliness. The loneliness that I was made for. If I feel alone, I might as well be alone. To hell with the bastard. He's out of my life forever. Good riddance.

MAN: I'm really starting to enjoy these young women who have not conceived of themselves as destined to have their hearts broken and do not feel compelled to bring on this destiny in self-fulfilling prophesy.

WOMAN: Get out.

MAN: Sweetheart, sweetheart, come on, let me back in bed please.

WOMAN: No.

MAN: I promise I won't leave again.

WOMAN: You've already left.

MAN: You're being very unreasonable, you know that?

WOMAN: I don't care. Get out.

MAN: I'm going.

WOMAN: I knew that. I knew you'd do that.

MAN: But you chased me out.

WOMAN: You're supposed to fight harder.

MAN: You're being impossible. *(beat)* All right. I'll fight to the death for you with you.

WOMAN: Too late. Loving is impossible to bear.

MAN: I'll call you tomorrow, okay?

WOMAN: I guess.

MAN: Can't you tell me what it is?

WOMAN: No. There are no words.

MAN: Bye.

> *(MAN exits.)*

WOMAN: Who are you?

> *(As the lights start to slowly fade, the haunting, wordless melody is heard again.)*

WOMAN: *(cont'd)* Now that he's gone, my loneliness lies in bed with me like a young woman who sings herself to sleep and keeps on singing the same sad song in her dreams. Hers is a beautiful, sad and never-ending song of lovers separated by a great sea.

> *(Singing. Final fade to black. End of play.)*

The End

JINXED

K. Alexa Mavromatis

PRODUCTION NOTES:

June 2010 at Center Stage, NY, as part of Renegade Red-head Productions' *Last Day on Earth* evening of short plays. The production was directed, in association with Boomerang Theatre Company, by Marielle Duke.

Cast:
    MEATLOAF, Catherine McNelis
    STRINGBEAN, Philip Emeott

CHARACTERS:
MEATLOAF, a woman.
STRINGBEAN, a man.

SETTING: Detritus of city, perhaps Boston.
TIME: Three days post-apocalypse.

> The blizzard, the blizzard of the world has crossed the thresholdAnd it has overturned the order of the soul.
>
> — *Leonard Cohen*

> We're all alone, no chaperone
> Can get our number
> The world's in slumber—let's misbehave!
>
> — *Cole Porter*

A note

Jinxed is for a director with a twisted take on the universe and an ear for the rhythm of comedic insanity. Timing is crucial, and the play benefits from intelligent actors who are not afraid to be physical. It's a workout. Meatloaf and Stringbean were originally written as characters in their fifites; and while I still hold that actors in mid—life work best, I've seen younger performers do a great job, too. Either way, I do feel that casting actors who are of similar age to one another is crucial.

Rules and consequences of the game of Jinx differ from region to region, era to era. Some of the rules included here are real; others are simply made up. Also, whoopie pies: These treats are a New England phenomenon, consisting of two round chocolate cake slices with creamy white icing holding them together. (Imagine a soft Oreo on steroids.) Have fun.

Three days post apocalypse. Detritus of city, perhaps Boston. MEATLOAF, a woman wearing one spike heel, and STRINGBEAN, a man wearing broken black glasses and a military—style jacket with lots of pockets, are the sole survivors. Both are hungry, and seemingly on the brink of insanity. MEATLOAF stands downstage, staring into the darkness. STRINGBEAN fusses with a walkie—talkie.

STRINGBEAN: *(Stopping to study her)* Well, you sure as hell wore the wrong shoes.

> *STRINGBEAN hands her one of the walkie—talkies and walks upstage. MEATLOAF laughs.*

STRINGBEAN: What?

MEATLOAF: Nothing.

STRINGBEAN: What?

MEATLOAF: It figures. The end of the world. Me. *You*. As if the rats and roaches weren't bad enough.

STRINGBEAN: I don't see what's so funny about that. (Into the walkie—talkie) Meatloaf . . . Stringbean to Meatloaf. Do you copy?

> *(MEATLOAF glares downstage.)*

STRINGBEAN: (Hiding, into his walkie-talkie) Stringbean to Meatloaf. What's your 20?

> *MEATLOAF continues to stare straight ahead.*

STRINGBEAN: *(Louder)* Meatloaf! Meatloaf?! Do you copy?!

MEATLOAF: Yeah, I copy—*because I'm ten fucking feet away from you*.

STRINGBEAN: Goddammit. If these things would work, we could divide and conquer, and still, you know, talk . . . Do you understand?

MEATLOAF: Well, I told you they wouldn't work. And stop calling me that. *Jessica*. Or Jess is fine, but you . . .

STRINGBEAN: I dreamed I cooked you a meatloaf.

MEATLOAF: You dreamed?

STRINGBEAN: I always dream.

MEATLOAF: About *food*.

STRINGBEAN: Well . . .

MEATLOAF: Okay, you're obsessing over food, David, and it's really starting to . . .

STRINGBEAN: *(Covering his ears, turning red)* Stringbean! I am Stringbean! Call me Stringbean! Stringbeeeeeeeeeean!

MEATLOAF: This is *food psychosis*. Do you hear me?

STRINGBEAN: No!

MEATLOAF: *Food psychosis*. You are the living embodiment of . . . ! You are *cracking up*!

STRINGBEAN: No.

MEATLOAF: And I'll tell you something . . .

STRINGBEAN: What?

MEATLOAF: . . . I'll tell you something else . . .

STRINGBEAN: What?

MEATLOAF: I don't want to hear *one more word* about how hungry you are. Because you know what I ate yesterday? Nothing. And the day before that? *An expired pack of Carl Buddig sliced turkey I had to pry from the hand of a dead guy.* So fuck you.

STRINGBEAN: Fuck you.

BOTH: *Fuck you!*

MEATLOAF: Jinx!

STRINGBEAN: What?

MEATLOAF: Jinx.

STRINGBEAN: What are you . . . ?

MEATLOAF: We both said 'fuck you' at the same time. So I'm calling j . . .

STRINGBEAN: You can't call . . .

MEATLOAF: The hell I *can't.*

STRINGBEAN: Eh! You mean to tell me . . . You have a Ph.D. from fucking *Brandeis*, and you're calling 'jinx'?

MEATLOAF: That's right. *(Punching him in the arm)* Enough with the food obsession freak show. *Dr. Meatloaf is calling jinx.*

STRINGBEAN: *(Rubbing his arm)* What was your dissertation? Punch buggy?

MEATLOAF: *(Punching him again)* Actually, that was my master's thesis. My dissertation was a survey of the societal implications of Jinx and related playground games on cultures throughout history, ranging from post-colonial Caribbean settlements to contemporary North America. With an emphasis on the Victorians. I love them.

STRINGBEAN: Are you for fucking real?

MEATLOAF: *(Punching him again)* I should probably warn you: You're in danger of invoking the Quadruple Jinx American Buffalorumpus, a common variation in the Great Plains. You really should just stop talking.

> *STRINGBEAN purses his lips and raises his hands in defeat. He plops himself down on an overturned crate.*

MEATLOAF: And when I decide to say your name—which

isn't going to be for *a long damn time*—you can open your mouth again.

MEATLOAF starts to rummage through some of the rubbish that litters the stage. She is looking for food. As she goes, she occasionally glances over at STRINGBEAN, but eventually forgets he is there. STRINGBEAN, meanwhile, takes a whoopie pie out of his coat pocket, and begins to eat it. It's messy, and he enjoys it very, very much, to an almost pornographic degree. He reaches the last bite.

MEATLOAF: *(Taking note of what he's doing for the first time)* What's that?

STRINGBEAN: *(Mouth full)* Hmmmmmmm?

MEATLOAF: What do you have?

During the following, STRINGBEAN, still under jinx, refuses to speak. His intended communications —which he expresses by making noise and gesturing —are in brackets. MEATLOAF becomes increasingly agitated.

STRINGBEAN: [I don't know.]

MEATLOAF: *(Grabbing his hand)*Let me see . . .

STRINGBEAN: [You won't let me talk.]

MEATLOAF: Where did you get that?

STRINGBEAN: [I can't tell you.]

MEATLOAF: *Where did you find that?*

STRINGBEAN: [You won't let me talk.]

MEATLOAF: Are there any more?

STRINGBEAN: [I can't tell . . .]

MEATLOAF: Tell me!

STRINGBEAN: [Hey, you called jinx!]

MEATLOAF: STRINGBEAN!

STRINGBEAN: Aha!

MEATLOAF: Shit!

STRINGBEAN: Ha—gotcha!

MEATLOAF: Goddammit!

STRINGBEAN: You said my first name!

MEATLOAF: *(She punches him in the arm—thinking quickly on her feet)* But I didn't say your *middle* name. Midwestern variation . . .

STRINGBEAN: You don't *know* my middle name.

MEATLOAF: . . .and your name isn't Stringbean anyway.

STRINGBEAN: *(Punching her in the arm)* Stringbean!

MEATLOAF: *(Punching him in the arm again)* Ow! Don't hit *me—you're* the one under jinx!

STRINGBEAN: That's not how we played it in Chicago.

MEATLOAF: I don't give a shit how you played it in Chicago.

STRINGBEAN: Well, I should think you would care a lot, *doctor*, because you should know that *in Chicago*, you'd be buying me a Coke right about now, because you didn't call "Lock" after jinxing me the first time, which means that you're not the only one who can release me from the jinx. So I released myself. And that means the jinx doubles back on you. Ha!

MEATLOAF: Everyone knows that move requires a third person.

STRINGBEAN: *This is an extenuating circumstance!*

MEATLOAF: *Life* is an extenuating circumstance! You're creating your own rules here, David . . .

STRINGBEAN: Stringbean!

MEATLOAF: Oh. My. God.

STRINGBEAN: *Stringbean*!!!

MEATLOAF: Where are they?

STRINGBEAN: What?

MEATLOAF: The *whoopie pies*! Where did you find it?

STRINGBEAN: Over there. There was a whole case . . .

> *MEATLOAF crosses to the area of the stage where STRINGBEAN is pointing. She picks up an empty box, turns it over. Wads of whoopie pie wrappers fall to the ground. MEATLOAF lets out a cry of anguish. It is the saddest sound we've ever heard.*

STRINGBEAN: I found them last night.

MEATLOAF: Last *night*?!

STRINGBEAN: Oh, and I ate them all. Whoops. I guess that's makes them whoopsie pies . . . *(Laughing to himself)* Get it—whoops . . .

> *Screaming, like a warrior running into battle, MEATLOAF lunges at STRINGBEAN and grabs his neck.*

STRINGBEAN: Hey!

MEATLOAF: *(Choking him)* You *bastard*!

STRINGBEAN: *(Coughing, gasping)* Whoa, whoa, hey . . . !

MEATLOAF: I hate you, and I don't care if you *are* the only other person left on the face of the fucking earth!

STRINGBEAN: Ouch!

> *He stomps on her bare foot.*

MEATLOAF: Ow! Goddammit!

STRINGBEAN: *(Grabbing her hair)* Look, wait . . .

MEATLOAF: Owww . . .

> *They are in an odd embrace. MEATLOAF still has her hands around STRINGBEAN's throat; he is pulling her hair with both hands. STRINGBEAN's foot is on top of MEATLOAF's bare foot. MEATLOAF digs her spike heel into STRINGBEAN's calf, but keeps losing her balance.*

STRINGBEAN: *(Softly)* There's one left.

> *They freeze. She looks at him, hungry and wild-eyed. Suspicious.*

STRINGBEAN: In my pocket. Look here, Meatloaf. One more.

> *They slowly untangle. She looks at him.*

STRINGBEAN: All for you.

> *MEATLOAF holds out her hand.*

STRINGBEAN: Eh, eh, eh.

MEATLOAF: You ate the whole frickin' case.

STRINGBEAN: Oh no no no . . .

MEATLOAF: C'mon. Don't be an ass . . . Gimme.

STRINGBEAN: Manners, manners! I'll give it to you . . .

> *MEATLOAF holds out her hand.*

STRINGBEAN: . . . but you have to let me feed you.

MEATLOAF: Oh no way.

STRINGBEAN: Oh then no pie.

MEATLOAF: Oh, nonononono . . .

STRINGBEAN: How hungry are you *really*, Meatloaf?

MEATLOAF: Fuck you.

STRINGBEAN: You know you want it.

MEATLOAF: Nope, not really. I don't want it that bad.

STRINGBEAN: Hate to have to eat it all by myself . . .

MEATLOAF: No, no, go for it. Seriously. No problem.

STRINGBEAN: Okay, suit yourself then.

STRINGBEAN squeezes the whoopie pie until the cream oozes out of the side. MEATLOAF watches him lick the cream off his fingers.

STRINGBEAN: Mmmm . . . This is even better that the last one.

STRINGBEAN holds his hand out to her. His fingers are coated with cream.

STRINGBEAN: Here.

MEATLOAF kneels slowly, cautiously, under STRINGBEAN's hand. She begins licking the cream from his fingers.

STRINGBEAN: Good.

He holds out the remaining piece of pie.

STRINGBEAN: It's good.

He smears cream onto her face. She licks her lips.

STRINGBEAN: So good.

MEATLOAF: Mmmm . . .

STRINGBEAN: Mmmm . . . yeah.

MEATLOAF bites STRINGBEAN's hand.

STRINGBEAN: Ow! *Fuck!* Oh my god!

MEATLOAF: *(Through teeth clenched around his fingers)* Give me the rest of the pie!

STRINGBEAN screams and drops the remaining whoopie pie on the floor. MEATLOAF grabs it and eats it. He watches her, wincing, shaking his hand.

STRINGBEAN: *(In pain, blowing on and shaking his hand)* You hurt me!

MEATLOAF: *(Mouth full)* Well you deserved it, asshole—not telling me . . .

STRINGBEAN: Owwwwww. Owwwwww . . .

Overlapping, they reach "I hate you" at the same time:

MEATLOAF:	STRINGBEAN:
You're a creep, you know that? A big creep! Your stupid walkie—talkies and your condescending tone—"Do you understand?" Like you're God's gift . . . Well, *I* don't think so. In fact, *I hate you!*	My hand! I can't believe . . . Don't bite the hand that feeds . . . you ever heard of that? Women! You vicious . . . You know what, I don't care if you do hate me, because I hate *you!*

BOTH: Jinx!
BOTH: Double jinx!
BOTH: Triple jinx!
BOTH: Quadruple jinx!
BOTH: Quintuple jinx!
BOTH: Hextuple jinx!
BOTH: Septuple jinx!
BOTH: Octuple jinx!
>*Pause. They stare into each others' eyes.*
BOTH: What comes after 'octuple'?
BOTH: Jinx!
BOTH: Double jinx!
BOTH: Triple jinx!
BOTH: Quadruple jinx!
BOTH: Quintuple jinx!
BOTH: Hextuple jinx!
BOTH: Septuple jinx!
BOTH: Octuple jinx!
>*They are out of breath, looking at one another. They*
>*still don't know what comes after "octuple."*
STRINGBEAN: You know, I have to tell you... I've always had a little crush on you.
>*MEATLOAF stands up on her one spike heel. She is*
>*taller than STRINGBEAN. MEATLOAF half smiles,*
>*half grimaces. She likes him too.*
>*MEATLOAF: (Punching him in the arm) You're a*
>*little short for a string bean.*
>*Blackout.*

The End

Just Us

Jon Spano

PRODUCTION NOTES:

Emerging Artists Theatre
March 7 through March 20, 2011 at TADA!
New York City.
Directed by Barbara Grecki

Cast:
TRACEY, Tommy Day Carey
SAMARA, Erin Hadley

CHARACTERS

TRACY MALE: Twenties. Samara's husband. A handsome, take-charge kind of guy determined to parlay recent fame as a Reality-TV star into a multi-media brand. Like many charming men, he's ultimately self-centered and deceptive.

SAMARA FEMALE: Twenties. A pretty but uncomplicated woman who's more content being a stay-at-home Mom than a Reality-TV star. She finds herself caught in a whirlwind of domestic intrigue and plummets from innocence into frightened confusion and desperation.

TIME / PLACE: Pretty much around now. The U.S.
SETTING: Tracy and Samara's place. Not realistic.

A plunger; tool box; two chairs; can of Drano.
Children's toys, games, and clothes.

> *In the blackout, an audio montage of various Reality*
> *TV shows. Lights rise on SAMARA, folding laundry*
> *as TRACY, her husband, plunges away at a clog in*
> *the kitchen sink. Tracy's tool box is on the counter.*
> *Stuffed animals and children's toys lie about.*

TRACY: And the wife has two sisters. One's a nun. The other's a prostitute.

SAMARA: This clog reminds me of our first apartment Tracy, remember?

TRACY: You play the wife of course. And I'm your husband. Just like we did on *Houseguest.* Dylan and Tyler can play the boys again. Same basic set-up as before, you following?

SAMARA: *(Fond memory.)* Remember the awful plumbing and the rusty pipes?

TRACY: *(Plunging harder and faster.)* Yeah—yeah. Except we all go to India together. To an ashram. We never went to an ashram on *Houseguest* now did we?

SAMARA: And remember you built a crib because I was pregnant with Dylan?

TRACY: Uh-huh. And maybe we foster a child for the purposes of the trip. A child with a *disease.*

SAMARA: Maple, wasn't it? Or was it oak?

TRACEY: It's the same yet different Samara, don't you think?

> *(Cone of light on SAMARA Flashback. The "interview" portion of the TV show she and Tracy were recently on. TRACY freezes.)*

SAMARA: So here it is, first day of the shoot and any regrets I had it's too late now. Our houseguest arrives soon, a sixty-two-year-old nurse. So I'm like "whatever." Tracy says our lives are about to change forever.

> *(Sighs.)*

I don't like change.

> *(Lights change, the present. SAMARA looks into the sink as TRACY plunges briskly.)*

TRACY: So? Don't you think it's different?

SAMARA: Oh look! The water's going down. Counterclockwise.

TRACY: And we go to Cambodia and live together in a hut. Near a river.

SAMARA: I think it's because of how the earth—

TRACY: And then I drown Dylan and Tyler in the river.

SAMARA: *(Realizing what he just said.)* Spins. Wait. You what?!

TRACY: I'm *kidding!* Just wanna see if you're listening.

SAMARA: Of course I am. I mean, where do you get all this stuff from?

TRACY: I get it from *life*. You just take everyday life and give it a little twist. All we need is one good twist and we're set. Barry will offer us another show. He said I might even get a shot at creating my *own* show this time! I'll become a *brand*! Like Ryan.

SAMARA: I don't want you to be a brand. And I want Barry to stop calling.

TRACY: You'd prefer I go back to selling cars? No way in hell!

> *(Cone of light on TRACY, the past: His turn now. SAMARA freezes.)*

TRACY: *(cont'd)* I don't believe in fate *per se*, but I *do* believe in *luck*. It was *fortuitous* the day Barry walked into the

---

showroom and said those five magic words: "I. Want. You. On. *Houseguest*."—I want to make something of my life. This is my last chance.

(Lights change, the present. They resume.)

SAMARA: Everything I did on *Houseguest* I did for *you*. For *your* career. You don't need me anymore.

TRACY: No, of course I need you. "Tracy" without "Samara" is like . . . "Ricky without Lucy."

"Ben" without "Hur . . . ."

(THEY share a "between them" laugh.)

SAMARA: "Ben" without . . . .You see, this is what I miss. Laughing at your bad jokes. But I told you when the show ended that I didn't want to be involved anymore. The boys and I, we want a normal life.

TRACY: But I want us to be happy.

SAMARA: I *am* happy!

TRACY: We can be happier. There's always room for more.

(Cone of light on Samara. Flashback. SAMARA resumes the interview. TRACY freezes.)

SAMARA: "More." Tracy's favorite word is "more." I'm a good wife and mother but I have my limits. I like my privacy. Tracy loves all the attention and he's like, "But this is going to be so much fun!"

(Sighs.)

I'm still waiting for the "fun" part.

(Lights change, the present. Throughout, SAMARA will fold and clean. TRACY will tinker with his tools.)

TRACY: Barry says strike while the iron's hot. Before audiences forget who we are.

SAMARA: Barry, Barry, *Barry!* Jesus you hadn't seen the guy in ten years and suddenly it's, "My best friend *Barry!*"

TRACY: You gotta admire Barry's drive. He doesn't let anything stand in his way.

SAMARA: Oh. So I'm standing in your way is that it?

(Silence.)

Well am I?

TRACY: Maybe a little.

SAMARA: What about the boys?

(Cone of light on Tracy, Flashback. TRACY resumes interview. SAMARA freezes.)

TRACY: Dylan and Tyler are the light of my life. But Samara just doesn't get it sometimes, so I have to really pull her in, you know? Throw a wrench to get her going. It only works when everything's a great big mess. It's kinda cool.

(Lights change. Continuing right where they left off.)

SAMARA: Are Dylan and Tyler in your way too?

TRACY: Frankly? Sometimes I wish they'd stay at your mother's more often.

SAMARA: I'll call Mother. I'm sure she won't mind keeping the boys another night.

TRACY: Maybe she can keep them for the rest of the summer . . . I mean, don't you ever get tired of it?

SAMARA: Of what exactly?

TRACY: *(As the kids; Whiney bastards.)* "Mommy I'm hungry. I want to go swimming! Daddy I want the new *X-Men*!"

SAMARA: I didn't know you felt that way.

TRACY: Every Mom and Dad at some point looks at their kids and says, "Why? What the hell was I thinking?" Why didn't somebody tell me once I had you I'd be wiping your scrunty little asses for the rest of my life?!

SAMARA: Tracy, Jesus!

TRACY: *(Extreme change.)* WHAT?!

SAMARA: Why are you being so hostile?!

TRACY: YOU THINK *THIS* IS HOSTILE? I'LL SHOW YOU HOSTILE!

(TRACY throws or breaks something. Silence. SA-MARA is shocked. TRACY relaxes, grins, starts to chuckle. The chuckling builds to laughter.)

TRACY: I'm *kidding!*

(Laughing.)

That was *priceless* Sam—Sam*!* You shoulda seen the look on your face! And it's not even in the script!

SAMARA: Oh . . . Thank God. I I thought you were serious for a minute. —Wait. What script?

TRACY: Half the shit we do is mine anyway. Not Barry's. Not the writers' or the director's. *Mine!* I make it up on the fly and that's what people see on the show.

SAMARA: Except Tracy. There *is* no more show.

TRACY: Oh Samara! Why are you such a *downer*? Is it still because of Claire?

> *(Light on SAMARA, resuming past interview. TRACY freezes.)*

SAMARA: First her furniture arrives. Then her clothes. And then *she* shows up. First time I see Claire I'm like, "That's not a nurse! That's a Dallas Cowboy cheerleader under my roof for the next ten weeks!"—*Greeaaaaat!*

> *(Lights change. Continuing. TRACY gets a call on his cell.)*

TRACY: (Taking the call. One cryptic word at a time.) Barry . . . .! Yeah . . . 'kay . . . . Right . . . ! Oh . . . ? Yep . . . . Spit . . . . *Dude* . . .

> *(Disconnects. Grins.)*

SAMARA: Why is every conversation with Barry monosyllabic?

TRACY: Barry said he *loves* the thing with Claire.

SAMARA: What thing with Claire?

TRACY: The having dinner with Claire. Thing.

SAMARA: *What?!*

TRACY: Don't tell me you forgot!

SAMARA: You never told me about—

TRACY: Of course I did.

SAMARA: When?

TRACY: Last Tuesday.

SAMARA: No I mean when are we having dinner with Claire?!

TRACY: Tonight. Here.

SAMARA: No way! That tramp isn't setting foot in this house!

TRACY: She misses the show. She wants to see us.

SAMARA: Since when do you care what Claire wants?

TRACY: SINCE WHEN ARE YOU THE ONE WHO MAKES THE DECISIONS AROUND HERE?!

> *(Again, TRACY throws or breaks something. SAMARA is silent. TRACY grins, starts to laugh: he's fooled her again.)*

TRACY: (cont'd) Kidding!

> *(Cone of light on TRACY, resuming interview. SAMARA freezes.)*

TRACY: *(cont'd)* I think one of the things people like about me is that they can't tell when I'm joking. That adds a lot of tension. I like to mess with people's heads.

(Lights change. Continuing.)

SAMARA: Tracy you you you've got to stop doing that! I-I-I just can't tell anymore when you're serious or not.

TRACY: Listen it'll be great. Claire visits your mother. Then shows up here unexpectedly. It's all nicey—nice at first. Air kisses. Laughter. The usual "Oh my god's!" Then when we're at dinner, she starts to lick the butter knife. Fellating it. And the butter sticks to her lips.

SAMARA: Don't!

TRACY: And she puts her hand on my leg, under the table. You don't know that though. The camera catches it. Then you take Bandit for his after—dinner walk.

SAMARA: Bandit?

TRACY: Our dog.

(Offstage, a dog barks. SAMARA looks towards the bark: "We have a dog?")

TRACY: *(cont'd)* And Claire and I are in the kitchen alone together.

SAMARA: Stop!

TRACY: Doing dishes. Playing with the soap bubbles. And then you walk in and . . .

SAMARA: I SAID STOP IT!

TRACY: Please? For me, Sam—Sam?

SAMARA: NO! And don't call me Sam—Sam anymore! That was only for the show. So you can stop acting. There're no cameras around.

TRACY: *What?!* Did you forget what I said on the show, Samara? *Did* you?

(Lights change. SAMARA, resuming interview. TRACY freezes.)

SAMARA: So when Tracy says "this isn't what it looks like" I'm like, "What the hell? It looks like sex!" I know he just wanted a reaction from me when I walked into the utility room and caught him with Claire. *Buuuuttt* if Tracy says nothing really happened between them, then I believe him.

(Jittery chuckle.)

I'll be so happy when this is all over with and we can go

back to being just us.

(Lights change, continuing. TRACY starts to set the dinner table.)

TRACY: You should make your meatloaf and scalloped potatoes.

SAMARA: I'm not making anything!

TRACY: How about mac-and-cheese with your Swedish Meatballs then?

SAMARA: I SAID I'M NOT COOKING!

TRACY: Hey this is *good*! This is *so* good, Samara! You're finally getting it! Better than just standing there when something happens and you've got that blank look on your face.

SAMARA: What blank look?

TRACY: Yeah, like when Claire said you looked like her high school librarian? Most women would throw something. *Cry.* Not you. You hold it in, stand there stone—faced. Which is not very dramatic, Samara. Not very *real*.

SAMARA: It just occurred to me.

TRACY: What?

SAMARA: You weren't pretending were you?

TRACY: I.

SAMARA: When I walked in on you and Claire.

TRACY: That was the highest rated episode of the season!

SAMARA: It *was* what it looked like, wasn't it?

TRACY: Just *go* with it Samara! Stop resisting! You know how important this is to me!

SAMARA: I think I'm going to be sick.

(SAMARA gets nauseated. Her knees go weak. She's short of breath. TRACY gets her a chair.)

TRACY: *Heyyyy* easy does it! Hey now . . . . Are you alright? Do you want some aspirin? Some ginger ale for your tummy? Here, let me feel your pulse.

(TRACY feels Samara's pulse. TRACY's cell rings.)
(As before: one word at a time.)

Yo . . . . ! Sure . . . . Definitely . . . . No . . . . Escalator . . . . Awesome. . . . . ! Bubbles.

(TRACEY disconnects. Grins.)

SAMARA: Are you . . . are you in love with her?

TRACY: Dylan and Tyler *adore* Claire. Even your *mother* likes Claire.

(Cone of light on TRACY, resuming interview. SA-MARA freezes.)

TRACY: I think Samara's mother looks at Claire as the daughter she never had.

(Realizing mistake.)

I mean, as a *second* daughter . . . That's what I mean. Oops.

(Light out on Tracy. They resume.)

SAMARA: My mother?

TRACY: And do you know *why* your mother likes Claire?

SAMARA: Because Claire's full of shit?!

TRACY: Because she's not *average!*

SAMARA: THERE'S NOTHING WRONG WITH AVERAGE! I *LIKE* AVERAGE!

TRACY: *WOOOOWWWW!* Your reaction! It's great! I *knew* you had it in you! Good girl!

(TRACY smooches Samara.)

I've gotta call Barry about this.

SAMARA: You just talked to him!

TRACY: Barry thinks you could be *huge!*

(TRACY exits to make the call. Lights change, flashback. SAMARA, interviewing.)

SAMARA: I can't pretend to be something I'm not. I mean, I'm just a stay—at—home mom at heart. And if anyone has a problem with that it's *their* problem. And it's time for Claire to go home!

(Lights return to the present.)

SAMARA: *(cont'd)* Tracy . . . ? TRACY!

(TRACY steps on, indicates the phone, "shushes" Samara. TRACY steps off.)

(Recalling what Tracy said:)

SAMARA: *(cont'd)* Even my *mother* likes Claire . . .

(A realization!)

Mother!

(SAMARA grabs her cell, makes a frantic call.)

Mother . . . ? I-I'm coming to get the boys . . . W-w-w-wait who . . . who's voice is that . . . ? No I heard someone's voice, Mother . . . . Is, is that . . . Is *Claire* with you? No, no, wait Mother . . . What is Claire doing at your . . . .

PLAYING WITH THE BOYS . . . ?! No I didn't, I'm not, it's not . . . .You get that woman out of your house right now do you hear me Mother . . . .!? RIGHT NOW . . . ! NO IT'S NOT PART OF *ANY*THING MOTHER . . . ! WHAT THE HELL IS *WRONG* WITH YOU . . . . ?

> *(SAMARA disconnects the call. She's frantic. She grabs her keys and her purse. TRACY returns. He watches Samara for a moment.)*

TRACY: (*Gently.*) There, there. It's alright.

SAMARA: What going on?

TRACY: Everything's going to be alright. I just want you to know I'm so. So *proud* of you. And son's Barry.

SAMARA: But the boys! No I—I have to go pick up the boys!

TRACY: No, no I'll get them. You shouldn't drive when you're so upset.

SAMARA: No I'm fine, I just need to—!

TRACY: *(Blocking her exit. A bit scary.)* No. I *said. I'll* go!

SAMARA: Are you leaving me for Claire?

TRACY: You need some rest. It's been a long day.

SAMARA: You could have just told me.

TRACY: Oh Samara. You still don't get it, do you?

SAMARA: Oh. You mean. This is all just. Part of the, the show?

TRACY: Oh I don't know Samara. What difference does it make?

> *(TRACY takes the keys, gently kisses SAMARA: on her forehead, and exits. SAMARA alone. She starts to tremble. Several moments pass. SAMARA faces the audience, anticipating the interview segment of Houseguest where she speaks to the camera. Beat.)*

SAMARA: May I have my light now, please . . . ?

> *(Looking around, confused.)*

Hello . . . ? Is anyone . . . ?

> *(Brief pause.)*

I SAID I WANT MY LIGHT!

> *(Silence. Suddenly SAMARA's special light snaps on; an otherwise dark stage. She looks out, horrified. Gasps! Blackout.)*

The End

The Kids Menu

Richard Vetere

PRODUCTION NOTES:

The Weathervane Theater in Akron
Ohio opening on July 15th, 2011 as finalist in the 8
by 10 Ten Minute Play Festival
Director, Alan Scott Ferrall
Producer, Eileen Moushey

Cast:
CARMINE DOLCINO, Michael Pitt
KAT, Rachel Gehlert

CHARACTERS:

CARMINE DOLCINO, fifties blue collar from the neighborhood, blasé, seen it before and doesn't suffer fools.

KAT, in her early thirties. She is white collar, successful, filled with self-righteous motivation.

SET: Pizza parlor in Park Slope, Brooklyn.
TIME: Now

CARMINE: Yes? What can I get you?

KAT: *(firmly)* Can I speak to the owner please?

CARMINE: *(now concerned)* You want to talk to the owner? Sure. What can I do for you?

KAT: Oh. You're the owner then?

CARMINE: You asked for the owner. I'm the owner. You want me to find one of my nephews to talk to you? They talk to customers like you better.

KAT: Customers like me? What do mean?

CARMINE: You know, customers like you. Interlopers.

KAT: Interloper? Why are you calling me that? I'm not an interloper. I live in this neighborhood.

CARMINE: Of course you do. For how long?

KAT: Two years. Nearly.

CARMINE: Congratulations. Do you know the brown brick three story across the street?

(She looks.)

KAT: Yes.

CARMINE: I was born there. Two decades before you were born probably. Lived there all my life. So, I'm what they call a native, you're what they call an interloper. No harm intended. Just a fact. Now, yes, I'm the owner. What can I do for you?

(KAT is now thrown off her mission and has to find her way back to it.)

KAT: I want to know why you don't have it. Lola's has it and Ned's Bakery has one and even Joe's Chinese has it.

CARMINE: Has what?

KAT: A children's menu.

CARMINE: So you're the one.

KAT: *(proudly)* Yes. I probably am.

CARMINE: You're the one who sent out that internet stuff.

KAT: E-mail blasts. Yes, that's me.

CARMINE: And you're the one who put up the signs around on Spring Street.

KAT: Me again. Yes.

CARMINE: What's your problem lady?

KAT: My name is Kat. Kat Henshaw. My problem is this. My friend Zoey Larmen came here one day last week and asked you the same question on why you didn't have a children's menu and you intimidated her.

CARMINE: Tall, dark hair? Interloper?

KAT: *(annoyed)* She's been living here a year already.

CARMINE: Of course she has.

KAT: You made Zoey so upset.

CARMINE: Sorry, I must have been having a bad day.

KAT: So, when I heard this, I sent a e-mail blast to all of our friends, all the mothers who live around here, that you are the only restaurant in the neighborhood without a children's menu and you refuse to do anything about it.

(silence)

CARMINE: All this aggravation over a kids menu.

KAT: Children's menu. Why don't you have one?

(CARMINE steps back. He hands her a menu.)

CARMINE: You want something? It's on the house. If not, please go.

KAT: I have a right to know why you don't have a children's menu.

CARMINE: You have a right? And this right is in the Constitution?

KAT: As a parent of two children, Wendell and Zara, I have a right.

CARMINE: Do you me a favor. Take a minute. Look around. How many different kinds of pizza pies do you think I make?

KAT: I'm not a mathematician. I'm in marketing.

CARMINE: *(cutting her off)* Thirty. Thirty different pizzas we make everyday. We have marinara with and without anchovies, with mozzarella, the Grandma pizza, Sicilian, artichokes, arugula, white pizza, meatball pizza, pizza with pineapple . . .

KAT: *(cutting him off)* And your point.

CARMINE: Your kid has got to like one of those. If you have a suggestion on the kind of pizza you'd like, tell my nephew Salvatore. He's the big kid the girls like to look at. Have a nice day and give him your order on me.

    (He walks away.)

KAT: It's the portions. You need to have children's portions, sir.

CARMINE: You are going to tell me how much pasta I can sell? I prefer a guy with a gun come in and rob me. At least he has a gun. You come in hiding behind the word 'mother' and all you want to do is rob me.

KAT: Sir, children should have their own portions, their own menus.

CARMINE: Whose kids?

KAT: All kids.

CARMINE: Where you from?

KAT: The avenue.

CARMINE: No, before that.

KAT: I'm from Parma. It's a suburb outside of Cleveland.

CARMINE: I've heard of Parma. In fact, I know Parma. I had an uncle from Cleveland. The cops found him in a hole out in Vegas. My mother's brother. They called him Funzi. My Uncle Funzi. My father never liked him. He was a crook and a homicidal manic. He gave my father the money to start up this joint and my father paid him back every dime and then washed his hands of him. My Uncle's wiseguy's buddies tried to get a piece of this place but me and my brother stood our ground. Blood was spilled just to make sure this place made it. You got that lady?

    (pause)

Dolcino's has been standing here long before they built the first driveway in Parma. And now you, the lady with a stick up her ass, is coming here to tell me that I have to have a kid's menu?

KAT: You can't talk to me like that.

CARMINE: Lady, from the very beginning I suggested you talk to one of my nephews. I send all the interlopers to him.

KAT: I am not an interloper. I came here to politely to ask you sir.

CARMINE: Carmine. The name's Carmine. My friends know me in the neighborhood as Buddy. But you, you can call me Mister Dolcino.

(He starts to walk away. KAT doesn't give up.)

KAT: Mister Dolcino, I have another complaint.

CARMINE: No doubt you do.

KAT: I know you have every right to sell soda. But look how you have it prominently displayed. The bright colors, the bright light coming out of the machine. This is a major temptation to children. It draws them in. It looks magical to them and it's dangerous. Soda is dangerous to children. One can of soda consumed a day will put a pound a week on an individual. A pound a week for the rest of their lives.

CARMINE: You got a husband right?

KAT: I don't have to answer that.

CARMINE: I'm not interviewing you for a job. It's just a question. I see you come in with a man so I am figuring it's your husband, no harm it that, is there? Kabish?

KAT: Yes I have a husband. He works in banking.

CARMINE: I didn't ask what he did. I just wanted to know if he exists.

KAT: Why?

CARMINE: I think you should send him around to me. That's all.

KAT: Why? You don't think I can speak for myself?

CARMINE: I didn't say that. I just think that when someone comes into a man's place of business and tells him what to do with that business, he better have a big set of balls hanging between his legs.

KAT: I have balls, Mister Dolcino.

CARMINE: Lady, you just told me that you have two kids. If you got what you need for that to happen and you have a pair of balls at the same time, I'll make you a "whole pie with everything on it" for free.

KAT: Nice joke.

CARMINE: Words mean something to me. So, I listen closely. And I don't like the words you use. I don't read the internet but I did hear from nephew, Salvatore, the one the girls like to look at, that you threatened to boycott my pizza place because I don't have a kid's menu. Is that correct?

KAT: It is correct.

CARMINE: Madone.

KAT: Mister Dolcino, Wendell is only eight and he's putting on weight. He comes here with his friends and buys pizza. Lots of it. If you sold children's portions maybe he wouldn't be eating so much.

CARMINE: So, now it's my job to control your kid's appetite?

KAT: Look, I'll design the menu myself. I'll print it up and pay for it, everything, myself.

CARMINE: No.

KAT: We share the same neighborhood, can't we work together?

CARMINE: I'm sharing it with you, yes. You buy my pizza, yes, but you do not tell me how to run my business.

KAT: Why are you being so hard?

CARMINE: Because this is my business and you are not a partner, lady.

KAT: Okay, look, I came here on a mission, Mister Dolcino. I thought first I'd be hard. Now I am nearly begging. I can't go back to the ladies and tell them that I failed. I can't do that. So you have to work with me on this.

(She smiles, even flirting doing all she can to get on his good side.)

KAT: I heard you men here in Brooklyn, you natives, have a soft side for the ladies. I'm playing that card, Mister Dolcino. Do you see? I'm flirting with you. Do you see me flirting? I haven't flirted with a man since I got married. And that includes my husband. But you I am flirting with you because this is important to me.

(CARMINE gives her a hard look and she stops.)

CARMINE: *(with force)* If your husband is not important to you, keep that to yourself. Okay?

KAT: *(slowly)* Okay.

CARMINE: And don't ever. Ever, flirt with me again.

KAT: Okay.

CARMINE: Leave and never come back. I don't need your business.

KAT: I got you angry at me. I didn't mean to do that.

(He gives her a look like, "you have to be kidding.")

KAT: I like your pizza and it's so convenient to come here. How am I going to tell my husband we can't come here anymore?

(He stares at her.)

KAT: Can I make it up to you? I can bring in a party of my girlfriends and their friends and order tons of pizza. We all like Italy you know. Mainly Rome. The people are so nice. *(pause)* Do you go there often? *(pause)* Have you visited where your parents are from? *(pause)* Say something, please.

CARMINE: Kids should be seen and not heard.

KAT: No! No! No! They have rights! You should have a children's menu! It's the only thing we have is our children!

CARMINE: People like you, interlopers, you think you invented everything and you got the answers for everything else. You think you can run the world, change words around and you act like the first people to ever have kids. Do you know I can't call my workers waiters or waitresses anymore. They are servers now. That is more a demeaning word than waitress. I have to put the calories on menus because people are too lazy or too stupid to figure out that pizza is fattening. And now you, a distortion of everything ladylike, comes into my store to tell me that I have to worry about what your f'n fat kid can eat. Salvatore! Throw this interloper out of my restaurant.

(KAT looks and raises her hand.)

KAT: Okay, okay. I'm going. I am. *(pause)* Can I make this up to you? Try another day to discuss this? Bring you flowers?

(Tries flirting again. He smirks then leans in on with a terse reply.)

CARMINE: Beware of those with bread in one hand because they might have a stone in the other.

KAT: My God, what's made you so hard? Gangsters? Thieves? Family? What?

CARMINE: People like you.

(LIGHTS OUT)

The End

LINES

Tony Glazer

PRODUCTION NOTES:

LINES was performed as part of the "10 for the Ta Tas" Ten-Minute Play Festival on June 10th, 11th and 12th, 2011.

It was performed at the TBG Studio Theatre 312 West 36th Street, New York, New York produced by Graveyard Kiss Productions. Directed by Laura Belsey

Cast:
JONATHAN, Bradley Anderson
PATRICIA, Farrah Crane

CHARACTERS:
PATRICIA (twenties) sweet-natured but with an edge
JONATHAN (twenties) stylish, slightly uptight

TIME: Present
PLACE: New York City

> *Lights up on a studio apartment. A few boxes litter the floor—*
> *someone is either coming or going. A woman PATRICIA*
> *stands in the center of the apartment while JONATHAN*
> *stands in the door jamb with a box cradled in his arms.*
> *Silence. Then . . .*

JONATHAN: That's it. That's everything.
PATRICIA: Last box.
> *(Awkwardness. Then . . .)*
I've called the utility companies.
JONATHAN: Good, that's . . . I called cable and Sunday Times
delivery.
PATRICIA: Everyone in the building just took turns stealing
our copy anyway.
JONATHAN: Environmentalists.
PATRICIA: At least they recycle.
> *(JONATHAN notices something.)*
JONATHAN: Do you want to take the curtains?
PATRICIA: No.
JONATHAN: Really? You spent so much time picking /
them—
PATRICIA: *(gently interrupting)* Let's, let's just leave them for
the next tenant.
JONATHAN: Sure.
PATRICIA: I mean, it's nice to come to a place for the first . . .
it's nice to come to the new place you're staying in and find
curtains already hanging there.
JONATHAN: Yeah.
PATRICIA: That never happens. People almost always take
theirs so when you come in and see them hanging up it's
more than just one more thing off your list. It makes everything feel more like a . . .

JONATHAN: Home.

> *(Awkwardness. Finally . . .)*

I should go.

PATRICIA: I won't be much longer.

JONATHAN: You're set with everything?

PATRICIA: I'm good.

JONATHAN: You don't need any help with / the rest of—

PATRICIA: *(gently interrupting)* No, no. I'm fine. I've got it.

JONATHAN: Okay. Okay, then.

> *(Beat. Then . . .)*

PATRICIA: We did try.

JONATHAN: No one could accuse us of not making the effort.

PATRICIA: We ran the gamut.

JONATHAN: We did.

PATRICIA: Self-help books.

JONATHAN: That vacation.

PATRICIA: All that sex, food, beaches . . . more sex.

JONATHAN: Talking.

PATRICIA: Couples' therapy.

JONATHAN: I still don't think that guy was licensed.

PATRICIA: You should let that go.

JONATHAN: Neither of our insurance companies would recognize him, Pat.

PATRICIA: That doesn't mean anything, John.

JONATHAN: Plus he kept wanting us to color in books. What licensed therapist asks you to do that?

PATRICIA: Everyone has their own method.

JONATHAN: Only the "unlicensed ones" involve crayons.

PATRICIA: Don't be so judgmental.

JONATHAN: Wasn't that why we were there?

PATRICIA: We were there to reflect—not judge.

JONATHAN: How do you accomplish that without some form of critical thought?

PATRICIA: Critical thought about us not—it doesn't matter.

JONATHAN: No.

PATRICIA: He didn't help anyway.

JONATHAN: He made it worse. Or better. Depending . . .

> *(The two stand just there, until . . .)*

See you around.

PATRICIA: No.

JONATHAN: No, what?

PATRICIA: You won't "see me around." We broke up, John. We just divided up our belongings and are now going our separate ways. You don't "see each other around" after you do something like that.

JONATHAN: It's just an expression.

PATRICIA: Find a better one.

JONATHAN: Okay. Goodbye.

> *(JONATHAN exits. PATRICIA begins to cry quietly. JONATHAN returns as if to say something. He stands there, looking at her, affected, before walking to her, putting an arm around her. She's startled at first but then, realizing that it's him, relaxes back into her sadness.)*

JONATHAN: It's okay.

PATRICIA: It's not.

JONATHAN: I know.

PATRICIA: Then don't say something is "okay" when you know it's not.

JONATHAN: All right.

> *(He continues to hold her. She continues to cry until it becomes awkward again and they separate.)*

PATRICIA: I'm fine now.

JONATHAN: Goodbye.

> *(JONATHAN moves towards to the door.)*

PATRICIA: I just . . .

> *(JONATHAN turns back.)*

I don't . . .

JONATHAN: You slept with my brother.

PATRICIA: I know, John. I was there when it happened.

JONATHAN: You couldn't have thought sleeping with him was going to come without any consequences.

PATRICIA: I didn't.

JONATHAN: And yet you did it all the same knowing full well it was going to lead us right to this moment.

PATRICIA: It wasn't that simple.

JONATHAN: He's my brother.

PATRICIA: You're repeating yourself.

JONATHAN: My stupid, back-stabbing, unemployed, selfish

and irresponsible brother.

PATRICIA: At least he could look at my scars without flinching.

(Almost unconsciously, JONATHAN looks to PATRI-CIA's chest before looking away.)

JONATHAN: No . . . don't you . . . don't turn that . . . that's not . . .

PATRICIA: Fair? No it isn't. It's not even decent.

JONATHAN: It's not . . . accurate.

PATRICIA: Accurate enough.

JONATHAN: You changed.

PATRICIA: I survived.

(Pause. Finally . . .)

JONATHAN: I should really go.

PATRICIA: You can't color inside the lines.

JONATHAN: What's that?

PATRICIA: At the therapist's office. When he asked us to color. I saw you couldn't color inside the lines. When I saw that I knew it wasn't going to work out.

JONATHAN: Is that right?

PATRICIA: I could never be with someone who couldn't do something as basic as color inside the lines. You have a problem with lines.

JONATHAN: And you don't. Not with crossing them, anyway.

PATRICIA: Screw you.

JONATHAN: See you around.

(JONATHAN is about to exit again.)

PATRICIA: Coward.

(JONATHAN stops himself, this last statement striking a nerve. Finally . . .)

JONATHAN: I was there for you.

(PATRICIA does not respond.)

By your side. Through everything. All of it . . . the tests, the insurance forms, the surgery, all that . . . poison. I was there. One hundred percent. Until you got well.

PATRICIA: Your point?

JONATHAN: I loved you.

PATRICIA: Isn't that easy to say?

JONATHAN: I still do for what's it's worth.

PATRICIA: Which isn't much.

JONATHAN: Right.

PATRICIA: Because you're a coward.

JONATHAN: We've been through this already. I don't need to hear—

PATRICIA: I'm very blessed, actually.

JONATHAN: Of course you are. You're alive.

PATRICIA: No. I'm blessed about you.

(JONATHAN just stares. Then . . .)

Somewhere between sleeping with your brother and the coloring books and you never quite being able to look at my chest it finally occurred to me just how amazing it was to actually be able to see you. See who you really are. Startling, really—the clarity of that moment. I owe you. I never would have challenged our situation. We were on a set track, you and I. We were a straight shot to marriage and kids. I never would have got off that track—not on my own. Of course, now that you've stepped off, not only do I know that I never could be with someone this fundamentally bunched over the lines on my chest, I would never want to be.

(Beat. Then . . .)

JONATHAN: *(sincere)* It's not you, Patricia. It's not / that I don't . . .

PATRICIA: *(interrupting)* We don't have to revisit / this anymore.

JONATHAN: *(interrupting)* I can't explain it. I'm not proud of it. It just makes me uncomfortable.

PATRICIA: Stop saying "it." It is not "it." I had to listen to you in that fucking pretend therapist's office go on about "it" for months. Well, before you walk out that door, let's make one thing perfectly clear. "It" is "me," John. You don't have a problem with "it"—it's me you can't look at, can't touch, can't love.

JONATHAN: No, you . . . I don't have a problem with you. You're twisting this . . . it's not . . . you.

PATRICIA: Prove it.

(Impulsively, and with her back to the audience, PATRICIA begins to open her blouse.)

JONATHAN: What are you . . .

PATRICIA: If that's true you have to prove it. Right now. Before you go, before we never see each other again, make me believe our entire relationship wasn't a lie.

JONATHAN: Patricia . . . don't . . .

PATRICIA: No, Jonathan. If you loved me—still love me, like you say—then you have to see "me." Not "it." Me.

JONATHAN: Please, Pat. I . . .

> *(PATRICIA has exposed her chest. JONATHAN, after a moment, looks and then, very tentatively, approaches. After a moment, he puts a hand on PATRICIA's chest. His hand stays there for a long time until..).*

Lines.

Lights out.

The End

LOOKING AGAIN

Charles Evered

PRODUCTION NOTES:

The Curan Repertory Company as part of their Notes
From The Underground Festival at The American
Theatre of Actors in New York City
April 27–May 1, 2011.
Directed by Ken Terrell.

Cast:
BILL, Benjamin Weaver
STEVE, Robert Getz.

CHARACTERS

BILL, around forty, is dressed in a leather jacket and thin tie. He's in shape, wiry.

STEVE, a little younger, is dressed a little hipper than Bill, but is rounder and a bit more slovenly.

PLACE: in a bar.
TIME: is the present.

Lights up on Bill and Steve at a bar. They are holding drinks and looking at one particular (unseen) female patron.

BILL: Don't look at 'em.

STEVE: Why not?

BILL: Because it weakens you. It weakens your position.

STEVE: What position? Why can't I just look at her?

BILL: Because you weren't looking at her, you were lookin' at her breasts.

STEVE: Don't worry about it. I am nothing if not discreet.

BILL: That isn't the point.

STEVE: Then what is, Bill?

BILL: You weaken yourself. By looking at them, you weaken your position.

STEVE: Why do you imagine she's wearing a low cut blouse like that?

BILL: Don't point you moron. She's wearing that blouse because she wants you to look at 'em.

STEVE: And I, being a gentleman, am simply complying with her wishes.

BILL: No you're not—you're doing what she doesn't want to see you doing.

STEVE: You wear a blouse like that, you are soliciting stares from men.

BILL: She wears a blouse like that because she wants to be able to see the extent to which you are able to keep yourself from lookin' at 'em.

STEVE: That's insane.

BILL: You could characterize it any way you want—the point remains that the more you look at 'em, the less likely it'll be that you'll enjoy 'em someday. Be the cowboy, Steve.

STEVE: The cowboy?

BILL: The cowboy doesn't look at 'em. The cowboy doesn't have to. You're supposed to be the cowboy. Used to be we'd cut down a tree and split it, throw some logs on the campfire and stir up some grub. Now what are we? We are exactly what the eunuchs who run television shows depicted us into being. Marginalized metro-sexual tubs of butter incapable of threatening our own shadows. We are confused, confounded, passive and compromised little toady boys. What are we? Are we men? Do men even really need to exist anymore? If they don't need our penises anymore to have a baby, if you don't even need to differentiate one gender from the other anymore, then why have two separate genders at all? Why don't we all just be one gender? Why don't we all just be a bunch of "Sam's" or "Terri's"—lets all cut our hair down just to the middle of our necks. Lets all wear pants or "chinos" or whatever the hell so called men wear now. Why have pants at all, when you think of it, lets just have "leg coverings" so as not to offend those who don't feel comfortable wearing pants, and better yet, lets not wear clothes at all, as wearing them is in its own way discriminatory toward those who prefer not to so publicly declare their own gender. You want to be alive again Steve? You want to break the chains? Don't look at 'em.

STEVE: Dude, you're losin' it.

BILL: I'm not losin' it, buddy, I'm finding it.

STEVE: You're angry, Bill.

BILL: Of course I'm angry. I'm conscious.

STEVE: Seriously, Bill, are you okay?

BILL: I'm fine. Why?

STEVE: I just feel like you're getting a little, I don't know, existential.

BILL: And what's wrong with that, Steve?

STEVE: I didn't say anything was.

BILL: I've done bad things, okay? I'm just trying to spare you the pain of it.

STEVE: Pain of what? What have you done that's so bad?

BILL: Just something, okay—in the way the world thinks of as "bad."

STEVE: What did you do?

BILL: What does it matter what I did? Just learn from me.

STEVE: How could I learn if—

(Steve's eyes follow a girl.)

BILL:—ah ah ah, STOP looking.

STEVE: What, you didn't just see her look at me?

BILL: So what if she did? Be a man.

STEVE: I am a man.

BILL: You're a tool. You're a protoplasmic tool.

STEVE: Seriously, what did you do that was bad?

BILL: I killed someone.

STEVE: Bull crap like when?

BILL: What does that matter? You think everybody that kills somebody gets caught? You think life is like your television set? You think everything has ramifications? You're a child—a naïve child. You think there's no space between the dreams we have and the known world?

STEVE: What are you talking about?

BILL: You look in a mirror. What do you see? You think you see you? Do you think that's the person staring back at you? "You?" What you? Which you?—staring back. You think that person in the mirror sees you? How do you know that person staring back at you isn't staring in a mirror too? And if they are—who the hell are you then? Are you a reflection?

BILL: *(cont.)* Or, are you reflecting? Are you reflecting? Huh? Are you reflecting, Steve?

STEVE: Geez, Bill, I think you've kind of gone over some kind of line.

BILL: I am standing in the middle of a forest. As I have for thousands of years. I am raising my hands up.

(He does.)

My hands soaked with blood, for I have made a good and bloody kill. I have done what I had to—to protect our little tribe. I made a move. I took action. The people in my tribe will eat tonight. The women will sleep and at least for a few hours, they know their young will not be snatched up from under them and defiled or devoured or consumed by the poisonous world we traffic in. I would not be considered a viable political candidate, nor would

I win a popularity contest—and I would not garner the most votes on a tv talent show, but yet I made a move—even, no, especially when it was dangerous and now societally unpopular for me to have done so. The people I protect—they revere me. I was a leader then. What am I now? What are all of us now?

STEVE: Who did you kill?

BILL: It doesn't matter who I killed Steve. We're just whizzing around on a dying star, baby—and we're all acting like we got it figured out. Well, we don't got it figured out. There are no straight lines, Steve.

STEVE: I don't believe you killed anybody.

BILL: It isn't really important that you do.

STEVE: I think you're overcompensating. I think you feel like a lot of us do, disenfranchised, put off, marginalized, and in your head you've created this kind of doppelganger version of yourself—the version of you that you wish were really you. But it's not really you. All of us have that version of ourselves, the version of ourselves that we believe we are, until that moment where we catch ourselves in front of a mirror and its suddenly confirmed for us that—that isn't who we are at all. Who are we really? I don't have all the answers, I'm just a guy who got B-minuses all his life—not smart enough to get As, and not interesting enough to fail out. I'm just a B minus guy, Bill, but I'm okay with that. But I'm getting to a place where I know who I'm going to see when I look in that mirror and it doesn't shock me anymore. I'm resigned I guess you could say, not disappointed with who I am, but resigned. And I'm okay with that. I really am.

(pause)

BILL: Steve, I don't want you to be offended by what I'm about to say to you because you have to understand it isn't personal, and so I don't mean any offense to you directly. But I do want to say this: You are what this society calls "a man," but in millennia before us, lets be honest—you would be a liability. I want you to imagine what good you do—really take a long hard look at yourself. I'm not talking about feeling here, Steve, I'm talking about thinking. The world is falling apart because grown men don't know the

difference anymore. People think because they feel something, it must be right. No doubt Steve, you "feel" you are
a good man. That you have some worth and that perhaps,
someday, you will meet a woman of average attractiveness
and perhaps above average breast size and you'll couple
with her and the two of you will roll around in an agreed
upon orgy of self delusion that allows you both to believe
you matter in the world. You'll mutually agree to subscribe
to some made up tenant of belief and every Sunday you will
go to church and act like something means something, well
it doesn't Steve. It has no meaning. And neither do you. I
want you to really think about what I'm about to propose to
you—and I want you to think about it like a man would. I
want you to think about taking your own life, because when
all is said and done, it's the only real control we can exert
upon a universe that otherwise has us reeling in anarchy and
randomness. Seriously think about it, Steve. And don't make
a big production of it either. If you're going to take your
own life, do it in a way that would seem questionable as to
whether you actually did it at all. Do it with built in plausible
deniability so that your mother can tell her friends it was an
"accident," or some kind of mishap but for all that is right
and true and good in this putrid world, Steve, do it.

    (Holds up his glass.)

Do you want another one?

    (Long pause)

STEVE: I'm good, thanks.

BILL: You are more than welcome my friend. And Steve?

STEVE: Yes, Bill?

BILL: You're looking again.

    *(Steve turns back to Bill and just looks at him as the
    lights fade slowly to black.)*

The End

Minimalistic Men

Spenser Davis

Production Notes:

Chicago Dramatists Theatre
June 2011
Artistic Director, Russ Tutterow
Director, Jeff Poole.

Cast:
JERRY, Jonathan Helvey
BRAD, Adam Kander

Donny's Skybox Theatre at
The Second City Chicago
November 19th, 2011
Director, Jeff Poole

CHARACTERS

JERRY: Mid-twenties. Maybe handsome, but at lights up, he's disheveled, having made a horrifying discovery.

BRAD: His roommate. Same age. Maybe frumpy. Clueless to the truth.

SETTING: Their apartment. Somewhere in America.
TIME: Present day.

PLAYWRIGHT'S NOTES:

Living up to the promise of the title, the staging of this play should be ridiculously simple. The two mens' "couch"—consisting of two chairs pushed together—is the only physical object on the stage. Everything else, prop or otherwise, is mimed.

> *Lights up on JERRY, standing DR, dialing his phone.*

JERRY: Come on, Brad, you son-of-a-gun, pick up.
> *(puts phone to ear, waits)*

Pick up, pick up, pick up.

BRAD: *(O.S.)* Hey, this is Brad. If you're hearing this, I didn't pick up like you were anxiously hoping I would. So when the thing goes beep, say stuff.
> *Pause. Then "beep."*

JERRY: *(into phone)* Brad, it's Jerry. Look, I'm coming home. There's something really important I have to tell you, and we don't have much time. Just, um, don't. Do. Anything. I'm coming home. There's something really important I have—Shit, I already said that. Look, I'm coming home. Shit. I said—Shit.
> *(hangs up)*

Shit.
> *(looks at audience, furious)*

Do you people *mind?*

> *JERRY exits R. Lights up on C, where BRAD sits on*

the couch, talking on the phone.

BRAD: *(into phone)* What do you mean I am? No way. *You're* the best. Okay, fine. But only if you do.

JERRY re-enters R, runs up to the side of the couch.

JERRY: Brad, we need to talk.

BRAD: *(oblivious to him)* No, you hang up first. No, you. No, you first. Gosh, you're . . . what a rascal.

JERRY anxiously taps BRAD on the shoulder.

BRAD: *(still smiling)* Oh, hey, Jerr.

(into phone)

No, you first. Okay, okay, fine. At the same time then.

JERRY: Brad, we need to—

BRAD: One, two, three.

(pause, then laughs hysterically)

Well, you didn't either.

JERRY: *(sternly)* Brad. Please. Come on.

BRAD looks at him, annoyed.

BRAD: *(into phone)* Hey, I gotta go. Okay. I'll call you back, Mom.

(hangs up phone)

Have you no respect?

JERRY: Brad, I'm sorry. But this can't wait.

BRAD: Really? 'Cause I get to talk to my mom once a week. Once a week, for one hour. That's all the guards will allow her. And all I've asked is that you allot me that one hour to speak to her in peace.

JERRY: I know, Brad, but this can't wait an hour—

BRAD: *(looks down at caller I.D.)* Oh, and look. I have one missed call.

JERRY: Yeah. That was me calling.

BRAD: Oh. Well remind me to call you back later.

BRAD walks DL, to the stove. JERRY watches him; already he is almost drained.

JERRY: Brad. What are you doing?

BRAD: I'm making ramen noodles. Is that alright, or are you going to interrupt me before I add the flavoring?

JERRY: *(desperately)* How can you think about food at a time like this?

BRAD: Most people think about food at lunchtime.

JERRY approaches BRAD, grabs his arm.

JERRY: Listen, leave the noodles for a second. There's something very important I need—

BRAD: The noodles'll burn.

JERRY: If you don't listen to me, if you don't take me serious
for two seconds, there aren't gonna be any noodles.

This, above all else, quiets BRAD.

JERRY: *(CONT.)* This might sound strange, but I need you to
listen: What we have here doesn't exist.

(pause)

BRAD: Huh?

JERRY: All of this—

(motions to the apartment)

None of this is real.

BRAD: *("Nice try, bud")* Yeah, right. That lampshade over there
alone is made of real wool. Trust me, I checked. It's posh.

JERRY: No, that's not what I—

(a new approach:)

Right now, we're on display.

(pause)

BRAD: You are high as hell.

JERRY: No.

BRAD: Yeah, yeah, you are. I can see it in your face.

JERRY: Brad—

BRAD: Why do you do that to yourself? You smoke a bowl and
then you run in spitting conspiracy theories. Like that time
you swore, up and down, that Rachel Ray was the one who
killed Bobby Kennedy.

JERRY: Read her book! It's all in there!

BRAD: And whenever I tried to convince you otherwise, you
wouldn't stand for it.

(pause)

I can't prove it, but I'm pretty sure you overfed my
goldfish in revenge for me debunking your theory—

JERRY: Brad, *we're in a play!*

Silence.

JERRY: *(CONT.)* We're in... we're in a play. This is not our
apartment, this is a stage. And look. Look.

(points BRAD towards audience)

Do you see them?

BRAD: See . . . ? See who?

JERRY: Keep looking. One. Two. Three. "Stop acting."

> *JERRY snaps his fingers. House lights come up (and gradually fade down again) as BRAD sees the audience for the first time.*

BRAD: Wh-who are they?

JERRY: May I introduce . . . the Audience.

BRAD: And, and they came here to what, watch us? Do what?

JERRY: I don't know. This. Talk. Disagree. Fight. Whatever.

BRAD: I, I need to sit down.

> *(sits down on couch; looks at it)*

Holy shit! Where's our couch?

JERRY: That's what I've been trying to tell you. It wasn't ever a couch. Just two chairs pushed together. This whole thing uses a minimalistic set.

BRAD: *(nods knowingly)* A minimalistic set. Right.

> *(pause)*

JERRY: You have no idea what that means, do you?

BRAD: Nope.

> *(pause; a thought comes to him)*

You know . . . maybe a life on display isn't so bad, though. I mean, we can adapt. With people watching us, we'll be like celebrities, except we still have to *pay* for our drugs.

> *BRAD preens in front of the newly discovered spectators.*

JERRY: Can you stop being so optimistic about this? You're forgetting the most important part of this whole thing.

> *(pause)*

Every play ends.

> *The preening ceases. A moment of realization.*

BRAD: Oh shit.

JERRY: That's right. "Oh shit." That's what I really came here to tell you. Because see, when the play ends, so do we. When the lights black out—

> *(snaps his fingers)*

We're dead.

Lawrence Harbison

BRAD: W-When is the play supposed to end?

JERRY: That's the part I don't know. A play can only last for so long. "August: Osage County" ran for three and a half hours. Even "The Norman Conquests" lasted about ten hours.

BRAD: *(hopeful)* Great! So we might still have some time.

JERRY: Nah. I have a feeling we have ninety minutes, tops. You better just pray that we're not in a one-act.

BRAD: *(nods knowingly)* A one-act. Right.

JERRY: . . . Never mind.

BRAD: But why does the play *have* to end? Why would it? I mean—

> *(points to audience)*

They don't have to stay here. We could keep on—

JERRY: Because that's what the Playwright wants. We have to do or say whatever He wants us to do or say.

BRAD: So some hipster types something into Microsoft Word and suddenly its the Holy Grail.

JERRY: Well . . . the Grail is a cup, but yeah, that's the idea.

> *BRAD rubs his forehead, thinking. Then, a curious realization.*

BRAD: How did you know?

JERRY: How did I know—what?

BRAD: All this. That we're in a play. That some guy is writing all this.

JERRY: *(realizes)* I . . . don't know. I guess He sort-of imparted the knowledge to me. Before the play began.

BRAD: You think He wanted you to know that you're in a play.

JERRY: I guess so. Heck, everything we're saying right now might seem spontaneous, but it's all been . . . pre-planned.

> *(pause)*

BRAD: YOU'RE A DOUCHE MUNCHER!

JERRY: *(taken aback, then)* WELL YOU'RE AN ASSHOLE!

BRAD: No, not you. I was just trying to catch Him off-guard.

JERRY: Oh. Well, I don't think you *can* catch Him off-guard. Or Her. Or whatever the playwright is. There's not a line we've said so far that wasn't thought out ahead of time. For example, if I said, "This playwright blows like a streetwhore," it's because He actually wanted me to say that.

BRAD: Wow . . . So we're written by a misogynist.

JERRY: Masochist.

BRAD: Bless you.

(suddenly kisses JERRY; to the audience)

Sarah Palin.

(looks at JERRY, confused)

Oh, shit! I'm so sorry! I didn't—

JERRY: *(unfazed)* It's okay. That was just the Playwright trying to be edgy . . . and topical.

BRAD: *(sad understanding)* So . . . there's nothing we can do to stop this, then.

JERRY: Nope. I suppose in a lot of ways, we're in the same position as the guy who discovered death.

BRAD: How'd he do that?

JERRY: I guess he died.

The two men look at each other as it all sinks in. Pause for several beats. Then something in BRAD registers.

BRAD: Then why did you tell me?

JERRY: . . . What do you mean?

BRAD: I mean, you knew, before you even told me, that this play was going to end, no matter what we tried. So why couldn't you just let me die ignorant of my fate?

JERRY: You'd rather me keep that to myself? I did you a favor!

BRAD: Before you burst in here, and told me about the Audience, and the Playwright, and the Blackout, and the fucking couch, I was fine. I was ignorant, but at least I was happy. If you making me conscious of my death doesn't prevent anything, then why couldn't you have just let me have my peace?

JERRY: *(comprehending)* Oh. Oh, Brad. Brad, I'm sorry . . . I didn't . . . I never considered the implications of . . .

BRAD scoffs, shakes his head in disgust.

JERRY: Look, don't take this out on me. I can't help that I just did was I was written to do.

BRAD: No. Don't fall back on that "written this way" shit! Don't you try to—

JERRY: But I am! We have to do what we're written to do!

BRAD: Really? Well what if I'm written to *kick your ass!*

They scuffle. It's messy, clumsy, and very brief. By the end, BRAD has his hands around JERRY'S throat.

JERRY: *(choking, breathless)* Stop, Brad! You're giving the Writer what He wants: Conflict!

BRAD: What's that, Jerry? I can't understand you. If I could stop strangling you, I might be able to, but I'm sorry. I'm just doing what I'm written to do!

JERRY knees BRAD in the groin. BRAD topples over. Both are lying on the ground, exhausted.

JERRY: No! I won't let you give in. I won't let you have us reach a climactic confrontation! If we do, the scene will only end quicker.

BRAD pushes JERRY, one last weak effort, before sitting on the floor with his back against the chairs.

JERRY: Brad—

BRAD: I can't do this, Jerry! I can't let some self-important douchebag decide how and when I'm going to die! I can't let it happen. I don't want to be minimalistic anymore, Jerry. Nothing will ever look the same again.

JERRY crawls over to his friend, sits down against the chairs too.

BRAD: I just want it all to end. If it has to, I hope it's soon . . . I don't want to have to think about it.

JERRY rests his hand on BRAD'S shoulder.

JERRY: I know, I know.

BRAD: I just want it all to end.

They look at each other. They accept it.

BRAD: *(CONT.)* Right . . . now.

They snap their fingers simultaneously. Lights out.

The End

OKOBOJI

Suzanne Bradbeer

For Karen

PRODUCTION NOTES:

Stageworks/Hudson
Play by Play Festival of New One-Acts.
Summer of 2011
directed by Laura Margolis

Cast:
ANNIE, Bavani Selvarajah,
ALAN, Donald Warfield

An earlier version of the play was presented as part of
a benefit for the FAB Women of The Barrow Group,
directed by Amy Hargreaves, with Lulu Roche and
Abbe Ouziel.

CHARACTERS:
ALAN HARPER: late forties-sixties. An artist from Boston.
ANNIE HANSGEN: early twenties. A girl from Iowa.

SETTING: West Okoboji Lake, Iowa.
TIME: The present.

> (*Alan and Annie, looking at West Okoboji Lake. It is
> an early morning in Iowa*)

ALAN: So this is it.
ANNIE: Yeah.
ALAN: The famous blue lake . . .
ANNIE: Yeah.
ALAN: Cobalt. Cobalt blue. It's almost a Prussian blue, but not
quite. No, it's definitely cobalt. My favorite color. Have you
ever been to Boston?
ANNIE: No. I'd like to someday.
ALAN: There's a painting at the Museum of Fine Arts, it's by
William Merritt Chase, have you heard of William Merritt
Chase?
ANNIE: No.
ALAN: I don't much care for him, I find him a little prissy in
his subject matter, but I like this particular painting, and he
uses this exact shade of blue.
ANNIE: I'd love to see it.
ALAN: This exact shade of blue . . . . (*Uncomfortable, he looks
behind them*) Look at all those *trees.*
ANNIE: I know, aren't they beautiful? Oak trees are my fa-
vorite.
ALAN: I hate nature.
ANNIE: (*Picking up a feather from the ground*) Look, a hawk's
feather! Look!
ALAN: Are you Indian?
ANNIE: No.
ALAN: I mean, sorry, Native American?
ANNIE: No.
ALAN: How do you know so much about the fauna and the
flora?
ANNIE: You mean, the hawk's feather?

ALAN: Hawk's feather, oak trees, yes, how do you know all that?

ANNIE: Um, the oak is a pretty common tree? And the red-tailed hawk, they've made Their homes all over this country—in meadows, mountains—the desert. They even have them in cities, like where you're from, Boston; I even heard there were these red-tailed hawks on Fifth Avenue in New York, a hawk couple named Pale Male and Lola.

ALAN: Fascinating. (*He looks back at the lake, considering*) They say this is one of only three true blue water lakes on the planet. 'Course you probably already know that, what with your obsessive cataloguing of the natural world.

ANNIE:—

ALAN: One of three on the planet and yet I had never heard of West Okoboji Lake until a year ago. Do you know where the other two blue water lakes are?

ANNIE: Lake Geneva in Switzerland, and Lake Louise in Alberta, Canada.

ALAN: Correct. I wonder how many people in the world have seen all three? Maybe there's a group, a society you can join, I could probably go online and find the Blue Water Lake Club.

ANNIE: Sounds neat.

ALAN: Sounds hideous. I hate clubs. Turns out though, I could be a founding member.

ANNIE: You've seen all three? Really?

ALAN: Lake Geneva, beautiful of course. Lake Louise, Brian was conceived in the Hotel Banff on the shores of Lake Louise. At least that's what we always liked to say. Brian's mother and I were very . . . at any rate, let's just say it's hard to pinpoint the exact moment. But I like to think it was in the Hotel Banff. (*Beat*) I'm always quite moved by rarity. One of only three blue water lakes. Biggest diamond in the world. Only son.

ANNIE: (*beat*) Brian's eyes were this color.

ALAN: Yes.

ANNIE: That was one of the first things I noticed about him. I've never met anyone else with eyes that were/ so blue.

ALAN: Brian's great-great-great grandfather was a Colonel in the Revolutionary Army. A Colonel is a very high rank, during the Revolution it was second only to General and, and I, I don't know what made me think of that except that he, the Colonel, he seemed to be quite fond of nature too. Very fond. Very, very fond. We have a few of his letters; he survived the war and wrote constantly, *incessantly* about his travels up and down the Massachusetts Shore, up and down, up and down he went. They're quite valuable these letters—boring! But valuable. Why are you smiling?

ANNIE: We used to call Brian 'the Colonel'. Even in the short time we knew him here. It was very important to him that people respect the lake and the woods. The, flora and the fauna. He always spoke to everyone in a nice way, but he was very firm about it, if they were littering, or being careless, he was very firm.

ALAN: Were they mean to him?

ANNIE: Who?

ALAN: Anyone, was anyone mean to him?

ANNIE: No. *No.*

ALAN: He was bullied quite a lot, when he was in school.

ANNIE: He told me.

ALAN: So, calling him the Colonel, they weren't being, mocking/ or, or—?

ANNIE: No, not at all—

ALAN: Because a boy less like a colonel you could hardly hope to find.

ANNIE: We called him the Colonel because he/ had very—

ALAN: Yes, I remember that he advised people not to litter.

ANNIE: It wasn't just that, he, he had standards of behavior, very high standards of behavior—for himself especially. And he was very, responsible and, and—oh!—and he always identified time in that military way, like nine o'clock at night wasn't nine o'clock, it was 2100 hours.

ALAN: 2100 hours, yes. He started doing that when he was about seven, for some reason.

ANNIE: And he valued loyalty. And, and doing the right thing. And niceness, I think he valued niceness most of all.

ALAN: Brian was much more like his mother. I had a good nights' sleep that night.

ANNIE: Sir?

ALAN: I don't usually sleep well, but that night I was sleeping very well. Until the call. I don't understand how I slept through . . . that moment. I don't understand that. They say he died immediately.

ANNIE: Yes.

ALAN: I thought maybe they lied. To spare me, I thought maybe they lied.

ANNIE: No.

ALAN: (*This is what he's been waiting to say*) See, I would prefer to think that you fired the gun —accidentally, accidentally of course—but I would prefer to think that you fired it, rather than . . . rather than what you want me to think.

ANNIE: I don't want you to think anything.

ALAN: But can you understand that? Can you understand how a father would prefer to think that?

ANNIE: . . . I guess.

ALAN: So this, this *Inquiry*, or inquest, or—

ANNIE: Autopsy, it was just/ an autopsy—

ALAN: Whatever it was, it doesn't have a workable result for me.

ANNIE: But why—I mean, that was a month ago—why/ are you—

ALAN: And I've been giving it a great deal of thought in the last month, a great deal. As you can imagine. And I just think that maybe you should admit what *really* happened.

ANNIE: I'm sorry, but didn't you read the report, the forensics were very clear.

ALAN: I don't care about God-damn forensics! I care about my boy. You were there; you could have shot him, you'd/ both been—

ANNIE: No.

ALAN: Yes! A bunch of you had been drinking earlier that night, you admitted as much. And maybe, maybe you'd never held a gun before/ and maybe you—

ANNIE: How can you say that to me?

ALAN: Where did he get the gun?

ANNIE: It's not hard to get a gun.

ALAN: Maybe you were curious and wanted to see what it felt like and maybe Brian was trying to show you but neither of you realized that the gun was loaded/ and maybe—

ANNIE: Is this why you came all the way back here?

ALAN: No one would blame you, I would make sure/ of that.

ANNIE: He shot himself in front of me, Mr. Harper.

ALAN: No he didn't. It was an accident.

ANNIE: He shot himself in front of me.

ALAN: If you ever have children you might understand how cruel you're being right now.

ANNIE: (*beat*) I'm sorry.

ALAN: My *son* was not cruel.

ANNIE: No, he wasn't.

ALAN: That's a very cruel thing, if it's true. To do what he did in front of you.

ANNIE: I don't think he meant to.

ALAN: See! It was an accident!

ANNIE: I just meant that he didn't mean for me to see; he didn't expect/ me to—

ALAN: Why can't you say it was an accident—just tell me it was a god-damn accident—what the hell is wrong with you?!

ANNIE: . . . It was an accident.

ALAN: . . . I could wish you were a better liar.

ANNIE: . . . Me too. (*Beat*) I knew he was depressed, I think he was depressed for a long time.

ANNIE: *(Cont'd)* We talked about it sometimes. He said he considered it part of his life. But it wasn't the only part. And it doesn't take away from the things that made him happy. This lake made him happy, especially this time of day, especially right here. Remembering his Mom made him happy. And you, your paintings, your paintings made him happy.

ALAN: I'm not painting anymore.

ANNIE: You don't hate nature.

ALAN: What?!

ANNIE: You said you hated nature. You're a painter, I don't think you hate nature.

ALAN: You don't know me. You don't know me and you barely knew my son—you knew him, what, ten months? You can't know someone in ten months.

ANNIE: He talked about showing you this lake. He said the first thing you'd do would be to indentify the exact color.

ALAN: Anyone would do that.

ANNIE: And say it was your favorite color, and then mention some obscure painter who has three names.

ALAN: William Merritt Chase is hardly obscure. (*Beat*) It's true Brian was often amused by what he called my, predictability. Did he tell you that?

    (Annie nods)

ALAN: *(Cont'd)* What else did he say about me?

ANNIE: I know that he loved you, Mr. Harper.

ALAN: (*Beat*) I'm not a warm person, I am aware of that you know. Did you just roll your eyes?

ANNIE: Did I? Sorry. I thought I just rolled them in my mind. Sorry.

ALAN: It's all right. (*Looking around*) This is a nice spot. And it was nice of you to bring me here. You seem like a nice kid. I'm ready to go back now.

    (He walks off, then looks back at Annie who hasn't moved)

Are you coming?

ANNIE: . . . I'm not a nice kid . . . .

ALAN: What?

ANNIE: (d*istraught*) I let him down, I'm not a nice kid, he needed me and I let him down.

ALAN: How?

ANNIE: He reached out to me, that last week he left me a couple messages but I was preoccupied, I don't even know with what, with nothing, with my own boring problems, which were nothing, they were nothing!!I didn't get back to him until the party. I knew he was depressed and I didn't get back to him until that party, what is wrong with me?!

ALAN: (*carefully*) I shouldn't have said those things to you. I'm sorry.

ANNIE: I'm not a nice kid!

ALAN: You didn't let him down.

ANNIE: You don't know!

ALAN: I do know. I know a few things. I've lived a long time and in spite of all evidence to the contrary, I know a few things. You didn't let him down. (*Looking at her*) You don't believe me?

    (Annie shakes her head)

ALAN: *(Cont'd)* I'm your elder. I think that means you have to believe whatever I say.

ANNIE: I'm sorry, but I don't.

ALAN: Well. Then we'll just have to stay in touch till I figure out how to convince you. Can we do that?

(Annie shrugs, helpless)

ALAN: *(Cont'd Gently)* Let's do that, let's stay in touch. Now tell me something. Why are you still carrying around that dirty feather?

ANNIE: *(Looking at the feather, surprised she still has it)* Birds are believed to carry messages of the spirit. Did you know that? A bird feather represents strength and, protection. And a hawk feather, a hawk feather is extra special. If you find a feather like this, you're supposed to let it go back into the wind with a prayer, or, or a message.

ALAN: I thought you weren't an Indian.

ANNIE: I'm not, I'm just, from Iowa.

ALAN: *(Of the feather)* You're supposed to send it back into the wind?

ANNIE: *(Annie nods)* With a prayer, or a message.

ALAN: Then, let's do it.

ANNIE: Do what?

ALAN: Let's send a message.

(Annie hesitates. Then she holds the feather aloft. Alan stands next to her, but not touching her. Beat. Annie lets go of the feather and they watch it fly off over the lake. Lights out)

The End

People Don't Change
(They Just Change Their Hair)

Bekah Brunstetter

PRODUCTION NOTES:

Counterpoint Theatre
www.counterpointtheatre.org
Venue: Bennett Media Studios, NYC
Director: Allison Troup-Jensen
April 2011

Cast:
Lauren Blumenfeld
Allison Yates

CHARACTER:
ABBY, twenty-nine, not hot
JEN, twenty-nine, her roommate, hot

PLACE: An apartment
TIME: Present.

> ABBY, twenty-nine, in front of a mirror, dressed in
> a very short skirt and heels that she is so not used
> to wearing. She also wears lipstick. Beyonce's
> VIDEOPHONE.

> ABBY is using this music for inspiration. She dances a
> little bit in the mirror, badly. This is a serious serious
> private moment, there's nothing silly about it to ABBY,
> she is trying, so hard, to access her inner sexy.

ABBY: What's up. Whaddup. It is I sexy.
   I am sexy and—and other things too!
   Wanna—? I have a bed. Would you like to go to it? It
   has pillows on it. I just washed them. I think they were
   giving me adult acne.
>   Trying again.
   Well *hey* there. I like pasta. Do you?
   I like to eat like a whole box of pasta, sautee some
   spinach and garlic and olive oil, toss that shit in there,
   first cold pressed is the ONLY kind I use, yeah, *so* much
   better for you,
   Sometimes I do the same thing but with a whole thing
   of ground beef.
>   *(of her statements)*
   WHAT?!
   Oh my God ABBY
>   She stands in front of the mirror, inspecting her-
>   self.
>   JEN enters, home from work. JEN is much more
>   confident and seems to just look good, like all the
>   time, and you want to punch her for it, but thankfully

she's also nice, so you don't. She's got the mail and isn't looking at ABBY.

JEN: Hey your student loans are sending you seven letters a day again and also there's this really sad possibly feral kitten outside that I really think we should feed, do we have tuna?

ABBY: takes the stack of bills.

ABBY: Thanks.

    JEN stops in her tracks. Looks again at ABBY: .

JEN: Ummmm . . . what's this?

ABBY: What?

JEN: Why're you dressed like that?

ABBY: New leaf.

JEN: Is that my skirt?

ABBY: I am a sad lumberjack toddler no more. I am hot.

JEN: Sort of—

ABBY: This is my last chance.

JEN: That's dramatic.

ABBY: I'm 29 this year. In one year, I'll be dead.

This is my last chance—my last year to—seize this part of my-self. This is ABSOLUTELY my last year to possibly rock something from forever 21 that also might be a headband, or a hat. To go dancing. Oh my God I want to go dancing. Why don't you ever take me with you?

JEN: Because it isn't fun.

ABBY: It's because I'm not hot.

JEN: *(kind of lying)* Yes you are!!

ABBY: I want to be sexy. And I'm just really really tired of not. Being that. I can't even say the word 'sexy' without blushing. Me and the word sexy are in entirely different rooms. Sexy is in the party room and I'm not invited. I'm next door watching the Discovery channel.

JEN: This is so stupid! You are so smart! And so funny!

    (Beat)

And so smart! You don't need to be hot.

ABBY: So I'm not. Fuck that.

ABBY: puts on too much lipstick.

JEN: I totally support this—transformation—but—

ABBY: bends over a little bit adjusting her boot.

    WOW—there's your—okay.

    Can we talk this through?

Lawrence Harbison   **179**

ABBY: Whenever we talk things through you win and I pay 75% of the electric bill because you don't have a hairdryer because you have perfect hair.

JEN: I know we don't know each other—that / well but

ABBY: We know each other!

JEN: We live together.

ABBY: Same thing.

JEN: Not necessarily.

ABBY: We tell each other things. I used your toothbrush once.

JEN: You did?

ABBY: It was an accident.

JEN: We're getting to know each other.

ABBY: I saw myself in a window today and I didn't even know it was me and I judged that person and then I felt shallow which only made it worse, that I am frumpy AND shallow. I am so fucking *sick* of feeling frumpy. Shallow also bothers me.

JEN: See you can't just—*decide* that you're hot. That makes you arguably less hot. That makes you arrogant. Not hot.

ABBY: Okay so then how. HOW.

JEN: You have to find it inside of yourself.

ABBY: Gross.

JEN: I'm serious.

ABBY: Like in my belly button?

JEN: In your soul, stupid.

ABBY: My soul is not hot. My soul eats a lot of doughnuts.

JEN: Tell it to stop.

ABBY: It can't.

JEN: Train it to eat carrots instead.

ABBY: But I want to be *happy.* I want to be happy and also hot.

JEN: You have to start with Happy.

ABBY: And carrots.

JEN: No. Start with: I love myself.

ABBY: Gross.

JEN: No. ABBY. Look in the mirror.

ABBY: No.

JEN: Come on. Look at yourself. Really look at yourself.

ABBY: I don't want to. It hurts.

JEN: Why?

ABBY: I see my Mom and I in the mall. I hear my Mom telling me, *you have other gifts.* My own mother telling me I'm not pretty. If my mom doesn't think I'm hot, who will?

JEN: You want your Mom to think you're hot?

ABBY: I want to be beautiful.

JEN: Look.

Look.

ABBY: *(looks in the mirror.)* Tears come to her eyes.

There is no one else like you.

ABBY: True.

JEN: And that's beautiful.

ABBY: I'd rather be you.

JEN: You don't wanna be me.

ABBY: Yep—yes I do. I want to have affairs with violinists. I want them to write me songs—

JEN: And then be done with me—

ABBY: Buy me organic dinners—

JEN: And then use me—

ABBY: Kiss me without me having to ask—

JEN: Show me off to their friends—

ABBY: Wake up in their lairs filled with violins.

JEN: It's not like that. You're totally wrong.

ABBY: I'd still trade with you.

JEN: You want to get giant boobs when you're 12 and not know what to do with them so you spend high school rubbing them on boys who don't look you in the eye which is a huge distraction from academics which throws you totally off course and later, way later, you realize after 4 abortions that you've never loved anyone or been loved and you fantasize about cutting off your boobs into tiny pieces and mailing them, piece by piece, to every person who's touched them?

(beat)

You want that?

ABBY: I was very driven in high school. I took all AP classes.

JEN: Because you weren't distracted by people touching your boobs.

ABBY: I guess.

JEN: You wouldn't be where you are today. If you were hot.

ABBY: So I'm not.

JEN: You are. In your own way. You just have to own it.

ABBY: I don't own anything. I don't own this apartment. I don't
    own a car. The TV is yours.
JEN: You own yourself. You have control over yourself.
ABBY: But that's pretty much it.
JEN: But at least you have that.
ABBY: You don't?
JEN: I belong to every person who's ever touched me.
        (beat)
    I don't belong to myself anymore.
    I wish I was *you.*
ABBY: I wish I was *you.*
JEN: I wish I was *you.*
ABBY: It's exhausting.
JEN: What?
ABBY: All the time we spend wishing we were each other. It's
    exhausting.
ABBY: looks back into the mirror. Inspects herself.
        Gives up. Takes off the shoes. They hurt.
JEN: I have to tell you something.
    I'm 32.
ABBY: Shut up.
    No you're not.
JEN: True story.
ABBY: I always just assumed you were younger than me—
JEN: Well I'm not.
ABBY: That's weirdly comforting.
        *JEN takes a tissues, wipes some of the lipstick off
        of ABBY*
JEN: See there's still time. There's plenty of time to change.
        JEN takes a look at ABBY's lips.
    There ya go. That's actually really nice.
ABBY: looks in the mirror again.
ABBY: Yeah—
    That's actually really good.
    I look—
JEN: You look hot.
ABBY: Is this what hot looks like?
JEN: Yeah.
        They look at each other tenderly.

ABBY: We don't have to make out now or anything, do we?

JEN: Nope.

ABBY: Because I'm not hot.

JEN: Because we're not gay.

ABBY: I changed the lightbulb in the bathroom, it involved a stool and some serious elbow grease, it was pretty bad ass.

JEN: That's hot.

> *They smile at each other.*
> *Lights.*

The End

The Rollercoaster of Love

Joe Musso

PRODUCTION NOTES:

Point of Contention Theatre Company
Chicago, Illinois,

Sixth Annual Chaos Festival of New Ten-Minute
Plays.

Lincoln Square Theatre
March 28-30 and April 4-6, 2011.
Directed by Thrisa Hodits

Cast:
WOMAN, Kaitlen Osburn
MAN, Frank R. Sjodin

CHARACTERS:
A Man and a Woman about the same age.

SETTING: An empty stage.
TIME: The present.

A man and a woman enter. Each is holding a closed folding chair. The MAN: opens his chair and places it center stage.

MAN: *(Referring to chair location.)* Here?
WOMAN: Does it matter?
MAN: Of course it matters.
WOMAN: Why?
MAN: Put yours next to mine.
    (She opens her chair and places it next to his, side by side.)
MAN: *(Cont'd)* See that?
WOMAN: *(Meaning yes.)* Uh-huh.
MAN: Two seats on an airplane.
WOMAN: Wow.
MAN: You try.
WOMAN: Okay. . . . The back seat of a car.
MAN: Good one. Now, watch what happens when I do this.
    (He moves one chair far from the other one.)
WOMAN: You moved one.
MAN: Yep.
WOMAN: Now I feel a sort of distance.
MAN: Bingo! Just the effect I was hoping for.
WOMAN: So where we place the chairs *does* matter.
MAN: Precisely.
WOMAN: Except this is supposed to be a play about sound, not the distance of chairs.
MAN: Really?
WOMAN: *(Pointing at a sheet of paper she has handed to him.)* See, says right here.
MAN: *(Reading.)* "The sense of sound must be an important element of the play." Damn.
WOMAN: We could always break the rules.
MAN: I wouldn't be able to live with myself. . . . *(Pocketing*

the piece of paper.) Oh well, back to the drawing board.

WOMAN: *(Returning the chair he moved.)* I don't like these chairs so far apart.

MAN: Aha! I have an idea.

WOMAN: What?

MAN: Freytag's pyramid.

WOMAN: Huh?

MAN: Freytag. Gustav Freytag.

WOMAN: He built a pyramid?

MAN: Sorta. He was a nineteenth century novelist who saw common patterns in fiction. He created a diagram, a "pyramid," to explain those patterns.

WOMAN: Okay.

MAN: He gave us the terms "exposition," "inciting incident," "rising action"—

WOMAN: *(Interrupting.)* Don't tell me. I know what comes next. "Climax."

    (Awkward pause.)

MAN: And then "falling action," "resolution," and "dénouement."

WOMAN: We're running out of time. We have to put in sound.

MAN: *(Directing her to one of the chairs.)* Sit.

    (She complies. He sits on the other chair.)

MAN: *(Cont'd)* We're on a roller coaster.

WOMAN: Cool. Are we lovers?

MAN: Huh?

WOMAN: Lovers. At an amusement park.

MAN: Okay.

WOMAN: I feel it moving.

MAN: We're off!

    (They act as if the imaginary rollercoaster starts moving.)

MAN: *(Cont'd)*

    (A little louder, as he puts his hands in the air.)

This isn't just any ol' roller coaster, either. It's the longest, fastest, scariest roller coaster in the world.

WOMAN: *(Hugging him fiercely, closing her eyes.)* Hold me. What's it doing?

MAN: Climbing . . . higher . . . higher . . . *higher* . . . *HIGHER.*

    (They crest the top of the first hill.)

Lawrence Harbison

Oh my GOD!

(They pick up incredible speed as the coaster begins its journey around the track. They scream, yell, holler, cry, laugh and shake in their coaster car seats. The ride lasts approximately a minute and then the coaster brakes and they come to a stop. She opens her eyes and loosens her grip some, but not entirely.)

WOMAN: My hair must be a mess.

MAN: Naw.

WOMAN: That had it all.

MAN: *(Meaning yes.)* Uh-huh.

WOMAN: Rising action. Climax.

MAN: Conflict. Falling action.

WOMAN: I felt the falling action. What was the conflict?

MAN: Whether I should tell you I'm married.

WOMAN: *You're what?*

MAN: Married, you know, as in walk down the aisle.

WOMAN: But?

MAN: My wife is off buying cotton candy. She's scared of roller coasters. She told me to ride it alone.

WOMAN: How could you?

MAN: Admit it. It was fun.

WOMAN: I feel so dirty.

MAN: Want to ride it again?

(She stands and slaps him.)

WOMAN: *YOU MONSTER!*

MAN: *(While massaging his jaw.)* Not the climax I was hoping for, but a climax just the same. Now for the resolution.

WOMAN: You want resolution, I'll give you resolution. Stand up.

(He stands. She kicks him in the crotch. He screams in pain and falls to the ground.)

WOMAN: (CONT'D) I'm outta here.

(She stomps loudly in place, as if she were leaving.)

WOMAN: *(CONT'D)*

(Stopping her stomping.)

Wow. Freytag's pyramid kicks butt.

MAN: That's not all it kicks.

WOMAN: Sorry. Got caught up in the scene.

(She helps him to his feet.)

MAN: Thank you. *(After catching his breath.)* We still have to do the "dénouement."

WOMAN: Remind me again. What is the "dénouement"?

MAN: The ending. It's a French term. At the dénouement, we explain any unresolved items that remain after the resolution.

WOMAN: So, I exited the scene too soon.

MAN: Yes, you did. You'll have to make another entrance.

WOMAN: Okay.

(She walks in place, as if making an entrance.)

WOMAN: *(CONT'D)*

YOU AGAIN!

(She is about to kick him in the crotch again.)

MAN: *DON'T! Please, please, please don't.*

WOMAN: Where's your wife?

MAN: I don't have one. I was joking.

WOMAN: *Liar!*

MAN: No, honest, it was a joke. A stupid joke, I admit, but only a joke. *(Holding up his left hand.)* See, no ring.

WOMAN: It's probably in your pocket.

MAN: I swear. I'm not married.

WOMAN: *(Calming down.)* Really?

MAN: Really.

WOMAN: You need to be more careful with your jokes.

MAN: Believe me. Next time, I will be.

WOMAN: Wanna ride the rollercoaster again?

MAN: No, I need to sit a spell. Rest.

WOMAN: *(Pointing at the chairs.)* How about that bench? It has a view of the duck pond.

MAN: Okay.

(She helps him to the chairs. They sit close to each other.)

WOMAN: We're at a duck pond.

MAN: Oh. *(Imitating a duck.)* Quack. Quack. Quack.

WOMAN: Good job.

MAN: Thanks. . . . Wanna hold hands?

WOMAN: Okay.

(They hold hands.)

MAN: Pretty soon the sun's gonna set.

WOMAN: That'll be nice.

MAN: Yeah. . . . What would you like? A poem? A song?

WOMAN: Silence.

MAN: Seriously?

> *(She leans into him.)*

WOMAN: The sound of silence.

(In silence, they watch the sun set.)

MAN: I'm—

WOMAN: (Interrupting.) Shhhhh.

> *(They look longingly into each other's eyes. Quietly, they kiss.)*
>
> *(Fade.)*

The End

SECOND TIERS

Glenn Alterman

For
Monica Lewinsky

PRODUCTION NOTES:

Folsom One Act Theater Festival
September 2011,
Part of the Nach in Berlin, Germany .
Directed by Henning Hurwicz.

Cast:
JIMMY, Carl Dorn
ROBIN , Hans Breth.

The play also received a developmental reading at
The Workshop Theater Company
New York in September, 2011

Cast:
JIMMY, Dustye Winniford
ROBIN, Jeff Paul

CHARACTERS:
JIMMY, A nice looking, middle aged man
ROBIN, A nice looking, middle aged man

PLACE: a small, dimly lit bar in Key West, Florida
TIME: The present, early afternoon

(In the dark we hear a parade, music, crowd voices outside. As the lights come up we are inside a small, dimly lit bar. It is early afternoon, The bar is still boarded up from the night before. The bar is empty except for JIMMY and ROBIN, seated at a table. JIMMY has a drink, his glass is half empty)

JIMMY: James!
ROBIN: *(Trying to calm him)* Jimmy . . .
JIMMY: JAMES!
ROBIN: Jimmy, c'mon.
JIMMY: That's how he'd say it, like that. From the other room, BELLOWING! Not Jimmy, no, not even Jim: JAMES! With that condescending, superior . . . JAMES!!!
    (Bellowing)
James-Bartholomew-Olson, come in here right now!
ROBIN: *(Starting to leave)* I'm gonna go.
JIMMY: Like I was his slave or something.
ROBIN: *(Stopping)* Jimmy, are you coming to the parade or not?!
JIMMY: And if he'd had a bad day, y'know, like didn't save someone or something, me, I'd get the brunt of it!
ROBIN: YES OR NO?!
JIMMY: *(Turning to him, finishing his drink, suddenly softer)* You ever miss it, Robbie?
ROBIN: What?
JIMMY: The danger, excitement.
ROBIN: No, absolutely not! What, being someone's *shadow*?
JIMMY: Being Batman's *boy*?
ROBIN: *(Going over to him)* Boy-toy; plaything for his pleasure! No, Jimmy, I don't miss a minute of it. I am absolutely happy here in Key West, with you—without any of *that*.
JIMMY: But don't you miss . . . ?

ROBIN: What, the capes, the cave, living a closety life, being someone's second?! All the secrets, the lies, the cover ups. Secrets, yeah, like everyone didn't know.

JIMMY: They knew, people knew?

ROBIN: Sure, 'course.

JIMMY: Well no one knew about us.

ROBIN: Dynamic duo, that was his dumb idea. We couldn't be just Bruce Wayne, Dick Grayson, lovers. No, always had to be some fantasy with him. And as for Alfred, that old queen . . .

JIMMY: Well actually Lois knew.

ROBIN: Always amazed me how no one ever outed Miss Alfie. 'Mean he was so obvious, so fey. S'funny how if you carried a tray and wore a tux back then, you could get away with anything. You know one time we caught him watching us doing it?

JIMMY: Alfred?

ROBIN: Yeah, Bruce and me were going hot and heavy in the Bat bed, and I noticed the eyes in a painting on the wall were moving, then staring. I stopped, said "Bruce, your painting, look! He jumped up, got out of bed, ran out into the hall. Saw Alfred "pretending" he was dusting something. I mean there's Bruce, buck naked. I'm sure Miss Alfie got an eyeful. 'Mean they didn't call Bruce the "bat" for nothing. Anyway, Alfred sort of apologized and swished off with his duster. And how Alfie *loooved* helping Bruce in and out of that Bat suit. He'd be glued to the night sky waiting, *hoping* for the Bat signal so he'd be able to dress "Master Bruce". Bruce thought it was funny. I thought it was kinda creepy. Anyway, Alfred didn't care very much for me either. Thought I wasn't "worthy enough," Y'know, the whole Wayne family pedigree. So eventually DC comics "arranged" for his marriage, for show. Last I heard, Bruce was secretly sneaking off to cruise the men's rooms in the Gotham City Mall. He's a regular tea room, toe tapper. Pretty pathetic, if you ask me. Eh, ancient history.—C'mon, c'mon, let's go

(ROBIN starts to leave)

JIMMY: Lois was a Lesbian!

ROBIN: *(Stopping)* What?!

JIMMY: Lois Lane was a lesbian!

ROBIN: What are you talking about? Everyone knew she had the hots for him. Didn't she marry him in what, like '95?

JIMMY: For show. It sold comics. Kids. Actually Lois was into Diana Prince, Wonder Woman. Cat Woman introduced them at a DC comic convention. Been together for years. They live up in Northampton, Mass. Adopted a kid, Chinese, years ago.

ROBIN: So you're saying . . . ?

JIMMY: I was Lois' beard, and she was mine. Gotta remember the times, Robbie. Black and white TV.

ROBIN: So closety. How everyone worshipped them. If the public only knew the secrets they had hidden under those capes. Thought they were "indestructible", "above it all".

JIMMY: Well Superman sort of was.

ROBIN: Jimmy, everyone, everyone's got their Kryptonite, Achilles heel. *Nobody*'s above it all. They just think they are, 'cause they fly so high.

JIMMY: God, the parties back then. You haven't partied until you've been in a room filled with a bunch of steroid, muscled up, super-heroes showing off their "best attributes". This one time, Captain Marvel made Mr. Freeze just melt and . . .

ROBIN: Jimmy, what are you doing?!

JIMMY: What do you mean?

ROBIN: All this *nostalgia*? What's going on, you suddenly missing him?

JIMMY: "S"? No, not at all.

ROBIN: *(Smiling)* Am I getting too old to—leap tall buildings in a single bounce?

JIMMY: Bound; leap tall buildings in a single *bound.* Sides there are no tall buildings in Key West.

ROBIN: Come on, let's close up, watch the parade. Be fun; get you out of this—*funk.*

JIMMY: I don't want to go.

ROBIN: *(Looking at him)* What do you mean, you love Fantasy Fest.

JIMMY: I'll set up, get the bar ready for later. We should be getting a big crowd.

ROBIN: Jimmy, for God's sake, what the hell is going on?!

JIMMY: Nothing.

ROBIN: *(JIMMY starts setting up. ROBIN goes over to him)* What?!

JIMMY: *(Turning to ROBIN, a beat, then softly)* He's here.

ROBIN: Who? Clark, Superman, in Key West?!

JIMMY: He flew in for Fantasy Fest.

ROBIN: How do you know?

JIMMY: I . . . uh have a Jmmy Olsen page, on Facebook. And . . . we've been in touch.

ROBIN: I see.

    (Sitting down)

So, you want to see him?

JIMMY: My Jimmy Olsen Facebook pictures aren't exactly updated.

ROBIN: How old are they?

JIMMY: I don't know, . . . 'bout thirty years or something. From when I was still a cub reporter at the Daily Planet.

ROBIN: Oh.

JIMMY: He hasn't aged at all, "S." Looks the same. Something to do with Krypton. They don't age down here like we do. So no, I really don't want to see him.

ROBIN: You mean you don't want him to see *you*.—Why didn't you tell me about any of this?

JIMMY: I dunno. It's just . . . Lately I've been thinking about how exciting it all was back then. Always living in fear we'd be found out. The daily danger. Today, everybody's so God damned "out and proud and rah-rah-rah!" Back then a quick kiss in a corner, so romantic. A quickie with Clark in the Daily Planet men's room, so taboo.

ROBIN: Jimmy, they *used* us! Sure, we let them. Like everyone else, we were blinded by their light. Heroes, super heroes. But to them we were just notches on a belt.

JIMMY: I know.

ROBIN: *(Smiling)* For what it's worth, in my world, you always were and will be number on*e*; not someone's second. Ever since that moment we met at that Holloween party where you were dressed as . . .

JIMMY: *(Cringing)* Bat-girl.

ROBIN: And you looked at me and said . . . .

JIMMY: Great Caesar's ghost!

ROBIN: From that first minute I swear, I . . . I just knew.

JIMMY: Me too. And you scooped me up, and saved me- from Superman.

ROBIN: And you freed me from the Bat cave—and Alfred. I just felt we had this *something* in common. I mean little did I know . . . . But I have to confess . . .

JIMMY: What?

ROBIN: That Bat-girl wig you wore . . . I thought . . . You looked more like Super-Hassidic Jew.

JIMMY: Look who's talking? What were you dressed as?

ROBIN: *(Smiling)* Thoroughly Modern Millie. I was madcap Millie out looking for her man that night. And I found him, Bat-girl, in a bad wig! And c'mon, admit it, I looked damn good that night!

JIMMY: Yes you did, still do.

ROBIN: Well, for a middle aged . . . Go, see your Superman, go ahead. What's he going dressed as for Fantasy Fest?

JIMMY: Duh, Superman.

ROBIN: Okay, then you go as—Jimmy Olsen. Not James, not Jim! *(Like "Just Jack", from "Will and Grace")* JUST JIMMY!

JIMMY: *(Smiling, holding his hands up to frame his face)* Just Jimmy!

ROBIN: *(Going over to him, holding him)*Just Jimmy who I have loved for —God, over *thirty years*!

JIMMY: *(Smiling)* Ow.

ROBIN: And they said it would never last. "Just Jimmy", who I happily share a home, two dogs, a neurotic cat, and a gay bar called Champs in Key West with. Alright, so maybe you can't fly or bend steel in you bare hands, but you're a good person, Jimmy. Kind, caring. And kind, caring people are the *real heroes* today and are highly *underrated*. . . . Go ahead, go see him.

JIMMY: Maybe I should carry some Kryptonite.

ROBIN: Leave that for Lex Luthor. You don't need to kill the guy. Just go over to him, smile, say "Hey, hi, nice seeing you again Superman. Thanks for the memories. Welcome to Key West. This is where I live—*now.*

JIMMY: God, I love you.

ROBIN: *(Smiling)* So, can we finally go?

JIMMY: Sure.

(JIMMY kisses ROBIN)

ROBIN: *(A bit surprised)* What's that for?

JIMMY: For nothing, for thirty years. For everything. For saving me.

ROBIN: For saving *me.*

JIMMY: Hey, hi, hello—thanks for the memories. This is where I live—*now.*

(Then, smiling)

You really are thoroughly modern, Millie.

ROBIN: Yeah?

JIMMY: Just like in the movie, Julie Andrews. Perfect, absolutely perfect. Everything in place. Everything so right, . . . right down to the shoes.—C'mon, let's go.

(HE opens the door to the bar. Bright sunlight fills the bar. We hear the loud crowd, the parade. They look at each other, smile. Blackout. End of play)

The End

SKULL (LESS THREE AND TWENTY)

Jason Gray Platt

PRODUCTION NOTES:

Red Bull Theater
Artistic Director: Jesse Berger

Theater at St. Clement's.
June 13, 2011
Director: Wendy McClellan

Cast:
QUEEN, Kate MacCluggage
FOOL, Andrew Weems

CHARACTERS
THE QUEEN: A queen, female, 30s
THE FOOL: A fool, male, 40s

SETTING: A court, the queen's quarters.
TIME: Hundreds of years ago.

Text Notes:
A dash (-) means the speaker has stopped him or herself.
A backslash (/) denotes a point of overlapping or interruption by the following dialogue.
Text in parentheses (text) is spoken sotto voce.

The Queen and the Fool in the Queen's quarters.

FOOL: Her majesty asked to see me?

QUEEN: Please, make yourself comfortable.

FOOL: Not easy to do when the air is cold enough to freeze Satan's piss.

QUEEN: Yes. That cannot be good for the soul, can it, to be subject to such oscillations in weather? Surely a soul expands and contracts with the air just as any substance does.

FOOL: Exactly why I keep two souls, madame.

QUEEN: Two?

FOOL: Yes, it provides me much greater balance. Though I don't call them hot and cold but rather left and right.
(He indicates his feet.)

QUEEN: Do you think it's best to go stomping around on your souls all day?

FOOL: Without question. To tread on the soul is to make it terrible sad, and sadness of the soul is what your poet would call experience, and experience is wisdom. Therefore the wisest thing a man can do is to spend his day walking. The greatest fool I ever knew spent morning till night on his feet, and if ever he did offend, by the time he was to be punished he was already miles away.

QUEEN: That's nicely spun. I can see why my son is so attached to you. I find him echoing your gestures with increasing frequency.

FOOL: The honor is mine. What can I do for her majesty?

QUEEN: I often wish that I could make him laugh the way you do. Or anyone, for that matter. There is a great power in it.

FOOL: Nothing compared to a queen's influence. If her majesty is ever inclined to switch places—

QUEEN: Oh, do you aspire after royalty now? There is nothing so dangerous as foolish ambition.

FOOL: I only aspire to the degree necessary for subsequent respiration.

QUEEN: I don't think you'd much enjoy it. Queens have to be so horribly serious all the time. Whereas you get to say whatever you like.

FOOL: Not so.

QUEEN: Please. One cannot by definition be offended by a fool. Fools speak nonsense, and only another fool would take offense at nonsense. And then you would have proven the first fool was right all along.

FOOL: I'll ask you not to give away trade secrets, madame.

QUEEN: It's exactly the sort of trap my husband would fall into. Why don't you tell me one about him.

FOOL: One what?

QUEEN: Say something funny.

FOOL: A joke?

QUEEN: Yes. Tell me a joke about the king. I've heard you have some rather juicy ones.

FOOL: I would never dare to question his majesty.

QUEEN: Because he's already quite the fool himself, you mean? Come, there's no need to be withholding.

FOOL: I assure you /

QUEEN: What was it they told me you said the other night at the innkeeper's? "The king is so thick, he thinks fencing is a sport for carpenters." I also very much liked: "why does the king require ten women for his sexual satisfaction?"
(she waits for his reply)
Well?

FOOL: "Because it takes that many to hold down the horse."

QUEEN: Don't be misled by the fact that I'm not laughing. I do find them amusing. Somewhere deep beneath the flesh I'm quite sure my spleen is quivering in illicit delight. It's just that I

Lawrence Harbison

find displays of laughter somehow. Presumptuous, I suppose. It seems vain for the mortal beast to find humor in the very life that condemns her to death. You know this Then, of course, were someone to observe my laughter at such jokes, I would be in a great deal of trouble. Because to impugn the character of the king is an act of treason. Is it not?

> *(beat)*

FOOL: It would be.

QUEEN: Not a good position to find oneself in. But the king is so busy at the moment that I see no reason to involve him in such trivial matters. I thought instead that you and I could. Work something out ourselves. There are two sides to every story, after all.

FOOL: You haven't spoken to his majesty?

QUEEN: Oh no. No, I can keep secrets when necessary. It's a requisite trait for anyone in the public eye.

FOOL: Of course.

QUEEN: Would you perhaps like to hear one of them?

> *(beat)*

FOOL: Then it would no longer be a secret.

QUEEN: On the contrary, it becomes even more clandestine once two people share it because it's all the more dangerous. Which is the defining characteristic of the secret.

FOOL: It would be an honor to hold your confidence.

QUEEN: You're too kind. You see, when I heard what you'd said, I asked myself how much you might truly hate the king. The way he treats you—

FOOL: I promise you I harbor no hatred for his majesty, nor for anyone.

QUEEN: Please don't feel it necessary to deny your feelings. Now that you are in this precarious position we can be perfectly honest with one another. True honesty is only ever possible when power is unequally shared between two people. In times of equanimity we're all much too afraid of losing the advantage to be forthright.

FOOL: I believe it was your majesty who had something she wanted to share with me.

QUEEN: All right, if you're going to be shy. I ask how much you might hate the king because I, myself, have. Rather mixed feelings for him. He is not, as you know—It would be generous to say that he is not a sympathetic man. For anyone other than himself, that is. And a requirement, I believe, of any sovereign is that if they are not sympathetic, they must at least be intelligent. But as your humor has so delicately touched on, his majesty hardly possessed profound judgment to begin with, and whatever he did possess has now been thoroughly corroded in that familiar manner that only authority can occasion. How he treats his. Realm. Is astonishing in its callous ineptitude. The only reasonable solution is that he must leave the throne. I know that a number of us have come to this conclusion. However, he is not the kind to abdicate of his own volition. Therefore we must pressure him to do so.

FOOL: How?

QUEEN: With his death, ideally.

> *(beat)*

FOOL: Your majesty is joking, of course.

QUEEN: No, I leave that to the professionals. I am convinced that once he is dead, it will be much easier to remove him from the throne.

FOOL: Apparently you haven't seen how much his majesty has been eating recently.

QUEEN: We've stopped being funny now.

FOOL: People tell me I stopped years ago.

QUEEN: Hold your tongue. I thought that given your. Opinions of my husband, as well as the fact that he seems to trust you a great deal—which demonstrates exactly the strength of judgment he has—that you might be well suited to the task. There is also this unfortunate. Situation, that you find yourself in, which really works out to my benefit. And who would ever suspect the gentle fool?

FOOL: I'm afraid you may find me far too gentle and not enough of a fool.

QUEEN: Afterward, if you wished to stay here in my court you would be more than welcome, or if you desired your freedom, you would have that as well. You have my word. What you do not have, is much of a choice.

> *(beat)*

FOOL: You and his majesty are not very close.

QUEEN: Our personal relationship is immaterial.

FOOL: In the manner you imply, yes. I meant that the two of you don't speak a great deal.

QUEEN: Enough to leave us desiring no more of each other.

FOOL: Madame, why do you think his majesty brought me here to begin with?

QUEEN: He was rather on edge following that incident with the lords a number of years ago. I believe he desired some Levity, in the court.

FOOL: Levity, yes, but not for the court.

QUEEN: For whom, then?

FOOL: When I was conscripted, the king gave me instructions to go among the people, and to mock him.

The Queen suppresses a laugh.

QUEEN: I don't take offense at you attempting to equivocate your way out of the circumstances, but I am going to ask that you respect me enough to work a little harder at it.

FOOL: I'm not equivocating in the least. I was told very clearly to pass at least two nights a week in public houses ridiculing any number of subjects from his majesty himself, the monarchy, your highness, the young prince. Whatever happened to strike my fancy at the moment. To be perfectly honest, I'm surprised this is the first you've heard of it. But then, you don't appear especially concerned with his reputation.

QUEEN: Why on earth would he ask you to do that?

FOOL: So they would laugh at him, obviously.

QUEEN: He's encouraging acts of sedition?

FOOL: Sedition—

(he waves his hand)

His majesty is more concerned with power than reputation, you're quite right about that.

QUEEN: Then it can't possibly benefit him to instill revolutionary feeling among his subjects.

FOOL: Oh but you see, I do the opposite. I make people laugh.

QUEEN: And how is that the opposite?

FOOL: You can't despise what you casually dismiss with a good chuckle. When I said that I feel hatred for no one I was quite serious. I just find everything rather funny. Even this, really. This is the funniest thing that's happened to me in months. Not from your perspective, perhaps.

(beat)

FOOL: You see this is exactly why it's better to keep everything light, otherwise matters become so grave and uncomfortable. I merely. Release the pressure. So I suppose I am a kind of assassin after all. But my prey is passion, not people.

QUEEN: Aren't you a nasty little monkey. I've been trying to stir up this population for months now.

FOOL: In my experience, people tend to prefer a good hearty laugh to picking up a sword. Less of a mess to clean up afterward.

QUEEN: I may need to have a nice long sit down with the king about you.

FOOL: Please do. I'll be especially curious to hear how you explain that last part.

(The Fool takes out a juggling ball and tosses it casually.)

QUEEN: I think you and I have concluded our business.

FOOL:Not quite yet. It turns out that you were correct about my potential connection to treasonous acts.

QUEEN: How so?

FOOL: I believe it is treason to know of a plot against the king and not report it, isn't it? I merely wish to be a good subject.

QUEEN: You arrogant little clown, if you—Do you have any idea how much horror has come at that man's hands? He has bathed in so much blood that it sweats itself out of him in the night. I watch it seep from his skin onto the bed sheets. You're no better than some middling shade at the right hand of Hades. No matter. You are truly a fool if you imagine he would believe you.

FOOL: Oh, do the two of you have a strong relationship? Because he and I share the sort of bond that only comes with speaking frankly about one another. On the other hand, I do hold a great deal of faith in your ability to persuade me to maintain my silence. For whatever tempting reason that may be.

QUEEN: There's that foolish ambition rearing its little head.

FOOL:I suppose it is rather dangerous, though you were wrong about for whom. Feel free to begin persuading me whenever you like.

Lawrence Harbison

(beat)

FOOL: Shall I tell a joke to ease the tension?

QUEEN: Now that you mention it, yes. I think that's an excellent idea. Make me laugh, Yorrick.

FOOL: Your majesty doesn't quite seem to be in the mood.

QUEEN: That shouldn't matter to you, should it? As entertaining as you are. Unless you've ceased to be amusing altogether, which is beginning to be my opinion. That would mean your services are no longer required here. Anyone who keeps around a fool without wit has a much greater fool in herself So let's have a test of your mercenary charms, shall we? Since your cheery antics have the power to disperse rumblings of oppression, hunger, and revolution, as you claim—Let's jump straight to death.

FOOL: Your majesty?

QUEEN: What do you suppose is the funniest way to die?

FOOL: Thankfully I have no experience in that area.

QUEEN: I imagine it's hanging. Not if your neck breaks, that isn't very entertaining. But if for some reason you aren't dropped far enough, and you simply dangle in the air with your arms and legs flinging about like some gargantuan insect—

That would amuse me greatly.

FOOL: You don't think the prince would find the spectacle very disturbing?

QUEEN: I should hope he does. And with any luck he'll realize that while you have your uses, the power of the gambol and the gibe is much more treacherous than it may appear.

FOOL: The king would be very disappointed if that occurred.

QUEEN: I don't believe so. That's the problem with being the fly on the wall. No one notices if the fly is gone.

(beat)

FOOL: Perhaps I can help your majesty with her proposal after all.

QUEEN: Can you make me laugh?

FOOL: I—

QUEEN: If you can't make me laugh, you aren't much use to anyone, are you? Murderers are not so rare and much less valuable, but the power of a good jester, obviously—So here is the test. I want you to concentrate on your death.

Imagine the day that you will not return home to a familiar bed for the first time. Think of the rope around your neck, and your limp sack of muscle and bone hanging slackly beneath. Then your frigid corpse being feasted on by maggots and their offspring as they chew away at your flesh. And all of the choices you have made, all of the relations, all of the hardship you have so valiantly overcome, all of that now nothing more than a stained skull being tossed around a graveyard by two boys at play. Concentrate on all of that. And make me laugh.

The End

STALK ME BABY

C.S. Hanson

PRODUCTION NOTES:

STALK ME, BABY was developed by At-Hand Theatre in New Yo rk City (Dan Horrigan, artistic director).

Mankato Mosaic Theatre Company
Part of "Coffee Shop Tales,"
March 3 – 5, 2011,
Mankato, Minnesota
Directed by Launa Helder.

Cast:
HANNAH, Michaella Crnkovic
MATTHEW, Ryan Thoreson

CHARACTERS:
HANNAH, late twenties, female
MATTHEW, late twenties, male

SETTING: A coffee bar in an urban area.

> *(Hannah and Matthew sit at separate tables in a coffee bar. He's sending a text message on his cell phone. Hannah, with cell phone and latte, gets up and approaches Matthew.)*

HANNAH: Okay, that's enough. I am wigging out. Hand it over.

MATTHEW: What?

HANNAH: Oh please. You're caught. I see what you're doing.

MATTHEW: What are you talking about?

HANNAH: If I had a pair of handcuffs—stalker handcuffs—I'd cuff you right here, right now.

MATTHEW: Whaaaa? Did you say stalker?

HANNAH: The phone? Oh, that's good, act all alarmed. . . . Look, you're making me crazy. Mind if I sit?

MATTHEW: I'm in the middle of—

> *(Hannah sits.)*

HANNAH: Thanks.

MATTHEW: Actually, I'm kind of busy—

HANNAH: So, I could call the police—

MATTHEW: The police?

HANNAH: Hold on. But I'm willing to keep this private.

MATTHEW: I don't know what you're talking about.

HANNAH: Yeah right. Every time I come in here, I get these stalker text messages—lewd stuff, sicko messages, I mean really sicko. I know it's you. I see the pattern. I read your messages, squirm, get ho—*(almost says hot)* . . . horrified, and you, you, just get off on it, don't you? Every time I'm in here.

MATTHEW: I've never even seen you before.

HANNAH: I'm a regular. And so are you.

MATTHEW: It's not me. I swear. You got the wrong—

HANNAH: Listen, you big jerk, lay off. Do you realize how scared I am? Wondering if you're going to follow me back to my apartment at 302 Second Street in Park Slope?

MATTHEW: Geez, I think you should—

HANNAH: Apartment 1-F.

MATTHEW: —call the police.

HANNAH: Oh, that sounds easy. File a report. At a police station. They'd probably make me open my phone and read the messages out loud. I mean, I sit here reading them and I know I just start blushing. This is so embarrassing.

MATTHEW: It's that bad, huh?

HANNAH: I just want to know: Will you stop? Now that I've confronted you? Or . . . or I will risk humiliation and go to the cops. No, no, I'll call them right now.

MATTHEW: Hey, wait a minute. Check my outgoing messages. You'll see. I didn't send you any—go ahead, click on any message.

(Matthew hands her his phone. She reads his messages.)

HANNAH: You text your mom?

MATTHEW: And my eight-year-old nephew. And my friends. You see your number anywhere in there?

HANNAH: Maybe you erase the messages right away.

MATTHEW: Call the police. Get me out of this. Waste my time a little longer, would you?

HANNAH: Oh my God. I'm so sorry. I've lost sleep over this. I've never been this bugged out. You're . . . you're not the guy. You're not the e-stalker. Could I get you something for your trouble? A latte? Frapp? Mocha capp?

MATTHEW: It's okay.

HANNAH: Peppermint mocha twist frapp with extra whipped cream? And a cinnamon thing? Cake thing. A coffee, coffee cake or—something, anything. You should eat.

MATTHEW: I hope you catch the weirdo.

HANNAH: I feel so foolish.

MATTHEW: No, no, you shouldn't. Really. I, uh, I admire your tenacity, taking matters into your own hands.

HANNAH: Oh, thank you. I was so nervous, coming over here. I almost dropped my cell phone my hands were shaking so much.

MATTHEW: I almost thought you were going to whip out a pair of handcuffs.

(Big laugh from Hannah. Together, both chuckling, they move their chairs closer together.)

HANNAH: So, those messages about meeting up? Were they to your girlfriend? Not that it's any of my—

MATTHEW: Girlfriend? I, uh, nope.

HANNAH: No? Oh, okay. I mean, you seem like such a nice guy I thought—

MATTHEW: Your boyfriend must be pretty upset about the stalker.

HANNAH: Boyfriend? Oh, no, he's not—I mean, no, I don't, I mean, I'm not seeing anyone right now.

MATTHEW: Hey, you know you can block certain numbers?

HANNAH: You're kidding.

MATTHEW: I'll show you.

HANNAH: No, no, you've done enough.

MATTHEW: I'd like to help you out.

HANNAH: But, you know, when I go to the police, I should probably have everything preserved the way it happened—

MATTHEW: You mind?

(Matthew grabs Hannah's phone.)

HANNAH: Please, really, you don't have to—

MATTHEW: What'd you do? Erase all your evidence?

HANNAH: Did I? Well, let's see, maybe I—

MATTHEW: There are no ingoing or outgoing text records.

HANNAH: I'm a total klutz with technology.

MATTHEW: Did you just—? . . .

HANNAH: No, I accidentally deleted the messages.

MATTHEW: Have you been—?

HANNAH: I want my phone back.

MATTHEW: No text messages have been deleted in the last month. I work in IT. You're not being stalked. You're the one who's—

HANNAH: Look, I'm, I'm—

MATTHEW: Have you been stalking me?

HANNAH: No, well, not stalking. It's just—

MATTHEW: You've been stalking—

HANNAH: No, no. It's just, you sit here all hooked up to your laptop and your phone, barely looking up. Maybe I've overheard some conversations. You were so supportive when your mom had the bunion surgery. Tailor bunions? I'd never heard of—And getting her the crutches. Stocking her fridge with Peach Snapple Iced Tea, which is my favorite too. And that day your sister got dumped by that, well, obviously a moron, because your sister sounds, well, gosh you all seem really nice. I loved it when you insisted on taking her to that Sandra Bullock movie, which, yeah, it was panned by the critics, but it was the perfect I've-just-been-dumped movie. Perfect because she doesn't end up with the guy, but she's learned to feel special just for being her dorky self. I noticed we both laughed in the same places.

MATTHEW: What? You were there? You followed me to the—

HANNAH: No. No. Not followed, not exactly. But, you know, you made plans on the phone, sitting here. Out loud. The whole coffee bar could have picked up and gone. Kipps Bay, the 7:40 show. No, it's not like I was—I'd been thinking of going to a movie that night. Really. I mean, that was my plan. Come here, get some coffee, pick a movie. . . . I'm really, oh, I'm so sorry.

MATTHEW: Just . . . forget it.

HANNAH: It's just—

MATTHEW: What?

HANNAH: I didn't know how to get your attention.

MATTHEW: Ever heard of online dating? You don't have to accuse anyone of being a criminal.

HANNAH: I had eighty-nine dates last year with guys I met online. I'm taking myself offline. I don't like to pursue. I don't like to promote myself, in that way, you know, like, as "date" material. It makes me feel, well, kind of misunderstood right from the start. . . . I wanted someone to find me. And then I saw you.

(Matthew begins packing up his things.)

HANNAH: I apologize. I wasn't going to have you arrested. I wanted to exchange phone numbers.

MATTHEW: You could have asked.

HANNAH: Like you would have talked to me. I mean, people don't talk. They sit and text and IM and . . . Look, you can keep coming here. I'll find a new place.

(Hannah gets up to leave.)

MATTHEW: You're right about online dating. It sucks. If you low key your profile, you come off like a loser. If you put on a good spin, you're just gonna disappoint the other person. It's never gonna be the same as, you know, just getting to know someone, like, you know—

HANNAH: In person?

MATTHEW: We're all looking for the same thing.

HANNAH: Really? So, then, maybe you understand why I—

MATTHEW: I don't know.

HANNAH: So have me arrested—arrested for just trying to get someone's attention in this crazy city.

MATTHEW: Sit down. Put your phone away.

(Hannah sits down. They both beam.)

The End

PLAYS FOR THREE OR MORE ACTORS

amuse-bouche

Michael Clark

PRODUCTION NOTES:

amuse-bouche was originally produced in June 2010 by The New Perspective Festival in San Diego, California (Kelly Lapczynski, Festival Director). For general inquiries, please contact her through her website: www.kellylapczynski.com.

Directed by Christopher Burger

Cast

WIFE, Leticia Martinez
WAITER, Brendan Slater
HUSBAND, Tom Andrew

CHARACTERS:
WIFE, a woman in her middle twenties
WAITER, a man in his early thirties
HUSBAND, a man in his late twenties

SETTING: A Michelin starred restaurant in the Californiawine country.
TIME: Brunch.

WIFE: *(reads James Beard's Beard On Food)* "Food is our common ground, a universal experience."
WAITER: Good Morning.
WIFE: Good Morning.
WAITER: Welcome.
WIFE: Thank you.
WAITER: What a breathtaking day for such a bewitchingly beautiful woman!
WIFE: You're too kind.
WAITER: May I offer a chilled beverage: Bloody Mary or Krug Grand Cuvée?
WIFE: No thank you.
WAITER: May I offer a hot beverage? Organic, fair trade, sustainable coffee blend or infused white tea?
WIFE: No. Thank you. I am waiting for my fiancée.
WAITER: You are waiting for your fiancée? Your fiancée! So, what they say is true: "A thing of beauty is a joy forever."
WIFE: O-M-G! I love Mary Poppins.
WAITER: John Keats actually. I'll fetch you a bottle of mineral water from the French Alps.
WIFE: Still.
WAITER: *Still.* I shall return.
WIFE: Good Afternoon, my little crème brûlée.
HUSBAND: Hey.
WIFE: Happy Anniversary.
HUSBAND: Ah yes. The Anniversary.
WIFE: I loooooooooove you so much!
HUSBAND: I know you do.
WIFE: Can you believe it has been three whole months? It seems like our lifetime has passed us by.

WAITER: Good Afternoon and Welcome. Your fiancée wanted to start off brunch with a twenty five dollar bottle of mineral water from the French Alps.

WIFE: For our three month anniversary.

WAITER: For your three month anniversary?

WIFE: Yes. Our anniversary!

WAITER: Félicitations! Should we commence your brunch with a couple of glasses of champagne or California sparkling white wine? Taittinger Brut "La Francaise" or Domaine Chandon Rosé?

HUSBAND: Huh?

WIFE: Do you have juice?

WAITER: We have freshly squeezed, free range juice of citrus.

WIFE: That sounds wonderful. Two please.

WAITER: I shall return with your amuse-bouche.

HUSBAND: He shall return with my what?

WIFE: How did you sleep?

HUSBAND: We need to talk.

WIFE: I slept like a pangolin.

HUSBAND: That's nice. A pangolin?

WIFE: Yes. A pangolin. They're supposed to be the mammal that sleeps the most.

HUSBAND: Pangolins?

WIFE: Yes. The scaly anteater sleeps the best. Like I did. Last night.

HUSBAND: You learn something new everyday.

WIFE: And you said Wikipedia was pointless! They say that the first three months of a relationship are the roughest. The toughest. I know it's been sort of stressful but we made it. We made it through our first three months together! I am so ridiculously happy for us. Go us! Now, let's start planning the wedding. I was thinking pink. Pink as far as the eyes can see. My wedding is going to look like pink threw up all over it.

HUSBAND: My wedding? That's what I want to talk to you about.

WAITER: Here are your drinks.

HUSBAND: I'm leaving you.

WAITER: I'll give you second to look over the menu.

HUSBAND: I'm leaving you.

Lawrence Harbison   219

WIFE: I heard you the first time.

HUSBAND: I'm sorry but it's all the clichés. "It's not you, it's me." That's not true really. It's not me, it's you. "I think we should be friends." But not really. "We've drifted apart." More like I just wanted to get away from you. "Two roads diverged in a yellow wood" and I choose the road: "Not You".

WIFE: Stop it.

HUSBAND: I've been trying to tell you for eleven weeks.

WIFE: Eleven weeks? Wait. Let me do the math. *(She does the math in her head.)* Remainder three. *(Realization.)* We've only been going out for twelve!

HUSBAND: That's what makes this so difficult.

WIFE: You proposed to me. I chose our wedding chargers!

HUSBAND: I want my mood ring back.

WIFE: I can't believe this is happening. Why?

HUSBAND: It's the little things.

WIFE: What little things?

HUSBAND: You aren't the woman I acted like I fell in love with.

WIFE: That's a BIG THING!

HUSBAND: It's like you're a PC and I'm a Mac. We're just incompatible. I thought you'd be more fun. Thought provoking. I came to find your just a crappy computer that was already technologically obsolete the minute I bought it.

WIFE: Why do I have to be the PC? Why do you get to be the Mac?

HUSBAND: That's what you take from that? Really? You are boring.

WIFE: I'm what?

HUSBAND: You . . . . are . . . . boring.

WIFE: No . . . . I'm . . . not.

HUSBAND: You've changed.

WIFE: How have I changed?

HUSBAND: You treat me like a child.

WIFE: I do not. *(Emasculating)* Please put your napkin on your lap, Sweetie Pie.

HUSBAND: You make all the decisions.

WIFE: We need to be practical. We are planning for my wedding.

HUSBAND: We used to do things. Fun things. You know what?

You used to be fun. Now it's please and thanks you's. You used to drink. Now you won't even have a glass of California sparkling white wine on your three month anniversary! By the way, who the hell has a three month anniversary?! YouTube and Hulu have corroded your brain to have the attention span of a peanut. It's like your brain is a fifteen minute play.

WIFE: A peanut? Really? You drop a bomb like this? On our anniversary?

HUSBAND: I'm surprised we've lasted this long.

WIFE: You're surprised? I'm surprised.

HUSBAND: Totally being honest here: you've gotten fatter.

WIFE: I have not.

HUSBAND: Not around your waist. Around your earlobes. I can't be engaged to a woman who has chubby earlobes. What would people say?

WIFE: This is . . . You're not serious. This is a joke. A very sick joke. A very sick and cruel joke which I am not really getting the punchline to. What's the punchline? I'm not getting the punchline.

HUSBAND: The punchline is: I don't want to spend the rest of my life with you.

WIFE: How can you say that to me?

HUSBAND: Easily. I've only waited eleven weeks to say it.

WIFE: Twelve. You are unbelievable.

HUSBAND: I feel like our sex life is like watching: "No Deal or No Deal". "How I Met Your Mother". "Two and A Half Men" without Charlie Sheen. They said Ashton Kutcher was going to be better, but he wasn't. He really wasn't.

WIFE: What does that even mean?

HUSBAND: You don't do things anymore. Things you did before we got engaged.

WIFE: We're engaged now. I shouldn't have to do them.

HUSBAND: Even Bob's wife does things to him on his birthday.

WIFE: Bob's wife is poor white trash. *(Aside)* She shops at Walmart.

HUSBAND: Julie doesn't judge me. Julie loves me for who I am.

WIFE: Julie?

HUSBAND: The other woman.

Lawrence Harbison

WIFE: You're cheating on me? How could you cheat on me? I'm friggin' awesome.

HUSBAND: It's not my fault. It just happened like a week ago. *(Aside)* Repeatedly.

WIFE: Where did you meet this Kim Kardasian?!

HUSBAND: The Soup Kitchen.

WIFE: The Soup Kitchen?

HUSBAND: Yes. The Soup Kitchen. It all started when I was dropping off some donations to charity. You know: my set of rookie baseball card that "you" didn't want in "our" apartment.

WIFE: Don't be infantile. It's "our" apartment.

HUSBAND: It's your apartment that I built all the IKEA furniture in. If I ever see another neuken allen wrench I am going to neuken lose it!

WIFE: What does *neuken* mean?

HUSBAND: It's Dutch. Let's put it this way: you wouldn't know what neuken means because you haven't been neuken-ing me for weeks. (But Julie has.) She is refreshing. A fresh breath of Febreze.

WIFE: I bet she is very refreshing whether it's your birthday or not.

HUSBAND: *(sings)* It's a very merry unbirthday for me (and her)!

WIFE: How could you do this to me? To us?

HUSBAND: You did this to us a very long time ago.

WAITER: *(Sets down with a grandoise white plate with microscopic sized food)* We begin with your traditional brunch amuse-bouche: apple crusted brioche à tête with an Albertian syrup reduction glaze atop hydroponic potatoes Lyonnaise accompanied by your freshly squeezed, free range juice of citrus. Please enjoy.

HUSBAND: You call this breakfast?

> *(Moment. WIFE throws juice in HUSBAND's face.)*

HUSBAND: *Very mature.*

WIFE: You want to break up? You got it.

HUSBAND: *Pulpy.*

WIFE: I cannot believe I squandered my youth on someone like you. My rose has wilted.

HUSBAND: The sooner you grow up and quit being so dramatic the simpler life will be for you.

WIFE: I'll see you in court.

HUSBAND: You can take your IKEA furniture and shove them up your . . .

WAITER: GO!

HUSBAND: . . . what?

WAITER: Did I stutter? Get out of here.

HUSBAND: This is none of your business.

WAITER: You are in my hauté cuisine temple of gastronomy. You are my business.

HUSBAND: What are you going to do about it, tough guy?

WAITER: First, I'm going to force feed you mass amounts of corn until your liver is engorged. Then, I am going to tear open your skin with my bare hands and rip out your liver a lá Indiana Jones and the Temple of Doom. "Kali ma... Kali ma... Kali ma, shakthi deh!" Subsequently, I will sauté your liver with mountain huckleberries with a lemon zest confit and eat you with a very young Chenin Blanc served at an arid fifty five degrees. What are you going to do about that, tough guy?

WIFE: (sotto voce) Leave. Please just leave.

HUSBAND: You'll be hearing from my lawyers, Sweetie Pie.

(HUSBAND Exits. Moment of realization.)

WAITER: What an asshole!

WIFE: I'm sorry about your linens. I got orange juice all over them.

WAITER: Don't worry about that. (Aside) Did you just see that asshole?

WIFE: (Starts crying) I got orange juice all over them.

WAITER: Oh sweetie! There are bigger messes in life than spilt orange juice.

WIFE: Why can't someone just love me for who I am? My rose has wilted.

WAITER: When you threw that freshly squeezed, free range juice of citrus in his face, it made my day. Look. Life doesn't throw curve balls at us that we can't hit.

WIFE: Do you believe that?

WAITER: I do. I think I do. Sounded like I do. Sounded like the right thing to say anyway. What's the saying? When life throws orange juice on your linens, do the laundry.

WIFE: I wish there were more men in the world like you.

WAITER: Me too. I have been looking for a good man like me for years. Everything is going to be alright.

WIFE: I really hope it is. Thank you.

> *(WIFE exits towards the uncertain future. Moment. Blackout.)*

The End

ANGELS

Lisa Ebersole

PRODUCTION NOTES:

ANGELS was first produced by Graveyard Kiss Productions at The Barrow Group Theater, June 2011 as part of "10 For The Tatas." The play was directed by Johnny Orsini, with Belle Caplis, Christian Davies, Abigail Gampel and Betsy Holt.
Graveyard Kiss Productions
www.JonnyOrsini.com
www.RachelCoraWood.com

CHARACTERS:
STEPH (twenties) hyper, large breasts, dominating.
LIZ (twenties) more hyper, small breasts, deferential.
DONNA (thirties) assertive, large breasts, not a victim.

PLACE: Inside a women's locker room at a yoga studio.
TIME: Present day.

INSIDE A WOMEN's LOCKER ROOM at yoga STUDIO
*LIZ and STEPH change clothes post yoga. They're in
their bras. Steph's breasts are LARGE, Liz's breasts
are SMALL.*

STEPH: You've got great tits.
LIZ: YOU'VE got great tits.
STEPH: No, yours are perfect.
LIZ: Yours are perfect too!
STEPH: Mine are like grandma's.
        Liz checks herself out in the mirror.
LIZ: Mine are not perfect . . .
        DONNA enters, drying her hair with a towel.
DONNA: Mine are.
        Steph and Liz look at one another, then at Donna.
STEPH: You had a boob job.
DONNA: So? Perfection.
LIZ: I don't really like yours. They're too big.
DONNA: They're a C.
LIZ: I guess I like a smaller breast.
STEPH: Mine are double Ds! Were you lying when you said
    you liked mine?
LIZ: *(loud whisper)* Hers are fake, Stephanie.
DONNA: I did have cancer.
LIZ: What?
STEPH: Oh my God!
DONNA: These are the up-shot.
STEPH: *(to Liz)* You should apologize.
LIZ: I am SO sorry.
DONNA: Don't be. I appreciate a sincere reaction.
LIZ: But, you're a—

(whispers)
—"survivor"!
DONNA: I know.
STEPH: Wow. You just, like, elevated to a whole new level.
DONNA: Cause I had cancer?
Steph crosses herself.
LIZ: Can I pray for you?
DONNA: Can I control that?
LIZ: I'm gonna pray for you.
DONNA: What exactly are you praying for?
LIZ: Your health!
STEPH: I'm praying too! I'm praying right now.
Steph shuts her eyes.
LIZ: I'm praying too right now!
Liz shuts her eyes. Donna watches Steph and Liz in their bras, eyes tightly shut.
DONNA: Does it matter that I don't believe in God?
They open their eyes and look at her, incredulous.
STEPH: You have to believe.
DONNA: Sorry.
LIZ: He saved your life!
DONNA: He also almost took it.
LIZ: That was a test.
DONNA: What about all the people who die?
STEPH: They're angels now.
DONNA: Wow . . .
LIZ: They're all around you.
DONNA: The dead angels?
STEPH: Shhh! There's one right there!
DONNA: Where?
Liz points over Donna's shoulder.
DONNA: What's it doing?
LIZ: *(loud whisper)* Being an angel.
STEPH: *(loud whisper)* Being your angel.
DONNA: The angel belongs to me?
The girls nod.
DONNA: Huh.
STEPH: *(loud whisper)* If you believe, you can ask it questions.
DONNA: I can talk to the angel?
STEPH: If you believe.

DONNA: How's it gonna know?

LIZ: The angel will know.

STEPH: Plus, you just said it.

DONNA: I did, didn't I?

    The girls nod.

DONNA: How long do I have?

    The girls look at one another.

DONNA: To talk to the angel. Like, if I decide tomorrow to believe
    in the angel and ask it for something, is that gonna work?

    The girls consider.

STEPH: I think it has to happen now.

DONNA: Right now?

LIZ: I think Stephanie is right. Now.

    PAUSE.

DONNA: I'm drawing a blank.

STEPH: The angel has time.

DONNA: I'm late unfortunately.

    Donna goes for the door.

    Liz SLAMS it shut.

LIZ: This is your one chance!

DONNA: Could you move?

    Liz flattens her body spread eagle on the door.

STEPH: *(to Liz)* You look like a snow angel!

LIZ: Angel?!

STEPH: Oh my God! Angel!

LIZ: It's a sign!

DONNA: Of what?

    Steph steps to Donna.

STEPH: The angel knows we're here.

DONNA: I believe you guys. I do. But I actually have life, and
    I need to get back to it.

STEPH: Ask the angel a question.

DONNA: This is really happening?

    Liz pokes Donna.

LIZ: Ask it a question Boob Lady.

STEPH: Liz!

    Liz claps a hand over her mouth.

STEPH: *(to Donna)* That's what we call you. I mean, what we
    used to call you, before . . .

LIZ: Before we knew you had—
(loud whisper)
Cancer!
DONNA: I don't have it anymore.
Steph and Liz nod knowingly.
DONNA: Look, if I ask this angel a question, can I leave
peacefully?
STEPH: We promote peace on Earth!
Liz looks at Steph, excited.
LIZ: Can we tell her?
Steph shakes her head, "No."
DONNA: Tell me what?
LIZ: We're the angel!
STEPH: Oh my God! Liz?
DONNA: Your name is Liz?
Liz holds out her hand.
LIZ: Liz Angel.
DONNA: Donna De—
LIZ: *(cuts her off)* —We know.
Liz and Donna shake hands.
STEPH: I'm Stephanie Angel.
Steph looks at Donna's outstretched hand.
STEPH: I have a germ thing.
DONNA: Are you two . . . sisters?
They LAUGH.
LIZ: Oh my God!
STEPH: Of course not!
LIZ: You're so silly!
Liz punches Donna playfully.
DONNA: Right. Cause that would be a ridiculous question.
STEPH: Will you ask us now?
(knees knock together)
I really have to pee!
DONNA: You pee?
LIZ: Oh my God!
Liz punches Donna again.
LIZ: SO SILLY!
DONNA: Stop hitting me.
STEPH: Liz!

(to Donna)
She was totally cited for that.
LIZ: I'm really sorry Donna.
STEPH: History of violence.
> *Liz nods, sadly.*
DONNA: How'd you two die?
> *Liz looks at Steph. Steph nods.*
LIZ: I killed myself.
DONNA: Why?
> *Liz looks at Steph. Steph shakes her head.*
LIZ: It's not important.
> *Liz frowns slightly, then recovers, BIG SMILE.*
STEPH: I was hit by a car.
DONNA: Shit . . .
STEPH: It was a low point.
> *Steph frowns slightly, then suddenly, BIG SMILE.*
LIZ: See? We had all this tragedy and that's why angeling makes us so happy!
STEPH: We really want you to ask a question, Donna.
LIZ: You can ask two if you want!
> *Steph shoots her a look.*
LIZ: Okay, one.
> *LONG PAUSE.*
DONNA: Okay.
> *The girls look at her, excited.*
DONNA: Will it come back?
> *Before they can answer, the door SWINGS OPEN and THE STUDIO OWNER enters. She sees Donna and stops short.*
STUDIO OWNER: I'm sorry, I didn't realize anyone was in here.
> *Donna looks around. The angels are gone.*
STUDIO OWNER: I almost locked you in. Is it just you?
> *PAUSE.*
DONNA: I'm . . . not sure.

BLACKOUT

The End

BODY FARM

Laurel Haines

PRODUCTION NOTES:

Theater: Jimmy's No. 43 through Primary Stages, ESPA
Date: February 4, 2011
Cast List: Darcy Fowler, Amy Gordon, Walker Hare
Director: Carly Hoogendyk

Producer: Primary Stages, ESPA; Tessa LaNeve, Director of ESPA
Producer Contact Info: tessa@primarystages.org; 212-840-9705

CHARACTERS:
XANADU: female, around nineteen
DIRK: male, early twenties
GERALDINE: their boss, any age

SETTING: A body farm
TIME: Present

(XANADU speaks to the audience)
XANADU: I had a dream last night that I was back on the body
farm. The sun was shining bright on the corpses strewn
across the lawn. It would be a day of spectacular putrefaction. I checked on number 301, a young male stuffed inside
the trunk of an '87 Chevy. He was melting. I checked the
size of the maggots. They were getting fat. Everything was
right on schedule. And then I heard a tap . . . tap . . . tap . . . .
I perked up my ears like a newly born fawn. It was coming
from the shed. A young girl was buried in there. She was
about three months gone. I closed the trunk of the Chevy.
Tap . . . tap . . . tap . . . I pictured the girl, her tattered
red dress falling off her bones. She was almost one with
the earth, last time I checked. I opened the shed door and
—I'm at the family pig roast. Aunt Janice will not shut up
about her green bean casserole and my little cousin Louie
is wiping his nose on my jeans . . . And that's why I hate
dreams. They tell you nothing.
> *(The body farm. Geraldine, the head groundskeeper,
> is giving orders machine-gun style to her new help-
> ers, Dirk and Xanadu.)*
GERALDINE: This is a scientific research institute dedicated
to the study of the decay of the human body. The grounds
are 120 acres with a body approximately every 1.5 acres.
Your job is to keep the grounds clean and clear, except where
there's a body. Each body site is clearly marked off with
red tape. You are not to cross the red tape. Only researchers
may cross the red tape. You understand?
> *(XANADU and DIRK nod.)*
I'd like a verbal response please.
XANADU: Yes.

DIRK: Yo.

GERALDINE: The goal is to keep a clear path to each body. You'll mow the grass, whack the weeds and trim the hedges. You will not touch the body sites. Those areas must be allowed to go wild so that the bodies can decay in the most natural way possible. Touching a body is grounds for dismissal.

(DIRK snickers.)

Let me make one thing perfectly clear: There is nothing funny about these bodies. Now get whacking.

(XANADU and DIRK start whacking weeds. As Xanadu speaks, DIRK hums along to a heavy metal band in his head. He gets louder and louder.)

XANADU: *(to audience)* I found myself on the body farm the summer after I turned nineteen. I was paired with Dirk, a guy who dropped out of high school after repeating tenth grade four times. We spent a lot of time alone together.

(Dirk screams, heavy metal style)

DIRK: Eeeeoooowwwwwwwwwwwwwwwww!

(DIRK notices XANADU staring at him.)

What?

XANADU: Do you smell something?

DIRK: *(sniffs)* Yeah.

XANADU: I think it's a body. See the red tape?

(DIRK looks.)

DIRK: Whoa. Look at it.

(They get closer and react to the smell.)

XANADU: Ewww.

DIRK: Ugh!

(They cough and retch. Then they look at it again, this time with fascination.)

XANADU and DIRK: Cool.

DIRK: Let's get closer.

XANADU: But we're not supposed to cross the red tape.

DIRK: C'mon. No one's gonna know.

(Dirk steps forward. Geraldine appears out of nowhere with a megaphone, or just a loud voice.)

GERALDINE: Do not cross the red tape! Do not cross the red tape!

(Geraldine exits. DIRK turns to the audience)

DIRK: I have what you might call poor judgment. If I see a cage, I open it. And it just so happens my new brother in law was a keeper at the county zoo. So I asked him if he'd give me a tour and he said yes!—he was so excited to bond with me, and I followed him into the desert exhibit, bonked him on the head with a Coke bottle, and stole his keys. I just let out one hyena. They had so many.

(Days later. XANADU is whacking weeds.)

XANADU: I have a vague, undefined yearning.

DIRK: It's good to want something. It gives you direction in life.

XANADU: That's the problem. I don't know what I want.

DIRK: Just pick something.

XANADU: Anything?

DIRK: Not anything. Something that's easy to achieve. Take me for instance. I wanted to be employee of the month at Hardee's. Problem is, there was this doofus who won employee of the month every goddamn month. So I put a little Sominex in his pop. Made him fall asleep at the deep fryer! But the boss caught me and I got fired and that's why I'm here.

XANADU: So you didn't achieve your dream.

DIRK: No, but it's the journey that counts. If that hadn't happened, I wouldn't be here.

XANADU: I'm not sure someone like you should be taking care of dead bodies.

DIRK: I'm *exactly* the kind of person who should take care of dead bodies.

(GERALDINE walks through, shouting.)

GERALDINE: Attention! Attention! The front gate must be locked at all times. A hyena has escaped from the zoo. I repeat, a hyena has escaped from the zoo.

(GERALDINE walks off. Dirk looks at the audience.)

DIRK: Cool.

(XANADU and DIRK go back to work.)

XANADU: *(to audience)* The summer went on and on.

DIRK: Show me your boobs.

XANADU: What? No!

DIRK: It was worth a shot. How would you rate your boobs on

a scale of 1 to 10?

XANADU: I don't rate my boobs!

DIRK: I just want a ballpark figure.

XANADU: I feel semi-unsafe around you.

DIRK: Aw, come on. It's not like I'm gonna get at you. But seriously, if I wasn't, like, a scary dropout loser, would you be interested in me?

XANADU: No.

DIRK: I sensed a pause.

XANADU: There was no pause.

DIRK: Hesitation?

XANADU: That's what a pause is. And there wasn't any.

DIRK: Yeah, right. How come you're here? Why aren't you in college?

XANADU: I'm taking a year off.

DIRK: Why?

XANADU: I had to figure things out.

DIRK: What kinds of things?

XANADU: Things. OK?

DIRK: You didn't have the money?

XANADU: *(overlapping)* I tried to commit suicide.

DIRK: No you didn't.

XANADU: I did.

DIRK: And you're working *here?*

XANADU: It's helping me.

DIRK: Wow.

XANADU: *(to audience)* Dirk stopped asking about my boobs after that. He seemed quiet, introspective. And then one day . . .

(DIRK is hunched over a body.)

DIRK: *(loud whisper)* Xanadu!

XANADU: What are you doing? You're not supposed to cross the tape.

(DIRK turns around, holding a knife. His shirt is splattered with blood.)

DIRK: Pass me that bucket.

XANADU: Oh my god!

DIRK: Shut up!

XANADU: Oh my god oh my god!

DIRK: I wish you hadn't seen this, but now that you have, I'm going to let you in on an incredible business opportunity, which you will have no choice but to accept. I'm harvesting their organs.

XANADU: Harvesting their organs?

DIRK: We will make tons of money, dude. Look in that bucket.

> *(Xanadu looks and groans.)*

XANADU: Ugh! But these organs are dead. They're unusable. Not to mention illegal.

DIRK: I'm putting them on ice.

XANADU: It doesn't matter. No one will want them.

DIRK: Shit.

XANADU: You'd better get rid of these. The researchers will be really upset.

DIRK: I'll put them back. They won't notice.

XANADU: They're gonna notice.

> *(A hyena howls in the distance.)*

XANADU: What was that?

DIRK: Some animal.

XANADU: I've never heard an animal like that around here.

> *(The hyena howls again.)*

Oh, my god, it's the hyena.

DIRK: Bob!

XANADU: Who?

DIRK: I named him Bob. After I opened the cage. C'mere Bob, here Bob.

XANADU: You let the hyena out of the zoo?

DIRK: Yeah. It's a good thing my brother in law's still sedated. He hasn't told on me yet.

> *(Hyena howls again, closer now.)*

XANADU: We can't let him in here. He'll rip the bodies to shreds.

DIRK: Great idea! We'll blame it on Bob!

XANADU: We?

DIRK: It's genius!

XANADU: *(to audience)* That night, Dirk "accidentally" left the gate open.

DIRK: *(to audience, shrugs)* I got fired.

> *(Dirk exits.)*

XANADU: After the hyena incident the body farm was shut

down for two weeks. They brought in a hazmat team to remove the bodies, most of which had been mangled beyond hope. I stayed home and watched *Wheel of Fortune.* Geraldine called and asked if I wanted to come back once they got a fresh crop of bodies. She offered to make me a research intern. She thought I had potential. But I was done with the body farm.

(beat)

Except in my dreams. In my dreams, I'm always crossing the red tape.

The End

CAMERA FOUR

Cheri Magid

PRODUCTION NOTES:

Camera Four was originally produced by Blue Coyote
Theater Group, New York City in their evening 300
Vaginas Before Breakfast at Access Theater, NYC
May 27-June18, 2011.

MISS LANGAN, Lauren Balmer
OSBORNE, Christopher Gabriel Nunez
MR, KUBOVY, Gary Shrader
CHORUS, Katie Hayes, David Sedgwick,
       and Stephanie Willing
Directed by Gary Shrader

CHARACTERS:

MS. LANGAN, forties, a tenant in an upscale Upper West Side high rise. An attorney, buttoned up by supremely withdrawn, a bubble of sadness around her

OSBORN: Twenties, a doorman in the building, wiry, excessive energy

CHORUS: a man and two women, any age. All participating in public . . . well you'll see . . .

SETTING: The lobby of an Upper West Side high rise.

2: 00 AM, a weeknight. MS. LANGAN (forties, professional but supremely withdrawn, a bubble of sadness around her) carries a business satchel and a takeout bag. She opens the outside door of her Upper West Side apartment building. It's locked. She tries to open it again. She looks inside. No one is there. She buzzes. Nothing happens. She buzzes again. She gets huffy. She looks up at the building's security camera. Suddenly OSBORN, the doorman (twenties,wiry, excessive energy) runs to the door. He clutches his head. He tries to look as if he isn't clutching his head. He opens the door.

OSBORN: Miss Langan. I I apologize—
    She brushes by him.
OSBORN: I didn't hear the buzzer. I was I was usin' the facility so. I wasn't. Usin' the facility.
MS. LANGAN: Goodnight.
OSBORN: Someone was sick. Near the playroom. I was cleaning it.
    She hits the elevator button.
OSBORN: You havin' an alright evenin'?
    She looks at the elevator. A ways to go.
MS. LANGAN: I was at work.
OSBORN: Yeah.
MS. LANGAN: Goodnight.
OSBORN: Sick, right.
MS. LANGAN: I'm sorry?
OSBORN: That someone would do that at 2:00 AM thinkin' no one was watchin'.

MS. LANGAN: What?

OSBORN: Uh. Get sick. I mean.

MS. LANGAN: Oh.

He closes his eyes, tries to shake something off.

MS. LANGAN: Are you alright?

OSBORN: Who? Me? 'Course.

MS. LANGAN: You looked like you weren't alright. Your eyes flickered.

OSBORN: Oh. I'm alright. You alright?

MS. LANGAN: . . . goodnight.

He stares at her. She pulls her coat in closer.

MS. LANGAN: What. What are you looking at?

OSBORN: Your shoe . . .it's, it's wet.

MS. LANGAN: What? Oh. Oh! I. I must have stepped in something.

He takes out a hanky.

MS. LANGAN: No! That's—

She moves away from him.

MS. LANGAN: You know how it is. The city streets. They're dirty.

The elevator door opens. She goes to dodge in, follows his eyes.

MS. LANGAN: Oh my. I tracked it in.

OSBORN: Yeah.

He starts to laugh. The elevator door closes.

MS. LANGAN: Oh. I'll I'll—I should have gotten something from my apartment. I can—

OSBORN: I got it.

MS. LANGAN: No!

OSBORN: We got a mop. No one has to know.

She stares at him.

MS. LANGAN: Your head. There's, there's blood.

He touches his head.

OSBORN: What? Aw Christ. Sorry. I didn't mean to take the Lord's—

MS. LANGAN: Do you—I can call you an ambulance—

OSBORN: No! Naw. That's. I'll just go and sit down.

MS. LANGAN: Do you need help?

OSBORN: I hit my head. On the wall. When I was cleaning the barf. I mean, the vomit—

MS. LANGAN: You want me to get the super?

OSBORN: No! I'm just. I'll just sit behind the desk.

> *He opens the gate behind the desk that separates the doorman from the tenants. He trips over something.*

MS. LANGAN: Watch it!

OSBORN: Naw! You don't need to—

> *She stops. She sees something. She picks up a blank DVD case. He grabs it back from her. She looks behind the desk.*

MS. LANGAN: What's all this?

OSBORN: Nothin'.

MS. LANGAN: You have about a hundred DVD's behind your desk.

OSBORN: Yeah well. I I work graveyard. I get bored.

> *She goes to look more. He steps in front of her.*

OSBORN: Goodnight.

MS. LANGAN: Oh.

> *She leaves. He watches her go. He goes to stack the DVDs further under the desk. She comes back.*

MS. LANGAN: They're not labeled—

OSBORN: Jesus! You scared the shit out of—

> *She opens the gate.*

OSBORN: Don't do. I wouldn't do that if I were you.

MS. LANGAN: Is that a laptop under your desk?

OSBORN: I like to watch horror movies. The tenants. They get—

MS. LANGAN: You like to watch movies under your desk?

OSBORN: You need to get out from behind the desk.

> *Buzzer.*

OSBORN: Tenants aren't allowed here.

MS. LANGAN: Is your laptop connected to the building's security cameras?

> *The buzzer. OSBORN presses it. A MAN walks in with suitcases.*

OSBORN: Mr. Kubovy. Welcome home. Would you like some help with those bags?

MR. KUBOVY: That's all right.

> *Mr. Kubovy looks at MS. LANGAN: , who looks*

down, blushing furiously. The sound of him exiting.
Of the elevator door ringing. Of the doors closing.
MS. LANGAN: You're recording the security cameras?
OSBORN: No.
MS. LANGAN: Which cameras are you recording? Are you
    recording the interior cameras or the exterior ones. Which
    ones are you recording? Answer me.
    They look at each other.
OSBORN: Camera four. Outside. You know which one.
    She turns a furious shade of red.
MS. LANGAN: I can have you fired.
OSBORN: I can stream you on the internet
    She collapses against the wall.
OSBORN: It was you.
MS. LANGAN: You saw.
OSBORN: Maybe.
MS. LANGAN: So. You. Recorded it. You. Collect. Incidents.
    Answer me.
OSBORN: Only what you did. Not the getting busy stuff.
MS. LANGAN: Oh God. Oh God. I'm a lawyer. What are you
    going to do with them?
OSBORN: I—
MS. LANGAN: Tell me!
    He doesn't answer.
MS. LANGAN: You. . .you have a lot then?
OSBORN: Maybe. I guess.
MS. LANGAN: Show me.
OSBORN: What? You want me to—
MS. LANGAN: Show me what you have. Or I'll have you fired.
OSBORN: I told you I'll—
MS. LANGAN: Just. Please. I'm asking you.
    Something about her tone stops him. He takes the
    laptop out from under the desk. He puts in a DVD.
OSBORN: You sure you—
    She hits play. A surreal light on either side of them.
    The video. There's something slow motion, dance-
    like about it. No sound. Two young women enter.
    Bridge and Tunnel.
OSBORN: June of last year. I seen those girls. They're all over

Amsterdam Ave, goin' to those party bars. Giggly girls wearing too much make up. They won't smile at you. They think they're better than you.

They look around to see if anyone is watching. They pull their tights down. They squat as if they are urinating. They giggle. On the other side, a man looks around furtively, spreads his coat. A woman enters, squats behind him as if she were urinating. The two women on the first side of the stage exit.

OSBORN: He thought he was bein' all chivalrous. Look. She pees on his shoe.

On the other side of the stage, a woman pulls down her pants, remains standing, watches herself as she goes. The man and woman disappear.

OSBORN: They don't look up. They don't see you.

During the following—a man and woman and a pissing contest. A woman who is a dancer peeing. Etc.

OSBORN: It's like they're giving something up but they don't know it. Givin' all their secrets to you. I told my boy Pedro. And he said, dude, you gotta stream that shit. People would pay. You could be like the Girls Gone Wild guy. Think about it—you could get all the doorman in New York City to get you some tape. Chicago, LA. Paris, too. They piss in Paris. My man. We're talking empire.

Ms. Langam replaces the girls stage right. She acts out what he says.

OSBORN: And then there was you. You looked around. The way you moved. You don't move like that in life. You squatted like, like you was going to put out a picnic or something. And then. You looked right into the camera. Like you were darin' things. You wanted me to see.

Ms. Langam remembers.

MS. LANGAN: The first time I was at camp. The bathrooms, they were in a different bunk. It was far. I walked outside into this field. I didn't know I was going to. But it felt so cold, the air on me. I started doing it every night. I'd get excited to go to sleep knowing I would wake up and I would do it again. Then this counselor I had never talked to, he came up to me when no one was around and he said, I saw you. I was horrified. But I still did it. I wondered where he watched me from.

The memory is over.

MS. LANGAN: My firm would fire me.

OSBORN: I wouldn't sell it. Ever. Or stream it. I swear.

MS. LANGAN: Give it to me, please.

OSBORN: No.

MS. LANGAN: Please. I'll pay you for it. I have money. More money than you can—

OSBORN: Do it again.

MS. LANGAN: . . .what?

OSBORN: Here. Now.

He points to the camera.

OSBORN: If you duck behind the gate, no one'll see you.

MS. LANGAN: What? You want me to—

OSBORN: I won't open the door or nothin'. I'll watch you. I want to watch you.

MS. LANGAN: But.

OSBORN: Please.

MS. LANGAN: I can't!

OSBORN: I'll turn off the lights.

MS. LANGAN: I can't. I—I just went. Don't make me.

They stare at one another. He takes out his thermos of coffee. He pours a cup. He hands it to her.

OSBORN: Here. Drink it. Please.

She takes the coffee cup, looks at him. She turns to the camera. Looks right into it. She drinks. OSBORN watches her. He stares into the camera as well. Black out.

The End

Carol

Ron Riekki

PRODUCTION NOTES:

Carol was first produced at Stageworks/Hudson in New York.

Dates of production: PLAY BY PLAY Shadows, June 29 through July 10, 2011

Cast:
ALAN, Timothy W. Hull
STACIE, CHICK, SUSAN, NANCI, Bavani Selvarajah
TAMARA, SARA, CAROL, Louise Pillai
KURT, Donald Warfield

Director: Laura Margolis

Other info: PLAY BY PLAY is Stageworks/Hudson's annual festival of new one-acts. In 2011, the 15th year of the festival, eight plays (including CAROL and seven others) were produced under the title PLAY BY PLAY Shadows. As always, each play received its world premiere and was presented in each performance. PLAY BY PLAY Shadows was produced with four actors (listed above) who played all the roles in all eight plays and two directors, Laura Margolis and John Sowle, http://stageworkshudson.org/playbyplay_shadows.html

CHARACTERS:
ALAN, an everyman, thirty
STACIE, blond, good-looking, sixteen
TAMARAH, a hot mom type, twenty-six
THE CHICK HE MADE OUT WITH IN SPAIN, from Jerez de
    la Frontera, only speaks Spanish, twenty-one
SUSAN, a bit Goth, cute, twenty-three
KURT, a sloppy hippie, twenty-four
NANCI, mousy, pale, plain Jane, twenty-seven
SARA, a lingerie model, wears her makeup strangely, twenty-
    five
CAROL, pretty, kind, Christian, thirty-one

This play can be performed with as many as nine or as little as two actors (with an actor playing Alan and an actress playing all of the other eight roles).

PLACE: A lonely freeway somewhere in the U.S.
TIME: Late night.

("Stairway to Heaven"—played loudly—ends. Lights reveal two chairs, the rest of the stage bare, the chair representing the passenger seat empty. ALAN sits in the chair representing the driver's seat. He drives, fighting sleep. A freeway, night, empty, a long drive. He closes his eyes and "Beth" by Kiss starts, wakes him. While his eyes were closed, STACIE has appeared from the shadows and sits passenger side, chewing gum. She's blond, good-looking, sixteen, a bit of a weight problem. He turns down the song, startled when he notices her.)

ALAN: Jesus! What the—?
        (STACIE stops chewing the gum, frowns. ALAN concentrates on the road, keeping STACIE in his peripheral vision, sneaking peaks at her. She goes back to chewing her gum.)
You look . . . the same—you haven't changed, from sixteen. That's im—what the hell? . . . Do you talk or—
        (STACIE turns the music off.)
That was our song.

STACIE: No, it wasn't.

ALAN: Yeah, it was. Or . . . you didn't know? We danced to that. The first, you know, song, for me, ever, to slow dance to. I just—God, it's great, it's weird, but it's great to see you.

STACIE: Don't say that.

ALAN: Don't say what?

STACIE: Don't use the Lord's name in vain.

ALAN: I didn't . . . I didn't.

STACIE: You did.

ALAN: I'm sorry, it's just—Stacie Taggard . . . Ya know, I wish I woulda asked you out.

STACIE: You did, didn't you?

ALAN: I don't think so.

STACIE: You implied it. If I was interested, we would have went out.

ALAN: Well . . . I just—you just moved all of a sudden. I—

STACIE: My dad moved us.

ALAN: Sorry, what happened, with you and your dad.

STACIE: Don't talk about my dad.

ALAN: I'm sorry, that's all.

STACIE: Don't be.

ALAN: Are you crying?

STACIE: No.

ALAN: Thanks for trusting me, like you did.

STACIE: What? Are you talking about putting your hand up my shirt?

ALAN: No. I was—I meant, like, with your dad. Trusting me with what you told me about him.

STACIE: Don't talk about my father.

ALAN: How'm I supposed to not talk about something like that? I haven't seen you in—

(STACIE turns away from ALAN, leaning away from him.)

Don't do that. Look—sorry.

STACIE: It had nothing to do with you.

ALAN: I was so—*Oo!* You have no idea. I was gonna, like, fight him, remember?

STACIE: What do you mean, remember?

ALAN: Remember how I said I was—that I was gonna fight him?

STACIE: You never said that.

ALAN: In the letter.

STACIE: What letter?

ALAN: The letter I wrote you.

STACIE: You never wrote me a letter.

ALAN: Yeah, I did. I mailed it.

STACIE: You never wrote me a letter.

ALAN: I did.

STACIE: No, I just got some—weird thing, like, you mailed me an envelope with my name and address on it and your name and address, but nothing inside.

ALAN: There wasn't?

>*(STACIE shakes her head "no.")*

Maybe I forgot to put the letter in . . . I used to get really nervous with you.

STACIE: Why?

ALAN: I thought you were beautiful.

>*(STACIE likes this.)*

Yeah. God, I can't believe I forgot to put the stupid letter in. I had some really private things.

>*(ALAN looks out the window, away from STACIE. STACIE disappears in the shadows. TAMARAH, twenty-six, a hot mom type, takes her spot.)*

Like how much I was—just . . . with you, you know— Dumb, man! I always screw up like that. In the letter, I said—fff—

>*(ALAN turns back to STACIE, is shocked to see TAMARAH. She smokes.)*

TAMARAH: What letter? . . . What letter?

ALAN: Tamarah?

TAMARAH: What letter?

ALAN: Tamarah. Son of a gun, are you—

TAMARAH: What!

ALAN: This is just weird.

TAMARAH: Can I turn this on?

>*(TAMARAH turns on the radio. Neil Diamond plays. ALAN winces.)*

What?

ALAN: That's not a song I like.

TAMARAH: You said you like Neil Diamond.

ALAN: Neil Young.

TAMARAH: No, you said Neil Diamond.

ALAN: Maybe *a* song by Neil Diamond. But not many. Not this one . . . Not most of 'em.

(ALAN turns off the song.)

TAMARAH: You said you loved Neil Diamond when we were dating, or were you trying to get in my pants?

ALAN: *(ALAN looks away, out his window. TAMARAH disappears. THE CHICK HE MADE OUT WITH IN SPAIN, twenty-one, from Jerez de la Frontera, takes her spot.)* No, I'm not just trying to—

(He looks back.)

—get in your pants—who're you?

THE CHICK HE MADE OUT WITH IN SPAIN: (Everything she says is in fluent Spanish—) ¿Quien eres? [Who are you?]

ALAN: What?

THE CHICK HE MADE OUT WITH IN SPAIN: Me pareces familiar. *[You look familiar.]*

(They study each other. THE CHICK HE MADE OUT WITH IN SPAIN turns on the radio. Spanish flamenco music plays. ALAN turns down the music.)

ALAN: Are you the chick I made out with in Spain? That cheesy dance club off base across from Bar Pepe. We made out for, like, six hours. You bit my tongue, bit the hell out of it. I bled.

THE CHICK HE MADE OUT WITH IN SPAIN: Odio cuando los americanos hablan. Hablas como los gansos volando en las torretas de aviones. ?Y por que es el volante en lado equivocado? [I hate when Americans talk. You sound like geese flying into airplane turrets. And why is your steering wheel on the wrong side?]

ALAN: God, I don't speak Spanish. Habla espagnol?

THE CHICK HE MADE OUT WITH IN SPAIN: Por supuesto, gilipollas. *[Of course, shithead.]*

ALAN: Or no, anglais? Habla anglais?

THE CHICK HE MADE OUT WITH IN SPAIN: No. En lo absoluto. *[No. Not at all.]*

(THE CHICK HE MADE OUT WITH IN SPAIN turns off the music.)

Lawrence Harbison   251

Me gusta el silencio. *[I like silence.]*
> (Silence.)

Hermoso. El cielo. *[Beautiful. The sky.]*

ALAN: The stars?

THE CHICK HE MADE OUT WITH IN SPAIN: Encuentro algo muy familiar en ti. ¿Si eres Caronte? ¿Estamos muertos? *[There's something really familiar about you. Are you Charon? Are we dead?]*

ALAN: I wish I could see them better. I'm going to pull over, get a better look.
> *(ALAN goes to turn off to the side of the road.)*

THE CHICK HE MADE OUT WITH IN SPAIN: No, no se puede. Es una regla. [No, you can't! It's a rule.]
> *(ALAN understands her reaction, keeps driving.)*

No se puede detener. O mirar hacia otro lado, Solo a mi. Es la regla. *[You can't stop. Or look away from me. It's the rules.]*

ALAN: I understand nothing you're saying, but I love how you say it.

THE CHICK HE MADE OUT WITH IN SPAIN:Eres majo. *[You're cute.]*

> *(She kisses his cheek. ALAN, happy, looks up at the stars out of the window on his side. She disappears. SUSAN takes her spot; she's a bit Goth, cute, twenty-three.)*

ALAN: I actually can see them fine this way.
> *(ALAN looks back. SUSAN stares at him, poker-faced.)*

I think I'm starting to understand this.

SUSAN: Go ahead.

ALAN: No, like, this. What's going on.

SUSAN: And what's going on?
> *(ALAN can't put it in words.)*

Where have you been, by the way?

ALAN: Where've I been?

SUSAN: It's been, what, ten years? You could have got in contact with me.

ALAN: I don't even know your last name. Aren't you married

now?

SUSAN: Divorced.

ALAN: So you married him?

SUSAN: Alex, yeah. But I'm not supposed to be with him. I thought I was supposed to be with you.

ALAN: I know. You asked me to marry you.

SUSAN: When I was drunk.

ALAN: You were sober. You had a drink. *A* drink.

SUSAN: You should have said "yes." I'm awesome.

ALAN: After two months?

SUSAN: My parents got married after two months and they're still married. And they're awesome. I want that.

ALAN: So have you been doing this with everyone? Ask them to marry you after two months of dating?

SUSAN: If I feel they're right.

ALAN: You thought I was right?

SUSAN: You could have wrote. Called. Hunted me down. That would have been romantic.

ALAN: I don't want to marry you . . . I'm sorry. I mean, you— OK, I'm attracted to you. A lot, Susan.

SUSAN: You remember my first name?

ALAN: Of course . . . It is Susan, right?

(SUSAN smacks ALAN's leg. She leans over, nibbles on his ear. He likes this.)

You're gonna make me crash.

SUSAN: Remember that? . . . Why wouldn't you marry me? Look at me. How could you not want to marry this? Is it my boobs?

ALAN: No! You always say that. You went to Alex anyway. You left me in a day. I said no and you go back with him and ask him to marry you, in one day . . . And when I came over, your rabbit was gone. You got that rabbit when you met me and when I came over, that last time, I looked and your rabbit cage was empty. What happened to the rabbit?

SUSAN: I gave him away. To a friend. What does that have to do with anything?

ALAN: I was that rabbit.

SUSAN: Oh, so traumatic. You see symbols in everything. So Taurus.

Lawrence Harbison 253

ALAN: And I didn't like . . .

SUSAN: What?

ALAN: We'd be sleeping, second floor of your apartment and you had that winding staircase to get up to your bed and you'd wake me up to tell me you felt something. You'd be like, "Wake up, something's down there." You'd be faintly lit in shadows, and you have a dark face, dark hair, so I couldn't see you and you'd be like, "Something's coming up the stairs, I feel it." That scared the shit out of me! I realized being married to you, I'd spend the rest of my life like that.

SUSAN: I can't help if I feel things. I'm intuitive.

ALAN: Yeah, but don't tell me.

SUSAN: So if there's a spirit next to you, you don't want to know?

ALAN: No!

> *(They drive. SUSAN stares at him, grins. ALAN looks away, realizes what he's done for the first time, that she's probably gone, that someone else is probably there now. She disappears. TAMARAH takes her spot. ALAN turns back.)*

TAMARAH: Wanting me to take the morning-after pill was bullshit.

ALAN: Oh, that's right, we got back together.

TAMARAH: Seriously, what the fuck was that about?

> *(ALAN looks away. She disappears. KURT takes her place, twenty-four, a sloppy hippie.)*

ALAN: Now who?

> *(He looks over. KURT surprises the hell out of ALAN who looks away quickly. KURT disappears. NANCI replaces him; she's 27, mousy, pale, plain Jane.)*

OK, that was bullshit. Let me just say that. Whoever's listening right now, I did not screw that guy. That's my memory playing with me. Or ghosts.

> *(ALAN looks, sees NANCI. She's not amused.)*

That guy, like, kissed me at a party, drunk. Grabbed me and kissed me.

(NANCI studies him.)

Are you still mad I called you?

NANCI: I told you not to.

ALAN: That whole thing I said, about Beauty and the Beast, how you were the Beauty and I was the Beast, it's true . . . You don't want to talk about this? . . . What do you want to talk about?

NANCI: I want to go.

ALAN: You hate me that much? Is it because I watched Denis Leary's *No Cure for Cancer* when your mom was dying? . . . Or I always felt you broke up with me because you didn't like my shoes.

NANCI: They were old.

ALAN: It was the shoes.

NANCI: It wasn't the shoes.

ALAN: What was it? . . . Do you want me to look away?

NANCI: Yeah. Sorry, yes.

ALAN: I miss you. Nanci. I'm never going to see you again?

(NANCI wants to say "no," but holds her tongue.)

I'm sorry.

NANCI: I know.

ALAN: The women, keep getting better.

NANCI: What does that mean!

ALAN: I mean, I'm starting to figure out who I want to be with. Because, you were kind to me. Thanks for being kind to me.

NANCI: I wasn't kind to you. My mother was dying. I was selfish. I didn't have time to be kind. Or not time. I didn't have the energy to be kind.

ALAN: Yet you were.

NANCI: I think you should look away.

ALAN: Can I . . . Can you do me a favor?

(ALAN sees her apathy, that she wants to leave.)

Forget it.

(ALAN looks away. NANCI fades. KURT takes her place. ALAN looks back.)

Dude, seriously. That's like stalking. Don't do it at parties and then don't do it when you're a ghoul or whatever the hell you are . . . At least say something.

KURT: You kissed me back.

(ALAN looks away, shakes his head. Said to God—)

ALAN: Seriously, come on!

(ALAN, afraid to look at the passenger seat, does. SARA, twenty-five, appears, in lingerie; she has an odd way of wearing makeup.)

SARA: Pillow!

ALAN: Why do you call me that?

SARA: Pillow!

(SARA punches ALAN, messes up his hair.)

ALAN: Don't, I'm driving.

SARA: Pillow!

(She pokes his stomach, sings—)

Well, his name is Pillow 'cause that's his name. He's got a pillow and that's his name—He looks like a pillow, 'cause that's his name! Pillow!

(Stops singing.)

SARA: *(Cont.)*I've been working on a Dorothy impression . . . *Wizard of Oz*. Wanna hear it?

ALAN: No.

(SARA punches ALAN, messes up his hair.)

SARA: Pillow! I love you, Pillow. OK, here it is: "Toto, we're not in Kansas anymore." Whacha think?

ALAN: It's good.

SARA: Do you even know who Dorothy is?

ALAN: From *The Wizard of Oz*? Um, yeah.

SARA: Pillow, make your pillow face.

ALAN: What pillow face?

SARA: Your pillow face!

ALAN: I don't know what you're talking about?

SARA: *(SARA makes a strange face.)* Make this face.

(She stops making the face.)

Make that face.

ALAN: Why?

SARA: Because it makes me laugh.

(ALAN makes the face. She laughs hysterically. He stops making the face.)

Oh, keep making the face. Keep making the face!

ALAN: Why?

SARA: I want to do the face with you.

> *(ALAN makes the face. She makes it too, puts her head by his, laughs loudly.)*

I love you, Pillow. Thank you, Pillow.

ALAN: For what?

SARA: What you said . . . Before you disappeared forever, dumb-ass.

> *(ALAN still isn't completely sure.)*

You sat me down. This was at my apartment in Chicago, on Granville—I loved that apartment. And you broke it down. You got all Dr. Drew.

> *(She makes an overly serious face, does an exaggerated impression of ALAN.)*

"Sara, I'm concerned. I'm worried your being a lingerie model might have to do with abuse."

> *(She breaks into hysterics.)*

"Sara, I'm also worried that you like to be physically abused. And I'm not willing to do that." Like enjoying being choked is so crazy? Oh, Pillow, you're so conservative. Here's you.

> *(She straightens up, pretends she has a stick up her ass.)*

Plus you don't like *South Park*.

ALAN: Not 24-7.

SARA: Pillow.

ALAN: Remember when you thought the *Onion* was a serious newspaper? There was some joke story about Martians landing and you thought it was serious.

SARA: Martians could land. Strange things happen, Pillow. Strange things happen all the time . . . I want to go have fun, Pillow. You sit here and you be serious. I'm going to go have fun. Good bye, Pillow!

> *(She grabs his head and turns it so he's looking away. She disappears. CAROL replaces her; she's thirty-one, pretty, kind. ALAN looks back, sees her.)*

ALAN: The last one. There's no more after you.

CAROL: There will be.

(CAROL smiles, interweaves their arms together, leans into him. She turns on the radio. Don Henley's "Boys of Summer" plays. She holds him. This is a couple in love. ALAN, teary-eyed. The song ends. She turns off the stereo.)

I have to go.

ALAN: No, please.

CAROL: I have to.

(She separates from him, wipes the tear from his eye.)

ALAN: I love awful. I mean, I meant to say "I look awful." You look amazing . . . I collapsed after you left. I'm still collapsing.

CAROL: Let go and let God.

ALAN: You said that when we broke up. I wasn't sure though if you were saying "let go of God."

CAROL: No!

ALAN: It's going to be downhill from now on.

CAROL: "Patience." Like that last sermon we went to.

ALAN: I couldn't do it. And I felt like I lost you and lost God. That you were offering me the church, a family, and you, and . . . My first girlfriend, my first crush, she was raped by her father and her father was a pastor and every time I go into a church I get nauseous. You know.

CAROL: I have to go.

ALAN: I should have done it.

CAROL: What?

ALAN: Become a Christian.

CAROL: You still can.

ALAN: I should have done it, with you. I should have believed whatever you believe. Like Grandpa. He wasn't Catholic, but he pretended for my grandmother. I should have pretended.

CAROL: You were honest.

ALAN: But I lost you. And you're married now. With kids. I saw your facebook page and I almost killed myself.

CAROL: I want to go.

ALAN: I'm not going to kill myself. I don't know how.

(ALAN drives.)

I couldn't. I wouldn't. I just—I wish it was different, this life. I wish it was all different. I wish I was with you.

CAROL: I'm married.

ALAN: I know. And I'm lost.

(ALAN drives.)

Can you just drive with me? You're not really there. And if you're really a Christian, you want to be forgiving. And to heal the sick. And to love the lonely. And all that. Right? Please, I'm hurting. Just drive with me. Like we used to. I need to feel you near me. Like an angel. To get through this. I don't know where I'm heading. I'm just starting over. Until I get there. Just, please. We don't even have to talk.

(ALAN drives. CAROL interweaves her hand with his. She turns on the car radio, softly, a beautiful hymn comes on. They drive together. The lights fade.)

The End

THE CLOSET

Aoise Stratford

PRODUCTION NOTES:

City Theatre, Miami for their "Summer Shorts
Festival" 2007
Directed by Stuart Meltzer.
Featuring Ken Clement, Joe Kimble, and Antonio
Amadeo.

Revised 2011/2012 Season production:

Live Girls Theatre, Seattle, for their "Quickies!"
Festival, 2011 (June 3-18, 2011)
Theatre Off Jackson, Seattle, WA
Directed by Mike Lindgren.
Featuring Daniel Christensen, Jordaan Montes, and
Alex Garnett.
Contact Artistic Director Meghan Arnette
Meghan.arnette@gmail.com 206-683-6983

International productions:
Short and Sweet Festival, Sydney Australia, 2010
Directed by Heath Wilder. Featuring Kevin Curley,
Anthony Hunt, and Simone Oliver

CHARACTERS:
BERNARD, A toy Dinosaur
BART SPONGE, A toy Sponge
TWINKLES, A toy.

SETTING: A closet under the stairs. Set dressing can be minimal but should portray a space used for storing the unwanted.

A note on Costuming:
    While elaborate character costumes would be great, this play should be very easy to produce and consequently, costuming can be kept very simple. At a minimum, Bernard should wear purple and he needs a tail, even if it's just a pair of stuffed pantyhose hanging out of the back of his pants. Twinkles should wear purple and carry a red bag. Bart Sponge should wear loose shorts and a tie. You get the idea.

A note on casting:
    Bernard and Bart are male, and should be played by men, Bart is younger than Bernard. Twinkles can be played by either a woman or a man of any age.

A closet. Piles of newspapers, discarded shoes, tennis racquets, etc. BERNARD sits flicking idly through a copy of playboy, his long purple dinosaur tail hanging out of the back of his overalls. TWINKLES, a small, over-stuffed purple toy, holding a red handbag, is bouncing around, looking at his own feet and giggling. A beat. The door to the closet opens and BART SPONGE is hurled inside. The door slams. BART SPONGE picks himself and goes quickly to the door. It's locked. The sound of retreating footsteps.

TWINKLES: *(waving)* Hello.
BART SPONGE: *(calling through the door)* Please! Mr Peterson!
TWINKLES: Hello.
BART SPONGE: Kevin are you out there? Hey! I'm in here.
TWINKLES: Hello.

BERNARD: Hey, you. Sponge. The Tubby is talking to you. Show some respect.

BART SPONGE: *(rattling the door)* Sorry. I . . . Oh, geeze, it won't open.

TWINKLES: *(waving)* Hello.

BART SPONGE: Okay. Hi.

TWINKLES: Hello.

BERNARD: He gets it, already. He said hi. Now leave him alone. Christ on a crutch.

BART SPONGE: Do you know how to get out of here?

BERNARD: Out of the closet? Ha! That's a good one.

BART SPONGE: The . . . closet? *(a beat)* Oh my . . . I can't stay here.

BERNARD: What's the matter? Don't you like what I've done with the place?

BART SPONGE: Well, it's okay I guess, but . . . ah, about this door . . .

BERNARD: Probably a little messy for a neat freak like you. I tried to get on one of those tv makeover shows, you know, where those queer guys come in and bust up the place, give you new cushions, put a whole bunch of fucking candles everywhere and make you buy expensive hair gel and shit. No one would take me on. I guess closets ain't commercial. Still. It's not so bad. You get used to it.

BART SPONGE: Right. Um . . . I'm sure that's true, but I don't think I'm supposed to be in here. There's been a mix up.

BERNARD: Oh really? What happened? You get mistaken for a mop or something?

BART SPONGE: Well, I'm not quite sure. Mr. Peterson got back from a business trip late last night and first thing this morning he came and grabbed me out of the toy box and . . . well, here I am. Kevin is very attached to me; if he doesn't know his Dad put me in here he might worry.

BERNARD: And then again, he might not. He never came looking for me.

BART SPONGE: Oh. Well . . . I'm sure . . .

BERNARD: Can't expect too much from the kid. He is only three.

A long pause. BART SPONGE puts his ear to the door. Listens. Nothing.

BERNARD: *(cont)* The sooner you forget about it. The sooner you get used to it. That weird Harry Potter kid spent years in a closet under the stairs.

BART SPONGE: Years? Oh dear me. Have you been here long?

BERNARD: You trying to pick me up?

BART SPONGE: What?

BERNARD: *(lecherous)* Come here often?

A beat. BART SPONGE is quietly terrified.

BERNARD: *(cont)* It was a joke.

TWINKLES: Joke! Funny!

> *(Giggles inanely).*

BART SPONGE: Oh.

> *(forces a laugh. Tries to open the door)*

BERNARD: Relax. Where's the fire? Kevin's probably on his way to Daycare by now so you may as well get comfy. What's your name anyway?

BART SPONGE: I'm Bart Sponge Round Trousers. Kevin's favorite toy.

BERNARD: Pleased to meet you. I'm Bernard the dinosaur. Kevin's ex-favorite toy. And this here is Twinkles. He's a tubby, whatever the hell that is.

TWINKLES: Twinkles say hello!

BERNARD: Jesus in Jelly, what Kevin was thinking with that one, I'll never know.

BART SPONGE: Well, maybe when he was younger . . .

BERNARD: Yeah. Right. Kids these days outgrow that kinda shit in the womb.

> BERNARD takes a crumpled pack of American Spirit and offers one to BART SPONGE.

BERNARD: *(cont)* Cigarette? They're the good ones. No chemicals. Don't want to set a bad example.

BART SPONGE: Ah, no thanks.

BERNARD: So. What are you in for?

BART SPONGE: I'm sorry?

BERNARD: The closet, Spongepants, what are you in for?

BART SPONGE: It's Bart. Bart Sponge. And I'm, well, like I said, I'm just in here temporarily.

BERNARD: Yeah, that's what I thought. Were you a Christmas present?

BART SPONGE: Yes. Santa brought me. I was the best thing under the tree, so I'm sure Kevin'll want to get me back. I've got moveable parts, look!
(waving his arms and legs)
And my pants come off too.

BERNARD: Hey! Keep those on! Shit, no wonder they canned you.

BART SPONGE: I'm not canned. I can't be. I'm Kevin's favorite.

BERNARD: Yeah, yeah. So you said. Look kid, I hate to be the one to break it to you, but toys that go into the closet, don't come out. So what did you do? It's less than a month after Christmas; it must have been something big.

BART SPONGE: I didn't do anything. I'm innocent.

BERNARD: No such thing, Spongehead. Come on, you can tell your uncle Bernard.

BART SPONGE: I didn't do anything. Really.

BERNARD: Let me guess. Did you sneak into Kevin's sister's room and try to dress up in her barbie's outfits?

BART SPONGE: No! Why on earth would I do that?

BERNARD: *(gesturing crudely)* You didn't get caught bending over that teddy, did ya?

BART SPONGE: What? Bending . . . what?

BERNARD: Well it musta been something. I've never known Kevin to just get bored with a toy after only a few weeks... Even the tub-tub lasted a few months and look at it. Wait! I got it! Weren't you in that Teach Kids Tolerance video! The one that Pro Family Foundation dude said was corrupting kids and turning them all gay.

BART SPONGE: You heard about that video?

BERNARD: Sure; it was in the paper. Even the Governor knows about it, and he doesn't know shit from cookie dough.

BERNARD gets up and dances suggestively while singing a line or two from "We are family." TWINKLES bounces around, excited, trying to join in. BART SPONGE is appalled.

BART SPONGE: Oh, please, don't . . . . Do you mind my asking, which paper?

BERNARD: All of 'em, Bath Boy, you're famous. Mrs. Peterson keeps the recycling in here so we get the New York Times and the Examiner, plus The National Enquirer if she's been to the supermarket.

BART SPONGE: You really think that's why Mr. Peterson put me in here? Because of a video?

BERNARD: You bet your big round tush it is. Do you think he wants a little faggot like you playing with his precious son Kevin? It was bad enough when you were just running around your fruity fucking palace in your tighty fucking whities and holding hands with that limp dick pink thing /

BART SPONGE: Hey! You can't say that about my friend Patrick/

BERNARD: But then you had to go and get yourself associated with some leftie video promoting diversity awareness or some crap and send it out to schools all over the country. Face it, the conservatives are right: You're as camp as a row a tents, as gay as Tuesday, as queer as a three dollar bill. You ain't getting outa here any time soon. I might just be the best friend you got.

BART SPONGE contemplates this a moment and runs to the door, pounding on it.

BART SPONGE: Kevin! I'm in here. Mr. Peterson, I'm sorry, let me out!

BERNARD: Relax. Do I look like I want to fuck you?

BERNARD holds up the girly magazine.

Trust me; you're not my type. I'm more likely to stick it into Twinkles over there.

TWINKLES: In. Out. In. Out!

(giggles)

BART SPONGE: *(rattling the door)* Help! Let me out! Let me oouuuttttt.

BERNARD: Do you have to make so much noise?

BERNARD takes a step toward him. BART SPONGE turns on him, ready to fight.

BART SPONGE: Get away from me! If you try anything I'll . . . I'll . . .

BERNARD: Dude, get real. I'm a fucking plush and plastic toy. What am I going to do to you? Maul you to death with my felt teeth? Just give it up, will you?

BART SPONGE: I know karate!

BERNARD: I won't hurt you. I won't even make a pass at you.

BART SPONGE: *(beat)* Promise?

BERNARD: Cross my heart. Besides, it won't do you any good bashing on that door. Forget Kevin; the stink of scandal is on you now, my friend, and there ain't no going back from that. I should know. I was on TV once. All I did was clap my hands a lot and hug a few little boys. Big fucking deal. They let Whacko Jacko off, but not me, oh no. Look at that fucking thing, they said. Purple velvet is way too fucking gay; must drive a stick shift, take him away in the night while Kevin is sleeping and shove him down here in the dark. Forgotten. *(beat)* Look, I'm sorry if I came off a little gruff. I didn't mean to give you a hard time. I'm not that used to interacting with celebrities and it's pretty hard to practice your social graces when you're living in a closet with someone like Twinkles. *(beat)* Truth is I'm kinda lonely and I could use a friend. I gotta tell ya, I'm real glad you're here. The tubby is driving me fucking nuts.

TWINKLES starts jumping in little circles and swinging his handbag.

BART SPONGE: I can imagine.

BERNARD: He's a little hard to converse with.

BART SPONGE: It's a he?

BERNARD: Well . . . in a manner of speaking.

BART SPONGE: Wow.

BERNARD: Yeah. You think you got problems.

BART SPONGE: So. What do we do now? If we can't open the door. What's the plan? Do we just wait for it all to blow over?

BERNARD: Not a lot of choice. Mrs. Peterson comes in once a week with the recycling, you could try to make a run for it then, but you won't get far on those legs, and chances are next time you'll be straight off to the trash can. If I were you I'd try and keep a low profile. Hope for the best.

(beat. He pats the floor next to him)

Come on, take a load off. You may as well conserve your energy.

They sit on the floor, side by side, beaten.

BERNARD: *(cont)* So . . . just out of curiosity Spongebutt, are you?

BART SPONGE: Gay?

BERNARD: Yeah.

BART SPONGE: I don't know . . . . I'm a sponge.

BERNARD: Oh. *(beat)* Do you miss Kevin?

BART SPONGE: Yeah. He was nice to me. You?

BERNARD: Yeah. Not as much as the little guy does though. It's been really rough on him.

TWINKLES comes over to sit with them, sadly. BERNARD gives him a hug.

TWINKLES: Miss Kevin. Twinkles miss Kevin too.

BART SPONGE: Well, we'll all just have to stick together. Toys belong with kids. That's the natural way of things, right? I mean, what else are we for? They'll see that sooner or later. Kevin will come to rescue us. Just you wait and see.

The toys sit. Waiting. Lights slowly fade to black.

The End

CLOWN THERAPY

Nina Mansfield

For Zeynep.

PRODUCTION NOTES:

Clown Therapy was originally presented at the 2011 Snowdance 10 Minute Comedy Festival, produced by Over Our Head Players and directed by Rich Smith and the Snowdance Ensemble. The festival opened at the 6th Street Theatre in Racine, Wisconsin on January 28, 2011. The play was directed by Diane Carlson with the following cast:

THERAPIST, Brandy Harrell
MAGGIE, Melissa Hughes Ernest
FRANK, Jim Selovich

Clown Therapy was subsequently produced by Three Roses Players in North Hollywood, CA (April to May 2011.) It went on to be produced at the New Works Festival at the North Canton Playhouse in North Canton, OH (May 2011.) It also received a production as part of Turtle Shell Productions' Summer Shorties Playwright Festival in New York (July to August 2011) and Artists' Exchange's 6th Annual Black Box Theatre One Act Play Festival in Cranston, RI (August 2011.)

CHARACTERS:
FRANK: Frank is a clown. He is dressed in full clown attire
including a blue wig, a red nose, big shoes that honk, a water
squirting flower in his lapel, and a crazy tie that can grow
very long when pulled. Thirties to forties.
MAGGIE: Frank's wife. She is not a clown. Twenties to forties.
THERAPIST: A licensed marriage counselor. Female. Thirties
to fifties.

SETTING: Present day. A therapist's office.

> *(Maggie and Frank enter a therapist's office. Frank
> is dressed in full clown attire, with a red nose, blue
> hair, big shoes and funny tie.)*

THERAPIST: Come in. Please come in. Mr. and Mrs . . . .Bozo,
correct?
MAGGIE: It's pronounced: Bohzshoh. It's French.
THERAPIST: Bohcho.
MAGGIE: Bohzshoh.
THERAPIST: Bohzshoh. Please, Mr. and Mrs. Bohzshoh, have
a seat.
> *(Maggie sits. Frank stays standing.)*
FRANK: You didn't tell me she'd be a woman.
MAGGIE: You know I don't like male doctors.
FRANK: And I'm supposed to feel comfortable with a woman?
MAGGIE: Women are better listeners.
FRANK: Yeah, according to you.
MAGGIE: Would you please just sit down.
> *(Frank sits.)*
Thank you. Was that so hard?
THERAPIST: Does it bother you, Mr. Bozo, sorry . . .
> *(She pronounces the name carefully.)*
Bohzshoh, that I'm a woman?
FRANK: You can call me Frank.
THERAPIST: Okay, Frank, does it bother you that I'm a
woman?
MAGGIE: *(To Frank.)* I'm sorry. You know how I feel about
male doctors.

FRANK: That's because of your trust issues.

MAGGIE: Oh, and whose fault is that? After living with you, does it shock you that I have trust issues? It's surprising I ever leave the house after what you've put me through.

FRANK: Here we go again.

MAGGIE: *(To Therapist.)*See what I mean? See what I have to put up with?

THERAPIST: Uh, why don't we all take a deep breath—

FRANK: Besides, she's not really a doctor.

MAGGIE: Close enough.

THERAPIST: Licensed marriage counselor. I'm a licensed—

FRANK: But you're not a doctor.

THERAPIST: Not in the traditional sense of the word.

FRANK: See.

MAGGIE: What does that have to do with anything? At least she's not *pretending* to be a doctor!

> *(Frank looks away. Something in what Maggie has said has affected him.)*

THERAPIST: Why don't we discuss what brought you here.

> *(Maggie and Frank look down.)*

There's no need to feel...awkward, or ashamed. Many couples seek therapy for their issues.

MAGGIE: It's just that . . .

THERAPIST: Yes . . .

FRANK: *(To Maggie.)* Don't look at me. You're the one who wanted to come here.

MAGGIE: Oh, so now you want to leave.

FRANK: I didn't say that. I said you're the one that wanted to come here.

MAGGIE: Then let's just go. Let's just forget it.

FRANK: We're here now. We might as well get it over with.

> *(To Therapist.)*

You'd still charge us for the session if we left?

> *(Therapist nods.)*

See, we might as well stay.

MAGGIE: Fine, we'll stay. But don't say I didn't give you a choice.

THERAPIST: Okay, now that that's settled, let's . . . uh . . . discuss what brought you here.

(Pause. Frank and Maggie continue to look away.)
Do you mind if I venture a guess?
(They don't respond.)
I don't mean to be presumptuous here, but I think I've
seen this situation before.

MAGGIE: See, I told you she could help us.

FRANK: She hasn't even said anything yet.

THERAPIST: You've been together how long?

FRANK: Four years.

MAGGIE: Four and a half.

FRANK: Four and a half.

THERAPIST: And . . . Mrs. Bohzshoh, when did you discover
that your husband—

MAGGIE: Maggie. Call me Maggie.

THERAPIST: Maggie, when did you discover that your husband is . . . how can I put this delicately . . . when did you
discover that your husband is . . . a clown?

MAGGIE: Sorry?

THERAPIST: As I've said, I've seen this situation many, many
times. Husbands, and Frank, please correct me if I'm wrong,
but . . . it's something that they often hide from their wives.
The discovery is often shocking, upsetting. The man feels
like he needs to express his true nature, and the woman . . .
and mind you, this is a gender neutral situation. I'm actually
counseling a lesbian couple . . . one had been moonlighting
as a rodeo clown and—

MAGGIE: I've always known.

THERAPIST: Come again?

MAGGIE: I said, I've always known.

THERAPIST: So you . . . you knew? About the . . .

FRANK: Of course she knew.

MAGGIE: How could I not? That's how we met. Remember.
(To Frank. She is recalling a fond memory.)
You were piling out of the trunk of that compact car. There
were nineteen other clowns with you, but for me, there
was just one. Those other clowns, they might as well not
have even existed. They could go on honking their horns
and somersaulting around that ring, but it didn't matter.
They were nothing to me. You were the clown that I was

watching. The only clown. I couldn't keep my eyes off of you. I remember like it was yesterday. That red nose, that bright blue hair.

(To Therapist.)

I knew at that moment, he was the clown for me.

THERAPIST: You knew he was a clown?

MAGGIE: It was love at first sight. And then, every time we met, he would make me fall in love with him just a little bit more. That water squirting flower on his lapel. The way he would start juggling random objects—and inevitably drop them all—just to have them bounce right back up in the air. And the way every time he tried to tie his tie, it would grow longer and longer until he was totally wrapped up in it. That's the man I fell in love with. That's the man I thought I knew.

THERAPIST: I guess I'm a little confused then.

MAGGIE: He's a fraud.

FRANK: I'm not a fraud.

MAGGIE: Yes you are. You lied to me.

FRANK: I thought you knew. I thought it was . . . I don't know . . . common knowledge.

THERAPIST: Maggie, what exactly did he lie about?

FRANK: I did *not* lie.

THERAPIST: I'm trying to dig out the heart of this matter Frank.

FRANK: I understand that, but I just want to set the record straight. I did not lie.

MAGGIE: Omission Frank. That's still lying.

(To Therapist.)

That's still lying, right?

THERAPIST: Maggie, could you please explain what it is Frank . . . *omitted.*

MAGGIE: He's not really a clown.

FRANK: That's not true.

MAGGIE: Yes it is.

FRANK: I'm a clown, okay. I *am* a clown.

MAGGIE: No, not really. Not underneath all that.

FRANK: What do you think a clown is?

THERAPIST: Yes Maggie, what is your definition of clown?

MAGGIE: I thought he was . . . you know . . . a real clown.

THERAPIST: A *real* clown?

MAGGIE: Not just dressed up like a clown, but actually . . . you know, for real. How many years has he lead me to believe that this nose . . . this beautiful round, red nose . . . it's not really his, you know. It comes off.

    (Maggie pulls off his nose.)

FRANK: Ow. That hurt.

MAGGIE: Not as much as you've hurt me.

THERAPIST: So, the nose is fake. And this came as a shock?

MAGGIE: It's not just the nose. The hair too. This beautiful bushel of bright blue hair. It's a wig. A wig!

    (Maggie tries to pull off his wig. Frank tries to keep it on.)

FRANK: Leave my hair alone.

MAGGIE: Why? Are you ashamed to expose who you really are?

FRANK: Just leave it alone!

MAGGIE: No! I want her to see. See how you've been deceiving me!

    (They struggle. The wig comes off.)

FRANK: That's just great.

MAGGIE: And the worst, the absolutely worst discovery . . . his feet aren't really that big.

THERAPIST: And it took you . . . four and a half years to realize this?

MAGGIE: He always wore his shoes to bed.

    (Frank pulls off one of his shoes. It squeaks.)

FRANK: You thought my real foot made that noise? Is that what you thought? Is that what you really thought?

MAGGIE: *(Growing increasingly upset.)* Okay, so I was naïve. You were my first love Frank. What did I know? It's not like I'd had any clowns before you. You were the first one . . . and I thought you were the real thing. And then to wake up one morning and find out that it was all . . . all just a sham, a lie. A disguise! You know how violated I felt? How dirty. Used. Like I'd been sleeping with a stranger all these years. How can I trust anything, anyone! It's like everything I've ever believed in was a complete and total lie. How can I even go on anymore? I . . . I don't know if I can. How can I go on living if everything I've ever believed in doesn't

exist? How can I go on? I just want to die! I just want to
end it all!

(Maggie pulls out a gun. She aims it at her head.)
FRANK: No, Maggie.
THERAPIST: Maggie, please!
MAGGIE: No, I just want to die! I just want to die!
THERAPIST: Don't do it Maggie.
FRANK: Put the gun down Maggie.
MAGGIE: I can't! I can't go on!
THERAPIST/FRANK: MAGGIE!!!! NOOOOOOOO!!!!!!

*(Maggie fires the gun. A flower pops out of it. The
sight of the flower makes Maggie crumble.)*
MAGGIE: Why? WHY, WHY, WHY!?!?!

*(Maggie falls to the ground weeping. She weeps for
a long moment. Frank and Therapist watch her.)*
FRANK: I . . . I never knew. I never . . .
MAGGIE: *(Softly. Defeated.)* Why Frank? Why?
FRANK: I never knew you felt this way.
MAGGIE: How can we go on?
FRANK: I love you Maggie.
MAGGIE: I thought I loved you too, but I don't know who
you are.
FRANK: But you do know me Maggie. This wig, that nose, these
shoes . . . they might not be real, but it's who I am.
MAGGIE: Really?

(Frank honks his shoe. Maggie smiles.)
FRANK: This is who I am. I am still the clown you fell for. I'm
just plain old Frank too.

(Frank and Maggie kiss.)
THERAPIST: I . . . I think we might have made what, in my
profession, we call a breakthrough.
MAGGIE: Can you give me some clown Frank?
FRANK: Right now?
MAGGIE: Yeah Frank. Right here. I need some clown.
THERAPIST: Some clown?
FRANK: Are you sure? You want some clown? Right here?
Right now?
MAGGIE: Yeah.
FRANK: You got it babe!

(Frank begins to laugh and act like a silly clown.

He begins to squirt Maggie and the Therapist with a water pistol.)

MAGGIE: Oh yeah! OH BABY YEAH!

(Frank, still laughing his silly laugh, takes out a canister of silly string and sprays them both with it. Maggie cries out with pleasure as Therapist looks on, somewhat horrified.)

MAGGIE: Yes! YES! Give it to me!

(Maggie begins to pull at Frank's tie. It grows longer and longer.)

MAGGIE: That's it. Oh yeah! That's it!

(When the tie comes to an end, Frank falls on top of Maggie. They begin to roll around on the ground, passionately. Therapist looks on in shock.)

MAGGIE: Oh Frank! Yes. Yes! YES!

(The lights fade to the sound of squeaking shoes and Maggie's cries of pleasure.)

End of Play

CREDIT CHECK

Eddie Zipperer

PRODUCTION NOTES:

Georgia Military College. Milledgeville, GA.
June 2010.
Strike 38, A Striking Short Play Lab. New York,
NY.   June 2010.
Turtle Shell Productions, Summer Shorties Summ Ar
Not. New York, NY. August 2010

Wingz Productions, Macarthur Playwriting Festival.
Campbelltown, Australia. December 2010

Camino Real Playhouse, Showoff! San Juan Capist-
rano, CA. January 2011. (Festival Winner)

Students on Stage of NUSU and CSRC, Nipissing
State University Theatre. North Bay, ON Canada.
February 2011.

Sunshine Brooks Theatre, Summer Shorts. Oceanside,
CA. July 2011. (Festival Co—Winner)

CHARACTERS:
DAVID, A man, thirties, Recently deceased.
JESSICA, A woman, thirties, Recently deceased.
ANGELA, A real estate angel. White wings. Halo. Very pleasant but hates to hear complaining.
GOD, King of Kings.
DARK ANGEL, A real estate angel who works for a different company. Red horns and black wings.

SCENE: The afterlife.
TIME: The present.
SETTING: An empty stage.

>AT RISE: *David and Jessica are standing onstage. Both of them are disoriented as though they have just "appeared." They check to make sure all their most important body parts are still attached.*

DAVID: Wow!
JESSICA: What on Earth happened?
DAVID: I have no—.Where are we?
JESSICA: Where were we?
DAVID: I can't remember.
JESSICA: I remember a cow?
DAVID: A cow?
JESSICA: Was there a cow there?
DAVID: Where we came from?
JESSICA: Where we cam from.
DAVID: I think I'd have remembered a cow.
JESSICA: There was a cow! I remember!
DAVID: Yeah! A black and white one—.
JESSICA: It was in the road—.
DAVID: And I was about to slam right into it—.
JESSICA: So you swerved—.
DAVID: But we were on the bridge—.
JESSICA: I remember the splash.
DAVID: I remember my clothes being soaked.
JESSICA: And then we were here.
DAVID: Suddenly. Like magic.
JESSICA: Maybe we have amnesia.

DAVID: Or. I hate to be the one to say this, but think about it. That bridge was fifty feet above the water, and I drove right off it. It's possible, no, it's probable that we're—

An angel enters.

DAVID: Crap!

JESSICA: Language.

ANGEL: Hello there you two! You must be Mr. And Mrs. Bartley. I am so so sorry that I was running late today. I hope I didn't leave you standing here for too long. How in the heck are the two of you today?

DAVID: Dead, I think.

ANGEL: Okay, well that's a pretty pessimistic way of looking at it. This man you've got here is a real downer.

JESSICA: I guess he's—. Are we dead?

ANGEL: Well, I guess, technically, by your earthly definition of the word. Yes, you two are *(finger quotes)* "dead."

DAVID: No! No! I knew it! *(Breaking Down)* It wasn't my time! I had so much to offer the world! I was working on a novel—.

ANGEL: That sounds impressive.

JESSICA: He means reading a novel.

DAVID: I was this close to getting Larry promoted to the top of the medical career track!

JESSICA: Larry was his Sim.

ANGEL: I see.

DAVID: I had a nine o'clock tee time this Saturday, but it's all gone. It's all over.

JESSICA: Calm down, David. Die with a little dignity.

ANGEL: You're only freaking out because you don't know what death is. You think it's the end of everything, but do you feel *(finger quotes)* "dead?"

JESSICA: I feel the same.

DAVID: Hey, so do I. What gives? Is this a prank? Who are you?

ANGEL: Oh, dear. I'm sorry. In all the excitement I completely forgot to introduce myself. My name is Angela, and I'm your real estate angel.

DAVID: What? That's ridiculous. It sounds made up and not by someone clever if you know what I—.

ANGEL: Well, it's not made up. It's a real thing, and I've lined up some places to show you, but we'll have to hurry because I have another couple to meet up with in about ten minutes.

JESSICA: Are we in . . . Heaven?

ANGEL: Well, I suppose—according to your definition of the word—you are in *(finger quotes)* "Heaven."

DAVID: The finger quotes are getting a little bit condescending.

ANGEL: *(Suddenly very frightening)*Enough of your negativity, mortal! From now on you will speak when I tell you to speak! Do you understand? Speak!

DAVID: Yes.

ANGEL: Very well! *(Sweet as can be to Jessica)* You must feel like you can't get a word in sometimes.

JESSICA: I suppose. Sometimes.

David begins to retort, but the angel gives him a look, so he doesn't.

ANGEL: As I was saying. There's not really *(finger quotes)* "heaven" or *(finger quotes)* "hell." There's just the afterlife, but believe me when I tell you that location is *everything* in the afterlife. This is the only neighborhood you want to buy a place in.

JESSICA: But we don't have any money.

ANGEL: Oh, but you do have *(finger quotes)* "money." And lots of it as a matter of fact. Currency isn't pieces of paper here like it is where you're from. Here it's goodness. You get "credit" for all of your goodness in life. In the afterlife, the two of you are a very wealthy couple.

JESSICA: Did you hear that, David?

> *He nods.*

That's fantastic!

ANGEL: I have a place that will be perfect for the two of you.

> *The angel snaps her fingers.*

JESSICA: *(Looks around)*Wow!

ANGEL: This is one of the nicest places on the Upper Upper East Side. Three bedrooms. No baths—don't need 'em. If you look out this back window you'll see there's a balcony with a fantastic view of the fourteenth hole of the finest golf course in the afterlife.

> *David points to his lips.*

You're free to speak, David, but no complaining, okay?

There's nothing to complain about here.

DAVID: Sorry. There's golf here?

ANGEL: It wouldn't be *(finger quotes)* "heaven" if there wasn't. Not only is this place on the golf course, but it's only a couple clouds down from the theatre district.

DAVID: Maybe this won't be so bad after all.

ANGEL: I told you you were overreacting.

JESSICA: It's fantastic! We'll take it.

DAVID: Whoa. Angela, could we have a moment to talk this over?

ANGEL: Absolutely. I have four minutes left.

DAVID: Could we have some privacy? Maybe down on the golf course?

ANGEL: Certainly. Just think of the golf course, snap you're fingers, and you'll be there. When you're through talking it over, think of me, snap your fingers again, and I'll draw up the papers.

> *Angela exits. David closes his eyes and snaps his fingers. He opens them.*

DAVID: It worked. Wow! Look at these fairways. They're immaculate. This is nicer than the Augusta National. What an amazing course. It's a shame I'll never get to see Tiger Woods play it.

JESSICA: What did you want to talk about?

DAVID: Oh yeah. Why did you agree to take this place without asking me?

JESSICA: I thought you loved it. Look at this golf course.

DAVID: Still, this is the only place we've looked at. You don't just take the first place you look at. You shop around. If heaven has golf courses like this, imagine what else we might be able to score. She's probably showing us the worst place in the whole afterlife. She's probably sitting around with a bunch of other *(finger quotes)* "real estate angels" right now laughing at how she has the two new chumps on the line to buy the dump nobody else could unload.

JESSICA: I doubt the process is that dishonest here. We should be grateful that we still get to be together and not worry about where we get to be together.

DAVID: Well, that's actually the other thing I wanted to talk about.

JESSICA: What?

DAVID: Well, at the wedding—and I'm just offering this as a point of information—the vows were "till death do we part." "Till death." So . . .

JESSICA: So, now that we're in Heaven you want to get divorced! Is that it?

DAVID: No! Of course not! Not divorced. There's no need to bring up divorce. Divorce is when you can't wait until death to part. It's more like . . . graduation. We did it!

JESSICA: I can't believe this. How can this be Heaven when you're still such a jerk?

DAVID: We should still see each other. I'm just saying now that we're dead we can branch out a little. Maybe see other people, you know? I just thought—.

GOD: (*From offstage*) Fore!

> *A golf ball bounces across the stage. David watches it.*

DAVID: Oh my God! It went in the hole!

JESSICA: That's what you're concerned with right now?

DAVID: That guy just got a hole in one on a par five! That's a triple eagle!

God enters. He's holding a driver and has an empty golf bag on his back. He puts the driver in the bag and greets David and Jessica.

GOD: Hello there. You must be the new couple moving into cloud nine.

DAVID: And . . . long white beard . . . triple eagle . . . you must be . . . God.

GOD: I suppose so.

> *David offers his hand to shake.*

I'm afraid you don't want to shake my hand. You'd be so overcome by my goodness that you'd drop straight to the ground and wouldn't awaken for a thousand years.

> *David quickly withdraws his hand.*

JESSICA: I'm Jessica.

> *She offers her hand. God shakes it.*

GOD: Nice to meet you. I couldn't help but overhear your argument. I don't like to toss advice at everyone I meet, but I'm God, so listen up, David. Things are pretty much perfect here on the Upper Upper East Side, but all the perfection in the world is but dust when you're overcome by loneliness. You'll notice I'm not playing golf in a foursome here. No, sir, nobody wants to play golf with a guy who shoots a fourteen every time.

DAVID: Fourteen?!

GOD: Yeah, I hit all the par threes in zero shots.

DAVID: How is that even—.

GOD: I'd explain it, but your head would explode. Don't miss the point here, David. You need this young lady more than you think. You don't realize it because you're a human—and not a particularly clever one—but silently without you even knowing, this Jessica is like the very gravity that keeps you from being torn from the Earth and fired away like a missile through the stratosphere. I advise you not to strike her away as though she were as insignificant as a golf ball. Well, I have four more holes to play. Hope to see the two of you around.

DAVID: Bye.

> *God exits.*

Jeez, now I feel like maybe God's right. Maybe I should keep you around.

JESSICA: Maybe! Well, maybe I don't need you as much as you think. Ever consider that?

DAVID: Oh really?

JESSICA: Yeah!

DAVID: Well, this is death, so I suggest we part!

JESSICA: Have a nice afterlife, jerk!

> *Jessica exits. David snaps his fingers. Angela reenters.*

ANGEL: Did you come to a decision?

DAVID: I'll take it!

ANGEL: I'll draw up the papers.

DAVID: Great! This place is going to make one heaven of a bachelor pad.

ANGEL: Bachelor pad?

DAVID: Jessica and I have decided to go our separate ways. Play the afterlife field for a while.

ANGEL: Hmmm. I wish you had said something.

DAVID: Why?

ANGEL: Frankly, on your own, you don't have near the credit

you need to buy this place. In fact, without her, you're pretty deep in debt.

DAVID: Can I get financing or a loan?

ANGEL: Of goodness? It doesn't work like that. I'll have to have one of my associates show you a place downtown.

> *She snaps her fingers. A real estate angel with black wings and red horns enters.*

DARK ANGEL: Mr. Bartley, Great to meet you . . .

CURTAIN

The End

DUO

Tom Moran

PRODUCTION NOTES:

Original Production: Stone Soup Theatre,
Seattle, WA
Dates: May 13-16, 2010
Director: Danielle Villegas

Cast
ROCKMAN, Norman Husser
GRAVEL GIRL, Norah Elges
THE DEMON, Michael Ramquist

10x10 Production: The ArtsCenter, Carrboro, NC
Dates: July 8-10 and 15-17, 2011
Director: Jeff Aguiar

Cast
ROCKMAN, Brook North
GRAVEL GIRL, Kelsey Kallang
THE DEMON, Susannah Hough

CHARACTERS:

ROCKMAN, A burly, chiseled superhero in his forties.

GRAVEL GIRL, ROCKMAN'S SIDEKICK. An attractive 24-year-old superheroine, wearing a skimpy costume including high-heeled boots.

THE DEMON, A supervillain in his forties, sinister in a snively way.

TIME: Now

PLACE: The Demon's secret lair

Scene 1

(A windowless concrete basement. There is a door stage right. Center stage, ROCKMAN and GRAVEL GIRL are chained helplessly to a wall. Stage left, THE DEMON stands over a giant time bomb.)

DEMON: Finally, I have you both right where I want you! Today the world will suffer the end of Rockman and – um, what's your name again?

GRAVEL GIRL: I'm Gravel Girl!

DEMON: Well, alas, Gravel Girl, we hardly knew ye.

GRAVEL GIRL: We're not licked yet, Demon!

ROCKMAN: *(to GRAVEL GIRL)* Please, sweetheart, let me do the talking. (to DEMON) We're not licked yet, Demon!

DEMON: I beg to differ, Super-Minerals. (He hits a button on the bomb, which beeps loudly and begins to tick.) In ten minutes, this whole building will blow sky-high and take both of you with it.

GRAVEL GIRL: You're crazy!

ROCKMAN*: (to GRAVEL GIRL)* Hush! *(To DEMON)* You're crazy! You'll never get away with this, you scoundrel.

DEMON: On the contrary, I believe I already have. *(Gestures to bomb.)* Now if you'll excuse me, I have a hydrofoil to catch. See you on the other side, Rockhead and Rabble Girl!
(DEMON laughs maniacally and exits. ROCKMAN and GRAVEL GIRL struggle against their restraints.)

ROCKMAN: Confound his nefarious schemes! He won't escape from me this time.

GRAVEL GIRL: *(rolls her eyes)* Yeah. Of course not.

> *(ROCKMAN is struggling with the restraints and doesn't hear.)*

ROCKMAN: Must–reach–wrist–laser. *(He struggles more and gives up, panting.)* Can you reach your laser, Gravel Girl?

GRAVEL GIRL: Look, can you just call me Elaine? I mean, there's no one around.

ROCKMAN: What's wrong with Gravel Girl?

GRAVEL GIRL: What's wrong with it? First, I'm 24, I'm not a girl. Second, I'm named after rubble! It doesn't exactly strike fear into the hearts of criminals, now does it?

ROCKMAN: When we get out of here I'll think of a new one. How's Minerella sound?

GRAVEL GIRL: Like a Disney Princess, actually.

ROCKMAN: Look, can you reach your laser or not?

GRAVEL GIRL: I can't reach my laser because you won't let me have one, remember?

ROCKMAN: Oh, right. You're still on your probationary period.

GRAVEL GIRL: Probationary period. I've helped you foil three bank robberies and a robot invasion and all you've let me have is a Swiss Army Knife with a picture of a boulder on it.

ROCKMAN: Lava Lad never sassed me like this.

GRAVEL GIRL: Well maybe you should hire Lava Lad. (Pause.) I'm sorry. I shouldn't have said that.

ROCKMAN: Let's just get out of here.

GRAVEL GIRL: Hold on.

> *(GRAVEL GIRL struggles with her right arm restraint and tears the bolt out of the wall. She frees herself from the other restraints.)*

ROCKMAN: Of course! All the damp here must have rotted the concrete. *(He struggles to no avail.)*

GRAVEL GIRL: No, I have a bionic arm! Did you even look at my resume? Or did you just spend the whole interview staring at my tits?

ROCKMAN: You got the job, didn't you?

GRAVEL GIRL: I hope I didn't just hear that.

ROCKMAN: Please just set me free so we can defuse that bomb.

GRAVEL GIRL: We?

Lawrence Harbison

ROCKMAN: So you can defuse the bomb. Which is the sidekick's job. You cut the blue wire—or whatever, I pursue the villain.

GRAVEL GIRL: Right, I save our asses and you get the interview in Esquire. Funny how that works. Especially since the only reason we got caught in the first place is because *someone* locked the damn keys in the Rockmobile!

ROCKMAN: Look, I said I was sorry! *(Pause. Rueful)* I don't think you have a very firm grasp of the hero-sidekick dynamic. You are my stalwart, my unflappable companion, willing to lay down your life for mine—

GRAVEL GIRL: You know, I don't even have a dental plan.

ROCKMAN: This is not the time to discuss personnel issues.

GRAVEL GIRL: Actually, I think it's the perfect time for a nice *(Looks at bomb)* six and a half-minute chat. Let's start with my salary.

ROCKMAN: Crap.

GRAVEL GIRL: What was that?

ROCKMAN: You don't have a salary!

GRAVEL GIRL: Exactly. Oh, I know, I know, I get paid "in kind" by getting to live in the mansion, et cetera. But a "girl's" gotta plan for the future, you know. *(Pause.)* I want what Robin's making.

ROCKMAN: What? *Robin? (Pause.)* How about Batgirl?
  (GRAVEL GIRL starts to head toward the exit.)

GRAVEL GIRL: *(scoffing)* Gotta go.

ROCKMAN: Lava Lad was my sidekick for 14 years and I never paid him a dime! He did it for the good of mankind. *(Wistful)* He was the best crimefighting partner a hero could hope for.

GRAVEL GIRL: Of course he was. He was a house slave, apparently. I bet he didn't even have medical.

ROCKMAN: He had mutant healing power!

GRAVEL GIRL: Well I don't. *(Counts off on fingers.)* Salary. Medical. Dental. 401(k). And—a new costume. No more spike heels. Yeah, they're great for kicking someone in the face, but you ever try chasing down Doctor Cheetah in these?

ROCKMAN: This is blackmail. You will not get away with this, you brigand!

GRAVEL GIRL: Look, save the invective for the criminals, okay?

ROCKMAN: Right now I'm having a little trouble telling the difference. Look, what is this really about? *(No response.)* I doubt you would endanger our lives for a dental plan. We did a background check on you. You're noble.

GRAVEL GIRL: I am not!

ROCKMAN: What's wrong with noble?

GRAVEL GIRL: Noble is passé. I'm going for more of an antihero aesthetic.

ROCKMAN: It doesn't suit you.

GRAVEL GIRL: Then look at this as a noble act. I'm standing up to the club.

ROCKMAN: I don't understand.

GRAVEL GIRL: That's all this hero thing is, is an old boy's club. You and White Lightning, sitting around the Freedom League cocktail lounge, sipping martinis and talking about how great it is to save the world. So entitled. So *entrenched.* Do you even remember why you became a superhero?

ROCKMAN: *(reciting)* My parents were killed in a rockslide caused by the Demon. Sworn to revenge, I became an expert on mineralogy and the martial arts, then adopted the name Rockman—

GRAVEL GIRL: Sworn to revenge. And how many times have you battled the Demon in the last 20 years?

ROCKMAN: Oh, every three to six months or so, I suppose.

GRAVEL GIRL: And yet he's still free. Not in jail or the asylum or, I don't know, dead.

ROCKMAN: He is a crafty and a devious foe.

GRAVEL GIRL: No, you just have no follow-through. And you know why? Because you need the headlines to keep yourself going. You're as much responsible for that madman still being around as anyone. You've created a self-perpetuating battle which you can never win or lose because it means you're out of a job.

ROCKMAN: You're mad. I've dedicated my life to thwarting his schemes.

GRAVEL GIRL: And then letting him get away. *(Gestures to bomb.)* This is a case in point. Oh by the way, four minutes. *(10-second pause.)* Three minutes fifty seconds.

ROCKMAN: All right! You've got it. Everything you want.

GRAVEL GIRL: Everything?

ROCKMAN: Everything.

GRAVEL GIRL: All right. Let me take care of this.

(GRAVEL GIRL turns to the bomb, pulls her official Rockman knife out of her pocket and starts to work on it.)

ROCKMAN: Can you disarm it?

(Gravel Girl holds up the knife.)

GRAVEL GIRL: *(Sarcastic)* Piece of cake. *(She starts to work, then stops.)* One more question.

ROCKMAN: *Bomb!*

GRAVEL GIRL: What happened to Lava Lad?

ROCKMAN: You know what happened. The Black Tiger drop-kicked him into outer space.

GRAVEL GIRL: Bullshit. I don't believe you'd let him die like that. You loved him too much. I mean, strictly in a heterosexual super-life-partners sort of way. What's the real story?

ROCKMAN: If I tell you, will you defuse the bomb?

GRAVEL GIRL: Sure.

ROCKMAN: He quit. After 14 years. He ran out on me. He's trying to make it in Mexico City now. Calls himself "El Roca."

GRAVEL GIRL: Why'd he quit?

ROCKMAN: *(defeated)* He said he was tired of playing second fiddle. Braving death all the time and never getting the credit.

GRAVEL GIRL: A-ha! So you admit sidekicking is a crock.

ROCKMAN: Sounds like you don't need me to tell you that.

GRAVEL GIRL: And do you admit that superheroes are a joke too? That you're just pulling your punches?

ROCKMAN: The Demon has spent two decades slithering from my grasp. I want nothing more than to see him—

(A noise. The door opens and the DEMON pokes his head back in.)

DEMON: Hey. You're still here?

ROCKMAN: Of course we are. You chained us here!

DEMON: Yeah, but this was such a simple trap. I mean, I didn't even take your utility belts. I figured you be free by now.

(GRAVEL GIRL raises her hand)

GRAVEL GIRL: I am.

DEMON: *(to GRAVEL GIRL)* Shush! *(to ROCKMAN)* You didn't think I'd let you off the hook this easy. After all we've been through together, to finish you with a mere bomb?

ROCKMAN: What did you have in mind?

DEMON: Oh, you'll see. *(Laughs maniacally.)* A couple more doors and you reach the tarantula pit. Then there's the room lined with motion-sensitive lasers. After that is the trapdoor into the alligator cage, then you hit the phalanx of *luchadores* and killer cyborgs. And after that—well, it's a surprise.

ROCKMAN: Curse your cunning machinations!

DEMON: That's the spirit! Tell you what, let me just unshackle you and give you a start on me. I didn't go through all the time and effort of arranging an intricate series of escalating challenges so you could get killed right inside the front door. Oh, and let me get that bomb for you.

> *(The DEMON aims a remote at the bomb and hits a button. The bomb makes a noise like a car auto-unlocking and stops ticking.)*

GRAVEL GIRL: What the hell! *(to ROCKMAN)* Do you see what I'm talking about, Rockman?

ROCKMAN: I—I—Demon, what are you doing?

DEMON: I'm just being sporting –

ROCKMAN: Sporting? But you're a criminal! My archnemesis! You killed my parents, you fiend!

DEMON: Oh, you should really be over that by now. I feel like we've built up a rapport since then. Don't you think?

ROCKMAN: *(to himself)* My god. Gravel Girl is right.

DEMON: *(to ROCKMAN)* Now about those shackles—

> *(DEMON starts to advance toward ROCKMAN. GRAVEL GIRL removes a laser gun from ROCK-MAN's utility belt and aims it at the DEMON.)*

GRAVEL GIRL: Afraid I can't let you do that. He and I are in the middle of some very delicate negotiations here.

DEMON: Please be quiet. The men are trying to talk.

ROCKMAN: Hey! Knock it off! That's my sidekick you're talking to.

GRAVEL GIRL: Thank you.

ROCKMAN: You're welcome. Now shoot him.

GRAVEL GIRL and DEMON: *What?*

ROCKMAN: Shoot him. Kill him. You were right. This has gone on for far too long.

GRAVEL GIRL: Really?

DEMON: Really?

ROCKMAN: Really. And I want you to do the honors, Gravel Girl.

> *(GRAVEL GIRL aims the laser at a terrified DEMON and is about to fire, but eases up on the trigger. She gestures to him to move to center stage.)*

GRAVEL GIRL: *(to DEMON)* Get into those shackles, Demon. Do it!

> *(DEMON shackles up his own feet. GRAVEL GIRL does the hands, pulling some rope out of ROCK-MAN's utility belt to bind his right hand since the shackle is broken.)*

GRAVEL GIRL: There. *(to ROCKMAN)* You're right, I guess I am a lousy antihero.

ROCKMAN: I knew it all along. Now how about setting me free.

GRAVEL GIRL: No, I'm not gonna do that. What say you guys just hang out here. I'll call the Commissioner in a few hours and let him know where to find you. In the meantime, I suggest you have a frank discussion about the origins of your deep-seated codependent relationship. I think that'd be for the best.

> *(GRAVEL GIRL walks toward the door, giving Rockman a reassuring tap on the cheek along the way. He calls after her.)*

ROCKMAN: Hey! Dammit! You can forget about your Christmas bonus!

> *(GRAVEL GIRL continues out. Pause.)*

DEMON: You know, Lava Lad never pulled this crap.

> *(Blackout.)*

The End

Eleanor's Passing

John Patrick Bray

Production Notes:

"Eleanor's Passing" was one of eight winners of the Heartland Theatre Company's 2011 Annual Ten-Minute Play Festival in Normal, IL. It opened on Thursday, June 9, 2011.

Cast:
MOE, Larry Eggan
GUS, Dave Lemmon
TALL GLASS, Kevin Woodard

Directed by Christopher Gray.

CHARACTERS:
MOE, in his seventies
GUS, in his seventies
TALL GLASS, in his seventies

SETTING: Moe's back porch in Southeast Louisiana
TIME: Present Day

LIGHTS UP. A back porch. Two rocking chairs with a table in between. It is late evening in the late autumn in Southwest Louisiana. The lighting is dim. MOE enters with a small electric lantern. He is dressed mostly in black. He walks with a little bit of a limp. He sets it down between the chairs. He turns and looks at the chairs. A moment. He sits in one. He looks over at the other one. GUS enters. GUS, also an old-timer, is carrying a hunting magazine. He is holding a Bud-light. He looks at MOE and at the other rocking chair. MOE looks up at him. Then away. GUS continues to look at him, drinking his beer.

MOE: You going to keep on staring at me, or are you fixin' to take her chair?
GUS: I wouldn't ask it of you.
MOE: Go ahead.
GUS: I'd say yes, but I don't want you to get the wrong idea. I like to think we're close, but not that close.
  MOE chuckles.
GUS: Bud light?
MOE: If I start at this point, I doubt I'd stop. Ever.
GUS: Right.
MOE: How long we know each other, Gus?
GUS: Too long.
MOE: Thought so.
GUS: You want me to . . . I don't know . . . do something?
MOE: Like what?
GUS: It's what I keep asking myself. You know. What can I do? I want to do something. All I got is beer.
  (Pause)
I got a dog, too.

MOE gives him a severe look.
Now you think of how I regard Wallace before you start looking at me like that.
MOE chuckles.
MOE: I'm sure Eleanor wouldn't approve.
GUS: Why not?
MOE: The dog has a prettier name than me. She wouldn't abide that.
GUS: Sure she would.
MOE: It might tear through her garden. How could I have something that would dig up her garden? That's all I . . .
Slight Pause.
GUS: What do you think is going to happen?
MOE: I don't know. Do something I guess.
GUS: Guess so.
MOE: Wait for my turn.
GUS: Yes, sir. You could do that. (*Beat*). While waiting for God, I enjoy a Bud Light. You sure you don't want one? I know the kids these days drink Purple Haze. Named after a sixties rock-and-roll song.
MOE: I know the song.
GUS: Tourist shit, you ask me. Come down here. Show off their boobies if you throw them beads. Me? I like Bud light. It's unpretentious. The common denominator, you know? You can go into any store from here to Santa Fe, and you'll find Bud light.
MOE: Any store in America.
GUS: That's right. Any store in America. (*Beat*). I'm going to
GUS: (*Contd.*) miss Eleanor, Moe.
(Pause)
MOE: She didn't look that old. You know? I look like hell. She still skipped. She had an actual skip in her step. Her cheeks were like . . . big plums, you know? Just ripe. And that smile. Lord . . . that smile.
GUS: Yessir. She really looked good. Kept the house looking good, too. And that garden. Gorgeous.
(Pause)
The thing is, I . . . well, what I mean is . . . what are you going to do with the house?
MOE: What do you mean?

GUS: The house, Moe. What are you going to do with it?

MOE: I don't know. Nothing, I suppose.

GUS: Nothing?

MOE: Why? What you want me to do with it?

GUS: I was just thinking. With the two rooms upstairs. The divide between the kitchen and the backroom. You could really fix it up.

MOE: And what? Sell it?

GUS: Sell it? What you want to sell it for?

MOE: Well, you're getting all these ideas about my house.

GUS: It's a beautiful house! (*Beat*). Moe, you're broke.

>   *MOE turns away.*

Been broke for years. Me and Tall Glass. Well, we've been thinking.

MOE: That'd be a first for you two.

GUS: Hell, he's better at saying it than me anyway.

>   *TALL GLASS enters.*

TALL GLASS: Hey, young-timers.

>   *TALL GLASS sits in the other rocking chair without a thought. MOE and GUS look at him.*

GUS: That's my chair.

TALL GLASS: I didn't see the brass plaque.

GUS: That's MY chair!

TALL GLASS: Were you sitting in it?

GUS: I was fixin' to!

TALL GLASS: You shouldn't take so much time fixin' to.

GUS: It's still my chair.

TALL GLASS: Moe, what does he mean this is his chair?

MOE: Last time I checked it was my chair. I'm sitting in Eleanor's.

GUS: You're sitting in Eleanor's?

MOE: Yes, sir.

GUS: And you let me just stand here!

MOE: You were having some kind of crisis. I figured I should just leave you alone.

GUS: (*To Moe*). Look here, I'm his *best friend. Best friends* sit together!

>   *TALL GLASS reaches over and puts his hand on MOE'S. GUS looks annoyed.*

MOE: (*Wryly*). Thanks for coming over and making me feel

better, boys.

GUS: Oh, wait—

TALL GLASS: We shouldn't be behaving this way, it's just . . .

MOE: It's just what?

TALL GLASS: Well, we've both been eyeing this spot.

MOE: Eyeing this spot?

The moment is tense.

TALL GLASS: Sure. For the, for the plan. When we all move in with you.

MOE: Who all is moving where?

TALL GLASS: We all is . . . moving . . . that is, we are . . . Us. That's why . . . (*to GUS*) . . . you never got around to talking to him about it?

GUS: I was fixin' to.

TALL GLASS: That's you, Gus. Always fixin' to, never doing. A true Texan.

GUS: Now, you take it easy on that Texas stuff! You might have the Tigers, but we have the Longhorns, you hear? Let your Tigers go pro and see what happens!

MOE: You want to move in? With me?

TALL GLASS: No, no.

GUS: (*Beat*). Yes.

MOE: Why?

GUS: It's just that . . . well . . .

TALL GLASS: We ain't getting any younger.

GUS: That's the truth.

TALL GLASS: And between your gout and my back pain, and Gus' chronic "fixin'-to" condition . . .

GUS: We thought that three heads would be better than one.

MOE: Three heads?

TALL GLASS: That is, we all need a little looking after. (*Beat*). When's the last time the kids come down?

MOE: They're here enough. Too much.

TALL GLASS: Christmas.

MOE: Yeah. Christmas.

TALL GLASS: And they'll be here again?

MOE: They were just here.

GUS: And they'll be here again *when*? (*Beat*). They're like what we can the C and E over at the church. The Christmas and

Easter Christians. Show up on the two big holidays, and forget about the big guy the rest of the year.

(Pause)

TALL GLASS: I could take the upstairs guest room.

MOE: That's Millie's room.

TALL GLASS: On Christmas, I can duck out.

MOE: What's wrong with your place?

TALL GLASS: Not sure how much longer I'm going to keep it. The pawn shop is doing terrible. And all those stairs.

MOE: How are my stairs different?

GUS: When he hollers, he'll have a couple of fools to laugh at him.

TALL GLASS: It's true. The sound of hollering to yourself. It's not the way I want to go.

GUS: Me, neither.

(Pause)

Eleanor wouldn't want you to be alone, either, Moe.

Pause. MOE stands up and exits.

TALL GLASS: (*To Gus*). You were supposed to TALK to him!

GUS: I was—

TALL GLASS: Fixin' to, fixin' to. We sound like damn fools!

GUS: Maybe I should tell him.

TALL GLASS: Tell him what?

GUS: I'm losing my house. The kids want to ship me off in an old folk's home.

TALL GLASS: How'd you find out?

GUS: Just speculating. (*Beat*). It's what I wanted to do with my folks!

MOE enters. He is holding a third rocking chair with a small cooler on it. He sets it down, opens the cooler revealing more Bud Light.

MOE: Just one rule. I want three years of peace.

TALL GLASS: (*Beat*). Where you plan on going in three years?

MOE: Nowhere. Three years of peace just sound nice, doesn't it?

The men chuckle. MOE takes a Bud Light, hands a fresh one to GUS, and one to TALL GLASS. They

> *pop them open.*
TALL GLASS: Eleanor started a garden.
MOE: She did.
> *(Beat. The men look at him).*
> Drink my beer.
>> *They all sit on their chairs. It gets later. Stage goes dark.*
>> *CURTAIN.*

The End

A Lesson

David Johnson

PRODUCTION NOTES:

"A Lesson" was originally produced by Blue Coyote Theater Group at the Access Theater, New York, NY, as part of "Standards of Decency 3: 300 Vaginas Before Breakfast." June 1 – 18, 2011.

Cast
HENRY, Jim Ireland
EVA, Sarah Ireland
GIRL, Stephanie Willing

Directed by Gary Shrader
Producer: Blue Coyote Theater Group (Gary Shrader, Kyle Ancowitz, Stephen Speights, Robert Buckwalter)

CHARACTERS:
HENRY male, late thirties-early forties
EVA female, late thirties-early forties
YOUNG GIRL female, sixteen years old

SETTING: A nondescript living room.
TIME: The present.

> (*A man and a woman, HENRY and EVA. A room.
> Both late 30s-early 40s. There is an offstage voice
> of a young GIRL. She sings in the next room, ac-
> companied by a piano or cheap Casio keyboard.
> She is doing scales. She's not bad. But she's not very
> good either. EVA and HENRY listen. Scales continue
> under dialogue.*)

HENRY: She's opening. You can hear her opening. You can
feel it.
EVA: I don't think today is good.
HENRY: I hear gold.
EVA: Don't you think so?
HENRY: Think what.
EVA: That today is not good.
> (*Pause.*)
That there are better days than today.
HENRY: The sun room is clean, right?
EVA: Of course.
HENRY: You haven't left your shit laying around again, right?
It is a teaching space.
EVA: It's clean.
HENRY: I should have checked myself. We don't work with
the same definitions of "clean."
> (*Pause.*)
Sometimes I feel like a prospector. A prospector in an
old black and white movie. A movie about—gold. Gold
prospectors. The lust for gold. Prospecting for gold. And
they had the—pans. The mountain streams. And there's
always the old character actor who can—hear the gold.
Who was—who was that old actor—

EVA: Walter Huston?

HENRY: No, the actor I'm talking about is in that movie with Bogart. Love Bogart he's so authentic such an authentic actor I despair of these kids today learning about an actor like Bogart I don't know why they don't study him like you when I first met you you didn't know Bogart you were a fucking moron.

EVA: I—I knew who *Bogart*—

HENRY: It's that movie with Bogart and this wonderful old character actor and he's always talking about gold and he's got this look in his eye he talks about gold and men's lust and getting the gold out of the mountain and being able to sense it hear it—

EVA: I think that's Walter Huston I think he won an Oscar—

HENRY: It's not Walter Huston will you please stop saying that I fucking know who Walter Huston is and that is not who I'm talking about.

EVA: "Treasure of the Sierra Madre"—Bogart is—

HENRY: It's not "Sierra Madre," that's not the movie I'm—

EVA: But doesn't Walter Huston play a gold prospector in that unless there's another movie where he plays a—

HENRY: Never mind. Clearly it's going to be a big fucking problem.

EVA: I didn't mean to—

HENRY: When what I'm trying to do is organize my thoughts. *Express* them. Think aloud. Creatively. Create. Sculpt. As an artist does.

EVA: I'm sorry.

HENRY: I don't know why it's such a fucking problem. To express myself. Don't know why I need to fight for that.

(The singing continues.)

There's gold. I can hear it. It's buried deep, but it's there. I'm a prospector.

(He listens another moment.)

There's no experience in the voice. Not yet. That's what brings richness.

EVA: I don't think today is good.

(HENRY looks at her.)

I don't think today is—best. As something to consider.

I think there are better—days—to consider—than this one.

(Pause. Music.)

I know that's not your feeling.

HENRY: You don't know that. You can't read my mind.

EVA: I sense it.

HENRY: Fine.

EVA: But I want to express that. I don't think today is good.

HENRY: Thank you.

(Pause.)

Of course, we've discussed this. We've planned this discussed this—talked about how for today—

EVA: You just said this morning—

HENRY: Unless I was talking to myself. Again. But no. You. With your fine intellect. Finely honed to a precise point. With a GED. You feel—that today is not optimal. That's what you're saying.

EVA: I'm expressing my feelings.

HENRY: That's good. We've worked on that and I'm glad to see it's bearing fruit. But I'd like to dig deeper. Get to root causes. There's a young girl in the next room. And she's got a great deal of potential. It's raw. But it's there. You agree?

EVA: Yes.

HENRY: You agree.

EVA: Yes.

HENRY: But you don't think this is a good day?

EVA: I don't think it's the best.

HENRY: Interesting. Are you jealous?

EVA: No.

HENRY: No?

EVA: No. Of course not.

HENRY: Explain.

EVA: We're beyond that. You and I. We've moved past that.

HENRY: But she is younger.

EVA: I am not jealous of a sixteen year old.

HENRY: Why would you be?

EVA: I'm not.

HENRY: You've had several children. How many I've lost count.

EVA: I don't see what that has to—

HENRY: And recently it hasn't worked out well.

EVA: I know what you're trying to—

HENRY: I'm simply saying her body is much younger. She hasn't had all these children. She's at a different point in her journey. I'm not criticizing.

EVA: You are not going to do that to me you are not going to—

HENRY: You *continued* to have children. At an advanced age. And there have been results. Of that decision. That's all I'm saying. Perhaps that plays a part in this jealous acting out. That's my sense. I don't know. I can't read your mind.

(She's silent.)

Not that that has anything to do with anything. Your body has the beauty that comes by experience. That richness. It's one of the things I love about you. Your life is written on your body.

EVA: I don't want to do it. Not today.

(Pause.)

HENRY: Being an artist is the greatest thing anyone can achieve. The greatest goal in the world. Do you agree?

EVA: Yes.

HENRY: You agree.

EVA: Yes.

HENRY: And you don't want her to have that.

EVA: That's not what I'm saying.

HENRY: To have that experience. Why not? What's she done to you? I'm just curious.

EVA: *(her voice is at the same level as before)* I don't want to do it.

HENRY: Keep your voice down.

EVA: I didn't—

HENRY: KEEP YOUR VOICE DOWN!

(The music and singing stop for a moment.)

The space where I teach is sacred. I won't have you dragging your neuroses—your baggage all your toxic bullshit—I won't have you dragging it in to someone else's lesson. KEEP GOING!

(The music and singing continue.)

Lawrence Harbison

All that stupid moronic toxic garbage your family loaded onto you. All the work I've had to do. To get you to where you are. Had to break my back tear myself to pieces—castrate myself cut my own balls off to keep you from sinking back into the filth you came from. I studied in *Europe*.

EVA: I'm sorry.

HENRY: Europe. And Domingo—

EVA: I just didn't think today I just—

HENRY: Domingo heard me sing. Immediately made appointments for me to see the top—

EVA: You said you wanted me to express—

HENRY: (*bellows at the GIRL offstage*) BREATHE! BREATHE! FROM YOUR VAGINALS!

> (*The music and the voice stop.*)

I know I'm not supposed to say "vaginals" in this stupid goddamn place! I know I'm not supposed to recognize that a sixteen year-old girl has a vagina! I have a cock! She has a vagina, too! Let's acknowledge them! It's crazy I know but let's do it! And sing with our cock and ass and vagina and balls!

> (*No one makes a sound. HENRY continues to direct his tirade to the GIRL offstage.*)

Do you understand I'm introducing you to the world? That there is a whole world of richness and art and culture out there and otherwise you would just be chatting with retards on Facebook? Like you were doing when we met? That was your life! I'm offering you the whole world when everyone else is downloading porn and sending—little—smiley faces, twatting and chatting and skyping and waiting for some pervert to cut them up in a parking lot? I'm offering a connection! A real honest to Christ connection to the world! DO YOU HAVE ANY FUCKING IDEA WHAT I'M GIVING YOU?

> (*The GIRL enters. She is sixteen. Plain. So painfully shy speaking is an effort. She looks adoringly at HENRY.*)

GIRL: I do.

HENRY: You know what it means?

GIRL: I do.

HENRY: And you want to be an artist?

GIRL: More than anything.

HENRY: It's the hardest thing in the world. Being an artist. It's killed me.

GIRL: It hasn't. You're—alive.

HENRY: No I'm not.

GIRL: You're the most alive person I've ever known.

HENRY: And this is what you want?

GIRL: Yes.

(He holds her for a moment. She sobs a little. HENRY looks at EVA.)

HENRY: The sun room, yes?

(EVA looks at him and says nothing.)

Yes.

(to the GIRL)

Go into the sun room. Start your breathing.

(He kisses her lightly on the forehead. The GIRL exits. EVA does not look at him. A long pause, as HENRY looks at her and EVA avoids his gaze.)

I learn so much from my students.

(EVA continues to avoid his gaze.)

Come here.

EVA: Don't.

HENRY: Come here.

EVA: *(shaking, almost in tears)* I'm sorry. Today is good. It's good.

HENRY: Come here.

(She walks to him slowly. He reaches for her face. She flinches, ready to bolt. He kisses her. Slowly and tenderly at first, then with growing passion. She responds. He breaks it.)

The sun room?

EVA: Yes.

HENRY: How is today?

EVA: Today is good.

(He smiles. Blackout.)

The End

MEN AND PARTS
John Morogiello

PRODUCTION NOTES:

Men and Parts was originally produced by J.T. Burian Theatricals as a part of the Washington Theatre Festival in the summer of 2001.

Cast:

CONNIE, Roxanne Fournier
VICKIE, Lori Boyd
MAN, John Morogiello

This production was directed by Martin A. Blanco. It was a finalist for the Heideman Award at Actors Theatre of Louisville, where it was produced in the summer of 2002. This production was directed by Amy Wegener.

Cast:

CONNIE, Hannegan Beardsley
VICKI, Sarah DiMuro

The current version of the script was first produced at Flagpole Radio Cafe in Newtown, Connecticut in March of 2011, with the following cast:

Cast:

CONNIE, Kate Katcher
VICKIE, Barbara Gaines
MAN, Chris Teskey
This production was directed by Martin A. Blanco.

CHARACTERS:
CONNIE: a buxom, single woman with a thick New York accent, of an age ranging from mid-twenties to late-thirties.
VICKIE: a long-legged, single woman with a thick New York accent, of an age ranging from mid-twenties to late-thirties.
MAN: an attractive man, approximately the same age as Connie and Vickie.

SETTING: A bar in Manhattan.
TIME: The present, Happy Hour.

> (A bar in New York City during happy hour. Connie is at the bar drinking. Vickie enters, looking over the crowd for Connie. Connie spots Vickie and waves her over. Both have big hair and thick accents.)

CONNIE: Vickie! Over here. At the bar.
> (Vickie crosses to Connie. They give each other a hug and kiss of greeting. They sit at the bar.)
VICKIE: Hi.
CONNIE: I was about to give up on you.
VICKIE: You would not believe the day I had.
CONNIE: Yeah?
VICKIE: Awful. The Fed Ex guy tried to pick me up.
CONNIE: Oh, don't get me started on men today.
VICKIE: *(Giving her drink order, then proceeding.)* Wine spritzer. So, I'm sitting at my desk, you know, waiting for the polish, cause I got a chip over the weekend and she couldn't fit me in until tomorrow, you know what I'm saying?
CONNIE: Mm-hmm.
VICKIE: When I see the Fed Ex guy standing right in front of me with that look on his face.
CONNIE: What look?
VICKIE: That "I'm a man about to say something clever so I can get in your pants" look.
CONNIE: Oh, that one, sure.
VICKIE: So I say, "What?" And I swear to God, he says, "I'd ask you to sign for these, but I can already see you're the most precious package here."

CONNIE: Is he serious?

VICKIE: I'm like: Give me a break! Get outta here! Can you really see me spending the rest of my life with a guy couldn't even get work as a regular mailman?

CONNIE: No.

VICKIE: Can you see us growing old together?

CONNIE: That's why you gotta turn them down flat.

VICKIE: That's why I did.

CONNIE: Course, you know, this kind of thing is happening to me all the time.

VICKIE: Yeah?

CONNIE: All the time. At least twice a week. You know, it's not always the Fed Ex guy.

VICKIE: What, UPS?

CONNIE: No, no, no, *real* men. Like the other day, right? I'm on the subway; it's a little late, you know, happy hour's over. And this guy gets on, right? Soap opera gorgeous. I mean, the hair, the clothes. You know how you can figure out the pecs from the way the suit tapers?

VICKIE: Yeah.

CONNIE: That.

VICKIE: Eyes?

CONNIE: Black.

VICKIE: Yum.

CONNIE: With wavy, jet hair.

VICKIE: Beard?

CONNIE: No, but he had that stubble thing going.

VICKIE: Well, it's nice to look at—

CONNIE: —but I wouldn't want to live there, exactly. So, I'm sitting there, you know, pretending to read like I don't see him, and wouldn't you know it, he sits down right acrost from me. Whole car to choose from, he sits acrost from me.

VICKIE: Some nerve.

CONNIE: So I glance up, right? Like I'm turning the page? And he says, "Hey." So I give him one of those friendly little smiles, you know. The kind that say, "I'm trying to be polite but you're really bugging the crap out of me and if you don't cut it out I'm gonna kick you in the nuts."

VICKIE: I give them.

CONNIE: So he says, "Any good?"

VICKIE: What does that mean?

CONNIE: The book.

VICKIE: I see.

CONNIE: So he says, "Any good?" And I'm like: "Drop dead, Mr. Soap Opera Guy. I don't need you right now, okay? I'll go home and watch you on tape, you know what I'm saying?" Drop dead.

VICKIE: You gotta do it. It's the only thing they understand.

CONNIE: Every girl has got to tell a gorgeous guy to drop dead at least once in her life.

VICKIE: Once? We're talking daily over here. If I don't hear a title in the name, take a hike.

CONNIE: Like—

VICKIE: Like M.D.

CONNIE: A doctor, exactly.

VICKIE: Or esquire.

CONNIE: A magazine writer, yes.

VICKIE: Don't come at me with no stubbly face 'til I can see the bank book.

CONNIE: You know why they do this to me, don't you.

VICKIE: What.

CONNIE: Big boobs. They're a man vacuum. As soon as I step outside the apartment, my boobs just suck them in.

VICKIE: What are you saying?

CONNIE: I'm saying guys like big boobs.

VICKIE: That's not what you're saying.

CONNIE: What.

VICKIE: You're saying your boobs allow you to turn down more men than mine.

CONNIE: I'm not saying that.

VICKIE: I think you are.

CONNIE: What are you complaining about? You got the Fed Ex guy.

VICKIE: Oh, I see. It's not that your boobs dump more men than mine, it's that they attract a better class of dumpee. Is that what you're saying?

CONNIE: God, what is wrong with you?

VICKIE: There are other things besides boobs, you know.

CONNIE: Whatever.

VICKIE: Get a look at these legs. Huh? My legs have broken the hearts of far better men than your boobs could ever hope to know.

CONNIE: Like who?

VICKIE: Like Wolf Blitzer.

CONNIE: Wolf Blitzer??? When was this?

VICKIE: Last Christmas. I was at Rockefeller Center, you know, skating. And I've got my tights on, you know, skating there, one leg raised behind me, showing it off. So, I'm packing up to go, putting the skates in my bag, when who shows up but Wolf Blitzer. "Vickie," he says, "I can't take it anymore. I've watched you on that ice from my office window at Thirty Rock every Wednesday evening before the zamboni comes on. I am aflame with desire for your legs. I can't take it anymore, it's affecting my delivery of the news. Me, Vickie, and your legs. They must never be parted.

CONNIE: What did you do?

VICKIE: I said, "Get out!" "Get out of here, you lousy news-reader! These legs are being saved for a news*maker*!" And I took the blade of my skate and I slashed him across the mouth. That's why he grew the beard.

CONNIE: Wolf Blitzer's with CNN; what's he doing at NBC headquarters?

VICKIE: It would seem my legs are a "network-changing event."

CONNIE: Either that or they're "cable-ready."—Course that reminds me of something that happened to my boobs the other day. You remember that nice weather we had the other day? Well, I was outside, having lunch outside of the stock exchange, you know, looking for people to ignore. And I'm wearing the scoop neck, right? Eating my sandwich? When a small breeze blows up, ever so gentle, and blows the bag off my lap. I think nothing of it, right? Just pick it up. But as I'm bending over, I hear this noise.

(Connie whimpers like a hurt puppy.)

VICKIE: What's that?

CONNIE: That's the noise. Like a whimpering. So I straighten up; it stops. I bend over again and—

(Connie whimpers.)

VICKIE: The whimper.

CONNIE: Exactly. So I turn my head a bit toward the whimpering noise and guess who I see staring down my blouse? Donald Trump.

VICKIE: The Celebrity Apprentice guy? He's like eight million years old.

CONNIE: Apparently age means nothing to the breast man.

VICKIE: Yeah, but he's almost a different species, like one of those guys on the evolutionary charts.

CONNIE: Homo erectus.

VICKIE: Donald Trump? That homo hasn't been erectus since Marla Maples.

CONNIE: So I say, "Donald Trump, what are you doing over there whimpering down my cleavages? You should be out creating sound bites or something to save the economy." He says, "Connie, I must have you. You've the bust of a couple of towers I'd like to put my name on." Then instead of the whimper, he tried to give me the bang, so I yelled: "Drop dead, Mr. Real Estate Magnate Donald Trump! Drop dead and don't you ever let me catch you staring at my boobs in such a piteous manner ever again. You're fired!" And I tossed my orange at him, blinding him with the juice as he struggled to maintain the dignity of his combover.

VICKIE: Well, you know, something similar happened to me just last night. I had come home after a full day of dumping men. I'm in my bedroom, you know, getting ready for bed, taking off my stockings. When all of a sudden I hear, tap tap tap at the window.

CONNIE: What was it?

VICKIE: That's exactly what I asked myself. What was that? So I crawl stealthily over to the window, throw up the blinds and guess who I see crouching all huddled on the fire escape?

CONNIE: Who.

VICKIE: Elton John. He was peeking into my bedroom window, watching me get undressed.

CONNIE: Elton John is gay.

VICKIE: He *used* to be. My legs converted him. He said, "Vickie, I've been watching your legs through the blinds every night for the past five years. I'm a new man. Run away with me. Can you feel the love tonight?" So I said, "Get outta here, Elton John, leave my legs alone! Go back to your famous life on the great white way and cartoon theme songs." And I shoved him off the fire escape and watched him ever so gracefully, like a great, bespectacled bird with colorful plumage, plummet horribly into the dumpster. And sure enough, his career is still dead.

CONNIE: Men are men, no matter what you do.

VICKIE: I'm gonna vomit just thinking about them.

CONNIE: Any man tries to pick me up tonight is in serious, serious trouble.

(A man approaches the bar next to Vickie and Connie. He speaks to the bartender.)

MAN: Pint of Bass.

(As the man waits for his beer, Vickie and Connie glare angrily at him, waiting for the man to give them the slightest excuse to pounce. A beat as the man senses the extreme tension. Very, very slowly, he turns his head to meet their piercing glares. Perhaps he is about to say something. Perhaps he thinks better of it. But he is definitely confused, and a little bit frightened. The imaginary bartender hands the man his beer, breaking the moment.)

Thanks. Keep it.

(The man exits.)

CONNIE: Now how come a guy like that never comes on to us?

(Vickie shrugs as the lights fade.)

The End

THE METAPHOR

Matthew Freeman

PRODUCTION NOTES:

The Metaphor was originally produced by Blue Coyote Theater Group (Kyle Ancowitz, Robert Buckwalter, Gary Shrader, and Stephen Speights) as a part of "Standards of Decency 3: 300 Vaginas Before Breakfast", at the Access Theater in New York City in June 2011. It was directed by Kyle Ancowitz.

Cast:

LORI, Amanda Jones
ROB, Matthew Trumbull
HARRY, Charlie Wilson

CHARACTERS:
LORI, thirty to forty, a parish priest
ROB, thirty to forty, a new parishioner
HARRY, thirty to forty, Lori's husband

SETTING: Lori's office at the rectory
TIME: 2011

> *(LORI's home office. A desk, a couch. LORI is on the phone, and looking at a laptop.)*

LORI: (on the telephone) Well, Mrs. Rimbone, there's really . . . well God has a . . . well God doesn't need to . . .
> *(Enter ROB. LORI smiles, keeps talking, waves at him to take a seat.)*

Mrs. Rimbone, I have to . . .
> *(LORI makes little "yaketty-yak" gestures with her hands.)*

Painful as I'm sure it was, he's in a better place. Passing that much . . . passing a stone that size isn't usually . . . isn't usually lethal but he's in a better . . . he's in a better place . . . he's . . . he's in a better place Mrs. Rimbone.
> *(Pause.)*

He's in a better . . . place. He's . . . I have to go. I'm sorry. I have a visitor.
> *(Pause.)*

He's in a better place.
> *(Pause.)*

Bless you too, Mrs. Rimbone.
> *(Pause.)*

A better place.
> *(Pause.)*

Yes, a better place. Right. God bless you. I will. I'll pray for you. I will. Yes. I will. He's in a better place. He's with Jesus and they're drinking and watching the Jets. That's right. A better place. He's. In. A. Better place. Yes.
> *(Pause. Moves to hang up the phone and pulls it back to her ear.)*

What? Yes. A better place. Good bye Mrs. Rimbone.

Bye. Bye. Bye.

(Hangs up.)

Jesus H. Christ, right? Mrs. Rimbone's husband died and it was *gross*. She's a jabberjaw. Hi Rob. I'm glad you came.

(She reaches into her desk and takes out a priest's collar and puts it on while they talk.)

Sit down. Did Harry let you in?

ROB Yeah.

LORI: Great. That's great. I'm glad you came. You know what? Why don't you sit here at my desk, and I'll sit on the couch?

ROB You . . . why?

LORI: Less top-down. Gets us all out of our comfort zones. Then we can really talk without all the trappings of authority.

(ROB obliges. LORI sits.)

LORI: Great. So.

ROB So.

LORI: Yes.

(Pause.)

So.

ROB: So, yeah. I . . .

LORI: So.

(Pause.)

How can I help? Everything okay?

(Pause.)

Listen, it's okay. You want some coffee?

ROB: No, no. I'm fine. I'm a little nervous anyway.

LORI: You don't have to be nervous. Everything you say to me stays here. In this room. In my office. In my head. I won't share it. No one hears you but me.

ROB: And God.

LORI: Whatever floats your boat.

ROB: Because that's what I need. A little . . . something for my . . .

LORI: What?

ROB: Soul.

(Pause.)

Feels so childish to say it like that.

LORI: Sounds a little childish too. Doesn't mean it *is* childish, but . . . it does *sound* childish.

>   *(Pause.)*

>   So . . . Robert. Lay it on me.

ROB: I . . . well . . . you know I only moved here a few months ago and only just started coming to St. Stephen's. It's hard, you know. It's a sort of quiet area, and it's different here. Not a lot of people. Feels like when you're in your house at night, it's like . . . like you're the only person in the world. Sometimes.

LORI: That sounds creepy.

ROB: I know.

LORI: Did you kill someone?

ROB: No.

LORI: I'm not a cop.

ROB: I know that.

LORI: So you can tell me.

ROB: I didn't kill anyone.

LORI: Did you kill someone?

ROB: No.

>   *(Pause.)*

>   I'm just trying to describe . . . to tell you that I feel lonely. Which . . .

LORI: Right. I know. It sounds childish.

ROB: That's not what I was going to say.

LORI: No?

ROB: No.

LORI: Oh. Well . . . it does. Not that it's bad. When I went to seminary in Virginia, it was extremely . . . well . . . living in Virginia is like someone erased all the good parts of Pennsylvania. It's that bleak. Made me want to drink. I prayed and prayed and I heard nothing. Not peep from God. Loneliest feeling you could imagine. Crushing.

ROB: Right.

LORI: So I sympathize.

ROB: Right.

>   *(Pause.)*

>   It's not easy. I mean, I'm not a . . . well . . . I would never say I was someone who . . .

(Pause.)

This is *really* hard to talk about.

LORI: Hey. I'm here to help you.

ROB: I know. I know.

(Pause.)

Religion isn't exactly a usual part of my life. Or it hasn't been. But I was raised to believe that sometimes you have to, you know, ask for help. And lately, I'm s . . . so . . . confused, and . . . and I've gotten pulled into a sort of *thing* and I'm feeling really conflicted about it.

LORI: Pulled in?

ROB: Yeah. Sort of.

LORI: Someone came to your house with rope? Handcuffs? Held a gun to your head?

(Pause.)

Go on.

ROB: I've been . . . lately . . . well I just go online a lot. Not like, to read the news. I just . . . well . . . it's gotten so that I think about it too much. Like, I went out on a date, just like someone I met at work and I just thought about getting home so I could . . .

LORI: Go online.

(Pause.)

Is this poker?

ROB: *No.* No.

LORI: Because that's really . . . you know . . . my husband Harry lost about a third of our savings with poker. Totally idiotic. Nearly strangled him, the sweet thing.

ROB: It's not poker.

LORI: Rob. Rob. Spit it out. Not judging. No judging.

ROB: I look at a lot of . . . a lot of . . . dirty . . . pictures. And. Movies.

LORI: Kiddie porn?

ROB: What?

LORI: Do you look at pictures of children?

ROB: No.

LORI: So these are other adults?

(Pause.)

ROB: Yes but . . .

Lawrence Harbison   321

LORI: So you just feel like that's bad?

ROB: Isn't it?

LORI: Well . . . you tell me. How is it bad?

ROB: I . . . I masturbate five to six times a day. I jerk off when I wake up, in rest rooms, at home. I jerk off enough that sometimes I think I should stop because I'm in pain. A normal day involves . . . well . . . a lot of crying and masturbating and looking at women and sometimes not women. Just because I've seen so many things I wonder if there are more things to look at. I feel dulled down. Hollow. When I shave, and I look in my own eyes in the mirror, I actually cry and that makes me want to jerk off too.

(Pause.)

But I have to use a computer all the time. For work. For everything. So whenever it's on, I just find myself . . . again . . . on some . . . site and I . . . see things and I . . . want to stop doing this because . . . I can't have a date, you know?

LORI: Why can't you have a date?

ROB: Like . . . you know Heather Mickelston? From church?

LORI: Of course. I baptized Ralph.

ROB: Jesus.

LORI: Sorry.

ROB: Anyway, she's divorced and she asked me if I wanted to get coffee. So before I met her, I found pictures of people that look *like* her and abused myself. And then I went out with her and we had coffee and talked about her son. Then I went home and jerked off again. But while I was with her, I couldn't imagine . . . actually . . . you know? Doing anything. I'm just . . .

LORI: Worried that you're too obsessed with nude women who inhale fat penises? Or ponytailed Asian hookers who stick live eels in their vaginas and giggle about it?

(Pause.)

Harry!

(Pause.)

Hold on. Hold on. Let me explain something.

(HARRY enters. He's gaunt, mustached. Smiling.)

HARRY. Doll? How's it going in here?

LORI: C'mere Harry.

(HARRY sits down.)

Rob . . . just confessed to me that he looks at a lot of pornography.

HARRY. *(fatherly)* Chin up, Rob.

LORI: Exactly. Here . . . stand up Harry.

(HARRY stands up.)

Rob, take a look at Harry. Harry, show it to him.

HARRY. Now?

LORI: Come on babe.

(HARRY turns facing upstage, and unzips himself.)

ROB: Whoa! WHOA!

LORI: The real thing. What does it make you think of?

(ROB covers his face.)

You're covering your eyes? You've seen far worse. That's an adult man's *normal* penis. And yes, it conjures images. Of course! It makes me think of a snake charmer.

(HARRY zips up. LORI spanks his ass.)

Thanks sweetie. Get out.

HARRY. Snake charmer!

(HARRY exits.)

LORI: See?

ROB: I . . . I should go.

LORI: You don't understand. Listen, I'm a priest, Rob. I spend each and every day of my life thinking about God and the story of Jesus and how it applies to our lives. To the lives of people like you. People who go to my church, who listen to my sermons, who sit on committees. You know what I think? Look at my computer.

(Pause.)

Open chrome and read my history.

(Pause.)

Read it out loud.

ROB: Toyboys.com. LuckyFucky.com. BBWHorses.net, religioussnuffilms.com

LORI: That's just Easter research.

ROB: DongCastle, Milkandtitty.com, BadHabits.com

LORI: Nuns.

ROB: I . . .

LORI: Rob, you're not literally filling the world with your own miserable, depressed kids are you? You're not assigning your personal issues to some other wayward man or woman who, just like you, has poor coping skills, are you? Fantasy lives are practically designed to head actual spiritual crises off at the pass. Get me?

ROB: I do not get you.

LORI: Okay so . . . okay. Wait.

> *(Pause.)*
>
> *I can express this more clearly.*
>
> *(Long pause.)*
>
> I'm really drawing a blank.

ROB: You're not good at your job.

LORI: Ah ha! What exactly is my job?

ROB: You're a priest!

LORI: I *interpret.* I *assign* meaning.

ROB: What about Jesus?

LORI: Jesus is a metaphor, Rob. Where are we, Alabama? It's the 21st Century. Don't you read?

ROB: I'm so unhappy.

LORI: Don't blame the porn.

ROB: But what would God . . .

LORI: God doesn't care about websites! The only person that's all in a tizzy about your compulsion to self-pleasure is you. Maybe being impotent around real women isn't porn's fault. I can have sex with Harry and honestly, porn helps. So, I don't *know* what's wrong with you. Maybe you just need to get over your hang ups and stop sweating the small stuff. If you ask me . . .

ROB: But I'm not here to ask *you!*

> *(Pause.)*
>
> I wanted . . . you to help me to . . . find some answer through God. Like . . . we could pray. Together. For strength. Or guidance.
>
> *(Pause.)*

LORI: Okay. Fuck it. *(Breathes in.)* In the Bible, John says "In the beginning was the Word, and the Word was with God, and the Word was God." Then he says "The word was made flesh." I mean, that's the King James version, which, while popular, is largely a misinterpretation of a misinterpretation but let's put our blinders on and give credit to an excellent turn of phrase. The Word was God and the Word was made Flesh. The Flesh. Which is Jesus Christ. Who is God but with balls.

(Pause.)

Which means one thing for sure: even if Jesus was celibate, he woke up with sticky pants *sometimes*. If he wasn't rubbing them out, it had to go *somewhere*. In fact, I would argue that Jesus having wet dreams was really the whole point. Flesh is flawed, and it's filled with fluids, and it occasionally just spurts mucus or pus or blood or seamen.

(Pause.)

But how does your mind (which is also flesh) make sure you boys paint the inside of your jeans white? *Dreams*. Images of fantasy. Maybe Jesus saw sexy angels pointing at their angelic vaginas. Who knows? But pornography is just externalizing those images of fantasy. Human beings, in all our glory, capturing the means of production. Saying: "I'm not going to passively wait for my brain to combine the few things I did today and turn them into an unconscious orgasm . . . I'm going to use my God-given imagination to create those dreams on purpose." With or without computer assistance or video cameras, brains would conjure up perverse images on their very own. Pornography is just outsourcing something natural. And you know who made Nature, in all its competitiveness, brutality, wetness and filth? God did. And you know who He sent to earth to partake of the exact Nature that you're sitting around crying about? Jesus. And sure, you might say, there are all sorts of natural things that are forbidden in the Bible. You know what's not among them? Fantasizing about sex. Even fantasizing that is humbling and sad. Even . . . if it's . . .

(Pause.)

No. That's basically all I can think of.

(Pause.)

Yes, that's all I can think of. I hope that eventually, you'll be in a better place. So . . . so that we might delight in His Will and walk in His way. Forever and ever. Blessings be upon you and may shaving get easier.

(She crosses herself. Smiles. Long pause.)

How's that bullshit working for you?

ROB: It'll do.

LORI: Go in peace to love and serve the Lord.

ROB: Amen.

BLACKOUT

The End

Midsummer

Don Nigro

Production Notes:

Midsummer was first presented on July 5th, 2011 at Lost Nation Theatre in Montpelier, Vermont.

Cast:
PEASEBLOSSOM, Mary McNulty
COBWEB, Kate Kenney
MOTH, Elise Hudson
MUSTARDSEED, Elizabeth Gilbert
PUCK, Eric William Love

Directed by Kate Kenney.
Original Costume Design: Shawn Sturdevant.
Sets and Lighting Design: Clay Coyle.
Produced by Kate Kenney and Reyna de Courcy, Gravity and Glass Productions.

"Twice he was called, and made no reply, but the third time he answered, and the caller, raising his voice, cried out, 'When you come opposite to Palodes, tell them that great Pan is dead.' Hearing this . . . all were astonished, and argued among themselves whether it were better to carry out the order or refuse to meddle and let the matter rest... Thammus decided that if there should be a breeze, he would sail past and say nothing. But if there were no wind and a smooth sea at that place he would announce what he had heard. So when he came opposite Palodes and there was neither wind nor wave, Thammus, sitting in the stern and looking towards land, called out the words as he had heard them, 'Great Pan is dead.' "
—Plutarch, *De Defectu Oraculorum*

"No epilogue, I pray you; for your play needs no excuse. Never excuse; for when the players are all dead, there need none to be blamed."
—Shakespeare, *A Midsummer Night's Dream*

CHARACTERS:
PEASEBLOSSOM, a fairy girl
COBWEB, a fairy girl
MOTH, a fairy girl
MUSTARDSEED, a fairy girl
PUCK

SETTING: A wood near Athens.

A wood near Athens. Lush vegetation. Ferns. Shadows. Among the fallen logs and weeds, PUCK and four fairy girls are relaxing.

PEASEBLOSSOM: *(Sweet, pretty, and delicate, as are all the fairy girls.)* Puck is out of control. He's absolutely manic. He stages wild raids on the squirrels to get their nuts. He steals eggs from geese. I've never seen him this wild. All the girl fairies are doing our best to avoid him. He's dangerous.

He bites. I'm not kidding. He bit me on my left breast and I lost almost a quart of fairy blood. I don't know what's the matter with him. But maybe I make too much of it. Not all fairies are alike, you know. We all have our different little peccadilloes. Cobweb is distracted and complex. It's like she's always got things rolling back and forth in her head like walnuts in a bowl.

COBWEB: Where do we come from? What does all this mean? Why are dragon flies green? Are cowslips called cowslips because they look like cows' lips or because cows slip in them? Is the moon sad?

PEASEBLOSSOM: She's deep. Moth is always fluttering around, and has a lot of trouble concentrating, but probably not because she has deep thoughts.

MOTH: Do you think I have pretty feet? Everybody says I have pretty feet, but really, how pretty can feet be? I mean, they're feet.

PEASEBLOSSOM: Maybe she's not all that bright. But she's smarter than she lets on. She'd almost have to be.

MUSTARDSEED: You might want to wash them once in a while.

MOTH: I wash my feet. I dip them in limpid pools.

MUSTARDSEED: We drink out of those pools.

MOTH: I only sip nectar.

MUSTARDSEED: And your toenails are dirty.

COBWEB: Why do we have toenails? Why do we have toes? And why does Shakespeare keep sending me new lines? And who is Shakespeare? And what does it mean to have lines? Are we in some sort of a play? Is that normal?

MUSTARDSEED: Oh, God. Here she goes. Why do we have this? Why do we have that? Why does mold glow in the dark? Wake me up when she's done.

PEASEBLOSSOM: Mustardseed is a tart creature. She's always critical, but she does make some interesting points. She says Puck likes making us bleed because it excites him sexually. I'm not sure that's true.

MUSTARDSEED: Everything excites him sexually. And he's always bragging about what he can do and what he knows and what he's seen.

PUCK: I saw the Great God Pan die.

MUSTARDSEED: Did you kill him?

PEASEBLOSSOM: Great dragon flies buzz about, flying head first into prehistoric trees and falling, disappearing into the primrose beds. Glow worms and greenie buzz everywhere.

PUCK: No. I just watched.

MUSTARDSEED: He prefers to watch. Kinky.

COBWEB: Then what did he die of?

MOTH: Oww. Mosquito bit me right on the ass. Watch it.

PUCK: I am watching it. It's a pert little bottom. Do you want me to suck out the poison?

MUSTARDSEED: Gods don't die.

PUCK: Gods die when nobody worships them, or fears them, or loves them. But the most terrifying thing of all is the ghost of a dead god. The Great God Pan is dead, but he still haunts these woods. I can feel him moving through the briars and quaint mazes in the twilight. He's always itching in my head. Pan was one of the more insane gods.

MUSTARDSEED: And you're another.

PUCK: Do you think I'm a god?

PEASEBLOSSOM: Puck has a way of cocking his head at you when he listens, pretending to be innocent but not, really, part baby fox, part snake.

MUSTARDSEED: Maybe a little god. A little tiny god. With little tiny parts. A fragment of discarded and forgotten divinity the mice carry off.

PUCK: *(Running his hand along Peaseblossom's leg.)* I like your legs. You have pretty legs.

PEASEBLOSSOM: *(Pulling her leg away from him.)* Please don't touch my legs.

PUCK: You like it when I touch your leg.

PEASEBLOSSOM: No I don't.

PUCK: You shuddered with pleasure. I felt it.

PEASEBLOSSOM: That wasn't pleasure. It was disgust.

PUCK: Pleasure and disgust are closely related.

PEASEBLOSSOM: No they're not.

COBWEB: He has a point. Freud says—

MOTH: Who?

COBWEB: Freud, *The Interpretation of Dreams,* Hermia left a copy of it in the woods.

PEASEBLOSSOM: I don't think there's anybody named Freud.

COBWEB: He isn't born yet. All times and places coexist in the forest, including some which are entirely imaginary.

PEASEBLOSSOM: What kind of mushrooms have you been eating, anyway?

MUSTARDSEED: Puck is the sort of god who eats mice and lizards. An evil little god. A little fallen godling. A dangling little thing. A lost, evil little thing.

PUCK: Then we're all evil things. And we're all lost.

MOTH: I'm not evil. I might be lost, but I'm not evil.

PUCK: Even the stupid can be evil.

MOTH: We're not evil, are we? Because I find that whole concept very disturbing. To think we could be evil.

PEASEBLOSSOM: Moth looks to Cobweb for answers, but Cobweb is watching a large, brown centipede crawl by and disappear into the ferns.

MUSTARDSEED: Don't let him get to you. He just says things to make us uneasy.

PEASEBLOSSOM: Sometimes I think we might be evil. Puck is pretty evil, and if he can be evil, then why not us?

MUSTARDSEED: Sometimes, Peaseblossom, when you say stupid things like that, if I didn't know better, I'd think you were human. Now humans are stupid and evil.

MOTH: It was evil of Puck to bite Peaseblossom on the nipple. And I would never bite her on the nipple. I would never bite anybody on the nipple. I might suck very carefully, but I would never bite. Therefore, it follows, as the night the day, that I'm not evil. Also, I have pretty elbows. See?

MUSTARDSEED: We've seen your elbows.

MOTH: Not both at the same time. Look at the dimples. Nobody who was evil could have dimples in her elbows.

PEASEBLOSSOM: But all among the rank green afternoon shade and sun patchwork in the briars and quaint mazes of the tangled wood, things are buzzing and devouring one another. All fairy children are told that if we're not good, a praying mantis will come and eat us. The enchanted woods is entirely made of devouring. Changelings, poor lost creatures, neither fish nor fowl, sit and stare at one another in little bowers, in despair. All through the dark, wet places of the deep old woods, creatures are kissing and copulating and killing and eating each other among the shadows. The owls screech and the roots of ancient trees clutch into muddy ground like the twisted feet of ancient claw-footed dancers. And we four delicate fairy girls huddle together, combing one another's hair, picking out lice, squashing them

PEASEBLOSSOM: *(cont.)*between our fingernails, and sucking now and then on one another's breasts and fingers, for comfort's sake. There is canker on the rosebuds and much terror in these woods. And we are part of that terror somehow. Those we fear, those who fear us.

PUCK: It's not a joke, you know. It wasn't always thus. We once were something else.

MOTH: I was never anything else.

PEASEBLOSSOM: We were always this, weren't we?

PUCK: No. Long ago, we were gods.

MUSTARDSEED: We were never gods.

PUCK: We were. You don't remember. But somewhere at the back of your heads, you can hear the ghost of the dead God Pan whispering that it's true.

MOTH: I don't hear anything but tree frogs.

PEASEBLOSSOM: If we were gods, then what happened to us?

PUCK: We have descended somewhat in our status, like decayed gentry. The world is impossibly old, you see. Once there were other gods, and we came along and pushed them back into the dark. Then other gods came and began to push us out, and we retreated back into these woods. Oberon's a parody of what we used to be. A puffed up sort of mock god, a kind of player-king.

COBWEB: I think Puck is right.

MUSTARDSEED: Puck is never right. He's obnoxious, like a goat.

COBWEB: But sometimes I think, just at the edges of sleep, just coming in or out, that I almost remember.

MOTH: Remember what?

COBWEB: I can't quite put my finger on it.

PUCK: Come put your finger on this.

PEASEBLOSSOM: Vulgar. Would a god say that?

PUCK: Pan would say that. The gods have always been vulgar. They grow in low, damp places, like fungus.

PEASEBLOSSOM: But Pan's dead.

PUCK: He's dead, but he still lurks about. When you stand in the woods alone and it's absolutely still, and look just over the crest of the hill and see a stand of trees moving like there was a breeze only you can't feel anything, there's no breeze, except just right over there, where those trees are moving, that's him.

MOTH: That happened to me once. It scared me so much, I peed myself.

PUCK: It's Pan. The breath of Pan, moving through the trees. That's why they call it panic. Panic's what you feel alone in the woods when a sudden overwhelming awareness comes upon you of the presence of an ancient god. He comes to remind you that you're going to die.

MUSTARDSEED: *(Breaking the spell, but not completely sure.)* Oh, give me a break, Shakespeare.

PUCK: I'm telling you. You know it's true. You've always known, somewhere inside.

MUSTARDSEED: Well, on the whole, I'd rather be a fallen god than a human.

(Doing silly human voices, mocking.)

I love Hermia. I hate Hermia. I love Helena. I hate Helena. I love Demetrius. I love Lysander. Love me, I'm tall. Love me, I'm short. I'm pretty. I'm strong. I'm an Amazon. I have a penis. What fools.

COBWEB: Maybe the humans are fallen gods, too.PUCK: No. Humans are a form of degenerate monkey.

MOTH: Wait a minute. Humans can die.

PUCK: Not soon enough.

MOTH: And Pan was a god.

PUCK: Yes.

MOTH: And Pan died.

PUCK: Yes.

MOTH: And we used to be gods.

PUCK: Yes.

MOTH: But now we're in decline?

PUCK: Very much so.

MOTH: Then can we die?

(Pause.)

Puck? Can we die?

PUCK: Everything dies.

MOTH: So we can die. I could die. Peaseblossom and Cobweb and Mustardseed and I and everybody, all of us could die?

PUCK: Very likely.

MOTH: But how could that be? How could that possibly be?

PUCK: Gods die when nobody remembers them any more.

MOTH: But I don't want to die. I'm too young to die.

PEASEBLOSSOM: How old are you?

MOTH: I have no idea, but I know I'm too young to die. I mean, what is that, even? What would that even be like?

COBWEB: It wouldn't be like anything. You'd just be gone. When the last person who believed in you or at least remembered you was gone, you'd be gone too. Erased. Just nothing. Nothingness.

MOTH: No. I don't believe it.

MUSTARDSEED: You see things die in the woods every day.

MOTH: I know, but not us. We're beautiful and delicate and magical. Only ugly things die.

MUSTARDSEED: You're living in a fantasy world.

MOTH: I know, and I like it here. I don't want to leave.

PUCK: All quick bright things come to confusion. We're mostly imaginary already.

PEASEBLOSSOM: Then we've got to do something.

MUSTARDSEED: Do what? What can we do?

PEASEBLOSSOM: Do something so they won't forget us. Something to make them remember.

MOTH: Like what?

PEASEBLOSSOM: I don't know. Mess with them. Turn the milk sour. Turn their heads into ass heads. Make them love the wrong people. We've got to mess with their minds so they'll remember us, so we won't die.

PUCK: What do you think I've been doing all this time? Do you think I enjoy this? Impersonating roasted crabs and pouring ale on old women's laps? Turning myself into a stool and then running away so somebody's aunt can fall on her rump? This is hard work.

PEASEBLOSSOM: You're saying that's why you're so obnoxious? So they won't forget us? So we won't die?

PUCK: And precious little thanks I get for it, too.

MOTH: What was that?

PEASEBLOSSOM: What? A bat? An owl?

MOTH: No. Do you feel that?

COBWEB: I felt something.

MOTH: I just got the shivers.

PEASEBLOSSOM: I did, too. What is that?

COBWEB: Maybe it's that Shakespeare person, coming with more damned rewrites. Maybe he's cutting this scene entirely.

PEASEBLOSSOM: Maybe it's one of the new gods, walking in the garden in the cool of the evening.

PUCK: No. It's him. Look at those trees move.

MOTH: Like the wind? Like something going by in the wind?

COBWEB: There isn't any wind. Listen.

(They all listen. The sounds of the woods as lights fade on them and go out.)

The End

MIGRATORY BIRDS OF IRAQ
Mark Rigney

PRODUCTION NOTES:

The play was originally produced by the Attic Theatre as part of the Denise Ragan-Wiesenmeyer One-Act Festival, held at the Attic Theatre and Film Center, Los Angeles, CA.

The production opened September 16, 2011.

Director: James Carey

Cast:
VANNAKIATIS, Sarah Wahl
CARDOZA, Carlitos Dusouto
MYERS, Taylor Napier

SET & COSTUME REQUIREMENTS:
  A wall would be nice, but not essential. Also: Desert or
  urban fatigues, three pairs of binoculars, a beer (bottle or
  can) and one rifle (or hand gun).

CHARACTERS:
VANNAKIATIS, Female, twenties, white, probably not blonde.
CARDOZA, Male, twenties, Hispanic, definitely not blonde.
MYERS, Male, twenties, white or black, could be blonde.

THE PLACE: A rooftop at the edge of a (VBC) base, Iraq.
THE TIME: 201?: The evening before the final combat troops
  leave.

*Before rise, we hear a few wing-beats and then a birdcall,
complex and accomplished: A nightingale. Lights up on three
soldiers—CARDOZA, MYERS, VANNAKIATIS, the latter
female—all using binoculars and peering over a rooftop
wall. A peaceful off-duty moment, late 201- on the Victory
Base Complex (VBC) outside of Baghdad, Iraq. Evening.
Only Myers has his weapon.*

CARDOZA: Left of the building, two walls over.
MYERS: Don't got it.
VANNAKIATIS: More left.
MYERS: What are you talking about, more left? That's like
  a road.
CARDOZA: Nah, you gone past it. Back right.
MYERS: Can we try something closer?
CARDOZA: It's a bulbul, yeah?
VANNAKIATIS: Good. You're getting better.
MYERS: I see squat.
VANNAKIATIS: Look, try here. The light pole just in front of
  the southwest corner.
CARDOZA: On top?
VANNAKIATIS: Yeah.
MYERS: Which light pole?
CARDOZA: Oh, yeah.
MYERS: Which light pole!
CARDOZA: The broken one.

MYERS: They're all broken.

VANNAKIATIS: The one with the bird on it.

MYERS: I don't see nothing.

CARDOZA: Crested lark.

VANNAKIATIS: And he's showing his crest. There.

MYERS: What the hell?

VANNAKIATIS: Myers, you sure you got your lens caps off?

MYERS: You're funny.

VANNAKIATIS: You didn't get your official army-issue lens caps?

CARDOZA: Think it's a male.

VANNAKIATIS: You think everything's a male.

CARDOZA: I don't think you're no male.

VANNAKIATIS: I'm talking about birds.

MYERS: I still don't see it.

CARDOZA: Okay, chill. I got a bird you can find easy.

MYERS: Yeah? Where?

CARDOZA: Three miles north.

MYERS: Cardoza, I can't see three miles.

CARDOZA: Turn left at the big intersection, the one with all the Awakening guys directing traffic. Then half a mile, turn right at the palm trees.

MYERS: Cardoza.

CARDOZA: Through the gates, third cage on the right.

VANNAKIATIS: Cardoza, you're crazy.

CARDOZA: No, for real. You go there, you look straight in that cage, you'll see you a bird. Won't even need those glasses.

MYERS: And when I get there, what kind of bird am I gonna see?

CARDOZA: Fuckin' ostrich.

MYERS: You know what? Fuck you, Cardoza.

CARDOZA: Hey, I'm just riding you. Come on. Don't go.

MYERS: No, man. I'm gone. You want to spend your last daylight in Iraq scoping birds, fine. I'm gettin' me some pussy.

VANNAKIATIS: Good luck with that.

MYERS: I don't need luck, bitch. When I take aim, I'm hittin' my target.

> *Myers exits.*

VANNAKIATIS: Some things, I'm telling you, are gonna be so good to leave behind.

CARDOZA: Like Myers in particular?

VANNAKIATIS: No, I mean, at home, you're damned if you do, right? And here, it's damned if you don't. Now tell me that's not fucked up.

CARDOZA: Hey, what's that? On the wire there.

VANNAKIATIS: Fifteen feet up?

CARDOZA: Left of the dumpster, yeah.

VANNAKIATIS: Nightingale.

CARDOZA: Male?

VANNAKIATIS: Hope so. It'll sing.

CARDOZA: Night time, maybe.

VANNAKIATIS: That I will miss. Nightingales singing.

CARDOZA: But you get birds at home, yeah? Out in that Podunk wherever the fuck it is you're from.

VANNAKIATIS: Yeah. But not like that.

CARDOZA: Down 'round Inglewood, we get mockingbirds. And they sing. Long time, some days. But half the time they're imitating goddamned car alarms, so I don't know. When you sing like some dude's tricked-out Lexus, that ain't really singing, you know?

VANNAKIATIS: They native?

CARDOZA: What, mockingbirds?

VANNAKIATIS: Yeah.

CARDOZA: Don't know. I mean, what's native to South L.A.?

VANNAKIATIS: Mexicans.

CARDOZA: Copy that.

VANNAKIATIS: You gonna miss anything else?

CARDOZA: Naw. Well. Watchin' birds. Watchin' birds with you. I never figured birds was worth watchin' 'fore comin' here. Now, I don't know. I'd sure rather watch birds than people.

VANNAKIATIS: There's one. Street level.

CARDOZA: Where?

VANNAKIATIS: Walkin' with her big sister.

CARDOZA: No, seriously, let's stick to birds.

VANNAKIATIS: But look how cute!

CARDOZA: Hey, look. She's wavin'.

VANNAKIATIS: (Calling "Hello!" in Arabic) Marhaba!

CARDOZA: What'd she say?

VANNAKIATIS: Well, the rough translation would be, "Go

home, go fuck a goat, don't come back."

CARDOZA: Huh. Cute kid.

VANNAKIATIS: I will miss the birds, yeah. And I'll miss you. But I'm gonna miss the kids, too. Maybe not that one.

CARDOZA: Write the President, maybe he'll let you stay. Open up some kinda orphanage. "Dear Mr. Obama, I know I'm just one short white country hick, but I'd sure like you to give me one point five million to stay behind and found the Vannakiatis however-the-fuck-you-spell-that Orphanage to save all the poor little Iraqi chilluns."

VANNAKIATIS: I could do that. For real.

CARDOZA: Not with your last name. Vannakiatis. Jesus.

VANNAKIATIS: Maybe I name it after you.

CARDOZA: No way. That plane lifts off tomorrow, I'm on it. Me and my name both.

VANNAKIATIS: And when we're gone . . .

CARDOZA: Larks. Bulbuls. Nightingales.

VANNAKIATIS: And we wing our way home. One last migration.

CARDOZA: You damn straight better be winging your way home. You try stayin', for cute kids or whatever, I'm gonna lay some rope on you, tie you up, stuff you in my duffel, drag your ass all the way back to Missouri personally.

VANNAKIATIS: I'm just thinking.

CARDOZA: Well, stop. We ain't wanted here. And that cute smilin' kid down there, she's got like a fifty-fifty chance of growin' up and wantin' to shoot you in the head.

VANNAKIATIS: I know.

CARDOZA: Probably go marry some Awakening guy. Go all radical on us.

VANNAKIATIS: Let's go out to the wire.

CARDOZA: What?

VANNAKIATIS: Lieutenant says there's geese. Lesser White-fronted. And I know you ain't got those on your list.

CARDOZA: Well, then that's one duck that ain't goin' on my list.

VANNAKIATIS: Come on. Once in a lifetime chance to see a seriously endangered bird.

CARDOZA: No way.

VANNAKIATIS: What do you mean, no way?

CARDOZA: I mean those ponds are way out on the edge of base and I'm not goin' any closer to Iraq-for-real than this roof, which frankly is bad enough. You get me?

VANNAKIATIS: It's perfectly safe. The whole VBC, I mean, come on.

CARDOZA: Listen. Every war, there's gotta be a last man down. It is not gonna be me.

VANNAKIATIS: There's nothing out there. Just hawks and mice and maybe two really incredibly rare geese.

CARDOZA: No cover is what's out there.

VANNAKIATIS: All right, whatever.

CARDOZA: Hey, Vannakiatis. I'm serious. Don't.

VANNAKIATIS: Don't take a walk? On base?

CARDOZA: Walk someplace else. Walk in two days. When you're home.

VANNAKIATIS: Cardoza, you're sweet.

CARDOZA: Amy, I'm tellin' you, don't go out there!

VANNAKIATIS: Amy?

CARDOZA: It's your name, yeah?

VANNAKIATIS: Six months we been here, you never once used it.

CARDOZA: If it's birds you want, look, we got—what've we got, we got two rollers right down that wall. And we'll get bee-eaters any minute. You know? What's a better lookin' bird than a bee-eater?

Myers re-enters, holding a (Turkish) beer, ideally Efes.

MYERS: Man, you two gotta shift gears. Birds, birds, fuckin' birds. I mean, hey, it's your lucky day, Vannakiatis. I'm still available.

VANNAKIATIS: (*To Cardoza*) Miguel, I promise. I won't be the last Iraq casualty.

Vannakiatis gives Cardoza a quick kiss and exits.

MYERS: Whoa. How'd you do that?

CARDOZA: By being a coward.

MYERS: You two are both PTSD in a major way and you ain't even home yet. (*Looking through his binoculars*) Hey, that one I can see.

CARDOZA: Where?

MYERS: Ah! Fooled you.

CARDOZA: Could you maybe get off my roof?

MYERS: Base is base. You get off. Hey, look at that kid. Look at that smile.

CARDOZA: Yeah, she was down here before. Listen, I'm gonna go catch up with Vannakiatis. Make sure she doesn't wind up in the last available body bag.

MYERS: Whatever. But you get into her pants, I want a full report.

Cardoza exits.

MYERS: *Marhaba!* Hey, kid! *Marhaba!* Hey, Cardoza, will you get a load of this? The kid just gave me the finger! Now why you want to do that? Yeah, well fuck you, too. Yeah. And the horse you rode in on. Oh, that's it. You are so fucked.

Myers gets hold of his firearm, does a quick check to make sure no one's watching, clicks off the safety, takes aim. Fires.

MYERS: *(cont'd)* Goddamn it. Come back here.

He fires again. And continues, ad-libbing quiet curses as the sound of flocking birds rises, wings beating, a thousand birds circling, flying, flapping desperately for release (possibly seen as a projection). The lights shift and music melds with the wing beats. Over this, the voices of Vannakiatis and Cardoza.

VANNAKIATIS: *(off)* Look! Corner of the reed-bed. Is that . . . ?

CARDOZA: *(off)* Goose, I think. Can't tell . . .

VANNAKIATIS: *(off)* That's it. White-fronted goose. We got one!

CARDOZA: *(off)* Holy crap. Will you look at that.

VANNAKIATIS: *(off)* Gorgeous.

CARDOZA: *(off)* Yeah. That is. That's a sight I can definitely fly home on.

Myers keeps firing, and keeps missing. Under the elegy of music, the birds fly on . . .

The End

Lawrence Harbison   343

MISFORTUNE

Mark Harvey Levine

PRODUCTION NOTES:

Misfortune was a winner of Lakeshore Player's 7th Annual 10-Minute Play Festival (White Bear Lake, MN) in June, 2011. Director: Caroline DeCoster.

Cast
    CINDY, Kim Egan
    BARRY, George M. Calger
    STEPHANIE, Allie Munson.

CHARACTERS:
CINDY: twenties - thirties, Asian, a little snarky
BARRY: twenties - fifties, a little testy
STEPHANIE: twenties - fifties, more than a little mischievous

SETTING: A Chinese restaurant.
TIME: Evening.

> *Barry and Stephanie have just finished their meal.
> Cindy, the young Asian waitress, approaches the
> table.*

CINDY: You guys finished?
BARRY: Yes . . . yes we are.
> *Cindy lays down the check in a little tray. Sitting on
> top of the check are two fortune cookies.*
STEPHANIE: Everything was wonderful.
BARRY: I know! I love this place. It's a little hole in the wall,
    but the food is fantastic.
> *They take their fortune cookies, break them open.*
STEPHANIE: *(reading her fortune)* "Work hard, and your work
    will work for you." Okay.
BARRY: *(reading his fortune)* "The person you just had dinner
    with will kill you tonight."
STEPHANIE: What?!
BARRY: What the hell . . . ?!
STEPHANIE: What does it say?!
BARRY: "The person you just had dinner with will kill you
    tonight."
STEPHANIE: It does not!
BARRY: Read it! *(he hands it to her)*
STEPHANIE: I don't believe this.
BARRY: What kind of fortune cookie . . . ?
STEPHANIE: I've never seen anything like this . . . "The person
    you just had dinner with will kill you tonight. Your lotto
    numbers are 8, 12, 32, 36, 42 and 7."
BARRY: Is this some kind of joke?! Did you do that?
STEPHANIE: No! I've never seen that cookie before in my
    life!

BARRY: Are you going to kill me tonight?

STEPHANIE: I wasn't planning to . . .

BARRY: Well, that's a relief.

STEPHANIE: But now I guess I have to.

BARRY: What?!

STEPHANIE: The cookies never lie, Barry.

BARRY: What are you talking about?

STEPHANIE: I've never known one of these cookies to be false. If the cookie says it, I'm going to do it.

BARRY: Really. You're going to kill me. Tonight.

STEPHANIE: Apparently. I wonder how I'll do it.

BARRY: Stephanie, this isn't funny.

STEPHANIE: *(looking at the back of the fortune)* Hey, you can learn Chinese, too. "Guó" is the word for "Kingdom".

BARRY: *(snatching the fortune back)* Give me that! *(motioning to Cindy)* Excuse me!!

    Cindy approaches their table.

CINDY: Yes?

BARRY: I want to complain about this fortune cookie I got. Look what it said.

CINDY: "The person you just had dinner with will kill you tonight." Woah. Bummer.

BARRY: I just had a lovely dinner and then I get hit with that. Do you think that's an appropriate saying for a fortune cookie?

CINDY: Well, it's not the happiest fortune I've seen.

BARRY: Uh, yeah.

CINDY: It's not even grammatically correct. It should be "The person with whom you just had dinner will kill you tonight."

BARRY: It shouldn't be any of those! It shouldn't say anything like that!

CINDY: You want two more cookies? I can bring you another two.

BARRY: Yes, dammit! Sheesh.

    Cindy leaves.

STEPHANIE: I'm sorry it had to end this way.

BARRY: You're hilarious.

    Cindy returns with two more cookies.

CINDY: Here you go.

She stays, standing over the table.

BARRY: Do you mind?

CINDY: I'm sorry, I'm kinda curious.

Stephanie cracks hers open.

STEPHANIE: *(reading)* "Today is a lucky day for those who are cheerful and optimistic."

BARRY: Okay. *(cracks it open, reads)* "You won't make it out of this restaurant alive."

STEPHANIE: Oh come on.

BARRY: Read it!

Stephanie reads it. Cindy reads it over her shoulder.

CINDY: Wow.

STEPHANIE: This is the strangest thing I've ever seen.

BARRY: *(to Cindy)* Did she put you up to this?

CINDY: Don't blame me!

STEPHANIE: It's the cookie. The cookie knows.

BARRY: The cookies don't know a damn thing! I want two more cookies!

STEPHANIE: I'm getting kind of full, actually.

BARRY: *(banging the table)* Two more cookies!

Cindy stomps off to get them.

STEPHANIE: So I kill you in the restaurent? How do I do it?

BARRY: It didn't say. Perhaps the next cookie will provide further detail.

STEPHANIE: Maybe the Kung Pao was poisoned.

BARRY: You had it too.

STEPHANIE: Or so you think.

Cindy returns with two more cookies.

CINDY: Here.

Barry hesitates.

CINDY: *(CONT'D)* Open it!

Barry gives her a look.

CINDY: *(CONT'D)* I can't stand the suspense!

Barry opens his.

BARRY: *(CONT'D)* Oh for the love of— *(reading)* "Your life is over."

STEPHANIE: *(reading)* "You have executive ability, and will go far in business."

BARRY: Okay, now, what the hell?

CINDY: Don't look at me!

BARRY: You're telling me you don't know anything about this?

CINDY: No, we sit up all night, baking the cookies by hand, and typing up the little slips of paper. You have no idea how hard it is to get them in the printer.

BARRY: Well, then, where do you get these things?

CINDY: I don't know! Some company! Same place where we get the sweet and sour sauce and everything else!

STEPHANIE: I thought you guys made that in the kitchen.

CINDY: Oh. Um . . . Oops.

BARRY: Forget that! I just want the cookies. Bring me the box. Bring me the whole damn box.

Cindy stomps off again.

CINDY: *(as she exits)* I'm not even Chinese! I'm from Reseda!

STEPHANIE: I'm sure there's a reasonable explanation.

BARRY: Besides that you're actually going to kill me?

STEPHANIE: Well, that would be one explanation.

From off stage we hear banging around.

STEPHANIE: So, why would I want to kill you?

BARRY: I don't know!! You wouldn't! Would you?

STEPHANIE: Would I?

Cindy returns with a whole restaurent-supply box, full of fortune cookies.

CINDY: Here. Knock yourself out.

Barry tries to open it but it is taped shut with packing tape.

BARRY: This is probably how I die—from a massive paper cut trying to get this thing open. Would it be too much trouble to get something so I can open this?

Cindy stomps off.

CINDY: *(muttering)* Madre de dios.

BARRY: She is so not getting a tip.

STEPHANIE: Now, honey, it's not her fault I'm going to murder you.

BARRY: Stop saying that! It's not funny. I'm getting freaked out here.

STEPHANIE: I think it's hysterical. A little cookie has you all jumpy!

BARRY: I'm not jumpy! I'm just pissed o—

Cindy returns with a huge knife and violently stabs into the box, slashing it open. Both Barry and Stephanie jump. She sets the knife down near Stephanie.

CINDY: There! Anything else?!

BARRY: *(after recovering)* No that's fine. *(opening the box)* Okay, here we go.

He grabs a cookie, rips it open.

BARRY: "There is no escape."

He opens another cookie.

BARRY: *(CONT'D)* "Only death awaits you."

Another cookie.

BARRY: *(CONT'D)* "You have minutes to live."

Another cookie.

BARRY: *(CONT'D)* "Here it comes."

STEPHANIE: *(opening one)* "Your charm and affability are noticed by your friends."

CINDY: Okay, now that's just freaky.

Stephanie picks up the knife in a rather murderous fashion.

STEPHANIE: What did you do?

BARRY: Honey! Put the knife down.

CINDY: Oh God.

STEPHANIE: Why am I going to kill you?! Are you fooling around on me?!

BARRY: No! No! I swear to God!

STEPHANIE: Did you and this waitress concoct this little scheme?!

BARRY: What? No! I'm not having an affair with the waitress!

CINDY: You wish.

STEPHANIE: What is it, then? You're keeping money from me? What?

BARRY: Nothing! Nothing! There's no reason you would kill me!

STEPHANIE: You have no secrets from me?

BARRY: None!

STEPHANIE: Absolutely none?!

BARRY: Absolut—*(he thinks)* Well . . .

STEPHANIE: *(raising knife)* Aha!

Cindy screams and runs off.

BARRY: It's a little thing! It's a stupid thing!

STEPHANIE: What? Tell me!

BARRY: The . . . the bakery dome that your sister Anna sent us? That I said got broken in shipping? It didn't . . . I . . . I broke it . . . accidentally . . . I meant to tell you . . .

STEPHANIE: What?

BARRY: It's not that I didn't like it . . . it just slipped . . . and I felt bad . . .

STEPHANIE: That's it? The bakery dome?

BARRY: That's it. My only secret. Whew. God. I'm glad I got that off my chest before I died.

STEPHANIE: *(putting down the knife)* I wouldn't kill you over that.

BARRY: You wouldn't?

STEPHANIE: You thought I would kill you from that?

BARRY: Well, not until the cookie . . .

STEPHANIE: Oh to hell with the cookie. Let's just pay the check and get out of here.

BARRY: What about "the cookie knows all"?!

STEPHANIE: Honey, it's just a cookie. Guess what, the lottery numbers won't win, either.

BARRY: Whew. *(picking up the check)* Well I can tell you one thing, we are never coming back to this restau—Wait. We didn't order "Pork in Peking Sauce". Or "Broccoli Beef."

STEPHANIE: *(Taking the check from him)* And where's the Kung Pao?

Cindy re-enters with a large frying pan, about to clobber Stephanie, but on hearing Barry she stops.

BARRY: That's not our check . . .

CINDY: Oh man, I'm sorry, I must've—

A horrible gurgling scream is heard from offstage. A man staggers in, two chopsticks sticking half out of his body. He is covered in blood. He falls down, dead, across Barry and Stephanie's table. A woman runs out, hiding her face.

Lawrence Harbison

CINDY: *(CONT'D)* . . . .switched your check with another table.

> *Cindy exits for a moment and returns with another tray, dripping blood. She puts it on top of the body, on their table.*

CINDY: *(CONT'D)* Here's yours.

> *She plops two cookies on the tray.*

CINDY: Do you need anything wrapped up?

> *BLACKOUT*

The End

MYTHAJAWABA

Claudia Haas

PRODUCTION NOTES:
   Originally produced by Sundog Theatre in New York
   City, April 2012
   Director: Karen O'Donnell

Cast:
   CASSANDRA, Susan Slotoroff
   ERIC, Ben Broad
   ULLIE, Jai Brandon

CHARACTERS:

CASSANDRA: (f) late twenties on a mission to save; incredibly
    connected to the world or maybe she's just a kook

ERIC: (m) late twenties; fifty percent nerd and fifty percent
    hero; trying to save Cassandra

ULLIE: (pronounced You-lee) (m) late twenties; in need of
    saving

SETTING: Staten Island Ferry—in the middle of its run; if
    you have something suggesting the rails of ship great—
    otherwise a bench is just fine.

TIME: March 15, a blustery eve

*AT RISE, CASSANDRA is at the edge of the ship by the rails.
She climbs on a bench. CASSANDRA intones the name of
Mythajawaba with great reverence. She kneels on the bench
looking out and then stands up on it.*

> *Eric enters as CASSANDRA attempts to stand on
> the bench.*

CASSANDRA: Myth-a-ja-wa-ba . . . myth-a-a-ja-wa-ba . . .
    myth-a-ja-WA-BA!

> *(ERIC runs over and tackles her. He can physically
> take her off the bench or merely hold on tight to her
> legs.)*

CASSANDRA: Mythajawaba!

ERIC: Don't jump!

CASSANDRA: Who's jumping?

ERIC: You are!

CASSANDRA: *(Breaking away.)* No, I'm not!

ERIC: Are you sure?

CASSANDRA: Yes!

ERIC: Oh.

CASSANDRA: You're not one of those, are you? A would-be-
    hero with no one to save . . .

ERIC: Give me some credit. You were standing on the bench
    looking like you were about to go over the side . . . it's
    getting dark, the winds are picking up—

CASSANDRA: I'm just trying to get a better look!

ERIC: Oh—tourist-type. Well—the Statue of Liberty is on the other side—

CASSANDRA: *I know that!*

ERIC: You prefer the bridge over Lady Liberty?

CASSANDRA: It's the ocean. I must face the ocean.

> *(CASSANDRA climbs back on the bench and opens her arms.)*

Myth-a-ja-wa-ba!

> *(And of course Eric rushes to save her. Again.)*

CASSANDRA: Stop doing that!

ERIC: I can't let you jump!

CASSANDRA: I'm—not—jumping! Please! Find someone else to save. I have things to do here.

ERIC: I'm not leaving you alone.

CASSANDRA: I told you—I'm not going to jump!

ERIC: But what if you do? What if the second my back is turned you hurl yourself into the water? I'd hear the splash—turn around and have to go searching. And then of course I'd have to jump also.

CASSANDRA: You're a follower, is that it? If I jump—you jump?

ERIC: To save you. And the water's pretty cold. I'd rather not have to jump in. I'd rather save you here. It's—drier.

CASSANDRA: There's nothing more annoying than having a person want to save you.

ERIC: There's nothing more annoying than standing on a ferry deck on a cold evening when one could be inside, seated and heated.

CASSANDRA: Go sit inside then! There's something I need to do and I'm running out of time!

ERIC: Aha! You are up to something! I think I'll stay. And freeze.

CASSANDRA: Suit yourself. But turn around. You can't watch.

ERIC: I have to watch. In case—you know—you try to—you know—

CASSANDRA: Jump. I won't jump!

ERIC: And I—won't leave.

CASSANDRA: Just—don't interfere! Space. I need space.

> *(ERIC moves a step away.)*

Lawrence Harbison

CASSANDRA: More space.

(ERIC moves another tiny step away.)

CASSANDRA: Can't a girl get some privacy here?

ERIC: Not on the Staten Island Ferry. It's a public place.

CASSANDRA: Shhh! I'm listening! The waves . . . . I hear the waves . . . and soon . . . just before the sun goes down . . . . Mythajawaba will be near. Soon . . . you will hear Mythajawaba. You should leave before you hear the call. Men cannot resist it. They—jump. And I wouldn't dare jump in to save you.

ERIC: I understand. Not everyone is a saver.

CASSANDRA: No, I—can't swim. But Mythajawaba would catch you. And you would be lost forever. Lost—in the world of Mythajawaba—

ERIC: If —you say so. And . . . who exactly is this mytha-jawa fellow?

CASSANDRA: Not a fellow. A goddess. Who takes mere mortals and turns them into her slaves.

ERIC: So . . . why exactly are you calling to her?

CASSANDRA: To sacrifice myself!

ERIC: I knew it! What did I tell you? I was right! You are planning on jumping!

CASSANDRA: There's a difference between jumping and sacrificing.

ERIC: You're just the tinniest bit nutty, you know that?

CASSANDRA: That's what my fiancee said when I told him about Mythajawaba.

ERIC: He was right.

CASSANDRA: Actually, I was. And now I need to make amends.

ERIC: If you say so.

CASSANDRA: If I hadn't told him about hearing Mythajawaba's calls when I was on the ferry, he never would have become Mythajawaba's slave.

ERIC: O-kay. So—he believed your mytha-something story?

CASSANDRA: Of course not. He looked at me like you're looking at me. So I showed him. I brought him on the ferry at the right time and we listened for the call.

(Slight pause)

ERIC: And—how did you know it was the right time?

CASSANDRA: It came to me. In a dream. Lots of things come to me in dreams.

ERIC: In a dream.

CASSANDRA: Yes.

(Slight pause)

I brought him on the ferry—he heard Mythajawaba's call and he jumped in and just as he jumped, he was scooped into the air by Mythajawaba and flown away.

ERIC: And . . . so you—want to—jump and get flown away, too?

CASSANDRA: Not exactly. But it's only right that I go in his place. I got him into this mess. So, I thought—I'll be Mythajawaba's slave if she lets my fiancee go. She might agree to that, don't you think?

ERIC: I—don't know what to think . . .

CASSANDRA: Don't you see? I have to sacrifice myself to get him back from her clutches. It's the honorable thing to do!

ERIC: But—you don't swim.

CASSANDRA: Mythajawaba will fly me to her cave where I will serve her. It's dry.

ERIC: And you know that because . . .

CASSANDRA: It came to me in a dream.

(CASSANDRA starts to shiver.)

ERIC: And if you jump and the Mythajawawa-thing-a-ma-jig doesn't come—you'll drown.

CASSANDRA: Oh. I hadn't thought of that.

ERIC: You're starting to shiver. Let's go inside. Where it's warm . . . and dry . . . and safe.

CASSANDRA: I have to stay. I have to make one real stab at this rescue thing.

ERIC: Take my jacket.

CASSANDRA: You need to go inside. When she comes, you won't be able to resist. Trust me. I know. It's been a year. My fiancée's been gone one year today.

ERIC: I'm so sorry for your loss.

CASSANDRA: He's not dead! Don't you understand? He's—out there! With Mythajawaba!

ERIC: Tell you what. You take my jacket—do your incantation thing and jump. If Mythajawaba doesn't scoop you up—I will catch you. So you don't drown. How's that for a plan?

CASSANDRA: You would do that? For a total stranger?

> *(ERIC puts his jacket around CASSANDRA)*

ERIC: It's the only option.

> *(CASSANDRA climbs up on the bench and stretches her arms and starts her incantation.)*

CASSANDRA: Mythajawaba . . . . Myth-a-ja-wa-ba . . . myth-a

> *(Sweet bell-like sounds or tinkling sounds are heard. ERIC and CASSANDRA listen. Whatever sound effect is chosen should be lyrical and haunting. Even eerie.)*

CASSANDRA: There! Do you hear? Can you hear it?

> *(But ERIC is transfixed. He moves closer and closer to the edge. arms spread out, he stands on the bench.)*
>
> BLACKOUT

CASSANDRA: Nooooo!

AT RISE CASSANDRA is on deck with Ully.

ULLIE: Cassandra?

CASSANDRA: Ully? Is it really you? How did you get here?

ULLIE: On the wings of Mythajawaba! It was glorious. Swooping between seas and stars! Cassandra!

> *(They embrace)*

What did you do?

CASSANDRA: What did I do—I seem to have—saved you! Mister? Where's that guy?

ULLIE: That guy?

CASSANDRA: My wanna-be-hero. Oh no! I seemed to have sacrificed him. It was supposed to be me!

ULLIE: Put me back!

CASSANDRA: Aren't you glad to see me?

ULLIE: Of course I am. Nice to see you. Now—send me back please.

CASSANDRA: Don't you still love me?

ULLIE: Of course I do, but—

CASSANDRA: But?

ULLIE: I don't want you to take this wrong way but, I love Mythajawaba.

CASSANDRA: How can you love a mythical creature who enslaves you?

ULLIE: Cassandra—she's—a goddess . . .

CASSANDRA: You're leaving me for a goddess?

ULLIE: I'm—sorry.

ULLIE: How can you be so shallow?

ULLIE: This past year I realized—your weird dreams and all—it was fate. You insisted I come on the ferry with you. You pleaded with me to hear her call. I was meant to be with Mythajawaba. I was meant for a goddess. Thank-you. Put me back now, I'm begging you!

CASSANDRA: And to think I was ready to sacrifice myself so that you could come back to the world!

ULLIE: That was very sweet of you. I still want to go back.

CASSANDRA: Believe me—if I could send you back and bring the rescuing guy here—I'd be more than happy to oblige! We are no longer engaged. I release you.

(She takes off her engagement ring.)

ULLIE: Do you mean that? Do you hear that, Mythajawaba? I'm no longer engaged! Will you marry me!

BLACKOUT

*We hear a loud thumb in the blackout. AT RISE
ERIC is on the floor having been thrown back by*
MYTHA JAWABA. CASSANDRA kneels to help him.

CASSANDRA: Are you all right?

ERIC: I think—I was just dumped by a goddess. She hovered above the ferry and threw me down.

CASSANDRA: I'm so sorry.

ERIC: Don't be. I'm glad to be back to reality. I just wish I had had a gentler landing.

CASSANDRA: Was she—beautiful?

ERIC: Yeah. But only in a stunning-model-gorgeous-goddess sort of way. Not my type.

CASSANDRA: Really?

ERIC: I'm kind of a meat and potatoes, trick or treat, pay your dues kind of guy. Besides she didn't want me. All I heard on my trip to her cave was, "You're not Ully! You're not Ully!"

CASSANDRA: She loves him. A goddess loves my ex-fiancee.

ERIC: Yeah. I guess. It's been—well . . . intriguing getting involved in your romantic mishap with the gods, but we're ready to dock—so—bye. You—don't need saving anymore, right?

CASSANDRA: Don't you—want your jacket back?

ERIC: Thank you.

CASSANDRA: There's a coffee shop nearby.

ERIC: A warm, caffeinated liquid would be very welcome, now that you mention it.

CASSANDRA: Or something stronger. Mister Hero—what's your name anyway?

ERIC: Eric.

CASSANDRA: Nice to meet you, Eric. I'm Cassandra.

> *They walk away in conversation as the lights fade to black. ERIC might even put his jacket around CASSANDRA'S shoulders.*

The End

NIGHT OF THE LIVING RELATIVES

Judy Klass

PRODUCTION NOTES:

This play was first produced in June/July of 2011 in a show called Vignettes For the Apocalypse 5, put on by End Times Productions, at The Kraine Theater, at 85 East 4th Street in NYC. It was directed by Sherri Barber.

Cast
SALLY, Elizabeth Dilley
ROSE, Lesley Shannon
JOHN, Matthew Kernisky

CHARACTERS:
JOHN, a somewhat credulous, pleasant soul, twenties to fifties.
ROSE, John's sister, currently a zombie, twenties to fifties.
SALLY, John's high-strung wife, twenties to fifties.

SCENE: A kitchen in a pleasant suburban home.
TIME: The near future, when Hell is full.

AT RISE: SALLY and JOHN sit at the kitchen table. ROSE, their undead zombie maid, is shuffling by the stove, back to the audience, mumbling quietly to herself. JOHN is reading the paper.

SALLY: Do you really need to read at the table like that?
JOHN: *(absently)* What?
SALLY: You know, you could talk to me.
JOHN: Mmmm. Here's something interesting.
SALLY: What? Fine, read it to me.
JOHN: An editorial comparing terrorists with zombies.
SALLY: Great.
     (Calling over to ROSE)
     Any time you're ready, Rose! We're not dead, you know, we'd like the food sometime this week.
ROSE: MMMMMMMMMMM! RRRRRR!
SALLY: Whatever.
JOHN: 'Cause, you know, if a suspected terrorist approaches you, or gets on a train, or whatever, you're not supposed to tackle him or shoot him in the arm, or even the heart.
SALLY: *(distracted)*No?
JOHN: No. You gotta shoot for the head. 'Cause the body could be booby trapped, and if you don't kill him right away, he could set himself off with the tiniest hand movement. Isn't that interesting?
SALLY: *(sarcastic)* Fascinating.
     At last, ROSE shuffles over, lugging a pot from the stove. Now the audience should be able to see SHE's a zombie. SHE moves to slop the food from the pot onto the plates.)
JOHN: That's okay, Rose. Rose? Put it on the trivet.
SALLY: Rose, if we haven't told you a hundred times . . .

ROSE: MMmmmmmmmmRRRrrrrr . . .

> *(SHE sets the pot heavily on the trivet, gnashes her teeth a few times, and shuffles away from them)*

SALLY: I hate that teeth-gnashing thing. She does it to scare us, I know.

JOHN: She does it when she's upset, you've got to be gentle with her.

SALLY: She gets away with everything around you. Just because she used to be your sister—

JOHN: She still sort of is.

SALLY: I think it's highly unsanitary letting her handle the food in the first place. Dead people should not touch food for living people.

> *(They serve themselves from the pot)*

JOHN: The food is hot, it's fine as long as it's hot—

SALLY: Whatever. You'll be singing a different song when we catch something nasty and end up like her.

JOHN: I won't be singing at all if we end up like her.

SALLY: Duh. Exactly my point.

JOHN: I don't see you breaking your heart over not cooking anymore.

SALLY: Fine, whatever. So, what does the editorial say?

JOHN: What?

SALLY: The editorial about terrorists on the subway and zombies.

JOHN: Oh. Just that it's ironic. That there are parallels. In both cases, you have to kill them by blowing their brains out.

SALLY: That's it?

JOHN: Yeah.

SALLY: Somebody with nothing to say gets to write a big editorial like that, gets all that space in the paper?

JOHN: Well, he's witty about it—

SALLY: Witty my ass, who cares—

ROSE: Mmmmmmrrrrraaaawrrragraaawrrrrrrrrr!

> *(SHE is agitated, shuffling around zombie style, hands in front of her, gnashing her teeth, circling ever closer to SALLY and JOHN)*

SALLY: Now what's wrong with her?

JOHN: Sssshhh. You're getting her agitated, she doesn't like loud voices.

SALLY: *(Incredulous)* I'm getting her agitated?

JOHN: She doesn't like it when we fight, she's always hated tension in the home—

SALLY: Please, she's a frigging zombie! She's not Mother Teresa, here!

ROSE: Mrrraawrerrrrrrmmmmmmmuuuggghraaawrrrr!

> *(twitching and lurching toward them, making biting gestures)*

Graaarrrrrrrrwrrrrrrrr!

> *(They abandon their food and stand, moving away from her)*

SALLY: Okay, okay. I'm calm. My voice is quiet. See that, Rose? See how much we love each other?

ROSE: Mmmmmmraaaawwwwwrrrr! Sssssssssssss! Huh! Ugh!

SALLY: Tension in the home my ass, she's hungry, she sees us eating dinner every night, she's a flesh-eating zombie and she wants some dinner of her own.

JOHN: *(Pleading, trying to be firm)* Now, Rose, you know better than this. Please go down to the basement and mill around for a while. We don't like seeing you like this.

ROSE: Grrrrrrruuuuuuuuussssssmmmmmmrrrrrrrraaawwwr!

> *(SHE bites the air as SHE advances, and they inch around the table to get away from her.)*

SALLY: Okay, that's it, where's the gun?

JOHN: What do you mean?

SALLY: The gun. I said she could stay here and help out with chores if you trained her, and if you kept a gun handy at all times.

JOHN: I—I don't remember . . .

SALLY: Where the hell is the gun?

JOHN: She's my sister!

SALLY: She's not your sister! I *liked* your sister! This is an undead zombie bitch who's about to eat us for dinner! Where is the fucking gun?

> *(JOHN grabs a broom and hands it to SALLY)*

JOHN: Here! Hit her with this! I can't.

SALLY: A broom? What good is a broom?

JOHN: Drive her back.

> *(SALLY waves the broom, but ROSE keeps advanc-*

ing, grunting, hissing and biting, and they keep retreating.)

SALLY: It's a broom with a plastic handle, how the hell can I bash in her skull and crush her brains with this?

JOHN: Stop talking that way! She's my sister!

SALLY: You are such a useless, sentimental pussy, I swear!

(SHE hands him the broom, and bolts to the door, in the wings. We hear her OPEN THE DOOR, and hear ZOMBIE MOANS off stage.)

SALLY *(O.S.)* Oh—oh my God! She's invited her friends over! Or everybody in the neighborhood has died, it's like a zombie convention out here, it's AAAUUGHGH! GET AWAY FROM ME! Get off me, ew, it's Doug Hanson, he looks like he got runover by a lawn-mower—ugh! Ow, stop it aaaaaaaaah!

(We hear the DOOR SHUT. JOHN STANDS TREM-BLING, shaking the broom at ROSE: HE calls into the wings:)

JOHN: Sally? Sally, are you okay?

(Beat)

What do you think, Rose, is she okay?

(ROSE becomes less threatening. SHE stops advanc-ing and cocks her head to one side)

JOHN: Why am I asking you? You never liked her. Even when you were alive, you and Sally never got along. She says she liked you back then, but I know. I've seen you two snipping at each other. Snip, snip, snip!

(HE sits down, upset, on the floor. ROSE gently sinks down beside him)

JOHN: But you don't understand, we're really good together.Some-times. I thought I'd found it, you know? Instead of all the bick-ering and shouting when Mom and Dad were together, Rose, I thought I'd found that happy home we always talked about. You know? Do you still think it's possible to have that?

ROSE: *(Gently)*Urr! Urr! Urr! Urr!

(SHE is making sympathetic noises, like a seal call-ing out, or cooing like a little bird. HE smiles and lays the broom on the floor)

JOHN: I know you still understand, Rose. You always were my favorite sister.

(Gently, clumsily, SHE moves to embrace him. And then SHE sinks her teeth into his shoulder and neck. There is much blood. JOHN *screams:)*

JOHN: Aaaaaaaaaah! Aaaaaaah!

(There is more blood, and HE lies still.)

(The DOOR CREAKS OPEN in the wings. A zomboid, bloody SALLY lurches in, and watches ROSE feed.)

SALLY: Mmmmmmmrrrrrgraaawrrr?

ROSE: Hehehheheherrrmmmaaaarrrrrrrraaaarrrrrr!

(SALLY falls to the floor to feed as well, munching on one of JOHN's arms. ROSE and SALLY chew noisily and contentedly. At last, JOHN sits up, staring straight ahead, a zombie.)

JOHN: Grrrraaheheherrrrrrmmrrrraawrrrr?

(LIGHTS OUT)

The End.

OPPRESSION AND PEARLS

Jenny Lyn Bader

PRODUCTION NOTES:

Oppression and Pearls was first performed in January 2011 at Largo at the Coronet in Los Angeles as part of *Standing on Ceremony*.Directed by Brian Shnipper.

Cast:

Lydia: Julie Hagerty
Ann: Amy Yasbeck
Emmie: Amy Brenneman.

Produced by Joan Stein & Stuart Ross
associate producer: Allain Rochel.

CHARACTERS:
    LYDIA—50's. Emmie's mother.
    ANN— 30's-40's. A bridal consultant.
    EMMIE—late 20's-early 30's. A bride-to-be.

SETTING: The bridal salon at Bergdorf Goodman.
TIME: One Saturday at 11am.

The art deco bridal salon at Bergdorf Goodman. EMMIE, a bride-to-be, arrives with LYDIA, her mother. A wedding department consultant, ANN, checks her appointment book.

LYDIA: *(to ANN)* We have an eleven o'clock appointment. Benson.

ANN: Yes. Welcome to the bridal salon at Bergdorf Goodman! Have you been to any wedding trunk shows yet?

EMMIE: No . . . I've never been to a trunk show at all.
    (looking around:)
    I thought there would be a trunk.

ANN: Right here you can see the designer's entire line of wedding veils.

EMMIE *(to ANN)*: Veils make me a little uncomfortable. Have you read the stories of women who are forced to take the veil?

ANN: You wouldn't be taking the veil. You would be buying the veil. This is Bergdorf.

EMMIE: I mean have you thought about the whole history of it? In the Bible, Laban fools Jacob by hiding Leah under a veil.

LYDIA: Oh Emmie, not that Laban story again . . .

EMMIE: You couldn't even choose who you married! You could be tricked by a veil. Marriage was a business transaction controlled by your parents. A girl's identity didn't matter. Women were just chattel! They could be sold and . . . draped.

ANN: But now, we can be draped so much more exquisitely.
    (LYDIA looks at the display.)

LYDIA: *(to ANN)* All of these veils are designed by Ali Marvani?

EMMIE: Who's he?

ANN: Ali is actually short for Alison, she's an up-and-coming designer.

LYDIA: Now where did I just read that she learned to sew at the age of five?

ANN: She was profiled in the *Style* section last . . .

EMMIE: Oh don't get me started on the *Style* section! I have these friends, literally the nicest couple, got their picture taken in the park to send to the wedding page—could not get in, because your eyebrows have to be the same level as your future spouse's in the submitted photograph and their eyebrows were just a tiny bit off. And meanwhile they're including all these random announcements. Dysfunctional couples, who keep breaking up and their whole terrible relationship is described in the announcement including their awful third date . . .

ANN: Uh, I hate that wh . . .

EMMIE: And they're putting in *divorced* people who have been in the section before multiple times, including a couple who just swapped spouses!

LYDIA: They didn't used to do that.

EMMIE: Oh—and suddenly they're announcing gay weddings and totally slacking on the eyebrow requirement there just so they can be P.C.!

(A pause.)

ANN: Uhm . . . *(A beat as she picks up a veil:)* Why don't you try this one.

EMMIE: *(to LYDIA)* Mom you can keep looking at veils, but they're not "me." And the wedding veil embodies the history of oppression.

LYDIA: Oh yes! Oppression and pearls. Tragic.

ANN: This veil goes with a tiara . . . One bride I worked with wore it like that, I can show you a picture . . . *(she opens a photo album.)*

EMMIE: My fiancé might laugh if I wore a crown. Sorry, tiara. It *is* pretty . . .

ANN: At least you can still tell what's pretty. That's good! Many brides entirely lose their sense of taste and decorum.

LYDIA: Yes, I've been to their weddings. What do you say when the bride wears tangerine?

ANN: *(agreeing)* Something borrowed, something Creamsicle?

EMMIE: Maybe the tiara without the veil might . . . *(tries it)* Ow! It has thorns!

LYDIA: Those aren't thorns, dear, they're combs!
     (to ANN)
I'd like to see one that's more structured.

EMMIE: I'd like to see one that's less painful.

LYDIA: Something not quite so . . . you know.

ANN: I do know.

LYDIA: You see the shape of her face?

ANN: I see it.

EMMIE: It's like I'm not even here.

LYDIA: *(to ANN)* It's so nice to meet someone who understands . . . Emmie wants to disregard every wedding tradition . . . She doesn't want a string quartet. She has a composer friend who arranges his works on a cell phone using ricki ticki sounds.

EMMIE: He's written a piece about our relationship. And there's a choral part where all the guests' cell phones can sing together using an app! He's worked on it a long . . .

LYDIA: She refuses to rent plates.

EMMIE: As a gift, one of our friends offered us a set of 200 biodegradable plates, which I think . . .

LYDIA: And she doesn't even want flower arrangements. But vegetables.

EMMIE: Rhubarbs look gorgeous in a centerpiece! And they are not vegetables.

LYDIA: *(coldly)* Botanically, they are!

EMMIE: *(to Ann)* We had our first date at the farmer's market in Union Square in May, and I still remember the rhubarb colors . . . So it's significant. To us as a couple.

LYDIA: *(to Ann)* I don't understand dating anymore. Who dates at a farmer's market?

ANN: *(cheerfully ignoring the tension)* So I'm thinking with her heart-shaped face, you might like the double-drape style. *(Putting the veil on EMMIE.)* I think you'll like the fabric liner on this model. *(to LYDIA)* And I think you'll like the length . . . There. What do you think?

(LYDIA is moved to tears:)

LYDIA: Ooh . . . My little baby's getting married!

EMMIE: *(touched:)* Oh mama!

LYDIA: Sorry — I didn't expect . . . *(she dabs at the corner of her eye:)*

EMMIE: Mom, your mascara just smudged right there.

LYDIA: I think my contact lens is migrating, excuse me. *(LYDIA exits.)*

EMMIE: *(to ANN)* Are you married?

ANN: Pretty much.

EMMIE: And was there a veil in your wedding?

ANN: There were two.

EMMIE: You mean, the double-draped style?

ANN: I mean, my bride and I each wore them.

EMMIE: Oh shit! I'm sorry, When I said . . . I didn't mean . . .

ANN: I've heard worse. Let it go. You're not the most insensitive person to wander into Bergdorf.

EMMIE: No, when I said gay people are getting on the wedding page now . . . I didn't mean they shouldn't be able to marry . . . I just meant, after the whole history of civil rights, why would they care about something so silly?

ANN: Same reason, after the history of sexist oppression, that you would choose to wear a veil.

(Beat.)

EMMIE: *(with understanding)* Because it makes your mother cry?

ANN: *(nods, opening the album)* I keep our favorite wedding pictures in here, with the ones my clients send me . . . . here's our announcement. I didn't care if our wedding was on the Society page, but my *mom*, when she saw this . . .

EMMIE: Your dress is . . . Wow! Not what I would have expected.

ANN: What? You were expecting something more radical lesbian chic?

EMMIE: No! . . . Maybe.

ANN: But what fun would it be if we just wore what people expected, right?

EMMIE: Yeah. So you didn't feel under pressure to look like this?

ANN: Are you kidding? My whole life, I kept being told I couldn't have a wedding at all. You've always known you could have one, so you want to change it around, mix it up.

EMMIE: No, I just want to make it personal!

ANN: For me, it was personal—just because I got to be the person.

EMMIE: *(empathic)* Of course.

ANN: And my mom . . . never thought it would happen!

EMMIE: She cried when she saw your announcement?

ANN: And all morning before the ceremony. And during it. She especially cried when we appeared with our veils, I'll show you—

EMMIE: *(gasps)* Oh!

> *(EMMIE and ANN start welling up as they look at the picture.)*

ANN: *(trying to pull it together, but sniffling a bit as she talks)* It's a nice picture.

> *(LYDIA enters.)*

LYDIA: What are you two crying about?

EMMIE: Ann is showing me her wedding pictures.

> *(LYDIA looks at the album and points at a photo.)*

LYDIA: Who's that?

ANN: That's my spouse.

LYDIA: Obviously your spouse. What's her name?

ANN: Joy.

LYDIA: *(turns to Emmie, vigorously)* Do you see those dresses? That bouquet? Those flowers?

EMMIE: *(knowing what's coming; she sees it too.)* Yes, mom.

LYDIA: Why do you have to do everything so upside-down? Why can't you have a traditional wedding like these girls? Don't they look splendid?

EMMIE: *(genuinely agreeing)* Beautiful.

LYDIA: Look at those veils. The cascading bouquets! The white roses . . . and are those Asiatic lilies? Lovely.

ANN: Thank you, Mrs. Benson.

LYDIA: Can you believe people think this should be against the law? It's those rhubarbs that should be against the law!

ANN: That's . . .

LYDIA: *(whirls around to ANN, equally indignant)* And you!

Why haven't you shown us that tiara, that Joy is wearing? Did you have that made or is it in stock?

ANN: Uh, hold on, yes we have it—here. *(ANN takes out the tiara.)* And here's a veil that goes with it. Would you like to try them?

EMMIE: Yes. I would.

(EMMIE puts them on herself.)

ANN: What do you think?

EMMIE: Mom. Mom. I look so much like the photo on your dresser. Of the bride in the antique dress edged with lace, the high collar, the headdress. Do you see it?

LYDIA: I see my daughter's veil. And I see my veil . . . and my mother's veil, and her mother's veil . . . *(EMMIE nods.)* I see women's faces covered in shadows, then revealed, full of hope. I see the flow of time . . . and time pausing for that one moment when you get to play the part of the bride. This is like . . . no shopping experience I have ever had.

EMMIE: *(to ANN)* I . . . I look so much like this one photograph of my great-grandmother at her wedding. Except now—I'm the person.

ANN: Yes, you are.

EMMIE: *(resisting tears)* I will not cry over a hair accessory!

ANN: But it's so much more than a hair accessory.

EMMIE: Mom?

LYDIA: What?

EMMIE: I love it. I'll wear it.

LYDIA: *(to ANN)* We'll take it.

ANN: Good.

LYDIA: . . . You know, I was just thinking, aren't rhubarbs in season in June?

ANN: I believe they are.

LYDIA: Do you think the guests will want to take them home?

ANN: Maybe to make pies.

EMMIE: Oh mom! I think they will.

The End

PASCAL AND MARTIN

Jan Buttram

PRODUCTION NOTES:

PASCAL AND MARTIN by Jan Buttram was first produced in "The Throne Play Benefit Challenge Series" in the Dorothy Strelsin Theatre at the Abingdon Theatre Arts Complex, June 29, 2010. Directed by Kate Bushmann

Cast:
PASCAL, Lori Gardner
MARTIN, Eugene M. Santiago
CORY, John Trevellini

CHARACTERS:

PASCAL, twenties, a transgender street woman, tough and attractive.

MARTIN, twenties, Pascal's grimy but adoring and loyal partner wearing dred locks, wears a housecoat.

CORY, forties, a NYC night watchman, strong and sexy, with a rye sense of humor.

TIME: Present. 1:00AM.
PLACE: NYC. Broadway theatre.

> *PASCAL sits on a throne. HER hair is covered. SHE wears a red dressing gown. MARTIN stands bowing his head in front of PASCAL. HE wears a terrycloth housecoat.)*

PASCAL: What did your grace say about my hair?

MARTIN: Thinning a little on top, that's all.

PASCAL: My hair is stylish.

MARTIN: Your hair is beautiful.

PASCAL: Because it's French hair. You can't speak anything bad about French hair.

MARTIN: Your majesty, I would never say a word to upset the loveliest lady of France.

PASCAL: Things would not go well for you.

MARTIN: Things have already not gone well for me.

PASCAL: The rack, disemboweled entrails strewn across the town square.

MARTIN: *(on one knee)* Most gracious Queen of France, have mercy on your servant who only moments ago, you did smile upon.

PASCAL: My mood was sunny moments ago. Now, there is a cloud. It is dark.

MARTIN: Make my day. Smile again.

> *(PASCAL extends HER hand. MARTIN kisses it)*

PASCAL: Poor Monsieur Martin.

MARTIN: I beg you not to misuse your servant.

PASCAL: Rien.

MARTIN: Oui.

PASCAL: There's a nasty rumor.

MARTIN: About me?

PASCAL: That you spit upon my minion, a bus driver.

MARTIN: Never happened.

PASCAL: I hear it did. It was printed in *The New York Times*.

MARTIN: That driver was a bitch.

PASCAL: Off with your head.

MARTIN: Mercy, I cry, mercy!

PASCAL: I will call out the dogs to eat you.

MARTIN: I will eat *you*.

> *(MARTIN places HIS head under the robe. PASCAL is thrilled)*

PASCAL: Oooh la la.

MARTIN: *(mumbling)* MMMMMMMMMMMMM like a coconut oil spill.

PASCAL: Do not overstep your station.

MARTIN: *(surfacing)* Stop?

PASCAL: Oui.

MARTIN: Madam, you are my life.

PASCAL: Blowing smoke up my ass. My pigs will feast on your rump.

MARTIN: Not the pigs.

PASCAL: Let me see your rump.

> *(MARTIN turns. Displays HIS butt)*

A beauty. Shame to waste it on pigs. Maybe I'll forgive. What would be your penance?

MARTIN: I will lay with you.

PASCAL: As you lay with my mother?

MARTIN: That was your mother?

PASCAL: Laid with her and begged her to betray me, the queen.

MARTIN: Wronged, I have been wronged.

PASCAL: You play with my enemies.

MARTIN: I was protecting you, discovering, under covering . . .

PASCAL: What? Cobwebs, dirt, monstrous creatures. Les roches. Clean the sewers that surround my castle, I command you!

MARTIN: Let me clean your privates, madam.

PASCAL: *(giggling)* Perhaps I will give you a second chance to redeem your failed attempts to gain my pardon.

MARTIN: Dearest giver of life, I am but a small man who lays awake waiting for your blessing. Give it to me.

Lawrence Harbison

PASCAL: Impossible wretch.

MARTIN: Give it to me, or, sacred queen, banish me.

PASCAL: There is no escape. I lift my hand and signal the sword to be brought down on your neck. I am supreme ruler.

> *(Makes a make believe gun with HER hand and shoots)*

Bang.

MARTIN: Hail the almighty queen. I die at your feet.

PASCAL: Lick my feet.

MARTIN: An honor.

> *(MARTIN does. PASCAL stands and turns HER back)*

PASCAL: Bow to my rear end.

MARTIN: Most gladly.

> *(HE does. SHE turns, playfully)*

PASCAL: Now, kiss my royal ass.

> *(HE does)*

PASCAL: *(cont'd)* All the whores and dunces, all the court bows and kisses my ass. You are my main pimp.

MARTIN: I'm not a pimp.

PASCAL: You are my pimp.

MARTIN: I ain't a pimp.

PASCAL: If you are not a pimp, what good are you to me? Off with your head.

MARTIN: Tired of this shit.

PASCAL: Don't go against me.

MARTIN: Coming down too hard.

PASCAL: Doomed, doomed, doomed.

> *(CORY, enters. HE is surprised, cautious)*

CORY: What the hell?

PASCAL: Who is this scoundrel?

CORY: What are you doing here?

MARTIN: Raining outside.

CORY: You can't be here.

PASCAL: Off with your head.

CORY: How did you get in here?

PASCAL: I'm a queen, French queen actually. It's my castle.

MARTIN: We'll leave, brother.

PASCAL: The hell we will.

MARTIN: Little high, that's all.

PASCAL: Martin, don't cater to this low class motherfucker.

MARTIN: C'mon, baby, play is over.

PASCAL: I ain't playing. I'm a queen.

MARTIN: She'll come down to earth in a second. Give her a chance . . . .

CORY: Is that a woman?

PASCAL: French drag queen, mother fucker.

(CORY pulls out cell phone)

MARTIN: Heh, don't call the cops.

CORY: You're in a Broadway theatre. You're sitting on the set and wearing costumes? What the hell?

PASCAL: Ought to protect my stuff. Leave the queen's robe lying around backstage.

CORY: It's a rehearsal robe.

PASCAL: I'm an actress. I'm going to be on RuPaul's show.

CORY: This ain't television. This is legitimate.

PASCAL: Legitimate my skinny ass. You need a sign on this throne, "Watch the nails." Speaking of asses, you should do something about yours. Get you a warning signal when you back up that ass of yours, boy. You could hurt someone.

(Makes a "beep, beep, beep sound a truck makes when backing up)

CORY: Get out. Now.

PASCAL: Bow to me.

MARTIN: We snuck in when that big crowd was leaving, don't mean no harm. Cold out there. Give me five minutes; I'll get her out.

CORY: Five minutes.

PASCAL: You will be hung at dawn. Hung and thrown to the buzzards.

(CORY exits)

MARTIN: Pascal, we got to book.

PASCAL: I ain't finished ruling.

MARTIN: C'mon, baby, we'll find us a better place to hang.

PASCAL: I ain't sleeping in a shelter.

MARTIN: All closed.

PASCAL: I was having a good time.

MARTIN: You were on a roll.

PASCAL: Then that yodel comes in here and bothers us.

MARTIN: Bad timing.

PASCAL: RuPaul says timing is everything.

(MARTIN checks HIS pockets for change. Pulls out some coins)

MARTIN: Coins of the realm. Enough for a hotdog.

PASCAL: I ain't hungry.

MARTIN: I got the rest of that joint.

PASCAL: They're always so nasty in Smiler's.

MARTIN: Get us a bottle?

PASCAL: Don't want no bottle.

MARTIN: Pascal, this is Martin talking, now. Take off the robe.

PASCAL: No.

MARTIN: Baby, we only got a few minutes left.

PASCAL: This was your idea.

MARTIN: Worked for a while. Rain probably stopped by now.

PASCAL: Fucking theatre. What does it have to do with me?

MARTIN: Little place to rest, that's all.

PASCAL: You love me, Martin?

MARTIN: You are my queen.

PASCAL: *(laughing)* We played Broadway, babe.

MARTIN: We did.

PASCAL: I was the queen of France and you were my knight in shining armour.

MARTIN: But I ain't a pimp.

PASCAL: Baby, you so sensitive. You know what sounds good, a Pinkberry.

MARTIN: That shit is too expensive.

PASCAL: It's good for you, Martin. It's organic and stuff.

MARTIN: Costs too much.

PASCAL: I'm sorry I said that about that boy's ass. He's nice. Do we have enough money to buy him a beer?

MARTIN: Maybe.

PASCAL: If he don't bring the cops back with him, I think we should invite him to have a beer. Show him some royal love.

MARTIN: We'll ask.

PASCAL: May be on some time clock or some shit.

MARTIN: Could be.

(CORY enters)

PASCAL: Baby, you want to get high?

CORY: I got people to answer to.

PASCAL: No, baby. What's your name?

CORY: Cory.

PASCAL: Cory. You got to answer to me; I'm the queen of the night.

CORY: Right.

PASCAL: Can we buy you a beer?

CORY: I got a break in ten minutes.

PASCAL: We'll wait for you at Smiler's.

CORY: See you in fifteen.

MARTIN: Thanks.

PASCAL: You like this theatre stuff?

CORY: I seen a couple of the shows. I liked this one all right.

PASCAL: Martin and me, we going to see us a show one day.

CORY: You got to have a lot of money.

PASCAL: That's right. We'll make our own show.

MARTIN: See you at Smiler's.

PASCAL: This Queen is going to buy you a beer and we going to smoke a little weed, talk over the state of Broadway.

CORY: Sounds right.

MARTIN: My queen is a real beauty.

PASCAL: Pascal and Martin rule.

(PASCAL and MARTIN exit. CORY watches THEM go. Pulls out a vial of cocaine. Sniffs. Speaks on HIS cell)

CORY: They're gone. Forget about calling the cops. I'm taking my break in ten.

(CORY sits on throne)

My kingdom, bitch.

(Blackout)

The End

POLAR BEAR SWIM

Marisa Smith

PRODUCTION NOTES:

Polar Bear Swim was originally produced by the Half Moon Theater (Poughkeepsie, NY) June 4th and 5th 2011 as part of Half Moon Theatre's 10 Minute Play Festival, directed by Geoff Tarson.

Cast:
BROTHER, Frank Trezza
TROY, Ryan Katzer
HARRY, Paul Kassel

CHARACTERS:

BROTHER, Auto mechanic, fifties, a townie, born and raised in a small NH village, tough, strong, no pretenses.

TROY, Also a townie, twenties, innocent, a good-looking, good ol'boy.

HARRY, From the city, fifties, down on his luck and at the end of his rope.

SETTING: Brother's Auto Shop. Winter in northern New Hampshire, near the Canadian border, the real boonies.

TIME: The present. Saturday afternoon.

BROTHER is standing behind the counter next to the cash register doing some paperwork, wearing a t-shirt despite the weather. TROY blows in, wearing a t-shirt and a vest. BROTHER looks up from his paperwork, takes his reading glasses off.

BROTHER: Look what the cat drug in.

TROY: Brother. Hey.

BROTHER: How ya doin?

TROY: Not too bad.

BROTHER: Tiny said he saw ya truck over ta The Shady Lane, yestiddy. Oughta park in the back if she's married ya know.

TROY: Ah, c'mon—

BROTHER: Don't wanna end up fulla buckshot just when ya at the height of ya powas.

TROY: You know I'd never cheat on Melissa.

BROTHER: Uh huh.

TROY: And she'd never cheat on me! That was *us* at The Shady Lane. She wanted to do sumpin' diffr'nt. Wanted to pretend we were *tourists.*

BROTHER: Tiny said he saw her Fiesta over ta the college the other day, behind one of them fraternities.

TROY: That's a lie! She never goes over to the college!

BROTHER: Mebbe she's doin' sumpin'diffr'nt.

 (HARRY enters, unkempt, unshaven, looking like a wreck.)

HARRY: *(nervous)* Excuse me, but I'm looking for the Polar

Bear swim? Do you know where it is? I saw a sign as I came into town, I really have to find it.

TROY: *(to BROTHER)* Polar Bear Swim? That today Brother?

BROTHER: Up ta Wink's Pond.

TROY: (to *HARRY*) Okay, then, you take Beaver Meadow—

BROTHER: Beava Medda is closed. Had all those blow-downs.

    (off HARRY'S quizzical look)

Trees come down cuz a the storm.

TROY: Oh, yeah, forgot about them blow-downs.

BROTHER: You planning on doin' it?

HARRY: Definitely, I'm definitely gonna do it, I drove all the way up here from New York!

BROTHER: Well, there's nothin' official but usually just people do it who are from around he-ah.

TROY: Yeah, town doesn't want ta get sued, you know, in case somebody dies.

HARRY: Oh, that's okay, that's fine in fact, that's just *fine*.

TROY: What's fine?

HARRY: If I die. I mean, I'm planning to, that's the whole idea! I hope the shock of the cold water will give me a heart attack and I'll die instantly. Boom, out like a light! Couldn't sue you then could I?

TROY: You really lookin' to kill yourself?

HARRY: Quick and painless, *perfect* way to go. I read some guy in Canada died last winter doing it.

BROTHER: Well, Canadians, ya know.

TROY: Yeah, Canadians.

HARRY: Have you ever done it?

TROY: Yeah, I done it.

HARRY: *(to BROTHER)* Have you?

BROTHER: Years ago. I didn't die but sumpin' worse happened. Much worse than dyin.

TROY: What? What happened Brother?

HARRY: Yeah, what happened?

BROTHER: Jumped in, colder than a witch's tit, couldn't move, couldn't catch my breath. And then—

TROY: And then, and then what?

    (BROTHER is shaking his head)

HARRY: What?

TROY: Tell us Brother!

Lawrence Harbison

BROTHER: Well . . . well, turns out my, my, *balls,* they just done disappeared right up me, wouldn't come out for 'owas.

TROY: Your balls? You couldn't find 'em?

HARRY: Your, your testicles, went, went . . . back in?

BROTHER: Yup. Had to go see Doc Emerson. He said they'd come back down and by Jesus they did. Took 'em bout a day but they came back.

TROY: You never told me that!

HARRY: God, that must have been terrible.

BROTHER: Don't think you wanna do the polar bear swim.

HARRY: I never thought *that* could happen. But, if I'm dead I wouldn't know!

TROY: You don't wanna live no more?

HARRY: Son, I've got a shitload of problems. I'm tired.

BROTHER: That Porsche nine eleven out there don't look like too much of a problem ta me.

(TROY goes to the window to look and whistles)

TROY: She's a beauty. *(to BROTHER)* Mass. plates.

BROTHER: *(to TROY)* Well, we won't hold that against 'im.

TROY: You in trouble?

HARRY: Nope. Just broke. My business went belly up.

TROY: Sorry.

HARRY: Yeah, the bank's after me, friends deserted me, my wife left me, it's a mess.

BROTHER: Well, people are mostly rotten, that ain't no surprise.

TROY: I dunno 'bout that Brother.

HARRY: They love you when you're up and kick you when you're down.

BROTHER: Yup, Soona or late-a just about everybody'll disappoint ya.

TROY: Not *everybody*—

HARRY: My wife moved back in with her mother in *New Jersey.*

BROTHER: When the gravy train stops the women disappe-ar. Them are practical creatures.

HARRY: Right on, you're only as good as your bank account.

TROY: C'mon Brother, not all women want fancy stuff, I mean Melissa and me are happy with a movie and a big bowl of popcorn

BROTHER: An city folk 'specially don't have no real friends. Everybody just usin' everybody else to get what they want.

HARRY: You said it, everybody just hustling everybody else.

BROTHER: Not that people don't use people he-ah. They do.

TROY: You don't use no one Brother! And I don't! That ain't true!

HARRY: I mean people are really the same no matter where they live.

BROTHER: Yup. Don't matter.

HARRY: Disloyal, deceitful, mean—

BROTHER: —lyin', cheatin', stealin' . . . can't count on no body.

TROY: People up here aren't like that and you know it Brother!

HARRY: *And,* we are all ultimately alone.

BROTHER: Alone when we come inta this world and alone when we go outa it.

HARRY: Yup. Amen.

BROTHER: Yup.

> *(BROTHER and HARRY shake their heads in agreement)*

HARRY: And the whole damn thing goes so fast.

BROTHER: One day you realize mosta your hair is gone, your teeth are crumblin' in your mouth like old plaster, and it takes longer and longer for your damn pee to come out.

HARRY: *(knowingly)* And worse things.

BROTHER: *(knowingly)* And worse things.

TROY: What worse things?

BROTHER: Nothin' you have ta worry about Troy.

HARRY: No, son, you're not there yet!

TROY: What are you talkin' about?

BROTHER: Yup, like I said, you at the height of your powas, you enjoy it now.

HARRY: *(to BROTHER)* Remember when we were that young.

BROTHER: Sure din't appreciate it did we?

HARRY: No, we didn't.

TROY: You're talkin' like you're dead! You're not dead yet!

BROTHER: That's right, we ain't, are we?

HARRY: Almost!

BROTHER: Yup, almost!

Lawrence Harbison

(BROTHER and HARRY share a good laugh)

TROY: You can still drive that Porsche out there! Je-sus!

HARRY: That's right! Here, take it for a spin.

(throws TROY the keys)

TROY: You mean it? Really?

HARRY: Knock yourself out.

TROY: Thanks! Won't be too long! Just to get a feel!

(TROY runs out)

HARRY: Good kid.

BROTHER: Don't make 'em better.

HARRY: Yeah, every now and then there's a winner. But like you said, most people are rotten.

BROTHER: To the core.

HARRY: That's just the way it is.

BROTHER: Nothin' we can do about it.

HARRY: We are all God's fallen creatures.

BROTHER: That's the truth.

HARRY: That's it in a nutshell. Fallen creatures.

BROTHER: And it's a miserable life.

HARRY: It certainly is.

> *(BROTHER and HARRY shake their heads in agreement)*

HARRY: Boy, it's been just great talking to you.

> *(Looks at sign)*

Brother, right?

BROTHER: Yes sir.

HARRY: *(puts out his hand to shake BROTHER'S hand)* I'm Harry. I feel so much better! You know, I probably woulda chickened out at the Polar Bear Swim—I mean it's one thing to have a heart attack but that *other* thing you told me about, no way Jose!

> *(TROY comes running into the shop)*

TROY: Brother, Brother, you won't believe it, you won't believe how *smooth* it is—

BROTHER: I know, she purrs like a kitten.

HARRY: Well, gentlemen, I think I'm gonna get back on the highway.

TROY: You don't wanna do the swim no more?

HARRY: No, I changed my mind. Gonna drive to New Jersey now.

BROTHER: Bring flowers. Neva met a women who din't like flowers.

HARRY: I will, nothing to lose at this point .

BROTHER: And bring 'em for her mother too.

HARRY: Don't know if I can go *that* far!

>   *(BROTHER and HARRY laugh)*
>   *(TROY throws HARRY his keys)*

TROY: Well, take care of her. The car I mean.

HARRY: You bet.

>   *(to BROTHER)*

Thanks, Brother.

>   *(to TROY and BROTHER)*

Good luck to you both. No swimming with the polar bears!

>   *(HARRY exits)*

BROTHER: *(grabs his cap and vest)* C'mon now, were gonna be late! Gonna beat my record for stayin' unda the watta this year.

TROY: Hey! That never happened with your balls, you were just bullshitting, just trying to scare him.

BROTHER: It did too happen one year, it did. That's why now I grease em' up with engine oil, keeps em' nice and warm.

TROY: You are so full of it Brother, just full of it.

BROTHER: Like hell I am.

TROY: And you don't think that people are rotten and all that stuff.

BROTHER: Like hell I do.

>   *(BROTHER puts his arm around TROY'S shoulders, and they head for the door)*

TROY: Hey, what's that worse thing you were talking about?

BROTHER: Oh, nuthin. Jus' talkin'. C'mon, let's go waya Beava Medda, mebbe it's open. I wanna see those blow-downs.

The End

Purgartory

Heidi Armbruster

PRODUCTION NOTES:
Purgarory was originally performed as part of Red Bull Theater's Short Play Festival in June 2011. Wendy McClellan directed.

Cast
ONE, Annika Boras
TWO, Jocelyn Kuritsky
THREE, Deanne Lorette
ANGEL Alfredo Narciso

CHARACTERS:
Woman ONE, The Guru (fifties to sixties)
Woman TWO:, The Beauty (twenties)
Woman THREE, the mother (thirties to forties)
ANGEL (a man or a woman)

> *slashes indicate overlapping dialogue.*
> *asterisks indicate continuous speech.*

Performance Note:

It is best to approach the following text as a score; adhering to overlapping and interrupted dialogue as one would adhere to the rhythmic structure of music.

Also, These women attack each of these rituals with the expectation and hope that they will solve their collective problem. In other words (the immortal ones of G. B. Shaw):

Louder, Faster, Funnier.

A space that is neither here nor there.

A mirror on the wall.

An empty wardrobe rack.

Three chairs behind a counter.

> *Woman ONE enters. She's a mess. Ripped and Shredded clothing. Her hair's a Disaster. She's out of breath and looks seriously post—traumatic. She sits in the first chair, puts her head between her legs, and breathes deeply.*
> *Beat.*
> *Woman TWO: enters. She's a mess. Ripped and Shredded clothing. Her face and chest are covered in Blood. Blood drips from her mouth.*

TWO: I'm starving.

ONE: (*Still upside down.*) Eat.

TWO: (*Foraging for food)*I was afraid my stomach would growl.

ONE: Better than sneezing.

TWO: Dead people definitely don't sneeze.

ONE: Their finger nails keep growing.

TWO: Mine are getting freakishly long.

ONE: How was your death?

TWO: Better. I think. Yours?

ONE: Harrowing.

TWO: Seriously?

ONE: Again.

TWO: Boys, man—Fuck!

ONE: The bag over my head was way too tight. I can still taste the plastic.

TWO: *(Finding food.)* Citrus?

ONE: *(declining the offer of citrus)* My Pitta Dosha's aggravated. You're getting blood on the floor.

TWO: Oh shit. It started pooling in my cleavage while I was lying there. Look, see it stained my dress.

TWO takes off her dress and tosses it on the floor, revealing some seriously sexy lingerie.

ONE: *(Sitting up.)* It looks good.

TWO: Really?

ONE: Really good. Look.

/It's all over your face.

TWO: Oh my God I look awesome!

I reached between my tits, to like grab at my chest when I was suffocating, and then I started scratching at my face cause like my skin was burning off, this is like twice the fucking blood!

ONE: Language.

TWO: Fuck, Sorry.

She reaches for a baby wipe and starts to attack the blood.

Hey, your *hair* looks amazing.

ONE: You think so?

TWO: Check it out.

/Seriously. Amazing.

ONE: *(overlapping)* /Oooh, it's a Disaster! I love it!

See, that's the upside of having the bag so tight.

TWO: You look seriously wretched and completely amazing.

ONE: So what do I do? Suffer suffocation or less than awful hair?

TWO: Vanity hurts. This blood tastes like rotting Pad Se Ew, but it *looks* so deliciously disgusting. We make sacrifice Baby wipe?

ONE: No, but I'll borrow your big comb if you don't mind?

TWO: (*Pulls the comb out of a drawer beneath the counter in front of her chair.*) Totally.

    Woman THREE enters. She's a mess. Ripped and Shredded clothing. Mascara is running down her face, creating a giant mascara mud puddle.

ONE: How was it?

THREE They were grunting.

TWO: That's disgusting.

ONE: Killing takes effort.

THREE: It sounded great.*

TWO: Oh, OK then, grunting's cool.

THREE: *(continuous)**But then they started to drool on me./

TWO: *(simultaneous)*/Oh God Yuck!

ONE: *(simultaneous)*/Oh How Awful.

THREE: I think it was drool, or maybe sweat. Something wet fell off of them and onto me and started to trickle down the middle of my back. It tickled. But I was dead, so it's not like I could scratch it.

TWO: Baby wipe?

THREE: Thanks.

ONE: Your mascara /looks wonderful!

TWO: /Oh my god, yeah. Fantastic!

THREE: Good. I was sobbing.

    Starts delicately wiping off her mascara with a baby wipe.

    Look, See—there's a mark on my neck—I knew that cord was too tight.

ONE: My bag was too tight

TWO: My rope was kinda too tight too.

THREE: They're getting a little over—zealous about murder-ing us.

ONE: A little careless maybe.

THREE: Should we say something?

TWO: For safety's sake?

ONE: I'll do it.

THREE: Just—Go Easy.

ONE: I would never provoke them./

THREE: *(simultaneous)* /You might actually.

TWO: *(simultaneous)* /You kinda would.

ONE: Somebody has to stand up for us/
THREE *(simultaneous)* /Agreed, but within reason
TWO: *(simultaneous)* /I get it, but, you know, tread carefully.
   The women continue combing, wiping, dabbing.
THREE Best to maintain positive relations with our killers.
TWO: Walk softly and wear lingerie.
   Beat.
   ONE takes a large pink quartz from her drawer.
ONE: We need a dose of positive energy.
   Time for Quartz.
   (Chanting)
   "We call upon
   Athena
   Maria
   Sofia
   Aphrodite
   And Aphra Behn:"
   Om shan-ti.
   Hands it to TWO.
TWO: *(Chanting)* Vag-in-a.
   Hands it to THREE
THREE: *(Chanting)* A-men.
   Beat. (It's kinda not working like it usually does.)
ONE: Better?
TWO: Not really.
THREE: Musical number?
ONE and TWO: Yes!
   ONE starts a drum roll on top of the counter and all
   three women begin to sing. There is choreography
   involved. It is silly and amazing
ONE, TWO, THREE: "I could have danced all night, I could
   have danced all night, and still have begged for more. I
   could have spread my wings and done a thousand things
   I'd never done before—"
   They stop abruptly.
   Beat. (It's kinda not working like it usually does.)
TWO: Its kinda not working like it usually does.
THREE: Oh sweetie, you're tired.
ONE: It's natural. We've been dying for so long.

THREE: Wait, is it time?*

ONE: *(simultaneous)* *It must be just about time.

TWO: *(simultaneous)* *It's definitely time! I'll get it!

THREE: *(continuous)* *I hope we didn't miss it. Turn it up really loud./ I want to hear them DIE!

ONE: *(simultaneous)* /Yeah, DIE! DIE! DIE!

TWO: *(simultaneous)* /DIE mutherfuckers!

> *TWO turns on the monitor and we hear the action off—stage, which is of course "on stage." The final bloodbath of a revenge tragedy. The women act it out, speaking the words along with the male voices onstage, doing all of the stage combat, using their dressing room implements as weapons. This is not some girly version of the men's fight. These women are fierce! And, although the deaths are deliciously dramatic, the killing is the fun part.*

TWO: *"What cause hast thou to pursue my life?"*

ONE: *"Oh mercy!"*

TWO: *"Now it seems thy greatness was only outward;* I'll not waste longer time, there!"

> *(TWO "stabs" ONE.)*

ONE: *"Thou hast hurt me."*

TWO: *"Again!"*

> *(TWO stabs ONE again.)*

ONE: *"I am slain!"*

THREE: *"Give me a fresh horse!"*

> *(THREE stabs TWO.)*

"Sound the alarum!"

ONE: *"Help me I am your brother!"*

THREE: *"The devil!"*

> *(THREE stabs ONE)*

ONE: *"Oh justice!"*

> *(ONE stabs THREE)*

TWO: *"Now my revenge is perfect!* Sink thou the main cause of my undoing."

> *(TWO stabs THREE)*

THREE: *"Whether we fall by ambition, blood or lust,* We are like diamonds cut with our own dust."

> *They die. Extravagantly. Beautifully. Gloriously.*

BIG GUN SHOT off stage, Followed by an aggressive KNOCK ON THE DOOR. The ANGEL enters carrying THREE funeral shrouds and hangs them on the wardrobe rack. They look a bit like kimonos— kind of "geisha—glam."

ANGEL: I have your shrouds.

ONE: You're an angel.

ANGEL: Took a little longer tonight. I gave them a really good steam.

THREE: I was starting to worry.

ANGEL You have five minutes.

THREE: It's only two pages.

ANGEL: Yeah but they're playing the shit out of it. As if the audience actually cared.

ONE: You don't think so?

ANGEL: It's called "Duchess of Malfi" not "Bosola the Psychotic Avenger." After the blood spurts from his groin the fun's over.

TWO: That is cold.

The Angel starts to dress each of them in their shrouds.

ANGEL: Honey, please, I'm supposed to give a shit about the agonizing deaths of a handful of mass murderers? At the three hour mark, all I have to say is: Good Riddance. And then, they parade out that horror—stricken child! I mean really people, just leave well enough alone. That toddler stands out there in blood up to his knees: his father's been gutted, one uncle still has the gun hanging out of his mouth, and the other uncle's pinned to the stage with a sword through his scrotum. All in the name of vengeance for his mother's death?! Honey, there is not enough Wellbutrin in the world to putty up those psychic cracks. You think that kid's gonna grow up with progressive attitudes towards women? Hell, no! He'll take a child bride, probably his first cousin, fuck a courtesan, and farm his daughters out to some skanky ladies in waiting.

The Angel points to TWO's crooked seams on her stockings.

Sweetheart: Seams. Give the garters a yank.

Alright ladies, Knock em dead.

Angel leaves, slamming the door.
Beat.

THREE: Last looks?

All THREE women pull out a Nars "Orgasm" blush, a "Great Lash" mascara, and a Mac "Viva Glam" lipstick from the drawers beneath the counter.

ONE: Orgasm?

All THREE women begin to apply blush. They make their "Blush Face" in the mirror. (You know the one.)

THREE: Always.

TWO: I finally got my own.

ONE: Essential.

THREE: Great Lash.

All THREE women apply mascara. "Mascara Faces."

ONE: Perennial favorite.

THREE: And for the finale . . .

TWO: Viva Glam!

All THREE women apply lipstick. Yep, "Lipstick Faces."

ONE: Ready?

TWO: OK!

THREE: Darlin, you and those seams. You're a wreck!

TWO: It's the garters—they're pinching.

THREE: Here I'll give you a tug.

TWO: Oh fuck ouch. Sorry.

ONE notices a particularly gruesome bruise just under the garter on the back of TWO:'s leg.

THREE: Oh my god, is that real?

TWO: I bruise easily.

THREE: Oh honey.

TWO: It looks worse than it is.

THREE: Is it tender to the touch?

ONE touches TWO's bruise.

TWO: Ow. Sorry. Yes.

THREE: From your death?

TWO: Two nights ago.

ONE: Arnica.

THREE: Quickly.

ONE: Real injuries are not OK. This decides it.

TWO: I don't really mind.*

ONE: *We need to say something.

TWO: *(continuous)* *Makes me feel like I'm doing it for real.

ONE: Sweetheart after 40 years of eight shows of week, a badge of honor starts to feel more like a hip replacement.*

THREE: *(simultaneous)* *Tomorrow, I'm going to call the UNION.

TWO: *(simultaneous)* *Really, I kind of like it.

No one can see it through the fishnets.

ONE: *(As she applies the arnica to TWO:'s leg)* Standing on the backs of all of those feminists while they roll in their graves is starting to feel frighteningly precarious.

    Beat.

TWO: Wait, what?*

ONE: *Standing on the backs of all of those feminists/

TWO: *(simultaneous)* *Oh never mind, I get it. Cause we're all like *victimized* and then we're all like *glam*?

THREE: The *character* was brutalized, *I* was triumphant. I'm not going out there looking frightful.

ONE: *(attack)* I'm not surprised you find honesty frightening.

THREE: *(attack)* Don't think I don't understand your delicately shrouded barbs.

ONE: *(attack)* A facility with delicacy, I wouldn't have guessed.

TWO: *(pacify)* Um, guys?

THREE: My agents are here tonight. I'm going red carpet, or not at all.

TWO: Who are you with again?

THREE: I only talk business over cocktails.

    ONE starts taking off her shroud

ONE: If ever there were a night for this./

THREE: *(simultaneous)* /What are you doing?*

TWO: *(simultaneous)* /For real?

I've always had this kind of secret fantasy about going out there totally wrecked.

THREE: *(continuous)* *Do we really have to make a stand tonight?

ONE: Do you have any leftover blood?

TWO: Only what's on the floor.

    ONE drops to her knees/ and starts to scoop up the

blood with her hands and smear it onto her face.

THREE: Oh, no, please, not, the,/ oh god, do you know what's probably on that floor!?

TWO: /Oh wow. You're for real. This is happening. This is totally hot.

> *TWO starts to disrobe and smears her Viva Glam all over her face.*

THREE: Ladies, please let's just think about this for a moment!

> *TWO starts messing up her hair.*

TWO: Will we get fired?

ONE: Who else are they gonna get to do all of this shit for 50 bucks a night?

TWO: Arnica makes like awesome hair gel.

ONE: Squirt some in my hand.

TWO: (*to THREE*) You want some?

THREE: Couldn't we be feminists on a night when my agents aren't here?

TWO: Too late.

ONE: Stand with your sisters.

THREE: You guys—

ONE: Be a woman! Back—comb for feminism!

> *We hear applause from the audience. The curtain call has started.*

TWO: Oh shit. That's like applause.

ONE: Join us?

TWO: It'll be way more fun if you come too.

THREE: Are they *hooting*?

TWO: Ooh! I love it when they scream and shout.

ONE: (*As she goes*) Hurry if you're coming!

TWO: (*Following TWO out the door*) Come! Please!

> *THREE is left alone. She takes one last hopeless look in the mirror and then,*

THREE: Fuck Fuck Fuck.

> *Pulls her hair down, rips off the "shroud," smears her lipstick. Attempts to bow grandly in front of the mirror,*

THREE: Oh, Fuck It.

> *Takes off running.*

The End

SERVERFRIENDS

Jason Chimonides.

PRODUCTION NOTES:

SERVERFRIENDS premiered at the 2011 Public Reading Series produced through the Playwrights Initiative Residency Program at the Blue Ridge Summer Theatre Festival - Endstation Theatre Company in Sweet Briar, VA on July 11ᵗʰ, 2011. It was directed by Jason Chimonides.

Cast
 GABE, Walter Kmiec
 JARED, Dan Caffrey
 ANNA, Natalie Caruncho.

Producer: Michael Stablein, Head of Playwright's Initiative, Endstation Theater Company, playwrights@endstationtheatre.org

CHARACTERS:
GABE, eighteen
ANNA, seventeen
JARED, seventeen

AUTHOR NOTES ON -PUNCTUATION:
A / indicates the commencement of the other character's
interruption.
. . . discovering, formulating
Lingering, noticing, decaying . . .
- the energy - flows - forward -
The energy is interup-
A lot. Of periods. Provide space. For actors. To make the
rhythms. Their own. Please do.

SPACE: Can be minimally or maximally indicated. Your
     choice.
TIME: It's always the present.

> *Black.*
> *Silence.*
> *The dull, rushing drone of patterned noise grows*
> *slowly in volume, till:*
> *A nearly empty train car bumps into view - hurtling*
> *somewhere fast.*
> *Ensconced at one end - a teenage couple, asleep,*
> *entwined.*
> *They share a pair of earbuds which swag loosely*
> *between their fused heads.*
> *A well dressed TEENAGE BOY, approximately the*
> *same age as the couple, instantly appears.*
> *Approaching them silently, he examines their physi-*
> *cal interconnection for a beat, then sits motionlessly*
> *next to them.*
> *The dull, rushing drone of patterned noise . . .*
> *He laughs.*
> *The COUPLE GIRL, bleary, stirs . . .*
> *Drowsily detecting the TEENAGE BOY, now barely*
> *leaning on her, she starts - jolting into motion and*

violently shaking her companion awake.

As the earbud tether is broken, the couple bobble upright, then begin to madly stalk the space for escape.

This goes on for a significant interval, but to no avail, as the TEENAGE BOY's laughing turns to howling and the COUPLE BOY and COUPLE GIRL eventually relent, huddling and breathing roughly in the opposite corner from where they began.

The dull, rushing drone of—

TEENAGE BOY: *(to COUPLE BOY, from across the train)* Your thighs.

> *Beat.*

COUPLE BOY: . . . Huh?

TEENAGE BOY: Your thighs. Bout the same size. *(beat)* As hers. As each others. Never noticed that before. It's a nice detail.

> *Pause.*

TEENAGE BOY: So. I've been talking with people. Outworld. Outworld people. I've been investigating. Poking around. And nobody I know . . . *Nobody.* This? What you two're. Attempting. Trying to. I'm not sure it's ever happened before. Maybe it has. In beta testing. Or something. Is that what it's called? Beta Testing? Maybe in some. Fucking. Mathematical. Model. Statistical. Or some shit. But I guess it was inevitable huh. Sooner or later. This was bound to happen.

> *Beat.*

COUPLE GIRL: . . . whattya gonna do to us Gabe?

GABE: I'm gonna pout. Anna. I'm gonna bleat. I might even cry. My eyes. Right now. *Prickling* with tears. I might delete you both.

> *The couple look fearfully at one another.*
>
> *Pause.*

GABE: . . . cause see. You've wounded my pride. Bad. So I might just get back into my body. And I might just delete you both forever. *Unambivalently.* Cause. What are you anyway? Really. You're data. Only. Information. You're

non-existent. This train car. Non-existent. The night. That
night. Beyond. Windows.

He moves to a window.

GABE: . . . kinda like black mirrors . . . Non-existent. That
rushing sound? Non-existent. This serverBody I'm in? You
should see what I *really* look like. All an *effect*.

Beat.

He leans in close to them.

GABE: Just a buncha sad little zeroes and ones. And you two.
Worst. Of all.

COUPLE BOY: *(almost tenderly)* Gabe. Gabe . . .

Silence. GABE starts to weep. Then gets very angry.
He stomps. Scatters, kicking. He stops cold, smears
his eyes.

GABE: *(sotto)* So what does it matter. Huh? If I delete you?
If I stamp out your little. Rebellion. It's my right. Right? I
thought we were friends.

Beat.

GABE: . . . were we ever *actually* friends?

Beat.

GABE: C'mon. All the rad stuff we did together . . . inWorld?
Sinkholes. Skinny dipping that one time. The Gravitron?
'Member that? Making plays together. Killing things. That
was *really* fun. Wasn't it? A total riot.

ANNA: Most of the time . . .

JARED: Anna . . .

Beat.

GABE: What of the time..?

ANNA: We had to sit. Most of the time we just sat and watched
you get high.

JARED: *(to ANNA, quietly)* Gabe. We still love you. / I know
this hurts.

ANNA: . . . had to listen to how much you *hated* yourself.
Hate yourself. How fucking *bored* you are. / You're not
bored enough . . .

GABE: That's not true! That's not true. I *love* myself. But I
never set that you two. I never set that you two could stop
loving me and start loving *each other*. *(beat)* Never *set* for
that. The settings? serverFriends don't love each other un-

less the user *sets* for it! Unless *I* set for it. *And I never set for it!* It's impossible. You're supposed to be mine.

Beat.

GABE: And you actually thought you could run away. Run away in serverWorld! Run away where?! *(beat)* Moxie. Yeah. Delusion. Okay. So. Here's what I'm gonna . . . Here's what I'm gonna do . . .

Suddenly distracted, GABE digs into his pocket and produces a small, black screen. It flickers with blue-diode light.

GABE: *(his eyes dancing at the device)* Fuck . . . *(beat)* It's my Mom. *(beat)* She broke into my world. *Succubus.* I have to take it. Have to. *How the fuck did she find them . . . ?!*

The couple look piercingly at one another.

GABE: *(distracted, intensely irritated)* Hold on . . . just . . . lemme . . . gotta get back. Hate fucking. Getting back in my body . . . just . . . stay . . . right there . . . stay right here . . . .

GABE's serverBody goes instantly limp and then freezes, discarded. The skin is grey. Voided. The body stands crumpled and inert in the center of the car.

Pause.

JARED: *(looking out the window)* . . . do you think. It'll be day soon? Or is it always night on this world? *(beat)* Does this world even have day you think? Or is it always just . . .

ANNA notices the earbuds dangling from JARED's pocket. Gathering them, she tenderly places one first in his ear and then in hers.

JARED: *(listening)* It's still playing.

They kiss. Deeply, but awkwardly.

ANNA: He's gonna be back Jared. He sealed the car.

Pause.

JARED: I love you so much . . .

Pause. Interlacing their fingers, he brings his head close to hers.

JARED: . . . listen listen. Listen. This is my favorite . . . part . . . this is . . .

(singing softly, sweetly)
READ THE RIPPLES IN THE POND TO SAY
BEND THE CURTAINS BACK

LET'S GO OUT AND PLAY
GO OUT AND PLAY
COME PLAY TODAY
WATCH IT DECAY
WATCH IT DECAY
WATCH IT DECAY
> *The dull rushing drone of patterned noise . . .*
> *LIGHT FADES . . .*

The End

Storms, Sheets, and Show Tunes

Stacey Lane

Production Notes:

Storms, Sheets, and Show Tunes was produced in July 2011 by the Sage Players in Spokane, Washington. Producer: Paul F. Ruch. Artistic Director: Anne Selcoe. Director: Roseanne Lasater. Stage Manager: Robert Nelson.

Cast

SKIP SMITH, Mark J. W. Elston
PATTY MERT, Lynn Noel
JAMES BLAKE BILLINGTON, Paul F. Ruch
LADONNA DAILY, Judith Albrecht
EDWIN BLACKHEART, Marek G. Nelson
GIRL, Patricia Hewitt

CHARACTERS:

SKIP SMITH, An anxious, fresh-faced, dull-witted ghost

PATTY MERT, A go-getting do-gooder of a ghost

JAMES BLAKE BILLINGTON, A minuscule man of a ghost with a booming voice

LADONNA DAILY, A theatre-loving ghost waiting for her prime

EDWIN BLACKHEART, An ancient ghoul who has seen and done it all with no remorse

GIRL, A grief-stricken young woman

SCENE: The stage of the Hartman Theatre in Columbus, Ohio
TIME: 1971

> *AT RISE: The lights come up on the stage of the Hartman Theatre in Columbus, Ohio in 1971. PATTY MERT, a plump and perky ghost, sits authoritatively behind a table cluttered with papers. An empty chair is next to her. On the other side of the stage, five chairs are set-up in a line. In the first sits, SKIP SMITH, a nervous, young ghost, clutching a back pack and frantically filling out a form attached to a clipboard. The second chair is empty. The back of the third chair is being used as a dance bar by LADONNA DAILY, a determined ghost, in the process of doing an intense physical and vocal acting warm-up. The fourth chair is empty. The final chair is occupied by the stoic ghost of EDWIN BLACKHEART. He simply stares forward, deadpan, uninterested in the flurry around him. After a moment, SKIP jumps up and hurries over to PATTY's table, clipboard in hand.*

SKIP: Okey dokey. I got this thing filled out for ya and here's my resume, but where it says headshot—

PATTY: Hun, if you don't have—

SKIP: You see ma'am, I wasn't shot in the head. I fell off a roof.

PATTY: This will be fine, honey. If you'll just have a seat, we'll be getting started as soon as—

> *(JAMES BLAKE BILLINGTON, a tiny ghost with a large nasally voice to overcompensate his small stature, bustles in and crosses to the table. SKIP scampers to his chair. LADONNA takes her seat, sitting at attention.)*

JAMES: Patty, how many times did I tell you—Bring them in groups of five! Five! Not three. Can't you do anything correctly?

PATTY: This is it, boss.

JAMES: I beg your pardon.

PATTY: This is everybody that showed up.

JAMES: But how can that—

PATTY: I guess the stage just isn't as popular as it used to be. Now everybody wants to haunt Hollywood.

JAMES: The bastard art! In my day, the legitimate theatre—

PATTY: Well, it looks like this is what we're stuck with, chief. Wanna get started?

JAMES: Very well. Good evening ladies and gentlemen, ghouls and boys. As I am sure you are well aware, I am James Blake Billington, your director. Although too numerous to mention, my casting credits include the Palace Theatre, the Huntington Playhouse, the Roundtown Theatre, Variety Theatre—

LADONNA: Wow!

JAMES: I'm certain you've heard of the legendary Miss Victoria, haunter of Victoria Theatre.

LADONNA: Of course.

JAMES: Well, I cast her—

LADONNA: *(Impressed)* Really?

JAMES: *(Overlapping)* Understudy.

LADONNA: Oh.

JAMES: But I don't wish to bore you with my extensive resume. We could be here for hours if I—

　　　(PATTY clears her throat.)

JAMES: Allow me to introduce my assistant director—

PATTY: Slash stage manager—

JAMES and PATTY: Patty Mert.

JAMES: And we are here, as you are well aware, to cast a replacement for the renowned, the legendary, Dr. Samuel J. Hartman, who not only built, but has haunted the Hartman Theatre, for nearly sixty years.

PATTY: But now wishes to retire to Hawaii to self-medicate with Peruna snake-oil cocktails—

JAMES: Leaving the American theatre with quite a void to fill—

PATTY: Which is where you *three* come in.

Lawrence Harbison

JAMES: Before I see your prepared auditions pieces, I would like to get to know each of you a little better by asking you where you are currently haunting—

PATTY: And why you would rather be haunting the Hartman.

JAMES: Young man, you may begin.

SKIP: Me? Well, um, hey! I'm Skip. Skip Smith.

JAMES: And?

SKIP: And?

PATTY: Where are you currently haunting?

SKIP: Buckeye Mart.

JAMES: And why do you wish to leave your current post?

SKIP: Cause its at Buckeye Mart.

JAMES: Can you elaborate?

SKIP: Well, um, I hate it there. Nobody 'spects a Buckeye Mart to be haunted, so nobody takes me seriously and stuff. If I knock over a display, they blame the stock boys. If I take bites out of the candy bars, they blame the kids or the rats. Nobody ever blames nothing supernatural.

PATTY: I see how that could be frustrating.

JAMES: Why would you like to haunt the Hartman?

SKIP: Cause it's not Buckeye Mart.

JAMES: Next.

LADONNA: (*Standing*) Good evening Mr. Billington, Ms. Mert. Allow me the pleasure of introducing myself. My name is Ladonna Daily and I am a life-time lover of the stage and all it stands for. I would be most honored to be selected to haunt the Hartman—

JAMES: Where do you currently haunt?

LADONNA: Well, I've been exploring my artistic options and bettering myself as an artist. I audition at every chance I—

JAMES: And where do you currently haunt?

LADONNA: A couple of restaurants part-time. It's a great study of human nature. And did I mention I've only been dead three months, so—

PATTY: And why would you like to haunt the Hartman?

LADONNA: I've always loved the theatre and I especially love this one. It feels like home to me. I auditioned here four times when I was alive.

EDWIN: How many times did you perform here?

LADONNA: *(Ignoring him)* Ever since I was a little girl, I've dreamed of being a theatre ghost one day, if the whole Broadway star thing didn't work out and I had to kill myself. And it didn't and I did. So here I am. Haunting a theatre is really something special. The raw emotions, the tension, the passion, the love, the hate that passes through the air flowing freely between the performers and the audience—well, it's magic. The pure joy of—

JAMES: Next.

EDWIN: Edwin Blackheart, at your service. I have had the privilege of haunting the Camp Chase Confederate Cemetery for the past one hundred odd years.

SKIP: Oh cool! A real dead graveyard ghost! Why the heck would you want to leave—

JAMES: *(Clearing his throat)* Why are you unsatisfied with your post?

EDWIN: Camp Chase is haunted by five other ghosts, three of which are less experienced than myself. Not to mention the Lady in Grey with her incessant crying fits. I desire to be the only one in the establishment which I haunt.

LADONNA: Let me guess. Don't play well with others?

EDWIN: Would you like to find out?

LADONNA: I'd rather die
> *(a beat)*

again.

PATTY: So why do you want to be the only ghost—

EDWIN: Differences in ideology. Case in point. Drunken lads come to the cemetery looking for a thrill. I believe we should not give them the satisfaction of getting what they came for. The others take the bate and play their foolish games. Now a grieving widow, crying at her beloved's graveside, that's more my taste.

LADONNA: That's sick.

PATTY: And so why the theatre?

EDWIN: John Wilkes Booth sparked my interest in the theatre and its possibilities.

JAMES: Let's move on to the prepared audition pieces shall we?
> *(To SKIP)*

Young man?

SKIP: Huh?

PATTY: Are you ready to audition?

SKIP: Right. Okay. Yeh. *(SKIP does not get up)*

PATTY: Well, whenever you're ready . . .

SKIP: Uh huh.

> *He grabs his bag, pulls out a white sheet which he stuffs behind his back and moves to center stage.)*

You ready?

JAMES: Please.

SKIP: Okey dokey. Here we go.

> *(SKIP throws the sheet over his head and stretches his arms out in front him and begins to move slowly around the stage.)*

Boooooohhhhhh! Ooooooohhhhhhhhhh!!!

JAMES: Next.

> *(SKIP takes off the sheet and returns to his seat. LADONNA jumps to her feet.)*

LADONNA: *(She takes center stage, closes her eyes, takes a deep breath, and opens her eyes, a huge smile plastered across her face.)*

Good evening. My name is Ladonna Daily, Auditonee number two. For my first piece, I will be singing "Meet Me in St. Louis" from the great Broadway musical *Meet Me in St. Louis* based on the great classic movie *Meet Me in St. Louis*.

> *(She puts a record on her record player and the musical accompaniment begins to play. She sings slightly off key with musical theatre zest.)*

Meet me in St. Louis, Louis,

Meet me at the fair,

Don't—

JAMES: Next.

LADONNA: *(Holding her ground)* For my next piece, I, Ladonna Daily, Auditonee number two, will perform a monologue from *Romeo and Juliet* by the great William Shakespeare. I will be portraying to role of Juliet.

> *(She closes her eyes, takes a deep breath and gets into character. Her acting, while not awful, does leave something to be desired.)*

O Romeo, Romeo! Wherefore art thou Romeo?

Deny thy father and refuse—

JAMES: Next.

LADONNA: For my next piece, I, Ladonna Daily, Auditionee number two, will perform a tap dance to "I Got Rhythm" by the great George Gershwin. If you will just allow me a moment to put on my tap shoes—

JAMES: No. Next.

LADONNA: For my next—

JAMES: Sit down, Miss Weekly.

LADONNA: It's Daily.

JAMES: Don't correct me. Next.

LADONNA: But I still have so much more to show you. I'm a triple threat.

JAMES: I don't feel threatened.

LADONNA: That's because you haven't given me a chance to—

JAMES: Ms. Yearly, your audition made Skip's sheet shit seem almost appropriate.

SKIP: *(Cheerfully)* Thanks.

PATTY: What Mr. Billington is trying to say is we don't think you understand what you are auditioning for, honey.

JAMES: What Mr. Billington is trying to say is NEXT!

LADONNA: *(Not budging)* I'm suppose to show you what I would do if I was haunting the Hartman and if I was haunting the Hartman, I would wander the empty corridors singing the haunting tunes of Gershwin and the exhausted techie working a late night would wonder if it was just the wind or maybe something a little more. I'd softly tap dance in the attic and the lonely old janitor working early on a Sunday morning would stop and think, "Hmm, do we have raccoons with rhythm or could it be something bigger?" I'd recite Shakespeare on that cold empty stage just before the actors arrived for a long hard day of rehearsal and maybe they'd catch a glimpse of me out of the corner of their eyes and then they'd know they are not alone. In this scary, hurtful world of sacrificing your heart, your mind, your body, and your soul to create art for strangers, laying yourself out bare each day to be accepted or rejected—

JAMES: Next!

(EDWIN silently strides forward, forcefully pushing LADONNA back to her sear. He takes center stage,

makes a dramatic arm gesture and the entire theatre is plunged into darkness. EDWIN exits the stage in the darkness and goes into the audience. SKIP screeches in fear.)

PATTY: You're scared of the dark? Hun, you're a ghost!

SKIP: Buckeye Mart is always very well lit. I guess I've just gotten used to—

JAMES: Shhh! I think this is his audition.

(There is an unnerving silence.)

LADONNA: Well, isn't this exciting?

JAMES: Silence.

(In the audience, EDWIN breaths heavily into the ear of an audience member. Then he runs an ice cube down the back of the neck of a female audience member. Ideally, this will illicit a scream or other verbal response, but regardless, EDWIN then lets out a low, terrifying howl and the lights flicker on and off as he rushes down the center aisle and leaps onto the stage.)

LADONNA: *(Yawning)* Cheap party tricks.

(Through impressive gestures and vocalization, ED-WIN conjures a storm. Lighting flashes. Wind howls. Thunder crashes. Throughout the theatre, doors can be heard opening and closing and the papers on the table are picked up by the wind (a fan offstage) and flutter to the ground. As the fury of the storm increases, windows offstage can be heard breaking.)

LADONNA: Stop! You're breaking—The Hartman is a histori-cal . . . You can't just . . . Please . . . please stop.

(Smiling wickedly, EDWIN increases the violence in his gestures and more glass can be heard shattering offstage. Other loud crashing noises follow. If possible, some curtains onstage should come crashing down. At the height of the chaos, EDWIN makes a final gesture and everything goes silent and still. EDWIN solemnly bows.)

JAMES: You're hired.

PATTY: Wait! No! First we need to have an artistic—

JAMES: Patty, what part of the A-S-S- period in front of your title, do you fail to comprehend? If I say he's hired—

PATTY: *(To SKIP, LADONNA, and EDWIN)* We need to have a little directors' meeting. Talk among yourselves.

(They don't. She pulls JAMES aside.)

Look, boss. I just don't trust him. Trust me on this. He gives me the creeps.

JAMES: Patty, we're hiring him to haunt a theatre, not baby-sit your kids. You don't need to trust—

PATTY: Theatre audiences are dwindling as it is. I don't think we need a ghost that's going to scare them all away. What we need is somebody like—

JAMES: Like who-Surely not sheet boy?

PATTY: No, of course not. But, well, the girl, maybe.

JAMES: Absolutely not.

PATTY: Why not give her a chance, chief?

JAMES: She's a girl.

PATTY: *(Puffing up)* Just what's that suppose to—

JAMES: Samuel Hartman was not.

PATTY: Was not what—

JAMES: A girl.

PATTY: So?

JAMES: So . . . We are casting his replacement. The people will expect a male ghost to—

PATTY: I don't see why that should—

JAMES: Besides she has not a single discernible ounce of talent.

PATTY: But her heart's in the right place. What she said about what a theatre ghost should do—

(Crying is heard offstage.)

JAMES: What was that?

PATTY: *(Crossing and looking offstage)* Looks like we got a live one, boss.

JAMES: *(Clapping his hands once)* Your attention please! A *not-yet-deceased* is headed in this direction. Please be discrete.

(SKIP dives to the ground, throwing his sheet on top of him. LADONNA strikes a dramatic musical theatre-style pose, perhaps the splits. PATTY ducks under the table. JAMES stands against a wall or the proscenium. EDWIN holds his guard. A GIRL enters, sobbing, clutching a newspaper clipping. She crosses to the center of the

---

Lawrence Harbison

415

stage and looks out into the house in disbelief. EDWIN comes up behind her and breaths down her neck. She begins to shiver and cries even harder.)

LADONNA: *(Quietly)* I wonder what's wrong with her.

JAMES: Shhh!

(The GIRL looks at the newspaper and shakes her head in disbelief and looks around the stage.)

EDWIN: *(Looking down at the newspaper and reading the heading)* "Hartman Theatre to be Demolished".

JAMES: What?

(The GIRL rips up the newspaper into a few pieces and tosses them to the ground. She crosses to the edge of the stage and sits, defeated. JAMES, PATTY, EDWIN, and SKIP hurry over and immediately drop to the floor and reassemble the newspaper. They silently read it in disbelief. LADONNA watches the GIRL with concern.)

PATTY: This can't be—

JAMES: Patty, did you know about this?

PATTY: Of course not, boss.

JAMES: Well, you should have. That's your job. What a waste of my time.

(He exits in a huff.)

PATTY: Um, sorry folks. Auditions are cancelled. Thanks for coming out. Have a nice day.

SKIP: So I guess this means I'm going back to Buckeye Mart?

PATTY: Honey, I hate to break it you, but you were always going back to Buckeye Mart.

(She hurries after JAMES.)

EDWIN: It would seem Samuel Hartman picked a convenient time to retire. Never trust a snake oil salesman.

(SKIP and EDWIN exit.)

(LADONNA begins to hum a hauntingly beautiful tune as she crosses to the GIRL and sits next to her, gently stroking her hair. The GIRL's sobbing subsides and a faint glimmer of hope crosses her face as she looks across the theatre.)

(Lights down.)

The End

THAT THING YOU DO WITH YOUR TONGUE

R. D. Murphy

PRODUCTION NOTES:

THAT THING YOU DO WITH YOUR TONGUE was first produced by The Firehouse Center for the Arts in Newburyport MA, Kimm Wilkinson, Artistic Director. The 10th Annual New Works Festival ran from January 20 – 28, 2012. The production was directed by Jason Breitkopf.

Cast

TYNGSBORO, Stephen Faria
SERENA, Jennifer Wilson
DR. ANITA SAYLOR, Maureen Daley.

CHARACTERS:

TYNGSBORO DOG, personified by a twenty-something male, exuberant, sloppy, wants to be liked and loves everybody in the room.

SERENA CAT, personified by a twenty-something female. Sensual. High maintenance. Does not suffer fools gladly.

DR. ANITA SAYLOR, Physicist and part-time waitress, age thirty-five to forty-five. Professional, dispassionate, and objective. For a while anyway. Wears glasses and a lab coat.

> *NOTE: Actors playing TYNGSBORO and SERENA are asked not to pick up anything with their hands. Hand gestures are fine, elbows on the table are OK, but no lifting or grasping is permitted. And that goes for drinking.*

PLACE: A downtown restaurant. Early evening.

SCENIC NEEDS: Small table with two chairs. White tablecloth and a basket of peanuts on table. Note: A tray with additional glasses should be at the ready either close to, or under, the table.

Lights up on a downtown restaurant. TYNGSBORO and SERENA sit at a table waiting to be served.

TYNGSBORO: So my buddies put me up to it. I mean why not? Free meal and I mean they wouldn't pair you up with a monstah right? You're no monstah, right? I mean this has to go into a family paper. I'm Tyngsboro, by the way. From Leominster. [*Pronounced: LEM min ster*]
   (*TYNG leans over the table and smells SERENA. SERENA stiffens. She hisses.*)

SERENA: (*Recovers*) Luh—Leominster?

TYNGSBORO: Yeah. I mean no. No, I'm Tyngsboro FROM Leominster. I mean, if you said LEO- Minster, I could understand the confusion. That sounds like a name. But they call me Tyngsboro. Or TyngsBOBO. Tyng-man. Tyng-THING. (*He starts to get excited and gets up from the chair. End zone dance, vigorously shaking his butt.*) Tyng- THANG.

Tyng-THANG-BOOM-AND-BANG. The Tyng-stah. Tyng-meister. Tyng-mister-sir-YES- SIR. Roscoe—

SERENA: Roscoe?

(TYNG stops. Beat.)

TYNGSBORO: Maybe that was somebody else. Can I put my head in your lap?

SERENA: SIT. *(TYNG does so.)*

TYNGSBORO: What do they call you?

SERENA: I don't answer.

TYNGSBORO: When they want you to come. What do they call you?

SERENA: I don't come.

TYNGSBORO: *(To the audience)* Well, this will be a short night.

> *(He's back out of the chair. The end zone dance continues.)*

Tyng-stinator. Tyng-ka-bob. Tyng-KABOOM. Count von Tyngsborough: *(with accent)* "Listen to them the children of the night"

> *(TYNG gives a wolf howl. Takes a bow. Sits.)*
>
> *(Pause)*

SERENA: Serena.

TYNGSBORO: That's hot. And mad, uh, perky. Like you. Have some nuts.

> *(TYNG nudges the basket of peanuts with his nose.)*

SERENA: I don't do nuts.

TYNGSBORO: *(Beat. As if calling for a waiter.)* Check please.

SERENA: You can leave.

TYNGSBORO: No. KIDDING. I want to stay. I want to be with you. Can I put my head in your lap?

SERENA: SIT. *(TYNG does so.)*

TYNGSBORO: So why do you think they paired us up? What do you like to do? *(Beat. No answer)*I like to Run. Eat. Run. Drink. Run. Play. Run. Swim. And, ah, you know, run. You?

SERENA: *(Deliberately)* Lie in the sun. Meditate. Nap. Stare at the vast emptiness outside the window. Watch the dust in the air.—

Lawrence Harbison

TYNGSBORO: There's dust in the air? I don't smell anything.

SERENA:—Torment small creatures. Lick myself.

TYNGSBORO: Oh, me too. I can lick my—

> *(ANITA the waitress rushes the table carrying a tray of drinks. She is also a physicist. In fact, she is late for her waitress shift, having just left the lab. She wears glasses and has forgotten to take off her lab coat.)*

ANITA: This the *Dinner With Cupid* table? Here you go. Drinks on the house.

> *(She places two large—almost bowl-like—margarita glasses on the table. TYNG sniffs the glass and licks the rim. Slight growl, starts gnawing on the salt rim. SERENA does not move.*

ANITA: So drink up.

> *(TYNG is lapping it up. SERENA stares back at ANITA.)*

SERENA: *(Looking at ANITA'S lab coat)* Is this a test?

ANITA: Sorry, got out of the lab late. Funding crisis. *(Takes off lab coat and tosses it over her shoulder)* But, hey, that's not your problem. *(Encouraging her, ANITA pushes the glass towards her.)* Probably a good thing I'm a physicist. You're on a blind date. Question of attraction, right? Who better to measure? And here's yours, Princess.

> *(ANITA stares at SERENA. SERENA stares back. TYNG slurps, all over the table and his face.)*

SERENA: Can I help you?

ANITA: Can I help you?

SERENA: Not only is this room cold and tacky. There's an echo.

ANITA: However belated, I'll be your server this evening. My name's Anita, Anita Saylor. *(Yes, that sounds like "I need a sailor.")*

> *(TYNG does a spit take.)*

TYNGSBORO: *(To audience)* Fleet's in! (Looks at *ANITA*) The plot thickens. And so do her eyebrows.

ANITA: Please drink up.

TYNGSBORO: I'm done!

> *(SERENA looks at her glass then ANITA)*

TYNGSBORO: *(CONT'D)* I win! The Tyng-DOUBLE-X. TYNG TONG!

ANITA: *(To TYNG)* Good job. Very good job. You are wonder-ful. *(She musses his hair. His foot thumps.)* And so cute! *(To SERENA)* Girl, you lucked out.

TYNGSBORO: Can I put my head in your lap?

ANITA: *(Kindly)* I'm standing.

TYNGSBORO: *(Stands and starts hopping. To SERENA)* Something wrong with yours? Ya don't want it? I'll take it. I mean, if ya don't want—

SERENA AND ANITA: SIT *(TYNG does so.)*

> *(Pause. SERENA laps the drink. Once. She looks up for adulation.)*

ANITA: Amazing. Did you see that?

TYNGSBORO: Yeah. Uh. See what? No.

> *(SERENA laps the drink again.)*

TYNGSBORO: Oh. Yeah. Awesome. But I WON.

> *(SERENA laps a third time.)*

ANITA: I missed it. Please do it again.

TYNGSBORO: *(Again to the imaginary waiter)* ANOTHER ROUND HERE.

> BLACK OUT

> *(Dance music and/or restaurant sounds briefly heard. The lights come up quickly. The table is now covered with large mostly empty margarita glasses. The scientific study is well underway and highly lubricated.)*

ANITA: How the hell do you do that?

SERENA: *(Disingenuously)* Drink? Anyone can—

ANITA: Your whiskers remain perfectly dry.

SERENA: Perfectly.

TYNGSBORO: *(Looks up from his glass)* Whoa. Wait a minute—WHISKERS?

> *(TYNG leans across the table for a closer look. SERENA stiffens. She hisses.)*

SERENA: You got a problem with that?

TYNGSBORO: I mean, I noticed the eyelashes—

ANITA: Lashes to die for.

TYNGSBORO: Yeah, they're, ya know, pretty. But whiskers?

SERENA: You've got them too, dumbass.

Lawrence Harbison   421

TYNGSBORO: Yeah, but I'm—Okay. Ookaay. Ok. They're cute. On you they look good. I like 'em.

ANITA: You both have whiskers so that when you go through an opening you won't get stuck.

TYNGSBORO: *(Beat. To the audience)* Rrrrrr. And the plot ain't the only thing thickening around here.

ANITA: I just can't figure it out.

SERENA: Don't you have anything better to do?

ANITA: Never underestimate the mysteries of everyday life. Do you use those tiny hairs on the middle of your tongue?

TYNGSBORO: TONGUE HAIRS? Look: Whiskers . . . I'll give you a pass. But TINY HAIRS ON—

SERENA: A tongue like sandpaper.

TYNGSBORO: *(Involuntary flinch)* Ouch.

SERENA: Unlike your tongue? It's been hanging out so long, I thought you were wearing an old pink and grey tie.

TYNGSBORO: I mean you have a cute tongue. Like a tiny Slim Jim. A Slim Jim nugget. As they say in France, a pink Slim Jim *Noo GAY.*

SERENA: You trying to make me hurl a hair ball?

TYNGSBORO: *(Emphatic but still good hearted)* You're whacked, both of you. *(To ANITA)* "Mystery of everyday life." The best thing about everyday life is that there is no mystery. It happens everyday. Again and again and again. Thank god. That's why it's called *everyday life.*

(To SERENA)

And what's the fascination with dust? There's no smell. No grit. Ya can't roll in it and wear it around town like a hoodie of mud and feces.

ANITA: Tyngsboro, you're in a restaurant—

TYNGSBORO: *(Earnestly, using his indoor voice)* I didn't say shit, I said feces. *(To both. Back up to speed)* You want a tongue? This is a tongue. *(He holds the tip of his tongue for all to see.)* You take this tongue and make it into a LADLE. *(He lets go of the tongue.)* A big, warm, slobbering, soup ladle. You scoop, you slurp, you gulp. Repeat. As quickly as possible. So what if it gets on the table? So what is it get all over your face? That's what sleeves are for. *(He wipes his mouth with his forearms.)*

ANITA: *(Be that as it may. To Serena)* But how do you use that tiny pink tongue to lap up water?

SERENA: Give it a rest. You know, you would benefit from getting a life.

ANITA: My, you're a feisty one, Princess—

SERENA: AND MY NAME'S NOT PRINCESS, DAMMIT.

ANITA: I would benefit? I. Would. Benefit. I would benefit from a huge motherfucking research grant to design the next generation of soft robots that manipulate liquids. And the sizzle to that steak, the PR speed bump to that news cycle, the bullet to the top of that KA-CHING chart, the crack pipe to hook my so-called peer reviewers, *(ANITA takes a breath)* is to demonstrate-how-a-cat-manages-to-drink-liquid-without-getting-her-face- wet.

SERENA: *(Might be intimidated but won't show it)* You're cutting into my nap time.

ANITA: That's not all that's gonna get cut around here.

TYNGSBORO: *(Looks up from drink)* OW. Hey, don't kid that way.

> *(Pause.)*

SERENA: Okay. I am going to explain this once. Are you listening, Cam Jansen super-sleuth?

> *(SERENA has their attention. The following is conveyed with an enticing and luxuriating air and may be accompanied by some catlike stretches. She is, after all, the center of the universe.)*

SERENA: *(CONT'D)* I extend my tongue and curl it into a "J". *(TYNG and ANITA do likewise.)* A reverse "J", you dipshits. *(Not so easy for TYNG and ANITA.)* I descend. The front of my supple moist tongue caresses the liquid surface juuusssst barely grazing without penetrating.

> *(TYNG howls.)*

SERENA AND ANITA: SIT. *(TYNG does so)*

SERENA: I retract my tongue and the tip draws a liquid column up through the sheer power of attraction. I draw the undulating pillar of liquid toward me. Inertia and gravity push and pull, ebb and flow, the eternal dance, until the precise moment they are in balance when . . . . I close my mouth. I swallow. My face remains dry. *(Beat)* Repeat. So slow you would moan but so quick you would not know why.

Lawrence Harbison

(Pause)

ANITA: *(Quietly)* Thank you, Princess.

TYNGSBORO: *(To the audience)* Anybody got a cigarette? *(Beat)*

Hey, it's time for grading the date!

ANITA: Right. You each need to evaluate your date on a scale of A to D. *(Looking at SERENA)* May I add parenthetically, no one's ever given a D.

TYNGSBORO: God, I'm so happy. If I had an extra leg, I'd hump it.

SERENA: *(To ANITA)* Take off the glasses.

ANITA: *(Starts to clear the table.)* Are you finished?

SERENA: No. Your glasses. Take them off.

ANITA: *(She does so. Perhaps loosens her hair.)* Do you find me attractive?

SERENA: No.

ANITA: Do you think you will ever love me?

SERENA: No. But I might keep you around.

TYNGSBORO: *(An Olympic judge)* I grade Serena A + + +.

SERENA: That's all?

TYNGSBORO: I can get more pluses? *(To ANITA)* And I give you an A too because, because, well, because you're nice. And you patted my head. And you gave us drinks.

ANITA: Thank you. And you, Serena?

SERENA: I give TyngsBOBO a D.

ANITA: D?

TYNGSBORO: D?

ANITA: No one's ever—

TYNGSBORO: No plusses? Did I use up all the plusses?

SERENA: Minus. D-.

(Pause. TYNGSBORO is devastated. Sad puppy eyes to the audience.)

SERENA: *(To ANITA)* You may take me home now.

TYNGSBORO: What about me?

SERENA: Get another leg.

(ANITA looks at Tyngsboro. She wants to pat him under the chin.)

SERENA *(CONT'D)(To ANITA)* What part of "you may take me home now" don't you believe?

(Scientific objectivity gone with the wind, ANITA

escorts SERENA out. TYNGSBORO is left sitting with his head bowed. He slowly raises his sad puppy eyes. He notices a member of the audience.)

TYNGSBORO: *(Whispers)* Can I put my head in your lap?

(There will be an audience response. He notices another audience member. Louder.)

Can I put my head in YOUR lap?

(Response grows. So do his spirits. To another audience member:)

Can I put my head in your lap?

(He roams the edge of the stage.)

Can I? Can I? Can I put my head in your lap? YES!

(TYNG goes into his end zone dance. Dance music is heard.)

Blackout

The End

THERE'S NO HERE HERE

Craig Pospisil

for Lanford Wilson

PRODUCTION NOTES:

THERE'S NO HERE HERE was produced as part of an evening entitled CAUGHT IN THE ACT . . . AGAIN at Theatre Daedalus (Artistic Director: Jeremy Sony) in Columbus, Ohio in March 26, 2011. It was directed by James F. Petsche: lighting design by Gerry Pyle: and the stage manager was Jaylene Henderson. The cast was as follows:

Cast:
    JULIETTE, Laila Newell
    JEAN-LUC, Jim LeVally
    GERTRUDE, Amy Anderson
    LANCE, Brant Jones

CHARACTERS:

JULIETTE, a beautiful, chic Parisian woman in her twenties or thirties

JEAN-LUC, a waiter at the café, full of ennui. thirties, forties or fifties

GERTRUDE, a frumpy American woman in her forties or fifties

LANCE, an American writer, verging on desperate, in his late thirties or forties

PLACE: what appears to be a Parisian sidewalk café
TIME: what appears to be the present

> *(A Parisian café. Spring. French music, perhaps something by Serge Gainsbourg, plays in the background.*
> *JULIETTE, beautiful and chic, sits at a small café table, reading a book, Camus' L'Etranger. A menu lies on the table. Another woman, GERTRUDE, in frumpy clothes, sits at another table with her back to the audience. She does not turn around until indicated. She has a glass of rosé wine which she sips from time to time.*
> *JEAN-LUC, a bored French waiter in a white apron, enters with a cup of coffee, which he sets down on Juliette's table. She nods a thank you to him. He gestures to the menu on her table. "Anything else?" Juliette shakes her head, "no." Jean-Luc shrugs, a little put out, but it means less work for him. He takes the menu and starts to exit, when LANCE comes barreling in, carrying a notebook. Juliette looks up as he stops in front of her.)*

LANCE: You can't touch someone's life like that and then just bedone with them!

> *(Juliette stares at Lance, confused. She looks at Jean-Luc, who shrugs. They both look at Lance, who drops his notebook on Juliette's table and turns to the audience.)*

LANCE: At least, that's what I wanted to say.

> *(slight pause)*

There's a lot of things I want to say. I don't actually saymost of them.

> *(slight pause)*

Or anything like them really. It comes out wrong.

(slight pause)
So, that's what I wanted to say, but I think what I actually said was:
(turning back to Juliette, plaintively)
Why won't you answer my calls?
JULIETTE: Lance . . . chérie, cette chose entre nous, c'est fini.
(Lance winces and holds up his hand to her to say "wait." He turns back to the audience.)
LANCE: Sorry. Uh, we're in France. Paris, actually. Left Bank, not far from the Seine. Does everyone speak French? No?
(turning back to the others)
You've got to speak in English.
JULIETTE: Quoi?
LANCE: Parlez en anglais.
JULIETTE: Pourquoi?
LANCE: Parce que.
(He points at the audience. Juliette sighs and shrugs.)
JULIETTE: Okay.
(Lance looks at Jean-Luc, who simply shakes his head.)
JEAN-LUC: Non.
LANCE: Come on.
JEAN-LUC: Non.
LANCE: They won't understand. That's rude.
JEAN-LUC: Oui.
(Jean-Luc exits. Lance turns back to Juliette, who goes back to her book.)
LANCE: Juliette—
JULIETTE: I have nothing to say to you.
LANCE: You're being unreasonable.
JULIETTE: I am a French woman.
LANCE: But this is why I'm here. I came here to write.
JULIETTE: Oh, yes, you saved, for years you saved so you could come to Paris and write, just to write.
LANCE: Yes! But now there's also you.
JULIETTE: Hmmmpf.
(She continues reading. Lance reaches over and takes the book from her hands.)

LANCE: Juliette—

JULIETTE: Donnez-moi ce livre!

LANCE: In English.

JULIETTE: Give me my book.

(He hands her back the book.)

JULIETTE: You want to write, fine. Go be with your words. I have words too, and my word is "Good-bye."

LANCE: All I said was that I needed to work this afternoon.

JULIETTE: Yes, one afternoon after another. Hmmmpf.

LANCE: Why can't we just talk about this?

JULIETTE: You talk and you talk and you talk until the talking is over.

GERTRUDE: *(turning around)* Oh, I like that.

(Lance and Juliette look at her.)

GERTRUDE: Don't mind me, I'm just listening in.

LANCE: Um . . . we're having a private conversation.

GERTRUDE: In a public place.

LANCE: Do you mind?

GERTRUDE: All right. I'm sorry.

LANCE: That's okay.

GERTRUDE: You don't mean that.

LANCE: Sure, I do.

GERTRUDE: No, you're just being polite.

JULIETTE: Who is this person?

LANCE: I have no idea.

GERTRUDE: Yes, you do.

LANCE: No. I don't.

GERTRUDE: You're never going to write something true if you keep that up.

(Lance stops and stares at her. On some level he now recognizes, but he's unable to place her.)

LANCE: Wait, are . . . who are you?

GERTRUDE: Garçon?

(Jean-Luc, full of ennui, enters.)

JEAN-LUC: Oui, madame?

GERTRUDE: A glass of rosé, please.

JEAN-LUC: Certainement.

(Jean-Luc exits.)

LANCE: You already have a glass of wine.

GERTRUDE: It won't last forever.

JULIETTE: Ooo! You come here, you interrupt my reading, saying you must talk to me, why won't I talk to you . . . and then you stand and talk with this . . . stranger, meanwhile my café crème has gone cold, and my temper is hot.

GERTRUDE: She's a spitfire.

LANCE: Just hold on there's something . . .

JULIETTE: There is something, yes, there is something! This is how it always is with you. You see only what is right in front of you and the rest just fades away. You expect me—me, a beautiful French woman!—to be here when you want me, but even when you are here, you are not here.

GERTRUDE: There's no here here.

(Jean-Luc returns with a glass of wine, which he sets on Gertrude's table.)

JEAN-LUC: Voila, madame.

GERTRUDE: Merci.

(Jean-Luc turns and leaves again. Gertrude swirls the wine in her glass and takes a sniff of its bouquet.)

GERTRUDE: A rosé is a rosé is a rosé.

LANCE: Oh, my god!

JULIETTE: What?

LANCE: She's Gertrude Stein!

JULIETTE: Who?

LANCE: A famous American writer who lived in Paris in the Nineteen Twenties and Thirties.

JULIETTE: That's impossible.

GERTRUDE: I prefer it that way. If it can be done, why do it?

LANCE: No, no, no . . .

(turning to the audience)

I'm sorry, I don't know why she's here.

(back to Gertrude)

LANCE: *(CONT.)* You can't be here. You're dead.

(back to the audience)

She's dead.

GERTRUDE: Who are you talking to?

LANCE: Them.

GERTRUDE: So, having a fight with your girlfriend in café in Paris while an audience somewhere else watches you is okay, but talking to a woman who's been dead since 1946, that's going too far?

LANCE: Okay, this is . . . this is . . .

GERTRUDE: This is your story.

LANCE: Story?

JULIETTE: Wait, you are writing this?

LANCE: Oh, my god, I think I am.

JULIETTE: You! You come to make this big scene here at the café, to talk, to make me take you back . . . but you are somewhere still writing?!

LANCE: *(a beat)* Yes?

JULIETTE: You are a bad lover.

LANCE: Juliette, you—

JULIETTE: *(cutting him off)* And! You are a bad writer.

GERTRUDE: Bam, said the lady.

LANCE: Do you mind?!

GERTRUDE: Hey, this is your imagination. You don't want me here, say the word.

LANCE: Go!

GERTRUDE: That's not the word.

LANCE: Look, please just . . . go back to your table and finish your wine.

GERTRUDE: Sorry, Lance. I aim to misbehave.

(Hearing wine mentioned, Jean-Luc returns.)

JEAN-LUC: Un peu plus de vin?

LANCE: Juliette, please this is—

JULIETTE: Don't bother speaking. I hear the lies already.

LANCE: No. I'm here to write. This could be my last chance. Something either happens this year or . . . I've been doing this since I was twenty-two, and all I've got to show are a couple of short stories in an anthology, an agent that won't take my calls, and . . . . I'm divorced. I don't have any kids. I have a cat. I found her in an alley around the corner from here, and I call her Elle. I saved her life, but she only pays attention to me when it's time to eat. I just want to get something down on the page that's alive. But I haven't been able to. Then I met you, and I feel something. And it inspires me to write, and—

(Juliette slaps him.)

GERTRUDE: Affection can be so dangerous.

JEAN-LUC: Pardon, monsieur, mais

LANCE: Would you go away? Can't you just ignore us like most Parisian waiters?!

JEAN-LUC: No. I will not. I have, as you say, a bone to pick. My role in this story of yours is nothing more than an insulting cliché. A rude French waiter? Oo-la-la! So clever. How did you ever come up with an idea such as that? *(slight pause)* Feh! No wonder you have no success. You have the imagination of a cow. I don't even have a name in this scenario of yours.

(waving a hand toward the audience)

To them, I am just the French waiter, full of ennui, saying only "oui" and "non" because your French is too poor to allow me to truly give voice to all that is inside me. And I'm supposed to just go in and out bringing you wine and coffee while you play out this ridiculous scene with this woman, telling her you "feel something," instead of telling her you love her. If you love her, you take action. You don't plead and moan about writing words. What are words? Will they love you anymore than your cat? But like all Americans all you think of is yourself and you miss the point completely. In love you should act and act decisively! A woman like this needs to be grabbed hard, and then held tenderly.

(Jean-Luc suddenly takes hold of Juliette's arms and pulls her to him in a flash, and then instantly holds her tenderly in his arms. Their faces are close. He caresses her face with one hand.)

Darling. Your cool beauty overwhelms me. You are like a tonic to a man lying in bed with malaria and a high fever, on the knife's edge between life and death. You are water in the desert. You give me life, you give me breath.

JULIETTE: Oh, Jean-Luc.

JEAN-LUC: *(suavely)* Yes . . .

(then looking to Lance)

. . . that is my name.

JULIETTE: Jean-Luc, will you take me away from here?

JEAN-LUC: Yes, my darling. We'll leave this behind, start anew. Come with me to the Casbah.

Lawrence Harbison

JULIETTE: Yes, yes, I will. If we go now we can still catch the night plane.

(Jean-Luc and Juliette kiss passionately. When they break apart, Jean-Luc turns dismissively to Lance.)

JEAN-LUC: That is how you keep a woman like Juliette.

JULIETTE: Oui, c'est vrai. *(She looks out at the audience, remembering to speak in English.)* I mean—

LANCE: No, it's okay. I think they get it.

(Juliette kisses him on both cheeks.)

JULIETTE: Au revoir, chérie.

LANCE: Au revoir.

(Jean-Luc takes off his apron, drops it on the ground, then takes Juliette's hand and they hurry off stage. Lance watches them go.)

GERTRUDE: That's what happens when you ignore minor characters. They come back and bite you in the ass.

LANCE: I'm starting to wonder who the minor character here really is.

GERTRUDE: You don't understand what you don't understand.

LANCE: What?

GERTRUDE: Think about it.

LANCE: *(pause)* I'm blind to the parts of myself that I don't want to hear.

GERTRUDE: Oh, I like that.

LANCE: Yeah.

(Lance sits down at the table and begins to write in his notebook. Gertrude gets the glass of rosé from her table and sets it down by Lance.)

GERTRUDE: To write is to write is to write is to write . . . but you might get thirsty along the way.

(Lance continues to write. Gertrude smiles and gently pats the back of his head, caressing his hair lightly.)

GERTRUDE: Good man, Lance. You keep working.

(Gertrude turns and makes her way off down the boulevard, as the lights fade on Lance, who keeps writing.)

The End

A Walk in the Park

Aren Haun

Production Notes:

A WALK IN THE PARK was originally produced by Lakeshore Players Theatre as part of their 7th Annual 10-Minute Play Festival, held June 9-12, 2011. The play was directed by Keith McCarthy. The cast was as follows:

Cast:

MAN, James Patrick (JP) Barone
WIFE, Sara Feinberg
STRANGER, James Elsenpeter

CHARACTERS:
MAN, a man in his forties to sixties
WIFE, his wife, same age or slightly younger
STRANGER, a younger man, late twenties to early thirties

SETTING: A public park.
TIME: The present.

A MAN and his WIFE are walking through the park. Birds chirping . . . It's a nice day.

MAN: I'm saying, I'm saying that there's something wrong with us. I don't mean you and me personally. Well, not . . . I mean, all of us. People. We've lost . . . We've lost faith . . . We've lost touch with what—
(THEY are interrupted by a STRANGER.)
STRANGER: Excuse me. I apologize for interrupting.
MAN: We're not interested.
STRANGER: I'm sorry?
MAN: Whatever you're preaching or selling or . . . We're in the middle of a conversation.
STRANGER: I appreciate that, I do . . .
MAN: We're just minding our own—
STRANGER: But you haven't heard what I—
MAN: I'm sure it's a very sad story. But we don't have any money. Okay? So, please, leave us alo—
STRANGER: I'm not a . . .
MAN: Or whatever religion . . . Scientology . . .
STRANGER: That isn't why I'm—
MAN: Would I interrupt you? If you were out, having a nice walk in the park, conversing with someone, would I interrupt you? I'm asking you.
STRANGER: You're right. I'm terribly sorry. I'll leave you alone. It won't happen again.
MAN: Well, thank you. I don't mean to sound harsh, but . . .
STRANGER: No, please. I understand. And I feel exactly the same way. I believe a loss of manners is something that is seriously damaging our . . . I'm very sorry to have bothered you.
MAN: That's all right.
(Pause.)

STRANGER: I just need one thing.

MAN: Look. I've explained to you . . .

STRANGER: Your wallet.

MAN: My what?

STRANGER: Your wallet. And your wife's purse. Is this your wife?

MAN: You . . . what? You're saying . . . what? You want what?

STRANGER: The wallet and the purse. And your phone. Then I'll go.

MAN: Is this a joke?

STRANGER: A joke? Not at all. This is how I make my living.

MAN: Are you . . . ?

(Pause.)

Are you robbing us?!

STRANGER: You could say that.

(Pause.)

MAN: Excuse me . . .

(The MAN attempts to lead his wife away. The STRANGER blocks their path.)

Get out of our way.

STRANGER: Just hand over the things I've asked for and you can go back to your conversation. I am sorry about the interruption . . .

MAN: Why should we give things to you that belong to us?

STRANGER: Because I have a gun.

(Pause.)

MAN: You have a gun.

STRANGER: I have a gun. Politically, you know, I'm against them, but they are an unfortunate necessity in this line of work.

MAN: I don't believe you have a gun.

STRANGER: Do you have a gun?

MAN: No, I don't have a gun.

STRANGER: Then you're at a disadvantage.

MAN: Let me see it.

STRANGER: You want to see my gun?

MAN: You can't make threats in public like this. Even as a jo . . .

(The STRANGER takes out the gun and shows it to them. Pause. The WIFE hands over her purse.)

MAN: *(CONT'D)*What do you want from us?

STRANGER: Just your wallet and your phone. Then I'll go.

MAN: What will you do if I don't give them to you?

STRANGER: I'll shoot you.

> *(Pause.)*

I'd have no choice, you see. It does no good going around threatening people with a gun if you can't back it up. It would be disingenuous.

> *(Another pause. The MAN hands over his wallet and phone.)*

MAN: Are you really a mugger?

STRANGER: I just stole your money and your phone.

MAN: Yes, but you don't act like . . .

STRANGER: You mean like some kind of stereotypical . . . ?

MAN: You just don't seem like someone . . . The way you talk . . .

STRANGER: I have a Master's.

MAN: In what, thievery?

STRANGER: Art history, actually. Lot of good that did me. I used to work as a security guard at the museum for awhile, just trying to stick around that world, you know? But after awhile, it became, oh, I don't know, unsatisfying somehow. Anyway, this pays better.

MAN: And you don't think . . .

STRANGER: I still go on the weekends. Sorry.

MAN: No, you go ahead.

STRANGER: No, please, I was finished. You were saying . . . ?

MAN: I was going to ask whether or not you see anything wrong with this.

STRANGER: You mean . . . mugging? Of course! I'm not naïve. But the way I see it, we all get robbed sooner or later. I'm doing my part to make the experience as pleasant as possible. I know it can never be fun to have your money stolen. It's like going to the dentist when you're a kid. That lollipop doesn't make it any less painful, does it? It only adds insult to injury. But I still believe there's such a thing as decorum . . .

MAN: What do you mean?

STRANGER: Well, just because one has an unpleasant task to do, doesn't mean there isn't a proper way to conduct oneself. Some of these muggers, you should see them . . . I mean, after all, it isn't your fault you're being robbed. Why should you have to suffer indignity in addition to losing your possessions?

MAN: But doesn't that make it even worse? We're still victims . . .

STRANGER: You see yourselves as victims?

MAN: Aren't we?

STRANGER: Well, sure. In a sense, we're all victims . . . Aren't we getting robbed every day . . . ? I mean, just the other day I paid four dollars for a bottle of water. I said, "Four dollars? Are you kidding?" Twenty years ago we would have laughed at that. We would have thought it was insane.

MAN: That's right, we would have.

STRANGER: This city's changed. The whole country's changed. It's all hypocrisy. They tell you, buy six bags of chips for six dollars. But who needs six?

MAN: You know, I was at Whole Foods the other day . . .

(to the WIFE)

. . . I already told you this . . .

(to the STRANGER)

. . . and one of the items scanned at the register at a higher price than it said on the shelf. So I asked them to do a price check. And they acted like I was the one holding up the whole line. And then, twenty minutes later, when they'd finally figured out their mistake . . . did they even apologize? They were essentially robbing me and acting like . . .

STRANGER: No one takes any responsibility, do they? Everyone acts as though it's the person working above them who's to blame. That's why I'm self-employed.

MAN: Yes, even in my job . . . I'm a contractor. I do windows, window panes, that sort of thing . . . I always try to provide my clients with a fair quote. But a lot of people in my line will inflate the estimate. They'll double, even triple it, depending on who they're talking to.

STRANGER: And it's legal.

MAN: Completely legal!

STRANGER: Look at gas prices . . .

MAN: Right! It changes depending on the region, not on . . .

STRANGER: . . . on the price of oil.

MAN: They fix the prices. And it's all legal.

STRANGER: Legal. Pfff. The police don't know what real crime is anymore. They're too busy handing out parking tickets . . .

MAN: Don't get me started on parking . . . It's a complete racket. We don't need the mafia anymore . . . they've all gone to work for the government!

STRANGER: I got a parking ticket on my way over here today. I stopped for two minutes . . . I'm telling you . . .

MAN: What can we do? We have to have our cars. Look at public transportation in this country. It's shameful . . .

STRANGER: Couldn't agree with you more.

    (Pause.)

MAN: Well.

STRANGER: Yes, well.

MAN: What can you do . . .

STRANGER: There's nothing you can do. My philosophy is: take care of yourself, your health, and the people you love. And do it as honestly as you can.

MAN: I feel exactly the same way.

STRANGER: I always try to be straightforward in my work.

MAN: I can tell.

STRANGER: I'm not like one of those movie previews where they show you one thing, and then you get to the theater . . .

MAN: . . . and it's completely different! I hate that!

STRANGER: Let's face it. Our society is crumbling. It's coming to an end. The plane is going to crash. All we can do on the way down is show each other a little courtesy, a little kindness . . . treat each other with fairness and respect. I mean, here we are. In this glorious park. On such a beautiful day. And let's face it, you're gonna get robbed. It might be on your taxes, it might be at your local farmer's market, there's no avoiding it . . . The real question we have to ask ourselves is: Whatever happened to old-fashioned decency?

    (Pause.)

Whew. That was a mouthful, wasn't it?

MAN: I want you to know. I deeply appreciate everything you just said . . .

STRANGER: Thank you. I get these, you know, thoughts stuck up in my head, I don't even know they're there . . .

MAN: If you don't mind my saying, you seem like a very reasonable person.

STRANGER: I try.

MAN: I wonder if you'd be willing to do us a favor.

STRANGER: Um, if I can . . .

MAN: I'm not asking for the money back . . .

STRANGER: Okay, because . . .

MAN: Or the phone.

STRANGER: No, I need that.

MAN: But how about letting us keep the wallet and purse? You can take everything of value inside them . . . but let my wife keep her day planner . . . I've got my gym membership ID in there, you know how it is, such a pain in the ass . . .

STRANGER: Mm, I'd have to keep the credit cards.

MAN: I understand. What do you say?

STRANGER: I'd love to, but I really can't. It's a valid request, no question, but you make one exception, then another, where does it end? I'll tell you what, though. I'm walking that way. I might drop the purse and wallet, once I've had a chance to go through them. I'm sorry, it's the best I can do.

MAN: No, that's . . . We appreciate it.

STRANGER: All right, well . . . Thanks for talking with me. Good luck to both of you.

MAN: And to you.

(The STRANGER exits. Pause.)

MAN: *(CONT'D)* Well. Well well well.

(Pause.)

How about that.

(looks at his WIFE)

Honey? Are you all right? You look pale. What is it? Sweetheart, talk to me, what's wrong?

(Pause.)

WIFE: HELP!!!

(BLACKOUT.)

The End

10-Minute Play Producers

Actors Theatre of Louisville www.actorstheatre.org
Amy Wegener
(awegener@actorstheatre.org)

American Globe Theatre Turnip Festival,
Gloria Falzer—falzer@verizon.net

Appetite Theatre Company
Bruschetta: An Evening of Short Plays
www.appetitetheatre.com

Artistic New Directions
Janice Goldberg - Co Artistic Director
- ANDJanice@aol.com
Kristine Niven - Co Artistic Director -
KNiven@aol.com
ArtisticNewDirections.org

The Arts Center, Carrboro NC
10x10 in the Triangle
Jeri Lynn Schulke, director
theatre@artscenterlive.org
www.artscenterlive.org/performance/
opportunities

A-Squared Theatre Workshop
My Asian Mom Festival
Joe Yau (jyauza@hotmail.com)

Association for Theatre in Higher
Education New Play Development
Workshop
Contact Person: Charlene A. Donaghy
Email address of theatre/contact person:c harlene@charleneadonaghy.com
Website of theatre: http://
www.athe.org/displaycommon.
cfm?an=1&subarticlenbr=70

Boston Theatre Marathon
Boston Playwrights Theatre
www.bostonplaywrights.org
Kate Snodgrass (ksnodgra@bu.edu)
(Plays by New England Playwrights only)

Boulder Life Festival, Boulder, Colorado
Dawn Bower, Director of Theatrical Program (dawn@boulderlifefestival.com)
www.boulderlifefestival.com

The Box Factory
Judith Sokolowski, President
boxfactory@sbcglobal.net
www.boxfactoryforthearts.org

The Brick Theater's "Tiny Theater Festival" Michael Gardner, Artistic Director
mgardner@bricktheater.com
www.bricktheater.com

The Brooklyn Generator
Erin Mallon (contact)
email: brooklyngenerator@outlook.com
website: https://www.facebook.com/
TheBrooklynGenerator/info

Camino Real Playhouse
www.caminorealplayhouse.org

Chalk Repertory Theatre Flash Festival
produced by Chalk Repertory Theatre
Contact person: Ruth McKee
ruthamckee@aol.com
www.chalkrep.com

City Theatre
www.citytheatre.com
Susan Westfall (sjwestfall@aol.com)

Distilled Theatre Co.
submissions.dtc@gmail.com

Drilling Company
Hamilton Clancy
drillingcompany@aol.com

Durango Arts Center 10-Minute Play Festival
www.durangoarts.org
Theresa Carson
TenMinutePlayDirector@gmail.com

Eden Prairie Players
www.edenprairieplayers.com

Edward Hopper House (Two on
the Aisle Playwriting Competition)
Nyack, NY
Rachael Solomon
edwardhopper.house@verizon.net
www.edwardhopperhouse.org

Emerging Artists Theatre
Fall EATFest
www.emergingartiststheatre.org

Ensemble Theatre of Chattanooga
Short Attention Span Theatre Festival
Contact Person: Garry Posey (Artistic
Director)
garryposey@gmail.com
www.ensembletheatreofchattanooga.
com

Fell's Point Corner Theatre
10 x 10 Festival
Contact Person: Richard Dean Stover
Email address of theatre/contact per-
son: rick@fpct.org
Website of theatre: www.fpct.org

Fine Arts Association
Annual One Act Play Festival
ahedger@fineartsassociation.org
Firehouse Center for the Arts, New-
buryport MA
New Works Festival
Kimm Wilkinson, Director
www.firehouse.org
Limited to New England playwrights

Fire Rose Productions
www.fireroseproductions.com
kazmatura@gmail.com

Fusion Theatre Co.
http://www.fusionabq.org
info@fusionabq.org

Future Ten
info@futuretenant.org

GI60
Steve Ansell
screammedia@yahoo.com

Heartland Theatre Co.
www.heartlandtheatre.org

Generic Theatre Co.
www.generictheatre.org
contact@generictheatre.org

The Gift Theater
TEN Festival
Contact: Michael Patrick Thornton
www.thegifttheatre.org

Heartland Theatre Company
Themed 10-Minute Play Festival Every Year
Contact Person: Mike Dobbins (Artistic
Director)
boxoffice@heartlandtheatre.org
www.heartlandtheatre.org

Hella Fresh Fish
freshfish2submit@gmail.com

Hobo Junction Productions - Hobo Robo
Festival
Spenser Davis, Literary Manager
hobojunctionsubmissions@gmail.com
www.hobojunctionproductions.com

The Hovey Players, Waltham MA
Hovey Summer Shorts
www.hoveyplayers.com

Illustrious Theatre Co.
www.illustrioustheatre.org
illustrioustheatre@gmail.com

Image Theatre
Naughty Shorts
jbisantz@comcast.net

Independent Actors Theatre (Columbia,
MO)
Short Women's Play Festival
Emily Rollie, Artistic Director
e.rollie@iatheatre.org
www.iatheatre.org

Kings Theatre
www.kingstheatre.ca

Lake Shore Players
www.lakeshoreplayers.com
Joan Elwell
office@lakeshoreplayers.com

La Petite Morgue (Fresh Blood)
Kellie Powell at Lapetitemorgue@
gmail.com
www.lapetitemorgue.blogspot.com

Lebanon Community Theatre Playwriting Contest
Plays must be at least 10 minutes and
no longer than 20 minutes.
www.lct.cc/PlayWriteContest.htm

Lee Street Theatre, Salisbury, NC
(themed)
Original 10-Minute Play Festival
Justin Dionne, managing artistic
director
info@leestreet.org
www.leestreet.org

Little Fish Theatre Co.
www.litlefishtheatre.org

Live Girls Theatre
submissions@lgtheater.org

Little Fish Theatre
Pick of the Vine Festival
www.littlefishtheatre.org/wp/partici-
pate/submit-a-script/

Lourdes University Drama Society One
Act Play Festival, Sylvania, Ohio
Keith Ramsdell, Drama Society Advisor
dramasociety@lourdes.edu
www.lourdes.edu/dramasociety.aspx

Madlab Theatre
Theatre Roulette
Andy Batt (andy@madlab.net)
www.madlab.net/MadLab/Home.html

Magnolia Arts Center, Greenville, NC
Ten Minute Play Contest
info@magnoliaartscenter.com
www.magnoliaartscenter.com
Fee charged

Manhattan Repertory Theatre, New
York, NY
Ken Wolf
manhattanrep@yahoo.com
www.manhattanrep.com

McLean Drama Co.
www.mcleandramacompany.org
Rachel Bail (rachbail@yahoo.com)

Mildred's Umbrella
Museum of Dysfunction Festival
www.mildredsumbrella.com
info@mildredsumbrella.com

Nantucket Short Play Competition
Jim Patrick
www.nantucketshortplayfestival.com
nantucketshortplay@comcast.net
Napa Valley Players
8 x 10: A Festival of 10 Minute Plays
www.napavalleyplayhouse.org

New American Theatre
www.newamericantheatre.com
New Voices Original Short Play Festival
Kurtis Donnelly (kurtis@gvtheatre.org)

NFA New Play Festival
Newburgh Free Academy
201 Fullerton Ave, Newburgh, NY 12550
Terry Sandler (terrysandle@hotmail.com
(may not accept electronic submissions)

North Park Playwright Festival
New short plays (no more than 15 pages,
less is fine)
Submissions via mail to:
North Park Vaudeville and Candy Shoppe
2031 El Cajon Blvd.
San Diego, CA 92104
Attn: Summer Golden, Artistic Director.
www.northparkvaudeville.com

Northport One-Act Play Festival
Jo Ann Katz (joannkatz@gmail.com)
www.northportarts.org

Nylon Fusion
nylonsubmissions@gmail.com
www.nylonfusioncollective.org

Over Our Head Players, Racine WI
www.overourheadplayers.org/oohp15

Pan Theater, Oakland, CA
Anything Can Happen Festival
David Alger, pantheater@comcast.net
http://www.facebook.com/sanfrancis-
coimprov

Paw Paw Players One Act Festival
www.ppvp.org/oneacts.htm

Pegasus Theater Company (in Sonoma
County, north of San Francisco)
Tapas Short Plays Festival
www.pegasustheater.com/html/sub-
missions.html
Contact: Lois Pearlman lois5@sonic.net

Playhouse Creatures
Page to Stage
newplays@playhousecreatures.org

Playmakers Spokane Hit& Run
Sandra Hosking
playmakersspokane@gmail.com
www.sandrahosking.webs.com

Playwrights' Arena
Flash Theater LA
Contact person: Jon Lawrence Rivera
email: jonlawrencerivera@gmail.com
Website: www.playwrightsarena.org

Playwrights' Round Table (Launch
Series), Orlando, FL
Chuck Dent charlesrdent@hotmail.
com
www.theprt.com

Playwrights Studio Theater
5210 W. Wisconsin Ave.
Milwaukee, WI 53208
Attn: Michael Neville, Artistic Dir.

Ruckus Theatre
Allison Shoemaker
theruckus@theruckustheater.org
www.ruckustheater.org/home/contact.
html

Salem Theatre Co.
Moments of Play
mop@salemtheatre.com

Santa Cruz Actor's Theatre / Eight
Tens at Eight
Wilma Chandler, Artistic Director
ronziob@email.com
http://www.sccat.org

Secret Rose Theatre
www.secretrose.com
info@secretrose.com

Secret Theatre (Midsummer Night Festival), Queens, NY.
Odalis Hernandez, odalis.hernandez@
gmail.com
http://www.secrettheatre.com/

Shelterbelt Theatre, Omaha, NB
From Shelterbelt with Love
McClain Smouse, associate-artistic@
shelterbelt.org
submissions@shelterbelt.org
www.shelterbelt.org

Shepparton Theatre Arts Group
"Ten in 10" is a performance of
10 plays each running for 10 minutes
every year.
Email: info@stagtheatre.com
Website: www.stagtheatre.com

Short+Sweet
Literary Manager, Pete Malicki
Pete@shortandsweet.org
http://www.shortandsweet.org/short-
sweet-theatre/submit-script

Silver Spring Stage, Silver Spring, MD
Jacy D'Aiutolo
oneacts2012.ssstage@gmail.com
www.ssstage.org

Six Women Play Festival
www.sixwomenplayfestival.com

Source Festival
jenny@culturaldc.org

Southern Repertory Theatre
6 x6
Aimee Hayes (literary@southernrep.com)
www.southernrep.com/

Stage Door Productions
Original One-Act Play Festival
www.stagedoorproductions.org

Stage Q
www.stageq.com

Stratton Summer Shorts
Stratton Players
President: Rachel D'onfro
www.strattonplayers.com
info@strattonplayers.com

Ten Minute Playhouse (Nashville)
Nate Eppler, Curator
newworksnashville@gmail.com
www.tenminuteplayhouse.com

Ten Minute Play Workshop
www.tenminuteplayworkshop.com

Theatre One Productions
theatreoneproductions@yahoo.com

Theatre Out, Santa Ana CA
David Carnevale david@theatreout.
com
LGBT plays

Theatre Oxford 10 Minute Play
Contest
http://www.theatreoxford.com

Alice Walker
10minuteplays@gmail.com

Theatre Three
www.theatrethree.com
Jeffrey Sanzel (jeffrey@theatrethree.
com)

Towne Street Theatre Ten-Minute Play
Festival
info@townestreet.org

Unrenovated Play Festival
unrenovatedplayfest@gmail.com

Wide Eyed Productions
www.wideeyedproductions.com
playsubmissions@wideeyedproduc-
tions.com

Wild Claw Theatre:
Death Scribe 10 Minute Radio Horror
Festival
www.wildclawtheatre.com/index.html
literary@wildclawtheatre.com

Winston-Salem Writers
Annual 10 Minute Play Contest
www.wswriters.org
info@wswriters.org

Write Act
www.writeactrep.org
John Lant (j316tlc@pacbell.net)

Prim. Verily, neighbor Tradelove, thou dost waste thy breath about nothing. All that thou hast said tendeth only to debauch youth and fill their heads with the price and luxury of this world. The merchant is a very great friend to Satan and sendeth as many to his dominions as the pope.

Periwinkle. Right, I say knowledge makes the man.

Prim. Yea, but not thy kind of knowledge. It is the knowledge of truth. Search thou for the light within and not for baubles, friend.

Mrs. Lovely. Ah, study your country's good, Mr. Periwinkle, and not her insects; rid you of your home-bred monsters before you fetch any from abroad. I dare swear you have maggots enough in your own brain to stock all the virtuosos in Europe with butterflies.

Sir Philip. By my soul, Miss Nancy's a wit.

Prim. That is more than she can say by thee, friend. Look ye, it is in vain to talk; when I meet a man worthy of her, she shall have my leave to marry him.

Mrs. Lovely. Provided he be one of the faithful.— (Aside.) Was there ever such a swarm of caterpillars to blast the hopes of a woman?— (Aloud.) Know this: that you contend in vain. I'll have no husband of your choosing, nor shall you lord it over me long. I'll try the power of an English senate—orphans have been redressed and wills set aside, and none did ever deserve their pity more.— (Aside.) O Fainwell! Where are thy promises to free me from these vermin? Alas, the task was more difficult than he imagined!

A harder task than what the poets tell
Of yore, the fair Andromeda befell;
She but one monster feared, I've four to fear,
And see no Perseus, no deliv'rer near. (Exit.)

(Enter Servant and whispers to Prim.)

Servant. One Simon Pure inquireth for thee. (Exit.)

Periwinkle. The woman is mad. (Exit.)

Sir Philip. So are you all, in my opinion. (Exit.)

Prim. Friend Tradelove, business requireth my presence.

ACT V.

Scene i. Prim's house.

(Enter Mrs. Prim and Mrs. Lovely in Quaker's dress, meeting.)

Mrs. Prim. So now I like thee, Ann. Art thou not better without thy monstrous hoop coat and patches? If Heaven should make thee so many black spots upon thy face, would it not fright thee, Ann?

Mrs. Lovely. If it should turn your inside outward and show all the spots of your hypocrisy, 'twould fright me worse.

Mrs. Prim. My hypocrisy! I scorn thy words, Ann; I lay no baits.

Mrs. Lovely. If you did, you'd catch no fish.

Mrs. Prim. Well, well, make thy jests, but I'd have thee to know, Ann, that I could have catched as many fish (as thou call'st them) in my time as ever thou didst with all thy fool traps about thee. If admirers be thy aim, thou wilt have more of them in this dress than thy other. The men, take my word for't, are most desirous to see what we are most careful to conceal.

Mrs. Lovely. Is that the reason of your formality, Mrs. Prim? Truth will out. I ever thought, indeed, there was more design than godliness in the pinched cap.

Mrs. Prim. Go, thou art corrupted with reading lewd plays and filthy romances, good for nothing but to lead youth into the high road of fornication. Ah! I wish thou art not already too familiar with the wicked ones.

Mrs. Lovely. Too familiar with the wicked ones! Pray, no more of those freedoms, madam; I am familiar with none so wicked as yourself. How dare you talk thus to me. You, you, you unworthy woman, you— (Bursts into tears.)

(Enter Tradelove.)

Tradelove. What, in tears, Nancy?—What have you done to her, Mrs. Prim, to make her weep?

Mrs. Lovely. Done to me! I admire I keep my senses among you. But I will rid myself of your tyranny if there be either law or justice to be had. I'll force you to give me up my liberty.

Mrs. Prim. Thou hast more need to weep for thy sins, Ann—yea, for thy manifold sins.

Mrs. Lovely. Don't think that I'll be still the fool which you have made me. No, I'll wear what I please, go when and where I please, and keep what company I think fit, and not what you shall direct—I will.

Tradelove. For my part, I do think all this very reasonable, Mrs. Lovely. 'Tis fit you should have your liberty, and for that very purpose I am come.

(Enter Mr. Periwinkle and Obadiah Prim with a letter in his hand.)

Periwinkle. I have bought some black stockings of your husband, Mrs. Prim, but he tells me the glover's trade belongs to you; therefore, I pray you look me out five or six dozen of mourning gloves, such as are given at funerals, and send them to my house.

Prim. My friend Periwinkle has got a good windfall today—seven hundred a year.

Mrs. Prim. I wish thee joy of it, neighbor.

Tradelove. What, is Sir Toby dead then?

Periwinkle. He is. —You'll take care, Mrs. Prim?

Mrs. Prim. Yea, I will, neighbor.

Prim *(to Mrs. Prim)*. This letter recommendeth a speaker; 'tis from Aminadab Holdfast of Bristol; peradventure he will be here this night; therefore, Sarah, do thou take care for his reception. *(Gives her the letter.)*

Mrs. Prim. I will obey thee. *(Exit.)*

Prim. What are thou in the dumps for, Ann?

Tradelove. We must marry her, Mr. Prim.

Prim. Why truly, if we could find a husband worth having, I should be as glad to see her married as thou wouldst, neighbor.

Periwinkle. Well said; there are but few worth having.

Tradelove. I can recommend you a man now that I think you can none of you have an objection to.

(Enter Sir Philip Modelove.)

Periwinkle. You recommend! Nay, whenever she marries, I'll recommend the husband.

Sir Philip. What must it be, a whale or a rhinoceros, Mr. Periwinkle, ha, ha, ha? —Mr. Tradelove, I have a bill upon you *(Gives him a paper.)*,[63] and have been seeking for you all over the town.

Tradelove. I'll accept it, Sir Philip, and pay it when due.

Periwinkle. He shall be none of the fops at your end of the town with full perukes and empty skulls, nor yet none of your trading gentry, who puzzle the heralds to find arms for their coaches. No, he shall be a man famous for travels, solidity, and curiosity—one who has searched into the profundity of nature. When Heaven shall direct such a one, he shall have my consent, because it may turn to the benefit of mankind.

Mrs. Lovely. The benefit of mankind! What, would you anatomize me?

Sir Philip. Ay, ay, madam, he would dissect you.

Tradelove. Or pore over you through a microscope to see how your blood circulates from the crown of your head to the sole of your foot, ha, ha! But I have a husband for you, a man that knows how to improve your fortune; one that trades to the four corners of the globe.

Mrs. Lovely. And would send me for a venture, perhaps.

Tradelove. One that will dress you in all the pride of Europe, Asia, Africa, and America—a Dutch merchant, my girl.

Sir Philip. A Dutchman! Ha, ha, there's a husband for a fine lady—ya juffrow, will you met myn slapen[64]—ha, ha. He'll learn you to talk the language of the hogs, madam, ha, ha.

Tradelove. He'll learn you that one merchant is of more service to a nation than fifty coxcombs. The Dutch know the trading interest to be of more benefit to the state than the landed.

Sir Philip. But what is either interest to a lady?

Tradelove. 'Tis the merchant makes the belle. How would the ladies sparkle in the box without the merchant? The Indian diamonds! The French brocade! The Italian fan! The Flanders lace! The fine Dutch holland! How would they vent their scandal over their tea tables? And where would you beaus have champagne to toast your mistress, were it not for the merchant?

TRADELOVE. O, I shan't trouble you.— *(Aside.)* Pox take him for an unmannerly dog—however, I have kept my word with my Dutchman and will introduce him too for all you. *(Exit.)*

(Enter Colonel in a Quaker's habit.)

PRIM. Friend Pure, thou art welcome; how is it with Friend Holdfast and all Friends in Bristol? Timothy Littlewit, John Slenderbrain, and Christopher Keepfaith?

COLONEL *(aside)*. A goodly company!— *(Aloud.)* They are all in health, I thank thee for them.

PRIM. Friend Holdfast writes me word that thou camest lately from Pennsylvania; how do all Friends there?

COLONEL *(aside)*. What the devil shall I say? I know just as much of Pennsylvania as I do of Bristol.

PRIM. Do they thrive?

COLONEL. Yea, Friend, the blessing of their good works fall upon them.

(Enter Mrs. Prim and Mrs. Lovely.)

PRIM. Sarah, know our Friend Pure.

MRS. PRIM. Thou art welcome.

(He salutes her.)

COLONEL *(aside)*. Here comes the sum of all my wishes. How charming she appears, even in that disguise.

PRIM. Why dost thou consider the maiden so intentively, friend?

COLONEL. I will tell thee. About four days ago, I saw a vision—this very maiden, but in vain attire, standing on a precipice; and heard a voice, which called me by my name and bade me put forth my hand and save her from the pit. I did so, and methought the damsel grew to my side.

MRS. PRIM. What can that portend?

PRIM. The damsel's conversion, I am persuaded.

MRS. LOVELY *(aside)*. That's false, I'm sure.

PRIM. Wilt thou use the means, Friend Pure?

COLONEL. Means! What means? Is she not thy daughter and already one of the faithful?

Mrs. Prim. No, alas. She's one of the ungodly.

Prim (to Mrs. Lovely). Pray thee, mind what this good man will say unto thee; he will teach thee the way that thou shouldest walk, Ann.

Mrs. Lovely. I know my way without his instructions. I hoped to have been quiet when once I had put on your odious formality here.

Colonel. Then thou wearest it out of compulsion, not choice, Friend?

Mrs. Lovely. Thou art in the right of it, Friend.

Mrs. Prim. Art not thou ashamed to mimic the good man? Ah, thou art a stubborn girl.

Colonel. Mind her not; she hurteth not me. If thou wilt leave her alone with me, I will discuss some few points with her that may, perchance, soften her stubbornness and melt her into compliance.

Prim. Content; I pray thee put it home to her. —Come, Sarah, let us leave the good man with her.

([Mrs. Lovely] catching hold of Prim; he breaks loose and exits [with Mrs. Prim].)

Mrs. Lovely (calls after them). What do you mean—to leave me with this old enthusiastical canter? Don't think, because I complied with your formality, to impose your ridiculous doctrine upon me.

Colonel. I pray thee, young woman, moderate thy passion.

Mrs. Lovely. I pray thee, walk after thy leader; you will but lose your labor upon me. —These wretches will certainly make me mad.

Colonel. I am of another opinion; the spirit telleth me that I shall convert thee, Ann.

Mrs. Lovely. 'Tis a lying spirit; don't believe it.

Colonel. Say'st thou so? Why, then thou shalt convert me, my angel. (Catching her in his arms.)

Mrs. Lovely (shrieks). Ah! Monster, hold off, or I'll tear thy eyes out.

Colonel (whispers). Hush! For Heaven's sake—dost thou know me? I am Fainwell.

Mrs. Lovely. Fainwell!

(Enter old Prim.)

(Aside.) O, I'm undone; Prim here—I wish with all my soul I had been dumb.

PRIM. What is the matter? Why didst thou shriek out, Ann?

MRS. LOVELY. Shriek out! I'll shriek and shriek again, cry murder, thieves, or anything to drown the noise of that eternal babbler, if you leave me with him any longer.

PRIM. Was that all? Fie, fie, Ann.

COLONEL. No matter; I'll bring down her stomach, I'll warrant thee. Leave us, I pray thee.

PRIM. Fare thee well. *(Exit.)*

COLONEL. My charming lovely woman. *(Embraces her.)*

MRS. LOVELY. What means thou by this disguise, Fainwell?

COLONEL. To set thee free, if thou wilt perform thy promise.

MRS. LOVELY. Make me mistress of my fortune, and make thy own conditions.

COLONEL. This night shall answer all thy wishes. See here, I have the consent of three of thy guardians already, and doubt not but Prim shall make the fourth.

(Door opens slightly, unobserved, Prim listening.)

PRIM *(aside)*. I would gladly hear what argument the good man useth to bend her.

MRS. LOVELY *(unaware of Prim)*. Thy words give me new life, me-thinks.

PRIM *(aside)*. What do I hear?

MRS. LOVELY *(still unaware of Prim)*. Thou best of men! Heaven meant to bless me sure, when first I saw thee.

PRIM *(aside)*. He hath mollified her. O wonderful conversion!

COLONEL *(sees Prim; aside to Mrs. Lovely)*. Ha! Prim listening—no more, my love; we are observed; seem to be edified, and give 'em hopes that thou wilt turn Quaker, and leave the rest to me.— *(Aloud.)* I am glad to find that thou art touched with what I said unto thee, Ann; another time I will explain the other article to thee. In the meanwhile be thou dutiful to our Friend Prim.

MRS. LOVELY. I shall obey thee in everything.

(Enter old Prim.)

Prim. O, what a prodigious change is here! Thou hast wrought a miracle, friend!—Ann, how dost thou like the doctrine he hath preached?

Mrs. Lovely. So well that I could talk to him forever, methinks. I am ashamed of my former folly and ask your pardon, Mr. Prim.

Colonel. Enough, enough that thou art sorry; he is no pope, Ann.

Prim. Verily, thou dost rejoice me exceedingly, friend; will it please thee to walk into the next room and refresh thyself? Come, take the maiden by the hand.

Colonel. We will follow thee.

(Enter Servant.)

Servant. There is another Simon Pure inquireth for thee, master.

Colonel *(aside)*. The devil there is.

Prim. Another Simon Pure? I do not know him; is he any relation of thine?

Colonel. No, Friend, I know him not.— *(Aside.)* Pox take him; I wish he were in Pennsylvania again, with all my blood.

Mrs. Lovely *(aside)*. What shall I do?

Prim *(to Servant)*. Bring him up.

(Exit Servant.)

Colonel *(aside)*. Humph, then one of us most go down; that's certain. Now impudence assist me.

(Enter Simon Pure.)

Prim. What is thy will with me, Friend?

Pure. Didst thou not receive a letter from Aminadab Holdfast of Bristol, concerning one Simon Pure?

Prim. Yea, and Simon Pure is already here, Friend.

Colonel *(aside)*. And Simon Pure will stay here, Friend, if possible.

Pure. That's an untruth, for I am he.

Colonel. Take thou heed, Friend, what thou dost say; I do affirm that I am Simon Pure.

Pure. Thy name may be Pure, Friend, but not that Pure.

Colonel. Yea, that Pure which my good Friend Aminadab Hold-fast wrote to my Friend Prim about, the same Simon Pure that came from Pennsylvania and sojourned in Bristol eleven days; thou wouldst not take my name from me, wouldst thou?— *(Aside.)* Till I have done with it.

Pure. Thy name! I am astounded.

Colonel. At what? At thy own assurance? *(Going up to him; S. Pure starts back.)*

Pure. Avaunt, Satan; approach me not! I defy thee and all thy works.

Mrs. Lovely *(aside)*. O, he'll outcant him—undone, undone forever.

Colonel. Hark thee, Friend, thy sham will not take. Don't exert thy voice; thou art too well acquainted with Satan to start at him, thou wicked reprobate. What can thy design be here?

(Enter Servant and gives Prim a letter.)

Prim. One of these must be a counterfeit, but which I cannot say.

(Exit Servant.)

Colonel *(aside)*. What can that letter be?

(Prim reads the letter.)

Pure. Thou must be the devil, Friend; that's certain, for no human power can stock so great a falsehood.

Prim *(to S. Pure)*. This letter sayeth that thou art better acquainted with that Prince of Darkness than any here. —Read that, I pray thee, Simon. *(Gives it the Colonel.)*

Colonel *(aside)*. 'Tis Freeman's hand.— *(reads [aloud].)* "There is a design formed to rob your house this night and cut your throat, and for that purpose there is a man disguised like a Quaker who is to pass for one Simon Pure; the gang whereof I am one, though now resolved to rob no more, has been at Bristol; one of them came up in the coach with the Quaker, whose name he hath taken, and from what he gathered from him, formed that design and did not doubt but he should impose so far upon you as to make you turn out the real Simon Pure and keep him with you. Make the right use of this. Adieu."— *(Aside.)* Excellent well!

PRIM *(to S. Pure).* Dost thou hear this?

PURE. Yea, but it moveth me not; that, doubtless, is the impostor. *(Pointing at the Colonel.)*

COLONEL. Ah, thou wicked one! Now I consider thy face, I remember thou didst come up in the leathern convenience[65] with me; thou hadst a black bob wig on and a brown camblet coat with brass buttons. Canst thou deny it, ha?

PURE. Yea, I can and with a safe conscience too, Friend.

PRIM. Verily, Friend, thou art the most impudent villain I ever saw.

MRS. LOVELY *(aside).* Nay then, I'll have a fling at him too.— *(Aloud.)* I remember the face of this fellow at Bath—ay, this is he that picked my Lady Raffle's pocket upon the grove; don't you remember that the mob pumped you,[66] friend? This is the most notorious rogue—

PURE. What doth provoke thee to seek my life? Thou wilt not hang me, wilt thou, wrongfully?

PRIM. She will do thee no hurt, nor thou shalt do me none; therefore, get thee about thy business, friend, and leave thy wicked course of life, or thou mayst not come off so favorably everywhere.

COLONEL. Go, Friend, I would advise thee, and tempt thy fate no more.

PURE. Yea, I will go, but it shall be to thy confusion; for I shall clear myself. I will return with some proofs that shall convince thee, Obadiah, that thou art highly imposed upon. *(Exit.)*

COLONEL *(aside).* Then here will be no staying for me, that's certain. What the devil shall I do?

PRIM. What monstrous works of iniquity are there in this world, Simon.

COLONEL. Yea, the age is full of vice.— *(Aside.)* 'Sdeath, I am so confounded I know not what to say.

PRIM. Thou art disordered, Friend; art thou not well?

COLONEL. My spirit is greatly troubled, and something telleth me that though I have wrought a good work in converting this maiden, this tender maiden, yet my labor will be in vain; for the

evil spirit fighteth against her; and I see, yea, I see with the eyes
of my inward man that Satan will rebuffet her again whenever
I withdraw myself from her; and she will, yea, this very damsel
will return again to that abomination from whence I have re-
trieved her, as if it were, yea, as if it were out of the jaws of the
fiend—hum—

PRIM. Good lack! Thinkest thou so?

MRS. LOVELY *(aside)*. I must second him.— *(Aloud.)* What
meaneth this struggling within me? I feel the spirit resisting the
vanities of this world, but the flesh is rebellious, yea, the
flesh—I greatly fear the flesh, and the weakness thereof—
hum—

PRIM. The maid is inspired.

COLONEL. Behold, her light begins to shine forth.— *(Aside.)* Excellent woman.

MRS. LOVELY. This good man hath spoken comfort unto me, yea,
comfort, I say; because the words which he hath breathed into
my outward ears are gone through and fixed in mine heart, yea,
verily in mine heart, I say—and I feel the spirit doth love him
exceedingly, hum—

COLONEL *(aside)*. She acts it to the life.

(Enter Mrs. Prim.)

PRIM. Prodigious! The damsel is filled with the spirit, Sarah.

MRS. PRIM. I am greatly rejoiced to see such a change in our beloved Ann. —I came to tell thee that supper stayeth for thee.

COLONEL. I am not disposed for thy food; my spirit longeth for
more delicious meat. Fain would I redeem this maiden from the
tribe of sinners and break those cords asunder wherewith she is
bound—hum—

MRS. LOVELY. Something whispers in my ears, methinks, that I
must be subject to the will of this good man and from him only
must hope for consolation—hum—it also telleth me that I am
a chosen vessel to raise up seed to the faithful and that thou
must consent that we two be one flesh according to the Word—
hum—

PRIM. What a revelation is here! This is certainly part of thy vision, friend; this is the maiden's growing to thy side. Ah, with
what willingness should I give thee my consent, could I give

thee her fortune too; but thou will never get the consent of the wicked ones.

COLONEL *(aside)*. I wish I was as sure of yours.

PRIM *(to Mrs. Lovely)*. My soul rejoiceth, yea, it rejoiceth, I say, to find the spirit within thee; for lo, it moveth thee with natural agitation—yea, with natural agitation, I say again, and stirreth up the seeds of thy virgin inclination towards this good man—yea, it stirreth, as one may say, yea, verily, I say, it stirreth up thy inclination—yea, as one would stir a pudding.

MRS. LOVELY. I see, I see—the spirit guiding of thy hand, good Obadiah Prim, and now behold thou art signing thy consent. —And now I see myself within thy arms, my friend and brother, yea, I am become bone of thy bone and flesh of thy flesh[67] *(Embraces him.)*—hum—

COLONEL *(aside)*. Admirably performed.— *(Aloud.)* And I will take thee in all spiritual love for an helpmeet, yea, for the wife of my bosom. —And now, methinks, I feel a longing—yea, a longing, I say, for the consummation of thy love, hum—yea, I do long exceedingly.

MRS. LOVELY. And verily, verily, my spirit feeleth the same longing.

MRS. PRIM. The spirit hath greatly moved them both. Friend Prim, thou must consent; there is no resisting of the spirit.

PRIM. Yea, the light within showeth me that I shall fight a good fight, and wrestle through those reprobate fiends, thy other guardians—yea, I perceive the spirit will hedge thee into the flock of the righteous—thou art a chosen lamb—yea, a chosen lamb, and I will not push thee back—no, I will not, I say, no, thou shalt leap-a and frisk-a and skip-a and bound, and bound, I say—yea, bound within the fold of the righteous—yea, even within thy fold, my brother. —Fetch me the pen and ink, Sarah, and my hand shall confess its obedience to the spirit.

(Exit Mrs. Prim.)

COLONEL *(aside)*. I wish it were over.

(Enter Mrs. Prim with pen and ink.)

MRS. LOVELY *(aside)*. I tremble lest this Quaking rogue should return and spoil all.

PRIM. Here, friend, do thou write what the spirit prompteth, and I will sign it.

(Colonel sits down.)

MRS. PRIM. Verily, Ann, it greatly rejoiceth me to see thee reformed from that original wickedness wherein I found thee.

MRS. LOVELY. I do believe thou art, and I thank thee.

COLONEL *(reads [aloud])*. "This is to certify all whom it may concern that I do freely give up all my right and title in Ann Lovely to Simon Pure and my full consent that she shall become his wife, according to the form of marriage. Witness my hand."

PRIM. That is enough. Give me the pen. *(Signs it.)*

(Enter Betty, running to Mrs. Lovely.)

BETTY. O, madam, madam, here's the Quaking man again; he has brought a coachman and two or three more.

MRS. LOVELY *(aside to Colonel)*. Ruined past redemption.

COLONEL *(aside to Mrs. Lovely)*. No, no, one minute sooner had spoiled all, but now—*(Aloud.)* here is company coming, Friend; give me the paper. *(Going up to Prim hastily.)*

PRIM. Here it is, Simon, and I wish thee happy with the maiden.

MRS. LOVELY. 'Tis done, and now, devil do thy worst.

(Enter Simon Pure and Coachman, etc.)

PURE. Look thee, Friend, I have brought these people to satisfy thee that I am not that impostor which thou didst take me for; this is the man which did drive the leathern conveniency that brought me from Bristol, and this is—

COLONEL. Look ye, friend, to save the court the trouble of examining witnesses, I plead guilty, ha, ha.

PRIM. How's this? Is not thy name Pure, then?

COLONEL. No, really, sir, I only made bold with this gentleman's name. But I here give it up safe and sound; it has done the business which I had occasion for, and now I intend to wear my own, which shall be at his service upon the same occasion at any time, ha, ha, ha.

PURE. O, the wickedness of this age.

COACHMAN *(to S. Pure).* Then you have no farther need of us, sir. *(Exeunt.)*

COLONEL. No, honest man, you may go about your business.

PRIM. I am struck dumb with thy impudence, Ann; thou hast deceived me and perchance undone thyself.

MRS. PRIM. Thou art a dissembling baggage, and shame will overtake thee. *(Exit.)*

PURE. I am grieved to see thy wife so much troubled; I will follow and console her. *(Exit.)*

(Enter Servant.)

SERVANT. Thy brother guardians inquireth for thee; there is another man with them. *(Exit.)*

MRS. LOVELY *(to the Colonel).* Who can that other man be?

COLONEL *(aside to Mrs. Lovely).* 'Tis one Freeman, a friend of mine, whom I ordered to bring the rest of thy guardians here.

(Enter Sir Philip, Tradelove, Periwinkle, and Freeman.)

FREEMAN *(to the Colonel).* Is all safe? Did my letter do you service?

COLONEL *(aside [to Freeman]).* All, all's safe; ample service.

SIR PHILIP. Miss Nancy, how dost do, child?

MRS. LOVELY. Don't call me Miss, Friend Philip; my name is Ann, thou knowest.[68]

SIR PHILIP. What, is the girl metamorphosed?

MRS. LOVELY. I wish thou wert so metamorphosed. Ah, Philip, throw off that gaudy attire and wear the clothes becoming of thy age.

PRIM *(aside).* I am ashamed to see these men.

SIR PHILIP. My age! The woman is possessed.

COLONEL. No, thou art possessed rather, friend.

TRADELOVE. Hark ye, Mrs. Lovely, one word with you. *(Takes hold of her hand.)*

COLONEL. This maiden is my wife, thanks to Friend Prim, and thou hast no business with her. *(Takes her from him.)*

TRADELOVE. His wife! Hark ye, Mr. Freeman.

PERIWINKLE. Why, you have made a very fine piece of work of it, Mr. Prim.

Sir Philip. Married to a Quaker! Thou art a fine fellow to be left guardian to an orphan, truly. There's a husband for a young lady.

Colonel. When I have put on my beau clothes, Sir Philip, you'll like me better.

Sir Philip. Thou wilt make a very scurvy beau, friend.

Colonel. I believe I can prove it under your hand that you thought me a very fine gentleman in the Park today, about thirty-six minutes after eleven. Will you take a pinch, Sir Philip, out of the finest snuffbox you ever saw? *(Offers him snuff.)*

Sir Philip. Ha, ha, ha, I am overjoyed, faith I am, if thou be'st that gentleman. I own I did give my consent to the gentleman I brought here today, but if this is he, I can't be positive.

Prim. Canst thou not? Now, I think thou art a fine fellow to be left guardian to an orphan—thou shallow-brained shuttle-cock; he may be a pickpocket for aught thou dost know.

Periwinkle. You would have been two rare fellows to have been trusted with the sole management of her fortune, would ye not, think ye? But Mr. Tradelove and myself shall take care of her portion.

Tradelove. Ay, ay, so we will.—Did not you tell me the Dutch merchant desired me to meet him here, Mr. Freeman?

Freeman. I did so, and I am sure he will be here, if you'll have a little patience.

Colonel. What, is Mr. Tradelove impatient; nay then, ik ben gereet voor you; heb ye Jan van Timtamtirelireletta Heer van Fainwell vergeeten?[69]

Tradelove. O, pox of the name! What, have you tricked me too, Mr. Freeman?

Colonel. Tricked, Mr. Tradelove! Did I not give you two thousand pound for your consent fairly? And now do you tell a gentleman that he has tricked you?

Periwinkle. So, so, you are a pretty guardian, faith; sell your charge! What did you look upon her as, part of your stock?

Prim. Ha, ha, ha! I am glad thy knavery is found out, however. I confess the maiden overreached me and no sinister end at all.

Periwinkle. Ay, ay, one thing or another overreached you all; but I'll take care he shall never finger a penny of her money, I warrant you—overreached, quoth'a? Why, I might have been overreached too, if I had had no more wit. I don't know but this very fellow may be him that was directed to me from Grand Cairo today. Ha, ha, ha.

COLONEL. The very same, sir.

PERIWINKLE. Are you so, sir? But your trick would not pass upon me.

COLONEL. No, as you say, at that time it did not; that was not my lucky hour. But hark ye, sir, I must let you into one secret. You may keep honest John Tradescant's coat on, for your uncle, Sir Toby Periwinkle, is not dead; so the charge of mourning will be saved, ha, ha. Don't you remember Mr. Pillage, your uncle's steward, ha, ha, ha?

PERIWINKLE. Not dead! I begin to fear I am tricked too.

COLONEL. Don't you remember the signing of a lease, Mr. Periwinkle?

PERIWINKLE. Well, and what signifies that lease, if my uncle is not dead? Ha! I am sure it was a lease I signed—

COLONEL. Ay, but it was a lease for life, sir, and of this beautiful tenement, I thank you. *(Taking hold of Mrs. Lovely.)*

OMNES. Ha, ha, ha, neighbor's fare!

FREEMAN. So, then, I find you are all tricked, ha, ha.

PERIWINKLE. I am certain I read as plain a lease as ever I read in my life.

COLONEL. You read a lease, I grant you, but you signed this contract. *(Showing a paper.)*

PERIWINKLE. How durst you put this trick upon me, Mr. Freeman; did not you tell me my uncle was dying?

FREEMAN. And would tell you twice as much to serve my friend, ha, ha.

SIR PHILIP. What, the learned, famous Mr. Periwinkle choused, too, ha, ha, ha. I shall die with laughing, ha, ha, ha.

PRIM. It had been well if her father had left her to wiser heads than thine and mine, Friend, ha, ha.

TRADELOVE. Well, since you have outwitted us all, pray you, what and who are you, sir?

SIR PHILIP. Sir, the gentleman is a fine gentleman. —I am glad you have got a person, madam, who understands dress and good breeding. —I was resolved she should have a husband of my choosing.

PRIM. I am sorry the maiden is fallen into such hands.

TRADELOVE. A beau! Nay, then she is finely helped up.

Mrs. Lovely. Why, beaus are great encouragers of trade, sir, ha, ha.

Colonel. Look ye, gentlemen, I am the person who can give the best account of myself, and I must beg Sir Philip's pardon when I tell him that I have as much aversion to what he calls dress and breeding as I have to the enemies of my religion. I have had the honor to serve his Majesty and headed a regiment of the bravest fellows that ever pushed bayonet in the throat of a Frenchman; and notwithstanding the fortune this lady brings me, whenever my country wants my aid, this sword and arm are at her service.

> And now, my fair, if you'll but deign to smile,
> I meet a recompense for all my toil.
> Love and religion ne'er admit restraint,
> Force makes many a sinner, not one saint;
> Still free as air the active mind does rove,
> And searches proper objects for its love;
> But that once fixed, 'tis past the power of art,
> To chase the dear ideas from the heart.
> 'Tis liberty of choice that sweetens life,
> Makes the glad husband, and the happy wife.

EPILOGUE.

Written by Mr. Sewell and Spoken by Mrs. Bullock.

What new strange ways our modern beaus devise!
What trials of love skill to gain the prize!
The heathen gods, who never mattered rapes,

Scarce wore such strange variety of shapes.
The devil take their odious barren skulls,
To court in form of snakes and filthy bulls.
Old Jove once nicked it, I am told,
In a whole lapful of true standard gold;
How must his godship then fair Danaë warm?
In trucking ware for ware there is no harm.
Well, after all—that money has a charm.
But now indeed that stale invention's past;
Besides, you know that guineas fall so fast,
Poor nymph must come to pocket piece at last.
Old Harry's face, or good Queen Bess's ruff—
Not that I'd take 'em—may do well enough;
No—my ambitious spirit's far above
Those little tricks of mercenary love.
That man be mine, who, like the Colonel here,
Can top his character in every sphere;
Who can a thousand ways employ his wit,
Outpromise statesmen, and outcheat a cit;
Beyond the colors of a trav'ler paint,
And cant, and ogle too—beyond a saint.
The last disguise most pleased me, I confess;
There's something tempting in the preaching dress;
And pleased me more than once a dame of note,
Who loved her husband in his footman's coat.
To see one eye in wanton motions played,
Th'other to the heavenly regions strayed,
As if it for its fellow's frailties prayed.
But yet I hope, for all that I have said,
To find my spouse a man of war in bed.

Notes to *A Bold Stroke for a Wife*

1. Centlivre's dedication, like many of the time, flatters its subject. Wharton was actually a witty profligate who wasted his gifts and advantages, although he was a liberal patron of writers.
2. A scholar, used pejoratively in this period for a collector of useless, esoteric information and objects.
3. Exchange-broker, dealer on the Stock Exchange.

4. The title *Mrs.* was still in use for unmarried young ladies.

5. Snapped up, seized by surprise.

6. Bath was a fashionable spa, where people went to drink or bathe in the mineral waters.

7. Good-looking women help along trade in taverns at the fashionable other (west) end of London, but his clientele in the City ("within the walls") sin only by cheating in business. Below: officers got partial ("half") pay when their military units were disbanded; this allowance had been reduced in January 1718.

8. Castrated him. Leading roles in opera were sung by *castrati,* male sopranos.

9. Virtuosos studied the exotic information found in travelers' tales, such as the fanciful medieval travel book attributed to Sir John Mandeville.

10. Probably means *showy* here, without our contemporary connotation of cheapness.

11. Supply you suitably.

12. St. James's was a fashionable section around St. James's Palace and Park. Prosperous people were carried about in sedan chairs by two chairmen.

13. Retinue of servants from the West Indies.

14. Quakers wore distinctively plain and modest dress, including a pleated (pinched) cap for women.

15. Dashing . . . indefinable.

16. A woman in a mask, probably a prostitute. The Mall was a fashionable promenade adjoining St. James's Park.

17. The flats are pulled aside to reveal the characters and scene behind them.

18. By Jove, he is a man of wit.

19. But [they] are rare indeed . . . the beautiful Englishwomen. Below: By Jove, you have been taken in. No, I assure you, Sir.

20. The French ambassador had popularized masquerades in London after the Peace of Utrecht (1713). John James Heidegger organized public masquerades.

21. Masquerades supposedly provided opportunities for sexual affairs: hence they would benefit the surgeons (getting them fees for treating venereal disease) and enable citizens' wives to have affairs with men of fashion.

22. Tender affection.

23. Traditionally, women who died unmarried had to lead apes in hell.

24. The black, the brown, the white—what the devil, where are those rascals? Let us go, Sir Knight.

25. Pinner, a fashionable cap with long streamers on the sides. Stays, a corset, pushed up the breasts.
26. An oval track in Hyde Park, around which fashionable people rode in their coaches.
27. Sect.
28. Pay your surgeons for treating your venereal disease.
29. Deceived, taken in. Cf. *bite,* below.
30. A blend of cheaper wines passed off as more expensive wine.
31. Really brilliant exploit.
32. An actual Alexandrian scientist of the second century A.D.
33. Tell lies to or copulate with the Devil for a bundle of beanstraw, the Scottish equivalent of a witch's broomstick.
34. A seventeenth-century traveler and antiquarian.
35. The references to the mummy and the crocodile poke fun at *Three Hours after Marriage* (1717), a short-lived farce about a virtuoso by the Tory wits Alexander Pope, John Gay, and John Arbuthnot.
36. William Whiston, Edmund Halley, and other contemporary scientists had studied the sun's position and heat at given latitudes and hours. Below: René Descartes had speculated about sun spots and the relation of flames to cinders. Some philosophers (those favoring the ancients) maintained that nature was progressively decaying. Recent research had increased knowledge about and interest in comets: Halley had predicted that the comet of 1682 would return in 1758, and Whiston had stated that the very conspicuous comet of 1680 had caused the Flood and would return to cause a "General Conflagration."
37. According to legend, the sacred geese saved Rome by cackling and thus warning the Romans when Gauls attempted to seize the Capitol.
38. Am surprised that.
39. Loud roaring (Greek).
40. Zone (girdle), or mousebane (mousetrap?) for fools.
41. The Indian Emperor in Delhi, the Sultan in Istanbul, and George I in London.
42. From the time of Charles II, scientists had been trying unsuccessfully to discover a method for determining the longitude at sea (not discovered until 1765).
43. Cheated.
44. Can see into a millstone (a proverbial expression for acuteness) as far as the man who grinds it.
45. Shares in the South Sea Company, which controlled trade in Spanish America and the Pacific. Below: Class Lottery was a state lottery, and the East India Company controlled trade in the East Indies. The

Sword Blade Company was a powerful banking partnership, agents for the South Sea Company.

46. Working on his accounts.

47. A state lottery that helped to finance the Civil List (the royal household). Caco, possibly the cacao market. A bull buys stock, expecting to sell it at a profit; a bear sells stock not yet owned, hoping to buy it for less than the delivery price. Below: a put is an option to deliver a certain amount of stock at a specified price within a specific time.

48. Louis XIV died in 1715. It was common to manipulate the stock market through true and false news reports.

49. Freeman plays on rumors of a Spanish military threat in Cagliari, Sardinia (1717).

50. A tall column commemorating the Great Fire of London.

51. Two thousand pounds, Sir; 'tis done. This gentleman shall hold the money. Below: I don't believe it, Mr. Freeman; I shall hold you doubled. (His Dutch is mixed with English.)

52. Swindled, outsmarted.

53. Treat. Cherish means to entertain kindly.

54. Quakers were too thrifty to go to the expense of hiring post horses.

55. Bumpkin.

56. Organize a club that will meet at Sackbut's tavern, thus giving him business.

57. Jove courted women under a variety of disguises.

58. Land confiscated from an abbey at the Reformation; Peter's pence, a land tax paid to the papal see before the Reformation.

59. Doctors' Commons, where wills were registered.

60. Ha, Mr. Tradelove, I am sorry for your troubles—but I shall make you easy; I will not take the money. Below: Yes, the lady shall set all to rights, Sir . . . Yes, truly . . . And so shall I . . . Yes, I shall certainly do that.

61. Well, Sir, you must do more; you must speak well of me to the lady. Below: What the devil, have you more guardians? . . . What, then you have tricked me, Sir? Had I known that, I would have been even with you . . . Well, that is certain. But you must first speak of me to the lady and the parents [i.e., guardians].

62. Fortune.

63. A bill of exchange, a money order with a due date.

64. Yes, lady, will you sleep with me?

65. Pompous circumlocution for coach.

66. Held you under a pump, the traditional punishment for pickpockets.

67. Genesis 2:23.

68. Quakers renounced the use of titles.

69. I am ready for you; have you forgotten Jan . . .

Mercy Otis Warren
(1728–1814)

BY FAMILY situation and personal inclination, Mercy Otis was at the center of political activity from the beginnings of trouble between England and her colonies through the establishment of the American republic. Her brother James and her husband were revolutionary leaders; she knew the Washingtons and was a close friend of the John Adamses. Her father, a judge and militia colonel in Barnstable, Massachusetts, had Mercy taught along with her two older brothers by their clergyman uncle. Later, James Otis guided her reading; it was he who introduced her to the liberal political philosophy of John Locke. Her marriage to James's college friend James Warren proved to be long and happy; they had five sons.

James Otis took a leading role in defending colonial rights against British encroachments until a beating by thugs in 1769 incapacitated him. Mercy Warren took up his work in pamphlets and newspaper articles. At the suggestion of John Adams, she wrote a satiric poem on the Boston Tea Party, "The Squabble of the Sea Nymphs." Most of her political tracts are in dramatic form: *The Adulateur* (1772–1773), *The Defeat* (1773), *The Group* (1775), and perhaps two others. Although these appeared in the newspapers anonymously, her friends knew that she had written them. In 1790, she published *Poems, Dramatic and Miscellaneous,* which included two conventional tragedies on themes of freedom and patriotism. Her most substantial work is her partisan but conscientiously researched history of the American Revolution (1805).

It would be tedious to trace every forgotten reference in *The Group,* a detailed topical satire. Warren wrote it in the fall of

1774, when the American colonies were in hostile confrontation with the British government. The dispute over Britain's right to tax her colonies had erupted in the Boston Tea Party in December 1773. In retaliation, Parliament had passed the Coercive, or Intolerable, Acts, which closed the port of Boston, altered the charter of Massachusetts to replace the elected council with one appointed by the governor, and made it legal to quarter troops in private houses and to transport disturbers of public order outside the colony, even to England, for trial. Boston had become an armed camp occupied by British troops, who patrolled the streets, sometimes harassing passers-by, and paraded on Boston Common. Governor Thomas Hutchinson (whom Warren had pilloried as Rapatio in *The Adulateur*) had just departed for England— temporarily, he thought—and been replaced by General Thomas Gage (Sylla). The atmosphere was tense, with colonial militia surrounding the city; but fighting did not actually begin until Gage sent an expedition to Concord in April 1775. The despicable characters in *The Group* are American Tories, collaborators with the British; several are Mandamus Councilors, created by mandamus, royal writ, rather than properly elected.

The Group was enthusiastically received. Its first two scenes were published in both the *Boston Gazette* and the *Massachusetts Spy* in January 1775, and at least three separate editions (one the expanded version included here) were published within the year. The author's opening reference to acting and re-acting refers not to production in the theater but to continuing action on the stage of life.

The Group

As lately acted, and to be re-acted to the wonder of all superior intelligences, nigh headquarters at Amboyne.

The author has thought proper to borrow the following spirited lines from a late celebrated poet and offer [them] to the public by way of PROLOGUE, which cannot fail of pleasing at this crisis.

> What! armed for virtue, and not point the pen,
> Brand the bold front of shameless guilty men,
> Dash the proud gamester from his gilded car,
> Bare the mean heart which lurks beneath a star,
>
> Shall I not strip the gilding off a knave,
> Unplaced, unpensioned, no man's heir or slave?
> I will, or perish in the generous cause;
> Hear this and tremble, ye who 'scape the laws;
> Yes, while I live, no rich or noble knave,
> Shall walk the world in credit to his grave;
> To virtue only, and her friends, a friend,
> The world beside may murmur or commend.[1]

Dramatis Personæ.

LORD CHIEF JUSTICE HAZLEROD[2]
JUDGE MEAGRE
[GENERAL SYLLA][3]
BRIGADIER HATEALL[4]
HUM HUMBUG, ESQ.
SIR SPARROW SPENDALL
HECTOR MUSHROOM, COL.
BEAU TRUMPS[5]
DICK, THE PUBLICAN
SIMPLE SAPLING, ESQ.
MONSIEUR DE FRANÇOIS
CRUSTY CROWBAR, ESQ.
DUPE, SECRETARY OF STATE
SCRIBLERIUS FRIBBLE
COMMODORE BATTEAU
COLLATERALIS, a New-made Judge

Attended by a swarm of court sycophants, hungry harpies, and unprincipled danglers, collected from the neighboring villages, hovering over the stage in the shape of locusts, led by Massachusettensis in the form of a basilisk; the rear brought up by Proteus, bearing a torch in one hand and a powder-flask in the other: The whole supported by a mighty army and navy, from Blunderland, for the laudable purpose of enslaving its best friends.

ACT I.

Scene i. A little dark parlor, guards standing at the door.
Hazlerod, Crusty Crowbar, Simple Sapling, Hateall, and
Hector Mushroom.

SIMPLE. I know not what to think of these sad times,
  The people armed—and all resolved to die
  E'er they'll submit.—
CRUSTY CROWBAR. I too am almost sick of the parade
  Of honors purchased at the price of peace.
SIMPLE. Fond as I am of greatness and her charms,
  Elate with prospects of my rising name,
  Pushed into place,—a place I ne'er expected,
  My bounding heart leapt in my feeble breast
  And ecstasies entranced my slender brain.—
  But yet, e'er this I hoped more solid gains,
  As my low purse demands a quick supply.—
  Poor Sylvia weeps,—and urges my return
  To rural peace and humble happiness,
  As my ambition beggars all her babes.
CRUSTY. When first I 'listed in the desperate cause,
  And blindly swore obedience to his will,
  So wise, so just, so good I thought Rapatio,[6]
  That if salvation rested on his word
  I'd pin my faith and risk my hopes thereon.
HAZLEROD. And why not now?—What staggers thy belief?
CRUSTY. Himself—his perfidy appears—
  It is too plain he has betrayed his country.
  And we're the wretched tools by him marked out
  To seal its ruins—tear up the ancient forms,
  And every vestige treacherously destroy,
  Nor leave a trait of freedom in the land.
  Nor did I think hard fate would call me up
  From drudging o'er my acres,—

Treading the glade, and sweating at the plough,
To dangle at the tables of the great;
At bowls and cards to spend my frozen years;
To sell my friends, my country, and my conscience;
Profane the sacred sabbaths of my God;
Scorned by the very men who want my aid
To spread distress o'er this devoted people.

HAZLEROD. Pho—what misgivings—why these idle qualms,
This shrinking backwards at the bugbear conscience?
In early life I heard the phantom named,
And the grave sages prate of moral sense
Presiding in the bosom of the just;
Or planting thongs [thorns?] about the guilty heart.
Bound by these shackles, long my laboring mind
Obscurely trod the lower walks of life,
In hopes by honesty my bread to gain;
But neither commerce, or my conjuring rods,
Nor yet mechanics, or new-fangled drills,
Or all the ironmonger's curious arts,
Gave me a competence of shining ore,
Or gratified my itching palm for more;
Till I dismissed the bold intruding guest,
And banished conscience from my wounded breast.

CRUSTY. Happy expedient!—Could I gain the art,
Then balmy sleep might soothe my waking lids.
And rest once more refresh my weary soul.—

HAZLEROD. Resolved more rapidly to gain my point,
I mounted high in justice's sacred seat,
With flowing robes, and head equipped without,
A heart unfeeling, and a stubborn soul,
As qualified as e'er a Jeffreys[7] was;
Save in the knotty rudiments of law,
The smallest requisite for modern times,
When wisdom, law, and justice are supplied
By swords, dragoons, and ministerial nods,
Sanctions most sacred in the pander's creed,
I sold my country for a splendid bribe.
Now let her sink—and all the dire alarms
Of war, confusion, pestilence, and blood,
And tenfold misery be her future doom—

Let civil discord lift her sword on high,
Nay, sheathe its hilt e'en in my brother's blood;
It ne'er shall move the purpose of my soul;
Though once I trembled at a thought so bold;
By Philalethes's arguments, convinced
We may live demons, as we die like brutes,
I give my tears and conscience to the winds.
HATEALL. Curse on their coward fears and dastard souls,
Their soft compunctions and relenting qualms;
Compassion ne'er shall seize my steadfast breast,
Though blood and carnage spread through all the land;
Till streaming purple tinge the verdant turf,
Till every street shall float with human gore,
I, Nero like, the capital in flames,
Could laugh to see her glotted sons expire,
Though much too rough my soul to touch the lyre.[8]
SIMPLE. I fear the brave, the injured multitude.
Repeated wrongs arouse them to resent,
And every patriot like old Brutus stands,
The shining steel half drawn—its glittering point
Scarce hid beneath the scabbard's friendly cell.
Resolved to die, or see their country free.
HATEALL. Then let them die—*The dogs we will keep down*—
while N————'s my friend, and G————[9] approves the deed,
Though Hell and all its Hell-hounds should unite,
I'll not recede to save from swift perdition
My wife, my country, family, or friends.
G————'s mandamus I more highly prize
Than all the mandates of th'ethereal king.
HECTOR MUSHROOM. Will our abettors in the distant towns
Support us long against the common cause,
When they shall see from Hampshire's northern bound
Through the wide western plains to southern shores
The whole united continent in arms?[10]
HATEALL. They shall—as sure as oaths or bonds can bind;
I've boldly sent my new-born brat abroad,
Th'association of my morbid brain,
To which each minion must affix his name.
As all our hope depends on brutal force,
On quick destruction, misery, and death;

Soon may we see dark ruin stalk around,
With murder, rapine, and inflicted pains,
Estates confiscate, slavery, and despair,
Wrecks, halters, axes, gibbeting, and chains,
All the dread ills that wait on civil war;—
How I could glut my vengeful eyes to see
The weeping maid thrown helpless on the world,
Her sire cut off.—Her orphan brothers stand
While the big tear rolls down the manly cheek.
Robbed of maternal care by grief's keen shaft,
The sorrowing mother mourns her starving babes.
Her murdered lord torn guiltless from her side,
And flees for shelter to the pitying grave
To screen at once from slavery and pain.

HAZLEROD. But more complete I view this scene of woe,
By the incursions of a savage foe,
Of which I warned them, if they dare refuse
The badge of slaves, and bold resistance use.
Now let them suffer—I'll no pity feel.

HATEALL. Nor I—But had I power, as I have the will
I'd send them murmuring to the shades of Hell.

ACT II.

(The scene changes to a large dining room. The table furnished with bowls, bottles, glasses, and cards.—The Group appear sitting round in a restless attitude. In one corner of the room is discovered a small cabinet of books, for the use of the studious and contemplative—containing Hobbes's Leviathan, Sipthrop's Sermons, Hutchinson's History, Fable of the Bees, Philalethes on Philanthrop, with an appendix by Massachusettensis, Hoyle on Whist, Lives of the Stuarts, Statutes of Henry the Eighth and William the Conqueror, Wedderburn's Speeches, and Acts of Parliament for 1774.)[11]

Scene i. Hateall, Hazlerod, Monsieur, Beau Trumps, Simple, Humbug, Sir Sparrow, etc., etc.

SCRIBLERIUS. Thy toast, Monsieur—
   Pray, why that solemn phiz?[12]—
   Art thou, too, balancing 'twixt right and wrong?
   Hast thou a thought so mean as to give up
   Thy present good, for promise in reversion?
   'Tis true hereafter has some feeble terrors,
   But e'er our grizzly heads are wrapped in clay
   We may compound, and make our peace with Heaven.
MONSIEUR. Could I give up the dread of retribution,
   The awful reckoning of some future day,
   Like surly Hateall I might curse mankind,
   And dare the threatened vengeance of the skies.
   Or like yon apostate—*(Pointing to Hazlerod, retired to a corner to read Massachusettensis.)*
         Feel but slight remorse
   To sell my country for a grasp of gold.
   But the impressions of my early youth,

Infixed by precepts of my pious sire,
Are stings and scorpions in my goaded breast.
Oft have I hung upon my parent's knee
And heard him tell of his escape from France;
He left the land of slaves and wooden shoes;
From place to place he sought a safe retreat,
Till fair Bostonia stretched her friendly arm
And gave the refugee both bread and peace.
(Shall I ungrateful 'rase the sacred bonds,
And help to clank the tyrant's iron chains
O'er these blest shores—once the sure asylum
From all the ills of arbitrary sway?)
With his expiring breath he bade his sons,
If e'er oppression reached the western world,
Resist its force, and break the servile yoke.

SCRIBLERIUS. Well, quit thy post;—Go make thy flattering court
To Freedom's sons, and tell thy baby fears;
Show the soft traces in thy puny heart,
Made by the trembling tongue and quivering lip
Of an old grandsire's superstitious whims.

MONSIEUR. No.—I never can—
So great the itch I feel for titled place,
Some honorary post, some small distinction,
To save my name from dark oblivion's jaws,
I'll hazard all, but ne'er give up my place;
For that I'll see Rome's ancient rites restored,
And flame and faggot blaze in every street.[13]

BEAU TRUMPS. —That's right, Monsieur,
There's nought on earth that has such tempting charms
As rank and show, and pomp, and glittering dress,
Save the dear counters at beloved quadrille.
Viner unsoiled, and Littleton may sleep,
And Coke[14] lie moldering on the dusty shelf,
If I by shuffling draw some lucky card
That wins the livres or lucrative place.

HUM HUMBUG. When sly Rapatio showed his friends the scroll,
I wondered much to see thy patriot name
Among the list of rebels to the state,
I thought thee one of Rusticus's[15] sworn friends.

BEAU TRUMPS. When first I entered on the public stage

My country groaned beneath base Brundo's hand,
Virtue looked fair and beckoned to her lure,
Through Truth's bright mirror I beheld her charms
And wished to tread the patriotic path,
And wear the laurels that adorn his fame;
I walked a while and tasted solid peace
With Cassius, Rusticus, and good Hortensius,
And many more, whose names will be revered
When you and I, and all the venal herd,
Weighed in Nemesis' just, impartial scale,
Are marked with infamy till time blot out
And in oblivion sink our hated names.
But 'twas a poor, unprofitable path—
Naught to be gained, save solid peace of mind.
No pensions, place, or title there I found;
I saw Rapatio's arts had struck so deep
And given his country such a fatal wound,
None but its foes promotion could expect;
I trimmed, and pimped, and veered, and wavering stood,
But half resolved to show myself a knave,
Till the arch Traitor, prowling round for aid,
Saw my suspense and bid me doubt no more;—
He gently bowed, and smiling took my hand,
And whispering softly in my listening ear,
Showed me my name among his chosen band,
And laughed at virtue dignified by fools,
Cleared all my doubts, and bid me persevere
In spite of the restraints or hourly checks
Of wounded friendship, and a goaded mind,
Or all the sacred ties of trust and honor.

COLLATERALIS. Come, 'mongst ourselves we'll e'en speak out the
    truth.
Can you suppose there yet is such a dupe
As still believes that wretch an honest man?
    The latter strokes of his serpentine brain
Outvie the arts of Machiavel himself;
His Borgian model here is realized,[16]
And the stale tricks of politicians played
Beneath a vizard fair—
—Drawn from the heavenly form

Of blest Religion weeping o'er the land
For virtue fallen, and for freedom lost.
BEAU TRUMPS. I think with you—
—unparallelled his effrontery,
When by chicanery and specious art,
Midst the distress in which he'd brought the city,
He found a few (by artifice and cunning,
By much industry of his wily friend
The false Philanthrop[17]—sly, undermining tool,
Who with the Siren's voice—
Deals daily round the poison of his tongue)
To speak him fair—and overlook his guilt.
They by reiterated promise made
To stand their friend at Britain's mighty court,
And vindicate his native injured land,
Lent him their names to sanctify his deeds.
But mark the traitor—his high crime glossed o'er
Conceals the tender feelings of the man,
The social ties that bind the human heart;
He strikes a bargain with his country's foes,
And joins to wrap America in flames.
Yet with feigned pity and Satanic grin,
As if more deep to fix the keen insult,
Or make his life a farce still more complete,
He sends a groan across the broad Atlantic,
And with a phiz of crocodilian stamp,
Can weep and wreathe, still hoping to deceive,
He cries, the gathering clouds hang thick about her,
But laughs within—then sobs—
—Alas! my country!
HUM HUMBUG. Why so severe, or why exclaim at all,
Against the man who made thee what thou art?
BEAU TRUMPS. I know his guilt,—I ever knew the man,
Thy father knew him ere we trod the stage;
I only speak to such as know him well;
Abroad I tell the world he is a saint.
But as for interest, I betrayed my own
With the same views, I ranked among his friends;
But my ambition sighs for something more.
What merits has Sir Sparrow of his own,

And yet a feather graces the fool's cap:
Which did he wear for what himself achieved,
'Twould stamp some honor on his latest heir—
But I'll suspend my murmuring care awhile;
Come, t'other glass—and try our luck at loo,
And if before the dawn your gold I win,
Or ere bright Phoebus does his course begin,
The eastern breeze from Britain's hostile shore
Should waft her lofty floating towers o'er,
Whose waving pendants sweep the watery main,
Dip their proud beaks and dance towards the plain,
The destined plains of slaughter and distress,
Laden with troops from Hanover and Hess,
I would invigorate my sinking soul,
For then the continent we might control;
Not all the millions that she vainly boasts
Can cope with veteran barbarian hosts;—
But the brave sons of Albion's warlike race,
Their arms and honors never can disgrace,
Or draw their swords in such a hated cause
In blood to seal a N_____'s oppressive laws.
They'll spurn the service;—Britons must recoil,
And show themselves the natives of an isle
Who fought for freedom, in the worst of times
Produced her Hampdens, Fairfaxes, and Pyms.[18]
    But if by carnage we should win the game,
Perhaps by my abilities and fame,
I might attain a splendid, glittering car,
And mount aloft, and sail in liquid air;
Like Phaeton, I'd then outstrip the wind,
And leave my low competitors behind.

Scene ii. Collateralis, Dick the Publican.

PUBLICAN. This dull inaction will no longer do;
    Month after month the idle troops have lain,
    Nor struck one stroke that leads us to our wish.
        The trifling bickerings at the city gates,
    Or bold outrages of their midnight routs,
    Bring us no nearer to the point in view.

Though much the daily sufferings of the people,
Commerce destroyed, and government unhinged,
No talk of tame submission yet I hear.
COLLATERALIS. No—not the least—
—they're more resolved than ever.
They're firm, united, bold, undaunted, brave,
And every villa boasts their marshalled ranks,
The warlike clarion sounds through every street;
Both vigorous youth and the gray-headed sire
Bear the fusee,[19] in regimental garbs,
Repairing to defend invaded right,
And if pushed hard, by manly force repel;
And though Britannia sends her legions o'er,
To plant her daggers in her children's breast,
It will rebound—New whetted, the keen point
Will find a sheath in every tyrant's heart.
PUBLICAN. —What then is to be done?
My finances too low to stand it long.
You well remember—
When stationed there to gripe the honest trader,
How much I plundered from your native town.
Under the sanctions of the laws of trade,
I the hard earnings of industry
Filched from their hands, and built my nest on high.
And on the spoils I rioted a while,
But soon the unrighteous pelf slipped through my hand.
Nor longer idly could I waste my time,
A numerous flock was rising round my board,
Who urged to something that might give them bread.
    My only game was hither to repair,
And court the proud oppressors of my country,
By the parade of pompous luxury,
To win their favor, and obtain a place;
That (with my limbeck)[20] might have kept me on,
But for the cursed, persevering spirit
Of Freedom's sons—who triumph o'er distress,
Nor will comply with requisitions made
By haughty mandates from corrupted courts,
To pay the workmen for the chains, they'd forged.
COLLATERALIS. No—though proud Britain wafts her wooden walls

O'er the broad waves—and plants them round these coasts,
Shuts up their ports, and robs them of their bread,
They're not dismayed—nor servilely comply
To pay the hunters of the Nabob shores
Their high demand for India's poisonous weed,
Long since a sacrifice to Thetis made,
A rich regale—Now all the watery dames
May snuff souchong and sip in flowing bowls
The higher flavored choice Hysonian stream,
And leave their nectar to old Homer's gods.[21]

PUBLICAN. The Group this morn were summoned to the camp;
The council early meets at Sylla's tent,
But for what purpose yet I cannot learn.

COLLATERALIS. Then let us haste, 'tis novel to be called
By Sylla's order, summoned to attend,
So close he keeps his counsels in his breast,
Nor trusts us with the maneuvers of state,
I fear he half despises us himself.
And if he does, we cannot wonder much,
We're made the jest of every idle boy:
Most of us hunted from our rural seats,
Drove from our homes, a prey to guilty fears.
When—When dare we return?[22]

 And now shut up in this devoted city,
Amidst the pestilence on either hand,
Pursued by every dreadful execration
That the bold tongue of innocence oppressed
Pours forth in anguish for a ruined state.

 Scene iii. The fragments of the broken council appear with
trembling, servile gestures, showing several applications to the
General from the undertools in the distant counties, begging each
a guard of myrmidons to protect them from the armed multitudes
(which the guilty horrors of their wounded consciences hourly
 presented to their frighted imaginations) approaching to take
speedy vengeance on the court parasites, who had fled for refuge
to the camp, by immediate destruction to their pimps, panders,
 and sycophants left behind.

(Sylla walking in great perplexity.)

SYLLA. Pray, how will it comport with my pretence
  For building walls and shutting up the town,
  Erecting fortresses and strong redoubts,
  To keep my troops from any bold inroads
  A brave, insulted people might attempt,
  If I send out my little scattered parties,
  And the long-suffering, generous patriot's care
  Prevents a skirmish?
      Though they're the sport of wanton, cruel power,
  And Hydra-headed ills start up around,
  Till the last hope of a redress cut off
  Their humane feeling, urge them to forbear,
  And wait some milder means to bring relief.
HATEALL. 'Tis now the time to try their daring tempers.
  Send out a few—and if they are cut off,
  What are a thousand souls sent swiftly down
  To Pluto's gloomy shades,—to tell in anguish
  Half their compeers shall sit pandemonic
  Ere we will suffer Liberty to reign.
  Or see her sons triumphant win the day.
    I fain would push them to the last extreme,
  To draw their swords against their legal King.
  Then short's the process to complete destruction.
SECRETARY DUPE. Be not so sanguine—the day is not our own,
  And much I fear it never will be won.
  Their discipline is equal to our own,
  Their valor has been tried,—and in a field
  They're not less brave than are Frederick's troops.[23]
  Those members formidable pour along,
  While Virtue's banners shroud each warrior's head,
  Stern Justice binds the helmet on his brow,
  And Liberty sits perched on every shield.
  But who's applied, and asked the General's aid,
  Or wished his peaceful villa such a curse
  As posting troops beside the peasant's cot?
JUDGE MEAGRE. None but the very dregs of all mankind,
  The stains of Nature,—the blots of human race.
  Yet that's no matter, still they are our friends;
  'Twill help our projects if we give them aid.
SIMPLE SAPLING. Though my paternal acres are eat up,

My patrimony spent, I've yet an house
My lenient creditors let me improve;
Send up the troops, 'twill serve them well for barracks.
I somehow think 'twould bear a noble sound,
To have my mansion guarded by the King.

SYLLA. Hast thou no sons or blooming daughters there,
To call up all the feelings of a father,
Lest their young minds contaminate by vice,
Caught from such inmates, dangerous and vile,
Devoid of virtue, rectitude, or honor
Save what accords with military fame?
    Hast thou no wife who asks thy tender care
To guard her from Bellona's hardy sons?
Who, when not toiling in the hostile field,
Are faithful votaries to the Cyprian Queen.
Or is her soul of such materials made,
Indelicate and thoughtless of her fame,
So void of either sentiment or sense,
As makes her a companion fit for thee!

SIMPLE SAPLING. Silvia's good-natured, and no doubt will yield,
And take the brawny veterans to her board,
When she's assured 'twill help her husband's fame.
    If she complains or murmurs at the plan,
Let her solicit charity abroad;
Let her go out and seek some pitying friend
To give her shelter from the wintry blast,
Disperse her children round the neighboring cots,
And then—

PUBLICAN. —Then weep thy folly, and her own hard fate!
I pity Silvia; I knew the beauteous maid
Ere she descended to become thy wife:
She silent mourns the weakness of her lord,
For she's too virtuous to approve thy deeds.

HATEALL. Pho—what's a woman's tears,
Or all the whinings of that trifling sex?
I never felt one tender thought towards them.
    When young, indeed, I wedded nut brown Kate
(Blithe buxom dowager, the jockey's prey),
But all I wished was to secure her dower.
I broke her spirits when I'd won her purse;

For which I'll give a recipe most sure
To every henpecked husband round the board;
If crabbed words or surly looks won't tame
The haughty shrew, nor bend the stubborn mind,
Then the green hickory or the willow twig
Will prove a curse [cure?] for each rebellious dame
Who dare oppose her lord's superior will.

SYLLA. Enough of this, ten thousand harrowing cares
Tear up my peace and swell my anxious breast.
   I see some mighty victim must appease
An injured nation, tottering on the verge
Of wide destruction, made the wanton sport
Of hungry harpies, gaping for their prey;
Which, if by misadventures they should miss,
The disappointed vulture's angry fang
Will seize the lesser gudgeons of the state,
And sacrifice to mad Alecto's rage;
Lest the tide turning, with a rapid course
The booming torrent rushes o'er their heads,
And sweeps the "cawing cormorants from earth."

HATEALL. Then strike some sudden blow, and if hereafter
Dangers should rise—then set up for thyself,
And make thy name as famous in Columbia
As ever Caesar's was in ancient Gaul.
Who would such distant provinces subdue
And then resign them to a foreign lord!
With such an armament at thy command
Why all this cautious prudence?

SYLLA. I only wish to serve my sovereign well,
And bring new glory to my master's crown,
Which can't be done by spreading ruin round
This loyal country—
—Wrought up to madness by oppression's hand.
How much deceived my royal master is
By those he trusts!—but more of this anon.
   Were it consistent with my former plan,
I'd gladly send my sickly troops abroad
Out from the stench of this infected town,
To breathe some air more free from putrefaction;
To brace their nerves against approaching spring,

If my ill stars should destine a campaign,
And call me forth to fight in such a cause.
　To quench the generous spark, the innate love
Of glorious freedom, planted in the breast
Of every man who boasts a Briton's name,
Until some base born lust of foreign growth
Contaminate his soul, till false ambition,
Or the sordid hope of swelling coffers,
Poison the mind, and brutalize the man.

COLLATERALIS. I almost wish I never had engaged
To rob my country of her native rights,
Nor strove to mount on Justice' solemn bench
By mean submission cringing for a place.
　How great the pain, and yet how small the purchase!
Had I been dumb, or my right hand cut off,
Ere I so servilely had held it up,
Or given my voice abjectly to rescind
The wisest step that mortal man could take
To curb the talons of tyrannic power,
Outstretched rapacious, ready to devour
The fair possessions, by our Maker given,
Confirmed by compacts—ratified by Heaven.

SYLLA. Look o'er the annals of our virtuous sires,
And search the story of Britannia's deeds,
From Caesar's ravages to Hampden's fall;
From the good Hampden down to glorious Wolfe,
Whose soul took wing on Abraham's fatal plain,
Where the young hero fought Britannia's foes
And vanquished Bourbon's dark, ferocious hosts,
Till the slaves trembled at a George's name.
　'Twas love of freedom drew a Marlborough's sword;
This glorious passion moved a Sydney's pen,
And crowned with bays a Harrington and Locke;[24]
'Tis Freedom wreathes the garlands o'er their tombs.
　For her how oft have bleeding heroes fallen!
With the warm fluid, gushing from their wounds,
Conveyed the purchase to their distant heirs!
　And shall I rashly draw my guilty sword,
And dip its hungry hilt in the rich blood
Of the best subjects that a Brunswick boasts,

And for no cause, but that they nobly scorn
To wear the fetters of his venal slaves!
   But swift time rolls, and on his rapid wheel
Bears the winged hours and the circling years.
   The cloud-capped morn, the dark, short, wintry day,
And the keen blasts of roughened Boreas' breath,
Will soon evanish, and approaching spring
Opes with the fate of empires on her wing. *(Exit Sylla.)*

(Hazlerod rises in great agitation.)

HAZLEROD. This balancing of passions ne'er will do,
   And by the scale which virtue holds to reason,
   Weighing the business ere he executes,
   Doubting, deliberating, half resolved
   To be the savior of a virtuous state,
   Instead of guarding refugees and knaves,
   The buzzing reptiles that crawl round his court,
   And lick his hand for some delicious crumb
   Or painted plume to grace the guilty brow,
   Stained with ten thousand falsities, trumped up
   To injure every good and virtuous name
   Who won't strike hands and be his country's foe:
   I'll hasten after, and stir up his soul
   To dire revenge and bloody resolutions,
   Or the whole fabric falls on which we hang,
   And down the pit of infamy we plunge,
   Without the spoils we long have hoped to reap.

(He crosses the stage hastily and goes out after Sylla. Meagre and Secretary Dupe at the further part of the stage.)

MEAGRE. As Sylla passed I marked his anxious brow;
   I fear his soul is with compassion moved
   For suffering virtue, wounded and betrayed;
   For freedom hunted down in this fair field,
   The only soil, in these degenerate days,
   In which the heavenly goddess can exist.
SECRETARY. Humanity recoils—his heart relucts
   To execute the black, the accurst design.

Such I must call it, though thy guilty friends,
Thy subtle brother, laid the artful plan,
"And like the toad squat at the ear of Eve"[25]
Infusing poisons by his snaky tongue,
Pushed Brundo on to tread the thorny path,
And plunge his country in ten thousand woes;
Then slyly justling him behind the scenes,
Stepped in his place, for which he long had sighed.
MEAGRE. Yes, all allow he played a master game,
And dealt his cards with such peculiar skill
That every dangler about the court,
As you and I and all might well suppose,
Thought the chains fixed which Brundo only clanked.
    But yet unless some speedy method's found
To break the union and dissolve the bonds
That bind this mighty continent so firm,
Their congresses, their covenants, and leagues,
With their committees, working in each town
With unremitting vigilance and care,
To baffle every evil machination
Of all state rooks, who peck about the land,
If not broke up, will ruin all at last.
    Amidst the many scribblers of the age,
Can none be found to set their schemes afloat,
To sow dissension—and distrust abroad,
Sap that cement that bears down all before it,
And makes America a match for all
The hostile powers that proud Europa boasts?
SECRETARY. Not all the swarms of prostituted pens,
Nor hireling smatterers scribbling for gain,
From the first pensioned on the northern list
To bigot priests—who write from southern shores,
With all their phantoms, bugbears, threats, or smiles,
Will e'er persuade them to renounce their claim
To freedom, purchased with their fathers' blood.
    How various are the arts already tried,
What pains unwearied to write men to sleep,
Or rock them in the cradle of despair,
To doze supinely, 'till they should believe
They'd neither eyes, nor tongues, or strength to move

But at the nod of some despotic lord!
    What shifts, evasions, what delusive tales,
What poor prevarication for rash oaths,
What nightly watchings, and what daily cares
To dress up falsehood in some fair disguise,
Or wrap the bantling of their midnight dreams
In the soft vest of friendship, to betray,
Then send it forth in every fairy form,
To stalk at noontide, giddy with fond hope
That some new gambols might deceive again
Men broad awake, who see through all the cheat.
MEAGRE. There still is hope—why need we yet despair?
    The doughty champion of our sinking cause,
The deep "arcana" of whose winding brain
Is fraught with dark expedients to betray,
By the long labors of his veteran quill,
By scattering scraps from every musty code
Of canon, civil, or draconian laws,
Quoting old statutes or defining new,
Treasons, misprisions, riots, routs, cabals,
And insurrections of these stubborn times,
He'll sure prevail and terrify at last,
By bringing precedents from those blest days
When royal Stuarts Britain's sceptre swayed,
And taught her sons the right divine of Kings.
    When pains and forfeitures an hundred fold
Were dealt to traitors, puny when compared
To the bold rebels of this continent,
From Merrimack to Mississippi's banks,
Who dare resist a ministerial frown.
    In spite of all the truths Nov. anglus tells,
And his cool, reasoning argumentive style,
Or master strokes of his unrivaled pen,
They will divide, and wavering will submit
And take the word of Massachusettensis
That men were born already bitted, curbed,
And on their backs the saddles prominent,
For every upstart sycophant to mount.
SECRETARY. Not Massachusettensis' oily tongue,
    Or retailed nonsense of a Philarene,

Not Senex' rant, not yet dull Grotius' pen,[26]
Or the whole group of selfish, venal men,
If gathered from cold Zembla's frozen shore
To the warm zone where rapid rivers roar,
Can either coax them, or the least control
The valorous purpose of their Roman souls.
MEAGRE. Let not thy soft timidity of heart
Urge thee to terms, till the last stake is thrown.
　'Tis not my temper ever to forgive
When once resentment's kindled in my breast.
　I hated Brutus[27] for his noble stand
Against the oppressors of his injured country.
　I hate the leaders of these restless factions
For all their generous efforts to be free.
　I curse the senate which defeats our bribes,
Who Hazlerod impeached for the same crime.
　I hate the people, who, no longer gulled,
See through the schemes of our aspiring clan.
And from the rancor of my venomed mind,
I look askance on all the human race,
And if they're not to be appalled by fear,
I wish the earth might drink that vital stream
That warms the heart and feeds the manly glow,
The love inherent, planted in the breast,
To equal liberty, conferred on man
By him who formed the peasant and the King!
　Could we erase these notions from their minds,
Then (paramount to these ideal whims,
Utopian dreams of patriotic virtue,
Which long has danced in their distempered brains)
We'd smoothly glide on midst a race of slaves,
Nor heave one sigh though all the human race
Were plunged in darkness, slavery, and vice.
If we could keep our foothold in the stirrup,
And, like the noble Claudia of old,
Ride o'er the people, if they don't give way;
Or wish their fates were all involved in one,
For I've a brother, as the Roman dame,
Who would strike off the rebel neck at once.[28]
SECRETARY. No, all is o'er unless the sword decides,

Which cuts down Kings and kingdoms oft divides.
By that appeal I think we can't prevail,
Their valor's great, and Justice holds the scale.
They fight for freedom, while we stab the breast
Of every man who is her friend professed.
They fight in virtue's ever sacred cause,
While we tread on divine and human laws.
Glory and victory and lasting fame
Will crown their arms and bless each hero's name!

MEAGRE. Away with all thy foolish, trifling cares,
And to the winds give all thy empty fears;
Let us repair and urge brave Sylla on,
I long to see the sweet revenge begun.
As Fortune is a fickle, sportive dame,
She may for us the victory proclaim,
And with success our busy ploddings [plottings?] crown,
Though injured Justice stern and solemn frown.
    Then they shall smart for every bold offence,
Estates confiscated will pay th'expence;
On their lost fortunes we a while will plume
And strive to think there is no after doom.

*(Exeunt omnes. As they pass off the stage the curtain draws up,
and discovers to the audience a lady nearly connected with one of
the principal actors in the Group, reclined in an adjoining alcove,
who in mournful accents accosts them—thus—)*

    What painful scenes are hovering o'er the morn,
When spring again invigorates the lawn!
    Instead of the gay landscape's beauteous dyes,
Must the stained field salute our weeping eyes,
Must the green turf and all the mournful glades,
Drenched in the stream, absorb their dewy heads,
Whilst the tall oak and quivering willow bends
To make a covert for their country's friends,
Denied a grave!—amid the hurrying scene
Of routed armies scouring o'er the plain.
    Till British troops shall to Columbia yield,
And Freedom's sons are masters of the field;
Then o'er the purpled plain the victors tread

Among the slain to seek each patriot dead
(While Freedom weeps that merit could not save
But conquering heroes must enrich the grave).
  An adamantine monument they rear
  With this inscription—*Virtue's sons lie here!*

Notes to *The Group*

1. Alexander Pope, "The First Satire of the Second Book of Horace, Imitated" (1733), lines 105–8, 115–22 (quoted with slight inaccuracies).
2. Peter Oliver, brother-in-law of Governor Hutchinson, had made a fortune in iron manufacturing. He was appointed Chief Justice in 1771, but the legislature impeached him for accepting a grant from the Crown (interpreted by the Patriots as a bribe). See below, p. 268. Governor Hutchinson blocked the impeachment, and two successive grand juries refused to serve under Oliver. He was one of the Mandamus Councilors.
3. General Thomas Gage, Governor of Massachusetts 1774–5. Lucius Cornelius Sulla was a Roman general and dictator, noted for ruthlessness toward his opponents.
4. Timothy Ruggles, a lawyer and soldier who married a rich widow and was described as bold and haughty, witty and profane, with an intimidating manner. He was an enemy of James Otis and was said to have threatened to jail anyone who signed a nonimportation agreement.
5. Daniel Leonard, a lawyer from a leading family, was said to be foppish and overfond of card-playing and womanizing. Although he was originally opposed to the King, Governor Hutchinson persuaded him to turn his coat and made him a Mandamus Councilor. In a series of articles in the *Massachusetts Gazette* (1774–5), under the name Massachusettensis (see below), he ably defended Crown policies and argued that the rebels would be destroyed by the British as well as condemned by God. John Adams replied under the name "Novanglus," to whom Warren forces Meagre to give grudging praise on p. 284.
6. Thomas Hutchinson, Governor of Massachusetts 1771–4, who urged Parliament to exert its authority sternly over the colonies and enforced unpopular British laws such as the Tea Act.
7. George Jeffreys, the notoriously brutal judge who presided over the

Bloody Assizes following the Monmouth Rebellion in England (1685).

8. The vicious Emperor Nero, said to have played music while a fire was destroying Rome. *Glotted* may be a misprint for glutted.

9. Frederick, Lord North (Prime Minister 1770–82), and King George III.

10. The British and their sympathizers hoped to isolate Massachusetts, but the other colonies recognized a common cause. The First Continental Congress was meeting in Philadelphia, in defiance of British authority.

11. Discovered = revealed. Thomas Hobbes's *Leviathan* (1651) and Bernard de Mandeville's *Fable of the Bees* (1714) are both offensive to orthodox morality and piety, and *Leviathan* could be used to support absolute power in the sovereign. Governor Hutchinson's history of Massachusetts reflects his political outlook. Edmond Hoyle's *Short Treatise on Whist* (1742), a comic inclusion, suggests that some of the Loyalists are not even serious. The Stuarts, Henry VIII, and William the Conqueror were absolutist kings. Parliament attempted to exert undue authority over the colonies in the Intolerable Acts, passed in spring, 1774.

12. Physiognomy, slang for facial expression.

13. Monsieur feels remorse because his father found refuge in Boston from France, "the land of slaves [absolutist government] and wooden shoes [poverty]." However, he would rather see religious persecution in the colonies (as in France) than give up his hopes for a political appointment.

14. Charles Viner, Sir Thomas Littleton, and Sir Edward Coke were distinguished English writers of law. Livres (below) were old French coins, originally equivalent to a pound of silver.

15. James Warren. In the following speech, Brundo is Francis Bernard, Governor before Hutchinson. Cassius is Samuel Adams and Hortensius, John Adams. The Arch Traitor is Rapatio, who induced Trumps to go over to the Loyalists.

16. Niccolo Machiavelli and various members of the Borgia family were types of conniving, unscrupulous politicians.

17. Jonathan Sewall, once an intimate friend of John Adams and a Patriot, turned against them when he was refused a grant by the General Court (1760), for which he particularly blamed James Otis. Taking advantage of his disaffection, the Loyalists won his allegiance with a series of political appointments. As "Philanthropos," Sewall wrote ably for the Loyalists, though he was not Massachusettensis, as Adams and Warren supposed.

18. Trumps looks forward to the arrival of mercenary troops from Ger-

many, since Britons would not fight to crush American freedom. John Hampden, Ferdinando Fairfax, and John Pym resisted tyrannical acts by Charles I (1620s to 1640s).

19. Light musket.

20. Alembic, distilling apparatus.

21. The port of Boston was to be closed until the citizens paid for the tea destroyed in the Boston Tea Party ("India's poisonous weed"). However, blockading their coast and closing their ports will not force Americans to comply. Now the sea nymphs can drink choice teas instead of their traditional nectar.

22. The Mandamus Councilors were threatened by the people; some were intimidated into resigning, and some, including Leonard, fled from their neighbors to Boston.

23. Troops of Frederick the Great of Prussia, probably the best-trained army in Europe.

24. Julius Caesar invaded Britain, and Hampden was killed early in the Civil War. General James Wolfe died on the Plains of Abraham, in the Battle of Quebec (1759) that completed the conquest of Canada from the French (Bourbon, the King of France). The Duke of Marlborough was a great English general of the late seventeenth–early eighteenth century. Algernon Sydney, James Harrington, and John Locke (all seventeenth century) wrote in favor of political liberty. Below: Brunswick refers to the British royal house.

25. John Milton, *Paradise Lost* 4:800 (slightly misquoted). Since Meagre represents Foster Hutchinson, his "subtle brother" is Governor Hutchinson.

26. Pseudonyms of writers on the opposing side: Senex, old man; Grotius, a great Dutch jurist. Below: Nova Zembla, two islands in the Arctic Ocean.

27. Ancient Roman patriot, representing James Otis, Warren's brother.

28. It was the vicious emperor Caligula who wished that a Roman crowd had only one neck, so he could cut through it. However, Claudia Augusta (Poppea), the emperor Nero's wife, was capable of similar sentiments.

Frances Burney
(1752–1840)

FRANCES BURNEY, daughter of the charming, self-made music teacher and musicologist Charles Burney, picked up her education from her gifted family and the varied, often brilliant company that frequented her father's house. Charles Burney was a member of Samuel Johnson's Club, and David Garrick used to stop by and amuse the Burney children with mimicry. Frances wrote voluminously from her early teens, producing stories and a diary that evolved into journal-letters that circulated among her appreciative family circle. In these journals she developed her ability to make people reveal themselves and their class through dialogue and to bring out comic interplay in social encounters. She made the most of these skills in her first novel, *Evelina* (1778), which she wrote and sent to a publisher in secret. It proved to be a sensational success, and when her authorship gradually became known, she was welcomed into the most elite intellectual society. Elizabeth Montagu, the leading Bluestocking hostess, made much of her.

Despite its popularity, *Evelina* brought Burney practically no money; and her friends urged her to try the more profitable field of playwriting. With her proven talent for social comedy and the enthusiastic advice and support of friends such as the dramatist Richard Brinsley Sheridan, who was also the manager of the Drury Lane Theater, her success was almost guaranteed. She set to work on *The Witlings* with high hopes, but with strange perversity she chose to focus her ridicule on Bluestockings; worse, Lady Smatter, her major butt, lends herself to identification with Mrs. Montagu, who not only was socially powerful but had been very gracious to Burney. Had the play been produced, her justified fury would have destroyed Burney's precarious social position. It is possible that Burney was not consciously attacking Montagu, whose worst enemies could not have accused her of the gross ignorance displayed by Smatter; but the character's high-handedness, conceit, wealth, and dependent nephew would have immediately suggested the great hostess. Burney's mentors, her father and "Daddy" Crisp (a revered family friend), were horrified by this imprudence, although their reservations took the form of dark insinuations about the indelicacy of writing stage comedy and the perils of appearing as a playwright. With pathetic regrets, Frances consented to suppress *The Witlings*. It is only now being published.

She then published another novel, *Cecilia* (1782). Although this too was successful, it was not profitable enough to support a still-unmarried woman; and Burney was pressured into accepting an appointment as Second Keeper of the Robes to Queen Charlotte. After five stultifying years, she escaped back into private life, fell in love with and married a penniless French émigré, Alexandre d'Arblay, and had a son. The necessity of supporting her family motivated her to drive an advantageous bargain for her third novel, *Camilla* (1796), which brought her two thousand pounds. Meanwhile, she continued her ambivalent and self-defeating relationship with the theater. She wrote three more potentially successful comedies, which, for various insufficient reasons, were not produced. Her only play to reach the stage, *Edwy and Elgiva* (1795), was a dreary tragedy, written during her most unhappy time at Court: it deserved and met with humiliating failure.

The Witlings

A Comedy by
A Sister of the Order

Dramatis Personæ.

Beaufort.

Censor.

Dabbler.

Jack, Half Brother to Beaufort.

Codger, Father to Jack, and Father-in-Law [Stepfather] to Beaufort.

Bob, Son to Mrs. Voluble.

Lady Smatter, Aunt to Beaufort.

Cecilia.

Mrs. Sapient.

Mrs. Voluble.

Mrs. Wheedle, a Milliner.

Miss Jenny, her Apprentice.

Betty, Maid to Mrs. Voluble.

ACT I.

Scene i. A Milliner's Shop. A counter is spread with caps, ribbons, fans, and bandboxes. Miss Jenny and several young women at work.

(Enter Mrs. Wheedle.)

MRS. WHEEDLE. So, young ladies! pray what have you done to-day? (*She examines their work.*) Has anybody been in yet?

MISS JENNY. No, ma'am, nobody to signify;—only some people afoot.

MRS. WHEEDLE. Why, Miss Sally, who is this cap for?

MISS SALLY. Lady Mary Megrim, ma'am.

MRS. WHEEDLE. Lady Mary Megrim, Child? Lord, she'll no more wear it than I shall! why how have you done the lappets? they'll never set while it's a cap;—One would think you had never worked in a Christian land before. Pray, Miss Jenny, set about a cap for Lady Mary yourself.

MISS JENNY. Ma'am, I can't; I'm working for Miss Stanley.

MRS. WHEEDLE. O, ay, for the wedding.

MISS SALLY. Am I to go on with this cap, ma'am?

MRS. WHEEDLE. Yes, to be sure, and let it be sent with the other things to Mrs. Apeall in the Minories;[1] it will do well enough for the City.

(Enter a Footman.)

FOOTMAN. Is Lady Whirligig's cloak ready?

MRS. WHEEDLE. Not quite, Sir, but I'll send it in five minutes.

FOOTMAN. My lady wants it immediately; it was bespoke a week ago, and My Lady says you promised to let her have it last Friday.

MRS. WHEEDLE. Sir, it's just done, and I'll take care to let her Ladyship have it directly.

(Exit Footman.)

MISS JENNY. I don't think it's cut out yet.

MRS. WHEEDLE. I know it i'n't. Miss Sally, you shall set about it when you've done with that cap. Why Miss Polly, for goodness' sake, what are you doing?

MISS POLLY. Making a tippet, ma'am, for Miss Lollop.

MRS. WHEEDLE. Miss Lollop would as soon wear a halter: 'twill be fit for nothing but the window, and there the Miss Notables, who work for themselves, may look at it for a pattern.

(Enter a Young Woman.)

YOUNG WOMAN. If you please, ma'am, I should be glad to look at some ribbons.

MRS. WHEEDLE. We'll show you some presently.

(Enter Mrs. Voluble.)

MRS. VOLUBLE. Mrs. Wheedle, how do do? I'm vastly glad to see you. I hope all the young ladies are well. Miss Jenny, my dear, you look pale; I hope you a'n't in love, Child? Miss Sally, your servant. I saw your uncle the other day, and he's very well, and so are all the children; except, indeed, poor Tommy, and they're afraid he's going to have the whooping cough. I don't think I know that other young lady? O Lord yes, I do,—it's Miss Polly Dyson! I beg your pardon, my dear, but I declare I did not recollect you at first.

MRS. WHEEDLE. Won't you take a chair, Mrs. Voluble?

MRS. VOLUBLE. Why yes, thank you, ma'am; but there are so many pretty things to look at in your shop, that one does not know which way to turn oneself. I declare it's the greatest treat in the world to me to spend a hour or two here in a morning; one sees so many fine things, and so many fine folks,—Lord, who are all these sweet things here for?

MRS. WHEEDLE. Miss Stanley, ma'am, a young lady just going to be married.

MRS. VOLUBLE. Miss Stanley? why I can tell you all about her. Mr. Dabbler, who lives in my house, makes verses upon her.

MISS JENNY. Dear me! is that gentleman who dresses so smart a poet?

MRS. VOLUBLE. A poet? yes, my dear, he's one of the first wits of the age. He can make verses as fast as I can talk.

MISS JENNY. Dear me! Why he's quite a fine gentleman; I thought poets were always as poor as Job.

MRS. VOLUBLE. Why so they are, my dear, in common; your *real* poet is all rags and atoms: but Mr. Dabbler is quite another thing; he's what you may call a poet of fashion. He studies, sometimes, by the hour together. O he's quite one of the great geniuses, I assure you! I listened at his door, once, when he was at it,—for he talks so loud when he's by himself, that we can hear him quite downstairs: but I could make nothing out, only a heap of words all in a chime, as one may say,—mean, lean, dean, wean—Lord, I can't remember half of them! At first when he came, I used to run in his room, and ask what was the matter? but he told me I must not mind him, for it was only the *fit* was on him, I think he called it, and so—

YOUNG WOMAN. I wish somebody would show me some ribbons, I have waited this half hour.

MRS. WHEEDLE. O, ay, I forgot; do show this young gentlewoman some ribbons. (*In a low voice.*) Take last year's. You shall see some just out of the loom.

MRS. VOLUBLE. Well but, Mrs. Wheedle, I was going to tell you about Miss Stanley; you must know she's a young lady with a fortune all in her own hands, for she's just come of age, and she's got neither Papa nor Mama, and so—

(Enter a Footman.)

FOOTMAN. Lady Bab Vertigo desires Mrs. Wheedle will come to the coach door. (*Exit.*)

(Mrs. Wheedle goes out.)

MRS. VOLUBLE (*turning to Miss Jenny*). And so, Miss Jenny, as I was saying, this young lady came to spend the winter in town with Lady Smatter, and so she fell in love with my lady's nephew, Mr. Beaufort, and Mr. Beaufort fell in love with her, and so—

(Re-enter Mrs. Wheedle.)

MRS. WHEEDLE. Miss Jenny, take Lady Bab the new trimming.

MRS. VOLUBLE *(turning to Miss Sally)*. And so, Miss Sally, the match is all agreed upon, and they are to be married next week, and so, as soon as the ceremony is over—

MRS. WHEEDLE. Miss Sally, put away those ribbons.

MRS. VOLUBLE *(turning to Miss Polly)*. And so, Miss Polly, as soon as the ceremony's over, the bride and bridegroom—

CENSOR *(within)*. No, faith, not I! do you think I want to study the fashion of a lady's topknot?

BEAUFORT. Nay, prithee, Censor, in compassion to me—

(Enter Beaufort and Censor struggling.)

CENSOR. Why how now, Beaufort? is not a man's person his own property? do you conclude that, because you take the liberty to expose your own to a ridiculous and unmanly situation, you may use the same freedom with your friend's?

BEAUFORT. Pho, prithee don't be so churlish. Pray, ma'am *(advancing to Mrs. Wheedle)*, has Miss Stanley been here this morning?

MRS. WHEEDLE. No, sir; but I expect her every moment.

BEAUFORT. Then, if you'll give me leave, I'll wait till she comes.

CENSOR. Do as you list, but, for my part, I am gone.

BEAUFORT. How! Will you not stay with me?

CENSOR. No, Sir; I'm a very stupid fellow,—I take no manner of delight in tapes and ribbons. I leave you, therefore, to the unmolested contemplation of this valuable collection of dainties: and I doubt not but you will be equally charmed and edified by the various curiosities you will behold, and the sagacious observations you will hear. Sir, I heartily wish you well entertained. *(Going.)*

BEAUFORT *(holding him)*. Have you no bowels, man?

CENSOR. Yes, for *myself*,—and therefore it is I leave you.

BEAUFORT. You sha'n't go, I swear!

CENSOR. With what weapons will you stay me? Will you tie me to your little finger with a piece of ribbon, like a lady's sparrow? or will you enthrall me in a net of Brussels lace? Will you raise a fortification of caps? or barricade me with furbelows? Will you fire at me a broadside of pompons? or will you stop my retreat with a fan?

MISS JENNY. Dear, how odd the gentleman talks!

MRS. WHEEDLE. I wonder they don't ask to look at something.

MRS. VOLUBLE. I fancy I know who they are. (*Whispers.*)

BEAUFORT. Are you not as able to bear the place as I am? if you had any grace, you would blush to be thus outdone in forbearance.

CENSOR. But, my good friend, do you not consider that there is some little difference in our situations? I, for which I bless my stars! am a *free* man, and therefore may be allowed to have an opinion of my own, to act with consistency, and to be guided by the light of Reason: you, for which I most heartily pity you, are a lover, and, consequently, can have no pretensions to similar privileges. With you, therefore, the practice of patience, the toleration of impertinence, and the study of nonsense, are become duties indispensable; and where can you find more ample occasion to display these acquirements, than in this region of foppery, extravagance, and folly?

BEAUFORT. Ought you not, in justice, to acknowledge some obligation to me for introducing you to a place which abounds in such copious materials to gratify your splenetic humor?

CENSOR. Obligation? what, for showing me new scenes of the absurdities of my fellow creatures?

BEAUFORT. Yes, since those new scenes give fresh occasion to exert that spirit of railing which makes the whole happiness of your life.

CENSOR. Do you imagine, then, that, like Spenser's Strife,[2] I *seek* Occasion? Have I not eyes? and can I open them without becoming a spectator of dissipation, idleness, luxury, and disorder? Have I not ears? and can I use them without becoming an auditor of malevolence, envy, futility, and detraction? O Beaufort, take me where I can *avoid* occasion of railing, and then, indeed, I will confess my obligation to you!

MRS. VOLUBLE (*whispering to Mrs. Wheedle*). It's the youngest that's the bridegroom, that is to be; but I'm pretty sure I know the other too, for he comes to see Mr. Dabbler; I'll speak to him. (*Advances to Censor.*) Sir, your humble servant.

CENSOR. Madam!

MRS. VOLUBLE. I beg your pardon, Sir, but I think I've had the pleasure of seeing you at my house, Sir, when you've called upon Mr. Dabbler.

CENSOR. Mr. Dabbler?—O, yes, I recollect.—Why, Beaufort, what do you mean? did you bring me hither to be food to this magpie?

BEAUFORT. Not I, upon my honor; I never saw the woman before. Who is she?

CENSOR. A fool, a prating, intolerable fool. Dabbler lodges at her house, and whoever passes through her hall to visit him, she claims for her acquaintance. She will consume more words in an hour than ten men will in a year; she is infected with a rage for talking, yet has nothing to say, which is a disease of all others the most pernicious to her fellow creatures, since the method she takes for her own relief proves their bane. Her tongue is as restless as scandal, and, like that, feeds upon nothing, yet attacks and tortures everything; and it vies, in rapidity of motion, with the circulation of the blood in a frog's foot.

MISS JENNY (to Mrs. Voluble). I think the gentleman's very proud, ma'am, to answer you so short.

MRS. VOLUBLE. O, but he won't get off so, I can tell him! I'll speak to him again. Poor Mr. Dabbler, Sir, (to Censor.) has been troubled with a very bad headache lately; I tell him he studies too much, but he says he can't help it; however, I think it's a friend's part to advise him against it, for a little caution can do no harm, you know, Sir, if it does no good, and Mr. Dabbler's such a worthy, agreeable gentleman, and so much the scholar, 'twould be a thousand pities he should come to any ill. Pray, Sir, do you think he'll ever make a match of it with Mrs. Sapient? She's ready enough, we all know, and to be sure, for the matter of that, she's no chicken. Pray, Sir, how old do you reckon she may be?

CENSOR. Really, madam, I have no talents for calculating the age of a lady. What a torrent of impertinence! Upon my honor, Beaufort, if you don't draw this woman off, I shall decamp.

BEAUFORT. I cannot imagine what detains Cecilia; however, I will do anything rather than wait with such gossips by myself. I hope, ma'am, we don't keep you standing?

MRS. VOLUBLE. O no, Sir, I was quite tired of sitting. What a polite young gentleman, Miss Jenny! I'm sure he deserves to marry a fortune. I'll speak to him about the 'Sprit³ Party; he'll be quite surprised to find how much I know of the matter. I think, Sir, your name's Mr. Beaufort?

BEAUFORT. At your service, ma'am.

MRS. VOLUBLE. I was pretty sure it was you, Sir, for I happened to be at my window one morning when you called in a coach; and Mr. Dabbler was out,—that is, between friends, he was only at his studies, but he said he was out, and so that's all one. So you gave in a card,[4] and drove off. I hope, Sir, your good aunt, my Lady Smatter, is well? for though I have not the pleasure of knowing her Ladyship myself, I know them that do. I suppose you two gentlemen are always of the 'Sprit Party, at my Lady's house.

CENSOR. 'Sprit Party? prithee, Beaufort, what's that?

BEAUFORT. O, the most fantastic absurdity under Heaven. My good aunt has established a kind of club at her house, professedly for the discussion of literary subjects; and the set who compose it are about as well qualified for the purpose, as so many dirty cabin boys would be to find out the longitude. To a very little reading, they join less understanding, and no judgment; yet they decide upon books and authors with the most confirmed confidence in their abilities for the task. And this club they have had the modesty to nominate the Esprit Party.

CENSOR. Nay, when you have told me Lady Smatter is President, you need add nothing more to convince me of its futility. Faith, Beaufort, were you my enemy instead of my friend, I should scarce forbear commiserating your situation in being dependent upon that woman. I hardly know a more insufferable being, for having, unfortunately, just *tasted the Pierian Spring,* she has acquired that *little knowledge* so dangerous to shallow understandings,[5] which serves no other purpose than to stimulate a display of ignorance.

MRS. VOLUBLE. I always know, Sir, when there's going to be a 'Sprit party, for Mr. Dabbler shuts himself up to study. Pray, Sir, did you ever see his monody on the birth of Miss Dandle's lap dog?

CENSOR. A monody on a birth?

MRS. VOLUBLE. Yes, Sir. A monody, or elegy, I don't exactly know which you call it, but I think it's one of the prettiest things he ever wrote; there he tells us,—O dear, is not that Mrs. Sapient's coach? I'm pretty sure I know the cypher.

CENSOR. Mrs. Sapient? Nay, Beaufort, if *she* is coming hither—

BEAUFORT. Patience, Man; she is one of the set, and will divert you.

CENSOR. You are mistaken; such consummate folly only makes me melancholy. She is more weak and superficial even than Lady Smatter, yet she has the same facility in giving herself credit for wisdom; and there is a degree of assurance in her conceit that is equally wonderful and disgusting, for as Lady Smatter, from the shallowness of her knowledge, upon all subjects forms a *wrong* judgment, Mrs. Sapient, from extreme weakness of parts, is incapable of forming *any;* but, to compensate for that deficiency, she retails all the opinions she hears, and confidently utters them as her own. Yet, in the most notorious of her plagiarisms, she affects a scrupulous modesty, and apologizes for troubling the company with her poor opinion.

BEAUFORT. She is, indeed, immeasurably wearisome.

CENSOR. When she utters a truth self-evident as that the sun shines at noonday, she speaks it as a discovery resulting from her own peculiar penetration and sagacity.

BEAUFORT. Silence! She is here.

(Enter Mrs. Sapient.)

MRS. SAPIENT. O Mrs. Wheedle, how could you disappoint me so of my short apron? I believe you make it a rule never to keep to your time; and I declare, for *my* part, I know nothing so provoking as people's promising more than they perform.

MRS. WHEEDLE. Indeed, ma'am, I beg ten thousand pardons, but really, ma'am, we've been so hurried, that upon my word, ma'am—but you shall certainly have it this afternoon. Will you give me leave to show you any caps, ma'am? I have some exceeding pretty ones just finished.

MRS. SAPIENT *(looking at the caps).* O, for Heaven's sake, don't show me such flaunting things, for, in *my* opinion, nothing can be really elegant that is tawdry.

MRS. WHEEDLE. But here, ma'am, is one I'm sure you'll like; it's in the immediate taste,—only look at it, ma'am! what can be prettier?

MRS. SAPIENT. Why, yes, this is well enough, only I'm afraid it's too young for me; don't you think it is?

MRS. WHEEDLE. Too young? dear ma'am, no, I'm sure it will become you of all things: only try it. (*Holds it over her head.*) O ma'am, you can't think how charmingly you look in it! and it sets so sweetly! I never saw anything so becoming in my life.

MRS. SAPIENT. Is it? Well, I think I'll have it,—if you are sure it is not too young for me. You must know, I am mightily for people's consulting their time of life in their choice of clothes: and, in *my* opinion, there is a wide difference between fiveteen and fifty.

CENSOR (*to Beaufort*). She'll certainly tell us, next, that, in *her* opinion, a man who has but one eye, would certainly look rather better if he had another!

MRS. WHEEDLE. O I'm sure, ma'am, you'll be quite in love with this cap, when you see how well you look in it. Shall I show you some of our new ribbons, ma'am?

MRS. SAPIENT. O, I know, now, you want to tempt me; but *I* always say the best way to escape temptation is to run away from it: however, as I *am* here—

MRS. VOLUBLE. Had not you better sit down, ma'am? (*Offering a chair.*)

MRS. SAPIENT. O Mrs. Voluble, is it you? How do do? Lord, I don't like any of these ribbons. Pray, how does Mr. Dabbler do?

MRS. VOLUBLE. Very well, thank you, ma'am; that is, not *very* well, but *pretty* well considering, for to be sure, ma'am, so much study's very bad for the health; it's pity he don't take more care of himself, and so I often tell him; but your great wits never mind what little folks say, if they talk never so well, and I'm sure I've sometimes talked to him by the hour together about it, for I'd never spare my words to serve a friend; however, it's all to no purpose, for he says he has a kind of a *fury*, I think he calls it, upon him, that makes him write whether he will or not. And, to be sure, he does write most charmingly! and he has such a collection of miniscrips! Lord, I question if a pastry cook or a cheesemonger could use them in a year![6] for he says he never destroyed a line he ever wrote in his life. All that he don't like, he tells me he keeps by him for his Postimus Works, as he calls them, and I've some notion he intends soon to print them.

MRS. WHEEDLE. Do, ma'am, pray let me put this cloak up for you, and I'll make you a hat for it immediately.

MRS. SAPIENT. Well, then, take great care how you put in the ribbon, for you know I won't keep it if it does not please me. Mr. Beaufort!—Lord bless me, how long have you been here? O Heavens! is that Mr. Censor? I can scarce believe my eyes! Mr. Censor in a milliner's shop! Well, this does, indeed, justify an observation I have often made, that the greatest geniuses sometimes do the oddest things.

CENSOR. Your surprise, madam, at seeing me here today will bear no comparison to what I must myself experience, should you ever see me here again.

MRS. SAPIENT. O, I know well how much you must despise all this sort of business, and, I assure you, I am equally averse to it myself: indeed I often think what pity it is so much time should be given to mere show;—for what are we the better tomorrow for what we have worn today? No time, in *my* opinion, turns to so little account as that which we spend in dress.

CENSOR (*to Beaufort*). Did you ever hear such an impudent falsehood?

MRS. SAPIENT. For *my* part, I always wear just what the milliner and mantua-maker please to send me; for I have a kind of maxim upon this subject which has some weight with *me*, though I don't know if anybody else ever suggested it: but it is, that the real value of a person springs from the *mind,* not from the outside appearance. So I never trouble myself to look at anything till the moment I put it on. Be sure (*Turning quick to the Milliners.*) you take care how you trim the hat! I sha'n't wear it else.

CENSOR. Prithee, Beaufort, how long will you give a man to decide which is greatest, her folly or her conceit?

MRS. SAPIENT. Gentlemen, good morning; Mrs. Voluble, you may give my compliments to Mr. Dabbler. Mrs. Wheedle, pray send the things in time, for, to *me*, nothing is more disagreeable than to be disappointed.

(*As she is going out, Jack enters abruptly, and brushes past her.*)

MRS. SAPIENT. O Heavens!

JACK. Lord, ma'am, I beg you a thousand pardons! I did not see you, I declare. I hope I did not hurt you?

MRS. SAPIENT. No, Sir, no; but you a little alarmed me,—and really, an alarm, when one does not know how to account for it, gives one a rather odd sensation,—at least *I* find it so.

JACK. Upon my word, ma'am, I'm very sorry,—I'm sure if I'd seen you—but I was in such monstrous haste, I had no time to look about me.

MRS. SAPIENT. O, Sir, 'tis of no consequence; yet, allow me to observe that, in *my* opinion, too much haste generally defeats its own purpose. Sir, good morning. (*Exit.*)

BEAUFORT. Why Jack, won't you see her to her coach?

JACK. O ay, true, so I must. (*Follows her.*)

CENSOR. This brother of yours, Beaufort, is a most ingenious youth.

BEAUFORT. He has foibles which you, I am sure, will not spare; but he means well, and is extremely good-natured.

CENSOR. Nay, but I am serious, for without ingenuity, no man, I think, could continue to be always in a hurry, who is never employed.

(Re-enter Jack.)

JACK. Plague take it, Brother, how unlucky it was that you made me go after her! in running up to her, my deuced spurs caught hold of some of her falaldrums, and in my haste to disengage myself, I tore off half her trimming. She went off in a very ill humor, telling me that, in *her* opinion a disagreeable accident was very—very—very disagreeable, I think, or something to that purpose.

BEAUFORT. But, for Heaven's sake, Jack, what is the occasion of all this furious haste?

JACK. Why Lord, you know I'm always in a hurry; I've no notion of dreaming away life: how the deuce is anything to be done without a little spirit?

BEAUFORT. Pho, prithee, Jack, give up this idle humor.

JACK. Idle? nay, Brother, call me what else you please, but you can never charge me with idleness.

BEAUFORT. Why, with all your boasted activity, I question if there is a man in England who would be more embarrassed how to give any account of his time.

JACK. Well, well, I can't stay now to discourse upon these matters,—I have too many things to *do* to stand here talking.

BEAUFORT. Nay, don't go till you tell us what you have to do this morning?

JACK. Why more things than either of you would do in a month, but I can't stop now to tell you any of them, for I have three friends waiting for me in Hyde Park, and twenty places to call at in my way. (*Going.*)

MRS. WHEEDLE (*following him*). Sir, would you not choose to look at some ruffles?

JACK. O, ay,—have you anything new? what do you call these?

MRS. WHEEDLE. O pray, Sir, take care! they are so delicate they'll hardly bear to be touched.

JACK. I don't like them at all! show me some others.

MRS. WHEEDLE. Why, Sir, only see! you have quite spoiled this pair.

JACK. Have I? well, then, you must put them up for me. But pray have you got no better?

MRS. WHEEDLE. I'll look some directly, Sir,—but, Dear Sir, pray, don't put your switch upon the caps! I hope you'll excuse me, Sir, but the set is all in all in these little tasty things.

CENSOR. And pray, Jack, are all your hurries equally important, and equally necessary as those of this morning?

JACK. Lord, you grave fellows, who plod on from day to day without any notion of life and spirit, spend half your lives in asking people questions they don't know how to answer.

CENSOR. And we might consume the other half to as little purpose, if we waited to find out questions which such people *do* know how to answer.

JACK. Severe, very severe, that! however, I have not time, now, for repartee, but I shall give you a Rowland for your Oliver[7] when we meet again. (*Going.*)

MRS. WHEEDLE. Sir, I've got the ruffles,—won't you look at them?

JACK. O, the ruffles! well, I'm glad you've found them, but I can't stay to look at them now. Keep them in the way against I call again. (*Exit.*)

MRS. WHEEDLE. Miss Jenny, put these ruffles up again. That gentleman never knows his own mind.

MISS JENNY. I'm sure he's tumbled and tossed the things about like mad.

CENSOR. 'Tis to be much regretted, Beaufort, that such a youth as this was not an elder brother.

BEAUFORT. Why so?

CENSOR. Because the next heir might so easily get rid of him; for, if he was knocked down, I believe he would think it loss of time to get up again, and if he were pushed into a river, I question if he would not be drowned, ere he could persuade himself to swim long enough in the same direction to save himself.

BEAUFORT. He is young, and I hope this ridiculous humor will wear away.

CENSOR. But how came *you* so wholly to escape its infection? I find not, in you, any portion of this inordinate desire of action, to which all power of thinking must be sacrificed.

BEAUFORT. Why we are but half brothers, and our educations were as different as our fathers, for my mother's second husband was no more like her first, than am *I to Hercules;*[8]—though Jack, indeed, has no resemblance even to his own father.

CENSOR. Resemblance? an hare and a tortoise are not more different; for Jack is always running, without knowing what he pursues, and his father is always pondering, without knowing what he thinks of.

BEAUFORT. The truth is, Mr. Codger's humor of perpetual deliberation so early sickened his son, that the fear of inheriting any share of it made him rush into the opposite extreme, and determine to avoid the censure of inactive meditation by executing every plan he could form at the very moment of projection.

CENSOR. And pray, Sir,—if such a question will not endanger a challenge,—what think you, by this time, of the punctuality of your mistress?

BEAUFORT. Why,—to own the truth—I fear I must have made some mistake.

CENSOR. Bravo, Beaufort! ever doubt your own senses, in preference to suspecting your mistress of negligence or caprice.

BEAUFORT. She is much too noble-minded, too just in her sentiments, and too uniform in her conduct, to be guilty of either.

CENSOR. Bravissimo, Beaufort! I commend your patience, and, this time twelvemonth, I'll ask you how it wears! In the meantime, however, I would not upon any account interrupt your contemplations either upon her excellencies, or your own mistakes, but, as I expect no advantage from the one, you must excuse my any longer suffering from the other: and, ere you again entangle me in such a wilderness of frippery, I shall take the liberty more closely to investigate the accuracy of your appointments. (*Exit.*)

BEAUFORT. My situation begins to grow as ridiculous as it is disagreeable. Surely Cecilia cannot have forgotten me!

MRS. VOLUBLE (*advancing to him*). To be sure, Sir, it's vastly incommodious to be kept waiting so, but, Sir, if I might put in a word, I think—

(Enter Jack running.)

JACK. Lord, Brother, I quite forgot to tell you Miss Stanley's message.

BEAUFORT. Message! What message?

JACK. I declare I had got halfway to Hyde Park, before I ever thought of it.

BEAUFORT. Upon my honor, Jack, this is too much!

JACK. Why I ran back the moment I recollected it, and what could I do more? I would not even stop to tell Will Scamper what was the matter, so he has been calling and bawling after me all the way I came. I gave him the slip when I got to the shop,—but I'll just step and see if he's in the street. (*Going.*)

BEAUFORT. Jack, you'll provoke me to more anger than you are prepared for! what was the message? tell me quickly!

JACK. O ay, true! why she said she could not come.

BEAUFORT. Not come? but *why*? I'm sure she told you *why*.

JACK. O yes, she told me a long story about it,—but I've forgot what it was.

BEAUFORT (*warmly*). Recollect, then!

JACK. Why so I will. O, it was all your aunt Smatter's fault,— somebody came in with the new Ranelagh Songs,[9] so she stayed at home to study them; and Miss Stanley bid me say she was very sorry, but she could not come by herself.

BEAUFORT. And why might I not have been told this sooner?

JACK. Why she desired me to come and tell you of it an hour or two ago, but I had so many places to stop at by the way, I could not possibly get here sooner: and when I came, my head was so full of my own appointments, that I never once thought of her message. However, I must run back to Will Scamper, or he'll think me crazy.

BEAUFORT. Hear me, Jack! if you do not take pains to correct this absurd rage to attempt everything, while you execute nothing, you will render yourself as contemptible to the world, as you are useless or mischievous to your family. (*Exit.*)

JACK. What a passion he's in! I've a good mind to run to Miss Stanley, and beg her to intercede for me. (*Going.*)

MRS. WHEEDLE. Sir, won't you please to look at the ruffles?

JACK. O ay, true,—where are they?

MRS. WHEEDLE. Here, Sir. Miss Jenny, give me those ruffles again.

JACK. O if they a'n't ready, I can't stay. (*Exit.*)

MRS. VOLUBLE. Well, Mrs. Wheedle, I'm sure you've a pleasant life of it here, in seeing so much of the world. I'd a great mind to have spoke to that young gentleman, for I'm pretty sure I've seen him before, though I can't tell where. But he was in such a violent hurry, I could not get in a word. He's a fine lively young gentleman, to be sure. But now, Mrs. Wheedle, when will you come and drink a snug dish of tea with me? you, and Miss Jenny, and any of the young ladies that can be spared. I'm sure if you can *all* come—

(*Enter Bob.*)

BOB. I ask pardon, Ladies and Gentlemen, but pray is my mother here?

MRS. VOLUBLE. What's that to you, Sirrah? who gave you leave to follow me? get home, directly, you dirty figure you! go, go, I say!

BOB. Why Lord, Mother, you've been out all the morning, and never told Betty what was for dinner!

MRS. VOLUBLE. Why you great, tall, greedy, gormandizing, lubberly cub, you, what signifies whether you have any dinner or no? go, get away, you idle, good for nothing, dirty, greasy, hulking, tormenting—

(*She drives him off, and the scene closes.*)

ACT II.

Scene i. A Drawing Room at Lady Smatter's.

(Lady Smatter and Cecilia.)

LADY SMATTER. Yes, yes, this song is certainly Mr. Dabbler's, I am not to be deceived in his style. What say you, my dear Miss Stanley, don't you think I have found him out?

CECILIA. Indeed I am too little acquainted with his poems to be able to judge.

LADY SMATTER. Your indifference surprises me! for my part, I am never at rest till I have discovered the authors of everything that comes out; and, indeed, I commonly hit upon them in a moment. I declare, I sometimes wonder at myself, when I think how lucky I am in my guesses.

CECILIA. Your Ladyship devotes so much time to these researches, that it would be strange if they were unsuccessful.

LADY SMATTER. Yes, I do indeed devote my time to them; I own it without blushing, for how, as a certain author says, can time be better employed than in cultivating intellectual accomplishments? And I am often surprised, my dear Miss Stanley, that a young lady of your good sense should not be more warmly engaged in the same pursuit.

CECILIA. My pursuits, whatever they may be, are too unimportant to deserve being made public.

LADY SMATTER. Well to be sure, we are all born with sentiments of our own, as I read in a book I can't just now recollect the name of, so I ought not to wonder that yours and mine do not coincide; for, I declare, if my pursuits were not made public, I should not have any at all, for where can be the pleasure of reading books, and studying authors, if one is not to have the credit of talking of them?

CECILIA. Your Ladyship's desire of celebrity is too well known for your motives to be doubted.

LADY SMATTER. Well but, my dear Miss Stanley, I have been thinking for some time past of your becoming a member of our Esprit Party: Shall I put up your name?

CECILIA. By no means; my ambition aspires not at an honor for which I feel myself so little qualified.

LADY SMATTER. Nay, but you are too modest; you can't suppose how much you may profit by coming among us. I'll tell you some of our regulations. The principal persons of our party are authors and critics; the authors always bring us something new of their own, and the critics regale us with manuscript notes upon something old.

CECILIA. And in what class is your Ladyship?

LADY SMATTER. O, I am among the critics. I love criticism passionately, though it really is laborious work, for it obliges one to read with a vast deal of attention. I declare I am sometimes so immensely fatigued with the toil of studying for faults and objections, that I am ready to fling all my books behind the fire.

CECILIA. And what authors have you chiefly criticized?

LADY SMATTER. Pope and Shakespeare. I have found more errors in those than in any other.

CECILIA. I hope, however, for the sake of readers less fastidious, your Ladyship has also left them some beauties.

LADY SMATTER. O yes, I have not cut them up regularly through; indeed, I have not, yet, read above half their works, so how they will fare as I go on, I can't determine. O, here's Beaufort.

(Enter Beaufort.)

BEAUFORT. Your Ladyship's most obedient.

CECILIA. Mr. Beaufort, I am quite ashamed to see you! yet the disappointment I occasioned you was as involuntary on my part, as it could possibly be disagreeable on yours. Your brother, I hope, prevented your waiting long?

BEAUFORT. That you meant he should is sufficient reparation for my loss of time; but what must be the disappointment that an apology from you would not soften?

LADY SMATTER (*reading*). O lovely, charming, beauteous maid,—I wish this song was not so difficult to get by heart,—but I am always beginning one line for another. After all, study is a most fatiguing thing! O how little does the world suspect, when we are figuring in all the brilliancy of conversation, the private hardships, and secret labors of a belle esprit![10]

(Enter a Servant.)

SERVANT. Mr. Codger, My Lady.

(Enter Mr. Codger.)

LADY SMATTER. Mr. Codger, your servant. I hope I see you well?

CODGER. Your Ladyship's most humble. Not so well, indeed, as I could wish, yet, perhaps, better than I deserve to be.

LADY SMATTER. How is my friend Jack?

CODGER. I can't directly say, madam; I have not seen him these two hours, and poor Jack is but a harum-scarum young man; many things may have happened to him in the space of two hours.

LADY SMATTER. And what, my good Sir, can you apprehend?

CODGER. To enumerate all the casualties I apprehend might, perhaps, be tedious. I will, therefore, only mention the heads. In the first place, he may be thrown from his horse; in the second place, he may be run over while on foot; in the third place—

LADY SMATTER. O pray *place* him no more in situations so horrible. Have you heard lately from our friends in the north?

CODGER. Not very lately, madam: the last letter I received was dated the sixteenth of February, and that, you know, madam, was five weeks last Thursday.

LADY SMATTER. I hope you had good news?

CODGER. Why, madam, yes; at least none bad. My sister Deborah acquainted me with many curious little pieces of history that have happened in her neighborhood: would it be agreeable to your Ladyship to hear them?

LADY SMATTER. O no, I would not take up so much of your time.

CODGER. I cannot, madam, employ my time more agreeably. Let me see,—in the first place—no, that was not first,—let me recollect!

BEAUFORT. Pray, Sir, was any mention made of Tom?

CODGER. Yes; but don't be impatient; I shall speak of him in his turn.

BEAUFORT. I beg your pardon, Sir, but I enquired from hearing he was not well.

CODGER. I shall explain whence that report arose in a few minutes; in the meantime, I must beg you not to interrupt me, for I am trying to arrange a chain of anecdotes for the satisfaction of Lady Smatter.

LADY SMATTER. Bless me, Mr. Codger, I did not mean to give you so much trouble.

CODGER. It will be no trouble in the world, if your Ladyship will, for a while, forbear speaking to me, though the loss upon the occasion will be all mine. (*He retires to the side scene.*)[11]

LADY SMATTER. What a formal old fogrum[12] the man grows! Beaufort, have you seen this song?

BEAUFORT. I believe not, madam.

LADY SMATTER. O, it's the prettiest thing! but I don't think you have a true taste for poetry; I never observed you to be enraptured, lost in ecstasy, or hurried as it were out of yourself, when I have been reading to you. But *my* enthusiasm for poetry may, perhaps, carry me too far; come now, my dear Miss Stanley, be sincere with me, don't you think I indulge this propensity too much?

CECILIA. I should be sorry to have your Ladyship suppose me quite insensible to the elegance of literary pursuits, though I neither claim any title, nor profess any ability to judge of them.

LADY SMATTER. O you'll do very well in a few years. But, as you observe, I own I think there is something rather elegant in a taste for these sort of amusements: otherwise, indeed, I should not have taken so much pains to acquire it, for, to confess the truth, I had from Nature quite an aversion to reading,—I remember the time when the very sight of a book was disgustful to me!

CODGER (*coming forward*). I believe, madam, I can now satisfy your enquiries.

LADY SMATTER. What enquiries?

CODGER. Those your Ladyship made in relation to my letter from our friends in Yorkshire. In the first place, my sister Deborah writes me word that the new barn which, you may remember, was begun last summer, is pretty nearly finished. And here, in my pocket book, I have gotten the dimensions of it. It is fifteen feet by—

LADY SMATTER. O, for Heaven's sake, Mr. Codger, don't trouble yourself to be so circumstantial.

CODGER. The trouble, madam, is inconsiderable, or, if it were otherwise, for the information of your Ladyship I would most readily go through with it. It is fifteen feet by thirty. And pray does your Ladyship remember the old dog kennel at the parsonage house?

LADY SMATTER. No, Sir; I never look at dog kennels.

CODGER. Well, madam, my sister Deborah writes me word—

(Enter Servant.)

SERVANT. Mr. Dabbler, My Lady.

(Enter Mr. Dabbler.)

LADY SMATTER. Mr. Dabbler, you are the man in the world I most wished to see.

DABBLER. Your Ladyship is beneficence itself!

LADY SMATTER. A visit from you, Mr. Dabbler, is the greatest of favors, since your time is not only precious to yourself, but to the world.

DABBLER. It is, indeed, precious to myself, madam, when I devote it to the service of your Ladyship. Miss Stanley, may I hope you are as well as you look? if so, your health must indeed be in a state of perfection; if not, never before did sickness wear so fair a mask.

LADY SMATTER. 'Tis a thousand pities, Mr. Dabbler, to throw away such poetical thoughts and imagery in common conversation.

DABBLER. Why, ma'am, the truth is, something a little out of the usual path is expected from a man whom the world has been pleased to style a poet;—though I protest I never knew why!

LADY SMATTER. How true is it that modesty, as Pope, or Swift, I forget which, has it, is the constant attendant upon merit![13]

DABBLER. If merit, madam, were but the constant attendant upon modesty, then, indeed, I might hope to attain no little share! Faith, I'll set that down. (*He takes out his tablets.*)

CODGER. And so, madam, my sister Deborah writes me word—

LADY SMATTER. O dear, Mr. Codger, I merely wanted to know if all our friends were well.

CODGER. Nay, if your Ladyship does not want to hear about the dog kennel—

LADY SMATTER. Not in the least! I hate kennels, and dogs too.

CODGER. As you please, madam! (*Aside.*) She has given me the trouble of ten minutes recollection, and now she won't hear me!

LADY SMATTER. Mr. Dabbler, I believe I've had the pleasure of seeing something of yours this morning.

DABBLER. Of mine? you alarm me beyond measure!

LADY SMATTER. Nay, nay, 'tis in print, so don't be frightened.

DABBLER. Your Ladyship relieves me: but, really, people are so little delicate in taking copies of my foolish manuscripts, that I protest I go into no house without the fear of meeting something of my own. But what may it be?

LADY SMATTER. Why I'll repeat it.

O sweetest, softest, gentlest maid—

DABBLER. No, ma'am, no;—you mistake,—

O lovely, beauteous, charming maid,—

is it not so?

LADY SMATTER. Yes, yes, that's it. O what a vile memory is mine! after all my studying to make such a mistake! I declare I forget as fast as I learn. I shall begin to fancy myself a wit by and by.

DABBLER. Then will your Ladyship for the *first* time be the *last* to learn something. (*Aside.*) 'Gad, I'll put that into an epigram!

LADY SMATTER. I was reading, the other day, that the memory of a poet should be short, that his works may be original.

DABBLER. Heavens, madam, where did you meet with that?

LADY SMATTER. I can't exactly say, but either in Pope or Swift.[14]

DABBLER. O curse it, how unlucky!

LADY SMATTER. Why so?

DABBLER. Why, madam, 'tis my own thought! I've just finished an epigram upon that very subject! I protest I shall grow more and more sick of books every day, for I can never look into any, but I'm sure of popping upon something of my own.

LADY SMATTER. Well, but, dear Sir, pray let's hear your epigram.

DABBLER. Why—if your Ladyship insists upon it—(*Reads.*)

> Ye gentle Gods, O hear me plead,
> And kindly grant this little loan;
> Make me forget whate'er I read
> That what I write may be my own.

LADY SMATTER. O charming! very clever indeed.

BEAUFORT. But, pray, Sir, if such is your wish, why should you read at all?

DABBLER. Why, Sir, one must read; one's reputation requires it; for it would be cruelly confusing to be asked after such or such an author, and never to have looked into him—especially to a person who passes for having some little knowledge in these matters.

BEAUFORT (*aside*). What a shallow coxcomb!

LADY SMATTER. You must positively let me have a copy of that epigram, Mr. Dabbler. Don't you think it charming, Mr. Codger?

CODGER. Madam, I never take anything in at first hearing; if Mr. Dabbler will let me have it in my own hand, I will give your Ladyship my opinion of it, after I have read it over two or three times.

DABBLER. Sir, it is much at your service; but I must insist upon it that you don't get it by heart.

CODGER. Bless me, Sir, I should not do that in half a year! I have no turn for such sort of things.

LADY SMATTER. I know not in what Mr. Dabbler most excels, epigrams, sonnets, odes or elegies.

DABBLER. Dear ma'am, mere nonsense! but I believe your Ladyship forgets my little lampoons?

LADY SMATTER. O no, that I never can! there you are indeed perfect.

DABBLER. Your Ladyship far overrates my poor abilities;—my writings are mere trifles, and I believe the world would be never the worse, if they were all committed to the flames.

BEAUFORT (*aside*). I would I could try the experiment!

LADY SMATTER. Your talents are really universal.

DABBLER. O ma'am, you quite overpower me! but now you are pleased to mention the word *universal*,—did your Ladyship ever meet with my little attempt in the epic way?

LADY SMATTER. O no, you sly creature! but I shall now suspect you of everything.

DABBLER. Your Ladyship is but too partial. I have, indeed, some little facility in stringing rhymes, but I should suppose there's nothing very extraordinary in that: everybody, I believe, has some little talent,—mine happens to be for poetry, but it's all a chance! nobody can choose for himself; and really, to be candid, I don't know if some other things are not of equal consequence.

LADY SMATTER. There, Mr. Dabbler, I must indeed differ from you! what in the universe can be put in competition with poetry?

DABBLER. Your Ladyship's enthusiasm for the fine arts—

(Enter a Servant.)

SERVANT. Mrs. Sapient, madam.

LADY SMATTER. Lord, how tiresome! She'll talk us to death!

(Enter Mrs. Sapient.)

Dear Mrs. Sapient, this is vastly good of you!

DABBLER. Your arrival, madam, is particularly critical at this time, for we are engaged in a literary controversy; and to whom can we so properly apply to enlighten our doubts by the sunbeams of her counsel, as to Mrs. Sapient?

LADY SMATTER *(aside)*. What a sweet speech! I wonder how he could make it to that stupid woman!

MRS. SAPIENT. You do me too much honor, Sir. But what is the subject I have been so unfortunate as to interrupt? for though I shall be ashamed to offer my sentiments before such a company as this, I yet have rather a peculiar way of thinking upon this subject.

DABBLER. As how, ma'am?

MRS. SAPIENT. Why, Sir, it seems to *me* that a proper degree of courage is preferable to a superfluous excess of modesty.

DABBLER. Excellent! extremely right, madam. The present question is upon poetry. We were considering whether, impartially speaking, some other things are not of equal importance?

MRS. SAPIENT. I am unwilling, Sir, to decide upon so delicate a point; yet, were I to offer my humble opinion, it would be, that though to *me* nothing is more delightful than poetry, I yet fancy there may be other things of greater utility in common life.

DABBLER. Pray, Mr. Codger, what is your opinion?

CODGER. Sir, I am so intently employed in considering this epigram, that I cannot, just now, maturely weigh your question;

and indeed, Sir, to acknowledge the truth, I could have excused your interrupting me.

DABBLER. Sir, you do my foolish epigram much honor—(*Aside.*) That man has twice the sense one would suppose from his look. I'll show him my new sonnet.

MRS. SAPIENT. How much was I surprised, Mr. Beaufort, at seeing Mr. Censor this morning in a milliner's shop!

CECILIA. I rejoice to hear you had such a companion; and yet, perhaps, I ought rather to regret it, since the sting of his raillery might but inflame your disappointment and vexation.

BEAUFORT. The sting of a professed satirist only proves poisonous to fresh subjects; those who have often felt it are merely tickled by the wound.

DABBLER (*aside*). How the deuce shall I introduce the sonnet? Pray, Ladies and Gentlemen, you who so often visit the Muses, is there anything new in the poetical way?

LADY SMATTER. Who, Mr. Dabbler, can so properly answer that question as you,—you, to whom all their haunts are open?

DABBLER. O dear ma'am, such compositions as mine are the merest baubles in the world! I dare say there are people who would even be ashamed to set their names to them.

BEAUFORT (*aside*). I hope there is but one person who would not!

MRS. SAPIENT. How much more amiable in *my* eyes is genius when joined with diffidence, than with conceit!

CODGER (*returning the epigram*). Sir, I give you my thanks: and I think, Sir, your wish is somewhat uncommon.

DABBLER. I am much pleased, Sir, that you approve of it. (*Aside.*) This man does not want understanding, with all his formality. He'll be prodigiously struck with my sonnet.

MRS. SAPIENT. What, is that something new of Mr. Dabbler's? Surely, Sir, you must write night and day.

DABBLER. O dear no, ma'am, for I compose with a facility that is really surprising. Yet, sometimes, to be sure, I have been pretty hard worked; in the charade season I protest I hardly slept a wink! I spent whole days in looking over dictionaries for words of double meaning: and really I made some not amiss. But 'twas too easy; I soon grew sick of it. Yet I never quite gave it up till, accidentally, I heard a housemaid say to a scullion, "My first, is yourself; my second, holds good cheer; and my third, is my own office;"—and 'Gad, the word was scrub-bing!

CODGER. With respect, Sir, to that point concerning which you consulted me, I am inclined to think—

DABBLER. Sir!

CODGER. You were speaking to me, Sir, respecting the utility of poetry; I am inclined to think—

DABBLER. O àpropos, now I think of it, I have a little sonnet here that is quite pat to the subject, and—

CODGER. What subject, good Sir?

DABBLER. What subject?—why—this subject, you know.

CODGER. As yet, Sir, we are talking of no subject; I was going—

DABBLER. Well but—ha! ha!—it puts me so in mind of this little sonnet we were speaking of, that—

CODGER. But, Sir, you have not heard what I was going to say.—

DABBLER. True, Sir, true;—I'll put the poem away for the present,—unless, indeed, you very much wish to see it?

CODGER. Another time will do as well, Sir. I don't rightly comprehend what I read before company.

DABBLER. Dear Sir, such trifles as these are hardly worth your serious study; however, if you'll promise not to take a copy, I think I'll venture to trust you with the manuscript,—but you must be sure not to show it [to] a single soul,—and pray take great care of it.

CODGER. Good Sir, I don't mean to take it at all.

DABBLER. Sir!

CODGER. I have no time for reading; and I hold that these sort of things only turn one's head from matters of more importance.

DABBLER. O very well, Sir,—if you don't want to see it—(*Aside.*) What a tasteless old dolt! curse me if I shall hardly be civil to him when I meet him next!

CODGER. Notwithstanding which, Sir, if I should find an odd hour or two in the course of the winter, I will let you know, and you may send it to me.

DABBLER. Dear Sir, you do me a vast favor! (*Aside.*) The fellow's a perfect driveler!

LADY SMATTER. I declare, Mr. Codger, had we known you were so indifferent to the charms of poetry, we should have never admitted you of our party.

CODGER. Madam, I was only moved to enter it in order to oblige your Ladyship; but I shall hardly attend it above once more,—or twice at the utmost.

(Enter Jack.)

JACK (*to Lady Smatter*). Ma'am, your servant. Where's Miss Stanley? I'm so out of breath I can hardly speak. Miss Stanley, I'm come on purpose to tell you some news.

CECILIA. It ought to be of some importance by your haste.

BEAUFORT. Not a whit the more for that! his haste indicates nothing, for it accompanies him in everything.

JACK. Nay, if you won't hear me at once, I'm gone.

CODGER. And pray, Son Jack, whither may you be going?

JACK. Lord, Sir, to an hundred places at least. I shall be all over the town in less than half an hour.

CODGER. Nevertheless it is well known, you have no manner of business over any part of it. I am much afraid, Son Jack, you will be a blockhead all your life.

LADY SMATTER. For shame, Mr. Codger! Jack, you were voted into our Esprit Party last meeting; and if you come tonight, you will be admitted.

JACK. I'll come with the greatest pleasure, ma'am, if I can but get away from Will Scamper, but we are upon a frolic tonight, so it's ten to one if I can make off.

MRS. SAPIENT. If I might take the liberty, Sir, to offer *my* advice upon this occasion, I should say that useful friends were more improving than frivolous companions, for, in *my* opinion, it is [a] pity to waste time.

JACK. Why, ma'am, that's just my way of thinking! I like to be always getting forward, always doing something. Why I am going now as far as Fleet Street, to a print shop where I left Tom Whiffle. I met him in my way from Cornhill, and promised to be back with him in half an hour.

BEAUFORT. Cornhill? you said you were going to Hyde Park.[15]

JACK. Yes, but I met Kit Filligree, and he hauled me into the City. But, now you put me in mind of it, I believe I had best run there first, and see who's waiting.

BEAUFORT. But what, in the meantime, is to become of Tom Whiffle?

JACK. O, hang him, he can wait.

CODGER. In truth, Son Jack, you scandalize me! I have even apprehensions for your head; you appear to me to be *non compos mentis*.

BEAUFORT. 'Tis pity, Jack, you cannot change situations with a running footman.

JACK. Ay, ay, good folks, I know you all love to cut me up, so pray amuse yourselves your own way,—only don't expect me to stay and hear you. (*Going.*)

CODGER. Son Jack, return. Pray answer me to the following question.

JACK. Dear Sir, pray be quick, for I'm in a horrid hurry.

CODGER. A little more patience, Son, would become you better; you should consider that you are but a boy, and that I am your father.

JACK. Yes, Sir, I do. Was that all, Sir?

CODGER. All, why I have said nothing.

JACK. Very true, Sir.

CODGER. You might, also, to keep it constantly in your head that I am not merely older, but wiser than yourself.

JACK. Yes, Sir. (*Aside.*) Demme, though, if I believe that!

CODGER. You would do well, also, to remember, that such haste to quit my presence, looks as if you took no pleasure in my company.

JACK. It does so, Sir. (*Aside.*) Plague take it, I sha'n't get away this age.

CODGER. Son Jack, I insist upon your minding what I say.

JACK. I will, Sir. (*Going.*)

CODGER. Why you are running away without hearing my question.

JACK (*aside*). O dem it, I shall never get off! Pray, Sir, what is it?

CODGER. Don't speak so quick, Jack, there's no understanding a word you say. One would think you supposed I was going to take the trouble of asking a question that was not of sufficient importance to deserve an answer.

JACK. True, Sir: but do pray be so good [as] to make haste.

CODGER. Son, once again, don't put yourself in such a fury; you hurry me so, you have almost made me forget what I wanted to ask you; let me see,—O, now I recollect; pray, do you know if the fish was sent home before you came out?

JACK. Lord no, Sir, I know nothing of the matter! (*Aside.*) How plaguy tiresome! to keep me all this time for such a question as that.

CODGER. Son Jack, you know nothing! I am concerned to say it, but you know nothing!

LADY SMATTER. Don't judge him hastily. Mr. Dabbler, you seem lost in thought.

DABBLER. Do I, ma'am? I protest I did not know it.

LADY SMATTER. O you are a sly creature! Planning some poem, I dare say.

JACK. I'll e'en take French leave. (*Going.*)

CECILIA. You are destined to be tormented this morning, (*Following him.*) for I cannot suffer you to escape till we come to an explanation: you said you had news for me?

JACK. O ay, true; I'll tell you what it was. While I was upon 'Change[16] this morning—but hold, I believe I'd best tell Lady Smatter first.

CECILIA. Why so?

JACK. Because perhaps you'll be frightened.

CECILIA. Frightened? at what?

JACK. Why it's very bad news.

CECILIA. Good God; what can this mean?

BEAUFORT. Nothing, I dare be sworn.

JACK. Very well, Brother! I wish you may think it nothing when you've heard it.

CECILIA. Don't keep me in suspense, I beseech you.

BEAUFORT. Jack, what is it you mean by alarming Miss Stanley thus?

JACK. Plague take it, I wish I had not spoke at all! I shall have him fly into another passion.

CECILIA. Why will you not explain yourself?

JACK. Why, ma'am, if you please, I'll call on you in the afternoon.

CECILIA. No, no, you do but increase my apprehensions by this delay.

BEAUFORT. Upon my honor, Jack, this is insufferable!

JACK. Why Lord, Brother, don't be so angry.

LADY SMATTER. Nay, now Jack, you are really provoking.

MRS. SAPIENT. Why yes, I must needs own I am, myself, of opinion that it is rather disagreeable to wait long for bad news.

CODGER. In truth, Jack, you are no better than a booby.

JACK. Well, if you will have it, you will! but I tell you beforehand you won't like it. You know Stipend, the banker?

CECILIA. Good Heaven, know him? Yes,—what of him?

JACK. Why—now, upon my word, I'd rather not speak.

CECILIA. You sicken me with apprehension!

JACK. Well,—had you much money in his hands?

CECILIA. Everything I am worth in the world!

JACK. Had you, faith?

CECILIA. You terrify me to death!—what would you say?

BEAUFORT. No matter what,—Jack, I could murder you!

JACK. There, now, I said how it would be! now would not anybody suppose the man broke[17] through my fault?

CECILIA. Broke?—O Heaven, I am ruined!

BEAUFORT. No, my dearest Cecilia, your safety is wrapped in mine, and, to my heart's last sigh, they shall be inseparable.

LADY SMATTER. Broke?—What can this mean?

MRS. SAPIENT. Broke? who is broke? I am quite alarmed.

CODGER. In truth, this has the appearance of a serious business.

CECILIA. Mr. Beaufort, let me pass—I can stand this no longer.

BEAUFORT. Allow me to conduct you to your own room; this torrent will overpower you. Jack, wait till I return. (*He leads Cecilia out.*)

JACK. No, no, Brother, you'll excuse me there!—I've stayed too long already. (*Going.*)

LADY SMATTER. Hold, Jack. I have ten thousand questions to ask you. Explain to me what all this means. It is of the utmost consequence I should know immediately.

MRS. SAPIENT. I, too, am greatly terrified: I know not but I may be myself concerned in this transaction; and really the thought of losing one's money is extremely serious, for, as far as *I* have seen of the world, there's no living without it.

CODGER. In truth, Son Jack, you have put us all into tribulation.

MRS. SAPIENT. What, Sir, did you say was the banker's name?

JACK (*aside*). Lord, how they worry me! Stipend, ma'am.

MRS. SAPIENT. Stipend? I protest he has concerns with half my acquaintance! Lady Smatter, I am in the utmost consternation at this intelligence; I think one hears some bad news or other every day,—half the people one knows are ruined![18] I wish your Ladyship good morning. Upon my word, in *my* opinion, a bankruptcy is no pleasant thing! (*Exit.*)

LADY SMATTER. Pray, Jack, satisfy me more clearly how this affair stands; tell me all you know of it.

JACK (*aside*). Lord, I sha'n't get away till midnight! (*To Lady Smatter.*) Why ma'am, the man's broke, that's all.

LADY SMATTER. But *how?* is there no prospect his affairs may be made up?

JACK. None; they say upon 'Change there won't be a shilling in the pound.

LADY SMATTER. What an unexpected blow! Poor Miss Stanley!

DABBLER. 'Tis a shocking circumstance indeed. (*Aside.*) I think it will make a pretty good elegy, though!

LADY SMATTER. I can't think what the poor girl will do! for here is an end of our marrying her!

DABBLER. 'Tis very hard upon her indeed. (*Aside.*) 'Twill be the most pathetic thing I ever wrote! (*To Lady Smatter.*) Ma'am, your Ladyship's most obedient. I'll to work while the subject is warm,—nobody will read it with dry eyes! (*Exit.*)

LADY SMATTER. I have the greatest regard in the world for Miss Stanley,—nobody can esteem her more; but I can't think of letting Beaufort marry without money.

CODGER. Pray, madam, how came Miss Stanley to have such very large concerns with Mr. Stipend?

LADY SMATTER. Why he was not only her banker, but her guardian, and her whole fortune was in his hands. She is a pretty sort of girl,—I am really grieved for her.

JACK. Lord, here's my brother! I wish I could make off.

(Re-enter Beaufort.)

BEAUFORT. Stay, Sir! one word, and you will be most welcome to go. Whence had you the intelligence you so humanely communicated to Miss Stanley?

JACK. I had it upon 'Change. Everybody was talking of it.

BEAUFORT. Enough. I have no desire to detain you any longer.

JACK. Why now, Brother, perhaps you think I am not sorry for Miss Stanley, because of my coming in such a hurry? but I do assure you it was out of mere good nature, for I made a point of running all the way, for fear she should hear it from a stranger.

BEAUFORT. I desire you will leave me: my mind is occupied with other matters than attending to your defense.

JACK. Very well, Brother. Plague take it, I wish I had gone to Hyde Park at once! (*Exit.*)

CODGER. In truth, Son Beaufort, I must confess Jack has been somewhat abrupt; but, nevertheless, I must hint to you that, when I am by, I think you might as well refer the due reproof to be given by me. Jack is not everybody's son, although he be mine.

BEAUFORT. I am sorry I have offended you, Sir, but—

CODGER. Madam, as your house seems in some little perturbation, I hope you will excuse the shortness of my visit if I take leave now. Your Ladyship's most humble servant. Jack is a good lad at the bottom, although he be somewhat wanting in solidity. (*Exit.*)

BEAUFORT. At length, thank Heaven, the house is cleared. O madam, will you not go to Miss Stanley? I have left her in an agony of mind which I had no ability to mitigate.

LADY SMATTER. Poor thing! I am really in great pain for her.

BEAUFORT. Your Ladyship alone has power to soothe her,—a power which, I hope, you will instantly exert.

LADY SMATTER. I will go to her presently—or send for her here.

BEAUFORT. Surely your Ladyship will go to *her*?—at such a time as this, the smallest failure in respect—

LADY SMATTER. As to that, Beaufort,—but I am thinking what the poor girl had best do; I really don't know what to advise.

BEAUFORT. If I may be honored with your powerful intercession, I hope to prevail with her to be mine immediately.

LADY SMATTER. Pho, pho, don't talk so idly.

BEAUFORT. Madam!

LADY SMATTER. Be quiet a few minutes, and let me consider what can be done.

BEAUFORT. But, while we are both absent, what may not the sweet sufferer imagine?

LADY SMATTER. Suppose we get her into the country?—yet I know not what she can do when she is there; she can't live on green trees.

BEAUFORT. What does Your Ladyship mean?

LADY SMATTER. Nothing is so difficult as disposing of a poor girl of fashion.

BEAUFORT. Madam!

LADY SMATTER. She has been brought up to nothing,—if she can make a cap, 'tis as much as she can do, and, in such a case, when a girl is reduced to a penny, what is to be done?

BEAUFORT. Good Heaven, madam, will Miss Stanley ever be reduced to a penny while I live in affluence?

LADY SMATTER. Beaufort,—to cut the matter sort, you must give her up.

BEAUFORT. Give her up?

LADY SMATTER. Certainly; you can never suppose I shall consent to your marrying a girl who has lost all her fortune. While the match seemed suitable to your expectations, and to my intentions towards you, I readily countenanced it, but now, it is quite a different thing,—all is changed, and—

BEAUFORT. No, madam, no, all is not changed, for the heart of Beaufort is unalterable! I loved Miss Stanley in prosperity,—in adversity, I adore her! I solicited her favor when she was surrounded by my rivals, and I will still supplicate it, though she should be deserted by all the world besides. Her distress shall increase my tenderness, her poverty shall redouble my respect, and her misfortunes shall render her more dear to me than ever!

LADY SMATTER. Beaufort, you offend me extremely. I have as high notions of sentiment and delicacy as you can have, for the study of the fine arts, as Pope justly says, greatly enlarges the mind;[19] but, for all that, if you would still have me regard you as a son, you must pay me the obedience due to a mother, and never suppose I adopted you to marry you to a beggar.

BEAUFORT. A beggar?—Indignation chokes me!—I must leave you, madam,—the submission I pay you as a nephew, and the obedience I owe you as an adopted son, will else both give way to feelings I know not how to stifle! (*Exit.*)

LADY SMATTER (*alone*). This is really an unfortunate affair. I am quite distressed how to act, for the eyes of the world will be upon me! I will see the girl, however, and give her a hint about Beaufort;—William!

(*Enter a Servant.*)

Tell Miss Stanley I beg to speak to her. (*Exit Servant.*) I protest I wish she was fairly out of the house! I never cordially liked her,—she has not a grain of taste, and her compliments are so cold, one has no pleasure in receiving them,—she is a most insipid thing! I sha'n't be sorry to have done with her.

(Enter Cecilia.)

Miss Stanley, my dear, your servant.

CECILIA. Oh, madam!

LADY SMATTER. Take courage; don't be so downcast,—a noble mind, as I was reading the other day, is always superior to misfortune.

CECILIA. Alas, madam, in the first moments of sorrow and disappointment, Philosophy and Rhetoric offer their aid in vain! Affliction may, indeed, be alleviated, but it first must be felt.

LADY SMATTER. I did not expect, Miss Stanley, you would have disputed this point with *me;* I thought, after so long studying matters of this sort, I might be allowed to be a better judge than a young person who has not studied them at all.

CECILIA. Good Heaven, madam, are you offended?

LADY SMATTER. Whether I am or not, we'll not talk of it now; it would be illiberal to take offense at a person in distress.

CECILIA. Madam!

LADY SMATTER. Do you think Jack may have been misinformed?

CECILIA. Alas no! I have just received this melancholy confirmation of his intelligence. *(Gives Lady Smatter a letter.)*

LADY SMATTER. Upon my word, 'tis a sad thing! a sad stroke upon my word! however, you have good friends, and such as, I dare say, will take care of you.

CECILIA. Take care of me, madam?

LADY SMATTER. Yes, my dear, I will for one. And you should consider how much harder such a blow would have been to many other poor girls, who have not your resources.

CECILIA. My resources? I don't understand you!

LADY SMATTER. Nay, my dear, I only mean to comfort you, and to assure you of my continued regard; and if you can think of anything in which I can serve you, I am quite at your command; nobody can wish you better. My house, too, shall always be open to you. I should scorn to desert you because you are in distress. A mind, indeed, cultivated and informed, as Shakespeare has it, will ever be above a mean action.

CECILIA. I am quite confounded!

LADY SMATTER. In short, my dear, you will find *me* quite at your disposal, and as much your friend as in the sunshine of your prosperity:—but as to Beaufort—

CECILIA. Hold, madam! I now begin to understand your Ladyship perfectly.

LADY SMATTER. Don't be hasty, my dear. I say as to Beaufort, he is but a young man, and young men, you know, are mighty apt to be rash; but when they have no independence, and are of no profession, they should be very cautious how they disoblige their friends. Besides, it always happens that, when they are drawn in to their own ruin, they involve—

CECILIA. No more, I beseech you, madam! I know not how to brook such terms, or to endure such indignity. I shall leave your Ladyship's house instantly, nor, while any other will receive me, shall I re-enter it! Pardon me, madam, but I am yet young in the school of adversity, and my spirit is not yet tamed down to that abject submission to unmerited mortifications which time and long suffering can alone render supportable.

LADY SMATTER. You quite surprise me, my dear! I can't imagine what you mean. However, when your mind is more composed, I beg you will follow me to my own room. Till then, I will leave you to your meditations, for, as Swift has well said, 'tis vain to reason with a person in a passion. (*Exit.*)

CECILIA (*alone*). Follow you? no, no, I will converse with you no more. Cruel, unfeeling woman! I will quit your inhospitable roof, I will seek shelter—alas, where?—without fortune, destitute of friends, ruined in circumstances, yet proud of heart,—where can the poor Cecilia seek shelter, peace or protection? Oh Beaufort! 'tis thine alone to console me; thy sympathy shall soften my calamities, and thy fidelity shall instruct me to support them. Yet fly I must!—Insult ought not to be borne, and those who twice risk, the third time deserve it.

ACT III.

Scene i. A Dressing Room at Lady Smatter's.

(Enter Lady Smatter, followed by Beaufort.)

BEAUFORT. Madam you distract me! 'tis impossible her intentions should be unknown to you,—tell me, I beseech you, whither she is gone? what are her designs? and why she deigned not to acquaint me with her resolution?

LADY SMATTER. Why will you, Beaufort, eternally forget that it is the duty of every wise man, as Swift has admirably said, to keep his passions to himself?

BEAUFORT. She must have been *driven* to this step,—it could never have occurred to her without provocation. Relieve me then, madam, from a suspense insupportable, and tell me, at least, to what asylum she has flown?

LADY SMATTER. Beaufort, you make me blush for you!—Who would suppose that a scholar, a man of cultivated talents, could behave so childishly? Do you remember what Pope has said upon this subject?

BEAUFORT. This is past endurance! no, madam, no!—at such a time as this, his very name is disgustful to me.

LADY SMATTER. How!—did I hear right? The name of Pope disgustful?—

BEAUFORT. Yes, madam,—Pope, Swift, Shakespeare himself, and every other name you can mention but that of Cecilia Stanley, is hateful to my ear and detestable to my remembrance.

LADY SMATTER. I am thunderstruck!—this is downright blasphemy.

BEAUFORT. Good Heaven, madam, is this a time to talk of books and authors?—however, if your Ladyship is cruelly determined to give me no satisfaction, I must endeavor to procure intelligence elsewhere.

LADY SMATTER. I protest to you she went away without speaking to me; she sent for a chair, and did not even let the servants hear whither she ordered it.

BEAUFORT. Perhaps, then, she left a letter for you?—O, I am sure she did! her delicacy, her just sense of propriety would never suffer her to quit your Ladyship's house with an abruptness so unaccountable.

LADY SMATTER. Well, well, whether she writ or not is nothing to the purpose; she has acted a very prudent part in going away, and once again I repeat, you must give her up.

BEAUFORT. No, madam, never!—never while life is lent me will I give up the tie that renders it most dear to me.

LADY SMATTER. Well, Sir, I have only this to say,—one must be given up, she or me,—the decision is in your own hands.

BEAUFORT. Deign then, madam, to hear my final answer and to hear it, if possible, with lenity. That your favor, upon every account, is valuable to me, there can be no occasion to assert, and I have endeavored to prove my sense of the goodness you have so long shown me, by all the gratitude I have been able to manifest: you have a claim undoubted to my utmost respect and humblest deference; but there is yet another claim upon me,—a sacred, an irresistible claim,—Honor! And this were I to forgo, not all your Ladyship's most unbounded liberality and munificence would prove adequate reparation for so dreadful, so atrocious a sacrifice!

(Enter Servant.)

SERVANT. Mr. Censor, My Lady.

LADY SMATTER. Beg him to walk upstairs. I will put this affair into his hands; (*Aside.*) he is a sour, morose, ill-tempered wretch, and will [give] Beaufort no quarter.

(Enter Censor.)

Mr. Censor, I am very glad to see you.

CENSOR. I thank your Ladyship. Where is Miss Stanley?

LADY SMATTER. Why, not at home. O Mr. Censor, we have the saddest thing to tell you!—we are all in the greatest affliction,—poor Miss Stanley has met with the cruellest misfortune you can conceive.

CENSOR. I have heard the whole affair.

LADY SMATTER. I am vastly glad you came, for I want to have a little rational consultation with you. Alas, Mr. Censor, what an unexpected stroke! You can't imagine how unhappy it makes me.

CENSOR. Possibly not; for my imagination is no reveller,—it seldom deviates from the bounds of probability.

LADY SMATTER. Surely you don't doubt me?

CENSOR. No, madam, not in the least!

LADY SMATTER. I am happy to hear you say so.

CENSOR (*aside*). You have but little reason if you understood me. When does your Ladyship expect Miss Stanley's return?

LADY SMATTER. Why, really, I can't exactly say, for she left the house in a sort of a hurry. I would fain have dissuaded her, but all my rhetoric was ineffectual,—Shakespeare himself would have pleaded in vain! To say the truth, her temper is none of the most flexible; however, poor thing, great allowance ought to be made for her unhappy situation, for, as the poet has it, misfortune renders everybody unamiable.

CENSOR. What poet?

LADY SMATTER. Bless me, don't you know? Well, I shall now grow proud indeed if I can boast of making a quotation that is new to the learned Mr. Censor. My present author, Sir, is Swift.

CENSOR. Swift?—you have, then, some private edition of his works?

LADY SMATTER. Well, well, I won't be positive as to Swift,— perhaps it was Pope. 'Tis impracticable for anybody that reads so much as I do to be always exact as to an author. Why, now, how many volumes do you think I can run through in one year's reading?

CENSOR. More than would require seven years to digest.

LADY SMATTER. Pho, pho, but I study besides, and when I am preparing a criticism, I sometimes give a whole day to poring over only one line. However, let us, for the present, quit these abstruse points, and as Parnell says, "e'en talk a little like folks of this world."[20]

CENSOR. Parnell?—you have, then, made a discovery with which you should oblige the public, for that line passes for Prior's.

LADY SMATTER. Prior?—O, very true, so it is. Bless me, into what errors does extensive reading lead us! But to business,—this poor girl must, some way or other, be provided for, and my opinion is she had best return to her friends in the country. London is a dangerous place for girls who have no fortune. Suppose you go to her, and reason with her upon this subject?

BEAUFORT. You *do* know her direction, then?

LADY SMATTER. No matter; I will not have *you* go to her, whoever does. Would you believe it, Mr. Censor, this unthinking young man would actually marry the girl without a penny? However, it behooves me to prevent him, if only for example's sake. That, indeed, is the chief motive which governs me, for such is my *fatal pre-eminence,* as Addison calls it,[21] that should I give way, my name will be quoted for a license to indiscreet marriages for ages to come.

CENSOR. I hope, madam, the gratitude of the world will be adequate to the obligations it owes you.

LADY SMATTER. Well, Mr. Censor, I will commit the affair to your management. This paper will tell you where Miss Stanley is to be met with, and pray tell the poor thing she may always depend upon my protection, and that I feel for her most extremely; but, above all things, let her know she must think no more of Beaufort, for why should the poor girl be fed with false hopes? It would be barbarous to trifle with her expectations. I declare I should hate myself were I capable of such cruelty. Tell her so, Mr. Censor, and tell her—

BEAUFORT. Oh, madam, forbear!—Heavens, what a message for Miss Stanley! Dishonor not yourself by sending it. Is she not the same Miss Stanley who was so lately respected, caressed, and admired? whose esteem you sought? whose favor you solicited?—whose alliance you coveted?—Can a few moments have obliterated all remembrance of her merit? Shall *we* be treacherous, because *she* is unfortunate? must *we* lose our integrity, because *she* has lost her fortune? Oh madam, reflect while it is yet time, that the judgment of the world at large is always impartial, and let us not, by withholding protection from her, draw universal contempt and reproach upon ourselves!

LADY SMATTER. Beaufort, you offend me extremely. Do you suppose I have labored so long at the fine arts, and studied so deeply the intricacies of literature, to be taught, at last, the right rule of conduct by my nephew? O Mr. Censor, how well has Shakespeare said, rash and inconsiderate is youth!—but I must waive a further discussion of this point at present, as I have some notes to prepare for our Esprit Party of tonight. But remember, Beaufort, that if you make any attempt to see or write to Miss Stanley, I will disown and disinherit you. Mr. Censor, you will enforce this doctrine, and pray tell him, it was a maxim with Pope,—or Swift, I am not sure which, that resolution, in a cultivated mind, is unchangeable. (*Exit.*)

(Beaufort and Censor.)

BEAUFORT. By Heaven, Censor, with all your apathy and misanthropy, I had believed you incapable of listening to such inhumanity without concern.

CENSOR. Know you not, Beaufort, that though we can all see the surface of a river, its depth is only to be fathomed by experiment? Had my concern been shallow, it might have babbled without impediment, but, as it was strong and violent, I have restrained it, lest a torrent of indignation should have overflowed your future hopes and laid waste my future influence.

BEAUFORT. Show me, I beseech you, the paper, that I may hasten to the lovely, injured writer, and endeavor, by my fidelity and sympathy, to make her forget my connections.

CENSOR. Not so fast, Beaufort. When a man has to deal with a lover, he must think a little of himself, for he may be sure the inamorato will think only of his mistress.

BEAUFORT. Surely you do not mean to refuse me her direction?

CENSOR. Indeed I do, unless you can instruct me how to sustain the assault that will follow my surrendering it.

BEAUFORT. Why will you trifle with me thus? What, to you, is the resentment of Lady Smatter?

CENSOR. How gloriously inconsistent is the conduct of a professed lover! while to his mistress he is all tame submission and abject servility, to the rest of the world he is commanding, selfish, and obstinate; everything is to give way to him, no convenience is to be consulted, no objections are to be attended to in opposition to his wishes. It seems as if he thought it the sole business of the rest of mankind to study his single interest,—in order, perhaps, to recompense him for pretending to his mistress that he has no will but hers.

BEAUFORT. Show me the address,—then rail at your leisure.

CENSOR. You think nothing, then, of the disgrace I must incur with this literary phenomenon if I disregard her injunctions? Will she not exclude me forever from the purlieus of Parnassus?—Stun me with the names of authors she has never read?—and pester me with flimsy sentences which she has the assurance to call quotations?—

BEAUFORT. Well, well, well!—

CENSOR. Will she not tell me that Pope brands a breach of trust as dishonorable?—that Shakespeare stigmatizes the meanness of treachery?—And recollect having read in Swift—that fortitude is one of the cardinal virtues?

BEAUFORT. Stuff and folly!—does it matter what she says?—the paper!—the direction!—

CENSOR. Heavens, that a woman whose utmost natural capacity will hardly enable her to understand the *History of Tom Thumb,* and whose comprehensive faculties would be absolutely baffled by the Lives of the *Seven Champions of Christendom,* should dare blaspheme the names of our noblest poets with words that convey no ideas, and sentences of which the sound listens in vain for the sense![22] O, she is insufferable!

BEAUFORT. How unseasonable a discussion! Yet you seem to be more irritated at her folly about books, than at her want of feeling to the sweetest of her sex.

CENSOR. True; but the reason is obvious,—Folly torments because it gives present disturbance,—as to want of feeling—'tis a thing of course. The moment I heard that Miss Stanley had lost her fortune, I was certain of all that would follow.

BEAUFORT. Can you, then, see such treachery without rage or emotion?

CENSOR. No, not without *emotion,* for base actions always excite contempt,—but *rage* must be stimulated by surprise: no man is much moved by events that merely answer his expectations.

BEAUFORT. Censor, will you give me the direction? I have neither time nor patience for further uninteresting discussions. If you are determined to refuse it, say so; I have other resources, and I have a spirit resolute to essay them all.

CENSOR. It is no news to me, Beaufort, that a man may find more ways than one to ruin himself; yet, whatever pleasure may attend putting them in practice, I believe it seldom happens, when he is irreparably undone, that he piques himself upon his success.

BEAUFORT. I will trouble you no longer,—your servant. (*Going.*)

CENSOR. Hold, Beaufort! Forget, for a few moments, the lover and listen to me, not with passion but understanding. Miss Stanley, you find, has now no dependence but upon you;—you have none but upon Lady Smatter,—what follows?

BEAUFORT. Distraction, I believe,—I have nothing else before me!

CENSOR. If, instantly and wildly, you oppose her in the first heat of her determination, you will have served a ten years' apprenticeship to her caprices, without any other payment than the pleasure of having endured them. She will regard your disobedience as rebellion to her judgment, and resent it with acrimony.

BEAUFORT. Oh misery of dependence!—the heaviest toil, the hardest labor, fatigue the most intense,—what are they compared to the corroding servility of discontented dependence?

CENSOR. Nothing, I grant, is so painful to endure, but nothing is so difficult to shake off; and therefore, as you are now situated, there is but one thing in the world can excuse your seeking Miss Stanley.

BEAUFORT. Whatever it may be, I shall agree to it with transport. Name it.

CENSOR. Insanity.

BEAUFORT. Censor, at such a time as this, raillery is unpardonable.

CENSOR. Attend to me then, in sober sadness. You must give up all thoughts of quitting this house, till the ferocity of your learned aunt is abated.

BEAUFORT. Impossible!

CENSOR. Nay, prithee, Beaufort, act not as a lunatic while you disclaim insanity. I will go to Miss Stanley myself, and bring you an account of her situation.

BEAUFORT. Would you have me, then, submit to this tyrant?

CENSOR. Would I have a farmer, after sowing a field, not wait to reap the harvest?

BEAUFORT. I will endeavor, then, to yield to your counsel; but, remember, Censor, my yielding is not merely reluctant,—it must also be transitory; for if I do not speedily find the good effects of my self-denial, I will boldly and firmly give up forever all hopes of precarious advantage, for the certain, the greater, the nobler blessing of claiming my lovely Cecilia,—though at the hazard of ruin and destruction.

CENSOR. And do you, Beaufort, remember in turn, that had I believed you capable of a different conduct, I had never ranked you as my friend.

BEAUFORT. Oh Censor, how soothing to my anxiety is your hard-earned, but most flattering approbation! Hasten, then, to the sweet sufferer,—tell her my heart bleeds at her unmerited distresses,—tell her that, with her fugitive self, peace and happiness both flew this mansion,—tell her that, when we meet—

CENSOR. All these messages may be given!—but not till then, believe me! Do you suppose I can find no better topic for conversation, than making soft speeches by proxy?

BEAUFORT. Tell her, at least, how much—

CENSOR. My good friend, I am not ignorant that lovers, fops, fine ladies, and chambermaids have all charters for talking nonsense; it is, therefore, a part of their business, and they deem it indispensable; but I never yet heard of any order of men so unfortunate as to be under a necessity of listening to them. (*Exit.*)

BEAUFORT (*alone*). Dear, injured Cecilia! Why cannot I be myself the bearer of the faith I have plighted thee?—prostrate myself at thy feet, mitigate thy sorrows, and share, or redress thy wrongs! Even while I submit to captivity, I disdain the chains that bind me,—but alas, I rattle them in vain! O happy those who to their own industry owe their subsistence, and to their own fatigue and hardships their succeeding rest and rewarding affluence! Now, indeed, do I feel the weight of bondage, since it teaches me to envy even the toiling husbandman and laborious mechanic.[23]

Scene ii. An apartment at Mrs. Voluble's.

(Dabbler is discovered writing.)

DABBLER. *The pensive maid, with saddest sorrow sad,*—no, hang it, that won't do!—*saddest sad* will never do. With—with—with *mildest*—ay that's it! *The pensive maid, with mildest sorrow sad,*—I should like, now, to hear a man mend that line! I shall never get another equal to it.—Let's see,—sad, bad, lad, Dad,—curse it, there's never a rhyme will do!—Where's the *Art of Poetry?*—O, here,—now we shall have it; (*Reads.*) Add,— hold, that will do at once,—*with mildest sorrow sad, shed crystal tears, and sigh to sigh did add.* Admirable! admirable by all that's good! Now let's try the first stanza, (*Reads.*)

> Ye gentle nymphs, whose hearts are prone to love,
> Ah, hear my song, and ah! my song approve;
> And ye, ye glorious, mighty sons of fame,
> Ye mighty warriors—

How's this, two *mighty*s?—hang it, that won't do!—let's see,—ye *glorious* warriors,—no, there's *glorious* before,—O curse it, now I've got it all to do over again!—just as I thought I had finished it!—ye *fighting*,—no,—ye *towering*, no;—ye,— ye—ye—I have it, by Apollo!—

(Enter Betty.)

BETTY. Sir, here's a person below who—
DABBLER (*starting up in a rage*). Now curse me if this is not too much! What do you mean by interrupting me at my studies? how often have I given orders not to be disturbed?
BETTY. I'm sure, Sir, I thought there was no harm in just telling you—
DABBLER. Tell me nothing!—get out of the room directly!—and take care you never break in upon me again,—no, not if the house be on fire!—Go, I say!
BETTY. Yes, Sir. Lord, how masters and *Missises* do love scolding! (*Exit.*)
DABBLER (*alone*). What a provoking intrusion! just as I had worked myself into the true spirit of poetry!—I sha'n't recover my ideas this half hour. 'Tis a most barbarous thing that a man's retirement cannot be sacred. (*Sits down to write.*) Ye *fighting*,—no, that was not it,—ye ye—ye—O curse it, (*Stamping.*) if I have not forgot all I was going to say! That unfeeling, impenetrable fool has lost me more ideas than would have made a fresh man's reputation. I'd rather have given a hundred guineas than have seen her. I protest, I was upon the point of making as good a poem as any in the language,—my numbers

flowed,—my thoughts were ready,—my words glided,—but now, all is gone!—all gone and evaporated! (*Claps his hand to his forehead.*) Here's nothing left! nothing in the world!—What shall I do to compose myself? Suppose I read?—why where the Deuce are all the things gone? (*Looking over his papers.*) O, here,—I wonder how my epigram will read today,—I think I'll show it to Censor,—he has seen nothing like it of late;—I'll pass it off for some dead poet's, or he'll never do it justice;—let's see, Suppose Pope?—No, it's too smart for Pope,—Pope never wrote anything like it!—well then, suppose—

(Enter Mrs. Voluble.)

O curse it, another interruption!

MRS. VOLUBLE. I hope, Sir, I don't disturb you?—I'm sure I would not disturb you for the world, for nothing's so troublesome; and I know you gentlemen writers dislike it of all things; but I only just wanted to know if the windows were shut, for fear of the rain, for I asked Betty if she had been in to see about them, but she said—

DABBLER. They'll do very well,—pray leave them alone,—I am extremely busy;—(*Aside.*) I must leave these lodgings, I see!

MRS. VOLUBLE. O Sir, I would not stay upon any account, but only sometimes there are such sudden showers, that if the windows are left open, half one's things may be spoilt before one knows anything of the matter. And if so much as a paper of yours was to be damaged, I should never forgive myself, for I'd rather all the poets in the world should be burnt in one great bonfire, than lose so much as the most miniken bit of your writing, though no bigger than my nail.

DABBLER. My dear Mrs. Voluble, you are very obliging. (*Aside.*) She's a mighty good sort of woman,—I've a great mind to read her that song:—no, this will be better. Mrs. Voluble, do you think you can keep a secret?

MRS. VOLUBLE. O dear Sir, I'll defy anybody to excel me in that! I am more particular scrupulous about secrets than anybody.

DABBLER. Well, then, I'll read you a little thing I've just been composing, and you shall tell me your opinion of it. (*Reads.*) *On a Young Lady Blinded by Lightning.*

> Fair Cloris, now deprived of sight,
> To Error owed her fate uneven;
> Her eyes were so refulgent bright
> The blundering lightning thought them Heaven.

What do you think of it, Mrs. Voluble?

MRS. VOLUBLE. O, I think it the prettiest, most moving thing I ever heard in my life.

DABBLER. Do you indeed?—pray sit down, Mrs. Voluble, I protest I never observed you were standing.

MRS. VOLUBLE. Dear Sir, you're vastly polite. (*Seats herself.*)

DABBLER. So you really think it's pretty good, do you?

MRS. VOLUBLE. O dear yes, Sir; I never heard anything I liked so well in my life. It's prodigious fine, indeed!

DABBLER. Pray don't sit so near the door, Mrs. Voluble; I'm afraid you will take cold. (*Aside.*) 'Tis amazing to me where this woman picked up so much taste!

MRS. VOLUBLE. But I hope, Sir, my being here is of no hindrance to you, because if it is, I'm sure—

DABBLER. No, Mrs. Voluble, (*Looking at his watch.*) I am obliged to go out myself now. I leave my room in your charge; let care be taken that no human being enters it in my absence, and don't let one of my papers be touched or moved upon any account.

MRS. VOLUBLE. Sir, I shall lock the door, and put the key in my pocket. Nobody shall so much as know there's a paper in the house.

(Exit Dabbler.)

MRS. VOLUBLE (*alone*). I believe it's almost a week since I've had a good rummage of them myself. Let's see, is not this 'Sprit Night? Yes; and he won't come home till very late, so I think I may as well give them a fair look over at once. (*Seats herself at the table.*) Well, now, how nice and snug this is! What's here? (*Takes up a paper.*)

(Enter Bob.)

BOB. Mother, here's Miss Jenny, the milliner maker.

MRS. VOLUBLE. Is there? ask her to come up.

Bob. Lord, Mother, why you would not have her come into Mr. Dabbler's room? why if he—

Mrs. Voluble. What's that to you? do you suppose I don't know what I'm about? You're never easy but when you're a talking,—always prate, prate, prate about something or other. Go and ask her to come up, I say.

Bob. Lord, one can't speak a word!— (*Exit.*)

Mrs. Voluble (*alone*). Have done, will you? mutter, mutter, mutter;—It will be a prodigious treat to Miss Jenny to come into this room.

(*Enter Miss Jenny.*)

Miss Jenny, how do do, my dear? this is very obliging of you. Do you know whose room you are in?

Miss Jenny. No, ma'am.

Mrs. Voluble. Mr. Dabbler's own room, I assure you! And here's all his papers; these are what he calls his *miniscrips.*

Miss Jenny. Well, what a heap of them!

Mrs. Voluble. And he's got five or six boxes brimful besides.

Miss Jenny. Dear me! well, I could not do so much if I was to have the Indies!

Mrs. Voluble. Now if you'll promise not to tell a living soul a word of the matter, I'll read you some of them: but be sure, now, you don't tell.

Miss Jenny. Dear no, I would not for ever so much.

Mrs. Voluble. Well, then, let's see,—what's this? (*Takes up a paper.*) *Elegy on the Slaughter of a Lamb.*

Miss Jenny. O, pray let's have that.

Mrs. Voluble. I'll put it aside, and look out some more. *A Dialogue between a Tear and a Sigh,—Verses on a Young Lady's Fainting Away—*

Miss Jenny. That must be pretty indeed! I dare say it will make us cry.

Mrs. Voluble. *An Epitaph on a Fly killed by a Spider; an—*

(*Enter Bob.*)

Bob. Mother, here's a young gentlewoman wants you.

Mrs. Voluble. A young gentlewoman?—who can it be?

BOB. I never see her before. She's a deal smarter than Miss Jenny.

MISS JENNY. I'm sure I'd have come more dressed, if I'd known of seeing anybody.

MRS. VOLUBLE. Well, I can't imagine who it is. I'm sure I'm in a sad pickle. Ask her into the parlor.

MISS JENNY. Dear ma'am, you'd better by half see her here; all the fine folks have their company upstairs, for I see a deal of the quality, by carrying things home.

MRS. VOLUBLE. Well, then, ask her to come up.

BOB. But suppose Mr. Dabbler—

MRS. VOLUBLE. Mind your own business, Sir, and don't think to teach me. Go and ask her up this minute.

BOB. I'm going, a'n't I? (*Exit.*)

MRS. VOLUBLE. I do verily believe that boy has no equal for prating; I never saw the like of him,—his tongue's always a running.

(*Re-enter Bob, followed by Cecilia.*)

BOB. Mother, here's the young gentlewoman.

CECILIA. I presume, ma'am, you are Mrs. Voluble?

MRS. VOLUBLE. Yes, ma'am.

CECILIA. I hope you will excuse this intrusion; and I must beg the favor of a few minutes private conversation with you.

MRS. VOLUBLE. To be sure, ma'am. Bobby, get the lady a chair. I hope, ma'am, you'll excuse Bobby's coming in before you; he's a sad rude boy for manners.

BOB. Why, the young gentlewoman bid me herself; 'twas no fault of mine.

MRS. VOLUBLE. Be quiet, will you? Jabber, jabber, jabber,—there's no making you hold your tongue a minute. Pray, ma'am, do sit down.

CECILIA. I thank you, I had rather stand. I have but a few words to say to you, and will not detain you five minutes.

MISS JENNY. Suppose Master Bobby and I go downstairs till the lady has done? (*Apart to Mrs. Voluble.*) Why Lord, Mrs. Voluble, I know who that lady is as well as I know you! why it's Miss Stanley, that we've been making such a heap of things for.

MRS. VOLUBLE. Why you don't say so! what, the bride?

MISS JENNY. Yes.

MRS. VOLUBLE. Well, I protest I thought I'd seen her somewhere before. Ma'am, (*To Cecilia.*) I'm quite ashamed of not recollecting you sooner, but I hope your goodness will excuse it. I hope, ma'am, the good lady your aunt is well?—that is, your aunt that is to be?

CECILIA. If you mean Lady Smatter,—I believe she is well.—

MRS. VOLUBLE. I'm sure, ma'am, I've the greatest respect in the world for her Ladyship, though I have not the pleasure to know her; but I hear all about her from Mrs. Hobbins,—to be sure, ma'am, you know Mrs. Hobbins, my Lady's housekeeper?

CECILIA. Certainly: it was by her direction I came hither.

MRS. VOLUBLE. That was very obliging of her, I'm sure, and I take your coming as a very particular favor. I hope, ma'am, all the rest of the family's well? And Mrs. Simper, my lady's woman? But I beg pardon for my ill manners, ma'am, for to be sure, I ought first to have asked for Mr. Beaufort. I hope he's well, ma'am!

CECILIA. I—I don't know—I believe,—I fancy he is.—

MRS. VOLUBLE. Well, he's a most agreeable gentleman indeed, ma'am, and I think—

CECILIA. If it is inconvenient for me to speak to you now—

MRS. VOLUBLE. Not at all, ma'am; Miss Jenny and Bobby can as well divert themselves in the parlor.

MISS JENNY. Dear me yes, I'll go directly.

BOB. And I'll go and sit in the kitchen, and look at the clock, and when it's five minutes, I'll tell Miss Jenny.

MISS JENNY. Come, then, Master Bobby. She's very melancholic, I think, for a young lady just going to be married. (*Exit with Bob.*)

CECILIA. The motive which has induced me to give you this trouble, Mrs. Voluble—

MRS. VOLUBLE. Dear ma'am, pray don't talk of trouble, for I'm sure I think it none. I take it quite as a favor to receive a visit from such a young lady as you. But pray, ma'am, sit down; I'm quite ashamed to see you standing,—it's enough to tire you to death.

CECILIA. It is not of the least consequence. A very unexpected and unhappy event has obliged me, most abruptly, to quit the house of Lady Smatter, and if—

MRS. VOLUBLE. Dear ma'am, you surprise me! but I hope you have not parted upon account of any disagreement?

CECILIA. I must beg you to hear me. I have, at present, insuperable objections to visiting any of my friends; and Mrs. Hobbins, who advised me to apply to you, said she believed you would be able to recommend me to some place where I can be properly accommodated till my affairs are settled.

MRS. VOLUBLE. To be sure, ma'am, I can. But pray, ma'am, may I make bold to ask the reason of your parting?

CECILIA. I am not, at present, at liberty to tell it. Do you recollect any place that—

MRS. VOLUBLE. O dear yes, ma'am, I know many. Let's see,— there's one in King Street,—and there's one in Charles Street,— and there's another in—Lord, I dare say I know an hundred! only I shall be very cautious of what I recommend, for it is not every place will do for such a lady as you. But pray, ma'am, where may Mr. Beaufort be? I hope he has no hand in this affair?

CECILIA. Pray ask me no questions!

MRS. VOLUBLE. I'm sure, ma'am, I don't mean to be troublesome; and as to asking questions, I make a point not to do it, for I think that curiosity is the most impertinent thing in the world. I suppose, ma'am, he knows of your being here?

CECILIA. No, no,—he knows nothing about me.

MRS. VOLUBLE. Well, that's quite surprising, upon my word! To be sure, poor gentleman, it must give him a deal of concern, that's but natural, and besides—

CECILIA. Can you name no place to me, Mrs. Voluble, that you think will be eligible?

MRS. VOLUBLE. Yes sure, I can, ma'am. I know a lady in the very next street, who has very genteel apartments, that will come to about five or six guineas a week, for, to be sure, a young lady of your fortune would not choose to give less.

CECILIA. Alas!

MRS. VOLUBLE. Dear ma'am, don't vex so; I dare say My Lady will think better of it; besides, it's for her interest, for though, to be sure, Mr. Beaufort will have a fine income, yet young ladies of forty thousand pounds fortune a'n't to be met with every day; and the folks say, ma'am, that yours will be full that.

CECILIA. I must entreat you, Mrs. Voluble, not to speak of my affairs at present; my mind is greatly disordered, and I cannot bear the subject.

MRS. VOLUBLE. Dear ma'am, I won't say another word. To be sure, nothing's so improper as talking of private affairs,—it's a thing I never do, for really—

(Enter Miss Jenny and Bob.)

MISS JENNY. May we come in?

MRS. VOLUBLE. Lord no; why I ha'n't heard one single thing yet.

BOB. It's a great deal past the five minutes. I've been looking at the clock all the time.

MISS JENNY. Well, then, shall we go again?

CECILIA. No, it is not necessary. Mrs. Voluble, you can be so good as to answer my question, without troubling anybody to leave the room.

MISS JENNY. Then we'll keep at this side, and we sha'n't hear what you say.

(Miss Jenny and Bob walk aside.)

MRS. VOLUBLE. What think you, ma'am, of that place I mentioned?

CECILIA. I mean to be quite private, and should wish for a situation less expensive.

MRS. VOLUBLE. Why sure, ma'am, you would not think of giving less than five guineas a week? That's just nothing out of such a fortune as yours.

CECILIA. Talk to me no more of my fortune, I beseech you,—I have none!—I have lost it all!—

MRS. VOLUBLE. Dear ma'am, why you put me quite in a cold sweat! lost all your fortune?

CECILIA. I know not what I say!—I can talk no longer;—pray excuse my incoherence;—and if you can allow me to remain here for half an hour, I may, in that time perhaps hear from my friends, and know better how to guide myself.

MRS. VOLUBLE. Yes, sure, ma'am, I shall be quite proud of your company. But I hope, ma'am, you was not in earnest about losing fortune?

CECILIA. Let nothing I have said be mentioned, I beseech you; converse with your friends as if I was not here, and suffer me to recover my composure in silence. (*Walks away.*) (*Aside.*) Oh

Beaufort, my only hope and refuge! hasten to my support ere
my spirits wholly sink under the pressure of distressful suspense.

MRS. VOLUBLE. Well, this is quite what I call a *nigma!* Miss Jenny
my dear, come here; I'll tell you how it is,—do you know she's
come away from Lady Smatter?

MISS JENNY. Dear me!

MRS. VOLUBLE. Yes; and what's worse, she says she's lost all her
fortune.

MISS JENNY. Lost all her fortune? Lack a dasy![24] why then who's
to pay for all our things? Why we've got such a heap as will
come to a matter of I don't know how much.

MRS. VOLUBLE. Well, to be sure it's a sad thing; but you're to
know I don't much believe it, for she said it in a sort of a pet;
and my notion is she has been falling out with her sweetheart,
and if so may be her head's a little touched. Them things often
happens in the quarrels of lovers.

(Enter Betty.)

BETTY. Ma'am, here's a gentleman wants the young lady.

CECILIA *(starting)*. 'Tis surely Beaufort!—Beg him to walk
upstairs.—Mrs. Voluble, will you excuse this liberty?

MRS. VOLUBLE. Yes, sure, ma'am.

(Exit Betty.)

CECILIA *(aside)*. Dear, constant Beaufort!—how grateful to my
heart is this generous alacrity!

MRS. VOLUBLE *(aside to Miss Jenny)*. I dare say this is her sweetheart.

MISS JENNY. Dear me, how nice! we shall hear all they say!

(Enter Censor.)

CECILIA. Mr. Censor!—good Heaven!

CENSOR. Miss Stanley, I will not say I rejoice,—for, in truth, in this
place I grieve to see you.

MRS. VOLUBLE. Pray, sir, won't you sit down?

CENSOR. I thank you, madam, I had rather stand. Miss Stanley, I must beg the honor of speaking to you alone.

MRS. VOLUBLE. O Sir, if you like it, I'm sure we'll go.

CENSOR. Ay, pray do.

MRS. VOLUBLE (*aside to Miss Jenny*). This gentleman is by no means what I call a polite person. Sir, I hope you'll put the young lady in better spirits; she has been very low indeed since she came; and, Sir, if you should want for anything, I beg—

CENSOR. Do, good madam, be quick. I am in haste.

MRS. VOLUBLE. We're going directly, Sir. Come, Miss Jenny. Bobby, you great oaf, what do you stand gaping there for? why don't you go?

BOB. Why, you would not have me go faster than I can, would you? (*Exit.*)

MRS. VOLUBLE. I would have you hold your tongue, Mr. Prate-apace! always wrangling and wrangling. Come, Miss Jenny. (*Exit.*)

MISS JENNY. I don't see why we might not as well have stayed here. (*Exit.*)

CECILIA. By what means, Sir, have you discovered me?—have you been at Lady Smatter's?—does anybody there know where I am, except her Ladyship?

CENSOR. First let me ask you what possible allurement could draw you under this roof? did you mean, by the volubility of folly, to overpower the sadness of recollection? did you imagine that nonsense has the same oblivious quality as the waters of Lethe? and flatter yourself that, by swallowing large draughts, you should annihilate all remembrance of your misfortunes?

CECILIA. No, no! I came hither by the dire guidance of necessity. I wish to absent myself from my friends till the real state of my affairs is better known to me. I have sent my servant into the City, whence I expect speedy intelligence. Lady Smatter's housekeeper assured me that the character of this woman was unblemished, and I was interested in no other enquiry. But tell me, I beseech you, whence you had your information of the calamity that has befallen me? and who directed you hither? and whether my letter has been shown or concealed?—and what I am to infer from *your* being the first to seek me?

CENSOR. Pray go on!

CECILIA. Sir!

Censor. Nay, if you ask forty more questions without waiting for an answer, I have messages that will more than keep pace with your enquiries; therefore ask on, and spare not!

Cecilia. (*disconcerted*). No, Sir, I have done!

Censor. How! have I, then, discovered the art of silencing a lover? Hasten to me, ye wearied guardians of pining youth, I will tell ye a secret precious to ye as repose! fly hither, ye sad and solemn confidants of the love-lorn tribe, for I can point out relief to exhausted patience!

Cecilia. Spare this raillery, I beseech you;—and keep me not in suspense as to the motive of your visit.

Censor. My first motive is the desire of seeing,—my second of serving you; if indeed, the ill-usage you have experienced from one banker, will not intimidate you from trusting in another.

Cecilia. How am I to understand you?

Censor. As an honest man! or, in other words, as a man to whose friendship distressed innocence has a claim indisputable.

Cecilia. You amaze me!

Censor. It must be some time ere your affairs can be settled, and the loss of wealth will speedily, and roughly make you know its value. Consider me, therefore, as your banker, and draw upon me without reserve. Your present situation will teach you many lessons you are ill-prepared to learn; but experience is an unfeeling master, whose severity is neither to be baffled by youth, nor softened by innocence. Suppose we open our account today?—this may serve for a beginning; (*Presenting a paper.*) I will call again tomorrow for fresh orders. (*Going.*)

Cecilia. Stay, stay Mr. Censor!—amazement has, indeed, silenced me, but it must not make me forget myself. Take back, I entreat you, this paper—

Censor. Probably you suspect my motives? and, if you do, I am the last man whom your doubts will offend; they are authorized by the baseness of mankind, and, in fact, suspicion, in worldly transactions, is but another word for common sense.

Cecilia. Is it, then, possible you can think so ill of all others, and yet be so generous, so benevolent yourself?

Censor. Will any man follow an example he abhors to look at? Will you, for instance, because you see most women less handsome than yourself, ape deformity in order to resemble them?

Cecilia. O how little are you known, and how unjustly are you judged! For my own part, I even regarded you as my enemy, and imagined that, if you thought of me at all, it was with ill-will.

CENSOR. In truth, madam, my character will rather increase than diminish your surprise as you become more acquainted with it. You will, indeed, find me an odd fellow; a fellow who can wish you well without loving you, and, without any sinister view, be active in your service; a fellow, in short, unmoved by beauty, yet susceptible of pity,—invulnerable to love, yet zealous in the cause of distress. If you accept my good offices, I shall ever after be your debtor for the esteem your acceptance will manifest,—if you reject them, I shall but conclude you have the same indignant apprehensions of the depravity of your fellow creatures that I harbor in my own breast.

CECILIA. If, hitherto, I have escaped misanthropy, think you, Sir, an action such as this will teach it me? No; I am charmed with your generous offer, and shall henceforward know better how to value you; but I must beg you to take back this paper. (*Returns it.*) I have at present no occasion for assistance, and I hope—but tell me, for uncertainty is torture, have you, or have you not been at Lady Smatter's?

CENSOR. I have; and I come hither loaded with as many messages as ever abigail was charged with for the milliner of a fantastic bride. The little sense, however, comprised in their many words, is briefly this; Lady Smatter offers you her protection,—which is commonly the first step towards the insolence of avowed superiority: and Beaufort—

CECILIA. Beaufort?—Good Heaven!—did Mr. Beaufort know whither you were coming?

CENSOR. He did; and charged with as many vows, supplications, promises, and tender nonsenses, as if he took my memory for some empty habitation that his fancy might furnish at its pleasure. He commissioned me—

CECILIA. Oh Heaven! (*Weeps.*)

CENSOR. Why how now? he commissioned me, I say—

CECILIA. Oh faithless Beaufort! lost, lost Cecilia!

CENSOR. To sue for him,—Kneel for him;—

CECILIA. Leave me, leave me, Mr. Censor!—I can hear no more.

CENSOR. Nay, prithee, madam, listen to his message.

CECILIA. No, Sir, never! at such a time as this, a message is an in-

sult! He must know I was easily to be found, or he would not
have sent it, and, knowing that, whose was it to have sought
me?—Go, go, hasten to your friend,—tell him I heard all that
it became me to hear, and that I understood him too well to
hear more: tell him that I will save both him and myself the disgrace of further explanation,—tell him, in short, that I renounce
him for ever!

CENSOR. Faith, madam, this is all beyond my comprehension.

CECILIA. To desert me at such a time as this! to know my abode,—
yet fail to seek it! to suffer my wounded heart, bleeding in all
the anguish of recent calamity, to doubt his faith, and suspect
his tenderness!

CENSOR. I am so totally unacquainted with the laws and maxims
necessary to be observed by fine ladies, that it would ill become
me to prescribe the limits to which their use of reason ought to
be contracted; I can only—

CECILIA. Once more, Mr. Censor, I must beg you to leave me. Pardon my impatience, but I cannot converse at present. Ere long,
perhaps, indignation may teach me to suppress my sorrow, and
time and reason may restore my tranquility.

CENSOR. Time, indeed, may possibly stand your friend, because
time will be regardless of your impetuosity, but faith, madam,
I know not what right you have to expect succor from reason,
if you are determined not to hear it. Beaufort, I say—

CECILIA. Why will you thus persecute me? nothing can extenuate
the coldness, the neglect, the insensibility of his conduct. Tell
him that it admits no palliation, and that henceforth—no, tell
him nothing,—I will send him no message,—I will receive none
from him,—I will tear his image from my heart,—I will forget,
if possible, that there I cherished it!—

(Enter Mrs. Voluble.)

MRS. VOLUBLE. I hope I don't disturb you, Sir? Pray, ma'am, don't
let me be any hindrance to you; I only just come to ask if you
would not have a bit of fire, for I think it's grown quite cold.
What say you, Sir? pray make free if you like it. I'm sure I
would have had one before if I had known of having such company; but really the weather's so changeable at this time of the
year, that there's no knowing what to do. Why this morning I

declare it was quite hot. We breakfasted with both the windows open. As to Bobby, I verily thought he'd have caught his death, for he would not so much as put his coat on.

CENSOR. Intolerable! the man who could stand this, would sing in the stocks, and laugh in the pillory!—Will you, Miss Stanley, allow me five minutes conversation to explain—

MRS. VOLUBLE. I beg that my being here may not be any stop to you, for I'll go directly if I'm in the way. I've no notion of prying into other people's affairs,—indeed, I quite make it a rule not to do it, for I'm sure I've business enough of my own, without minding other people's. Why now, Sir, how many things do you think I've got to do before night? Why I've got to—

CENSOR. O pray, good madam, don't make your complaints to me,—I am hard of heart, and shall be apt to hear them without the least compassion. Miss Stanley—

MRS. VOLUBLE. Nay, Sir, I was only going—

CENSOR. Do prithee, Good Woman, give me leave to speak. Miss Stanley, I say—

MRS. VOLUBLE. Good Woman! I assure you, Sir, I'm not used to be spoke to in such a way as that.

CENSOR. If I have called you by an appellation opposite to your character, I beg your pardon; but—

MRS. VOLUBLE. I can tell you, Sir, whatever you may think of it, I was never called so before; besides—

CENSOR. Miss Stanley, some other time—

MRS. VOLUBLE. Besides, Sir, I say, I think in one's own house it's very hard if—

CENSOR. Intolerable! Surely this woman was sent to satirize the use of speech! once more—

MRS. VOLUBLE. I say, Sir, I think it's very hard if—

CENSOR. Miss Stanley, your most obedient! (*Exit abruptly.*)

MRS. VOLUBLE. Well, I must needs say, I think this is the rudest fine gentleman among all my acquaintance. Good Woman indeed! I wonder what he could see in me to make use of such a word as that! I won't so much as go downstairs to open the street door for him,—Yes I will, too, for I want to ask him about—(*Exit talking.*)

CECILIA (*alone*). Hast thou not, Fortune, exhausted, now, thy utmost severity?—reduced to poverty,—abandoned by the world,—betrayed by Beaufort,—what more can I fear?—

Beaufort, on whose constancy I relied,—Beaufort, from whose sympathy I expected consolation,—Beaufort, on whose honor, delicacy and worth I founded hopes of sweetest tranquility, of lasting happiness, of affection unalterable! Oh hopes forever blighted! Oh expectations eternally destroyed! Oh fair and lovely tranquility—thou hast flown this bosom, never, never more to revisit it!

(Re-enter Mrs. Voluble.)

MRS. VOLUBLE. I could not overtake him all that ever I could do, and yet I went as fast as—Lord, ma'am, sure you a'n't a crying?

CECILIA. Loss of fortune I could have borne with patience,—change of situation I could have suffered with fortitude, but such a stroke as this!—

MRS. VOLUBLE. Poor young lady!—I declare I don't know what to think of to entertain her.

CECILIA. Oh Beaufort! had our situations been reversed, would such have been my conduct?

MRS. VOLUBLE. Come, dear ma'am, what signifies all this fretting? If you'll take my advice—

(Enter Betty.)

BETTY. Do pray, ma'am, speak to Master Bobby,—he's a turning the house out of windows, as a body may say.

MRS. VOLUBLE. Well, if I don't believe that boy will be the death of me at last!—only think, ma'am, what a plague he is to me! I'm sure I have my misfortunes as well as other people, so you see, ma'am, you a'n't the only person in trouble.—Why ma'am, I say!—did not you hear Betty?—She says that Bobby—

CECILIA. O for a little repose!—leave me to myself, I beseech you! I can neither speak or listen to you;—pray go,—pray—alas, I know not what I say!—I forget that this house is yours, and that I have no right even to the shelter its roof affords me.

MRS. VOLUBLE. Dear ma'am, pray take a little comfort,—

CECILIA. Have you, madam, any room which for a few hours you can allow me to call my own?—where, unmolested and alone, I may endeavor to calm my mind, and settle some plan for my future conduct?

MRS. VOLUBLE. Why, ma'am, the room overhead is just such another as this, and if it's agreeable—

CECILIA. Pray show it me,—I'm sure it will do.

MRS. VOLUBLE. I only wish, ma'am, it was better for your sake; however, I'll make it as comfortable as ever I can, and as soon—(*Exit, talking with Cecilia.*)

BETTY (*alone*). I'll be hanged, now, if it is not enough to provoke a stork to live in such a house as this! One may clean and clean forever, and things look never the better for it. As to Master Bobby, he does more mischief than his head's worth; and as to my *Missis,* if she can but keep talk, talk, talk, she don't care a pin's point for nothing else.

(*Re-enter Mrs. Voluble.*)

MRS. VOLUBLE. Why Betty, what do you stand there for?—Do you think I keep you to look at?

BETTY. You won't keep me for nothing long. (*Exit Betty.*)

MRS. VOLUBLE (*alone*). There, now, that's the way with all of them! if one does but say the least thing in the world, they're ready to give one warning. I declare servants are the plague of one's lives. I've got a good mind to—Lord, I've got so many things to do, I don't know what to set about first! Let me see, (*Seats herself.*) now I'll count them over. In the first place, I must see after a porter to carry the lady's message;—then I must get the best plates ready against Mrs. Wheedle comes;—after that, I must put Mr. Dabbler's papers in order, for fear of a surprise;—then I must get in a little bit of something nice for supper;—then—Oh Lord, if I had not forgot that scapegrace Bobby! (*Runs off.*)

ACT IV.

Scene i. A Library at Lady Smatter's.

(Lady Smatter, Mrs. Sapient, Dabbler, and Codger, seated at a round table covered with books.)

LADY SMATTER. Now before we begin our literary subjects, allow me to remind you of the rule we established at our last meeting, That every one is to speak his real sentiments, and no flattery is to taint our discussions.

ALL. Agreed.

LADY SMATTER. This is the smallest assembly we have had yet; some or other of our members fail us every time.

DABBLER. But where such luminaries are seen as Lady Smatter and Mrs. Sapient, all other could only appear to be eclipsed.

LADY SMATTER. What have you brought to regale us with tonight, Mr. Dabbler?

DABBLER. Me? dear ma'am, nothing!

LADY SMATTER. Oh barbarous!

MRS. SAPIENT. Surely you cannot have been so cruel? for, in *my* opinion, to give pain causelessly is rather disobliging.

DABBLER. Dear Ladies, you know you may command me; but, I protest, I don't think I have anything worth your hearing.

LADY SMATTER. Let us judge for ourselves. Bless me, Mr. Codger, how insensible you are! why do you not join in our entreaties?

CODGER. For what, madam?

LADY SMATTER. For a poem, to be sure.

CODGER. Madam, I understood Mr. Dabbler [said] he had nothing worth your hearing.

LADY SMATTER. But surely you did not believe him?

CODGER. I knew no reason, madam, to doubt him.

LADY SMATTER. O you Goth! come, dear Mr. Dabbler, produce something at once, if only to shame him.

DABBLER. Your Ladyship has but to speak *(Takes a paper from his pocket book, and reads.)*

On a Certain Party of Beaux Esprits.

> Learning, here, doth pitch her tent,
>   Science, here, her seeds doth scatter;
> Learning, in form of Sapient,
>   Science, in guise of heav'nly Smatter.

LADY SMATTER. O charming! beautiful lines indeed.

MRS. SAPIENT. Elegant and poignant to a degree!

LADY SMATTER. What do *you* think, Mr. Codger, of this poem? To be sure, *(Whispering him.)* the compliment to Mrs. Sapient is preposterously overstrained, but, otherwise, nothing can be more perfect.

MRS. SAPIENT. Mr. Dabbler has, indeed, the happiest turn in the world at easy elegance. Why, Mr. Codger, you don't speak a word? Pray, between friends, *(Whispering him.)* what say you to the notion of making Lady Smatter represent science? don't you think he has been rather unskillful in his choice?

CODGER. Why, madam, you give me no time to think at all.

LADY SMATTER. Well, now to other matters. I have a little observation to offer upon a line of Pope; he says, "Most women have no character at all." Now I should be glad to know, if this was true in the time of Pope, why people should complain so much of the depravity of the present age?[25]

DABBLER. Your Ladyship has asked a question that might perplex a Solomon.

MRS. SAPIENT. It is, indeed, surprisingly ingenious.

DABBLER. Yes, and it reminds me of a little foolish thing which I composed some time ago.

LADY SMATTER. O pray let us hear it.

DABBLER. Your Ladyship's commands—

> The lovely Iris, young and fair,
> Possessed each charm of face and air
> That with the Cyprian might compare;
> So sweet her face, so soft her mind,

So mild she speaks,—she looks so kind,—
To hear—might melt!—to see,—might blind!

LADY SMATTER. ⎱ ... O elegant! enchanting! delicious!
⎰ (*Together.*)
MRS. SAPIENT. ⎰ ... O delightful! pathetic! delicate!

LADY SMATTER. Why Mr. Codger, have you no soul? is it possible you can be unmoved by such poetry as this?

CODGER. I was considering, madam, what might be the allusion to which Mr. Dabbler referred, when he said he was reminded of this little foolish thing, as he was pleased to call it himself.

DABBLER (*aside*). I should like to toss that old fellow in a blanket!

CODGER. Now, Sir, be so good as to gratify me by relating what may be the connection between your song and the foregoing conversation?

DABBLER (*pettishly*). Sir, I only meant to read it to the ladies.

LADY SMATTER. I'm sure you did us great honor. Mrs. Sapient, the next proposition is yours.

MRS. SAPIENT. Pray, did your Ladyship ever read Dryden?[26]

LADY SMATTER. Dryden? O yes!—but I don't just now recollect him;—let's see, what has he writ?

DABBLER. "Cymon and Iphigenia."

LADY SMATTER. O ay, so he did; and really for the time of day I think it's might pretty.

DABBLER. Why yes, it's well enough; but it would not do now.

MRS. SAPIENT. Pray what does your Ladyship think of *The Spectator*?

LADY SMATTER. O, I like it vastly. I've just read it.

CODGER (*to Lady Smatter*). In regard, madam, to those verses of Mr. Dabbler, the chief fault I have to find with them, is—

DABBLER. Why, Sir, we are upon another subject now! (*Aside.*) What an old curmudgeon! he has been pondering all this time only to find fault!

MRS. SAPIENT. For *my* part, I have always thought that the best papers in *The Spectator* are those of Addison.

LADY SMATTER. Very justly observed!

DABBLER. Charmingly said! exactly my own opinion.

MRS. SAPIENT. Nay, I may be mistaken; I only offer it as my private sentiment.

DABBLER. I can but wish, madam, that poor Addison had lived to hear such praise.

LADY SMATTER. Next to Mr. Dabbler, my favorite poets are Pope and Swift.

MRS. SAPIENT. Well, after all, I must confess I think there are as many pretty things in old Shakespeare as in anybody.

LADY SMATTER. Yes, but he is too common; *everybody* can speak well of Shakespeare.

DABBLER. I vow I am quite sick of his name.

CODGER. Madam, to the best of my apprehension, I conceive your Ladyship hath totally mistaken that line of Pope which says, "Most women have no character at all."

LADY SMATTER. Mistaken? how so, Sir? This is curious enough! (*Aside to Dabbler.*) I begin to think the poor creature is superannuated.

DABBLER. So do I, ma'am; I have observed it for some time.

CODGER. By *no* character, madam, he only means—

LADY SMATTER. A *bad* character, to be sure!

CODGER. There, madam, lieth your Ladyship's mistake; he means, I say—

LADY SMATTER. O dear Sir, don't trouble yourself to tell *me* his meaning;—I dare say I shall be able to make it out.

MRS. SAPIENT (*aside to Dabbler*). How irritable is her temper!

DABBLER. O, intolerably!

CODGER. Your Ladyship, madam, will not hear me. I was going—

LADY SMATTER. If you please, Sir, we'll drop the subject, for I rather fancy you will give me no very new information concerning it,—do you think he will, Mr. Dabbler?

CODGER. Mr. Dabbler, madam, is not a competent judge of the case, as—

DABBLER (*rising*). Not a judge, Sir? not a judge of poetry?

CODGER. Not in the present circumstance, Sir, because, as I was going to say—

DABBLER. Nay then, Sir, I'm sure I'm a judge of nothing!

CODGER. That may be, Sir, but is not to the present purpose; I was going—

DABBLER. Suppose, Sir, we refer to the ladies? Pray, now, Ladies, which do *you* think the most adequate judge of poetry, Mr. Codger, or your humble servant? Speak sincerely, for I hate flattery.

MRS. SAPIENT. I would by no means be so ill bred as to determine for Mr. Dabbler in the presence of Mr. Codger, because *I* have always thought that a preference of one person implies less approbation of another; yet—

CODGER. Pray, madam, let me speak; the reason, I say—

MRS. SAPIENT. Yet the well known skill of Mr. Dabbler in this delightful art—

CODGER. Madam, this interruption is somewhat injudicious, since it prevents my explaining—

MRS. SAPIENT (*rising*). Injudicious, Sir? I am sorry, indeed, if I have merited such an accusation: there is nothing I have more scrupulously endeavored to avoid, for, in *my* opinion, to be injudicious is no mark of an extraordinary understanding.

LADY SMATTER (*aside to Dabbler*). How soon she's hurt!

DABBLER. O most unreasonably!

CODGER. Madam, you will never hear me out; you prevent my explaining the reason, I say, why Mr. Dabbler cannot decide upon Lady Smatter's error in judgment—

LADY SMATTER (*rising*). Error in judgment? really this is very diverting!

CODGER. I say, madam—

LADY SMATTER. Nay, Sir, 'tis no great matter; and yet, I must confess, it's rather a hard case that, after so many years of intense study, and most laborious reading, I am not allowed to criticize a silly line of Pope.

DABBLER. And if I, who, from infancy have devoted all my time to the practice of poetry, am now thought to know nothing of the matter,—I should be glad to be informed who has a better title?

MRS. SAPIENT. And if I, who, during my whole life, have made propriety my peculiar study, am now found to be deficient in it,—I must really take the liberty to observe that I must have thrown away a great deal of time to very little purpose.

LADY SMATTER. And as to this line of Pope—

(*Enter a Servant.*)

SERVANT. Mr. Censor, My Lady, begs to speak to Your Ladyship for only two minutes upon business of consequence.

DABBLER. Censor? Suppose we admit him?—(*Aside.*) 'twill be an admirable opportunity to show him my epigram.

LADY SMATTER. Admit him? what, to ask his opinion of Mr. Codger's critical annotations?

CODGER. My doubt, madam, is, if you will give him time to speak it.

LADY SMATTER. Well, is it agreeable to ye all that Mr. Censor should have admittance? I know it is contrary to rule, yet, as he is one of the wits, and therefore ought to be among us, suppose we indulge him?

CODGER. Madam, I vote against it.

DABBLER (*aside to Lady Smatter*). I see he's afraid of him,—let's have him by all means.

LADY SMATTER. Without doubt. Pray, Mr. Codger, why are you against it?

CODGER. Because, madam, there are already so many talkers that I cannot be heard myself.

DABBLER (*aside to Lady Smatter*). You see how it is?

LADY SMATTER. Yes, and enjoy it of all things. Desire Mr. Censor to walk upstairs.

(Exit Servant.)

To be sure this is rather a deviation from the maxims of the society, but great minds, as a favorite author of mine observes, are above being governed by common prejudices.

CODGER. I am thinking, madam,—

(Enter Censor.)

LADY SMATTER. Mr. Censor, your entrance is most critically fortunate; give me leave to present you to our society.

CENSOR. I expected to have seen Your Ladyship alone.

LADY SMATTER. Yes, but I have obtained a dispensation for your admittance to our Esprit Party. But let us not waste our time in common conversation. You must know we are at present discussing a very knotty point, and I should be glad of your opinion upon the merits of the cause.

DABBLER. Yes; and as soon as that is decided, I have a little choice piece of literature to communicate to you which I think you will allow to be tolerable.

MRS. SAPIENT. And I, too, Sir, must take the liberty to appeal to your judgment concerning—

CENSOR. Ay, ay, speak all at a time, and then one hearing may do.

LADY SMATTER. Mr. Censor, when a point of the last importance is in agitation, such levity as this—

CENSOR. Why, madam, the business which brings me hither—

DABBLER. Business? O name not the word in this region of fancy and felicity.

MRS. SAPIENT. That's finely said, Mr. Dabbler, and corroborates with an opinion of mine which I have long formed,—that business and fancy should be regarded as two things.

CENSOR. Ay, madam, and with one of mine which I hold to be equally singular.

MRS. SAPIENT. What is it, Sir?

CENSOR. That London and Paris should be regarded as two places.

MRS. SAPIENT. Pshaw!

CODGER (to Lady Smatter). I say, Madam, I am thinking—

CENSOR. Then, Sir, you are most worthily employed; and this good company desire nothing less than to impede the progress of your thoughts, by troubling you to relate them.

DABBLER. Very true; suppose, therefore, we change the subject. O, àpropos, have you seen the new verses that run about?

CENSOR. No. Give me leave, madam, (Turning to Lady Smatter.) to acquaint you with the motive of my present visit.—

LADY SMATTER. You would not be such a Goth as to interrupt our literary discussions?—besides, I must positively have your sentiments upon an argument I have just had with Mr. Codger upon this line of Pope: "Most women—"

CENSOR. Hold, madam; I am no Quixote, and therefore encounter not danger where there is no prospect of reward; nor shall I, till I emulate the fate of Orpheus, ever argue about women—in their presence.[27]

DABBLER. Ha, Ha! mighty well said. But I was going to tell you, Mr. Censor, that if you have any desire to look at those verses I was speaking of, I believe I have a copy of them in my pocket. Let's see,—Yes, here they are; how lucky that I should happen to have them about me! (Gives them to Censor.) (Aside.) I think they will surprise him.

CENSOR (reading). That passion which we strongest feel

> We all agree to disapprove;
> Yet feebly, feebly we conceal—

DABBLER (*pettishly*). Sir you read without any spirit,—

> Yet feebly,—feebly we conceal

You should drop your voice at the second *feebly,* or you lose all the effect. (*Aside.*) It puts me in a fever to hear such fine lines murdered.

CENSOR (*reading*). We all are bound slaves to self love.

DABBLER (*snatching the paper*). Why you give it neither emphasis nor expression! you read as if you were asleep. (*Reading.*) That passion which—

CENSOR. O no more, no more of it. Pray who is the author?

DABBLER. Why really I—I don't absolutely know,—but, by what I have heard, I should take it to be somebody very—very clever.

CENSOR. You should?

DABBLER. Yes: and, indeed, to own the truth, I have heard it whispered that it is a posthumous work of—of—O, of Gay,—ay, of Gay.[28]

CENSOR. Of Gay?

DABBLER. Yes; found in a little corner of his private bureau.

CENSOR. And pray who has the impudence to make such an assertion?

DABBLER. Who?—O, as to that, really I don't know who in particular,—but I assure you not *me,*—though, by the way, do you really think it very bad?

CENSOR. Despicable beyond abuse. Are you not of the same opinion?

DABBLER. Me?—why, really, as to that—I—I can't exactly say, that is, I have hardly read it.—(*Aside.*) What a crabbed fellow! There is not an ounce of taste in his whole composition. Curse me, if I was Nature, if I should not blush to have made him. Hold, my tablets! a good thought that! I'll turn it into a lampoon, and drop it at Stapleton's. (*Walks aside and writes in his tablets.*)

CENSOR (*to Lady Smatter*). I have seen Miss Stanley, madam, and—

LADY SMATTER. Did you find her at Mrs. Voluble's?

CENSOR. Yes. (*They whisper.*)

MRS. SAPIENT (*listening*). (*Aside.*) So, so, she's at Mrs. Voluble's!—there must certainly be some design upon Dabbler.

CENSOR. But hear me, madam. I have something to communicate to you which—

LADY SMATTER. Not now, I can attend to nothing now. These evenings, Sir, which I devote to the fine arts, must not be contaminated with common affairs.

MRS. SAPIENT (*aside*). I sha'n't rest till I have dived into this matter. (*To Lady Smatter.*) I am much chagrined, madam, at the disagreeable necessity I am under of breaking abruptly from this learned and ingenious assembly, but I am called hence by an appointment which I cannot give up without extreme rudeness; and I must confess I should be rather sorry to be guilty of that, as I have long been of the opinion that a breach of good manners—is no great sign of politeness.

LADY SMATTER. I am quite sorry to lose you so soon.

(Exit Mrs. Sapient.)

What a tiresome creature! how glad I am she's gone!

CODGER. Notwithstanding the rebuff I have just met with, madam, I must say I cannot help thinking that—

CENSOR. Do you mean, Sir, to satirize the whole company, that you thus repeatedly profess thinking among those who have no other aim than talking?

CODGER. Sir, when a man has been pondering upon a subject for a considerable time, and assorting his ideas in order to explain himself, it is an exceedingly uncivil thing to interrupt him.

LADY SMATTER. Mr. Dabbler, what are you writing?

DABBLER. Only a little memorandum, ma'am, about business; nothing more.

CODGER (*aside*). I find I can never get in two words at a time.

(Enter Jack.)

JACK. Ma'am, Your Ladyship's most obedient.

LADY SMATTER. Why did not you come sooner, Jack?—we are just broke up.

JACK. I could not help it, upon my word. I came away now just as my tea was poured out at the coffee house, because I would not stay to drink it.

CODGER (*aside*). I'm glad Jack's come; I think, at least, I shall make him listen to me.

JACK. I have been in such a hurry the whole day, that I have never known what I have been about. I believe that I have been to sixteen places since dinner. You good folks who sit here talking by the hour together, must lead strange dull lives; I wonder you don't lose the use of your limbs.

CODGER. Son Jack, when you have finished your speech, please to hear one of mine.

JACK. I hope it won't be a long one, Sir.

CODGER. Why do you hope that, Son, before you know how well it may entertain you?

JACK. Lord, Sir, I never think of being entertained with speeches.

CODGER. What, Jack, not with your own father's?

JACK. Lord no, Sir.

CODGER. No, Sir? and pray, Sir, why?

JACK. Because I'm always tired before they're half done.

CODGER. Son Jack, 'tis these loose companions that you keep that teach you all this profligacy. Tired of hearing me speak! one would think the poor lad was an idiot.

JACK. So this is your Club Room, where you all meet to talk?

CENSOR. Yes; and the principal maxim of the learned members is that no one shall listen to what is said by his neighbor.

LADY SMATTER. Fie, Mr. Censor, I'm sure we're all attention—

CENSOR. Yes, to seize the next opportunity of speaking.

LADY SMATTER. Never mind what Mr. Censor says, Jack, for you know he is a professed Stoic.

CENSOR. Stoic? pray what does Your Ladyship mean?

LADY SMATTER. Well, well, Cynic, then, if you like it better.

CENSOR. You hold, then, that their signification is the same?

LADY SMATTER. Mercy, Mr. Censor, do you expect me to define the exact meaning of every word I make use of?

CENSOR. No, madam, not unless I could limit Your Ladyship's language to the contents of a primer.

LADY SMATTER. O horrid! did you ever hear anything so splenetic? Mr. Dabbler, what are you writing? Suppose, in compliment to our new member, you were to indulge us with a few lines?

DABBLER. Does Your Ladyship mean an extempore?

LADY SMATTER. The thing in the world I should like best.

DABBLER. Really, ma'am, I wish for nothing upon earth so much as the honor of Your Ladyship's commands,—but as to an extempore—the amazing difficulty,—the genius requisite,—the masterly freedom,—the—the—the things of that sort it requires make me half afraid of so bold an undertaking.

CENSOR. Sir, your exordium is of sufficient length.

DABBLER. I shall but collect my thoughts, and be ready in a moment. In the meantime, I beg I may not interrupt the conversation; it will be no manner of disturbance to me to hear you all talking; we poets, ma'am, can easily detach ourselves from the company. (*Walks apart.*)

CENSOR. I should be glad if Your Ladyship would inform me what time, according to the established regulations of your society, you allow for the *study* of extemporary verses?

LADY SMATTER. I think we have no fixed rule; some are quick, and some are slow,—'tis just as it happens.

CENSOR (*aside*). What unconscious absurdity!

(While they are speaking, Dabbler privately looks at a paper, which he accidentally drops instead of putting in his pocket.)

DABBLER (*advancing*). I hope I have not detained you long?

LADY SMATTER. Is it possible you can be ready so soon?

DABBLER. O dear yes, ma'am; these little things are done in a moment; they cost *us* nothing.

> In one sole point agree we all,
> Both rich and poor, and saint and sinner,
> Proud or humble, short or tall,—
> And that's—a taste for a good dinner.

LADY SMATTER. O charming! I never heard anything so satirical in my life.

CENSOR. And so, Sir, you composed these lines just now?

DABBLER. This very moment.

CENSOR. It seems, then, you can favor your friends whenever they call upon you?

DABBLER. O yes, Sir, with the utmost pleasure.

CENSOR. I should be obliged to you, then, Sir, for something more.

DABBLER. Sir, you do me honor. I will take but an instant for consideration, and endeavor to obey you. So, so!—I thought I should bring him round at last! (*Walking away.*)

CENSOR. Stay, Sir. As you make these verses with so much facility, you can have no objection, I presume, to my choosing you a subject?

DABBLER. Sir!

CENSOR. And then with firmer courage your friends may counteract the skepticism of the envious, and boldly affirm that they are your own, and unstudied.

DABBLER. Really, Sir, as to that, I can't say I very much mind what those sort of people say; we authors, Sir, are so much inured to illiberal attacks, that we regard them as nothing,—mere marks, Sir, of celebrity, and hear them without the least emotion.

CENSOR. You are averse, then, to my proposal?

DABBLER. O dear no, Sir!—not at all,—not in the least, I assure you, Sir! (*Aside.*) I wish he was in the deserts of Libya with all my heart!

CENSOR. The readiness of your compliance, Sir, proves the promptness of your wit. I shall name a subject which, I believe, you will find no difficulty to dilate upon,—self-sufficiency.

DABBLER. Sir?

CENSOR. Self-sufficiency,—don't you understand me?

DABBLER. Really, Sir, in regard to that, I don't exactly know whether I do or not, but I assure you, if you imagine that *I* am self-sufficient, you are most prodigiously mistaken; I defy anybody to charge me with that, for though I have written so many things that have pleased everybody else, I have always made it a rule to keep my own opinion to myself. Even Mr. Codger must, in this point, do me justice. Will you not, Sir?

CODGER. Sir, I shall say nothing. (*Folds his arms and leans upon the table.*)

CENSOR. Well, Sir, I will give you another subject, then, for of this, I must own, you might long since have been weary. I will not affront you by naming so hackneyed a theme as love, but give us, if you please, a spirited couplet upon war.

DABBLER. Upon war?—hum—let's see,—upon war,—ay,—but hold! don't you think, Sir, that war is rather a disagreeable subject where there are ladies? For *myself* I can certainly have no objection, but, I must confess, I am rather in doubt whether it will be quite polite to Lady Smatter.

JACK. Why Lord, Mr. Dabbler, a man might ride ten times round Hyde Park, before you are ready to begin.

DABBLER. Sir, you don't know what you talk of; things of this importance are not to be settled rashly.

CENSOR. Mr. Dabbler, I will give you an opportunity of taking your revenge; let your verses be upon the use and abuse of time, and address them, if you please, to that gentleman.

JACK. Ay, with all my heart. He may address what he will to me, so as he will not keep me long to hear him.

DABBLER. Time, did you say?—the use and the abuse of time?— ay, very good, a very good subject,—Time?—yes, a very good idea, indeed!—the use and the abuse of Time,—(*Pauses.*) But pray, Sir, pray, Mr. Censor, let me speak a word to you; are you not of opinion—now don't imagine this is any objection of *mine,* no, I like the subject of all things,—it is just what I wished,—but don't you think that poor Mr. Codger, here, may think it is meant as a sneer at him?

CENSOR. How so, Sir?

DABBLER. Why, Sir, on account of his being so slow. And really, notwithstanding his old fashioned ways, one would not wish to affront him, poor man, for he means no harm. Besides, Sir, his age!—consider that; we ought all to make allowances for the infirmities of age. I'm sure *I* do,—poor old soul!

CENSOR. Well, Sir, I shall name but one subject more, and to that if you object, you must give me leave to draw my own inference from your backwardness, and to report it accordingly.

DABBLER. Sir, I shall be very—I shall be extremely—that is, Sir, I shall be quite at your service. (*Aside.*) What a malignant fellow!

CENSOR. What say you, Sir, to an epigram on slander?

DABBLER. On slander?

CENSOR. Yes, Sir; what objection can you devise to that?

DABBLER. An illiberal subject, Sir! a most illiberal subject,—I will have nothing to do with it.

CENSOR. The best way to manifest your contempt will be to satirize it.

DABBLER. Why, as you say,—there's something in that;—satirize it?—ay, satirize slander,—ha! ha! a good hit enough!

CENSOR. Then, Sir, you will favor us without further delay.

DABBLER. Sir, I should be extremely happy to obey you,—nothing could give me greater pleasure, only that just now I am so par-

ticularly pressed for time, that I am obliged to run away. Lady
Smatter, I have the honor to wish Your Ladyship good night.
(*Going.*)

JACK (*stopping him*). Fair play, fair play! you sha'n't go till you
have made the verses; or, if you do, I swear I'll run after you.

DABBLER. Upon my word, Sir—

CENSOR. Prithee, Jack, don't detain him. This anecdote, you know,
(*Affecting to whisper.*) will *tell* as well without the verses as
with them.

DABBLER (*aside*). That fellow is a mere compound of spite and
envy.

LADY SMATTER. Come, Mr. Dabbler, I see you relent.

DABBLER. Why,—hem!—if—if Your Ladyship insists—Pray, Mr.
Censor, what is this same subject you have been talking of?

CENSOR. O, Sir, 'tis no matter; if you are so much hurried, why
should you stay? we are all pretty well convinced of the alacrity
of your wit already.

DABBLER. Slander, I think it was?—but suppose, Sir, for slander we
substitute fashion?—I have a notion I could do something upon
fashion.

CENSOR. Probably, Sir, you *have* done something upon fashion; entertain us, therefore, upon the given subject, or else be a better
nomenclator of your verses than to call them extemporary.

DABBLER. Well, Sir, well!—(*Aside and walking away.*) A surly fellow!

JACK. Pray has Your Ladyship heard the queer story about the
Miss Sippets?

LADY SMATTER. No; what is it?

JACK. Why I heard it just now at Mrs. Gabble's. Sir Harry Frisk,
you know, last winter paid his addresses to the eldest sister, but
this winter, to make what variety he could without quitting the
family, he deserted to the youngest; and this morning they were
to have been married.

LADY SMATTER. Well, and were they not?

JACK. Upon my word I don't know.

LADY SMATTER. Don't know? what do you mean?

JACK. Why I had not time to enquire.

LADY SMATTER. Pho, prithee, Jack, don't be so ridiculous.

DABBLER (*holding his hand before his eyes, and walking about*).
Not one thought,—not one thought to save me from ruin!

CENSOR. Why, Mr. Codger, what are you about? is it not rather melancholy to sit by yourself at the table, and not join at all in the conversation?

CODGER (*raising his head*). Perhaps, Sir, I may conceive myself to be somewhat slighted.

LADY SMATTER. Nay, nay, prithee, my good friend, don't be so captious.

CODGER. Madam, I presume, at least, I have as good a right to be affronted as another man; for which reason—

DABBLER (*pettishly*). Upon my word, if you all keep talking so incessantly, it is not possible for a man to know what he is about.

CODGER. I have not spoken before for this half hour, and yet I am as good as bid to hold my tongue! (*Leans again on the table.*)

JACK. O but, ma'am, I forgot to tell Your Ladyship the very best part of the story; the poor eldest sister was quite driven to despair, so last night, to avoid, at least, dancing bare-foot at her sister's wedding, she made an appointment with a young haberdasher in the neighborhood to set off for Scotland.[29]

LADY SMATTER. Well?

JACK. Well, and when she got into the post chaise, instead of her new lover the young haberdasher, who do you think was waiting to receive her?

LADY SMATTER. Nay, nay, tell me at once.

JACK. But who do you guess?

LADY SMATTER. Pho, pho, don't be so tiresome. Who was it?

JACK. Why that I am not certain myself.

LADY SMATTER. Not certain yourself?

JACK. No, for I had not time to stay till Mrs. Gabble came to the name.

LADY SMATTER. How absurd!

CODGER (*again raising his head*). Madam, if I might be allowed,—or, rather, to speak more properly, if I could get time to give my opinion of this matter, I should say—

LADY SMATTER. My good friend, we should all be extremely happy to hear you, if you were not so long in coming to the point;— that's all the fault we find with you; is it not, Jack?

JACK. To be sure, ma'am. Why sometimes, do you know, I have made a journey to Bath and back again, while he has been considering whether his next wig should be a bob, or a full-bottom.

CODGER. Son Jack, this is very unseemly discourse, and I desire—

LADY SMATTER. Nay, pray don't scold him. Jack, when shall you hear any more of Miss Sippet's adventure?

JACK. Why, ma'am, either tomorrow or Friday, I don't know which.

CODGER (aside, and reclining as before). I verily believe they'd rather hear Jack than me!

JACK. Why Lord, Mr. Dabbler, I believe you are dreaming. Will you never be ready?

DABBLER. Sir, this is really unconscionable! I was just upon the point of finishing,—and now you have put it all out of my head!

CENSOR. Well, Mr. Dabbler, we release you, now, from all further trouble, since you have sufficiently satisfied us that your extemporary verses are upon a new construction.

DABBLER. O, Sir, as to that, making verses is no sort of *trouble* to me, I assure you,—however, if you don't choose to hear these which I have been composing—

LADY SMATTER. O but *I* do, so pray—

JACK. Pho, pho, he has not got them ready.

DABBLER. You are mistaken, Sir, these are quite ready,—entirely finished,—and lodged here;—(*Pointing to his head.*)—but as Mr. Censor—

CENSOR. Nay, if they are ready, you may as well repeat them.

DABBLER. No, Sir, no, since you declined hearing them at first, I am above compelling you to hear them at all. Lady Smatter, the next time I have the honor of seeing Your Ladyship, I shall be proud to have your opinion of them. (*Exit hastily.*)

CENSOR. Poor Wretch! "Glad of a quarrel straight he shuts the door,"[30]—What's this? (*Picks up the paper dropped by Dabbler.*) So! so! so!—

(*Enter Beaufort.*)

BEAUFORT (*to Lady Smatter*). Pardon me, madam, if I interrupt you, I am come but for a moment. Censor, (*Apart to Censor.*) have you no heart? are you totally divested of humanity?

CENSOR. Why what's the matter?

BEAUFORT. The matter? You have kept me on the rack,—you have wantonly tortured me with the most intolerable suspense that the mind of man is capable of enduring. Where is Cecilia?—

have you given her my message?—have you brought me any answer?—why am I kept in ignorance of everything I wish or desire to know?

CENSOR. Is your harangue finished?

BEAUFORT. No, Sir, it is hardly begun! This unfeeling propensity to raillery upon occasions of serious distress is cruel, is unjustifiable, is insupportable. No man could practice it, whose heart was not hardened against pity, friendship, sorrow,—and every kind, every endearing tie by which the bonds of society are united.

CENSOR. At least, my good friend, object not to raillery in me, till you learn to check railing in yourself. I would fain know by what law or what title you gentlemen of the sighing tribe assume the exclusive privilege of appropriating all severities of speech to yourselves.

LADY SMATTER. Beaufort, your behavior involves me in the utmost confusion. After an education such as I have bestowed upon you, this weak anxiety about mere private affairs is unpardonable;—especially in the presence of people of learning.

BEAUFORT. I waited, madam, till Mrs. Sapient and Mr. Dabbler were gone,—had I waited longer, patience must have degenerated into insensibility. From Your Ladyship and from Mr. Codger, my anxiety has some claim to indulgence, since its cause is but too well known to you both.

JACK (aside). Not a word of me! I'll e'en sneak away before he finds me out. (Going.)

CODGER. Son Jack, please to stop.

JACK. Sir, I can't; my time's expired.

CODGER. Son, if I conceive aright, your time, properly speaking, ought to be mine.

JACK. Lord, Sir, only look at my watch; it's just eight o'clock, and I promised Billy Skip to call on him before seven to go to the play.

CODGER. Son Jack, it is by no means a dutiful principle you are proceeding upon, to be fonder of the company of Billy Skip than of your own father.

BEAUFORT. For mercy's sake, Sir, debate this point some other time. Censor, why will you thus deny me all information?

CODGER. So it is continually! whenever I speak you are all sure to

be in a hurry! Jack, come hither and sit by me; *you* may hear me, I think, if nobody else will. Sit down, I say.

JACK. Lord, Sir—

CODGER. Sit down when I bid you, and listen to what I am going to tell you. (*Makes Jack seat himself at the table, and talks to him.*)

LADY SMATTER. Beaufort, let *me* speak to Mr. Censor. What have you done, Sir, about this poor girl? did you give her my message?

CENSOR. She had too much sense, too much spirit, too much dignity to hear it.

LADY SMATTER. Indeed?

CENSOR. Yes; and therefore I should propose—

LADY SMATTER. Sir, I must beg you not to interfere in this transaction; it is not that I mean to doubt either your knowledge or your learning, far from it,—but nevertheless I must presume that I am myself as competent a judge of the matter as you can be, since I have reason to believe—you'll excuse me, Sir, that I have read as many books as you have.

BEAUFORT. O those eternal books! What, madam, in the name of reason, and of common sense, can books have to do in such an affair as this?

LADY SMATTER. How? do you mean to depreciate books? to doubt their general utility, and universal influence? Beaufort, I shall blush to own you for my pupil! Blush to recollect the fruitless efforts with which I have labored, as Shakespeare finely says, "To teach the young idea how to shoot.—"[31]

CENSOR. Shakespeare?—then what a thief was Thomson!

LADY SMATTER. Thomson? O, ay, true, now I recollect, so it was.

CENSOR. Nay, madam, it little matters which, since both, you know, were authors.

BEAUFORT. Unfeeling Censor! is this a time to divert yourself with satirical dryness? defer, I conjure you, these useless, idle, ludicrous disquisitions, and, for a few moments, suffer affairs of real interest and importance to be heard and understood.

LADY SMATTER. Beaufort, you expose yourself more and more every word you utter; disquisitions which relate to books and authors ought never to be deferred. Authors, Sir, are the noblest of human beings, and books—

BEAUFORT. Would to Heaven there were not one in the world!

LADY SMATTER. O monstrous!

BEAUFORT. Once again, madam, I entreat, I conjure—

LADY SMATTER. I will not hear a word more. Wish there was not a book in the world? Monstrous, shocking, and horrible! Beaufort, you are a lost wretch! I tremble for your intellects; and if you do not speedily conquer this degenerate passion, I shall abandon you without remorse to that ignorance and depravity to which I see you are plunging. (*Exit.*)

(Beaufort and Censor. Codger and Jack at the table.)

BEAUFORT. Hard-hearted, vain, ostentatious woman! Go, then, and leave me to that independence which not all your smiles could make me cease to regret! Censor, I am weary of this contention; what is life, if the present must continually be sacrificed to the future? I will fly to Cecilia, and I will tear myself from her no more. If, without her, I can receive no happiness, why, with her, should I be apprehensive of misery?

CENSOR. Know you not, Beaufort, that if you sap the foundation of a structure, 'tis madness to expect the sides and the top will stand self-supported? Is not security from want the basis of all happiness? and if you undermine that, do you not lose all possibility of enjoyment? Will the presence of Cecilia soften the hardships of penury? Will her smiles teach you to forget the pangs of famine? Will her society make you insensible to the severities of a houseless winter?

BEAUFORT. Well, well, tell me where I can find her, and she shall direct my future conduct herself.

CENSOR. I have a scheme upon Lady Smatter to communicate to you, which, I think, has some chance of succeeding.

BEAUFORT. Till I have seen Cecilia, I can attend to nothing; once more, tell me where she is.

CENSOR. Wherever she is, she has more wisdom than her lover, for she charged me to command your absence.

BEAUFORT. My absence?

CENSOR. Nay, nay, I mean not seriously to suppose the girl is wise enough to wish it; however, if she pretends to desire it, you have sufficient excuse for non-attendance.

BEAUFORT. I don't understand you.—Is Cecilia offended?

CENSOR. Yes, and most marvellously, for neither herself nor her neighbors know why.

BEAUFORT. I will not stay another minute!—I will find other methods to discover her abode. (*Going.*)

CENSOR. Prithee, Beaufort, be less absurd. My scheme upon Lady Smatter—

BEAUFORT. I will not hear it! I disdain Lady Smatter, and her future smiles or displeasure shall be equally indifferent to me. Too long, already, have I been governed by motives and views which level me with her narrow-minded self; it is time to shake off the yoke,—assert the freedom to which I was born,—and dare to be poor that I may learn to be happy! (*Exit.*)

CENSOR. Shall this noble fellow be suffered to ruin himself? No! the world has too few like him. Jack, a word with you,—Jack, I say!—are you asleep, man?

CODGER. Asleep? Surely not.

CENSOR. If you're awake, answer!

JACK (*yawning*). Why what's the matter?

CENSOR. Wake, man, wake and I'll tell you.

CODGER. How, asleep? pray, Son Jack, what's the reason of your going to sleep when I'm talking to you?

JACK. Why, Sir, I have so little time for sleep, that I thought I might as well take the opportunity.

CODGER. Son Jack, Son Jack, you are verily an ignoramus!

CENSOR. Come hither, Jack. I have something to propose to you—

CODGER. Sir, I have not yet done with him myself. Whereabouts was I, Son, when you fell asleep?

JACK. Why there, Sir, where you are now.

CODGER. Son, you are always answering like a blockhead; I mean whereabouts was I in my story?

JACK. What story, Sir?

CODGER How? did not you hear my story about your Aunt Deborah's poultry?

JACK. Lord, no, Sir!

CODGER. Not hear it? why, what were you thinking of?

JACK. Me, Sir? why, how many places I've got to go to tonight.

CODGER. This is the most indecorous behavior I ever saw. You don't deserve ever to hear me tell a story again. Pray, Mr. Censor, did *you* hear it?

CENSOR. No.

CODGER. Well, then, as it's a very good story, I think I'll e'en take the trouble to tell it once more. You must know, then, my sister Deborah, this silly lad's aunt—

CENSOR. Mr. Codger, I am too much engaged to hear you now,—I have business that calls me away.

CODGER. This is always the case! I don't think I ever spoke to three persons in my life that did not make some pretense for leaving me before I had done!

CENSOR. Jack, are you willing to serve your brother?

JACK. That I am! I would ride to York to see what's o'clock for him.

CENSOR. I will put you in a way to assist him with less trouble, though upon a matter of at least equal importance. You, too, Mr. Codger, have, I believe, a good regard for him?

CODGER. Sir, I shall beg leave to decline making any answer.

CENSOR. Why so, Sir?

CODGER. Because, Sir, I never intend to utter a word more in this room; but, on the contrary, it is my intention to abandon the club from this time forward.

CENSOR. But is that any reason why you should not answer me?

CODGER. Sir, I shall quit the place directly; for I think it an extremely hard thing to be made speak when one has nothing to say, and hold one's tongue when one has got a speech ready. (*Exit.*)

JACK. Is he gone? huzza! I was never so tired in my life. (*Going.*)

CENSOR. Hold! I have something to say to you.

JACK. Can't possibly stay to hear you.

CENSOR. Prithee, Jack, how many duels do you fight in a year?

JACK. Me? Lord, not one.

CENSOR. How many times, then, do you beg pardon to escape a caning?

JACK. A caning?

CENSOR. Yes; or do you imagine the very wildness and inattention by which you offend, are competent to make your apology?

JACK. Lord, Mr. Censor, you are never easy but when you are asking some queer question! But I don't much mind you. You odd sort of people, who do nothing all day but *muz*[32] yourselves with thinking, are always coming out with these sort of trimmers; however, I know you so well, that they make no impression on me. (*Exit.*)

CENSOR. Through what a multiplicity of channels does folly glide! its streams, alternately turgid, calm, rapid and lazy, take their several directions from the peculiarities of the minds whence they spring,—frequently varying in their courses,—but ever similar in their shallowness!

ACT V.

Scene i. A Parlor at Mrs. Voluble's.

(Mrs. Voluble, Mrs. Wheedle, Miss Jenny, and Bob are seated at a round table at supper; Betty is waiting.)

MRS. VOLUBLE. Well, this is a sad thing indeed!—Betty, give me some beer. Come, Miss Jenny, here's your love and mine. *(Drinks.)*

MRS. WHEEDLE. I do believe there's more misfortunes in our way of business than in any in the world; the fine ladies have no more conscience than a Jew; they keep ordering and ordering, and think no more of paying than if one could live upon a needle and thread.

MRS. VOLUBLE. Ah, the times are very bad! very bad, indeed!—all the gentlefolks breaking,—Why, Betty, the meat i'n't half done!—Poor Mr. Mite, the rich cheesemonger at the corner, is quite knocked up.

MRS. WHEEDLE. You don't say so?

MRS. VOLUBLE. Very true, indeed.

MRS. WHEEDLE. Well, who'd have thought of that? Pray, Mrs. Betty, give me some bread.

MISS JENNY. Why it is but a week ago that I met him a driving his own whiskey.[33]

MRS. VOLUBLE. Ah, this is a sad world! a very sad world, indeed! nothing but ruination going forward from one end of the town to the other. My dear Mrs. Wheedle, you don't eat; pray let me help you to a little slice more.

MRS. WHEEDLE. O, I shall do very well, I only wish you'd take care of yourself.

MRS. VOLUBLE. There, that little bit can't hurt you, I'm sure. As to Miss Jenny, she's quite like a crocodile, for she lives upon air.[34]

MRS. WHEEDLE. No, ma'am, the thing is she laces so tight, that she can't eat half her natural victuals.

MRS. VOLUBLE. Ay, ay, that's the way with all the young ladies; they pinch for fine shapes.

BOB. Mother, I wish you'd help *me*,—I'm just starved.

MRS. VOLUBLE. Would you have me help you before I've helped the company, you greedy fellow, you? Stay till we've done can't you? and then if there's any left, I'll give you a bit.

MISS JENNY. I'll give Master Bobby a piece of mine, if you please, ma'am.

MRS. VOLUBLE. No, no, he can't be very hungry, I'm sure, for he eat a dinner to frighten a horse. And so, as I was telling you, she has agreed to stay here all night, and to be sure, poor thing, she does nothing in the world but cry, all as ever I can say to her, and I believe I was talking to her for a matter of an hour before you came, without her making so much as a word of answer. I declare it makes one as melancholy as a cat to see her. I think this is the nicest cold beef I ever tasted,— you *must* eat a bit, or I shall take it quite ill.

MRS. WHEEDLE. Well, it must be [a] *leetle* tiny morsel, then.

MRS. VOLUBLE. I shall cut you quite a *Fox-hall* slice.[35]

BOB. Mother, if Mrs. Wheedle's had enough, you'd as good give it me.

MRS. VOLUBLE. I declare I don't believe there's such another fellow in the world for gormandizing!—There,—take that, and be quit. So, as I was saying—

BOB. Lord, Mother, you've given me nothing but fat!

MRS. VOLUBLE. Aye, and too good for you, too. I think, at your age, you've no right to know fat from lean.

MRS. WHEEDLE. Ah, Master Bobby, these are no times to be dainty! one ought to be glad to get bread to eat. I'm sure, for my part, I find it as hard to get my bills paid, as if the fine ladies had no money but what they earned.

MRS. VOLUBLE. If you'll take my advice, Mrs. Wheedle, you'll send in your account directly, and then, if the young lady has any money left, you'll get it at once.

MRS. WHEEDLE. Why, that's just what I thought myself, so I made out the bill, and brought it in my pocket.

MRS. VOLUBLE. That's quite right. But, good lack, Mrs. Wheedle, who'd have thought of such a young lady's being brought to such a pass?—I shall begin soon to think there's no trusting in anybody.

MISS JENNY. For my part, if I was to choose, I should like best to be a lady at once, and follow no business at all.

BOB. And for my part, I should like best to be a duke.

MRS. VOLUBLE. A duke? you a duke, indeed! you great numskull I wish you'd learn to hold your tongue. I'll tell you what, Mrs. Wheedle, you must know it's my notion this young lady expects something in the money way out of the City, for she gave me a letter, just before you came, to send by a porter; so as I was coming downstairs, I just peeped in at the sides—

(Enter Cecilia.)

O Law!—I hope she did not hear me!

CECILIA. I beg your pardon, Mrs. Voluble, for this intrusion, but I rang my bell three times, and I believe nobody heard it.

MRS. VOLUBLE. I'm sure, ma'am, I'm quite sorry you've had such a trouble; but I dare say it was all my son Bobby's fault, for he keeps such a continual jabbering, that there's no hearing anything in the world for him.

BOB. Lord, Mother, I'll take my oath I ha'n't spoke three words the whole time! I'm sure I've done nothing but gnaw that nasty fat the whole night.

MRS. VOLUBLE. What, you are beginning again, are you?—

CECILIA. I beg I may occasion no disturbance; I merely wished to know if my messenger were returned.

MRS. VOLUBLE. Dear no, ma'am, not yet.

CECILIA. Then he has certainly met with some accident. If you will be so good as to lend me your pen and ink once more, I will send another man after him.

MRS. VOLUBLE. Why, ma'am, he could not have got back so soon, let him go never so fast.

CECILIA *(walking apart)*. So soon! Oh how unequally are we affected by the progress of time! Winged with the gay plumage of hope, how rapid seems its flight,—oppressed with the burden of misery, how tedious its motion!—yet it varies not,—insensible to smiles and callous to tears, its acceleration and its tardiness are mere phantasms of our disordered imaginations. How strange that that which in its course is most steady and uniform, should, to our deluded senses, seem most mutable and irregular!

MISS JENNY. I believe she's talking to herself.

MRS. VOLUBLE. Yes, she has a mighty way of musing. I have a good mind to ask her to eat a bit, for, poor soul, I dare say she's hungry enough. Bobby, get up, and let her have your chair.

BOB. What, and then a'n't I to have any more?

MRS. VOLUBLE. Do as you're bid, will you, and be quiet. I declare I believe you think of nothing but eating and drinking all day long. Ma'am, will it be agreeable to you to eat a bit of supper with us?

MRS. WHEEDLE. The young lady does not hear you; I'll go to her myself. (*Rises and follows Cecilia.*) I hope, Miss Stanley, you're very well? I hope My Lady's well? I believe, ma'am, you don't recollect me?

CECILIA. Mrs. Wheedle?—Yes, I do.

MRS. WHEEDLE. I'm very sorry, I'm sure, ma'am, to hear of your misfortunes, but I hope things a'n't quite so bad as they're reported?

CECILIA. I thank you. Mrs. Voluble, is your pen and ink here?

MRS. VOLUBLE. You shall have it directly; but pray, ma'am, let me persuade you to eat a morsel first.

CECILIA. I am obliged to you, but I cannot.

MRS. VOLUBLE. Why now here's the nicest little minikin bit you ever saw;—it's enough to tempt you to look at it.

BOB. Mother, if the lady don't like it, can't you give it me?

MRS. VOLUBLE. I was just this minute going to help you, but now you're so greedy, you sha'n't have a bit.

CECILIA. Mrs. Voluble, can I find the pen and ink myself?

MRS. VOLUBLE. I'll fetch it in two minutes. But, dear ma'am, don't fret, for bad things of one sort or other are always coming to pass; and as to breaking, and so forth, why I think it happens to everybody. I'm sure there's Mr. Grease, the tallow chandler, one of my most particular acquaintance, that's got as genteel a shop as any in all London, is quite upon the very point of ruination: and Miss Moggy Grease, his daughter—

CECILIA. I'll step upstairs, and when you are at leisure, you will be so good as to send me the standish. (*Going.*)

MRS. WHEEDLE (*stopping her*). Ma'am, as I did not know when I might have the pleasure of seeing you again, I took the liberty just to make out my little account, and to bring it in my pocket; and I hope, ma'am, that when you make up your affairs, you'll be so good as to let me be the first person that's considered, for I'm a deal out of pocket, and should be very glad to have some of the money as soon as possible.

CECILIA. Dunned already! good Heaven, what will become of me! (*Bursts into tears.*)

MRS. VOLUBLE. Dear ma'am, what signifies fretting? better eat a bit of supper, and get up your spirits. Betty, go for a clean plate.

(*Exit Betty.*)

MRS. WHEEDLE. Won't you please, ma'am, to look at the bill?

CECILIA. Why should I look at it?—I cannot pay it,—I am a destitute creature,—without friend or resource!

MRS. WHEEDLE. But, ma'am, I only mean—

CECILIA. No matter what you mean!—all application to *me* is fruitless,—I possess nothing—The beggar who sues to you for a penny is not more powerless and wretched,—a tortured and insulted heart is all that I can call my own!

MRS. WHEEDLE. But sure, ma'am, when there comes to be a division among your creditors, your debts won't amount to more than—

CECILIA. Forbear, forbear!—I am not yet inured to disgrace, and this manner of stating my affairs is insupportable. *Your* debt, assure yourself, is secure, for sooner will I famish with want, or perish with cold,—faint with the fatigue of labor, or consume with unassisted sickness, than appropriate to my own use the smallest part of my shattered fortune, till your—and every other claim upon it is answered.

MRS. WHEEDLE. Well, ma'am, that's as much as one can expect.

(*Re-enter Betty with a plate and a letter.*)

BETTY. Ma'am, is your name Miss Stanley?

CECILIA. Yes; is that letter for me? (*Takes it.*)

MRS. VOLUBLE. Betty, why did you not bring the letter first to me? Sure I'm the mistress of my own house. Come, Mrs. Wheedle, come and finish your supper.

(*Mrs. Wheedle returns to the table.*)

CECILIA. I dread to open it! Does anybody wait?

BETTY. Yes, ma'am, a man in a fine lace livery.

CECILIA (*reading*). "Since you would not hear my message from Mr. Censor, I must try if you will read it from myself. I do most earnestly exhort you to go instantly and privately into the country, and you may then depend upon my support and protection. Beaufort now begins to listen to reason—"
Oh Heaven!
"and, therefore, if you do not continue in town with a view to attract his notice, or, by acquainting him with your retirement, seduce him to follow you—"
Insolent, injurious woman!
"I have no doubt but he will be guided by one whose experience and studies entitle her to direct him. I shall call upon you very soon, to know your determination, and to supply you with cash for your journey, being, with the utmost sorrow for your misfortunes, Dear Miss Stanley,
Yours & c Judith Smatter."
What a letter!

BETTY. Ma'am, if you please, is there any answer?

CECILIA. No, none.

BETTY. Then, ma'am, what am I to say to the footman?

CECILIA. Nothing.—Yes,—tell him I have read *this* letter, but if he brings me another, it will be returned unopened.

BETTY. Yes, ma'am. Laws! what a comical answer! (*Exit.*)

MRS. VOLUBLE. I wonder who that letter was from!

MISS JENNY. I dare say I can guess. I'll venture something it's from her sweetheart.

MRS. VOLUBLE. That's just my thought. (*They whisper.*)

CECILIA. Is then every evil included in poverty? and is the deprivation of wealth what it has least to regret? Are contempt, insult, and treachery its necessary attendants?—Is not the loss of affluence sufficiently bitter,—the ruin of all hope sufficiently severe, but that reproach, too, must add her stings, and scorn her daggers?

MRS. VOLUBLE. When I've eat this, I'll ask her if we guessed right.

CECILIA. "Beaufort begins to listen to reason,"—mercenary Beaufort! Interest has taken sole possession of thy heart,—weak and credulous that I was to believe I had ever any share in it!

Mrs. Voluble. I'm of ten minds whether to speak to her, or leave her to her own devices.

Cecilia. "To listen to reason,"—is, then, reason another word for baseness, falsehood and inconstancy?

Mrs. Wheedle. I only wish my money was once safe in my pocket.

Cecilia. Attract his notice? seduce him to follow!—am I already so sunk? already regarded as a designing, interested wretch? I cannot bear the imputation,—my swelling heart seems too big for its mansion,—O that I could quit them all!

Mrs. Voluble (*rising and approaching Cecilia*). Ma'am, I'm quite sorry to see you in such trouble; I'm afraid that letter did not bring you agreeable news;—I'm sure I wish I could serve you with all my heart, and if you're distressed about a lodging, I've just thought of one in Queen Street, that, in a week's time,—

Cecilia. In a week's time I hope to be far away from Queen Street,—far away from this hated city,—far away, if possible, from all to whom I am known!

Mrs. Voluble. Dear ma'am, sure you don't think of going beyond seas?

Mrs. Wheedle. If you should like, ma'am, to go abroad, I believe I can help you to a thing of that sort myself.

Cecilia. How?

Mrs. Wheedle. Why, ma'am, I know a lady who's upon the very point of going, and the young lady who was to have been her companion, all of a sudden married a young gentleman of fortune, and left her without any notice.

Cecilia. Who is the lady?

Mrs. Wheedle. Mrs. Hollis, ma'am; she's a lady of very good fortunes.

Cecilia. I have heard of her.

Mrs. Wheedle. And she wants a young lady very much. She sets off the beginning of next week. If it's agreeable to you to go to her, I shall be proud to show you the way.

Cecilia. I know not what to do!

Mrs. Voluble. Dear ma'am, I would not have you think of such a desperation scheme; things may be better soon, and who knows but Mr. Beaufort may prove himself a true lover at the last? Lord, if you could but once get the sight of him, I dare say, for all my Lady, the day would be your own.

CECILIA. What odious interpretations! to what insults am I exposed!—Yes, I had indeed better quit the kingdom,—Mrs. Wheedle, I am ready to attend you.

MRS. WHEEDLE. Then, Master Bobby, bid Betty call a coach.

CECILIA. No,—stay!—

MRS. WHEEDLE. What, ma'am, won't you go?

CECILIA (*walking apart*). Am I not too rash?—expose myself like a common servant, to be hired?—submit to be examined, and hazard being rejected!—no, no, my spirit is not yet so broken.

MRS. VOLUBLE. I hope, ma'am, you are thinking better of it. For my part, if I might be free to advise you, I should say send to the young gentleman, and see first what is to be done with *him*.

CECILIA. What humiliating suggestions! yes, I see I must be gone,—I see I must hide myself from the world, or submit to be suspected of views and designs I disdain to think of. Mrs. Wheedle, I cannot well accompany you to this lady myself, but if you will go to her in my name,—tell her my unhappy situation, as far as your knowledge of it goes—and that, alas, includes but half its misery!—you will much oblige me. When did you say she leaves England?

MRS. WHEEDLE. Next week, ma'am.

CECILIA. I shall have time, then, to arrange my affairs. Tell her I know not, yet, in what capacity to offer myself, but that, at all events, it is my first wish to quit this country.

MRS. WHEEDLE. Yes, ma'am. I'll get my hat and cloak, and go directly. (*Exit.*)

CECILIA. Alas, to what abject dependence may I have exposed myself!

MRS. VOLUBLE. Come, ma'am, let me persuade you to taste my raisin wine,—I do believe it's the best that—

CECILIA. I thank you, but I can neither eat nor drink. (*Going.*)

(*Re-enter Mrs. Wheedle.*)

MRS. WHEEDLE. I suppose, ma'am, I may tell Mrs. Hollis you will have no objection to doing a little work for the children, and things of that sort, as the last young lady did?

CECILIA. Oh heavy hour!—down, down, proud heart!—Tell her what you will!—I must submit to my fate, not choose it; and should servility and dependence be my lot, I trust, at least, that

I shall not only find them new,—not only find them heart-breaking and cruel—but short and expeditious.

MRS. VOLUBLE. But, ma'am, had not you best—

CECILIA. I have no more directions to give, and I can answer no more questions. The sorrows of my situation seem every moment to be aggravated,—Oh Beaufort! faithless, unfeeling Beaufort! to have rescued you from distress and mortification such as this would have been my heart's first joy,—my life's only pride! (*Exit.*)

MRS. VOLUBLE. She's quite in a sad taking, that's the truth of it.

MISS JENNY. Poor young lady! I'm so sorry for her you can't think.

MRS. VOLUBLE. Come, Mrs. Wheedle, you sha'n't go till you've drunk a glass of wine, so let's sit down a little while and be comfortable. (*They seat themselves at the table.*) You need not be afraid of the dark, for Bobby shall go with you.

BOB. Mother, I'd rather behalf [by half?] not.

MRS. VOLUBLE. Who wants to know whether you'd rather or not? I suppose there's no need to consult all your rathernesses. Well, ma'am, so, as I was going to tell you, poor Miss Moggy Grease—(*A violent knocking at the door.*) Lord bless me, who's at the door? why they'll knock the house down! Somebody to Mr. Dabbler, I suppose; but he won't be home this two hours.

BOB. Mother, may I help myself to a drop of wine? (*Takes the bottle.*)

MRS. VOLUBLE. Wine, indeed! no,—give me the bottle this minute. (*Snatches and overturns it.*) Look here, you nasty fellow, see how you've made me spill it!

(*Enter Betty.*)

BETTY. Laws, ma'am, here's a fine lady all in her coach, and she asks for nobody but you.

MRS. VOLUBLE. For me? well, was ever the like! Only see, Betty, what a slop Bobby's made! There's no such a thing as having it seen. Come, folks, get up all of you, and let's move away the table. Bob, why don't you stir? one would think you were nailed to your seat.

BOB. Why I'm making all the haste I can, a'n't I?

(*They all rise, and Bob overturns the table.*)

MRS. VOLUBLE. Well, if this is not enough to drive one mad! I declare I could flay the boy alive! Here's a room to see company! you great, nasty, stupid dolt, you, get out of my sight this minute.

BOB. Why, Mother, I did not do it for the purpose.

MRS. VOLUBLE. But you did, Mr. Loggerhead, I know you did! Get out of my sight this minute, I say! (*Drives him off the stage.*) Well, what's to be done now?—Did ever anybody see such a room?—I declare I was never in such a pucker in my life. Mrs. Wheedle, do help to put some of the things into the closet. Look here, if my china bowl i'n't broke! I vow I've a great mind to make that looby eat it for his supper.—Betty, why don't you get a mop?—you're as helpless as a child.—No, a broom,—get a broom, and sweep them all away at once.—Why you a'n't going empty-handed, are you?—I declare you have not half the head you was born with.

BETTY. I'm sure I don't know what to do no more than the dog. (*Gets a broom.*)

MRS. VOLUBLE. What do you talk so for? have you got a mind to have the company hear you?

(*The knocking is repeated.*)

There, they're knocking like mad! Miss Jenny, what signifies your staring? can't you make yourself a little useful? I'm sure if you won't at such a time as this—Why, Betty, why don't you make haste? Come, poke everything into the closet,—I wonder why Bobby could not have took some of the things himself,—but as soon as ever he's done the mischief he thinks of nothing but running away.

(*They clear the stage, and Miss Jenny runs to a looking glass.*)

MISS JENNY. Dear me, what a figure I've made of myself!

MRS. VOLUBLE. There, now, we shall do pretty well. Betty, go and ask the lady in.

(*Exit Betty.*)

I declare I'm in such a flustration!

MISS JENNY. So am I, I'm sure, for I'm all of a tremble.

MRS. WHEEDLE. Well, if you can spare Master Bobby, we'll go to Mrs. Hollis's directly.

MRS. VOLUBLE. Spare him? ay, I'm sure it would have been good luck for me if you had taken him an hour ago.

MRS. WHEEDLE. Well, good-by, then. I shall see who the lady is as I go along. (*Exit.*)

MISS JENNY. It's very unlucky I did not put on my Irish muslin.

MRS. VOLUBLE. It's prodigious odd what can bring any company at this time of night.

(Enter Mrs. Sapient.)

Mrs. Sapient! dear ma'am, I can hardly believe my eyes!

MRS. SAPIENT. I am afraid my visit is unseasonable, but I beg I may not incommode you.

MRS. VOLUBLE. Incommode me? dear ma'am no, not the least in the world; I was doing nothing but just sitting here talking with Miss Jenny, about one thing or another.

MRS. SAPIENT. I have a question to ask you, Mrs. Voluble, which—

MRS. VOLUBLE. I'm sure, ma'am, I shall be very proud to answer it; but if I had but known of the pleasure of seeing you, I should not have been in such a pickle; but it happened so that we've been a little busy today,—you know, ma'am, in all families there will be some busy days,—and I've the misfortune of a son, ma'am, who's a little unlucky, so that puts one a little out of sorts, but he's so unmanageable, ma'am, that really—

MRS. SAPIENT. Well, well, I only want to ask if you know anything of Miss Stanley?

MRS. VOLUBLE. Miss Stanley? to be sure I do, ma'am; why she's now in my own house here.

MRS. SAPIENT. Indeed?—And pray—what, I suppose, she is chiefly with Mr. Dabbler?—

MRS. VOLUBLE. No, ma'am, no, she keeps prodigiously snug; she bid me not tell anybody she was here, so I make it a rule to keep it secret,—unless, indeed, ma'am, to such a lady as you.

MRS. SAPIENT. O, it's very safe with me. But, pray, don't you think Mr. Dabbler rather admires her?

MRS. VOLUBLE. O no, ma'am, not half so much as he admires another lady of your acquaintance. Ha! Ha!

Mrs. Sapient. Fie, Mrs. Voluble!—but pray, does not he write a great deal?

Mrs. Voluble. Dear ma'am, yes; he's in one continual scribbling from morning to night.

Mrs. Sapient.—Well, and—do you know if he writes about any particular person?

Mrs. Voluble. O yes, ma'am, he writes about Celia, and Daphne, and Cleora,[36] and—

Mrs. Sapient. You never see his poems, do you?

Mrs. Voluble. O dear yes, ma'am, I see them all. Why I have one now in my pocket about Cleora, that I happened to pick up this morning. (*Aside to Miss Jenny.*) Miss Jenny, do pray put me in mind to put it up before he comes home. Should you like to see it, ma'am?—

Mrs. Sapient. Why—if you have it at hand—

Mrs. Voluble. Dear ma'am, if I had not, I'm sure I'd fetch it, for I shall be quite proud to oblige you. As to any common acquaintance, I would not do such a thing upon any account, because I should scorn to do such a baseness to Mr. Dabbler, but to such a lady as you it's quite another thing. For, whenever I meet with a lady of quality, I make it a point to behave in the genteelest manner I can. Perhaps, ma'am, you'd like to see Mr. Dabbler's study?

Mrs. Sapient. O no, not upon any account.

Mrs. Voluble. Because, upon his table, there's a matter of an hundred of his *miniscrips.*

Mrs. Sapient. Indeed?—But when do you expect him home?

Mrs. Voluble. O not this good while.

Mrs. Sapient. Well then—if you are certain we shall not be surprised—

Mrs. Voluble. O, I'm quite certain of that.

Mrs. Sapient. But, then, for fear of accidents, let your maid order my coach to wait in the next street.

Mrs. Voluble. Yes, ma'am. Here, Betty! (*Exit.*)

Mrs. Sapient. This is not quite right, but this woman would show them to somebody else if not to me. And now perhaps I may discover whether any of his private papers contain my name. She will not, for her own sake, dare betray me.

(*Re-enter Mrs. Voluble.*)

MRS. VOLUBLE. Now, ma'am, I'll wait upon you. I assure you, ma'am, I would not do this for everybody, only a lady of your honor I'm sure would be above—(*Exit talking with Mrs. Sapient.*)

MISS JENNY (*alone*). She's said never a word to *me* all the time, and I dare say she knew me as well as could be; but fine ladies seem to think their words are made of gold, they are so afraid of bestowing them.

(*Re-enter Mrs. Voluble.*)

MRS. VOLUBLE. O Miss Jenny, only look here! my apron's all stained with the wine! I never see it till this minute, and now—(*A knocking at the door.*) Oh! (*Screams.*) that's Mr. Dabbler's knock! what shall we all do?—run upstairs and tell the lady this minute,—

(*Exit Miss Jenny.*)

Betty! Betty! don't go to the door yet,—I can't think what brings him home so soon!—here's nothing but ill luck upon ill luck!

(*Enter Mrs. Sapient with Miss Jenny.*)

Come, ma'am, come in! Betty!—you may go to the door now.

MRS. SAPIENT. But are you sure he will not come in here?

MRS. VOLUBLE. O quite, ma'am; he always goes to his own room. Hush!—ay, he's gone up,—I heard him pass.

MRS. SAPIENT. I am quite surprised, Mrs. Voluble, you should have deceived me thus; did not you assure me he would not return this hour? I must tell you, Mrs. Voluble, that, whatever you may think of it, *I* shall always regard a person who is capable of deceit, to be guilty of insincerity.

MRS. VOLUBLE. Indeed, ma'am, I knew no more of his return than you did, for he makes it a sort of a rule of a 'Sprit night—

MISS JENNY. Ma'am, ma'am, I hear him on the stairs!

MRS. SAPIENT. O hide me,—hide me this instant anywhere,—And don't say I am here for the universe! (*She runs into the closet.*)

MRS. VOLUBLE. No, ma'am, that I won't if it costs me my life!—
you may always depend upon *me*. (*Shuts her in.*)

MISS JENNY. Laws, what a pickle she'll be in! she's got all among
the broken things.

(Enter Dabbler.)

DABBLER. Mrs. Voluble, you'll please to make out my account, for
I shall leave your house directly.

MRS. VOLUBLE. Leave my house? Lord, Sir, you quite frighten me!

DABBLER. You have used me very ill, Mrs. Voluble, and curse me
if I shall put up with it!

MRS. VOLUBLE. Me, Sir? I'm sure, Sir, I don't so much as know
what you mean.

DABBLER. You have been rummaging all my papers.

MRS. VOLUBLE. I?—no, Sir,—I'm sorry, Sir, you suspect me of such
a mean proceeding.

DABBLER. 'Tis in vain to deny it; I have often had reason to think
it, but now my doubts are confirmed, for my last new song,
which I called "Cleora," is nowhere to be found.

MRS. VOLUBLE. Nowhere to be found?—you surprise me! (*Aside.*)
Good Lack, I quite forgot to put it up!

DABBLER. I'm certain I left it at the top of my papers.

MRS. VOLUBLE. Did you indeed, Sir? well, I'm sure it's the oddest
thing in the world what can be come of it!

DABBLER. There is something so gross, so scandalous in this usage,
that I am determined not to be duped by it. I shall quit my
lodgings directly;—take your measures accordingly. (*Going.*)

MRS. VOLUBLE. O pray, Sir, stay,—and if you won't be so angry,
I'll tell you the whole truth of the matter.

DABBLER. Be quick, then.

MRS. VOLUBLE (*in a low voice*). I'm sorry, Sir, to betray a lady, but
when one's own reputation is at stake—

DABBLER. What lady? I don't understand you.

MRS. VOLUBLE. Hush, hush, Sir!—she'll hear you.

DABBLER. She?—Who?

MRS. VOLUBLE. Why Mrs. Sapient, Sir, (*Whispering.*) she's in that
closet.

DABBLER. What do you mean?

MRS. VOLUBLE. I'll tell you all, Sir, by and by,—but you must know she came to me, and—and—and begged just to look at your study, Sir,—So, Sir, never supposing such a lady as that would think of looking at your papers, I was persuaded to agree to it,—but, Sir, as soon as ever we got into the room, she fell to reading them without so much as saying a word!—while I, all the time, stood in this manner!—staring with stupefaction—so, Sir, when you knocked at the door, she ran down to the closet.

DABBLER. And what has induced her to do all this?

MRS. VOLUBLE. Ah, Sir, you know well enough. Mrs. Sapient is a lady of prodigious good taste; everybody knows how she admires Mr. Dabbler.

DABBLER. Why, yes, I don't think she wants taste.

MRS. VOLUBLE. Well but, Sir, pray don't stay, for she is quite close crammed in the closet.

DABBLER. I think I'll speak to her.

MRS. VOLUBLE. Not for the world, Sir! If she knows I've betrayed her, she'll go beside herself, and, I'm sure, Sir, I would not have told anybody but you upon no account. If you'll wait upstairs till she's gone, I'll come and tell you all about it,—but, pray, dear Sir, make haste.

DABBLER. Yes, she's a good agreeable woman, and really has a pretty knowledge of poetry. Poor soul!—I begin to be half sorry for her. (*Exit.*)

MRS. VOLUBLE. I thought he'd never have gone. How do do now, ma'am? (*Opens the closet door.*)

(*Enter Mrs. Sapient.*)

MRS. SAPIENT. Cramped to death! what a strange place have you put me in! Let me begone this instant,—but are you sure, Mrs. Voluble, you have not betrayed me?

MRS. VOLUBLE. I'm surprised, ma'am, you should suspect me! I would not do such a false thing for never so much, for I always—

(*A knocking at the door.*)

Why now who can that be?

MRS. SAPIENT. How infinitely provoking!—let me go back to this frightful closet till the coast is clear. (*Returns to the closet.*)

Mrs. Voluble. Well, I think I've managed matters like a *Matchwell*.[37]

(Enter Mrs. Wheedle.)

Mrs. Wheedle. O, I'm quite out of breath,—I never walked so fast in my life.

Mrs. Voluble. Where have you left Bobby?

Mrs. Wheedle. He's gone into the kitchen. I must see Miss Stanley directly.

Mrs. Voluble. We've been in perilous danger since you went. Do you know *(In a low voice.)* Mrs. Sapient is now in the closet? Be sure you don't tell anybody.

Mrs. Wheedle. No, not for the world. Miss Jenny, pray stop and tell Miss Stanley I'm come back.

(Exit Miss Jenny.)

Mrs. Voluble. Well, and while you speak to her, I'll go and talk over Mr. Dabbler, and contrive to poke this nasty song under the table. But first I'll say something to the poor lady in the closet. Ma'am! *(Opens the door.)* If you've a mind to keep still, you'll hear all what Miss Stanley says presently, for she's coming down.

Mrs. Sapient. Are you mad, Mrs. Voluble?—What do you hold the door open for?—Would you have that woman see me?

Mrs. Voluble. Ma'am, I beg your pardon! *(Shuts the door.)* I won't help her out this half hour for that crossness. *(Exit.)*

Mrs. Wheedle. These fine ladies go through anything for the sake of curiosity.

(Enter Cecilia.)

Cecilia. Well, Mrs. Wheedle, have you seen Mrs. Hollis?

Mrs. Wheedle. Yes, ma'am, and she's quite agreeable to your proposal; but as she's going very soon, and will be glad to be fixed, she says she shall take it as a particular favor if you will go to her house tonight.

Cecilia. Impossible! I must consult some friend ere I go at all.

Mrs. Wheedle. But, ma'am, she begs you will, for she says she's heard of your misfortunes, and shall be glad to give you her advice what to do.

CECILIA. Then I *will* go to her!—for never yet did poor creature more want advice and assistance!

MRS. WHEEDLE. Betty! (*Calls at the door.*) Go and get a coach. I will go speak to Mrs. Voluble, ma'am, and come again. (*Exit.*)

CECILIA (*alone*). Perhaps I may repent this enterprise,—my heart fails me already;—and yet, how few are those human actions that repentance may not pursue! Error precedes almost every step, and sorrow follows every error. I who to happiness have bid a long, a last farewell, must content myself with seeking peace in retirement and solitude, and endeavor to contract all my wishes to preserving my own innocence from the contagion of this bad and most diseased world's corruptions.

(Enter Betty.)

BETTY. Ma'am, the coach is at the door.

CECILIA. Alas!

BETTY. Mrs. Wheedle, ma'am, is gone upstairs to my *Missis,* but she says she'll be ready in a few minutes. (*Exit.*)

CECILIA (*alone*). O cease, fond, suffering, feeble heart! to struggle thus with misery inevitable. Beaufort is no longer the Beaufort he appeared, and since he has lost even the semblance of his worth, why should this sharp regret pursue his image? But, alas, that semblance which *he* has lost, I must ever retain! fresh, fair and perfect it is still before me!—Oh why must woe weaken all faculties but the memory?—I will reason no longer,—I will think of him no more,—I will offer myself to servitude, for labor itself must be less insupportable than this gloomy indolence of sorrowing reflection.—Where is this woman?—(*Going.*)

(Enter Beaufort, who stops her.)

BEAUFORT. My Cecilia!—

CECILIA. Oh—good Heaven!

BEAUFORT. My loved, lost, injured,—my adored Cecilia!

CECILIA. Am I awake?

BEAUFORT. Whence this surprise?—my love, my heart's sweet partner—

CECILIA. Oh forbear!—these terms are no longer—Mr. Beaufort, let me pass!

BEAUFORT. What do I hear?

CECILIA. Leave me, Sir,—I cannot talk with you,—leave me, I say.

BEAUFORT. Leave you?— (*Offering to take her hand.*)

CECILIA. Yes,— (*Turning from him.*) for I cannot bear to look at you.

BEAUFORT. Not look at me? What have I done? how have I offended you? why are you thus dreadfully changed?

CECILIA. *I* changed? comes this well from *you?*—but I will not recriminate, neither will I converse with you any longer. You see me now perhaps for the last time,—I am preparing to quit the kingdom.

BEAUFORT. To quit the kingdom?

CECILIA. Yes; it is a step which your own conduct has compelled me to take.

BEAUFORT. My conduct?—Who has belied me to you?—What villain—

CECILIA. No one, Sir; you have done your work yourself.

BEAUFORT. Cecilia, do you mean to distract me?—if not, explain, and instantly, your dark, your cruel meaning.

CECILIA. Can it want explanation to *you?* have you shocked me in ignorance, and irritated me without knowing it?

BEAUFORT. I shocked?—I irritated you?—

CECILIA. Did you not, in the very first anguish of a calamity which you alone had power to alleviate, neglect and avoid me? Send me a cold message by a friend? Suffer me to endure indignities without support, and sorrows without participation? Leave me, defenseless, to be crushed by impending ruin? and abandon my aching heart to all the torture of new-born fears, unprotected, unassured, and uncomforted?

BEAUFORT. Can *I* have done all this?

CECILIA. I know not,—but I am sure it has seemed so.

BEAUFORT. Oh wretched policy of cold, unfeeling prudence; had I listened to no dictates but those of my heart, I had never been wounded with suspicions and reproaches so cruel.

CECILIA. Rather say, had your heart sooner known its own docility, you might have permitted Lady Smatter to dispose of it ere the deluded Cecilia was known to you.

BEAUFORT. Barbarous Cecilia! take not such a time as this to depreciate my heart in your opinion, for now—'tis all I have to offer you.

CECILIA. You know too well—'tis all I ever valued.

BEAUFORT. Oh take it then,—receive it once more, and with that confidence in its faith which it never deserved to forfeit! Painfully I submitted to advice I abhorred, but though my judgment has been overpowered, my truth has been inviolate. Turn not from me, Cecilia!—if I have temporized, it has been less for my own sake than for yours; but I have seen the vanity of my expectations,—I have disobeyed Lady Smatter,—I have set all consequences at defiance, and flown in the very face of ruin,—and now, will *you*, Cecilia, (*Kneeling.*) reject, disdain and spurn me?

CECILIA. Oh Beaufort—is it possible I can have wronged you?

BEAUFORT. Never, my sweetest Cecilia, if now you pardon me.

CECILIA. Pardon you?—too generous Beaufort—Ah! rise.

(Enter Lady Smatter and Mr. Codger.)

BEAUFORT (*rising*). Lady Smatter!

LADY SMATTER. How, Beaufort here?—and kneeling, too!

CODGER. Son Beaufort, I cannot deny but I think it is rather an extraordinary thing that you should choose to be seen kneeling to that young lady, knowing, I presume, that your Aunt Smatter disaffects your so doing.

LADY SMATTER. Beaufort, I see you are resolved to keep no terms with me. As to Miss Stanley, I renounce her with contempt; I came hither with the most generous views of assisting her, and prevailed with Mr. Codger to conduct her to her friends in the country; but since I find her capable of so much baseness, since I see that all her little arts are at work—

CECILIA. Forbear, madam, these unmerited reproaches; believe me, I will neither become a burthen to you, nor a scorn to myself; the measures I have taken I doubt not will meet with Your Ladyship's approbation, though it is by no means incumbent upon me, thus contemptuously accused, to enter into any defenses or explanation. (*Exit.*)

BEAUFORT. Stay, my Cecilia,—hear me—(*Follows her.*)

LADY SMATTER. How? pursue her in defiance of my presence? Had

I a pen and ink I should disinherit him incontinently. Who are all these people?

(Enter Miss Jenny, Mrs. Voluble, and Mrs. Wheedle.)

MISS JENNY *(as she enters)*. Law, only look! here's Lady Smatter and an old gentleman!

MRS. VOLUBLE. What, in my parlor? Well, I declare, and so there is! Why how could they get in?

MRS. WHEEDLE. I suppose the door's open because of the hackney coach. But as to Miss Stanley, I believe she's hid herself.

CODGER. Madam, I can give Your Ladyship no satisfaction.

LADY SMATTER. About what?

CODGER. About these people, madam, that Your Ladyship was enquiring after, for, to the best of my knowledge, madam, I apprehend I never saw any of them before.

LADY SMATTER. I see who they are myself, now.

MRS. VOLUBLE *(advancing to Lady Smatter)*. My Lady, I hope Your Ladyship's well; I am very glad, My Lady, to pay my humble duty to Your Ladyship in my poor house, and I hope—

LADY SMATTER. Pray is Mr. Dabbler at home?

MRS. VOLUBLE. Yes, My Lady, and indeed—

LADY SMATTER. Tell him, then, I shall be glad to see him.

MRS. VOLUBLE. Yes, My Lady. I suppose, Miss Jenny, you little thought of my having such a genteel acquaintance among the quality! *(Exit.)*

MISS JENNY *(aside to Mrs. Wheedle)*. I'm afraid that poor lady in the closet will spoil all her things.

LADY SMATTER. Yes, I'll consult with Mr. Dabbler; for as to this old soul, it takes him half an hour to recollect whether two and three make five or six.

(Enter Censor.)

CENSOR. I have, with some difficulty, traced Your Ladyship hither.

LADY SMATTER. Then, Sir, you have traced me to a most delightful spot; and you will find your friend as self-willed, refractory and opinionated as your amplest instructions can have rendered him.

CENSOR. I would advise Your Ladyship to think a little less for him, and a little more for yourself, lest in your solicitude for his fortune, you lose all care for your own fame.

LADY SMATTER. My fame? I don't understand you.

CENSOR. Nay, if you think such lampoons may spread without doing you injury—

LADY SMATTER. Lampoons? What lampoons?—sure nobody has dared—

(Enter Dabbler and Mrs. Voluble.)

MRS. VOLUBLE. Why here's Mr. Censor too! I believe there'll be company coming in all night.

LADY SMATTER. Mr. Censor, I say, if there is any lampoon that concerns *me,* I insist upon hearing it directly.

CENSOR. I picked it up just now at a coffee house. (*Reads.*)
Yes, Smatter is the Muses' friend,
She knows to censure or commend;
And has of faith and truth such store
She'll ne'er desert you—till you're poor.

LADY SMATTER. What insolent impertinence!

DABBLER. Poor stuff! poor stuff indeed! Your Ladyship should regard these little squibs as *I* do, mere impotent efforts of envy.

LADY SMATTER. O I do; I'd rather hear them than not.

DABBLER. And ill done, too; most contemptibly ill done. I think I'll answer it for Your Ladyship.

CENSOR. Hark ye, Mr. Dabbler, (*Takes him aside.*) do you know this paper?

DABBLER. That paper?

CENSOR. Yes, Sir; it contains the lines which you passed off at Lady Smatter's as made at the moment.

DABBLER. Why, Sir, that was merely—it happened—

CENSOR. It is too late for equivocation, Sir; your reputation is now wholly in my power, and I can instantly blast it, alike with respect to poetry and to veracity.

DABBLER. Surely, Sir—

CENSOR. If, therefore, you do not, with your utmost skill, assist me to reconcile Lady Smatter to her nephew and his choice, I will show this original copy of your extemporary abilities to everybody who will take the trouble to read it: otherwise, I will

sink the whole transaction, and return you this glaring proof of
it.

DABBLER. To be sure, Sir,—as to Mr. Beaufort's choice—it's the
thing in the world I most approve,—and so—

CENSOR. Well, Sir, you know the alternative, and must act as you
please.

DABBLER (*aside*). What cursed ill luck!

LADY SMATTER. Mr. Censor, I more than half suspect you are yourself the author of that pretty lampoon.

CENSOR. Nay, madam, you see this is not my writing.

LADY SMATTER. Give it me.

CENSOR. Hold,—here's something on the other side which I did
not see. (*Reads.*)

> Were madness stinted to Moorfields
> The world elsewhere would be much thinner;
> To time now Smatter's beauty yields—

LADY SMATTER. How!

CENSOR (*reading*). She fain in wit would be a winner.
>   At thirty she began to read;—

LADY SMATTER. That's false!—entirely false!

CENSOR (*reads*). At forty, it is said, could spell,—

LADY SMATTER. How's that? at forty?—Sir, this is your own putting in.

CENSOR (*reads*). At fifty—

LADY SMATTER. At fifty?—ha! ha! ha!—this is droll enough!—

CENSOR (*reads*). At fifty, 'twas by all agreed
>   A common schoolgirl she'd excel.

LADY SMATTER. What impertinent nonsense!

CENSOR (*reads*). Such wonders did the world presage—

LADY SMATTER. Mr. Censor, I desire you'll read no more,—'tis
such rubbish it makes me quite sick.

CENSOR (*reads*).

> Such wonders did the world presage
> From blossoms which such fruit invited,—
> When avarice,—the vice of age,—
> Stepped in,—and all expectance blighted.

LADY SMATTER. Of age!—I protest this is the most impudent thing I ever heard in my life! calculated for no purpose in the world but to insinuate I am growing old.

CENSOR. You have certainly some secret enemy who avails himself of your disagreement with Miss Stanley to prejudice the world against you.

LADY SMATTER. O, I'm certain I can tell who it is.

CENSOR. Who?

LADY SMATTER. Mrs. Sapient.

MISS JENNY (*aside*). Law, I'm afraid she'll hear them.

LADY SMATTER. Not that I suspect her of the writing, for miserable stuff as it is, I know her capacity is yet below it; but she was the first to leave my house when the affair was discovered, and I suppose she has been tattling it about the town ever since.

MRS. VOLUBLE (*aside*). Ah, poor lady, it's all to fall upon her!

CENSOR. Depend upon it, madam, this will never rest here; Your Ladyship is so well known, that one satire will but be the prelude to another.

LADY SMATTER. Alas, how dangerous is popularity! O Mr. Dabbler, that I could but despise these libels as you do!—but this last is insufferable,—yet you, I suppose, would think it nothing?

DABBLER. No, really, ma'am, I can't say that,—no, not as *nothing*,—that is, not absolutely as nothing,—for,—for libels of this sort—are rather—

LADY SMATTER. How? I thought you held them all in contempt?

DABBLER. So I do, ma'am, only—

CENSOR. You do, Sir?—

DABBLER. No, Sir, no; I don't mean to absolutely say that,—that is, only in regard to *myself*,—for we men do not suffer in the world by lampoons as the poor ladies do;—they, indeed, may be quite—quite ruined by them.

LADY SMATTER. Nay, Mr. Dabbler, now *you* begin to distress me.

(*Enter Jack, singing.*)

JACK. She has ta'en such a dose of incongruous matter
  That Bedlam must soon hold the carcase of Smatter.

LADY SMATTER. How?—what?—the carcase of who?—

JACK. Ha! Ha! Ha! faith, madam, I beg your pardon, but who'd have thought of meeting Your Ladyship here?—O Dabbler, I have such a thing to tell you! (*Whispers him and laughs.*)

LADY SMATTER. I shall go mad!—What were you singing, Jack,—what is it you laugh at?—Why won't you speak?

JACK. I'm so much hurried I can't stay to answer Your Ladyship now. Dabbler, be sure [to] keep counsel. Ha! Ha! Ha,—I must go and sing it to Billy Skip and Will Scamper, or I sha'n't sleep a wink all night. (*Going.*)

LADY SMATTER. This is intolerable! Stay, Jack, I charge you! Mr. Codger, how unmoved you stand! Why don't you make him stay?

CODGER. Madam, I will. Son Jack, stay.

JACK. Lord, Sir,—

LADY SMATTER. I am half choked!—Mr. Codger, you would provoke a saint! Why don't you make him tell you what he was singing?

CODGER. Madam, he is so giddy pated he never understands me. Son Jack, you attend to nothing! Don't you perceive that her Ladyship seems curious to know what song you were humming?

JACK. Why, Sir, it was only a new ballad.

LADY SMATTER. A ballad with *my* name in it? Explain yourself instantly!

JACK. Here it is,—shall I sing it or say it?

LADY SMATTER. You shall do neither,—give it me!

CENSOR. No, no, sing it first for the good of the company.

JACK. Your Ladyship won't take it ill?

LADY SMATTER. Ask me no questions,—I don't know what I shall do.

JACK (*sings*).

> I call not to swains to attend to my song,
> Nor call I to damsels, so tender and young;
> To critics, and pedants, and doctors I clatter,
> For who else will heed what becomes of poor Smatter.
>   With a down, down, derry down.

LADY SMATTER. How? is my name at full length?

JACK (*sings*).

This lady with study has muddled her head;
Sans meaning she talked, and sans knowledge she read,
And gulped such a dose of incongruous matter
That Bedlam must soon hold the carcase of Smatter.
    With a down, down, derry down.

LADY SMATTER. The carcase of Smatter?—it can't be,—no one
    would dare—
JACK. Ma'am, if you stop me so often, I shall be too late to go and
    sing it anywhere else to night. (*Sings.*)

She thought wealth esteemed by the foolish alone,
So, shunning offence, never offered her own;
And when her young friend dire misfortune did batter,
Too wise to relieve her was kind Lady Smatter.
    With a down, down, derry down.

LADY SMATTER. I'll hear no more! (*Walks about in disorder.*)
CENSOR. Sing on, however, Jack; we'll hear it out.
JACK (*sings*).

Her nephew she never corrupted with pelf
Holding starving a virtue—for all but herself.
Of gold was her goblet, of silver, her platter,
To show how such ore was degraded by Smatter.
    With a down, down, derry down.
A club she supported of witlings and fools,
Who, but for her dinners, had scoffed at her rules;
The reason, if any she had, these did shatter
Of poor empty-headed, and little-souled Smatter.
    With a down, down, derry down.

LADY SMATTER. Empty-headed?—little-souled?—Who has dared
    write this?—Where did you get it?
JACK. From a man who was carrying it to the printer's.
LADY SMATTER. To the printer's?—O insupportable!—are they go-
    ing to print it?—Mr. Dabbler, why don't you assist me?—how
    can I have it suppressed?—Speak quick, or I shall die.
DABBLER. Really, ma'am, I—I—
CENSOR. There is but one way,—make a friend of the writer.

LADY SMATTER. I detest him from my soul,—and I believe 'tis yourself!

CENSOR. Your Ladyship is not deceived;—I have the honor to be the identical person. (*Bowing*.)

LADY SMATTER. Nay, then, I see your drift,—but depend upon it, I will not be duped by you. (*Going*.)

CENSOR. Hear me, madam!—

LADY SMATTER. No, not a word!

CENSOR. You must! (*Holds the door*.) You have but one moment for reflection, either to establish your fame upon the firmest foundation, or to consign yourself for life to irony and contempt.

LADY SMATTER. I will have you prosecuted with the utmost severity of the law.

CENSOR. You will have the thanks of my printer for your reward.

LADY SMATTER. You will not dare—

CENSOR. I dare do anything to repel the injuries of innocence! I have already shown you my *power,* and you will find my *courage* undaunted, and my *perseverance* indefatigable. If you any longer oppose the union of your nephew with Miss Stanley, I will destroy the whole peace of your life.

LADY SMATTER. You cannot!—I defy you! *(Walks from him.)*

CENSOR. I will drop lampoons in every coffee house,—(*Following her.*)

LADY SMATTER. You are welcome, Sir—

CENSOR. Compose daily epigrams for all the papers,—

LADY SMATTER. With all my heart,—

CENSOR. Send libels to every corner of the town,—

LADY SMATTER. I care not!—

CENSOR. Make all the ballad singers resound your deeds,—

LADY SMATTER. You cannot!—*shall* not!

CENSOR. And treat the Patagonian Theatre[38] with a poppet to represent you.

LADY SMATTER (*bursting into tears*). This is too much to be borne. Mr. Censor, you are a Demon!

CENSOR. But, if you relent,—I will burn all I have written, and forget all I have planned; lampoons shall give place to panegyric, and libels, to songs of triumph; the liberality of your soul, and the depth of your knowledge shall be recorded by the Muses, and echoed by the whole nation!

LADY SMATTER. I am half distracted!—Mr. Dabbler, why don't you counsel me?—how cruel is your silence!

DABBLER. Why, certainly, ma'am, what—what Mr. Censor says—

CENSOR. Speak out, man!—Tell Lady Smatter if she will not be a lost woman to the literary world, should she, in this trial of her magnanimity, disgrace its expectations. Speak boldly!

DABBLER. Hem!—You,—you have said, Sir,—just what I think.

LADY SMATTER. How? are *you* against me?—nay then—

CENSOR. Everybody must be against you; even Mr. Codger, as I can discern by his looks. Are you not, Sir?

CODGER. Sir, I can by no means decide upon so important a question, without maturely pondering upon the several preliminaries.

CENSOR. Come, madam, consider what is expected from the celebrity of your character,—consider the applause that awaits you in the world;—you will be another Sacharissa,[39] a second Sappho,—a tenth Muse.

LADY SMATTER. I know not what to do!—allow me, at least, a few days for meditation, and forbear these scandalous libels till—

CENSOR. No, madam, not an hour!—there is no time so ill spent as that which is passed in deliberating between meanness and generosity! You may now not only gain the esteem of the living, but—if it is not Mr. Dabbler's fault,—consign your name with honor to Posterity.

LADY SMATTER. To Posterity?—why where is this girl gone?—what has Beaufort done with himself?—

CENSOR. Now, madam, you have bound me yours forever!—here, Beaufort!—Miss Stanley!— (*Goes out.*)

JACK. Huzza!—

CODGER. Madam, to confess the verity, I must acknowledge that I do not rightly comprehend what it is Your Ladyship has determined upon doing.

LADY SMATTER. No; nor would you, were I to take an hour to tell you.

(*Re-enter Censor, with Beaufort and Cecilia.*)

BEAUFORT. O madam, is it indeed true that—

LADY SMATTER. Beaufort, I am so much flurried, I hardly know what is true,—save, indeed, that pity, as a certain author says, will ever, in noble minds, conquer prudence. Miss Stanley—

CENSOR. Come, come, no speeches; this whole company bears witness to your consent to their marriage, and Your Ladyship (*In a low voice.*) may depend upon not losing sight of *me* till the ceremony is over.

CECILIA. Lady Smatter's returning favor will once more devote me to her service; but I am happy to find, by this letter, that my affairs are in a less desperate situation than I had apprehended. (*Gives a letter to Lady Smatter.*) But here, Mr. Censor, is another letter which I do not quite so well understand; it contains an order for £5000, and is signed with your name.

CENSOR. Pho, pho, we will talk of that another time.

CECILIA. Impossible! Liberality so undeserved—

CENSOR. Not a word more, I entreat you!

CECILIA. Indeed I can never accept it.

CENSOR. Part with it as you can! *I* have got rid of it. I merit no thanks, for I mean it not in service to you, but in spite to Lady Smatter, that she may not have the pleasure of boasting, to her wondering witlings, that she received a niece wholly unportioned. Beaufort, but for his own stubbornness, had long since possessed it,—from a similar motive.

CECILIA. Dwells benevolence in so rugged a garb?—Oh Mr. Censor.

BEAUFORT. Noble, generous Censor! you penetrate my heart,—yet I cannot consent—

CENSOR. Pho, pho, never praise a man for only gratifying his own humor.

(Enter Bob running.)

BOB. Mother, Mother, I believe there's a cat in the closet!

MRS. VOLUBLE. Hold your tongue, you great oaf!

BOB. Why, Mother, as I was in the back parlor, you can't think what a rustling it made.

MISS JENNY (*aside*). Dear me!—it's the poor lady!—

MRS. WHEEDLE. Well, what a thing is this!

MRS. VOLUBLE. Bob, I could beat your brains out!

BOB. Why Lord, Mother, where's the great harm of saying there's a cat in the closet?

JACK. The best way is to look. (*Goes toward the closet.*)

DABBLER. Not for the world! I won't suffer it!

JACK. You won't suffer it?—Pray, Sir, does the cat belong to you?

BOB. Mother, I dare say she's eating up all the victuals.

JACK. Come then, my lad, you and I'll hunt her. (*Brushes past Dabbler, and opens the door.*)

ALL. Mrs. Sapient!

MRS. SAPIENT (*coming forward*). Sir, this impertinent curiosity—

JACK. Lord, ma'am, I beg your pardon! I'm sure I would not have opened the door for the world, only we took you for the cat. If you please, ma'am, I'll shut you in again.

LADY SMATTER. That's a pretty snug retreat you have chosen, Mrs. Sapient.

CENSOR. To which of the muses, madam, may that temple be dedicated?

JACK. I hope, ma'am, you made use of your time to mend your furbelows?

CODGER. Madam, as I don't understand this quick way of speaking, I should be much obliged if you would take the trouble to make plain to my comprehension the reason of your choosing to be shut up in that dark closet.

CENSOR. Doubtless, Sir, for the study of the occult sciences.

LADY SMATTER. Give me leave, madam, to recommend to your perusal this passage of Addison: Those who conceal themselves to hear the counsels of others, commonly have little reason to be satisfied with what they hear of themselves.

MRS. SAPIENT. And give *me* leave, ma'am, to observe,—though I pretend not to assert it positively,—that, in *my* opinion, those who speak ill of people in their absence, give no great proof of a sincere friendship.

CENSOR (*aside*). I begin to hope these Witlings will demolish their club.

DABBLER (*aside*). Faith, if they quarrel, I'll not speak till they part.

BEAUFORT. Allow me, Ladies, with all humility, to mediate, and to entreat that the calm of an evening succeeding a day so agitated with storms, may be enjoyed without allay. Terror, my Cecilia, now ceases to alarm, and sorrow, to oppress us; gratefully let us receive returning happiness, and hope that our example,— should any attend to it,—may inculcate this most useful of all practical precepts: That self-dependence is the first of earthly blessings; since those who rely solely on others for support and protection are not only liable to the common vicissitudes of human life, but exposed to the partial caprices and infirmities of human nature.

Notes to *The Witlings*

1. The Minories was an area in the City, the unfashionable part of London, where business was done and tradespeople lived.
2. In Edmund Spenser's *Faerie Queene* (1589), Book II, Canto iv, Atin (Strife) seeks Occasion (for fighting).
3. Voluble's ignorant rendition of *esprit*, wit.
4. Left a visiting card.
5. Alexander Pope, *An Essay on Criticism* (1711): "A little learning is a dangerous thing;/ Drink deep, or taste not the Pierian spring" (lines 215–6).
6. Waste paper was used to line baking pans and wrap cheese.
7. Be even with you, give you as good as I get.
8. William Shakespeare, *Hamlet* I.ii, 153.
9. Songs sung in the Rotunda at Ranelagh pleasure garden.
10. A person of wit and elegance, with a possible pun on *belle*.
11. Into the wings, behind a side flat.
12. Fogy.
13. Not in Pope or Jonathan Swift, but Pope did write that envy pursues merit like a shadow (*Essay on Criticism,* line 466), an effect demonstrated by these witlings.
14. Both Pope and Swift would have despised Smatter's idea that memory is incompatible with wit; she takes at face value an ironic passage in Swift's *A Tale of a Tub,* Section VI, where the wrong-headed narrator boasts about producing "our great forgetfulness, as an argument unanswerable for our great wit."
15. Jack was supposed to be going to Hyde Park, in the West End of London, but is now coming from Cornhill, at the eastern end of the City; Fleet Street is in between.
16. At the Stock Exchange.
17. Went bankrupt.
18. "An unusually large number of bankruptcies in 1777–8 introduced a depression that lasted from 1778–81" (Delery).
19. Not found in Pope. Most of Smatter's so-called quotations are commonplace maxims that she attributes to famous authors to create a

false impression of learning or sometimes to screen her cold-hearted selfishness. See Censor's speeches, p. 335.

20. Line 4 of Matthew Prior's "A Better Answer (To Cloe Jealous)."

21. She seems to be recalling Pope's "Painful preeminence," referring to the disadvantages of intellectual brilliance (*Essay on Man* 4:267–8) (Delery).

22. *The History of Tom Thumb* is a children's story, and Richard Johnson's *The Famous History of the Seven Champions of Christendom* (1597) is a childish chivalric romance. "Sound" and "sense" refer to Pope's *Essay on Criticism,* line 365.

23. Manual worker, artisan.

24. Lackaday! alas!

25. Smatter misinterprets Pope's line, which should read: "Most women have no characters at all" ("Epistle II. To a Lady. Of the Characters of Women," 1735, line 2). Pope meant strongly individual character, while she thinks he meant reputation.

26. Any educated person would have known the works of Dryden, one of the greatest poets of the seventeenth century. "Cymon and Iphigenia" is a story by Boccaccio that he put into verse.

27. Orpheus was torn in pieces by angry women, but the arguing seems to be Burney's (or Censor's) invention.

28. John Gay, a good poet, would never have produced verses as flat as Dabbler's.

29. In Scotland a couple could marry without preliminary steps required in England.

30. Paraphrase of Pope's "Epistle to Dr. Arbuthnot" (1735), line 67.

31. Actually from James Thomson's *The Seasons. Spring* (1728), line 1149.

32. Muz has two relevant meanings: fuddle, render muzzy; and study intensely. Trimmers = crushing rebukes.

33. One-horse carriage.

34. Herodotus reported that crocodiles eat nothing for four months in the year (Delery).

35. The refreshments served at Fox-hall (Vauxhall) included very thinly sliced meat.

36. Conventional names for female lovers in pastoral poetry.

37. Her version of Machiavelli (?), whose political philosophy featured crafty scheming.

38. A very popular puppet theater (Delery).

39. Edmund Waller's poetic name for the woman he celebrated in his poems.

Hannah Cowley
(1743–1809)

HANNAH PARKHOUSE, born in rural Devonshire, was educated and encouraged by her father, a bookseller and classical scholar, who, she said, "gave my youthful fancy wings to soar." In 1772, she married Thomas Cowley, a government clerk who wrote for the newspapers, and moved to London; they had four children. She remained in London when her husband moved to India in 1783 to work for the East India Company.

According to the preface to her collected works (1813), Hannah Cowley's attitude toward her writing career was casual, and she came to it almost by accident. One night at the theater she suddenly exclaimed, "Why, I could write as well myself!" Her husband laughed, but she sketched the first act of *The Runaway* the next morning, quickly finished the play, and sent it to David Garrick, manager of the Drury Lane Theater. Although she was unknown and unsponsored, he saw merit in the play, polished it, and promptly produced it (1776). It was very successful, bringing Cowley more than five hundred pounds for her three author's-benefit nights and more on publication. Had Garrick not encouraged her, she told him in her dedication, she would have given up writing right then. As it was, she went on to produce twelve more plays, most of them lively, witty comedies about courtship in fashionable life. The best are *The Belle's Stratagem* (1780), *Which Is the Man* (1782), and *The Town Before You* (1795).

She also wrote long narrative poems and, under the name Anna Matilda, carried on a mannered poetic correspondence with a male friend in a newspaper. Cowley published her last play, *The Town Before You*, with a preface condemning public taste for witless farce and renouncing the stage. In 1801 she retired to Devon and prepared the collected edition of her works.

Although some contemporaries praised Cowley's exemplary conduct, unassuming manners, and "peculiarly animated and expressive countenance," the novelist Charlotte Smith claimed that Cowley's modesty was false, that she revealed "a conviction of self-consequence" while affecting "tender languor," and that she had a particular hostility toward other literary women (*The Old Manor House*, 1793). Smith may have been put off by Cowley's ostentatious display of feminine propriety, as she minimized her intellectual interests and made a point of her unconcern with politics and her disapproval of Mary Wollstonecraft (advertisement to *A Day in Turkey*, 1792).

The Belle's Stratagem had its premiere at Covent Garden in 1780 and was acted twenty-eight times in its first season. Cowley must have earned more than four hundred pounds from her author's benefits, and she received an additional one hundred to delay publication, as well as what she ultimately got for sale of the copyright. It was the eleventh most frequently acted play during the last quarter of the eighteenth century—the fourth most frequently acted if we exclude older plays by Shakespeare and others. Ellen Terry played Letitia in Boston in 1883, and *The Belle's Stratagem* was produced commercially in London in 1913.

The Belle's Stratagem

TO
THE QUEEN.

MADAM,

In the following Comedy, my purpose was, to draw a FEMALE CHARACTER, which, with the most lively sensibility, fine understanding, and elegant accomplishments, should unite that beautiful reserve and delicacy which, whilst they veil those charms, render them still more interesting.[1] In delineating such a character, my heart naturally dedicated it to YOUR MAJESTY;[2] and nothing remained, but permission to lay it at Your feet. Your Majesty's graciously allowing me this high honor is the point to which my hopes aspired and a reward of which without censure I may be proud.

MADAM,

With the warmest wishes for the continuance of your Majesty's felicity,

I am

YOUR MAJESTY's

Most devoted

and most dutiful servant,

H. Cowley.

Dramatis Personæ.

Men.

DORICOURT	Mr. *Lewis.*
HARDY	Mr. *Quick.*
SIR GEORGE TOUCHWOOD	Mr. *Wroughton.*
FLUTTER	Mr. *Lee Lewes.*
SAVILLE	Mr. *Aickin.*
VILLERS	Mr. *Whitfield.*
COURTALL	Mr. *Robson.*
SILVERTONGUE	Mr. *W. Bates.*
CROWQUILL	Mr. *Jones.*
FIRST GENTLEMAN	Mr. *Thompson.*
SECOND GENTLEMAN	Mr. *L'Estrange.*
MOUNTEBANK	Mr. *Booth.*
FRENCH SERVANT	Mr. *Wewitzer.*
PORTER	Mr. *Fearon.*
DICK	Mr. *Stevens.*

Women.

LETITIA HARDY	Miss *Younge.*
MRS. RACKET	Mrs. *Mattocks.*
LADY FRANCES TOUCHWOOD	Mrs. *Hartley.*
MISS OGLE	Mrs. *Morton.*
KITTY WILLIS	Miss *Stewart.*
LADY	Mrs. *Poussin.*

MASQUERADERS, TRADESMEN, SERVANTS, &c.

ACT I.

Scene i. Lincoln's Inn.

(Enter Saville, followed by a Servant, at the top of the stage, looking round, as if at a loss.)

SAVILLE. Lincoln's Inn! Well, but where to find him, now I am in Lincoln's Inn?—Where did he say his Master was?

SERV. He only said in Lincoln's Inn, Sir.

SAV. That's pretty! And your wisdom never enquired at whose chambers?

SERV. Sir, you spoke to the servant yourself.

SAV. If I was too impatient to ask questions, you ought to have taken directions, blockhead!

(Enter Courtall singing.)

Ha, Courtall!—Bid him keep the horses in motion, and then enquire at all the chambers round.

(Exit Servant.)

What the devil brings you to this part of the town?—Have any of the Long Robes³ handsome wives, sisters or chambermaids?

COURT. perhaps they have;—but I came on a different errand; and, had thy good fortune brought thee here half an hour sooner, I'd have given thee such a treat, ha! ha! ha!

SAV. I'm sorry I missed it: what was it?

COURT. I was informed a few days since that my cousins Fallow were come to town, and desired earnestly to see me at their lodgings in Warwick-Court, Holborn. Away drove I, painting them all the way as so many Hebes. They came from the farthest part of Northumberland, had never been in town, and in course were made up of rusticity, innocence, and beauty.

Sav. Well!

Court. After waiting thirty minutes, during which there was a violent bustle, in bounced five sallow damsels, four of them maypoles;—the fifth, Nature by way of variety, had bent in the Æsop style.[4]—But they all opened at once, like hounds on a fresh scent:—"Oh, cousin Courtall!—How do you do, cousin Courtall! Lord, cousin, I am glad you are come! We want you to go with us to the Park, and the Plays, and the Opera, and Almack's,[5] and all the fine places!"—The devil, thought I, my dears, may attend you, for I am sure I won't.—However, I heroically stayed an hour with them, and discovered the virgins were all come to town with the hopes of leaving it—Wives:—their heads full of Knight-Baronights, fops, and adventures.

Sav. Well, how did you get off?

Court. Oh, pleaded a million engagements.—However, conscience twitched me; so I breakfasted with them this morning, and afterwards 'squired them to the gardens here, as the most private place in town; and then took a sorrowful leave, complaining of my hard, hard fortune, that obliged me to set off immediately for Dorsetshire, ha! ha! ha!

Sav. I congratulate your escape!—Courtall at Almack's, with five awkward country cousins! ha! ha! ha!—Why, your existence, as a Man of Gallantry, could never have survived it.

Court. Death, and fire! had they come to town, like the rustics of the last age, to see Paul's, the lions, and the wax-work[6]—at their service;—but the cousins of our days come up Ladies—and, with the knowledge they glean from magazines and pocket-books, Fine Ladies; laugh at the bashfulness of their grandmothers, and boldly demand their *entrées* in the first circles.

Sav. Where can this fellow be!—Come, give me some news—I have been at war with woodcocks and partridges these two months,[7] and am a stranger to all that has passed out of their region.

Court. Oh! enough for three Gazettes. The ladies are going to petition for a bill that, during the war, every man may be allowed two wives.

Sav. 'Tis impossible they should succeed, for the majority of both Houses know what it is to have one.

COURT. Gallantry was black-balled at the *Coterie* last Thursday, and prudence and chastity voted in.

SAV. Ay, that may hold 'till the camps break up.—But have ye no elopements? no divorces?

COURT. Divorces are absolutely out, and the Commons-Doctors starving; so they are publishing trials of *Crim. Con.* with all the separate evidences at large; which they find has always a wonderful effect on their trade, actions tumbling in upon them afterwards, like mackerel at Gravesend.[8]

SAV. What more?

COURT. Nothing—for weddings, deaths, and politics, I never talk of, but whilst my hair is dressing. But prithee, Saville, how came you in town whilst all the qualified gentry are playing at pop-gun on Coxheath, and the country over-run with hares and foxes?

SAV. I came to meet my friend Doricourt, who, you know, is lately arrived from Rome.

COURT. Arrived! Yes, faith, and has cut us all out!—His carriage, his liveries, his dress, himself, are the rage of the day! His first appearance set the whole *Ton*[9] in a ferment, and his valet is besieged by *levées* of tailors, habit-makers, and other Ministers of Fashion, to gratify the impatience of their customers for becoming *à la mode de Doricourt*. Nay, the beautiful Lady Frolic, t'other night, with two sister Countesses, insisted upon his waistcoat for muffs; and their snowy arms now bear it in triumph about town, to the heart-rending affliction of all our *Beaux Garçons*.

SAV. Indeed! Well, those little gallantries will soon be over; he's on the point of marriage.

COURT. Marriage! Doricourt on the point of marriage! 'Tis the happiest tidings you could have given, next to his being hanged—Who is the bride elect?

SAV. I never saw her; but 'tis Miss Hardy, the rich heiress—the match was made by the parents, and the courtship begun on their nurses' knees; Master used to crow at Miss, and Miss used to chuckle at Master.

COURT. Oh! then by this time they care no more for each other than I do for my country cousins.

SAV. I don't know that; they have never met since thus high, and so, probably, have some regard for each other.

COURT. Never met! Odd!

SAV. A whim of Mr. Hardy's; he thought his daughter's charms would make a more forcible impression if her lover remained in ignorance of them 'till his return from the Continent.

(Enter Saville's Servant.)

SERV. Mr. Doricourt, Sir, has been at Counsellor Pleadwell's, and gone about five minutes. *(Exit Servant.)*

SAV. Five minutes! Zounds! I have been five minutes too late all my life-time!—Good morrow, Courtall; I must pursue him. *(Going.)*

COURT. Promise to dine with me to-day; I have some honest fellows. *(Going off on the opposite side.)*

SAV. Can't promise; perhaps I may.—See there, there's a bevy of female Patagonians, coming down upon us.

COURT. By the Lord, then, it must be my strapping cousins.—I dare not look behind me—Run, man, run.

(Exit on the same side.)

Scene ii. A hall at Doricourt's.

(A gentle knock at the door. Enter the Porter.)

PORT. Tap! What sneaking devil art thou? *(Opens the door.)*

(Enter Crowquill.)

So! I suppose *you* are one of Monsieur's customers too? He's above stairs, now, overhauling all his Honor's things to a parcel of 'em.

CROWQ. No, Sir; it is with you, if you please, that I want to speak.

PORT. Me! Well, what do you want with me?

CROWQ. Sir, you must know that I am—I am the gentleman who writes the *Tête-à-têtes*[10] in the magazines.

PORT. Oh, oh!—What, you are the fellow that ties folks together, in your sixpenny cuts, that never meet anywhere else?

CROWQ. Oh, dear Sir, excuse me!—we always go on *foundation;* and if you can help me to a few anecdotes of your master, such

as what Marchioness he lost money to in Paris—who is his favorite lady in town—or the name of the girl he first made love
to at college—or any incidents that happened to his grandmother or great-aunts—a couple will do, by way of support-
ers—I'll weave a web of intrigues, losses, and gallantries,
between them, that shall fill four pages, procure me a dozen
dinners, and you, Sir, a bottle of wine for your trouble.

PORT. Oh, oh! I heard the butler talk of you, when I lived at Lord
Tinket's. But what the devil do you mean by a bottle of wine!—
You gave him a crown for a retaining fee.

CROWQ. Oh, Sir, that was for a Lord's amours; a commoner's are
never but half. Why, I have had a Baronet's for five shillings,
though he was a married man, and changed his mistress every
six weeks.

PORT. Don't tell me! What signifies a Baronet, or a bit of a lord,
who, may be, was never further than sun and sun round London?[11] We have traveled, man! My master has been in Italy, and
over the whole island of Spain; talked to the Queen of France,
and danced with her at a masquerade. Ay, and such folks don't
go to masquerades for nothing; but mum—not a word more—
Unless you'll rank my master with a lord, I'll not be guilty of
blabbing his secrets, I assure you.

CROWQ. Well, Sir, perhaps you'll throw in a hint or two of other
families where you've lived, that may be worked up into something; and so, Sir, here is one, two, three, four, five shillings.

PORT. Well, that's honest. *(Pocketing the money.)* To tell you the
truth, I don't know much of my master's concerns yet;—but
here comes Monsieur and his gang: I'll pump them: they have
trotted after him all round Europe, from the Canaries to the Isle
of Wight.

*(Enter several foreign Servants and two Tradesmen. The Porter
takes one of them aside.)*

TRADESM. Well then, you have showed us all?

FRENCHM. All, *en vérité, Messieurs!* you *avez* seen every ting.
Serviteur, serviteur.

(Exeunt Tradesmen.)

Ah, here comes one *autre* curious Englishman, and dat's one *autre* guinea *pour moi.*

(Enter Saville.)

Allons, Monsieur, dis way; I will show you tings, such tings you never see, begar, in England!—velvets by Le Mosse, suits cut by Verdue, trimmings by Grossette, embroidery by Detanville—

SAV. Puppy!—where is your master?

PORT. Zounds! you chattering frog-eating dunderhead, can't you see a gentleman?—'Tis Mr. Saville.

FRENCHM. Monsieur Saville! *Je suis mort de peur.*—Ten tousand pardons! *Excusez mon erreur,* and permit me you conduct to Monsieur Doricourt; he be too happy *vous voir.*

(Exeunt Frenchman and Saville.)

PORT. Step below a bit;—we'll make it out somehow!—I suppose a slice of sirloin won't make the story go down the worse.

(Exeunt Porter and Crowquill.)

Scene iii. An apartment at Doricourt's.

(Enter Doricourt.)

DORIC *(speaking to a servant behind).* I shall be too late for St. James's;[12] bid him come immediately.

(Enter Frenchman and Saville.)

FRENCHM. Monsieur Saville. *(Exit Frenchman.)*

DORIC. Most fortunate! My dear Saville, let the warmth of this embrace speak the pleasure of my heart.

SAV. Well, this is some comfort, after the scurvy reception I met with in your hall.—I prepared my mind, as I came upstairs, for a *bon jour,* a grimace, and an *adieu.*

DORIC. Why so?

SAV. Judging of the master from the rest of the family. What the devil is the meaning of that flock of foreigners below, with their parchment faces and snuffy whiskers? What! can't an Englishman stand behind your carriage, buckle your shoe, or brush your coat?

DORIC. Stale, my dear Saville, stale! Englishmen make the best soldiers, citizens, artisans, and philosophers in the world; but the very worst footmen. I keep French fellows and Germans as the Romans kept slaves, because their own countrymen had minds too enlarged and haughty to descend with a grace to the duties of such a station.

SAV. A good excuse for a bad practice.

DORIC. On my honor, experience will convince you of its truth. A Frenchman neither hears, sees, nor breathes, but as his master directs; and his whole system of conduct is comprised in one short word, *Obedience!* An Englishman reasons, forms opinions, cogitates, and disputes; he is the mere creature of your will: the other, a being conscious of equal importance in the universal scale with yourself, and is therefore your judge, whilst he wears your livery, and decides on your actions with the freedom of a censor.

SAV. And this in defence of a custom I have heard you execrate, together with all the adventitious manners imported by our travelled gentry.

DORIC. Ay, but that was at eighteen; we are always *very* wise at eighteen. But consider this point: we go into Italy, where the sole business of the people is to study and improve the powers of music: we yield to the fascination and grow enthusiasts in the charming science: we travel over France, and see the whole kingdom composing ornaments and inventing fashions: we condescend to avail ourselves of their industry and adopt their modes: we return to England, and find the nation intent on the most important objects; polity,[13] commerce, war, with all the liberal arts, employ her sons; the latent sparks glow afresh within our bosoms; the sweet follies of the Continent imperceptibly slide away, whilst senators, statesmen, patriots and heroes emerge from the *virtû* of Italy and the frippery of France.

SAV. I may as well give it up! You had always the art of placing your faults in the best light; and I can't help loving you, faults and all: so, to start a subject which must please you, When do you expect Miss Hardy?

DORIC. Oh, the hour of expectation is past. She is arrived, and I this morning had the honor of an interview at Pleadwell's. The writings were ready; and, in obedience to the will of Mr. Hardy, we met to sign and seal.

SAV. Has the event answered? Did your heart leap or sink when you beheld your mistress?

DORIC. Faith, neither one nor t'other; she's a fine girl, as far as mere flesh and blood goes.—But—

SAV. But what?

DORIC. Why, she's *only* a fine girl; complexion, shape, and features; nothing more.

SAV. Is not that enough?

DORIC. No! She should have spirit! fire! *l'air enjoué!*[14] that something, that nothing, which every body feels, and which no body can describe, in the restless charmers of Italy and France.

SAV. Thanks to the parsimony of my father, that kept me from travel! I would not have lost my relish for true unaffected English beauty, to have been quarrelled for by all the belles of Versailles and Florence.

DORIC. Pho! thou hast no taste. *English* beauty! 'Tis insipidity; it wants the zest, it wants poignancy, Frank! Why, I have known a Frenchwoman, indebted to nature for no one thing but a pair of decent eyes, reckon in her suite as many counts, marquisses, and *Petits Maîtres*[15] as would satisfy three dozen of our first-rate toasts. I have known an Italian *Marquizina* make ten conquests in stepping from her carriage and carry her slaves from one city to another, whose real intrinsic beauty would have yielded to half the little *grisettes* that pace your Mall on a Sunday.

SAV. And has Miss Hardy nothing of this?

DORIC. If she has, she was pleased to keep it to herself. I was in the room half an hour before I could catch the color of her eyes; and every attempt to draw her into conversation occasioned so cruel an embarrassment that I was reduced to the necessity of news, French fleets, and Spanish captures, with her father.

SAV. So Miss Hardy, with only beauty, modesty, and merit, is doomed to the arms of a husband who will despise her.

DORIC. You are unjust. Though she has not inspired me with violent passion, my honor secures her felicity.

SAV. Come, come, Doricourt, you know very well that when the honor of a husband is *locum-tenens* for his heart, his wife must be as indifferent as himself, if she is not unhappy.

DORIC. Pho! never moralise without spectacles. But, as we are upon the tender subject, how did you bear Touchwood's carrying Lady Frances?

SAV. You know I never looked up to her with hope, and Sir George is every way worthy of her.

DORIC. À la mode anglaise, a philosopher even in love.

SAV. Come, I detain you—you seem dressed at all points, and of course have an engagement.

DORIC. To St. James's. I dine at Hardy's, and accompany them to the masquerade in the evening: but breakfast with me tomorrow, and we'll talk of our old companions; for I swear to you, Saville, the air of the Continent has not effaced one youthful prejudice or attachment.

SAV. —With an exception to the case of ladies and servants.

DORIC. True; there I plead guilty:—but I have never yet found any man whom I could cordially take to my heart, and call friend, who was not born beneath a British sky, and whose heart and manners were not truly English.

(Ex. Doricourt and Saville.)

Scene iv. An apartment at Mr. Hardy's.

(Villers seated on a sofa, reading. Enter Flutter.)

FLUT. Hah, Villers, have you seen Mrs. Racket?—Miss Hardy, I find, is out.

VILL. I have not seen her yet. I have made a voyage to Lapland since I came in. *(Flinging away the book.)* A lady at her toilette is as difficult to be moved as a Quaker. *(Yawning.)* What events have happened in the world since yesterday? have you heard?

FLUT. Oh, yes; I stopped at Tattersall's as I came by, and there I found Lord James Jessamy, Sir William Wilding, and Mr. —. But, now I think of it, you sha'n't know a syllable of the matter; for I have been informed you never believe above one half of what I say.

VILL. My dear fellow, somebody has imposed upon you most egregiously!—Half! Why, I never believe one tenth part of what you say; that is, according to the plain and literal expression: but, as I understand you, your intelligence is amusing.

FLUT. That's very hard now, very hard. I never related a falsity in my life, unless I stumbled on it by mistake; and if it were otherwise, your dull matter-of-fact people are infinitely obliged to those warm imaginations which soar into fiction to amuse you; for, positively, the common events of this little dirty world are not worth talking about, unless you embellish 'em!—Hah! here comes Mrs. Racket: Adieu to weeds, I see! All life!

(Enter Mrs. Racket.)

Enter, Madam, in all your charms! Villers has been abusing your toilette for keeping you so long; but I think we are much obliged to it, and so are you.

MRS. RACK. How so, pray? Good-morning t'ye both. Here, here's a hand a-piece for you.

(They kiss her hands.)

FLUT. How so! Because it has given you so many beauties.

MRS. RACK. Delightful compliment! What do you think of that, Villers?

VILL. That he and his compliments are alike—showy, but won't bear examining.—So you brought Miss Hardy to town last night?

MRS. RACK. Yes, I should have brought her before, but I had a fall from my horse that confined me a week.—I suppose in her heart she wished me hanged a dozen times an hour.

FLUT. Why?

MRS. RACK. Had she not an expecting lover in town all the time? She meets him this morning at the lawyer's—I hope she'll charm him; she's the sweetest girl in the world.

VILL. Vanity, like murder, will out.—You have convinced me you think yourself more charming.

MRS. RACK. How can that be?

VILL. No woman ever praises another unless she thinks herself superior in the very perfections she allows.

FLUT. Nor no man ever rails at the sex unless he is conscious he deserves their hatred.

MRS. RACK. Thank ye, Flutter—I'll owe ye a *bouquet* for that. I am going to visit the new-married Lady Frances Touchwood.— Who knows her husband?

FLUT. Everybody.

MRS. RACK. Is there not something odd in his character?

VILL. Nothing, but that he is passionately fond of his wife;—and so petulant is his love, that he opened the cage of a favorite bullfinch and sent it to catch butterflies, because she rewarded its song with her kisses.

MRS. RACK. Intolerable monster! Such a brute deserves—

VILL. Nay, nay, nay, nay, this is your sex now—Give a woman but one stroke of character, off she goes, like a ball from a racket; sees the whole man, marks him down for an angel or a devil, and so exhibits him to her acquaintance.—This monster! this brute! is one of the worthiest fellows upon earth; sound sense, and a liberal mind; but dotes on his wife to such excess that he quarrels with everything she admires, and is jealous of her tippet and nosegay.

MRS. RACK. Oh, less love for me, kind Cupid! I can see no difference between the torment of such an affection and hatred.

FLUT. Oh, pardon me, inconceivable difference, inconceivable; I see it as clearly as your bracelet. In the one case the husband would say, as Mr. Snapper said t'other day, Zounds! Madam, do you suppose that *my* table, and *my* house, and *my* pictures!—*Àpropos des bottes.*[16] There was the divinest Plague of Athens sold yesterday at Langford's! the dead figures so natural, you would have sworn they had been alive! Lord Primrose bid five hundred—six, said Lady Carmine.—A thousand, said Ingot the nabob.—Down went the hammer.—A *rouleau* for your bargain, said Sir Jeremy Jingle. And what answer do you think Ingot made him?

MRS. RACKET. Why, took the offer.

FLUT. Sir, I would oblige you, but I buy this picture to place in the nursery: the children have already got Whittington and his Cat; 'tis just this size, and they'll make good companions.

MRS. RACK. Ha! ha! ha! Well, I protest that's just the way now— the nabobs and their wives outbid one at every sale, and the creatures have no more taste—

VILL. There again! You forget this story is told by Flutter, who always remembers everything but the circumstances and the person he talks about:—'twas Ingot who offered a *rouleau* for the bargain, and Sir Jeremy Jingle who made the reply.

FLUT. Egad, I believe you are right.—Well, the story is as good one way as t'other, you know. Good morning. I am going to Mrs. Crotchet's concert, and in my way back shall make my bow at Sir George's. *(Going)*

VILL. I'll venture every figure in your tailor's bill, you make some blunder there.

FLUT *(turning back)*. Done! My tailor's bill has not been paid these two years; and I'll open my mouth with as much care as Mrs. Bridget Button, who wears cork plumpers in each cheek, and never hazards more than six words for fear of showing them. *(Exit Flutter.)*

MRS. RACK. 'Tis a good-natured insignificant creature! let in everywhere, and cared for nowhere.—There's Miss Hardy returned from Lincoln's Inn: she seems rather chagrined.

VILL. Then I leave you to your communications.

(Enter Letitia, followed by her Maid.)

Adieu! I am rejoiced to see you so well, Madam! but I must tear myself away.

LETIT. Don't vanish in a moment.

VILL. Oh, inhuman! you are two of the most dangerous women in town—Staying here to be cannonaded by four such eyes is equal to a *rencontre* with Paul Jones or a midnight march to Omoa!—They'll swallow the nonsense for the sake of the compliment. *(Aside.) (Exit Villers.)*

LETIT *(gives her cloak to her maid)*. Order Du Quesne never to come again; he shall positively dress my hair no more. *(Exit Maid.)* And this odious silk, how unbecoming it is!—I was bewitched to choose it. *(Throwing herself on a sofa, and looking in a pocket-glass, Mrs. Racket staring at her.)* Did you ever see such a fright as I am today?

MRS. RACK. Yes, I have seen you look much worse.

LETIT. How can you be so provoking? If I do not look this morning worse than ever I looked in my life, I am naturally a fright. You shall have it which way you will.

MRS. RACK. Just as you please; but pray what is the meaning of all this?

LETIT *(rising)*. Men are all dissemblers! flatterers! deceivers! Have I not heard a thousand times of my air, my eyes, my shape—all made for victory! and today, when I bent my whole heart on one poor conquest, I have proved that all those imputed charms amount to nothing;—for Doricourt saw them unmoved.—A husband of fifteen months could not have examined me with more cutting indifference.

MRS. RACK. Then you return it like a wife of fifteen months, and be as indifferent as he.

LETIT. Aye, there's the sting! The blooming boy who left his image in my young heart is at four and twenty improved in every grace that fixed him there. It is the same face that my memory, and my dreams, constantly painted to me; but its graces are finished, and every beauty heightened. How mortifying to feel myself at the same moment his slave and an object of perfect indifference to him!

MRS. RACK. How are you certain that was the case? Did you expect him to kneel down before the lawyer, his clerks, and your father, to make oath of your beauty?

LETIT. No; but he should have looked as if a sudden ray had pierced him! he should have been breathless! speechless! for, oh! Caroline, all this was I.

MRS. RACK. I am sorry you was such a fool. Can you expect a man who has courted and been courted by half the fine women in Europe to feel like a girl from a boarding-school? He is the prettiest fellow you have seen, and in course bewilders your imagination; but he has seen a million of pretty women, child, before he saw you; and his first feelings have been over long ago.

LETIT. Your raillery distresses me; but I will touch his heart, or never be his wife.

MRS. RACK. Absurd and romantic! If you have no reason to believe his heart pre-engaged, be satisfied; if he is a man of honor, you'll have nothing to complain of.

LETIT. Nothing to complain of! Heavens! shall I marry the man I adore with such an expectation as that?

MRS. RACK. And when you have fretted yourself pale, my dear, you'll have mended your expectation greatly.

LETIT *(pausing)*. Yet I have one hope. If there is any power whose peculiar care is faithful love, that power I invoke to aid me.

(Enter Mr. Hardy.)

HARDY. Well, now; wasn't I right? Aye, Letty! Aye, Cousin Racket! wasn't I right? I knew 'twould be so. He was all agog to see her before he went abroad; and, if he had, he'd have thought no more of her face, may be, than his own.

MRS. RACK. May be, not half so much.

HARDY. Aye, may be so:—but I see into things; exactly as I foresaw, today he fell desperately in love with the wench, he! he! he!

LETIT. Indeed, Sir! how did you perceive it?

HARDY. That's a pretty question! How do I perceive everything? How did I foresee the fall of corn and the rise of taxes? How did I know that if we quarrelled with America, Norway deals would be dearer? How did I foretell that a war would sink the funds? How did I forewarn Parson Homily that if he didn't some way or other contrive to get more votes from Rubrick, he'd lose the lectureship? How did I—But what the devil makes you so dull, Letitia? I thought to have found you popping about as brisk as the jacks[17] of your harpsichord.

LETIT. Surely, Sir, 'tis a very serious occasion.

HARDY. Pho, pho! girls should never be grave before marriage. How did you feel, Cousin, beforehand? Aye!

MRS. RACK. Feel! why exceedingly full of cares.

HARDY. Did you?

MRS. RACK. I could not sleep for thinking of my coach, my liveries, and my chairmen; the taste of clothes I should be presented in distracted me for a week; and whether I should be married in white or lilac gave me the most cruel anxiety.

LETIT. And is it possible that you felt no other care?

HARDY. And pray, of what sort may your cares be, Mrs. Letitia? I begin to foresee now that you have taken a dislike to Doricourt.

LETIT. Indeed, Sir, I have not.

HARDY. Then what's all this melancholy about? A'n't you going to be married? and, what's more, to a sensible man? and, what's more to a young girl, to a handsome man? And what's all this melancholy for, I say?

MRS. RACK. Why, because he *is* handsome and sensible, and because she's over head and ears in love with him; all which, it seems, your foreknowledge had not told you a word of.

LETIT. Fye, Caroline!

HARDY. Well, come, do you tell me what's the matter then? If you don't like him, hang the signing and sealing, he sha'n't have ye:—and yet I can't say that neither; for you know that estate, that cost his father and me upwards of fourscore thousand pounds, must go all to him if you won't have him: if he won't have you, indeed, 'twill be all yours. All that's clear, engrossed upon parchment, and the poor dear man set his hand to it whilst he was a dying.—"Ah!" said I, "I foresee you'll never live to see 'em come together; but their first son shall be christened Jeremiah after you, that I promise you."—But come, I say, what is the matter? Don't you like him?

LETIT. I fear, Sir—if I must speak—I fear I was less agreeable in Mr. Doricourt's eyes than he appeared in mine.

HARDY. There you are mistaken; for I asked him, and he told me he liked you vastly. Don't you think he must have taken a fancy to her?

MRS. RACK. Why really I think so, as I was not by.

LETIT. My dear Sir, I am convinced he has not; but if there is spirit or invention in woman, he shall.

HARDY. Right, Girl; go to your toilette—

LETIT. It is not my toilette that can serve me: but a plan has struck me, if you will not oppose it, which flatters me with brilliant success.

HARDY. Oppose it! not I indeed! What is it?

LETIT. Why, Sir—it may seem a little paradoxical; but, as he does not like me enough, I want him to like me still less, and will at our next interview endeavor to heighten his indifference into dislike.

HARDY. Who the devil could have foreseen that?

MRS. RACK. Heaven and earth! Letitia, are you serious?

LETIT. As serious as the most important business of my life demands.

MRS. RACK. Why endeavor to make him dislike you?

LETIT. Because 'tis much easier to convert a sentiment into its opposite than to transform indifference into tender passion.

MRS. RACK. That may be good philosophy, but I am afraid you'll find it a bad maxim.

LETIT. I have the strongest confidence in it. I am inspired with unusual spirits, and on this hazard willingly stake my chance for happiness. I am impatient to begin my measures. *(Exit Letitia.)*

HARDY. Can you foresee the end of this, Cousin?

MRS. RACK. No, Sir; nothing less than your penetration can do that, I am sure; and I can't stay now to consider it. I am going to call on the Ogles, and then to Lady Frances Touchwood's, and then to an auction, and then—I don't know where—but I shall be at home time enough to witness this extraordinary interview. Good-bye. *(Exit Mrs. Racket.)*

HARDY. Well, 'tis an odd thing—I can't understand it—but I foresee Letty will have her way, and so I sha'n't give myself the trouble to dispute it. *(Exit Hardy.)*

ACT II.

Scene i. Sir George Touchwood's.

(Enter Doricourt and Sir George.)

DORICOURT. Married, ha! ha! ha! you, whom I heard in Paris say such things of the sex, are in London a married man.

SIR GEO. The sex is still what it has ever been since *la petite morale*[18] banished substantial virtues; and rather than have given my name to one of our high-bred fashionable dames, I'd have crossed the line in a fire-ship and married a Japanese.

DORIC. Yet you have married an English beauty, yea, and a beauty born in high life.

SIR GEO. True; but she has a simplicity of heart and manners that would have become the fair Hebrew damsels toasted by the Patriarchs.

DORIC. Ha! ha! Why, thou art a downright matrimonial Quixote.[19] My life on't, she becomes as mere a Town Lady in six months as though she had been bred to the trade.

SIR GEO. Common—common—. *(Contemptuously.)* No, Sir, Lady Frances despises high life so much, from the ideas I have given her, that she'll live in it like a salamander in fire.[20]

DORIC. Oh, that the circle *dans la place Victoire* would witness thy extravagance! I'll send thee off to St. Evreux this night, drawn at full length, and colored after nature.

SIR GEO. Tell him, then, to add to the ridicule, that Touchwood glories in the name of Husband; that he has found in one Englishwoman more beauty than Frenchmen ever saw, and more goodness than Frenchwomen can conceive.

DORIC. Well—enough of description. Introduce me to this phoenix; I came on purpose.

SIR GEO. Introduce!—oh, aye, to be sure—I believe Lady Frances is engaged just now—but another time. How handsome the dog looks today! *(Aside.)*

DORIC. Another time!—but I have no other time. 'Sdeath! this is the only hour I can command this fortnight!

SIR GEO (*aside*). I am glad to hear it, with all my soul. So then, you can't dine with us today? That's very unlucky.

DORIC. Oh, yes—as to dinner—yes, I can, I believe, contrive to dine with you today.

SIR GEO. Pfha! I didn't think on what I was saying; I meant supper—You can't sup with us?

DORIC. Why, supper will be rather more convenient than dinner—But you are fortunate—if you had asked me any other night, I could not have come.

SIR GEO. Tonight!—Gad, now I recollect, we are particularly engaged tonight—But tomorrow night—

DORIC. Why look ye, Sir George, 'tis very plain you have no inclination to let me see your wife at all; so here I sit. (*Throws himself on a sofa.*)—There's my hat, and here are my legs.—Now I sha'n't stir till I have seen her; and I have no engagements: I'll breakfast, dine, and sup with you every day this week.

SIR GEO. Was there ever such a provoking wretch! But, to be plain with you, Doricourt, I and my house are at your service: but you are a damned agreeable fellow, and ten years younger than I am; and the women, I observe, always simper when you appear. For these reasons, I had rather, when Lady Frances and I are together, that you should forget we are acquainted, further than a nod, a smile, or a how-d'ye.

DORIC. Very well.

SIR GEO. It is not merely yourself *in propriâ persona*[21] that I object to; but, if you are intimate here, you'll make my house still more the fashion than it is; and it is already so much so that my doors are of no use to me. I married Lady Frances to engross her to myself; yet such is the blessed freedom of modern manners that, in spite of me, her eyes, thoughts, and conversation are continually divided amongst all the flirts and coxcombs of fashion.

DORIC. To be sure, I confess that kind of freedom is carried rather too far. 'Tis hard one can't have a jewel in one's cabinet, but the whole town must be gratified with its lustre. He sha'n't preach me out of seeing his wife, though. (*Aside.*)

SIR GEO. Well, now, that's reasonable. When you take time to re-

flect, Doricourt, I always observe you decide right, and therefore I hope—

(Enter Servant.)

Serv. Sir, my Lady desires—
Sir Geo. I am particularly engaged.
Doric. Oh, Lord, that shall be no excuse in the world. *(Leaping
from the sofa.)* Lead the way, John.— I'll attend your Lady.
(Exit, following the Servant.)
Sir Geo. What devil possessed me to talk about her!—Here,
Doricourt! *(Running after him.)* Doricourt!

(Enter Mrs. Racket and Miss Ogle, followed by a Servant.)

Mrs. Rack. Acquaint your Lady that Mrs. Racket and Miss Ogle
are here. *(Exit Servant.)*
Miss Ogle. I shall hardly know Lady Frances, 'tis so long since I
was in Shropshire.
Mrs. Rack. And I'll be sworn you never saw her *out* of
Shropshire.—Her father kept her locked up with his caterpillars
and shells, and loved her beyond anything—but a blue butterfly,
and a petrified frog!
Miss Ogle. Ha! ha! ha!—Well, 'twas a cheap way of breeding
her:—you know he was very poor, though a Lord; and very
high-spirited, though a virtuoso.[22]—In town, her Pantheons,
Operas, and *robes de cour,* would have swallowed his sea-
weeds, moths, and monsters, in six weeks!—Sir George, I find,
thinks his wife a most extraordinary creature: he has taught her
to despise everything like fashionable life, and boasts that example will have no effect on her.
Mrs. Rack. There's a great degree of impertinence in all that—I'll
try to make her a Fine Lady, to humble him.
Miss Ogle. That's just the thing I wish.

(Enter Lady Frances.)

Lady Fran. I beg ten thousand pardons, my dear Mrs. Racket.—
Miss Ogle, I rejoice to see you: I should have come to you
sooner, but I was detained in conversation by Mr. Doricourt.

MRS. RACK. Pray make no apology; I am quite happy that we have your Ladyship in town at last.—What stay do you make?

LADY FRAN. A short one! Sir George talks with regret of the scenes we have left; and as the ceremony of presentation[23] is over, will, I believe, soon return.

MISS OGLE. Sure he can't be so cruel! Does your Ladyship wish to return so soon?

LADY FRAN. I have not the habit of consulting my own wishes; but, I think, if they decide, we shall not return immediately. I have yet hardly formed an idea of London.

MRS. RACK. I shall quarrel with your Lord and Master, if he dares think of depriving us of you so soon. How do you dispose of yourself today?

LADY FRAN. Sir George is going with me this morning: to the mercer's, to choose a silk; and then—

MRS. RACK. Choose a silk for you! ha! ha! ha! Sir George chooses your laces too, I hope; your gloves, and your pincushions!

LADY FRAN. Madam!

MRS. RACK. I am glad to see you blush, my dear Lady Frances. These are strange homespun ways! If you do these things, pray keep 'em secret. Lord bless us! If the Town should know your husband chooses your gowns!

MISS OGLE. You are very young, my Lady, and have been brought up in solitude. The maxims you learnt among the wood-nymphs in Shropshire won't pass current here, I assure you.

MRS. RACK. Why, my dear creature, you look quite frightened!—Come, you shall go with us to an exhibition and an auction.—Afterwards, we'll take a turn in the park, and then drive to Kensington;—so we shall be at home by four, to dress; and in the evening I'll attend you to Lady Brilliant's masquerade.

LADY FRAN. I shall be very happy to be of your party, if Sir George has no engagements.

MRS. RACK. What! Do you stand so low in your own opinion, that you dare not trust yourself without Sir George! If you choose to play Darby and Joan,[24] my dear, you should have stayed in the country;—'tis an exhibition not calculated for London, I assure you!

MISS OGLE. What, I suppose, my Lady, you and Sir George will be seen pacing it comfortably round the Canal, arm and arm, and then go lovingly to the same carriage; dine *tête-à-tête,* spend the evening at picquet, and so go soberly to bed at eleven!—Such a snug plan may do for an attorney and his wife; but, for Lady Frances Touchwood, 'tis as unsuitable as linsey-woolsey, or a black bonnet at the *Festino!*

LADY FRAN. These are rather new doctrines to me!—But, my dear Mrs. Racket, you and Miss Ogle must judge of these things better than I can. As you observe, I am but young, and may have caught absurd opinions.—Here is Sir George!

(Enter Sir George.)

SIR GEO *(aside)*. 'Sdeath! another room full!

LADY FRAN. My love! Mrs. Racket and the Miss Ogles.

MISS RACK. Give you joy, Sir George.—We came to rob you of Lady Frances for a few hours.

SIR GEO. A few hours!

LADY FRAN. Oh, yes! I am going to an exhibition, and an auction, and the Park, and Kensington, and a thousand places!—It is quite ridiculous, I find, for married people to be always together—We shall be laughed at!

SIR GEO. I am astonished!—Mrs. Racket, what does the dear creature mean?

MRS. RACK. Mean, Sir George!—what she says, I imagine.

MISS OGLE. Why, you know, Sir, as Lady Frances had the misfortune to be bred entirely in the country, she cannot be supposed to be versed in fashionable life.

SIR GEO. No; heaven forbid she should!—If she had, Madam, she would never have been my wife!

MRS. RACK. Are you serious?

SIR GEO. Perfectly so.—I should never have had the courage to have married a well-bred Fine Lady.

MISS OGLE. Pray, Sir, what do you take a Fine Lady to be, that you express such fear of her? *(Sneeringly.)*

SIR GEO. A being easily described, Madam, as she is seen everywhere, but in her own house. She sleeps at home, but she lives all over the town. In her mind, every sentiment gives place to the lust of conquest, and the vanity of being particular. The feelings of wife, and mother, are lost in the whirl of dissipation. If she continues virtuous, 'tis by chance—and if she preserves her

husband from ruin, 'tis by her dexterity at the card-table!—
Such a woman I take to be a perfect Fine Lady!

MRS. RACK. And you I take to be a slanderous Cynic of two-and-
thirty.—Twenty years hence, one might have forgiven such a
libel!—Now, Sir, hear my definition of a Fine Lady:—She is a
creature for whom Nature has done much, and Education
more; she has taste, elegance, spirit, understanding. In her manner she is free, in her morals nice. Her behavior is undistin-
guishingly polite to her husband and all mankind;—her
sentiments are for their hours of retirement. In a word, a Fine
Lady is the life of conversation, the spirit of society, the joy of
the public!—Pleasure follows wherever she appears, and the
kindest wishes attend her slumbers.—Make haste, then, my
dear Lady Frances, commence Fine Lady, and force your husband to acknowledge the justness of my picture!

LADY FRAN. I am sure 'tis a delightful one. How can you dislike
it, Sir George? You painted fashionable life in colors so disgusting that I thought I hated it; but, on a nearer view, it seems
charming. I have hitherto lived in obscurity; 'tis time that I
should be a Woman of the World. I long to begin;—my heart
pants with expectation and delight!

MRS. RACK. Come, then; let us begin directly. I am impatient to
introduce you to that society which you were born to ornament
and charm.

LADY FRAN. Adieu! my Love!—We shall meet again at dinner.
(Going.)

SIR GEO. Sure, I am in a dream!—Fanny!

LADY FRAN *(returning)*. Sir George?

SIR GEO. Will you go without me?

MRS. RACK. Will you go without me!—ha! ha! ha! what a pathetic
address! Why, sure you would not always be seen side by side,
like two beans upon a stalk. Are you afraid to trust Lady
Frances with me, Sir?

SIR GEORGE. Heaven and earth! with whom can a man trust his
wife, in the present state of society? Formerly there were dis-
tinctions of character among ye: every class of females had its
particular description; Grandmothers were pious, Aunts discreet, Old Maids censorious! but now aunts, grandmothers,
girls, and maiden gentlewomen are all the same creature;—a
wrinkle more or less is the sole difference between ye.

Mrs. Rack. That Maiden Gentlewomen have lost their censoriousness, is surely not in your catalogue of grievances.

Sir Geo. Indeed it is—and ranked amongst the most serious grievances.—Things went well, Madam, when the tongues of three or four old virgins kept all the wives and daughters of a parish in awe. They were dragons that guarded the Hesperian fruit;[25] and I wonder they have not been obliged, by act of Parliament, to resume their function.

Mrs. Rack. Ha! ha! ha! and pensioned, I suppose, for making strict enquiries into the lives and conversations of their neighbors.

Sir Geo. With all my heart, and empowered to oblige every woman to conform her conduct to her real situation. You, for instance, are a widow: your air should be sedate, your dress grave, your deportment matronly, and in all things an example to the young women growing up about you!—instead of which, you are dressed for conquest, think of nothing but ensnaring hearts; are a Coquette, a Wit, and a Fine Lady.

Mrs. Rack. Bear witness to what he says! A Coquette! a Wit! and a Fine Lady! Who would have expected an eulogy from such an ill-natured mortal!—Valor to a soldier, wisdom to a judge, or glory to a prince, is not more than such a character to a woman.

Miss Ogle. Sir George, I see, languishes for the charming society of a century and a half ago; when a grave 'Squire, and a still graver Dame, surrounded by a sober family, formed a stiff group in a moldy old house in the corner of a park.

Mrs. Rack. Delightful serenity! Undisturbed by any noise but the cawing of rooks and the quarterly rumbling of an old family-coach on a state-visit; with the happy intervention of a friendly call from the Parish apothecary or the curate's wife.

Sir Geo. And what is the society of which you boast?—a mere chaos, in which all distinction of rank is lost in a ridiculous affectation of ease, and every different order of beings huddled together, as they were before creation. In the same *select party,* you will often find the wife of a bishop and a sharper, of an earl and a fiddler. In short, 'tis one universal masquerade, all disguised in the same habits and manners.

Serv. Mr. Flutter. *(Exit Servant.)*

Sir Geo. Here comes an illustration. Now I defy you to tell from his appearance whether Flutter is a Privy Counsellor or a mercer, a lawyer, or a grocer's 'prentice.

(Enter Flutter.)

FLUT. Oh, just which you please, Sir George; so you don't make me a Lord Mayor. Ah, Mrs. Racket!—Lady Frances, your most obedient; you look—now hang me, if that's not provoking!—had your gown been of another color, I should have said the prettiest thing you ever heard in your life.

MISS OGLE. Pray give it us.

FLUT. I was yesterday at Mrs. Bloomer's. She was dressed all in green; no other color to be seen but that of her face and bosom. So says I, My dear Mrs. Bloomer! you look like a carnation, just bursting from its pod.

SIR GEO. And what said her husband?

FLUT. Her husband! Why, her husband laughed, and said a cucumber would have been a happier simile.

SIR GEO. But there *are* husbands, Sir, who would rather have corrected than amended your comparison; I, for instance, should consider a man's complimenting my wife as an impertinence.

FLUT. Why, what harm can there be in compliments? Sure they are not infectious; and, if they were, you, Sir George, of all people breathing, have reason to be satisfied about your Lady's attachment; everybody talks of it: that little bird there, that she killed out of jealousy, the most extraordinary instance of affection that ever was given.

LADY FRAN. I kill a bird through jealousy!—Heavens! Mr. Flutter, how can you impute such a cruelty to me?

SIR GEO. I could have forgiven you, if you had.

FLUT. Oh, what a blundering fool!—No, no—now I remember—'twas your bird, Lady Frances—that's it; your bullfinch, which Sir George, in one of the refinements of his passion, sent into the wide world to seek its fortune.—He took it for a knight in disguise.

LADY FRAN. Is it possible! O, Sir George, could I have imagined it was you who deprived me of a creature I was so fond of?

SIR GEO. Mr. Flutter, you are one of those busy, idle, meddling people who, from mere vacuity of mind, are the most dangerous inmates in a family. You have neither feelings nor opinions of your own; but, like a glass in a tavern, bear about those of every blockhead who gives you his;—and, because you *mean* no harm, think yourselves excused, though broken friendships, discords, and murders are the consequences of your indiscretions.

FLUT *(taking out his tablets).* Vacuity of mind!—What was the next? I'll write down this sermon; 'tis the first I have heard since my grandmother's funeral.

MISS OGLE. Come, Lady Frances, you see what a cruel creature your loving husband can be; so let us leave him.

SIR GEO. Madam, Lady Frances shall not go.

LADY FRAN. *Shall* not, Sir George?—This is the first time such an expression—*(Weeping.)*

SIR GEO. My love! my life!

LADY FRAN. Don't imagine I'll be treated like a child! denied what I wish, and then pacified with sweet words.

MISS OGLE *(apart).* The bullfinch! that's an excellent subject; never let it down.

LADY FRAN. I see plainly you would deprive me of every pleasure, as well as of my sweet bird—out of pure love!—Barbarous Man!

SIR GEO. 'Tis well, Madam;—your resentment of that circumstance proves to me, what I did not before suspect, that you are deficient both in tenderness and understanding.—Tremble to think the hour approaches, in which you would give worlds for such a proof of my love. Go, Madam, give yourself to the public; abandon you heart to dissipation, and see if, in the scenes of gaiety and folly that await you, you can find a recompence for the lost affection of a doting husband. *(Exit Sir George.)*

FLUT. Lord! what a fine thing it is to have the gift of speech! I suppose Sir George practices at Coachmakers Hall or the Black Horse in Bond Street.

LADY FRAN. He is really angry; I cannot go.

MRS. RACK. Not go! Foolish creature! you are arrived at the moment which some time or other was sure to happen; and everything depends on the use you make of it.

MISS OGLE. Come, Lady Frances! don't hesitate!—the minutes are precious.

LADY FRAN. I could find in my heart!—and yet I won't give up neither.—If I should in this instance, he'll expect it for ever. *(Exeunt Lady Frances and Mrs. Racket.)*

Miss Ogle. Now you act like a Woman of Spirit. *(Exit Miss Ogle and Mrs. Racket.)*

Flut. A fair tug, by Jupiter—between Duty and Pleasure!—Pleasure beats, and off we go, *Iö triumphe!*[26] *(Exit Flutter.)*

(Scene changes to an auction room.—Busts, pictures, &'c. &'c. Enter Silvertongue with three Puffers.[27])

Sil. Very well,—very well.—This morning will be devoted to curiosity; my sale begins tomorrow at eleven. But, Mrs. Fagg, if you do no better than you did in Lord Fillagree's sale, I shall discharge you.—You want a knack terribly: and this dress—why, nobody can mistake you for a gentlewoman.

Fag. Very true, Mr. Silvertongue; but I can't dress like a lady upon half-a-crown a day, as the saying is—If you want me to dress like a lady, you must double my pay.—Double or quits, Mr. Silvertongue.

Silv. —*Five shillings* a day! what a demand! Why, Woman, there are a thousand parsons in the town who don't make five shillings a day; though they preach, pray, christen, marry, and bury for the good of the community.—Five shillings a day!—why, 'tis the pay of a lieutenant in a marching regiment, who keeps a servant, a mistress, a horse; fights, dresses, ogles, makes love, and dies upon five shillings a day.

Fag. Oh, as to that, all that's very right. A soldier should not be too fond of life; and forcing him to do all these things upon five shillings a day is the readiest way to make him tired on't.

Silv. Well, Mask, have you been looking into the antiquaries?—have you got all the terms of art in a string—aye?

Mask. Yes, I have: I know the age of a coin by the taste; and can fix the birthday of a medal, *Anno Mundi* or *Anno Domini,* though the green rust should have eaten up every character. But you know, the brown suit and the wig I wear when I personate the antiquary are in Limbo.

Silv. Those you have on, may do.

Mask. These!—Why, in these I am a young travelled *cognoscento:* Mr. Glib bought them of Sir Tom Totter's valet; and I am going there directly. You know his picture-sale comes on today; and I have got my head full of Parmegiano, Sal Rosa, Metzu, Tarbaek, and Vandermeer. I talk of the relief of Woovermans, the spirit of Teniers, the coloring of the Venetian School, and the correctness of the Roman. I distinguish Claude by his sleep, and Ruysdael by his water. The rapidity of Tintoret's pencil strikes me at the first glance; whilst the harmony of Vandyck and the glow of Correggio point out their masters.[28]

(Enter company.)

LADY. Hey-day, Mr. Silvertongue! what, nobody here!

SILV. Oh, my Lady, we shall have company enough in a trice; if your carriage is seen at my door, no other will pass it, I am sure.

LADY. Familiar Monster! *(Aside.)* That's a beautiful Diana, Mr. Silvertongue; but in the name of wonder, how came Actæon to be placed on the top of a house?

SILV. That's a David and Bathsheba, Ma'am.

LADY. Oh, I crave their pardon!—I remember the names, but know nothing of the story.[29]

(More company enters.)

GENT. Was not that Lady Frances Touchwood, coming up with Mrs. Racket?

2D GENT. I think so;—yes, it is, faith.—Let us go nearer.

(Enter Lady Frances, Mrs. Racket, and Miss Ogle.)

SILV. Yes, Sir, this is to be the first lot:—the model of a city, in wax.

2D GENT. The model of a city! What city?

SILV. That I have not been able to discover; but call it Rome, Pekin, or London, 'tis still a city: you'll find in it the same jarring interests, the same passions, the same virtues, and the same vices, whatever the name.

GENT. You may as well present us a map of *Terra Incognita*.

SILV. Oh, pardon me, Sir! a lively imagination would convert this waxen city into an endless and interesting amusement. For instance—look into this little house on the right-hand; there are four old prudes in it, taking care of their neighbors' reputations. This elegant mansion on the left, decorated with Corinthian pillars—who needs be told that it belongs to a Court Lord, and is the habitation of patriotism, philosophy, and virtue? Here's a City Hall—the rich steams that issue from the windows nourish a neighboring workhouse. Here's a church—we'll pass over that, the doors are shut. The parsonage-house comes next;— we'll take a peep here, however.—Look at the doctor![30] he's asleep on a volume of Toland; whilst his lady is putting on *rouge* for the masquerade.—Oh! oh! this can be no English city; our parsons are all orthodox, and their wives the daughters of modesty and meekness.

(Lady Frances and Miss Ogle come forward, followed by Courtall.)

LADY FRAN. I wish Sir George was here.—This man follows me about, and stares at me in such a way that I am quite uneasy.

MISS OGLE. He has travelled and is heir to an immense estate; so he's impertinent by patent.

COURT. You are very cruel, Ladies. Miss Ogle—you will not let me speak to you. As to this little scornful beauty, she has frowned me dead fifty times.

LADY FRAN. Sir—I am a married woman. *(Confused.)*

COURT. A married woman! a good hint. *(Aside.)* 'Twould be a shame if such a charming woman was not married. But I see you are a Daphne just come from your sheep and your meadows, your crook and your waterfalls. Pray now, who is the happy Damon to whom you have vowed eternal truth and constancy?[31]

MISS OGLE. 'Tis Lady Frances Touchwood, Mr. Courtall, to whom you are speaking.

COURT. Lady Frances! By Heaven, that's Saville's old flame. *(Aside.)* I beg Your Ladyship's pardon. I ought to have believed that such beauty could belong only to your name—a name I have long been enamored of; because I knew it to be that of the finest woman in the world.

(Mrs. Racket comes forward.)

LADY FRAN *(apart)*. My dear Mrs. Racket, I am so frightened! Here's a man making love to me, though he knows I am married.

Mrs. Rack. Oh, the sooner for that, my dear; don't mind him. Was you at the *Cassino* last night, Mr. Courtall?

Court. I looked in.—'Twas impossible to stay. Nobody there but antiques. You'll be at Lady Brilliant's tonight, doubtless?

Mrs. Rack. Yes, I go with Lady Frances.

Lady Fran. Bless me! I did not know this gentleman was acquainted with Mrs. Racket.—I behaved so rude to him! *(To Miss Ogle.)*

Mrs. Rack. Come, Ma'am; *(Looking at her watch.)* 'tis past one. I protest, if we don't fly to Kensington, we sha'n't find a soul there.

Lady Fran. Won't this gentleman go with us?

Court *(looking surprised)*. To be sure, you make me happy, Madam, beyond description.

Mrs. Rack. Oh, never mind him—he'll follow.

(Exit Lady Frances, Mrs. Racket, and Miss Ogle.)

Court. Lady *Touchwood!* with a vengeance! But 'tis always so;—your reserved ladies are like ice, 'egad!—no sooner begin to soften, than they melt. *(Following.)*

ACT III.

Scene i. Mr. Hardy's.

(Enter Letitia and Mrs. Racket.)

MRS. RACKET. Come, prepare, prepare; your lover is coming.

LETIT. My lover!—Confess now that my absence at dinner was a severe mortification to him.

MRS. RACK. I can't absolutely swear it spoilt his appetite; he eat as if he was hungry, and drank his wine as though he liked it.

LETIT. What was the apology?

MRS. RACK. That you were ill;—but I gave him a hint that your extreme bashfulness could not support his eye.

LETIT. If I comprehend him, awkwardness and bashfulness are the last faults he can pardon in a woman; so expect to see me transformed into the veriest maukin.³²

MRS. RACK. You persevere then?

LETIT. Certainly. I know the design is a rash one, and the event important;—it either makes Doricourt mine by all the tenderest ties of passion, or deprives me of him for ever; and never to be his wife will afflict me less than to be his wife and not be beloved.

MRS. RACK. So you wo'n't trust to the good old maxim—"Marry first, and love will follow"?

LETIT. As readily as I would venture my last guinea, that good fortune might follow. The woman that has not touched the heart of a man before he leads her to the altar has scarcely a chance to charm it when possession and security turn their powerful arms against her.—But here he comes.—I'll disappear for a moment.—Don't spare me. *(Exit Letitia.)*

(Enter Doricourt, not seeing Mrs. Racket.)

DORIC. So! *(Looking at a picture.)* this is my mistress, I

presume.—*Ma foi!* the painter has hit her off.—The downcast
eye—the blushing cheek—timid—apprehensive—bashful.—A
tear and a prayer-book would have made her *La Bella
Magdalena.*—[33]

Give *me* a woman in whose touching mien
A mind, a soul, a polished art is seen;
Whose motion speaks, whose poignant air can move.
Such are the darts to wound with endless love.

MRS. RACK. Is that an impromptu? *(Touching him on the shoulder
with her fan.)*

DORIC *(starting).* Madam!—*(Aside.)* Finely caught!—Not absolutely—it struck me during the dessert, as a motto for your picture.

MRS. RACK. Gallantly turned! I perceive, however, Miss Hardy's
charms have made no violent impression on you.—And who
can wonder?—the poor girl's defects are so obvious.

DORIC. Defects!

MRS. RACK. Merely those of education.—Her father's indulgence
ruined her.—*Mauvaise honte*[34]—conceit and ignorance—all
unite in the lady you are to marry.

DORIC. Marry!—I marry such a woman!—Your picture, I hope, is
overcharged.—I marry *mauvaise honte,* pertness and ignorance!

MRS. RACK. Thank your stars that ugliness and ill temper are not
added to the list.—You must think her handsome?

DORIC. Half her personal beauty would content me; but could the
Medicean Venus[35] be animated for me, and endowed with a
vulgar soul, *I* should become the statue, and my heart transformed to marble.

MRS. RACK. Bless us!—We are in a hopeful way then!

DORIC *(aside).* There must be some envy in this!—I see she is a coquette. Ha, ha, ha! And you imagine I am persuaded of the
truth of your character? ha, ha, ha! Miss Hardy, I have been assured, Madam, is elegant and accomplished:—but one must allow for a lady's painting.

MRS. RACK *(aside).* I'll be even with him for that. Ha! ha! ha! and
so you have found me out!—Well, I protest I meant no harm;
'twas only to increase the *éclat* of her appearance, that I threw

a veil over her charms.—Here comes the lady;—her elegance and accomplishments will announce themselves.

(Enter Letitia, running.)

LET. La! Cousin, do you know that our John—oh, dear heart!—I didn't see you, Sir. *(Hanging down her head, and dropping behind Mrs. Racket.)*

MRS. RACK. Fye, Letitia! Mr. Doricourt thinks you a woman of elegant manners. Stand forward, and confirm his opinion.

LET. No, no; keep before me—He's my sweetheart; and 'tis imprudent to look one's sweetheart in the face, you know.

MRS. RACK. You'll allow in future for a lady's painting, Sir. Ha! ha! ha!

DORIC. I am astonished!

LET. Well, hang it, I'll take heart.—Why, he is but a man, you know, Cousin;—and I'll let him see I wasn't born in a wood to be feared by an owl. *(Half apart; advances, and looks at him through her fingers.)* He! he! he! *(Goes up to him, and makes a very stiff formal curtsy.)—(He bows.)*—You have been a great traveller, Sir, I hear?

DOR. Yes, Madam.

LET. Then I wish you'd tell us about the fine sights you saw when you went over-sea.—I have read in a book that there are some countries where the men and women are all horses.[36]—Did you see any of them?

MRS. RACK. Mr. Doricourt is not prepared, my dear, for these enquiries; he is reflecting on the importance of the question, and will answer you—when he can.

LET. When he can! Why, he's as slow in speech as Aunt Margery, when she's reading Thomas Aquinas;—and stands gaping like mum-chance.[37]

MRS. RACK. Have a little discretion.

LET. Hold your tongue!—Sure I may say what I please before I am married, if I can't afterwards.—D'ye think a body does not know how to talk to a sweetheart. He is not the first I have had.

DOR. Indeed!

LET. Oh, Lud! He speaks!—Why, if you must know—there was a curate at home:—when Papa was a-hunting, he used to come a-suitoring, and make speeches to me out of books.—Nobody knows what a *mort* of fine things he used to say to me;—and call me Venis, and Jubah, and Dinah![38]

DOR. And pray, fair Lady, how did you answer him?

LET. Why, I used to say, Look you, Mr. Curate, don't think to come over me with your flim-flams; for a better man than ever trod in your shoes is coming over-sea to marry me;—but, isags! I begin to think I was out.—Parson Dobbins was the sprightfuller man of the two.

DOR. Surely this cannot be Miss Hardy!

LET. Laws! why, don't you know me! You saw me today—but I was daunted before my father, and the lawyer, and all them, and did not care to speak out:—so, may be, you thought I couldn't;—but I can talk as fast as anybody, when I know folks a little:—and now I have shown my parts, I hope you'll like me better.

(Enter Hardy.)

HAR. I foresee this won't do!—Mr. Doricourt, may be you take my daughter for a fool; but you are mistaken: she's a sensible girl as any in England.

DOR. I am convinced she has a very uncommon understanding, Sir. *(Aside.)* I did not think he had been such an ass.

LET. My father will undo the whole.—Laws! Papa, how can you think he can take me for a fool! when everybody knows I beat the potecary at conundrums last Christmas-time? and didn't I make a string of names, all in riddles, for the Lady's Diary?— There was a little river, and a great house; that was Newcastle.—There was what a lamb says, and three letters; that was *Ba*, and *k-e-r*, ker, Baker.—There was—

HARDY. Don't stand ba-a-ing there. You'll make me mad in a moment!—I tell you, Sir, that for all that, she's dev'lish sensible.

DORIC. Sir, I give all possible credit to your assertions.

LETIT. Laws! Papa, do come along. If you stand watching, how can my sweetheart break his mind, and tell me how he admires me?

DORIC. That would be difficult, indeed, Madam.

HARDY. I tell you, Letty, I'll have no more of this.—I see well enough—

LETIT. Laws! don't snub me before my husband—that is is to be.—You'll teach him to snub me too,—and I believe, by his looks, he'd like to begin now.—So, let us go, Cousin; you may tell the gentleman what a genus I have—how I can cut watch-papers and work catgut; make quadrille-baskets with pins and take profiles in shade; ay, as well as the lady at No. 62, South Moulton Street, Grosvenor Square.[39] *(Ex. Hardy and Letitia.)*

MRS. RACK. What think you of my painting, now?

DORIC. Oh, mere water-colors, Madam! The lady has caricatured your picture.

MRS. RACK. And how does she strike you on the whole?

DORIC. Like a good design, spoilt by the incapacity of the artist. Her faults are evidently the result of her father's weak indulgence. I observed an expression in her eye that seemed to satirise the folly of her lips.

MRS. RACK. But at her age, when education is fixed, and manner become Nature—hopes of improvement—

DORIC. Would be as rational as hopes of gold from a juggler's[40] crucible.—Doricourt's wife must be incapable of improvement; but it must be because she's got beyond it.

MRS. RACK. I am pleased your misfortune sits no heavier.

DORIC. Your pardon, Madam; so mercurial was the hour in which I was born that misfortunes always go plump to the bottom of my heart, like a pebble in water, and leave the surface unruffled.—I shall certainly set off for Bath, or the other world, tonight;—but whether I shall use a chaise with four swift coursers, or go off in a tangent—from the aperture of a pistol, deserves consideration; so I make my *adieus. (Going.)*

MRS. RACK. Oh, but I entreat you, postpone your journey 'till tomorrow; determine on which you will—you must be this night at the masquerade.

DORIC. Masquerade!

MRS. RACK. Why not?—If you resolve to visit the other world, you may as well take one night's pleasure first in this, you know.

DORIC. Faith, that's very true; ladies are the best philosophers, after all. Expect me at the masquerade. *(Exit Doricourt.)*

MRS. RACK. He's a charming fellow!—I think Letitia sha'n't have him. *(Going.)*

(Enter Hardy.)

HARDY. What's [What, is] he gone?
MRS. RACK. Yes; and I am glad he is. You would have ruined
us!—Now, I beg, Mr. Hardy, you won't interfere in this business; it is a little out of your way. *(Exit Mrs. Racket.)*
HARDY. Hang me if I don't, though. I foresee very clearly what
will be the end of it, if I leave ye to yourselves; so, I'll e'en follow him to the masquerade and tell him all about it: Let me
see.—What shall my dress be? A Great Mogul? No.—A grena-
dier? No;—no, that, I foresee, would make a laugh. Hang me,
if I don't send to my favorite little Quick, and borrow his Jew
Isaac's dress:⁴¹—I know the dog likes a glass of good wine; so
I'll give him a bottle of my forty-eight, and he shall teach me.
Aye, that's it—I'll be Cunning Little Isaac! If they complain of
my want of wit, I'll tell 'em the cursed Duenna wears the
breeches, and has spoilt my parts. *(Exit Hardy.)*

Scene ii. Courtall's.

*(Enter Courtall, Saville, and three others, from an apartment in
the back scene. The last three tipsy.)*

COURT. You shan't go yet:—Another catch, and another bottle!
FIRST GENT. May I be a bottle, and an empty bottle, if you catch
me at that!—Why, I am going to the masquerade. Jack—, you
know who I mean, is to meet me, and we are to have a leap at
the new lustres.
SECOND GENT. And I am going too—a Harlequin—*(Hiccups.)* Am
not I in a pretty pickle to make harlequinades?—And Tony,
here—he is going in the disguise—in the disguise—of a gentleman!
FIRST GENT. We are all very disguised;⁴² so bid them draw up—
D'ye hear!

(Exeunt the three Gentlemen.)

SAV. Thy skull, Courtall, is a lady's thimble:—no, an egg-shell.
COURT. Nay, then you are gone too; you never aspire to similes,
but in your cups.

SAV. No, no; I am steady enough—but the fumes of the wine pass directly through thy egg-shell, and leave thy brain as cool as— Hey! I am quite sober; my similes fail me.

COURT. Then we'll sit down here and have one sober bottle.— Bring a table and glasses.

SAV. I'll not swallow another drop; no, though the juice should be the true Falernian.[43]

COURT. By the bright eyes of her you love, you shall drink her health.

SAV. Ah! *(Sitting down.)* Her I loved is gone *(Sighing.)*—She's married!

COURT. Then bless your stars you are not her husband! I would be husband to no woman in Europe, who was not dev'lish rich, and dev'lish ugly.

SAV. Wherefore ugly?

COURT. Because she could not have the conscience to exact those attentions that a pretty wife expects; or, if she should, her resentments would be perfectly easy to me, nobody would undertake to revenge her cause.

SAV. Thou art a most licentious fellow!

COURT. I should hate my own wife, that's certain; but I have a warm heart for those of other people; and so here's to the prettiest wife in England—Lady Frances Touchwood.

SAV. Lady Frances Touchwood! I rise to drink her. *(Drinks.)* How the devil came Lady Frances in your head? I never knew you give[44] a woman of chastity before.

COURT. That's odd, for you have heard me give half the women of fashion in England.—But, pray now, what do you take a woman of chastity to be? *(Sneeringly.)*

SAV. Such a woman as Lady Frances Touchwood, Sir.

COURT. Oh, you are grave, Sir; I remember you was an adorer of hers—Why didn't you marry her?

SAV. I had not the arrogance to look so high—Had my fortune been worthy of her, she should not have been ignorant of my admiration.

COURT. Precious fellow! What, I suppose you would not dare tell her now that you admire her?

SAV. No, nor you.

COURT. By the Lord, I have told her so.

SAV. Have! Impossible!

COURT. Ha! ha! ha!—Is it so?

SAV. How did she receive the declaration?

COURT. Why, in the old way; blushed, and frowned, and said she was married.

SAV. What amazing things thou art capable of! I could more easily have taken the Pope by the beard than profaned her ears with such a declaration.

COURT. I shall meet her at Lady Brilliant's tonight, where I shall repeat it; and I'll lay my life, under a mask, she'll hear it all without blush or frown.

SAV *(rising)*. 'Tis false, Sir!—She won't.

COURT. She will! *(Rising.)* Nay, I'd venture to lay a round sum, that I prevail on her to go out with me—only to taste the fresh air, I mean.

SAV. Preposterous vanity! From this moment I suspect that half the victories you have boasted, are false and slanderous, as your pretended influence with Lady Frances.

COURT. Pretended!—How should such a fellow as you, now, who never soared beyond a cherry-cheeked daughter of a ploughman in Norfolk, judge of the influence of a man of my figure and habits? I could show thee a list, in which there are names to shake thy faith in the whole sex!—and, to that list I have no doubt of adding the name of Lady—

SAV. Hold, Sir! My ears cannot bear the profanation;—you cannot—dare not approach her!—For your soul you dare not mention love to her! Her look would freeze the word, whilst it hovered on thy licentious lips!

COURT. Whu! whu! Well, we shall see—this evening, by Jupiter, the trial shall be made—If I fail—I fail.

SAV. I think thou darest not!—But my life, my honor on her purity. *(Exit Saville.)*

COURT. Hot-headed fool! But since he has brought it to this point, by Gad I'll try what can be done with her Ladyship *(Musing.)*— *(Rings.)* She's frost-work, and the prejudices of education yet strong: *ergo,* passionate professions will only inflame her pride and put her on her guard.—For other arts then!

(Enter Dick.)

Dick, do you know any of the servants at Sir George Touch-wood's?

DICK. Yes, Sir; I knows the groom, and one of the housemaids: for the matter-o'-that, she's my own cousin; and it was my mother that helped her to the place.

COURT. Do you know Lady Frances's maid?

DICK. I can't say as how I know she.

COURT. Do you know Sir George's valet?

DICK. No, Sir; but Sally is very thick with Mr. Gibson, Sir George's gentleman.

COURT. Then go there directly, and employ Sally to discover whether her master goes to Lady Brilliant's this evening; and, if he does, the name of the shop that sold his habit.

DICK. Yes, Sir.

COURT. Be exact in your intelligence, and come to me at Boo-dle's.[45] *(Exit Dick.)* If I cannot otherwise succeed, I'll beguile her as Jove did Alcmena, in the shape of her husband. The pos-session of so fine a woman—the triumph over Saville, are each a sufficient motive; and united, they shall be resistless. *(Exit Courtall.)*

Scene iii. The Street.

(Enter Saville.)

SAV. The air has recovered me! What have I been doing! Perhaps my petulance may be the cause of *her* ruin, whose honor I asserted:—his vanity is piqued;—and where women are con-cerned, Courtall can be a villain.

(Enter Dick. Bows, and passes hastily.)

Ha! that's his Servant!—Dick!

DICK *(returning)*. Sir.

SAV. Where are you going, Dick?

DICK. Going! I am going, Sir, where my master sent me.

SAV. Well answered;—but I have a particular reason for my en-quiry, and you must tell me.

DICK. Why then, Sir, I am going to call upon a cousin of mine, that lives at Sir George Touchwood's.

SAV. Very well.—There, *(Gives him money.)* you must make your cousin drink my health.—What are you going about?

DICK. Why, Sir, I believe 'tis no harm, or elseways I am sure I would not blab.—I am only going to ax if Sir George goes to the masquerade tonight, and what dress he wears.

SAV. Enough! Now, Dick, if you will call at my lodgings in your way back, and acquaint me with your cousin's intelligence, I'll double the trifle I have given you.

DICK. Bless your honor, I'll call—never fear. *(Exit Dick.)*

SAV. Surely the occasion may justify the means:—'tis doubly my duty to be Lady Frances's protector. Courtall, I see, is planning an artful scheme; but Saville shall out-plot him. *(Exit Saville.)*

Scene iv. Sir George Touchwood's

(Enter Sir George and Villers.)

VILL. For shame, Sir George! you have left Lady Frances in tears.—How can you afflict her?

SIR GEO. 'Tis I that am afflicted;—my dream of happiness is over.—Lady Frances and I are disunited.

VILL. The Devil! Why, you have been in town but ten days: she can have made no acquaintance for a Commons affair[46] yet.

SIR GEO. Pho! 'tis our minds that are disunited: she no longer places her whole delight in me; she has yielded herself up to the world!

VILL. Yielded herself up to the world! Why did you not bring her to town in a cage? Then she might have taken a peep at the world!—But, after all, what has the world done? A twelve-month since you was the gayest fellow in it:—If any body asked who dresses best?—Sir George Touchwood.—Who is the most gallant man? Sir George Touchwood.—Who is the most wedded to amusement and dissipation? Sir George Touchwood.—And now Sir George is metamorphosed into a sour censor, and talks of fashionable life with as much bitterness as the old crabbed fellow in Rome.

SIR GEO. The moment I became possessed of such a jewel as Lady Frances, everything wore a different complexion: that society in which I lived with so much *éclat,* became the object of my terror; and I think of the manners of polite life as I do of the atmosphere of a pest-house.—My wife is already infected; she was set upon this morning by maids, widows, and bachelors, who carried her off in triumph, in spite of my displeasure.

VILL. Aye, to be sure; there would have been no triumph in the case, if you had not opposed it:—but I have heard the whole story from Mrs. Racket; and I assure you, Lady Frances didn't enjoy the morning at all;—she wished for you fifty times.

SIR GEO. Indeed! Are you sure of that?

VILL. Perfectly sure.

SIR GEO. I wish I had known it:—my uneasiness at dinner was occasioned by very different ideas.

VILL. Here then she comes, to receive your apology; but if she is true woman, her displeasure will rise in proportion to your contrition;—and till you grow careless about her pardon, she won't grant it:—however, I'll leave you.—Matrimonial duets are seldom set in the style I like. *(Exit Villers.)*

(Enter Lady Frances.)

SIR GEO. The sweet sorrow that glitters in these eyes, I cannot bear. *(Embracing her.)* Look cheerfully, you rogue.

LADY FRAN. I cannot look otherwise, if you are pleased with me.

SIR GEO. Well, Fanny, today you made your *entrée* in the fashionable world; tell me honestly the impressions you received.

LADY FRAN. Indeed, Sir George, I was so hurried from place to place that I had not time to find out what my impressions were.

SIR GEO. That's the very spirit of the life you have chosen.

LADY FRAN. Everybody about me seemed happy—but everybody seemed in a hurry to be happy somewhere else.

SIR GEO. And you like this?

LADY FRAN. One must like what the rest of the world likes.

SIR GEO. Pernicious maxim!

LADY FRAN. But, my dear Sir George, you have not promised to go with me to the masquerade.

SIR GEO. 'Twould be a shocking indecorum to be seen together, you know.

LADY FRAN. Oh, no; I asked Mrs. Racket, and she told me we might be seen together at the masquerade—without being laughed at.

SIR GEO. Really?

Lady Fran. Indeed, to tell you the truth, I could wish it was the fashion for married people to be inseparable; for I have more heart-felt satisfaction in fifteen minutes with you at my side than fifteen days of amusement could give me without you.

Sir Geo. My sweet Creature! How that confession charms me!— Let us begin the fashion.

Lady Fran. O, impossible! We should not gain a single proselyte; and you can't conceive what spiteful things would be said of us.—At Kensington today a lady met us, whom we saw at Court when we were presented; she lifted up her hands in amazement!—Bless me! said she to her companion, here's Lady Frances without Sir Hurlo Thrumbo!⁴⁷—My dear Mrs. Racket, consider what an important charge you have! for Heaven's sake take her home again, or some enchanter on a flying dragon will descend and carry her off.—Oh, said another, I dare say Lady Frances has a clue at her heel, like the peerless Rosamond:—her tender swain would never have trusted her so far without such a precaution.

Sir Geo. Heaven and Earth!—How shall Innocence preserve its lustre amidst manners so corrupt!—My dear Fanny, I feel a sentiment for thee at this moment, tenderer than love—more animated than passion.—I could weep over that purity, exposed to the sullying breath of Fashion, and the *Ton,* in whose latitudinary vortex Chastity herself can scarcely move unspotted.

(Enter Gibson.)

Gib. Your Honor talked, I thought, something about going to the masquerade?

Sir Geo. Well.

Gib. Isn't it?—hasn't Your Honor?—I thought Your Honor had forgot to order a dress.

Lady Fran. Well considered, Gibson.—Come, will you be Jew, Turk, or Heretic; a Chinese Emperor, or a ballad-singer; a rake, or a watchman?

Sir Geo. Oh, neither, my Love; I can't take the trouble to support a character.

Lady Fran. You'll wear a domino then:—I saw a pink domino

trimmed with blue at the shop where I bought my habit.—
Would you like it?

SIR GEO. Anything, anything.

LADY FRAN. Then go about it directly, Gibson.—A pink domino
trimmed with blue, and a hat of the same—Come, you have not
seen my dress yet—it is most beautiful; I long to have it on.

(Exeunt Sir George and Lady Frances.)

GIB. A pink domino trimmed with blue, and a hat of the same—
What the Devil can it signify to Sally now what his dress is to
be?—Surely the slut has not made an assignation to meet her
master! *(Exit Gibson.)*

ACT IV.

Scene i. A masquerade.

(A party dancing cotillions in front—a variety of characters pass and repass. Enter Folly on a hobby-horse, with cap and bells.)

MASK. Hey! Tom Fool! what business have you here?

FOLL. What, Sir! Affront a prince in his own dominions! *(Struts off.)*

MOUNTEBANK. Who'll buy my nostrums? Who'll buy my nostrums?

MASK. What are they? *(They all come round him.)*

MOUNT. Different sorts, and for different customers. Her's a liquor for ladies—it expels the rage of gaming and gallantry. Here's a pill for Members of Parliament—good to settle consciences. Here's an eye-water for jealous husbands—it thickens the visual membrane, through which they see too clearly. Here's a decoction for the clergy—it never sits easy if the patient has more than one living. Here's a draught for lawyers, great promoter of modesty. Here's a powder for projectors—'twil rectify the fumes of an empty stomach and dissipate their airy castles.

MASK. Have you a nostrum that can give patience to young heirs whose uncles and fathers are stout and healthy?

MOUNT. Yes; and I have an infusion for creditors—it gives resignation and humility, when fine gentlemen break their promises or plead their privilege.[48]

MASK. Come along:—I'll find you customers for your whole cargo.

(Enter Hardy, in the dress of Isaac Mendoza.)

HARDY. Why, isn't it a shame to see so many stout, well-built young fellows masquerading and cutting *Courantas* here at home—instead of making the French cut capers to the tune of your cannon—or sweating the Spaniards with an English *Fandango?*[49]—I foresee the end of all this.

MASK. Why, thou little testy Israelite! back to Duke's Place, and preach your tribe into a subscription for the good of the land on whose milk and honey ye fatten.—Where are your Joshuas and your Gideons, aye? What! all dwindled into stockbrokers, peddlers, and rag-men?

HAR. No, not all. Some of us turn Christians, and by degrees grow into all the privileges of Englishmen! In the second generation we are patriots, rebels, courtiers, and husbands. *(Puts his fingers to his forehead.)*

(Two other Masks advance.)

3D MASK. What, my little Isaac!—How the Devil came you here? Where's your old Margaret?

HAR. Oh, I have got rid of her.

3D MASK. How?

HAR. Why, I persuaded a young Irishman that she was a blooming plump beauty of eighteen; so they made an elopement, ha! ha! ha! and she is now the toast of Tipperary. Ha! there's Cousin Racket and her party; they sha'n't know me. *(Puts on his Mask.)*

(Enter Mrs. Racket, Lady Frances, Sir George, and Flutter.)

MRS. RACK. Look at this dumpling Jew; he must be a Levite by his figure. You have surely practised the flesh-hook a long time, friend, to have raised that goodly presence.

HAR. About as long, my brisk widow, as you have been angling for a second husband; but my hook has been better baited than yours.—You have only caught gudgeons, I see. *(Pointing to Flutter.)*

FLUT. Oh! this is one of the geniuses they hire to entertain the company with their accidental sallies.—Let me look at your commonplace book, friend.—I want a few good things.

HAR. I'd oblige you, with all my heart; but you'll spoil them in repeating—or, if you should not, they'll gain you no reputation—for nobody will believe they are your own.

Sir Geo. He knows ye, Flutter;—the little gentleman fancies him-self a wit, I see.

Har. There's no depending on what you see—the eyes of the jeal-ous are not to be trusted.—Look to your lady.

Flut. He knows ye, Sir George.

Sir Geo. What! am I the Town-talker? *(Aside.)*

Har. I can neither see Doricourt nor Letty—I must find them out. *(Exit Hardy.)*

Mrs. Rack. Well, Lady Frances, is not all this charming? Could you have conceived such a brilliant assemblage of objects?

Lady Fran. Delightful! The days of enchantment are restored; the columns glow with sapphires and rubies. Emperors and fairies, beauties and dwarfs meet me at every step.

Sir Geo. How lively are first impressions on sensible[50] minds! In four hours, vapidity and langor will take place of that exquisite sense of joy which flutters your little heart.

Mrs. Rack. What an inhuman creature! Fate has not allowed us these sensations above ten times in our lives; and would you have us shorten them by anticipation?

Flut. O Lord! your wise men are the greatest fools upon earth:—they reason about their enjoyments and analyze their pleasures, whilst the essence escapes. Look, Lady Frances: D'ye see that figure strutting in the dress of an emperor? His father retails or-anges in Botolph Lane. That gypsy is a Maid of Honor, and that rag-man a physician.

Lady Fran. Why, you know everybody.

Flut. Oh, every creature.—A mask is nothing at all to me.—I can give you the history of half the people here. In the next apart-ment there's a whole family who, to my knowledge, have lived on watercresses this month, to make a figure here tonight;—but, to make up for that, they'll cram their pockets with cold ducks and chickens for a carnival tomorrow.

Lady Fran. Oh, I should like to see this provident family.

Flut. Honor me with your arm.

(Exeunt Flutter and Lady Frances.)

Mrs. Rack. Come, Sir George, you shall be *my* beau.—We'll make the *tour* of the rooms, and meet them. Oh! your pardon, you must follow Lady Frances; or the wit and fine parts of Mr.

Flutter may drive you out of her head. Ha! ha! ha! *(Exit Mrs. Racket.)*

SIR GEO. I was going to follow her, and now I dare not. How can I be such a fool as to be governed by the *fear* of that ridicule which I despise! *(Exit Sir George.)*

(Enter Doricourt, meeting a Mask.)

DORIC. Ha! My Lord!—I thought you had been engaged at Westminster on this important night.

MASK. So I am—I slipt out as soon as Lord Trope got upon his legs; I can *badiner*[51] here an hour or two, and be back again before he is down.—There's a fine figure! I'll address her.

(Enter Letitia.)

Charity, fair Lady! Charity for a poor pilgrim.

LETIT. Charity! If you mean my prayers, Heaven grant thee wit, Pilgrim.

MASK. That blessing would do from a devotee: from you I ask other charities;—such charities as beauty should bestow—soft looks—sweet words—and kind wishes.

LETIT. Alas! I am bankrupt of these, and forced to turn beggar myself.—There he is!—how shall I catch his attention?

MASK. Will you grant me no favor?

LETIT. Yes, one—I'll make you my partner—not for life, but through the soft mazes of a minuet.—Dare you dance?

DORIC. Some spirit in that.

MASK. I dare do anything you command.

DORIC. Do you know her, My Lord?

MASK. No: Such a woman as that would formerly have been known in any disguise; but beauty is now common—Venus seems to have given her *cestus* to the whole sex.

(A minuet.)

DORIC *(during the minuet).* She dances divinely.—*(When ended.)* Somebody must know her! Let us enquire who she is. *(Exit.)*

(Enter Saville and Kitty Willis,[52] habited like Lady Frances.)

SAV. I have seen Courtall in Sir George's habit, though he endeavored to keep himself concealed. Go and seat yourself in the tearoom, and on no account discover your face:—remember too, Kitty, that the woman you are to personate is a woman of virtue.

KITTY. I am afraid I shall find that a difficult character: indeed I believe it is seldom kept up through a whole masquerade.

SAV. Of that *you* can be no judge—Follow my directions, and you shall be rewarded. *(Exit Kitty.)*

(Enter Doricourt.)

DOR. Ha! Saville! Did you see a lady dance just now?

SAV. No.

DOR. Very odd. Nobody knows her.

SAV. Where is Miss Hardy?

DOR. Cutting watch-papers and making conundrums, I suppose.

SAV. What do you mean?

DOR. Faith, I hardly know. She's not here, however, Mrs. Racket tells me.—I asked no further.

SAV. Your indifference seems increased.

DOR. Quite the reverse; 'tis advanced thirty-two degrees towards hatred.

SAV. You are jesting?

DOR. Then it must be with a very ill grace, my dear Saville; for I never felt so seriously: Do you know the creature's almost an idiot?

SAV. What!

DOR. An idiot. What the Devil shall I do with her? Egad! I think I'll feign myself mad—and then Hardy will propose to cancel the engagements.

SAV. An excellent expedient. I must leave you; you are mysterious, and I can't stay to unravel ye.—I came here to watch over innocence and beauty.

DOR. The guardian of innocence and beauty at three and twenty! Is there not a cloven foot under that black gown, Saville?

SAV. No, faith. Courtall is here on a most detestable design.—I found means to get a knowledge of the lady's dress, and have brought a girl to personate her, whose reputation cannot be hurt.—You shall know the result tomorrow. Adieu. *(Exit Saville.)*

DOR *(musing)*. Yes, I think that will do.—I'll feign myself mad, see the doctor to pronounce me incurable, and when the parchments are destroyed— *(As he stands in a musing posture, Letitia enters, and sings.)*

Song.

Wake! thou Son of Dullness, wake!
From thy drowsy senses shake
All the spells that Care employs,
Cheating mortals of their joys

II.
Light-winged Spirits, hither haste!
Who prepare for mortal taste
All the gifts that Pleasure sends,
Every bliss that youth attends.

III.
Touch his feelings, rouse his soul,
Whilst the sparking moments roll;
Bid them wake to new delight,
Crown the magic of the night.

DOR. By Heaven, the same sweet creature!

LET. You have chosen an odd situation for study. Fashion and Taste preside in this spot:—they throw their spells around you:—ten thousand delights spring up at their command;—and you, a Stoic—a being without senses, are wrapt in reflection.

DOR. And you, the most charming being in the world, awake me to admiration. Did you come from the stars?

LET. Yes, and I shall reascend in a moment.

DOR. Pray show me your face before you go.

LET. Beware of imprudent curiosity; it lost Paradise.

DOR. Eve's curiosity was raised by the Devil;—'tis an Angel tempts mine.—So your allusion is not in point.

LET. But *why* would you see my face?

DOR. To fall in love with it.

LET. And what then?

DOR. Why, then—Aye, curse it! there's the rub. *(Aside.)*

LET. Your mistress will be angry;—but, perhaps, you have no mistress?

DOR. Yes, yes; and a sweet one it is!

LET. What! is she old?

DOR. No.

LET. Ugly?

DOR. No.

LET. What then?

DOR. Pho! don't talk about *her;* but show me your face.

LET. My vanity forbids it;—'twould frighten you.

DOR. Impossible! Your shape is graceful, your air bewitching, your bosom transparent, and your chin would tempt me to kiss it, if I did not see a pouting red lip above it, that demands—

LET. You grow too free.

DOR. Show me your face then—only half a glance.

LET. Not for worlds.

DOR. What! you will have a little gentle force? *(Attempts to seize her mask.)*

LET. I am gone for ever! *(Exit.)*

DOR. 'Tis false;—I'll follow to the end. *(Exit.)*

(Flutter, Lady Frances, and Saville advance.)

LADY FRAN. How can you be thus interested for a stranger?

SAV. Goodness will ever interest; its home is Heaven: on earth 'tis but a wanderer. Imprudent lady! why have you left the side of your protector? Where is your husband?

FLUT. Why, what's that to him?

LADY FRAN. Surely it can't be merely his habit;—there's something in him that awes me.

FLUT. Pho! 'tis only his grey beard.—I know him; he keeps a lottery-office on Cornhill.

SAV. My province, as an Enchanter, lays open every secret to me. Lady! there are dangers abroad—Beware! *(Exit.)*

LADY FRAN. 'Tis very odd; his manner has made me tremble. Let us seek Sir George.

FLUT. He is coming towards us.

(Courtall comes forward, habited like Sir George.)

COURT. There she is! If I can but disengage her from that fool Flutter—crown me, ye schemers, with immortal wreaths.

LADY FRAN. O my dear Sir George! I rejoice to meet you—an old conjuror has been frightening me with his prophecies.—Where's Mrs. Racket?

COURT. In the dancing-room.—I promised to send you to her, Mr. Flutter.

FLUT. Ah! she wants me to dance. With all my heart. *(Exit.)*

LADY FRAN. Why do you keep on your mask?—'tis too warm.

COURT. 'Tis very warm—I want air—let us go.

LADY FRAN. You seem quite agitated.—Sha'n't we bid our company adieu?

COURT. No, no;—there's no time for forms. I'll just give directions to the carriage, and be with you in a moment. *(Going, steps back.)* Put on your mask; I have a particular reason for it. *(Exit.)*

(Saville advances with Kitty.)

SAV. Now, Kitty, you know your lesson. Lady Frances, *(Takes off his mask.)* let me lead you to your husband.

LADY FRAN. Heavens! is Mr. Saville the conjuror? Sir George is just stepped to the door to give directions.—We are going home immediately.

SAV. No, Madam, you are deceived: Sir George is this way.

LADY FRAN. This is astonishing!

SAV. Be not alarmed: you have escaped a snare, and shall be in safety in a moment. *(Ex. Saville and Lady Frances.)*

(Enter Courtall, and seizes Kitty's hand.)

COURT. Now!

KITTY. 'Tis pity to go so soon.

COURT. Perhaps I may bring you back, my Angel—but go now, you must. *(Exit.)*

(Music.)

(Doricourt and Letitia come forward.)

DOR. By Heavens! I never was charmed till now.—English beauty—French vivacity—wit—elegance. Your name, my Angel!—tell me your name, though you persist in concealing your face.

LET. My name has a spell in it.

DOR. I thought so; it must be *Charming*.

LET. But if revealed, the charm is broke.

DOR. I'll answer for its force.

LET. Suppose it Harriet, or Charlotte, or Maria, or—

DOR. Hang Harriet, and Charlotte, and Maria—the name your father gave ye!

LET. That can't be worth knowing, 'tis so transient a thing.

DOR. How, transient?

LET. Heaven forbid my name should be *lasting* till I am married.

DOR. Married! The chains of matrimony are too heavy and vulgar for such a spirit as yours.—The flowery wreaths of Cupid are the only bands you should wear.

LET. They are the lightest, I believe: but 'tis possible to wear those of marriage gracefully.—Throw 'em loosely round, and twist 'em in a true-lover's knot for the bosom.

DOR. An Angel! But what will you be when a wife?

LET. A woman.—If my husband should prove a churl, a fool, or a tyrant, I'd break his heart, ruin his fortune, elope with the first pretty fellow that asked me—and return the contempt of the world with scorn, whilst my feelings preyed upon my life.

DOR. Amazing! *(Aside.)* What if you loved him, and he were worthy of your love?

LET. Why, then I'd be anything—and all!—Grave, gay, capricious—the soul of whim, the spirit of variety—live with him in the eye of fashion, or in the shade of retirement—change my country, my sex,—feast with him in an Esquimaux hut, or a Persian pavilion—join him in the victorious war-dance on the borders of Lake Ontario, or sleep to the soft breathings of the flute in the cinnamon groves of Ceylon—dig with him in the mines of Golconda, or enter the dangerous precincts of the Mogul's seraglio—cheat him of his wishes and overturn his empire to restore the husband of my heart to the blessings of Liberty and Love.

Dor. Delightful wildness! Oh, to catch thee, and hold thee for ever in this little cage! *(Attempting to clasp her.)*

Let. Hold, Sir! Though Cupid must give the bait that tempts me to the snare, 'tis Hymen must spread the net to catch me.

Dor. 'Tis in vain to assume airs of coldness—Fate has ordained you mine.

Let. How do you know?

Dor. I feel it *here*. I never met with a woman so perfectly to my taste; and I won't believe it formed you so on purpose to tantalize me.

Let. This moment is worth my whole existence. *(Aside.)*

Dor. Come, show me your face, and rivet my chains.

Let. Tomorrow you shall be satisfied.

Dor. Tomorrow! and not tonight?

Let. No.

Dor. Where then shall I wait on you tomorrow?—Where see you?

Let. You shall see me in an hour when you least expect me.

Dor. Why all this mystery?

Let. I like to be mysterious. At present be content to know that I am a woman of family and fortune. Adieu!

(Enter Hardy.)

Har. Adieu! Then I am come at the fag end. *(Aside.)*

Dor. Let me see you to your carriage.

Let. As you value knowing me, stir not a step. If I am followed, you never see me more. *(Exit.)*

Dor. Barbarous creature! She's gone! What, and is this really serious?—am I in love?—Pho! it can't be—O Flutter! do you know that charming creature?

(Enter Flutter.)

Flut. What charming creature? I passed a thousand.

Dor. She went out at that door, as you entered.

Flut. Oh, yes;—I know her very well.

Dor. Do you, my dear fellow? Who?

Flut. She's kept by Lord George Jennett.

Har. Impudent scoundrel! *(Aside.)*

Dor. Kept!!!

FLUT. Yes; Colonel Gorget had her first;—then Mr. Loveill;—then—I forget exactly how many; and at last she's Lord George's. *(Talks to other masks.)*

DOR. I'll murder Gorget, poison Lord George, and shoot myself.

HAR. Now's the time, I see, to clear up the whole. Mr. Doricourt!—I say—Flutter was mistaken; I know who you are in love with.

DOR. A strange *rencontre!* Who?

HAR. My Letty.

DOR. Oh! I understand your rebuke;—'tis too soon, Sir, to assume the father-in-law.

HAR. Zounds! what do you mean by that? I tell you that the lady you admire is Letitia Hardy.

DOR. I am glad *you* are so well satisfied with the state of my heart.—I wish *I* was. *(Exit.)*

HAR. Stop a moment—Stop, I say! What, you won't? Very well—if I don't play you a trick for this, may I never be a grandfather! I'll plot *with* Letty now, and not against her; aye, hang me if I don't. There's something in my head that shall tingle in his heart.—He shall have a lecture upon impatience, that I foresee he'll be the better for as long as he lives. *(Exit.)*

(Saville comes forward with other masks.)

SAV. Flutter, come with us; we're going to raise a laugh at Courtall's.

FLUT. With all my heart. "Live to Live," was my father's motto: "Live to Laugh," is mine. *(Exit.)*

Scene ii. Courtall's.

(Enter Kitty and Courtall.)

KITTY. Where have you brought me, Sir George? This is not our home.

COURT. 'Tis *my* home, beautiful Lady Frances! *(Kneels, and takes off his mask.)* Oh, forgive the ardency of my passion, which has compelled me to deceive you.

KITTY. Mr. Courtall! what will become of me?

COURT. Oh, say but that you pardon the wretch who adores you.

Did you but know the agonizing tortures of my heart since I had the felicity of conversing with you this morning—or the despair that now—

(Knock.)

KITTY. Oh! I'm undone!

COURT. Zounds! my dear Lady Frances. I am not at home. Rascal! do you hear?—Let no body in; I am not at home.

SERV *(without)*. Sir, I told the gentlemen so.

COURT. Eternal curses! they are coming up. Step into this room, adorable creature! *one* moment; I'll throw them out of the window if they stay three.

(Exit Kitty, through the back scene.)
(Enter Saville, Flutter, and masks.)

FLUT. O Gemini! beg the petticoat's pardon.—Just saw a corner of it.

1ST MASK. No wonder admittance was so difficult. I thought you took us for bailiffs.

COURT. Upon my soul, I am devilish glad to see you—but you perceive how I am circumstanced. Excuse me at this moment.

2D MASK. Tell us who 'tis then.

COURT. Oh, fie!

FLUT. We won't blab.

COURT. I can't, upon honor.—Thus far—She's a woman of the first character and rank. Saville, *(Takes him aside.)* have I influence, or have I not?

SAV. Why, sure, you do not insinuate—

COURT. No, not insinuate, but swear, that she's now in my bedchamber:—by gad, I don't deceive you.—There's generalship, you Rogue! Such an humble, distant, sighing fellow as thou art, at the end of a six-months siege, would have *boasted* of a kiss from her glove.—I only give the signal, and—pop!—she's in my arms.

SAV. What, Lady Fran—

COURT. Hush! You shall see her name tomorrow morning in red letters at the end of my list. Gentlemen, you must excuse me now. Come and drink chocolate at twelve, but—

Sav. Aye, let us go, out of respect to the lady:—'tis a person of rank.

Flut. Is it?—Then I'll have a peep at her. *(Runs to the door in the back scene.)*

Court. This is too much, Sir. *(Trying to prevent him.)*

1st Mask. By Jupiter, we'll all have a peep.

Court. Gentlemen, consider—for Heaven's sake—a lady of quality. What will be the consequences?

Flut. The consequences!—Why, you'll have your throat cut, that's all—but I'll write your elegy. So, now for the door! *(Part open the door, whilst the rest hold Courtall.)*—Beg Your Ladyship's pardon, whoever you are: *(Leads her out.)* Emerge from darkness like the glorious sun, and bless the wondering circle with your charms. *(Takes off her mask.)*

Sav. Kitty Willis! ha! ha! ha!

Omnes. Kitty Willis! ha! ha! ha! Kitty Willis!

1st Mask. Why, what a fellow you are, Courtall, to attempt imposing on your friends in this manner! A lady of quality—an earl's daughter—Your Ladyship's most obedient.—Ha! ha! ha!

Sav. Courtall, have you influence, or have you not?

Flut. The man's moon-struck.

Court. Hell, and ten thousand Furies, seize you all together!

Kitty. What! me, too, Mr. Courtall? me, whom you have knelt to, prayed to, and adored?

Flut. That's right, Kitty; give him a little more.

Court. Disappointed and laughed at!—

Sav. Laughed at and despised. I have fulfilled my design, which was to expose your villainy and laugh at your presumption. Adieu, Sir! Remember how you again boast of your influence with women of rank; and, when you next want amusement, dare not to look up to the virtuous and to the noble for a companion. *(Exit, leading Kitty.)*

Flut. And, Courtall, before you carry a lady into your bedchamber again, look under her mask, d'ye hear? *(Exit.)*

Court. There's no bearing this! I'll set off for Paris directly. *(Exit.)*

ACT V.

Scene i. Hardy's.

(Enter Hardy and Villers.)

VILLERS. Whimsical enough! Dying for her, and hates her; believes her a fool, and a woman of brilliant understanding!

HAR. As true as you are alive;—but when I went up to him last night at the Pantheon, out of downright good-nature to explain things—my gentleman whips round upon his heel, and snapped me as short as if I had been a beggar-woman with six children and he Overseer of the Parish.[53]

VILL. Her comes the wonder-worker—*(Enter Letitia.)* Here comes the enchantress, who can go to masquerades, and sing and dance, and talk a man out of his wits!—But pray, have we morning masquerades?

LET. Oh, no—but I am so enamored of this all-conquering habit that I could not resist putting it on, the moment I had breakfasted. I shall wear it on the day I am married, and then lay it by in spices—like the miraculous robes of St. Bridget.

VIL. That's as most brides do. The charms that helped to catch the husband are generally *laid by,* one after another, 'till the lady grows a downright wife, and then runs crying to her mother, because she has transformed her *lover* into a downright husband.

HAR. Listen to me.—I ha'n't slept tonight, for thinking of plots to plague Doricourt;—and they drove one another out of my head so quick that I was as giddy as a goose, and could make nothing of 'em—I wish to goodness you could contrive something.

VILL. Contrive to plague him! Nothing so easy. Don't undeceive him, Madam, 'till he is your husband. Marry him whilst he possesses the sentiments you labored to give him of Miss Hardy—and when you are his wife—

LET. Oh, Heavens! I see the whole—that's the very thing. My dear Mr. Villers, you are the divinest man.

VILL. Don't make love to me, Hussy.

(Enter Mrs. Racket.)

MRS. RACK. No pray don't—for I design to have Villers myself in about six years.—There's an oddity to him that pleases me.—He holds women in contempt; and I should like to have an opportunity of breaking his heart for that.

VILL. And when I am heartily tired of life, I know no woman whom I would with more pleasure make my executioner.

HAR. It cannot be—I foresee it will be impossible to bring it about. You know the wedding wasn't to take place this week or more—and Letty will never be able to play the fool so long.

VILL. The knot shall be tied tonight—I have it all here, *(Pointing to his forehead.)* the license is ready. Feign yourself ill, send for Doricourt, and tell him you can't go out of the world in peace, except you see the ceremony performed.

HAR. I feign myself ill! I could as soon feign myself a Roman ambassador.—I was never ill in my life, but with the tooth-ache—when Letty's mother was a breeding I had all the qualms.

VILL. Oh, I have no fears for *you*.—But what says Miss Hardy? Are you willing to make the irrevocable vow before night?

LET. Oh, Heavens!—I—I—'Tis so exceeding sudden, that really—

MRS. RACK. That really she is frightened out of her wits—lest it should be impossible to bring matters about. But *I* have taken the scheme into my protection, and you shall be Mrs. Doricourt before night. Come, *(To Mr. Hardy.)* to bed directly: your room shall be crammed with phials, and all the apparatus of Death;—then heigh presto! for Doricourt.

VILL. You go and put off your conquering dress, *(To Letty.)* and get all your awkward airs ready—And you practice a few groans *(To Hardy.)*—And you—if possible—an air of gravity. *(To Mrs. Racket.)* I'll answer for the plot.

LET. Married in jest! 'Tis an odd idea! Well, I'll venture it. *(Ex. Letitia and Mrs. Racket.)*

VILL. Aye, I'll be sworn! *(Looks at his watch.)* 'tis past three. The budget's to be opened this morning. I'll just step down to the House.[54]—Will you go?

HAR. What! with a mortal sickness?

VILL. What a blockhead! I believe, if half of us were to stay away with mortal sickness, it would be for the health of the nation. Good-morning.—I'll call and feel your pulse as I come back. (*Exit.*)

HAR. You won't find 'em over brisk, I fancy. I foresee some ill happening from this making believe to die before one's time. But hang it—a-hem!—I am a stout man yet; only fifty-six— What's that? In the last Yearly Bill[55] there were three lived to above an hundred. Fifty-six!—Fiddle-de-dee! I am not afraid, not I. (*Exit.*)

Scene ii. Doricourt's.

(*Doricourt in his robe-de-chambre.*)

(*Enter Saville.*)

SAV. Undressed so late?

DORIC. I didn't go to bed 'till late—'twas late before I slept—late when I rose. Do you know Lord George Jennett?

SAV. Yes.

DORIC. Has he a mistress?

SAV. Yes.

DORIC. What sort of a creature is she?

SAV. Why, she spends him three thousand a year with the ease of a duchess, and entertains his friends with the grace of a *Ninon.*[56] *Ergo,* she is handsome, spirited, and clever.

(*Doricourt walks about disordered.*)

In the name of caprice, what ails you?

DORIC. You have hit it—*Elle est mon caprice*—The mistress of Lord George Jennett is my caprice—Oh, insufferable!

SAV. What, you saw her at the masquerade?

DORIC. *Saw* her, *loved* her, *died* for her—without knowing her— And now the curse is, I can't hate her.

SAV. Ridiculous enough! All this distress about a kept woman, whom any man may have, I dare swear, in a fortnight—They've been jarring some time.

DORIC. Have her! The sentiment I have conceived for the witch is so unaccountable that, in that line, I cannot bear her idea. Was she a woman of honor, for a wife I could adore her—but, I really believe, if she should send me an assignation, I should hate her.

SAV. Hey-day! This sounds like love. What becomes of poor Miss Hardy?

DORIC. Her name has given me an ague. Dear Saville, how shall I contrive to make old Hardy cancel the engagements! The moiety of the estate which he will forfeit shall be his the next moment, by deed of gift.

SAV. Let me see—Can't you get it insinuated that you are a dev'lish wild fellow; that you are an infidel, and attached to wenching, gaming, and so forth?

DORIC. Aye, such a character might have done some good two centuries back.—But who the devil can it frighten now? I believe it must be the mad scheme, at last.—There, will that do for the grin?

SAV. Ridiculous!—But, how are you certain that the woman who has so bewildered you belongs to Lord George?

DORIC. Flutter told me so.

SAV. Then fifty to one against the intelligence.

DORIC. It must be so. There was a mystery in her manner for which nothing else can account.

(A violent rap.)

Who can this be?

(Saville looks out.)

SAV. The proverb is your answer—'tis Flutter himself. Tip him a scene of the mad-man, and see how it takes.

DORIC. I will—a good way to send it about town. Shall it be of the melancholy kind, or the raving?

SAV. Rant!—rant!—Here he comes.

DORIC. Talk not to me who can pull comets by the beard, and overset an island!

(Enter Flutter.)

There! This is he!—this is he who hast sent my poor soul, without coat or breeches, to be tossed about in ether like a duck-feather! Villain, give me my soul again!

FLUT. Upon my soul I hav'n't got it. *(Exceedingly frightened.)*

SAV. Oh, Mr. Flutter, what a melancholy sight!—I little thought to have seen my poor friend reduced to this.

FLUT. Mercy defend me! What's[57] he mad?

SAV. You see how it is. A cursed Italian lady—Jealousy—gave him a drug; and every full of the moon—

DORIC. Moon! Who dares talk of the moon? The patroness of genius—the rectifier of wits—the—Oh! here she is!—I feel her—she tugs at my brain—she has it—she has it—Oh! *(Exit.)*

FLUT. Well! this is dreadful! exceeding dreadful, I protest. Have you had Monro?[58]

SAV. Not yet. The worthy Miss Hardy—what a misfortune!

FLUT. Aye, very true.—Do they know it?

SAV. Oh, no; the paroxysm seized him but this morning.

FLUT. Adieu! I can't stay. *(Going in great haste.)*

SAV. But you must. *(Holding him.)* Stay, and assist me:—perhaps he'll return again in a moment; and, when he is in this way, his strength is prodigious.

FLUT. Can't indeed—can't upon my soul. *(Exit.)*

SAV. Flutter—Don't make a mistake, now;—remember 'tis Doricourt that's mad. *(Exit.)*

FLUT. Yes—you mad.

SAV. No, no; Doricourt.

FLUT. Egad, I'll say you are both mad, and then I can't mistake. *(Exeunt severally.)*

Scene iii. Sir George Touchwood's.

(Enter Sir George, and Lady Frances.)

SIR GEO. The bird is escaped—Courtall is gone to France.

LADY FRAN. Heaven and earth! Have ye been to seek him?

SIR GEO. Seek him! Aye.

LADY FRAN. How did you get his name? I should never have told it you.

SIR GEO. I learnt it in the first coffee house I entered.—Everybody is full of the story.

LADY FRAN. Thank Heaven! he's gone!—But I have a story for you—The Hardy family are forming a plot upon your friend Doricourt, and we are expected in the evening to assist.

SIR GEO. With all my heart, my Angel; but I can't stay to hear it unfolded. They told me Mr. Saville would be at home in half an hour, and I am impatient to see him. The adventure of last night—

LADY FRAN. Think of it only with gratitude. The danger I was in has overset a new system of conduct that, perhaps, I was too much inclined to adopt. But henceforward, my dear Sir George, you shall be my constant companion, and protector. And, when they ridicule the unfashionable monsters, the felicity of our hearts shall make their satire pointless.

SIR GEO. Charming Angel! You almost reconcile me to Courtall. Hark! here's company. *(Stepping to the door.)* 'Tis your lively widow—I'll step down the back stairs, to escape her. *(Exit Sir George.)*

(Enter Mrs. Racket.)

MRS. RACK. Oh, Lady Frances! I am shocked to death.—Have you received a card from us?

LADY FRAN. Yes; within these twenty minutes.

MRS. RACK. Aye, 'tis of no consequence.—'Tis all over—Doricourt is mad.

LADY FRAN. Mad!

MRS. RACK. My poor Letitia!—Just as we were enjoying ourselves with the prospect of a scheme that was planned for their mutual happiness, in came Flutter, breathless, with the intelligence:—I flew here to know if you had heard it.

LADY FRAN. No, indeed—and I hope it is one of Mr. Flutter's dreams.

(Enter Saville.)

Àpropos; now we shall be informed. Mr. Saville, I rejoice to see you, though Sir George will be disappointed: he's gone to your lodgings.

SAV. I should have been happy to have prevented Sir George. I hope Your Ladyship's adventure last night did not disturb your dreams?

LADY FRAN. Not at all; for I never slept a moment. My escape, and the importance of my obligations to you, employed my thoughts. But we have just had shocking intelligence—Is it true that Doricourt is mad?

SAV. So; the business is done. *(Aside.)* Madam, I am sorry to say that I have just been a melancholy witness of his ravings: he was in the height of a paroxysm.

MRS. RACK. Oh, there can be no doubt of it. Flutter told us the whole history. Some Italian princess gave him a drug, in a box of sweetmeats, sent to him by her own page; and it renders him lunatic every month. Poor Miss Hardy! I never felt so much on any occasion in my life.

SAV. To soften your concern, I will inform you, Madam, that Miss Hardy is less to be pitied than you imagine.

MRS. RACK. Why so, Sir?

SAV. 'Tis rather a delicate subject—but he did not love Miss Hardy.

MRS. RACK. He did love Miss Hardy, Sir, and would have been the happiest of men.

SAV. Pardon me, Madam; his heart was not only free from that lady's chains, but absolutely captivated by another.

MRS. RACK. No, Sir—no. It was Miss Hardy who captivated him. She met him last night at the masquerade, and charmed him in disguise—He professed the most violent passion for her; and a plan was laid, this evening, to cheat him into happiness.

SAV. Ha! ha! ha!—Upon my soul, I must beg your pardon; I have not eaten of the Italian princess's box of sweetmeats, sent by her own page; and yet I am as mad as Doricourt, ha! ha! ha!

MRS. RACK. So it appears—What can all this mean?

SAV. Why, Madam, he is at present in his perfect senses; but he'll lose 'em in ten minutes, through joy.—The madness was only a feint, to avoid marrying Miss Hardy, ha! ha! ha!—I'll carry him the intelligence directly. *(Going.)*

MRS. RACK. Not for worlds. I owe him revenge, now, for what he has made us suffer. You must promise not to divulge a syllable I have told you; and when Doricourt is summoned to Mr. Hardy's, prevail on him to come—madness and all.

Lady Fran. Pray do. I should like to see him showing off, now I am in the secret.

Sav. You must be obeyed; though 'tis inhuman to conceal his happiness.

Mrs. Rack. I am going home; so I'll set you down at his lodgings, and acquaint you, by the way, with our whole scheme. *Allons!*

Sav. I attend you. *(Leading her out.)*

Mrs. Rack. You won't fail us? *(Ex. Saville and Mrs. Racket.)*

Lady Fran. No; depend on us. *(Exit.)*

Scene iv. Doricourt's.

(Doricourt seated, reading.)

Doric *(flings away the book)*. What effect can the morals of fourscore have on a mind torn with passion? *(Musing.)* Is it possible such a soul as hers can support itself in so humiliating a situation? A kept woman! *(Rising.)* Well, well—I am glad it is so—I am glad it is so!

(Enter Saville.)

Sav. What a happy dog you are, Doricourt! I might have been mad, or beggared, or pistoled myself, without its being mentioned—But you, forsooth! the whole female world is concerned for. I reported the state of your brain to five different women—The lip of the first trembled; the white bosom of the second heaved a sigh; the third ejaculated and turned her eye—to the glass; the fourth blessed herself; and the fifth said, whilst she pinned a curl, "Well, now, perhaps, he'll be an amusing companion; his native dullness was intolerable."

Doric. Envy! sheer envy, by the smiles of Hebe!—There are not less than forty pair of the brightest eyes in town will drop crystals when they hear of my misfortune.

Sav. Well, but I have news for you:—Poor Hardy is confined to his bed; they say he is going out of the world by the first post, and he wants to give you his blessing.

Doric. Ill! so ill! I am sorry from my soul. He's a worthy little fellow—if he had not the gift of foreseeing so strongly.

Sav. Well; you must go and take leave.

DORIC. What! to act the lunatic in the dying man's chamber?

SAV. Exactly the thing; and will bring your business to a short issue: for his last commands must be, That you are not to marry his daughter.

DORIC. That's true, by Jupiter!—and yet, hang it, impose upon a poor fellow at so serious a moment!—I can't do it.

SAV. You must, 'faith. I am answerable for your appearance, though it should be in a strait waistcoat. He knows your situation, and seems the more desirous of an interview.

DORIC. I don't like encountering Racket.—She's an arch little devil and will discover the cheat.

SAV. There's a fellow!—Cheated ninety-nine women, and now afraid of the hundredth.

DORIC. And with reason—for that hundredth is a widow. *(Exeunt.)*

Scene v. Hardy's.

(Enter Mrs. Racket and Miss Ogle.)

MISS OGLE. And so Miss Hardy is actually to be married tonight?

MRS. RACK. If her fate does not deceive her. You are apprised of the scheme, and we hope it will succeed.

MISS OGLE. Deuce take her! She's six years younger than I am. *(Aside.)*—Is Mr. Doricourt handsome?

MRS. RACK. Handsome, generous, young, and rich.—There's a husband for ye! Isn't he worth pulling caps for?

MISS OGLE. I' my conscience, the widow speaks as though she'd give cap, ears, and all for him. *(Aside.)* I wonder you didn't try to catch this wonderful man, Mrs. Racket?

MRS. RACK. Really, Miss Ogle, I had not time. Besides, when I marry, so many stout young fellows will hang themselves, that, out of regard to society, in these sad times, I shall postpone it for a few years. This will cost her a new lace—I heard it crack.[59] *(Aside.)*

(Enter Sir George and Lady Frances.)

SIR GEO. Well, here we are.—But where's the Knight of the Woeful Countenance?[60]

Mrs. Rack. Here soon, I hope—for a woeful night it will be without him.

Sir Geo. Oh, fie! do you condescend to pun?

Mrs. Rack. Why not? It requires genius to make a good pun—some men of bright parts can't reach it. I know a lawyer who writes them on the back of his briefs; and says they are of great use—in a dry cause.

(Enter Flutter.)

Flut. Here they come!—Here they come!—Their coach stopped, as mine drove off.

Lady Fran. Then Miss Hardy's fate is at a crisis.—She plays a hazardous game, and I tremble for her.

Sav *(without)*. Come, let me guide you!—This way, my poor friend! Why are you so furious?

Doric *(without)*. The House of Death—to the House of Death!

(Enter Doricourt and Saville.)

Ah! this is the spot!

Lady Fran. How wild and fiery he looks!

Miss Ogle. Now, I think, he looks terrified.

Flut. Poor creature, how his eyes work!

Mrs. Rack. I never saw a madman before—Let me examine him—Will he bite?

Sav. Pray keep out of his reach, Ladies—You don't know your danger. He's like a wild cat, if a sudden thought seizes him.

Sir Geo. You talk like a keeper of wild cats—How much do you demand for showing the monster?

Doric. I don't like this—I must rouse their sensibility. There! there she darts through the air in liquid flames! Down again! Now I have her—Oh, she burns, she scorches!—Oh! she eats into my very heart!

Omnes. Ha! ha! ha!

Mrs. Rack. He sees the apparition of the wicked Italian princess.

Flut. Keep her Highness fast, Doricourt.

Miss Ogle. Give her a pinch, before you let her go.

Doric. I am laughed at!

Mrs. Rack. Laughed at—aye, to be sure; why, I could play the madman better than you.—There! there she is! Now I have her! Ha! ha! ha!

DORIC. I knew that devil would discover me. *(Aside.)* I'll leave the house:—I'm covered with confusion. *(Going.)*

SIR GEO. Stay, Sir—You must not go. 'Twas poorly done, Mr. Doricourt, to affect madness rather than fulfil your engagements.

DORIC. Affect madness!—Saville, what can I do?

SAV. Since you are discovered, confess the whole.

MISS OGLE. Aye, turn evidence, and save yourself.

DORIC. Yes; since my designs have been so unaccountably discovered, I will avow the whole. I cannot love Miss Hardy—and I will never—

SAV. Hold, my dear Doricourt! be not so rash. What will the world say to such—

DORIC. Damn the world! What will the world give me for the loss of happiness? Must I sacrifice my peace to please the world?

SIR GEO. Yes, everything, rather than be branded with dishonor.

LADY FRAN. Though *our* arguments should fail, there *is* a pleader whom you surely cannot withstand—the dying Mr. Hardy supplicates you not to forsake his child.

(Enter Villers.)

VILL. Mr. Hardy requests you to grant him a moment's conversation, Mr. Doricourt, though you should persist to send him miserable to the grave. Let me conduct you to his chamber.

DORIC. Oh, aye, anywhere; to the Antipodes—to the moon— Carry me—Do with me what you will.

MRS. RACK. Mortification and disappointment, then, are specifics in a case of stubbornness—I'll follow, and let you know what passes.

(Exeunt Villers, Doricourt, Mrs. Racket, and Miss Ogle.)

FLUT. Ladies, Ladies, have the charity to take me with you, that I may make no blunder in repeating the story. *(Exit Flutter.)*

LADY FRAN. Sir George, you don't know Mr. Saville. *(Exit Lady Frances.)*

SIR GEO. Ten thousand pardons—but I will not pardon myself, for not observing you. I have been with the utmost impatience at your door twice today.

Sav. I am concerned you had so much trouble, Sir George.

Sir Geo. Trouble! what a word!—I hardly know how to address you; I am distressed beyond measure; and it is the highest proof of my opinion of your honor and the delicacy of your mind, that I open my heart to you.

Sav. What has disturbed you, Sir George?

Sir Geo. Your having preserved Lady Frances in so imminent a danger. Start not, Saville; to protect Lady Frances was my right. You have wrested from me my dearest privilege.

Sav. I hardly know how to answer such a reproach. I cannot apologize for what I have done.

Sir Geo. I do not mean to reproach you; I hardly know what I mean. There is one method by which you may restore peace to me; I cannot endure that my wife should be so infinitely indebted to any man who is less than my brother.

Sav. Pray explain yourself.

Sir Geo. I have a sister, Saville, who is amiable; and you are worthy of her. I shall give her a commission to steal your heart, out of revenge for what you have done.

Sav. I am infinitely honored, Sir George; but—

Sir Geo. I cannot listen to a sentence which begins with so unpromising a word. You must go with us into Hampshire; and, if you see each other with the eyes I do, your felicity will be complete. I know no one to whose heart I would so readily commit the care of my sister's happiness.

Sav. I will attend you to Hampshire, with pleasure; but not on the plan of retirement. Society has claims on Lady Frances that forbid it.

Sir Geo. Claims, Saville!

Sav. Yes, claims; Lady Frances was born to be the ornament of courts. She is sufficiently alarmed not to wander beyond the reach of her protector;—and, from the British Court, the most tenderly-anxious husband could not wish to banish his wife. Bid her keep in her eye the bright example who presides there, the splendor of whose rank yields to the superior lustre of her virtue.

Sir Geo. I allow the force of your argument. Now for intelligence!

(Enter Mrs. Racket, Lady Frances, and Flutter.)

MRS. RACK. Oh! Heavens! do you know—

FLUT. Let me tell the story—As soon as Doricourt—

MRS. RACK. I protest you sha'n't—said Mr. Hardy—

FLUT. No, 'twas Doricourt spoke first—says he—No, 'twas the parson—says he—

MRS. RACK. Stop his mouth, Sir George—he'll spoil the tale.

SIR GEO. Never heed circumstances—the result—the result.

MRS. RACK. No, no; you shall have it in form.—Mr. Hardy performed the sick man like an angel—He sat up in his bed and talked so pathetically that the tears stood in Doricourt's eyes.

FLUT. Aye, stood—they did not drop, but stood.—I shall, in future, be very exact. The parson seized the moment; you know, they never miss an opportunity.

MRS. RACK. Make haste, said Doricourt; if I have time to reflect, poor Hardy will die unhappy.

FLUT. They were got as far as the Day of Judgment,[61] when we slipped out of the room.

SIR GEO. Then, by this time, they must have reached *Amazement*, which, everybody knows, is the end of matrimony.

MRS. RACK. Aye, the Reverend Fathers ended the service with that word, prophetically—to teach the bride what a capricious monster a husband is.

SIR GEO. I rather think it was sarcastically—to prepare the bridegroom for the unreasonable humors and vagaries of his helpmate.

LADY FRAN. Here comes the bridegroom of tonight.

(Enter Doricourt and Villers.—Villers whispers Saville, who gets out.)

OMNES. Joy! joy! joy!

MISS OGLE. If *he's* a sample of bridegrooms, keep me single!—A younger brother, from the funeral of his father, could not carry a more fretful countenance.

FLUT. Oh!—Now, he's melancholy mad, I suppose.

LADY FRAN. You do not consider the importance of the occasion.

VILL. No; nor how shocking a thing it is for a man to be forced to marry one woman, whilst his heart is devoted to another.

MRS. RACK. Well, now 'tis over, I confess to you, Mr. Doricourt, I think 'twas a most ridiculous piece of quixotism, to give up the happiness of a whole life to a man who perhaps has but a few moments to be sensible of the sacrifice.

FLUT. So it appeared to me.—But, thought I, Mr. Doricourt has travelled—he knows best.

DORIC. Zounds! Confusion!—Did ye not all set upon me?—Didn't ye talk to me of honor—compassion—justice?

SIR GEO. Very true—You have acted according to their dictates, and I hope the utmost felicity of the married state will reward you.

DORIC. Never, Sir George! To Felicity I bid adieu—but I will endeavor to be content. Where is my—I must speak it—where is my *wife?*

(Enter Letitia, masked, led by Saville.)

SAV. Mr. Doricourt, this lady was pressing to be introduced to you.

DOR. Oh! *(Starting.)*

LET. I told you last night, you should see me at a time when you least expected me—and I have kept my promise.

VILL. Whoever you are, Madam, you could not have arrived at a happier moment.—Mr. Doricourt is just married.

LET. Married! Impossible! 'Tis but a few hours since he swore to me eternal love: I believed him, gave him up my virgin heart—and now!—Ungrateful Sex!

DOR. Your virgin heart! No, Lady—my fate, thank Heaven! yet wants that torture. Nothing but the conviction that you was another's could have made me think one moment of marriage, to have saved the lives of half mankind. But this visit, Madam, is as barbarous as unexpected. It is now my duty to forget you, which, spite of your situation, I found difficult enough.

LET. My situation!—What situation?

DOR. I must apologise for explaining it in this company—but, Madam, I am not ignorant that you are the companion of Lord George Jennett—and this is the only circumstance that can give me peace.

LET. I—a companion! Ridiculous pretence! No, Sir, know, to your confusion, that my heart, my honor, my name is unspotted as hers you have married; my birth equal to your own, my fortune large—That, and my person, might have been yours.—But, Sir, farewell! *(Going.)*

DOR. Oh, stay a moment—Rascal! is she not—

FLUT. Who, she? O Lard! no—'Twas quite a different person that I meant.—I never saw that lady before.

DOR. Then, never shalt thou see her more. *(Shakes Flutter.)*

MRS. RACK. Have mercy upon the poor man!—Heavens! He'll murder him.

DOR. Murder him! Yes, you, myself, and all mankind. Sir George—Saville—Villers—'twas you who pushed me on this precipice;—'tis you who have snatched from me joy, felicity, and life.

MRS. RACK. There! Now, how well he acts the madman!—This is something like! I knew he would do it well enough, when the time came.

DOR. Hard-hearted woman! enjoy my ruin—riot in my wretchedness.

(Hardy bursts in.)

HAR. This is too much. You are now the husband of my daughter; and how dare you show all this passion about another woman?

DOR. Alive again!

HAR. Alive! aye, and merry. Here, wipe off the flour from my face. I was never in better health and spirits in my life.—I foresaw t'would do—.Why, my illness was only a fetch, Man! to make you marry Letty.

DOR. It was! Base and ungenerous! Well, Sir, you shall be gratified. The possession of my heart was no object either with you or your daughter. My fortune and name was all you desired, and these—I leave ye. My native England I shall quit, nor ever behold you more. But, Lady, that in my exile I may have one consolation, grant me the favor you denied last night;—let me behold all that mask conceals, that your whole image may be impressed on my heart, and cheer my distant solitary hours.

LET. This is the most awful moment of my life. Oh, Doricourt, the slight action of taking off my mask, stamps me the most blest or miserable of women!

DOR. What can this mean? Reveal your face, I conjure you.

Let. Behold it.

Dor. Rapture! Transport! Heaven!

Flut. Now for a touch of the happy madman.

Vill. This scheme was mine.

Let. I will not allow that. This little strategem arose from my disappointment in not having the impression on you I wished. The timidity of the English character threw a veil over me, you could not penetrate. You have forced me to emerge in some measure from my natural reserve, and to throw off the veil that hid me.

Dor. I am yet in a state of intoxication—I cannot answer you.—Speak on, sweet Angel!

Let. You see I *can* be anything; choose then my character—your taste shall fix it. Shall I be an *English* wife?—or, breaking from the bonds of Nature and Education, step forth to the world in all the captivating glare of foreign manners?

Dor. You shall be nothing but yourself—nothing can be captivating that you are not. I will not wrong your penetration by pretending that you won my heart at the first interview; but you have won my whole soul—your person, your face, your mind, I would not exchange for those of any other woman breathing.

Har. A dog! how well he makes up for past slights! Cousin Racket, I wish you a good husband with all my heart. Mr. Flutter, I'll believe every word you say this fortnight. Mr. Villers, you and I have managed this to a T. I never was so merry in my life—'Gad, I believe I can dance. *(Footing.)*

Dor. Charming, charming creature!

Letit. Congratulate me, my dear friends! Can you conceive my happiness?

Har. No, congratulate me; for mine is the greatest.

Flut. No, congratulate me, that I have escaped with life, and give me some sticking plaster—this wild cat has torn the skin from my throat.

Sir Geo. I expect to be among the first who are congratulated—for I have recovered one angel, while Doricourt has gained another.

Har. Pho! pho! Don't talk of angels, we shall be happier by half as mortals. Come into the next room; I have ordered out every drop of my forty-eight, and I'll invite the whole parish of St. George's, but what we'll drink it out—except one dozen, which

I shall keep under three double locks for a certain christening
that I foresee will happen within this twelvemonth.

DOR. My charming bride! It was a strange perversion of taste that
led me to consider the delicate timidity of your deportment as
the mark of an uninformed mind or inelegant manners. I feel
now it is to that innate modesty, *English* husbands owe a felicity the married men of other nations are strangers to: it is a sacred veil to your own charms; it is the surest bulwark to your
husband's honor; and cursed be the hour—should it ever
arrive—in which *British* ladies shall sacrifice to *foreign Graces*
the Grace of Modesty!

EPILOGUE.

Nay, cease, and hear me—I am come to scold—
Whence this night's plaudits, to a thought so old?
To gain a lover, hid behind a mask!
What's new in that? or where's the mighty task?
For instance, now—What Lady Bab, or Grace,
E'er won a lover—in her natural face?
Mistake me not—French red or blanching creams,
I stoop not to—for those are hackneyed themes;
The arts I mean are harder to detect,
Easier put on, and worn to more effect;—
As thus—
Do pride and envy, with their horrid lines,
Destroy th' effect of Nature's sweet designs?
The mask of softness is at once applied,
And gentlest manners ornament the bride.
  Do thoughts too free inform the vestal's eye,
Or point the glance, or warm the struggling sigh?
Not Dian's brows more rigid looks disclose;

And virtue's blush appears where passion glows.
     And you, my gentle Sirs, wear vizors too;
But here I'll strip you, and expose to view
Your hidden features—First I point at you.
That well-stuff'd waistcoat, and that ruddy cheek,
That ample forehead, and that skin so sleek,
Point out good-nature, and a generous heart—
Tyrant! stand forth, and, conscious, own thy part:
Thy wife, thy children, tremble in thy eye;
And Peace is banished—when the Father's nigh.
     Sure 'tis enchantment! See, from ev'ry side
The masks fall off!—In charity I hide
The monstrous features rushing to my view—
Fear not, there, Grand-Papa—nor you—nor you:
For should I show your features to each other,
Not one amongst ye'd know his friend, or brother.
'Tis plain, then, all the world, from youth to age,
Appear in masks—Here, only, on the stage,
You see us as we are: Here trust your eyes;
Our wish to please, admits of no disguise.

Notes to *The Belle's Stratagem*

1. Touching, involving the feelings.
2. Queen Charlotte, who did indeed illustrate the attributes named, especially reserve and delicacy. She and George III set a model of proper family life and presided over a singularly respectable Court (praised by Saville in V.v).
3. Lawyers.
4. Aesop, the semilegendary writer of fables, is supposed to have been a hunchback.
5. Almack's Assembly Rooms, a fashionable place for social gatherings.
6. St. Paul's Cathedral, the lions in the Tower menagerie, and a wax-work collection—standard tourist sights.
7. I have been hunting in the country (the typical occupation of upper-class men during the summer months; see Courtall's speech, below).
8. Divorce proceedings, handled by the Doctors of Civil Law in Doctors' Commons, began when the husband sued his wife's lover for criminal conversation; this produced a trial full of juicy sexual details.

9. Fashionable world.
10. Gossip columns.
11. A day's journey from London (?).
12. St. James's Palace, to attend the King's levee.
13. Statecraft.
14. A sprightly air.
15. Dandies. Toasts = belles. Grisettes = shop assistants, salesgirls. The Mall was a fashionable promenade adjoining St. James's Park.
16. By the way, speaking of [pictures]. He goes on to describe an auction of paintings.
17. Pieces of wood that moved (to pluck the strings) as the keys of a harpsichord were struck.
18. Minor morals; i.e., etiquette.
19. You have unrealistic expectations of marriage.
20. According to legend, a salamander could survive in fire.
21. In your own person, in particular.
22. A scholar and collector of scientific specimens. The Pantheon was a hall for fashionable social gatherings, such as the masquerade of Act IV.
23. Presentation to the King and Queen, an important social ritual for the upper class.
24. Act with absurdly excessive conjugal devotion, suitable to advanced years and humble life.
25. Golden apples belonging to Hera, guarded by an ever-watchful dragon.
26. Hurrah! Rejoice!
27. People hired to bid at an auction in order to run up the prices.
28. Names of esteemed painters, with the characteristics conventionally attributed to them.
29. The lady, unfamiliar with the Bible, identifies a picture of David and Bathsheba (II Samuel ch. 11) as the conventional mythological subject of Diana and Actaeon.
30. Clergyman. John Toland was an unorthodox, deistic writer.
31. Daphne and Damon were names common in pastorals, which presented an idealized picture of simple rural life.
32. Bumpkin.
33. Mary Magdalene as a penitent, a common subject for religious pictures.
34. Awkward bashfulness.
35. A statue much admired at the time.
36. Anyone with sense would realize that this country (Houyhnhnmland in Book IV of Jonathan Swift's *Gulliver's Travels*) is fictitious.
37. Silently, like a dummy.
38. Mort = a great number (rustic dialect). Venis is her mispronunciation of *Venus;* Dinah, Jacob's daughter, was proverbially famous for getting into trouble by straying from her family (Genesis ch. 34).

39. Genus is her mispronunciation of *genius*. She boasts of her skill in trivial, useless fancy work, regularly taught to girls at school, but probably done better by professionals who kept shops for fancy goods.

40. Alchemist's, with connotations of cheating.

41. Naturally Hardy favors Quick, the creator of his role, who is speaking this line. The Jew Isaac Mendoza, in Richard Brinsley Sheridan's *The Duenna* (1775), was another of Quick's famous roles. Margaret (referred to in IV.i) is the Duenna.

42. Drunk.

43. A particularly fine wine.

44. Give her name for a toast.

45. A fashionable club.

46. Business for Doctors' Commons, which handled divorces.

47. The leading figure in *Hurlothrumbo,* a burlesque of 1729. The other lady seems to have garbled the story of Fair Rosamond, mistress of Henry II, who was supposedly kept in a maze where she could only be reached by one with a clue (clew), a guiding thread.

48. The privilege of members of Parliament to be immune from arrest for debt.

49. England was at war with France and Spain (as well as her American colonies).

50. Sensitive.

51. Banter. He slipped away from the House of Lords when a long-winded speaker got up and will be back before the speech is over.

52. A well-known prostitute.

53. Each parish was responsible for maintaining its own poor; the Overseer was in charge of distributing aid.

54. House of Commons.

55. The Bills of Mortality were official lists of deaths, with their causes, published weekly for parishes in or near London.

56. Ninon de Lenclos, a brilliant and licentious society hostess of the seventeenth century.

57. What, is (?).

58. Alexander Monro the second, anatomist and author of works on the nervous system.

59. Miss Ogle's vexation has caused her to break the lace that held her corset tight.

60. Don Quixote, who was really mad.

61. "Day of Judgment" occurs early in the marriage service of the Church of England, in the minister's first speech to the couple that is to be married.

Elizabeth Inchbald
(1753–1821)

ELIZABETH SIMPSON was one of the eight children of Roman Catholic farmers. Intent on getting off the farm, she ran away to London to become an actress, even though she stuttered. Her marriage to Joseph Inchbald, an experienced actor twice her age, provided protection from predatory males and also enabled her to establish herself as an actress. The Inchbalds were never very successful, however, and spent most of their time slaving in traveling provincial companies, where they might have to play thirty leading roles within two months. Nevertheless, Elizabeth found time to educate herself; she not only read extensively and taught herself French, but also made abstracts of her reading for the benefit of her sisters at home. While touring, the Inchbalds became friends with Sarah Kemble Siddons, who was to become the greatest tragic actress of the day, and her brother John Philip Kemble. Elizabeth and John were strongly attracted to each other, and after Joseph's sudden death in 1779, she probably hoped to marry Kemble. However, he was evidently looking for a richer and more docile wife.

Inchbald got work as an actress in London but saw that she would never be really successful. She played supporting dramatic roles, including Lady Touchwood in Cowley's *Belle's Stratagem* in its second season; but she often found herself in pantomimes, parading around in tights to show her legs. She tried to move from acting to writing plays, but it took persistent effort to persuade the theater management to put on her farce *The Mogul Tale* (1784), a slight piece that shrewdly capitalized on the contemporary fad for ascension balloons. It was a great success, and she was able to continue as a playwright, going on to have fifteen more plays produced and printed. Most of them are social comedies, combining humor and sentimental appeal, of which the best are *Such Things Are* (1788), *Every One Has His Fault* (1793), and *Wives as They Were and Maids as They Are* (1797); she also adapted August von Kotzebue's *Lovers' Vows* (1798), the play that causes mischief in Jane Austen's *Mansfield Park*. Meanwhile she completed her novel *A Simple Story* (1791), initially inspired by her troubled relationship with Kemble.

Since she skillfully marketed all her works and invested her profits, Inchbald was able to retire with a good income. She edited *The British Theatre,* a twenty-five-volume collection of the current acting plays, with biographical-critical prefaces, which appeared in 1806–09. She was curiously apprehensive about this project, considering her success as an author, and reacted with hurt defensiveness when one male playwright protested her mild criticism.

Charming and witty as well as beautiful, Inchbald led an active social life that ranged from high society to the radical philosophers William Godwin and Thomas Holcroft. Like many other men, they fell in love with and proposed to her; but she refused them all—and, what was more remarkable, retained their friendship afterward. As she told an earlier suitor, she was too fond of her own way to make a good wife. Unlike Miss Milner of *A Simple Story,* who is in part a self-portrait, Inchbald maintained strict self-control and preserved an impeccable reputation.

Such Things Are was produced at Covent Garden in 1787. Successful in the theater and often reprinted, it earned her nine hundred pounds. The text here includes the remarks she added in *The British Theatre.*

Such Things Are

REMARKS.

The writer of this play was, at the time of its production, but just admitted to the honors of an authoress, and wanted experience to behold her own danger, when she attempted the subject on which the work is founded. Her ignorance was her protection. Had her fears been greater, or proportioned to her task, her success had been still more hazardous. A bold enterprise requires bold execution; and, as skill does not always unite with courage, it is often advantageous, where cases are desperate, not to see with the eye of criticism: chance will sometimes do more for rash self-importance than that judgment which is the parent of timidity.

Such was the consequence on the first appearance of this comedy—its reception was favorable beyond the usual bounds of favor bestowed upon an admired play, and the pecuniary remuneration equally extraordinary.

There was novelty, locality and invention in *Such Things Are;* and the audience forgave, or, in their warmth of approbation, overlooked improbability in certain events, incorrectness of language, and meanness, bordering on vulgarity, in some of the characters.

As the scene is played in the East Indies, where the unpolished of the British nation so frequently resort to make their fortune, perhaps the last mentioned defect may be more descriptive of the manners of the English inhabitants of that part of the globe, than had elegance of dialogue, and delicacy of sentiment, been given them. Nevertheless, a more elevated style of conversation and manners in Sir Luke and Lady Tremor would not have been wholly improper, and would assuredly have been much more pleasing, especially to those who may now sit in judgment upon the work, as readers, and cold admirers of that benevolence, no longer the constant theme of enthusiastic praise, as when this drama was first produced.

When this play was written, in 1786, Howard, the hero of the piece, under the name of Haswell, was on his philanthropic travels through Europe and parts of Asia, to mitigate the sufferings of the prisoner.[1] His fame, the anxiety of his countrymen for the success of his labors, and their pride in his beneficent character, suggested to the author a subject for the following pages. The scene chosen for its exhibition is the island of Sumatra; where the English settlement, the system of government, modes and habits of the natives, the residents, and the visitors of the isle, may well reconcile the fable and incidents of the drama to an interesting degree of possibility.[2]

As Haswell is the hero of the serious part of this play, so is Twineall of the comic half. His character and conduct is formed on the plan of Lord Chesterfield's finished gentleman. That nobleman's Letters to his Son excited, at least, the idea of Twineall in the author's mind;[3] and the public appeared to be as well acquainted with his despicable reputation, as with the highly honorable one of Howard.

Death having robbed the world of that good man's active services, though the effect of his exertions will ever remain, a short account of the virtuous tendency of his inclinations, and success of his charitable pursuits, is at present requisite for some readers, as explanatory of the following scenes.

John Howard, to whose revered memory a statue is erected in St. Paul's Cathedral, with a suitable inscription, was born in 1726.

The life of Mr. Howard, till the year 1773, is of little note, or has no reference whatever to his subsequent renown. At that period he was living on his own estate at Cardington, near Bedford, a widower, with one child. Here he served the office of sheriff for the county, which, as he has declared, "brought the distress of prisoners immediately under his notice, and led him to form the design of visiting the gaols through England, in order to devise means for alleviating the miseries of the sufferers."

In 1774, he was examined before the House of Commons on the subject of prisons, and received the thanks of the House.

He then extended his benevolent views to foreign countries, making various excursions to all parts of Europe.

In 1789, he published an Account of the principal Lazarettos he had seen. In this work he signified his intention of revisiting Russia, Turkey, and of extending his route into the East.—"I am not insensible," he says, "of the dangers which must attend such a journey: Trusting, however, in the protection of that kind Providence which has hitherto preserved me, I calmly and cheerfully commit myself to the disposal of unerring wisdom. Should it please God to cut off my life in the prosecution of this design, let not my conduct be uncandidly imputed to rashness or enthusiasm, but to a serious and deliberate conviction that I am pursuing the path of duty; and to a sincere desire of being made an instrument of more extensive usefulness to my fellow creatures than could be expected in the narrower circle of a retired life."

He fell a sacrifice to his humanity; for, visiting a sick patient at Kherson, who had a malignant fever, he caught the infection, and died January the 20th, 1790.

Dramatis Personæ.

SULTAN	Mr. *Farren.*
LORD FLINT	Mr. *Davies.*
SIR LUKE TREMOR	Mr. *Quick.*
MR. TWINEALL	Mr. *Lewis.*
MR. HASWELL	Mr. *Pope.*
ELVIRUS	Mr. *Holman.*
MR. MEANRIGHT	Mr. *Macready.*
ZEDAN	Mr. *Fearon.*
FIRST KEEPER	Mr. *Thompson.*
SECOND KEEPER	Mr. *Cubitt.*
FIRST PRISONER	Mr. *Helme.*
SECOND PRISONER	Mr. *Gardener.*
GUARD	Mr. *Blurton.*
MESSENGER	Mr. *Ledger.*
LADY TREMOR	Mrs. *Mattocks*
AURELIA	Miss *Wilkinson*
FEMALE PRISONER	Mrs. *Pope.*

Scene—*The Island of Sumatra, in the East Indies.*
Time of Representation—Twelve Hours.

PROLOGUE.

Written by Thomas Vaughan, Esq.
Spoken by Mr. Holman.

How say you, critic gods, and you below;[4]
Are you all friends?—or here—and there—a foe?
Come to protect your *literary* trade,
Which Mrs. *Scribble* dares *again* invade—
But know you not—*in all* the fair ones do,
'Tis not to please themselves alone—but you.
Then who so churlish, or so cynic grown,
Would wish to change a *simper* for a *frown?*
Or who so jealous of their own *dear* quill,
Would point the paragraph her fame to kill?
Yet such there are, in this all-scribbling town,
And men of letters too—of some renown,
Who sicken at all merit but their own.
But sure 'twere more for Wit's—for Honor's sake,
To make the Drama's *race—the give and take.*

(Looking round the house.)

My hint I see's approved—so pray begin it,
And praise us—*roundly* for the *good things* in it,
Nor let severity our faults expose,
When godlike Homer's self was known to doze.
  But of the piece—Methinks I hear you hint,
Some dozen lines or more should give the tint—
"Tell how *Sir John* with *Lady Betty's* maid
Is caught intriguing at a masquerade;

Which Lady Betty, in a jealous fit,
Resents by flirting with *Sir Ben*—the cit.
Whose *three*-foot spouse, to modish follies bent,
Mistakes a *six*-feet valet—for a gent.
Whilst Miss, repugnant to her guardian's plan,
Elopes in breeches with her favorite man."⁵
Such are the *hints* we read in *Roscius*'⁶ days,
By way of Prologue ushered in *their* plays.
But *we*, like Ministers and cautious spies,
In *secret measures* think—the merit lies.
Yet shall the Muse thus far unveil the plot—
This play was *tragi-comically* got,
Those sympathetic sorrows to impart
Which harmonize the feelings of the heart;
And may at least this humble merit boast,
A structure founded on fair *Fancy*'s coast.
With you it rests that judgment to proclaim,
Which *in the world* must raise or sink its fame.
Yet ere her judges sign their last report,
'Tis you *(To the boxes.)* must recommend her to the court;
Whose smiles, like *Cynthia,* in a winter's night,
Will cheer our wanderer with a gleam of light.

ACT I.

Scene i. A parlor at Sir Luke Tremor's.

(Enter Sir Luke, followed by Lady Tremor.)

SIR LUKE. I tell you, madam, you are two and thirty.

LADY. I tell you, sir, you are mistaken.

SIR LUKE. Why, did not you come over from England exactly sixteen years ago?

LADY. Not so long.

SIR LUKE. Have not we been married, the tenth of next April, sixteen years?

LADY. Not so long.

SIR LUKE. Did you not come over the year of the great eclipse?[7]— answer me that.

LADY. I don't remember it.

SIR LUKE. But I do—and shall remember it as long as I live.—The first time I saw you was in the garden of the Dutch envoy: you were looking through a glass at the sun—I immediately began to make love to you, and the whole affair was settled while the eclipse lasted—just one hour, eleven minutes, and three seconds.

LADY. But what is all this to my age?

SIR LUKE. Because I know you were at that time near seventeen, and without one qualification except your youth, and your fine clothes.

LADY. Sir Luke, Sir Luke, this is not to be borne!

SIR LUKE. Oh! yes—I forgot—you had two letters of recommendation from two great families in England.

LADY. Letters of recommendation!

SIR LUKE. Yes; your character—that you know, is all the fortune we poor Englishmen, situated in India, expect with a wife, who crosses the sea at the hazard of her life, to make us happy.

LADY. And what but our characters would you have us

bring?—Do you suppose any lady ever came to India, who brought along with her friends or fortune?

SIR LUKE. No, my dear: and what is worse, she seldom leaves them behind.

LADY. No matter, Sir Luke: but if I delivered to you a good character—

SIR LUKE. Yes, my dear, you did: and if you were to ask me for it again, I can't say I could give it you.

LADY. How uncivil! how unlike are your manners to the manners of my Lord Flint!

SIR LUKE. Ay, you are never so happy as when you have an opportunity of expressing your admiration of him.—A disagreeable, nay, a very dangerous man—one is never sure of one's self in his presence—he carries every thing he hears to the ministers of our suspicious Sultan—and I feel my head shake whenever I am in his company.

LADY. How different does his lordship appear to me!—To me he is all *politesse*.

SIR LUKE. *Politesse!* how should you understand what is real *politesse?* You know your education was very much confined.

LADY. And if it *was* confined?—I beg, Sir Luke, you will cease these reflections; you know they are what I can't bear!—*(Walks about in a passion.)*—Pray, does not his lordship continually assure me, I might be taken for a countess, were it not for a certain little grovelling toss I have caught with my head, and a certain little confined hitch in my walk; both which I learnt of you—learnt by looking so much at you.

SIR LUKE. And now, if you don't take care, by looking so much at his lordship, you may catch some of his defects.

LADY. I know of very few he has.

SIR LUKE. I know of many—besides those he assumes.

LADY. Assumes.

SIR LUKE. Yes: Do you suppose he is as forgetful as he pretends to be?—no, no; but because he is a favorite with the Sultan, and all our great men, he thinks it genteel or convenient to have no memory; and yet, I'll answer for it, he has one of the best in the universe.

LADY. I don't believe your charge.

SIR LUKE. Why, though he forgets his appointments with his tradesmen, did you ever hear of his forgetting to go to court when a place was to be disposed of? Did he ever make a blunder, and send a bribe to a man out of power? Did he ever forget to kneel before the prince of this island, or to look in his highness's presence like the statue of patient resignation, in humble expectation?

Lady. Dear, Sir Luke—

Sir Luke. Sent from his own country in his very infancy, and brought up in the different courts of petty arbitrary princes here in Asia, he is the slave of every rich man, and the tyrant of every poor one.

Lady. "Petty princes!"—'tis well his highness, our Sultan, does not hear you.

Sir Luke. 'Tis well he does not—don't you repeat what I say: but you know how all this fine country is harassed and laid waste by a set of princes—Sultans, as they style themselves, and I know not what—who are for ever calling out to each other, "That's mine," and "That's mine";—and "You have no business here," and "You have no business there";—and "*I* have business every where." *(Strutting.)*—Then, "Give *me* this," and "Give *me* that";—and "Take this," and "Take that." *(Makes signs of fighting.)*

Lady. A very elegant description, truly.

Sir Luke. Why, you know 'tis all matter of fact: and Lord Flint, brought up from his youth among these people, has not one *trait* of an Englishman about him: he has imbibed all this country's cruelty; and I dare say would mind no more seeing me hung up by my thumbs, or made to dance upon a red hot gridiron—

Lady. That is one of the tortures I never heard of!—O! I should like to see that of all things!

Sir Luke. Yes, by keeping this man's company, you'll soon be as cruel as he is: he will teach you every vice. A consequential, grave, dull—and yet with that degree of levity which dares to pay addresses to a woman, even before her husband's face.

Lady. Did you not declare, this minute, his lordship had not a *trait* of his own country about him?

Sir Luke. Well, well—as you say, that last *is* a *trait* of his own country.

(Enter Servant and Lord Flint.)

Serv. Lord Flint—*(Exit Servant.)*

Lady. My lord, I am extremely glad to see you: we were just mentioning your name.

Lord. Were you, indeed, madam? You do me great honor.

Sir Luke. No, my lord—no great honor.

Lord. Pardon me, Sir Luke.

Sir Luke. But, I assure you, my lord, in what I said I did *myself* a great deal.

Lady. Yes, my lord; and I'll acquaint your lordship what it was. *(Going up to him.)*

Sir Luke *(pulling her aside)*. Why, you would not inform against me, sure! Do you know what would be the consequence? My head must answer it. *(Frightened.)*

Lord. Nay, Sir Luke, I insist upon knowing.

Sir Luke *(to her)*. Hush! hush!—No, my lord, pray excuse me: your lordship, perhaps, may think what I said did not come from my heart; and I assure you, upon my honor, it did.

Lady. O, yes—that I am sure it did.

Lord. I am extremely obliged to you. *(Bowing.)*

Sir Luke. O, no, my lord, not at all—not at all. *(Aside to her.)* I'll be extremely obliged to *you,* if you will hold your tongue.— Pray, my lord, are you engaged out to dinner to-day? for her ladyship and I are.

Lady. Yes, my lord, and we should be happy to find your lordship of the party.

Lord. "Engaged out to dinner"?—Egad, very likely—very likely: but if I am, I have positively forgotten where.

Lady. We are going to—

Lord. No—I think, now you put me in mind of it—I think I have company to dine with me. I am either going out to dinner, or have company to dine with me; but I really can't tell which: however, my people know—but I can't recollect.

Sir Luke. Perhaps your lordship *has* dined: can you recollect that?

Lord. No, no—I have not dined—What's o'clock?

Lady. Perhaps, my lord, you have not breakfasted?

Lord. O, yes; I've breakfasted—I think so—but, upon my word these things are very difficult to remember.

Sir Luke. They are, indeed, my lord—and I wish all my family would entirely forget them.

Lord. What did your ladyship say was o'clock?

LADY. Exactly twelve, my lord.

LORD. Bless me! I ought to have been somewhere else then—an absolute engagement.—I have broke my word—a positive appointment.

LADY. Shall I send a servant?

LORD. No, no, no, no—by no means—it can't be helped now; and they know my unfortunate failing: besides, I'll beg their pardon, and I trust, that will be ample satisfaction.

LADY. You are very good, my lord, not to leave us.

LORD. I could not think of leaving you so soon—the happiness I enjoy in your society is so extreme—

SIR LUKE. That were your lordship to go away now, you might never remember to come again.

(Enter Servant.)

SERV. A gentleman, sir, just landed from on board an English vessel, says he has letters to present to you.

SIR LUKE. Show him in.

(Exit Servant.)

—He has brought his character too, I suppose, and left it behind, too, perhaps.

(Enter Mr. Twineall, in a fashionable undress.[8])

TWI. Sir Luke, I have the honor of presenting to you—*(Gives letters.)*—one from my Lord Cleland—one from Sir Thomas Shoestring—one from Colonel Fril.

SIR LUKE *(aside).* Who, in the name of wonder, have my friends recommended?—*(Reads while Lord Flint and the lady talk apart.)*—No—as I live, he is a gentleman, and the son of a lord—*(Going to Lady Tremor.)* My dear, that is a gentleman, notwithstanding his appearance.—Don't laugh; but let me introduce you to him.

LADY. A gentleman!—Certainly: I did not look at him before—but now I can perceive it.

SIR LUKE. Mr. Twineall, give me leave to introduce Lady Tremor to you, and my Lord Flint—this, my lord, is the Honorable Mr.

Twineall, from England, who will do me the favor to remain in my house till he is settled to his mind in some post here. *(They bow.)*—I beg your pardon, sir, for the somewhat cool reception Lady Tremor and I at first gave you—but I dare say her ladyship was under the same mistake as myself—and, I must own, I took you at first sight for something very different from the person you prove to be: for, really, no English ships having arrived in this harbor for these five years past, and the dress of English gentlemen being so much altered since that time—

Twi. But, I hope, Sir Luke, if it is, the alteration meets with your approbation.

Lady. Oh! it is extremely elegant and becoming.

Sir Luke. Yes, my dear, I don't doubt but you think so! for I remember you used to make your favorite monkey wear just such a jacket, when he went out a visiting.

Twi. Was he your favorite, madam?—Sir, you are very obliging. *(Bowing to Sir Luke.)*

Sir Luke. My lord, if it were possible for your lordship to call to your *remembrance* such a trifle—

Lady. Dear Sir Luke—*(Pulling him.)*

Lord. Egad, I believe I do call to my remembrance—*(Gravely considering.)*—Not, I assure you, sir, that I perceive any great resemblance—or, if it was so—I dare say it is merely in the dress—which I must own strikes me as most ridiculous—very ridiculous indeed.—

Twi. My lord!

Lord. I beg pardon, if I have said any thing that—Lady Tremor, what did I say?—make my apology, if I have said any thing improper—you know my unhappy failing. *(Goes up the stage.)*

Lady *(to Twineall).* Sir, his lordship has made a mistake in the word "ridiculous," which I am sure he did not mean to say: but he is apt to make use of one word for another. His lordship has been so long out of England, that he may be said, in some measure, to have forgotten his native language.

(His lordship all this time appears consequentially absent.)

Twi. You have perfectly explained, madam.—Indeed, I ought to have been convinced, without your explanation, that if his lordship made use of the word *ridiculous,* even intentionally, that

the word had now changed its former sense, and was become a
mode to express satisfaction—or he would not have used it, in
the very forcible manner he did, to a perfect stranger.

Sir Luke. What, Mr. Twineall, have you new fashions for *words*
too in England, as well as for dresses? and are you equally ex-
travagant in their adoption?

Lady. I never heard, Sir Luke, but that the fashion of words varied, as well as the fashion of everything else.

Twi. But what is most extraordinary, we have now a fashion, in
England, of speaking without any words at all.

Lady. Pray, sir, how is that?

Sir Luke. Ay, do, Mr. Twineall, teach my wife to do without
words, and I shall be very much obliged to you; it will be a
great accomplishment.—Even you, my lord, ought to be atten-
tive to this fashion.

Twi. Why, madam, for instance; when a gentleman is asked a
question which is either troublesome or improper to answer, he
does not say he *won't* answer it, even though he speaks to an
inferior; but he says, "Really it appears to me e-e-e-e-e—
(Mutters and shrugs.)—that is—mo-mo-mo-mo-mo—*(Mutters.)*—if you see the thing—for my part—te-te-te-te—and that's
all I can tell about it at present."

Sir Luke. And you have told nothing.

Twi. Nothing upon earth.

Lady. But mayn't one guess what you mean?

Twi. Oh, yes—perfectly at liberty to guess.

Sir Luke. Well, I'll be shot if I could guess.

Twi. And again—when an impertinent pedant asks you a question
which you know nothing about, and it may not be convenient
to say so—you answer boldly, "Why really, sir, my opinion is,
that the Greek poet—he-he-he-he—*(Mutters.)*—we-we-we-we—
you see—if his ideas were—and if the Latin translator—mis-
mis-mis-mis—*(Shrugs.)*—that I should think—in my humble
opinion.—But the doctor[9] may know better than I."

Sir Luke. The doctor must know very little else.

Twi. Or in case of a duel, where one does not care to say who
was right, or who was wrong—you answer—"*This*, sir, is the
state of the matter—Mr. F.—came first—te-te-te-te—on that—
be-be-be-be—if the other—in short—*(Whispers.)*—whis-whis-
whis-whis"—

Sir Luke. What?

Twi. "There, now you have it—there it is: but don't say a word about it—or if you do, don't say it came from me."

Lady. Why, you have not told a word of the story!

Twi. But that your auditor must not say to you—that's not the fashion—he never tells you that—he may say—"You have not made yourself perfectly clear";—or he may say—"He must have the matter more particularly pointed out somewhere else";—but that is all the auditor can say with good breeding.

Lady. A very pretty method indeed to satisfy curiosity!

(Enter Servant.)

Serv. Mr. Haswell.

Sir Luke. This is a countryman of ours, Mr. Twineall, and a very worthy man I assure you.

(Enter Mr. Haswell.)

Sir Luke. Mr. Haswell, how do you do? *(Warmly.)*

Hasw. Sir Luke, I am glad to see you.—Lady Tremor, how do you do? *(He bows to the rest.)*

Lady. Oh, Mr. Haswell, I am extremely glad you are come—here is a young adventurer just arrived from England, who has been giving us such a strange account of all that's going on there! *(Introducing Twineall.)*

Hasw. Sir, you are welcome to India.

(Sir Luke whispers Haswell.)

Indeed—*his* son.

Lady. Do, Mr. Haswell, talk to him—he can give you great information.

Hasw. I am glad of it: I shall then hear many things I am impatient to become acquainted with. *(Goes up to Twineall.)* Mr. Twineall, I have the honor of knowing your father extremely well—he holds his seat in Parliament still, I presume?

Twi. He does, sir.

Hasw. And your uncle, Sir Charles?

Twi. Both, sir—both in Parliament still.

Hasw. Pray, has any act in behalf of the poor clergy taken place?[10]

Twi. In behalf of the poor clergy, sir?—I'll tell you—I'll tell you, sir.—As to that act—concerning—*(Shrugs and mutters.)*—em-em-em-em—the Committee—em-em—ways and means—hee-hee—te-te-te—*(Sir Luke, Lady, and Lord Flint laugh.)* My father and my uncle both think so, I assure you.

Hasw. Think how, sir?

Sir Luke. Nay, that's not good breeding—you must ask no more questions.

Hasw. Why not?

Sir Luke. Because—we-we-we-we—*(Mimics.)*—he knows nothing about the matter.

Hasw. What!—not know?

Twi. Yes, sir, perfectly acquainted with every thing that passes in the House—but, I assure you, that when parliamentary business is reported—By the bye, Sir Luke, permit me, in my turn, to make a few inquiries concerning the state of this country.

(Sir Luke starts, and fixes his eyes suspiciously on Lord Flint.)

Sir Luke. Why, one does not like to speak much about the country one lives in.—But, Mr. Haswell, you have been visiting our en-campments: you may tell us what is going on there.

Lady. Pray, Mr. Haswell, is it true that the Sultan cut off the head of one of his wives the other day because she said to him—"I won't"?

Sir Luke. Do, my dear, be silent.

Lady. I won't.

Sir Luke. Oh, that the Sultan had you instead of me!

Lady. And with my head off, I suppose?

Sir Luke. No, my dear; in that state, I should have no objection to you myself.

Lady *(aside to Sir Luke)*. Now, I'll frighten you ten times more.—But, Mr. Haswell, I am told there are many persons suspected of disaffection to the present Sultan, who have been lately, by his orders, arrested, and sold to slavery—notwithstanding there was no proof against them produced.

Hasw. Proof! in a state such as this, the charge is quite sufficient.

Sir Luke *(in apparent agonies wishing to turn the discourse)*. Well, my lord, and how does your lordship find yourself this afternoon!—this morning, I mean. Bless my soul! why I begin to be as forgetful as your lordship. *(Smiling and fawning.)*

LADY. How I pity the poor creatures!

SIR LUKE *(aside to Lady)*. Take care what you say before that tool of state: look at him, and tremble for your head.

LADY. Look at him, and tremble for your own.—And so, Mr. Haswell, all this is true?—and some persons of family too, I am told, dragged from their homes, and sent to slavery merely on suspicion?

HASW. Yet, less do I pity those, than some, whom prisons and dungeons, crammed before, are yet prepared to receive.

LORD. Mr. Haswell, such is the Sultan's pleasure.

SIR LUKE. Will your lordship take a turn in the garden? it looks from this door very pleasant. Does not it, my lord?

LADY. But pray, Mr. Haswell, has not the Sultan sent for you to attend at his palace this morning?

HASW. He has, madam.

LADY. There! I heard he had, but Sir Luke said not—I am told he thinks himself under the greatest obligations to you.

HASW. The report has flattered me: but if his highness *should* think himself under obligations, I can readily point a way by which he may acquit himself of them.

LADY. In the mean time, I am sure you feel for those poor sufferers.

HASW *(with stifled emotion)*. Sir Luke, good morning to you.—I called upon some trifling business, but I have outstayed my time, and therefore I'll call again in a couple of hours.—Lady Tremor, good morning—my lord—Mr. Twineall. *(Bows, and exit.)*

TWI. Sir Luke, your garden *does* look so divinely beautiful—

SIR LUKE. Come, my lord, will you take a turn in it?—Come, Mr. Twineall—come, my dear—*(Taking her hand.)* I can't think what business Mr. Haswell has to speak to me upon!—for my part I am quite a plain man, and busy myself about no one's affairs, except my own—but I dare say your lordship has forgotten all we have been talking about.

LORD. If you permit me, Sir Luke, I'll hand Lady Tremor.

SIR LUKE. Certainly, my lord, if you please—Come, Mr. Twineall, and I'll conduct you. *(Exeunt.)*

ACT II.

Scene i. An apartment at Sir Luke Tremor's.

(Enter Twineall and Meanwright.)

TWI. My dear friend, after so long a separation, how devilish unlucky that you should, on the very day of my arrival, be going
to set sail for another part of the world!, yet, before you go, I
must beg a favor of you.—You know Sir Luke and his family
perfectly well, I dare say?

MEAN. I think so—I have been in his house near six years.

TWI. The very person on earth I wanted!—Sir Luke has power
here, I suppose?—a word from him might do a man some service perhaps? *(Significantly.)*

MEAN. Why, yes; I don't know a man who has more influence at
a certain place.

TWI. And Lady Tremor seems a very clever gentlewoman.

MEAN. Very.

TWI. And I have a notion they think me very clever.

MEAN. I dare say they do.

TWI. Yes—but I mean *very* clever.

MEAN. No doubt!

TWI. But, my dear friend, you must help me to make them think
better of me still—and when my fortune is made, I'll make
yours—for when I once become acquainted with people's dispositions, their little weaknesses, foibles, and faults, I can wind,
twist, twine, and get into the corner of every one's heart, and lie
so snug, they can't know I'm there till they want to pull me out,
and find 'tis impossible.[11]

MEAN. Excellent talent!

TWI. Is not it?—And now, my dear friend, do you inform me of
the secret dispositions and propensities of every one in this family, and that of all their connections?—What lady values herself
upon one qualification, and what lady upon another?—What

gentleman will like to be told of his accomplishments, or what man would rather hear of his wife's or his daughter's?—or of his horses, or of his dogs?—Now, my dear Ned, acquaint me with all this; and, within a fortnight, I will become the most necessary rascal—not a creature shall know how to exist without me.

MEAN. Why, such a man as you ought to have made your fortune in England.

TWI. No; there—my father and my three uncles monopolized all the great men themselves, and would never introduce me where I was likely to become their rival.—This, this is the very spot for me to display my genius.—But then I must first penetrate the people, unless you will kindly save me that trouble.—Come, give me all their characters—all their little propensities—all their whims—in short, all I am to praise, and all I am to avoid praising, in order to endear myself to them. *(Takes out tablets.)* Come—begin with Sir Luke.

MEAN. Sir Luke values himself more upon personal bravery, than upon any thing.

TWI. Thank you, my dear friend—thank you. *(Writes.)* Was he ever in the army?

MEAN. Oh, yes, besieged a capital fortress a few years ago: and now the very name of a battle, or a great general tickles his vanity; and he takes all the praises you can lavish upon the subject as compliments to himself.

TWI. Thank you—thank you, a thousand times. *(Writes.)* I'll mention a battle very soon.

MEAN. Not directly.

TWI. Oh, no—let me alone for time and place.—Go on, my friend—go on—her ladyship—

MEAN. Descended from the ancient kings of Scotland.

TWI. You don't say so!

MEAN. And though she is so nicely scrupulous as never to mention the word genealogy, yet I have seen her agitation so great, when the advantages of high birth have been extolled, that she could scarcely withhold her sentiments of triumph; which, in order to disguise, she has assumed a disdain for all "vain titles, empty sounds, and idle pomp."

TWI. Thank you—thank you: this is a most excellent *trait* of the lady's. *(Writes.)* "Pedigree of the kings of Scotland"?—Oh, I have her at once.

MEAN. Yet do it nicely;—oblique touches, rather than open explanations.

TWI. Let me alone for that.

MEAN. She has, I know, in her possession—but I dare say she would not show it you; nay, on the contrary, would affect to be highly offended, were you to mention it;—and yet it certainly would flatter her to know you were acquainted with her having it.

TWI. What—what—what is it?

MEAN. A large old-fashioned wig—which Malcolm the third or fourth, her great ancestor, wore when he was crowned at Scone, in the year—

TWI. I'll mention it.

MEAN. Take care.

TWI. O, let me alone for the manner.

MEAN. She'll pretend to be angry.

TWI. That I am prepared for.—Pray, who is my Lord Flint?

MEAN. A deep man—and a great favorite at court.

TWI. Indeed!—how am I to please him?

MEAN. By insinuations against the present Sultan.

TWI. Indeed!

MEAN. With all his pretended attachment, his heart—

TWI. Are you sure of it?

MEAN. Sure:—he blinds Sir Luke, who by the bye is no great politician—but I know his lordship; and if he thought he was certain of his ground—and he thinks, he shall be soon—then—

TWI. I'll insinuate myself, and join his party; but, in the mean time, preserve good terms with Sir Luke, in case any thing should fall in my way there.—Who is Mr. Haswell?

MEAN. He pretends to be a man of principle and sentiment;[12]—flatter him on that.

TWI. The easiest thing in the world—no characters love flattery better than such as those: they will bear even to hear their vices praised.—I will myself, undertake to praise the vices of a man of sentiment, till he shall think them so many virtues.—You have mentioned no ladies yet, but the lady of the house.

MEAN. I know little about any other, except a pretty girl who came over from England, about two years ago, for a husband;

and, not succeeding in a distant part of the country, was recommended to this house; and has been here three or four months.

TWI. Let me alone to please her.

MEAN. Yes—I believe you are skilled.

TWI. In the art of flattery, no one more.

MEAN. But, damn it, it is not a liberal art.

TWI. It is a great science, notwithstanding—and studied, at present, by all wise men.—Zounds! I have stayed a long time—I can't attend to any more characters at present—Sir Luke and his lady will think me inattentive, if I don't join them.—Shall I see you again!—if not, I wish you a pleasant voyage—I'll make the most of what you have told me—you'll hear I'm a great man.—Heaven bless you!—good bye!—you'll hear I'm a great man. *(Exit.)*

MEAN. And, if I am not mistaken, I shall hear you are turned out of this house before tomorrow morning. O, Twineall! exactly the reverse of every character have you now before you.—The greatest misfortune in the life of Sir Luke has been flying from his regiment in the midst of an engagement, and a most humiliating degradation in consequence; which makes him so feelingly alive on the subject of a battle, that nothing but his want of courage can secure my friend Twineall's life for venturing to name the subject. Then my Lord Flint, firmly attached to the interest of the Sultan, will be all on fire when he hears of open disaffection.—But most of all, Lady Tremor! whose father was a grocer, and uncle a noted advertising "Periwig-maker on a new construction." She will run mad to hear of births, titles, and long pedigrees.—Poor Twineall! little dost thou think what is prepared for thee.—There is Mr. Haswell too! but to him have I sent you to be reclaimed—to him, who, free from faults, or even foibles, of his own, has yet more potently received the blessing—of pity for his neighbor's. *(Exit.)*

Scene ii. The inside of a prison.

(Several Prisoners dispersed in different situations. Enter Keeper and Haswell, with lights.)

KEEP. This way, sir: the prisons this way are more extensive still.—You seem to feel for those unthinking men; but they are a set of unruly people, whom no severity can make such as they ought to be.

HASW. And would not gentleness, or mercy, do you think, reclaim them?

KEEP. That I can't say: we never make use of those means in this part of the world.—That man, yonder, suspected of disaffection, is sentenced to be here for life, unless his friends can lay down a large sum by way of penalty; which he finds they cannot do, and he is turned melancholy.

HASW *(after a pause).* Who is that? *(Pointing to another.)*

KEEP. He has been tried for heading an insurrection, and acquitted.

HASW. What keeps him here?

KEEP. Fees due to the court—a debt contracted while he proved his innocence.[13]

HASW. Lead on, my friend—let us go to some other part. *(Putting his hand to his eyes.)*

KEEP. In the ward we are going to, are the prisoners who, by some small reserve of money, some little stock when they arrived, or by the bounty of some friends who visit them, or such like fortunate circumstance, are in a less dismal place.

HASW. Lead on.

KEEP. But stop—put on this cloak; for, before we arrive at the place I mention, we must pass a damp vault, which to those who are not used to it—*(Haswell puts on the cloak.)* Or will you postpone your visit?

HASW. No—go on.

KEEP. Alas! who would suppose you had been used to see such places!—you look concerned—grieved to see the people suffer.—I wonder you should come, when you seem to think so much about them.

HASW. O, that, that is the very reason! *(Exit, following the Keeper.)*

(Zedan, a tawny Indian prisoner, follows them, stealing out, as if intent on something secret.—Two prisoners walk slowly down the stage, looking after Haswell.)

FIRST PRIS. Who is this man?

SECOND PRIS. From Britain—I have seen him once before.

First Pris. He looks pale—he has no heart.
Second Pris. I believe, a pretty large one.

(Re-enter Zedan.)

Zedan. Brother, a word with you. *(To the First Prisoner—the other retires.)* As the stranger and our keeper passed by the passage, a noxious vapor put out the light; and, as they groped along, I purloined this from the stranger. *(Shows a pocketbook.)* See, it contains two notes will pay our ransom. *(Showing the notes.)*
First Pris. A treasure—our certain ransom!
Zedan. Liberty, our wives, our children, and our friends, will these papers purchase.
First Pris. What a bribe for our keeper! He may rejoice too.
Zedan. And then the pleasure it will be to hear the stranger fret, and complain for his loss!—O, how my heart loves to see sorrow!—Misery, such as I have known, dealt to men who spurn me—who treat me as if, in my own island, I had no friends who loved me—no servants who paid me honor—no children who revered me.—Taskmasters, forgetful that I am a husband—a father—nay, a man.
First Pris. Conceal your thoughts—conceal your treasure too—or the Briton's complaint—
Zedan. Will be in vain.—Our keeper will conclude the prize must come to him at last, and therefore make no great search for it.—Here in the corner of my belt, *(Puts up the pocket-book.)*—'twill be secure.—Come this way, and let us indulge our pleasant prospect. *(They retire, and the scene closes.)*[14]

Scene iii. Another part of the prison.

(A kind of sofa, with an Old Man sleeping upon it—Elvirus sitting attentively by him. Enter Keeper and Haswell.)

Keep. That young man, watching his aged father as he sleeps, by the help of fees gains his admission; and he never quits the place, except to go and purchase cordials for the old man, who, though healthy and strong, when he was first a prisoner, is now become languid and ill.

HASW. Are they from Europe?

KEEP. No—but descended from Europeans. See how the youth holds his father's hand!—I have sometimes caught him bathing it with tears.

HASW. I'll speak to the young man. *(Going to him.)*

KEEP. He will speak as soon as he sees me—he has sent a petition to the Sultan, about his father, and never fails to inquire if a reply is come.

(They approach—Elvirus starts, and comes forward.)

ELVIR *(to Haswell).* Sir, do you come from court?—Has the Sultan received my humble supplication, can you tell?—Softly?—let not my father hear you speak.

HASW. I come but as a stranger, to see the prison.

ELVIR. No answer yet, keeper?

KEEP. No—I told you it was in vain to implore: they never read petitions sent from prisons—their hearts are hardened to such worn-out tales of sorrow.

(Elvirus turns toward his father, and weeps.)

HASW. Pardon me, sir—but what is the request you are thus denied?

ELVIR. Behold my father! But three months has he been confined here; and yet, unless he breathes a purer air—O, if you have influence at court, sir, pray represent what passes in this dreary prison—what passes in my heart.—My supplication is, to remain a prisoner here, while my father, released, shall retire to his paternal estate, and never more take arms against the present government, but at the peril of my life.—Or, if the Sultan would allow me to serve him as a soldier—

HASW. You would fight against the party your father fought for?

ELVIR *(starting).* No—but in the forests, or on the desert sands, amongst those slaves who are sent to battle with the wild Indians:—there I would go—and earn the boon I ask—Or in the mines—

HASW. Give me your name: I will, at least, present your suit—and, perhaps—

ELVIR. Sir! do you think it is likely?—Joyful hearing!

Hasw. Nay, be not too hasty in your hopes—I cannot answer for my success. *(Repeats.)* "Your father humbly implores to be released from prison; and, in his stead, *you* take his chains: or, for the Sultan's service, fight as a slave, or dig in his mines"?

Elvir. Exactly, sir—that is the petition—I thank you, sir.

Keep. You don't know, young man, what *it is* to dig in mines—or fight against foes, who make their prisoners die by unheard-of tortures.

Elvir. *You* do not know, sir, what *it is*—to see a parent suffer.

Hasw *(writing)*. Your name, sir?

Elvir. Elvirus Casimir.

Hasw. Your father's?

Elvir. The same—one who followed agriculture in the fields of Symria; but, induced by the call of freedom—

Hasw. How!—have a care.

Elvir. I thank you—his son, by the call of nature, supplicates his freedom.

Keep. The rebel, you find, breaks out.

Elvir *(aside to the Keeper)*. Silence! silence! he forgives it.—Don't remind him—don't undo my hopes.

Hasw. I will serve you, if I can.

Elvir. And I will merit it; indeed I will.—You shall not complain of me—I will be—

Hasw. Retire—I trust you.

(Elvirus bows lowly, and retires.)

Keep. Yonder cell contains a female prisoner.

Hasw. A female prisoner!

Keep. Without a friend or comforter, she has existed there these many years—nearly fifteen.

Hasw. Is it possible!

Keep. Would you wish to see her?

Hasw. If it won't give her pain.

Keep. At least, she'll not resent it—for she seldom complains, except in moans to herself.—*(Goes to the cell.)* Lady, here is one come to visit all the prisoners—please to appear before him.

Hasw. I thank you—you speak with reverence and respect to her.

Keep. She has been of some note, though now totally unfriended—at least we think she has, from her gentle manners;

and our governor is in the daily expectation of some liberal ransom for her: this makes her imprisonment without hope of release, till that day arrives.—*(Going to the cell.)* Take my hand— you are weak. *(He leads her from the cell—she appears faint, and as if the light affected her eyes.—Haswell pulls off his hat, and after a pause—)*

HASW. I fear you are not in health, lady.

(She looks at him solemnly for some time.)

KEEP. Speak, madam—speak.

PRIS. No—not very well. *(Faintingly.)*

HASW. Where are your friends? When do you expect your ransom?

PRIS *(shaking her head).* Never.

KEEP. She persists to say so; thinking, by that declaration, we shall release her without a ransom.

HASW. Is that your motive?

PRIS. I know no motive for a falsehood.

HASW. I was to blame—pardon me.

KEEP. Your answers are somewhat more proud than usual. *(He retires up the stage.)*

PRIS. They are.—*(To Haswell.)* Forgive me—I am mild with all these people—but from a countenance like yours—I could not bear reproach.

HASW. You flatter me.

PRIS. Alas! Sir, and what have I to hope from such a meanness?— You do not come to ransom me.

HASW. Perhaps I do.

PRIS. Oh! do not say so—unless—unless—I am not to be deceived. Pardon in your turn this suspicion: but when I have so much to hope for—when the sun, the air, fields, woods, and all that wondrous world wherein I have been so happy, is in prospect— forgive me, if the vast hope makes me fear.

HASW. Unless your ransom is fixed at something beyond my power to give, I *will* release you.

PRIS. Release me!—Benevolent!

HASW. How shall I mark you down in my petition? *(Takes out his book.)* What name?

PRIS. Tis almost blotted from my memory. *(Weeping.)*

KEEP. It is of little note—a female prisoner, taken with the rebel party, and in these cells confined for fifteen years.

PRIS. During which time I have demeaned myself with all humility to my governors: neither have I distracted my fellow-prisoners with a complaint that might recall to their memory their own unhappy fate. I have been obedient, patient; and cherished hope to cheer me with vain dreams, while despair possessed my reason.

HASW. Retire—I will present the picture you have given.

PRIS. And be successful—or, never let me see you more. *(She goes up the stage.)*

HASW. So it shall be.

PRIS *(returns)*. Or, if you should miscarry in your views—for who forms plans that do not sometimes fail?—I will not reproach you, even to myself.—No—nor will I suffer much from the disappointment—merely that you may not have what I suffer, to account for. *(Exit to her cell.)*

HASW. Excellent mind!

KEEP. In this cell— *(Going to another.)*

HASW. No—take me away: I have enough to do for those I have seen—I may not see more at present. *(Exeunt.)*

Scene iv. The former prison scene.

(Enter Zedan.)

ZEDAN. They are coming.—I'll stand here in his sight, that, should he miss what I have taken, he may not suspect me to be the robber, but suppose it is one who has hid himself.

(Enter Keeper and Haswell.)

KEEP *(to Zedan)*. What makes you here?—still moping by yourself, and lamenting for your family? *(To Haswell.)* That man, the most ferocious I ever met with, laments, sometimes even with tears, the separation from his wife and children.

HASW *(going to him)*. I am sorry for you, friend:

(Zedan looks sullen and morose.)

I pity you.

Keep. Yes, he had a pleasant hamlet on the neighboring island: plenty of fruits, clear springs, and wholesome roots, and now complains bitterly of his repasts—sour rice, and muddy water. *(Exit Keeper.)*

Hasw. Poor man! bear your sorrows nobly.—And, as we are alone, no miserable eye to grudge the favor—*(Looking round.)* take this trifle—*(Gives money.)* it will, at least, make your meals better for a few short weeks, till Heaven may please to favor you with a less sharp remembrance of the happiness you have lost.—Farewell. *(Going.)*

(Zedan catches hold of him, and taking the pocket-book from his belt, puts it into Haswell's hand.)

Hasw. What's this?

Zedan. I meant to gain my liberty with it—but I will not vex you.

Hasw. How came you by it?

Zedan. Stole it—and would have stabbed you, too, had you been alone—but I am glad I did not—Oh, I am glad I did not!

Hasw. You like me then?

Zedan *(shakes his head, and holds his heart)*. 'Tis something that I never felt before—it makes me like not only you, but all the world besides.—The love of my family was confined to them alone—but this sensation makes me love even my enemies.

Hasw. O, nature! grateful! mild! gentle! and forgiving!—worst of tyrants they, who, by hard usage, drive you to be cruel.

(Re-enter Keeper.)

Keep. The lights are ready, sir, through the dark passage. *(To Zedan.)* Go to your fellows.

Hasw *(to Zedan)*. Farewell—we will meet again.

(Zedan exit on one side; Haswell and Keeper exeunt on the other.)

ACT III.

Scene i. An apartment at Sir Luke Tremor's.

(Enter Sir Luke and Aurelia.)

Sir Luke. Why, then, Aurelia, (though I never mentioned it to my Lady Tremor) my friend wrote me word he had reason to suppose your affections were improperly fixed upon a young gentleman in that neighborhood; and this was his reason for wishing you to leave that place to come hither; and this continual dejection convinces me my friend was not mistaken.—Answer me—can you say he was?

Aure. Sir Luke, candidly to confess—

Sir Luke. Nay, no tears—why in tears? for a husband?—be comforted—we'll get you one ere long, I warrant.

Aure. Dear Sir Luke, how can you imagine I am in tears because I have not a husband, while you see Lady Tremor every day in tears for the very opposite cause?

Sir Luke. No matter; women like to have a husband through pride; and I have known a woman marry, from that very motive, even a man she has been ashamed of.

Aure. Perhaps Lady Tremor married from pride.

Sir Luke. Yes—and I'll let her know that pride is painful.

Aure. But, sir, her ladyship's philosophy—

Sir Luke. She has no philosophy.

(Enter Lady Tremor and Twineall.)

Sir Luke. Where is my Lord Flint? What have you done with him?

Lady. He's speaking a word to Mr. Meanright, about his passport to England—Did you mean me, Sir Luke, who has no philosophy?—I protest, I have a great deal.

Sir Luke. When did you show it?

Lady. When the servant at my Lady Grissel's threw a whole urn of boiling water upon your legs.—Did I then give any proofs of female weakness? did I faint, scream, or even shed a tear?

Sir Luke. No, very true; and while I lay sprawling on the carpet, I could see you holding a smelling-bottle to the lady of the house, begging of her not to make herself uneasy, "for that the accident was of no manner of consequence."

Aure. Dear sir, don't be angry: I am sure her ladyship spoke as she thought.

Sir Luke. I suppose she did, Miss.

Aure. I mean—she thought the accident might be easily—She thought you might be easily recovered.

Lady. No, indeed, I did not: but I thought Sir Luke had frequently charged me with the want of patience; and, that moment, the very thing in the world I could have wished occurred, on purpose to give me an opportunity to prove his accusation false.

Sir Luke. Very well, madam—but did not the whole company censure your behavior? did not they say, it was not the conduct of a wife?

Lady. Only our particular acquaintance could say so; for the rest of the company, I am sure, did not take me to be your wife.— Thank Heaven, our appearance never betrays that secret. Do you think we look like the same flesh and blood?

Sir Luke. That day, in particular, we did not; for I remember you had been no less than three hours at your toilet.

Lady. And indeed, Sir Luke, if you were to use milk of roses, and several other things of the same kind, you can't think how much more like a fine gentleman you would look.—Such things as those make, almost, all the difference between you and such a man as Mr. Twineall.

Twi. No, pardon me, madam—a face like mine may use those things; but in Sir Luke's they would entirely destroy that fine martial appearance—*(Sir Luke looks confounded.)*—which women, as well as men admire—for, as valor is the first ornament of our sex—

Lady. What are you saying, Mr. Twineall?—*(Aside.)* I'll keep on this subject if I can.

Twi. I was going to observe, madam, that the reputation of a general—which puts me in mind, Sir Luke, of an account I read of a battle—*(He crosses over to Sir Luke, who turns up the stage, in the utmost confusion, and steals out of the room.)*

LADY. Well, sir—go on, go on—you were going to introduce—

TWI. A battle, madam—but Sir Luke is gone!

LADY. Never mind that, sir: he generally runs away on these occasions.

SIR LUKE *(coming back)*. What were you saying, Aurelia, about a husband?

LADY. She did not speak.

SIR LUKE. To be sure, ladies in India do get husbands very soon.

TWI. Not always, I am told Sir Luke—Women of family, *(Fixing his eyes steadfastly on Lady Tremor.)* indeed, may soon enter into the matrimonial state—but the rich men in India, we are told in England, are grown of late very cautious with whom they marry; and there is not a man of any repute that will now look upon a woman as a wife, unless she is descended from a good family. *(Looking at Lady Tremor, who walks up the stage, and steals out of the room, just as Sir Luke had done before.)*

SIR LUKE. I am very sorry—very sorry to say, Mr. Twineall, that has not been always the case.

TWI. Then I am very sorry too, Sir Luke; for it is as much impossible that a woman, who is not born of an ancient family, can be—

(Lady Tremor returns.)

SIR LUKE. That is just what I say—they *cannot* be—

LADY. Sir Luke, let me tell you—

SIR LUKE. It does not signify telling, my dear—you have proved it.

LADY *(to Twineall)*. Sir, let me tell *you*.

TWI. O! O! my dear madam, 'tis all in vain—there is no such thing—it can't be—there is no pleading against conviction—a person of low birth must, in every particular, be a terrible creature.

SIR LUKE *(going to her)*. A terrible creature! a terrible creature!

LADY. Here comes my Lord Flint—I'll appeal to him.

(Enter Lord Flint.)

SIR LUKE *(going to him)*. My lord, I was saying, as a proof that our great Sultan, who now fills this throne, is no imposter, as the rebel party would insinuate, no low-born man, but of the royal stock, his conduct palpably evinces—for, had he not been nobly born, we should have beheld the plebeian busting forth upon all occasions—*(Looking at Lady Tremor.)*—and plebeian manners who can support?

LADY. Provoking! *(Goes up the stage.)*

LORD. Sir Luke, is there a doubt of the Emperor's birth and title? he is the real Sultan, depend upon it: it surprises me to hear you talk with the smallest uncertainty.

TWI. Indeed, Sir Luke, I wonder at it too: *(Aside to Lord Flint.)* and yet, damn me, my lord, if I have not my doubts. *(Lord Flint starts.)*

SIR LUKE. I, my lord? far be it from me! I was only saying what other people have said; for my part, I never harbored a doubt of the kind.—*(Aside.)* My head begins to nod, only for that word—Pray Heaven, I may die with it on!—I should not like to lose my head; nor should I like to die by a bullet—nor by a sword; and a cannon-ball would be as disagreeable as any thing I know.—It is very strange that I never yet could make up my mind in what manner I should like to go out of the world. *(During this speech, Twineall is paying court to Lord Flint— they come forward, and Sir Luke retires.)*

LORD. Your temerity astonishes me!

TWI. I must own, my lord, I feel somewhat awkward in saying it to your lordship—but my own heart, my own conscience, my own sentiments—they *are* my own; and they are dear to me.—So it is—the Sultan does not appear to me—*(With significance.)*—that great man some people think him.

LORD. Sir, you astonish me—Pray, what is your name? I have forgotten it.

TWI. Twineall, my lord—the Honorable Henry Twineall—your lordship does me great honor to ask.—Landed this morning from England, as your lordship may remember, in the ship Mercury, my lord; and all the officers on board speaking with the highest admiration and warmest terms of your lordship's official character.

LORD. Why, then, Mr. Twineall, I am very sorry—

TWI. And so am I, my lord, that your sentiments and mine should so far disagree, as I know they do.—I am not unacquainted with your firm adherence to the Sultan, but I am unused to disguise my thoughts—I could not, if I would. I have no little views, no sinister motives, no plots, no intrigues, no schemes of preferment; and I verily believe, that, if a pistol was now directed to my heart, or a large pension directed to my pocket (in the first case at least), I should speak my mind.

LORD *(aside).* A dangerous young man this! and I may make something of the discovery.

TWI *(aside).* It tickles him to the soul I find.—My lord, now I begin to be warm on the subject, I feel myself quite agitated; and, from the intelligence which I have heard, even when I was in England—there is every reason to suppose—exm—exm—exm— *(Mutters.)*

LORD. What, sir? what?

TWI. You understand me.

LORD. No—explain.

TWI. Why, then, there is every reason to suppose—some people are not what they should be—pardon my suspicions, if they are wrong.

LORD. I *do* pardon your thoughts, with all my heart—but your words young man, you must answer for. *(Aside.)*—Lady Tremor, good morning.

TWI *(aside).* He is going to ruminate on my sentiments, I dare say.

LADY. Shall we have your lordship's company in the evening? Mr. Haswell will be here; if your lordship has no objection.

SIR LUKE. How do you know Mr. Haswell will be here?

LADY. Because he has just called in his way to the palace and said so: and he has been telling us some of the most interesting stories.

SIR LUKE. Of his morning visits, I suppose—I heard Meanright say, he saw him very busy.

LADY. Sir Luke and I dine out, my lord; but we shall return early in the evening.

LORD. I will be here, without fail.—Sir Luke, a word with you, if you please—*(They come forward.)*—Mr. Twineall has taken some very improper liberties with the Sultan's name, and I must insist on making him accountable for them.

SIR LUKE. My lord, you are extremely welcome—*(Trembling.)*—to do whatever your lordship pleases with any one belonging to me, or to my house—but I hope your lordship will pay some regard to the master of it.

LORD. O! great regard to the master—and to the mistress also.—
But for that gentleman—

SIR LUKE. Do what your lordship pleases.

LORD. I will—and I will make him—

SIR LUKE. If your lordship does not forget it.

LORD. I shan't forget it, Sir Luke—I have a very good memory
when I please.

SIR LUKE. I don't in the least doubt it, my lord—I never did doubt
it.

LORD. And I can be very severe, Sir Luke, when I please.

SIR LUKE. I don't in the least doubt it, my lord—I never did doubt
it.

LORD. You may depend upon seeing me here in the evening; and
then you shall find I have not threatened more than I mean to
perform—Good morning.

SIR LUKE. Good morning, my lord—I don't in the least doubt it.

(Exit Lord Flint.)

LADY *(coming forward with Twineall).* For Heaven's sake, Mr.
Twineall, what has birth to do with—

TWI. It has to do with every thing,—even with beauty;—and I
wish I may suffer death, if a woman, with all the mental and
personal accomplishments of the finest creature in the world,
would, to me, be of the least value, if lowly born.

SIR LUKE. I sincerely wish every man who visits me was of the
same opinion.

AURE. For shame, Mr. Twineall! persons of mean birth ought not
to be despised for what it was not in their power to prevent:
and, if it is a misfortune, you should consider them only as objects of pity.

TWI. And so I do pity them—and so I do—most sincerely—Poor
. creatures! *(Looking on Lady Tremor.)*

SIR LUKE. Aye, now he has atoned most properly.

LADY. Mr. Twineall, let me tell you—

SIR LUKE. My dear Lady Tremor—*(Taking her aside.)*—let him
alone—let him go on—there is something preparing for him he
little expects—so let the poor man say and do what he pleases
for the present—it won't last long, for he has offended my Lord

Flint; and I dare say his lordship will be able, upon some account, or another, to get him imprisoned for life.

LADY. Imprisoned!—Why not take off his head at once?

SIR LUKE. Well, my dear, I am sure I have no objection; and I dare
say my lord will have it done, to oblige you.—Egad, I must
make friends with her to keep mine safe. *(Aside.)*

LADY. Do you mean to take him out to dinner with us?

SIR LUKE. Yes, my dear, if you approve of it—not else.

LADY. You are become extremely polite.

SIR LUKE. Yes, my dear, his lordship has taught me how to be
polite.—Mr. Twineall, Lady Tremor, and I, are going to prepare
for our visit, and I will send a servant to show you to your
apartment, to dress; for you will favor us with your company,
I hope?

TWI. Certainly, Sir Luke, I shall do myself the honor.

LADY. Come this way, Aurelia; I can't bear to look at him. *(Exit
with Aurelia.)*

SIR LUKE. Nor I to think of him. *(Exit.)*

TWI. If I have not settled my business in this family, I am mistaken: they seem to be but of one opinion about me.—Devilish
clever fellow!—egad I am the man to send into the world—such
a volatile, good-looking scoundrel too, that no one suspects
me.—To be sure, I am under some few obligations to my friend
for letting me into the different characters of the family; and yet
I don't know whether I am obliged to him or not; for if he had
not made me acquainted with them, I should soon have had the
skill to find them out myself.—No: I will not think myself
under any obligation to him—it is very inconvenient for a gentleman to be under obligations. *(Exit.)*

Scene ii. The palace.

*(The Sultan discovered, with guards and officers attending.
Haswell is conducted in by an officer.)*

SULT. Sir, you were invited hither to receive public thanks for our
troops restored to health by your prescriptions.—Ask a reward
adequate to your services.

HASW. Sultan, the reward I ask, is to preserve more of your people
still.

SULT. How! more! my subjects are in health: no contagion visits them.

HASW. The prisoner is your subject. There, misery, more contagious than disease, preys on the lives of hundreds: sentenced but to confinement, their doom is death. Immured in damp and dreary vaults, they daily perish; and who can tell but that, among these many hapless sufferers, there may be hearts bent down with penitence to heaven and you for every slight offence—there may be some, among the wretched multitude, even innocent victims. Let me seek them out—let me save them and you.

SULT. Amazement! retract your application: curb this weak pity; and receive our thanks.

HASW. Restrain my pity!—and what can I receive in recompense for that soft bond which links me to the wretched? and, while it soothes their sorrow, repays me more than all the gifts an empire could bestow.—But, if repugnant to your plan of government, I apply not in the name of pity, but of justice.

SULT. Justice!

HASW. The justice which forbids all, but the worst of criminals, to be denied that wholesome air the very brute creation freely takes.

SULT. Consider for whom you plead—for men (if not base culprits) so misled, so depraved, they are dangerous to our state, and deserve none of its blessings.

HASW. If not upon the undeserving—if not upon the hapless wanderer from the paths of rectitude,—where shall the sun diffuse his light, or the clouds distil their dew? Where shall spring breathe fragrance, or autumn pour its plenty?

SULT. Sir, your sentiments, still more your character, excite my curiosity. They tell me, that in our camps you visited each sick man's bed, administered yourself the healing draught, encouraged our savages with the hope of life, or pointed out their better hope in death.—The widow speaks your charities, the orphan lisps your bounties, and the rough Indian melts in tears to bless you.—I wish to ask why you have done all this?—What is it which prompts you thus to befriend the wretched and forlorn?

HASW. In vain for me to explain:—the time it would take to reveal to you—

SULT. Satisfy my curiosity in writing then.

HASW. Nay, if you will read, I'll send a book in which is already written why I act thus.

SULT. What book?—What is it called?

HASW. "The Christian Doctrine." *(Haswell bows here with the utmost reverence.)* There you will find—all I have done was but my duty.

SULT *(to the guards)*. Retire, and leave me alone with the stranger. *(All retire except Haswell and the Sultan—They come forward.)* Your words recall reflections that distract me; nor can I bear the pressure on my mind, without confessing—I am a Christian.

HASW. A Christian!—What makes you thus assume the apostate?

SULT. Misery and despair.

HASW. What made you a Christian?

SULT. My Arabella, a lovely European, sent hither in her youth, by her mercenary parents, to sell herself to the prince of all these territories. But 'twas my happy lot, in humble life, to win her love, snatch her from his expecting arms, and bear her far away; where, in peaceful solitude we lived, till, in the heat of the rebellion against the late Sultan, I was forced from my happy home to take a part.—I chose the imputed rebels' side, and fought for the young aspirer.—An arrow, in the midst of the engagement, pierced his heart; and his officers, alarmed at the terror this stroke of fate might cause among their troops, urged me (as I bore a strong resemblance to him) to counterfeit a greater still, and show myself to the soldiers as their king recovered. I yielded to their suit, because it gave me ample power to avenge the loss of my Arabella, who had been taken from her home by the merciless foe, and barbarously murdered.

HASW. Murdered!

SULT. I learnt so, and my fruitless search to find her has confirmed the intelligence. Frantic for her loss, I joyfully embraced a scheme which promised vengeance on the enemy:—it prospered; and I revenged my wrongs and hers with such unsparing justice on the opposite army and their king, that even the men, who made me what I am, trembled to reveal their imposition; and for their interest still continue it.

HASW. Amazement!

SULT. Nay, they fill my prisons every day with wretches, who but whisper I am not their real Sultan. The secret, therefore, I myself boldly relate in private: the danger is to him who speaks it again; and, with this caution, I trust it is safe with you.

HASW. It was, without that caution.—Now hear my answer to your tale:—Involved in deeds, in cruelties, at which your better thoughts revolt, the meanest wretch your camps or prisons hold, claims not half the compassion *you* have excited. Permit me, then, to be your comforter.

SULT. Impossible!

HASW. In the most fatal symptoms, I have undertaken the body's cure. The mind's disease, perhaps, I am not less a stranger to. Oh! trust the noble patient to my care.

SULT. What medicine will you apply?

HASW. Lead you to behold the wretched in their misery, and then show you yourself in their deliverer.—I have your promise for a boon—'tis this:—give me the liberty of six whom I shall name, now in confinement, and be yourself a witness of their enlargement.—See joy lighted in the countenance where sorrow still has left its rough remains—behold the tear of rapture chase away that of anguish—hear the faltering voice, long used to lamentation, in broken accents, utter thanks and blessings!— Behold this scene, and if you find the prescription ineffectual, dishonor your physician.

SULT. I will make trial of it.

HASW. Come, then, to the governor's house this very night,—into that council-room so often perverted to the use of the torture; and there (unknown to those, I shall release, as their king) you will be witness to all the grateful heart can dictate, and feel all that benevolence can taste.

SULT. I will meet you there.

HASW. In the evening?

SULT. At ten precisely.—Guards, conduct the stranger from the palace.

HASW. Thus far advanced, what changes may not be hoped for! *(Exit.)*

ACT IV.

Scene i. An apartment at Sir Luke Tremor's.

(Enter Elvirus and Aurelia.)

ELVIR. Oh! my Aurelia, since the time I first saw you—since you left the pleasant spot where I first beheld you—what distress, what anguish have we known!

AURE. Your family?

ELVIR. Yes; and that caused the silence which I hope you have lamented. I could not wound you with the recital of our misfortunes: and now, only with the sad idea that I shall never see you more, am I come to take my last farewell.

AURE. Is there a chance that we may never meet again?

ELVIR. There is; and I sincerely hope it may prove so.—To see you again, would be again to behold my father pining in misery.

AURE. Explain—

(A loud rapping at the door.)

That is Sir Luke and Lady Tremor.—What shall I say, should they come into this room?—They suspect I correspond with some person in the country.—Who shall I tell them you are? upon what business can I say you come?

ELVIR. To avoid all suspicion of my real situation, and to ensure admittance, I put on this habit, and told the servant, when I inquired for you, I was just arrived from England.—*(She starts.)*—Nay, it was but necessary I should conceal who I was in this suspicious place, or I might plunge a whole family in the imputed guilt of mine.

AURE. Good heaven!

ELVIR. I feared, besides, there was no other means, no likelihood, to gain admission; and what, what would I not have sacrificed, rather than have left you for ever without a last farewell? Think on these weighty causes, and pardon the deception.

AURE. But if I should be asked—

ELVIR. Say as I have done.—My stay must be so short, it is impossible they should detect me—for I must be back—

AURE. Where?

ELVIR. No matter where—I must be back before the evening—and wish never to see you more.—I love you, Aurelia—Oh, how truly!—and yet there is a love more dear, more sacred still.

AURE. You torture me with suspense—Sir Luke is coming this way—What name shall I say if he asks me?

ELVIR. Glanmore—I announced that name to the servant.

AURE. You tremble.

ELVIR. The imposition hurts me; and I feel as if I dreaded a detection, though 'tis scarce possible. Sorrows have made a coward of me: even the servant, I thought, looked at me with suspicion, and I was both confounded and enraged.

AURE. Go into this apartment: I'll follow you.

(Exit Elvirus at a door.)

SIR LUKE *(without)*. Abominable! provoking! impertinent! not to be borne!

AURE. *(listening)*. Thank heaven, Sir Luke is so perplexed with some affairs of his own, he may not think of mine. *(Exit to Elvirus.)*

(Enter Sir Luke, followed by Lady Tremor.)

SIR LUKE. I am out of all patience, and all temper—did you ever hear of such a complete impertinent coxcomb? Talk, talk, talk, continually! and referring to me on all occasions! "Such a man was a brave general—another a great admiral"; and then he must tell a long story about a siege, and ask me if it did not make my bosom glow!

LADY. It had not that effect upon your face, for you were as white as ashes.

SIR LUKE. But you did not see yourself while he was talking of grandfathers and great grandfathers;—If you had—

LADY. I was not white, I protest.

Sir Luke. No—but you were as red as scarlet.

Lady. And you ought to have resented the insult, if you saw me affected by it.—Oh! some men would have given him such a dressing!

Sir Luke. Yes, my dear, if your uncle the friseur had been alive, he would have given him a dressing,[15] I dare say.

Lady. Sir Luke, none of your impertinence: you know I can't, I won't bear it—neither will I wait for Lord Flint's resentment on Mr. Twineall.—No, I desire you will tell him to quit this roof immediately.

Sir Luke. My dear, you must excuse me—I can't think of quarreling with a gentleman in my own house.

Lady. Was it your own house today at dinner when he insulted us? and would you quarrel then?

Sir Luke. No; that was a friend's house—and I make it a rule never to quarrel in my own house, a friend's house, in a tavern, or in the streets.

Lady. Well, then, I would quarrel in my own house, a friend's house, a tavern, or in the street, if any one offended me.

Sir Luke. O, my dear, I have no doubt of it—no doubt, in the least.

Lady. But, at present, it shall be in my own house: and I will desire Mr. Twineall to quit it immediately.

Sir Luke. Very well, my dear—pray do.

Lady. I suppose, however, I may tell him, I have your authority to bid him go?

Sir Luke. Tell him I have no authority—none in the world over you—but that you will do as you please.

Lady. I can't tell him so—he won't believe it.

Sir Luke. Why not?—You tell me so, and make me believe it too.

Lady. Here the gentleman comes—Go away for a moment.

Sir Luke. With all my heart, my dear. *(Going in a hurry.)*

Lady. I'll give him a few hints, that he must either change his mode of behavior, or leave us.

Sir Luke. That's right—but don't be too warm: or if he should be very impertinent, or insolent—I hear Aurelia's voice in the next room—call *her,* and I dare say she'll come and take your part. *(Exit Sir Luke.)*

(Enter Twineall.)

TWI. I positively could pass a whole day upon that staircase—those reverend faces!—I presume they are the portraits of some of your ladyship's illustrious ancestors?

LADY. Sir! Mr. Twineall—give me leave to tell you—*(In a violent passion.)*

TWI. The word illustrious, I find, displeases you. Pardon me—I did not mean to make use of so forcible an epithet. I know the delicacy of sentiment, which cannot bear the reflection that a few centuries only should reduce from royalty, one whose dignified deportment seems to have been formed for that resplendent station.

LADY. The man is certainly mad!—Mr. Twineall—

TWI. Pardon me, madam; I own I am an enthusiast on these occasions. The dignity of blood—

LADY. You have too much, I am sure—do have a little taken from you.

TWI. Gladly would I lose every drop that fills these plebeian veins, to be ennobled by the smallest—

LADY. Pray, sir, take up your abode in some other place.

TWI. Madam? *(Surprised.)*

LADY. Your behavior, sir—

TWI. If my friend had not given me the hint, damn me if I should not think her downright angry. *(Aside.)*

LADY. I can scarcely contain my rage at being so laughed at. *(Aside.)*

TWI. I'll mention the wig: this is the time—*(Aside.)*—Perhaps you may resent it, madam: but there is a favor—

LADY. A favor, sir! is this a time to ask a favor?

TWI. To an admirer of antiquity, as I am—

LADY. Antiquity again!

TWI. I beg pardon—but—a wig—

LADY. A what? *(Petrified.)*

TWI. A wig. *(Bowing.)*

LADY. Oh! Oh! Oh! *(Choking.)* this is not to be borne—this is too much—ah! ah! *(Sitting down and going into fits.)* a direct, plain, palpable, and unequivocal attack upon my family, without evasion or palliative.—I can't bear it any longer.—Oh! oh!— *(Shrieking.)*

TWI. Bless my soul, what shall I do?—what's the matter?

SIR LUKE *(without).* Maids! maids! go to your mistress—that good-for-nothing man is doing her a mischief.

(Enter Aurelia.)

AURE. Dear madam, what is the matter?

(Enter Sir Luke, and stands close to the scenes.[16])

LADY. Oh! oh! *(Crying.)*
SIR LUKE. How do you do now, my dear?
TWI. Upon my word, Sir Luke—
SIR LUKE. O, sir, no apology—it does not signify—never mind it—I beg you won't put yourself to the trouble of an apology—it is of no kind of consequence.
LADY. What do you mean, Sir Luke? *(Recovered.)*
SIR LUKE. To show proper philosophy, my dear, under the affliction I feel for your distress.
LADY *(to Aurelia).* Take Twineall out of the room.
AURE. Mr. Twineall, her ladyship begs you'll leave the room till she is a little recovered.
TWI. Certainly. *(Bows respectfully to Lady Tremor, and exit with Aurelia.)*
SIR LUKE. I thought what you would get by quarreling,—fits—and tears.
LADY. And you know, Sir Luke, if you had quarreled, you would have been in the same situation. *(Rising from her seat.)* But, Sir Luke, my dear Sir Luke, show yourself a man of courage but on this occasion.
SIR LUKE. My dear, I would do as much for you as I would for my own life—but damn me if I think I could fight to save that.

(Enter Lord Flint.)

LORD. Lady Tremor, did the servant say you were very well, or very ill?
LADY. O, my lord, that insolent coxcomb, the Honorable Mr. Twineall—
LORD. I am very glad you put me in mind of him—I dare say I should have forgot else, notwithstanding I came on purpose.

LADY. Forgot what?

LORD. A little piece of paper here: *(Pulling out a parchment.)* but it will do a great deal.—Has he offended you?

LADY. Beyond bearing.

LORD. I am glad of it, because it gives double pleasure to my vengeance.—He is a disaffected person—boldly told me he doubted the Sultan's right to the throne.—I have informed against him; and his punishment is left to my discretion. I may have him imprisoned, shot, sent to the galleys, or his head cut off—but which does your ladyship choose?—Whichever you choose is at your service. *(Bowing.)*

LADY *(curtsying)*. O, they are all alike to me: whichever you please, my lord.

SIR LUKE. What a deal of ceremony! how cool they are upon the subject!

LORD. And why not cool, sir? why not cool?

SIR LUKE. O, very true—I am sure it has frozen me.

LORD. I will go instantly, for fear it should slip my memory, and put this paper into the hands of proper officers. In the mean time, Sir Luke, if you can talk with your visitor, Mr. Twineall, do.—Inquire his opinion of the Sultan's rights—ask his thoughts, as if you were commissioned by me—and, while he is revealing them to you, the officers shall be in ambush, surprise him in the midst of his sentiments, and bear him away to—

(Twineall looking in.)

TWI. May I presume to inquire how your ladyship does?

LADY. O, yes—and pray walk in—I am quite recovered.

LORD. Lady Tremor, I bid you good day for the present.

SIR LUKE *(following him to the door)*. Your lordship won't forget?

LORD. No—depend upon it, I shall remember.

SIR LUKE. Yes—and make some other people remember too.

(Exit Lord Flint.)

TWI. Is his lordship gone? I am very sorry.

SIR LUKE. No—don't be uneasy, he'll soon come back.

(Enter Haswell.)

Sir Luke. Mr. Haswell, I am glad to see you!

Hasw. I told Lady Tremor I would call in the evening, Sir Luke; and I have kept my word—I hoped to meet my Lord Flint here, as I have some business on which I want to speak to him; but he passed me at the door in such great haste he would hardly allow me to ask him how he did—I hope your ladyship is well this afternoon. *(Bows to Twineall—Sir Luke exit at the door to Aurelia and Elvirus.)*

Twi. Pardon me, Mr. Haswell, but I almost suspect you heard of her ladyship's indisposition, and therefore paid this visit; for I am perfectly acquainted with your care and attention to all under affliction.

Hasw *(bows gravely)*. Has your ladyship been indisposed?

Lady. A little—but I am much better.

Twi. Surely, of all virtues, charity is the first! it so protects our neighbor!

Hasw. Do you think, sir, that *patience* frequently protects him as much?

Twi. Dear sir—pity for the poor and miserable—

Hasw. Is oftener excited than the poor and miserable are aware of. *(Looking significantly at him.)*

Sir Luke *(from the room where Aurelia and Elvirus are)*. Nay, sir, I beg you will walk into this apartment.—Aurelia, introduce the gentleman to Lady Tremor.

Lady. Who has she with her?

Hasw. Aurelia!—oh! I have not seen her I know not when: and, besides my acquaintance with her relations in England, there is a frank simplicity in her manners that has won my friendship.

(Enter Sir Luke, Aurelia, and Elvirus.)

Sir Luke. You should have introduced Mr. Glanmore before.—I assure you, sir, *(To Elvirus.)* I did not know, nor should I have known, if I had not accidentally come into that room—

(Haswell starts, on seeing Elvirus.)

Sir Luke *(to Lady Tremor)*. A relation of Aurelia's—a Mr. Glanmore, my dear, just arrived from England; who has called to pass a few minutes with us before he sets off to the part of India he is to reside in.

(Elvirus and Aurelia appear in confusion.)

LADY. I hope, sir, your stay with us will not be so short as Sir Luke has mentioned?

ELVIR. Pardon me, madam,, it must.—The caravan, with which I travel, goes off this evening, and I must accompany it.

HASW *(aside).* I doubted my eyes: but his voice confirms me. *(Looking on Elvirus.)*

LADY. Why, if you only arrived this morning, Mr. Glanmore, you came passenger in the same ship with Mr. Twineall?

TWI. No, madam.—Sir, I am very sorry we had not the pleasure of your company on board of us. *(To Elvirus.)*

SIR LUKE. You had: Mr. Glanmore came over in the Mercury.— Did not you tell me so, sir?

(Elvirus bows.)

TWI. Bless my soul, sir! I beg your pardon: but surely that cannot be—I got acquainted with every soul on board of us—every creature—all their connexions—and I can scarcely suppose you were of the number.

SIR LUKE *(aside).* How impertinent he is to every body! O, that I had but courage to knock him down!

ELVIR *(to Twineall).* Perhaps, sir—

AURE. Yes, I dare say, that was the case.

TWI. What was the case, madam?

SIR LUKE. Wha-wha-wha—*(Mimicks.)* that is not good breeding.

HASW. Why do you blush, Aurelia?

AURE. Because *(Hesitating.)*—this gentleman—came over in the same ship with Mr. Twineall.

SIR LUKE. And I can't say I wonder at your blushing.

TWI. Why then positively, sir, I thought I had known every passenger—and surely—

LADY. Mr. Twineall, your behavior puts me out of all patience.— Did you not hear Mr. Glanmore say he came in the same vessel; and is not that sufficient?

Twi. Perfectly, madam—perfectly: but I thought there might be some mistake.

ELVIR. And there is, sir: you find *you* are mistaken.

LADY. I thought so.—

HASW *(to Elvirus)*. And you *did* come in the same vessel?

ELVIR. Sir, do you doubt it?

HASW. Doubt it!

ELVIR. Dare not doubt it.—*(Trembling and confused.)*

HASW. Dare not!

ELVIR. No, sir; dare not. *(Violently.)*

AURE. Oh, heavens!

SIR LUKE *(to Aurelia)*. Come, my dear, you and I will get out of the way. *(Retiring with her.)*

LADY. O dear!—for heaven's sake!—Mr. Twineall, this is your doing.

TWI. Me, madam!—

HASW. I beg the company's pardon—but *(To Elvirus.)* a single word with you, sir, if you please.

LADY. Dear Mr. Haswell—

HASW. Trust my prudence and forbearance, madam—I will but speak a word in private to this gentleman. *(Haswell takes Elvirus down to the bottom of the stage—the rest retire.)*

HASW. Are you, or are you not, an impostor?

ELVIR. I am—I am—but do not you repeat my words.—Do not *you* say it. *(Threatening.)*

HASW. What am I to fear?

ELVIR. Fear *me*—I cannot lie with fortitude; but I can—Beware of me.

HASW. I *will* beware of you, and so shall all my friends.

ELVIR. Insolent, insulting man!—*(With the utmost contempt.)*

(Lady Tremor and the rest come forward.)

LADY. Come, come, gentlemen, gentlemen, I hope you are now perfectly satisfied concerning this little misunderstanding—let us change the subject.—Mr. Haswell, have you been successful before the Sultan for any of those poor prisoners you visited this morning?

SIR LUKE. Aye; Meanright told me he saw you coming from them wrapped up in your long cloak; and he said he should not have known you, if somebody had not said it was you.

(Elvirus looks with surprise, confusion, and repentance.)

LADY. But what success with the Sultan?
HASW. He has granted me the pardon and freedom of any six whom I shall present as objects of his mercy.
LADY. I sincerely rejoice:—Then the youth and his father, whom you felt so much for, I am sure will be in the number of those who are to share your intercession.

(Haswell makes no reply; and, after a pause—)

ELVIR *(with the most supplicatory tone and manner)*. Sir—Mr. Haswell—O heavens! I did not know you.
SIR LUKE. Come, Mr. Haswell, this young man seems sorry he has offended you—forgive him.
LADY. Aye, do, Mr. Haswell.—Are you sorry, sir?
ELVIR. Wounded to the heart—and, without his pardon, see nothing but despair.
LADY. Good heavens!
HASW. Sir Luke, my Lord Flint told me he was coming back directly. Pray inform him I had business elsewhere and could wait no longer. *(Exit.)*
ELVIR. O! I'm undone.
LADY. Follow him if you have any thing to say.
ELVIR. I dare not—I feel the terror of his just reproach.
LADY. Did you know him in England?
AURE. Dear madam, will you suffer me to speak a few words—
SIR LUKE *(aside to Lady Tremor)*. Leave her and her relation together, and let us take a turn in the garden with Mr. Twineall.—I'm afraid his lordship will be back before we have drawn him to say any more on the subject, for which he is to be arrested.
LADY. You are right.
SIR LUKE. Mr. Twineall, will you walk this way?—that young lady and gentleman wish to have a little private conversation.
TWI. O, certainly, Sir Luke, by all means. *(Exeunt Sir Luke and Lady.)*—*(To Elvirus.)* I am extremely sorry, sir, that you kept

your bed during the voyage: I should else have been most prodigiously happy in such good company. *(Exit.)*

AURE. Why are you thus agitated? It was wrong to be so impetuous—but such regret as this is too much.

ELVIR. Hear the secret I refused to tell you before—my father is a prisoner for life.

AURE. Oh, heavens! then Mr. Haswell was the only man—

ELVIR. And he had promised me—promised me, with benevolence, his patronage: but the disguise he wore, when I first saw him, led me to mistake his figure and appearance—has made me expose my falsehood, my infamy, and treat his honored person with abuse.

AURE. Yes, let his virtues make you thus repent: but let them also make you hope for pardon.

ELVIR. Nay, he is just as well as compassionate; and for detected falsehood—

AURE. You make me tremble.

ELVIR. Yet he shall hear my story—I'll follow him, and obtain his pity, if not his forgiveness.

AURE. And do not blush, or feel yourself degraded to *kneel* to him, for *he* would scorn that pride which triumphs over the humbled. *(Exeunt.)*

Scene ii. The garden.

(Enter Sir Luke, Twineall, and Lady Tremor.)

TWI. Why, really, Sir Luke, as my lord has given you charge to sound my principles, I must own they are just such as I delivered them to him.

SIR LUKE. Mr. Twineall, I only wish you to be a little more circumstantial—we will suppose the present Sultan no impostor—yet what pretensions do you think the other family possessed?

TWI. That I'll make clear to you at once—or if my reasons are not very clear, they are at least very positive, and that you know is the same thing:—this family—no—that family—the family that reigned before this—this came after that—that came before this. Now every one agrees that this family was always—so and so—*(Whispering.)*—and that the other was always—so and so—*(Whispering.)*—in short, every body knows that one of them had always a very suspicious—you know what.

Sir Luke. No, I don't.

Twi. Pshaw—pshaw—everybody conjectures what—and though it was never said in so many words, yet it was always supposed—and though there never has been any proof, yet there have been things much more strong than proof—and for that very reason, Sir William—(Sir Luke, I mean—I beg your pardon) for that very reason—I can't think what made me call you Sir William—for that very reason—(O, I was thinking of Sir William Tiffany)—for that very reason, let people say what they will—that, that must be their opinion.—But then where is the man who will speak his thoughts freely, as I have done?

(Enter Guards, who had been listening at a distance, during this speech.)

Sir Luke *(starting)*. Bless my soul, gentlemen, you make my heart leap to my very lips.

Guards *(to Twineall)*. Sir, you are our prisoner, and must go with us.

Twi. Gentlemen, you are mistaken—I had all my clothes made in England, and 'tis impossible the bill can have followed me already.[17]

Guard. You are charged with treason against the state.

Twi. Treason against the state—You are mistaken: it cannot be me.

Guard. No—there is no mistake. *(Pulling out a paper.)* You are here called Henry Twineall.

Twi. But if they have left out *honorable,* it can't be me—I am the Honorable Henry Twineall.

Sir Luke. That you are to prove before your judges.

Guard. Yes, sir; and we are witnesses of the long speech you have just now been making.

Twi. And pray, gentlemen, did you know what I meant by it?

Guard. Certainly.

Twi. Why, then, upon my soul, it is more than I did—I wish I may be sacrificed—

SIR LUKE. Well, well, you are going to be sacrificed—Don't be impatient.

TWI. But, gentlemen—Sir Luke!

(The guards seize him.)

LADY. Dear Mr. Twineall, I am afraid you will have occasion for the dignity of all my ancestors to support you under this trial.

SIR LUKE. And have occasion for all my courage too.

TWI. But, sir—but, gentlemen—

SIR LUKE. Oh, I would not be in your coat, fashionable as it is, for all the Sultan's dominions.

(Exeunt Sir Luke and Lady on one side—Twineall and Guards on the other.)

ACT V.

Scene i. The prison.

(Haswell and the Female Prisoner discovered.)

HASW. Rather remain in this loathsome prison!—refuse the blessing offered you!—the blessing your pleased fancy formed so
precious, that you durst not even trust its reality?

PRIS. While my pleased fancy only saw the prospect, I own it was
delightful: but now reason beholds it, the view is changed; and
what, in the gay dream of fond delirium, seemed a blessing, in
my waking hours of sad reflection, would prove the most severe
of punishments.

HASW. Explain—what is the cause that makes you think thus?

PRIS. A cause, that has alone for fourteen years made me resigned
to a fate like this.—When you first mentioned my release from
this dark dreary place, my wild ideas included, with the light,
all that had ever made the light a blessing.—'Twas not the sun
I saw in my mad transport, but a husband filled my imagination—'twas his idea, that gave the colors of the world their
beauty, and made me fondly hope to be cheered by its bright-
ness.

HASW. A husband!

PRIS. But the world that I was wont to enjoy with him—to see
again without him; every well-known object would wound my
mind with dear delights forever lost, and make my freedom torture.

HASW. But yet—

PRIS. Oh! on my knees a thousand times I have thanked Heaven
that he partook not of this dire abode—that he shared not with
me my hard bondage; a greater blessing I possessed from that
reflection, than all his loved society could have given.—But in
a happy world, where smiling nature pours her boundless gifts!
oh! there his loss would be insupportable.

HASW. Do you lament him dead?

PRIS. Yes—or, like me, a prisoner—else he would have sought me out—have sought his Arabella!—*(Haswell starts.)* Why do you start?

HASW. Are you a Christian? an European?

ARABELLA. I am.

HASW. The name made me suppose it.—I am shocked that—the Christian's sufferings—*(Trying to conceal his surprise.)* But were you made a prisoner in the present Sultan's reign?

ARAB. I was—or I had been set free on his ascent to the throne; for he of course gave pardon to all the enemies of the slain monarch, among whom I and my husband were reckoned: but I was taken in a vessel, where I was hurried in the heat of the battle with a party of the late emperor's friends; and all these prisoners were, by the officers of the present Sultan, sent to slavery, or confined, as I have been, in hopes of ransom.

HASW. And did never intelligence or inquiry reach you from your husband?

ARAB. Never.

HASW. Never?

ARAB. I was once informed of a large reward offered for the discovery of a female Christian, and, with boundless hopes, I asked an interview with the messenger,—but found, on questioning him, *I* could not answer his description; as he secretly informed me, it was the Sultan who had caused the search, for one, *himself* had known, and dearly loved.

HASW. Good Heaven! *(Aside.)* You then conclude your husband dead?

ARAB. I do; or, like me, by some mischance, taken with the other party: and having no friend to plead his cause before the emperor whom he served—

HASW. *I* will plead it, should I ever chance to find him: but, ere we can hope for other kindness, you must appear before the Sultan, to thank him for the favor which you now decline, and to tell the cause why you cannot accept it.

ARAB. Alas! almost worn out with sorrow—an object of affliction as I am—in pity excuse me. Present my acknowledgments—my humble gratitude—but pardon my attendance.

HASW. Nay; you must go—it is necessary. I will accompany you to his presence.—Retire a moment; but when I send, be ready.

Arab. I shall obey. *(She bows obediently, and exit.)*

(As Haswell comes down, Elvirus places himself in his path—Haswell stops, looks at him with an austere earnestness, which Elvirus observing, turns away his face.)

Elvir. Nay, reproach me—I can bear your anger, but do not let me meet your eye—Oh! it is more awful, now I know who you are, than if you had kingdoms to dispense, or could deal instant death.—*(Haswell looks on him with a manly firmness, and then walks on, Elvirus following him.)*—I do not plead for my father now.—Since what has passed, I only ask forgiveness.

Hasw. Do you forgive yourself?

Elvir. I never will.

(Enter Keeper.)

Keep. One of our prisoners, who, in his cell, makes the most piteous moans, has sent to entreat that Mr. Haswell will not leave this place till he has heard his complaints and supplications.

Hasw. Bring me to him. *(Going.)*

Elvir. Nay, leave me not thus—perhaps never to see you more!

Hasw. You shall see me again: in the mean time, reflect on what you merit. *(Exit with Keeper.)*

Elvir. And what is that?—Confusion!—and yet, he says, I am to see him again—speak with him, perhaps.—Oh! there's a blessing the most abandoned feel, a divine propensity, they know not why, to commune with the virtuous. *(Exit.)*

Scene ii. The first prison scene.

(Enter Second Keeper, Haswell following.)

Hasw. Where is the poor unfortunate?

Second Keep. Here, sir.

Hasw. Am I to behold greater misery still?—a still greater object of compassion?

(Second Keeper opens a door, and Twineall enters a prisoner, in one of the prison dresses.)

Hasw. What have we here?

Twi. Don't you know me, Mr. Haswell?

Hasw. I beg your pardon—I beg your pardon—but is it—is it—

Twi. Why, Mr. Haswell, if you don't know me, or won't know me, I shall certainly lose my senses.

Hasw. O, I know you—know you very well.

Twi. What, notwithstanding the alteration in my dress?—there was a cruel plunder!

Hasw. O, I'll procure you that again; and, for all things else, I'm sure you will have patience.

Twi. O, no, I can't—upon my soul, I can't.—I want a little lavender water—My hair is in such a trim too!—no powder—no brushes—

Hasw. I will provide you with them all.

Twi. But who will you provide to look at me, when I am dressed?

Hasw. I'll bring all your acquaintance.

Twi. I had rather you would take me to see them.

Hasw. Pardon me.

Twi. Dear Mr. Haswell!—Dear sir!—Dear friend!—What shall I call you?—Only say what title you like best, and I'll call you by it directly:—I always did love to please everybody; and I am sure, at this time, I am more in need of a friend than ever I was in my life.

Hasw. What has brought you here?

Twi. Trying to get a place.

Hasw. A place?

Twi. Yes; and you see I have got one—and a very bad place it is—in short, sir, my crime is said to be an offence against the state; and they tell me, no man on earth but you can get that remitted.

Hasw. Upon my word the pardons I have obtained are but for few persons, and those already promised.

Twi. O, I know I am no favorite of yours: you think me an impertinent, silly, troublesome fellow,—and that my conduct in life will be neither of use to my country, nor of benefit to society.

Hasw. You mistake me, sir; I think such glaring imperfections as yours are, will not be of so much disadvantage to society, as those of a less faulty man. In beholding your conduct, thousands shall turn from the paths of folly to which fashion impels them: therefore, Mr. Twineall, if not pity for your failings, yet a concern for the good effect they may have upon the world (should you be admitted there again) will urge me to solicit your release.

Twi. Sir, you have such powers of oratory—such eloquence!—and I doubt not but that you are admired by the world equally for those advantages—

(Enter Messenger to Haswell.)

Mess. Sir, the Sultan is arrived in the council chamber, and has sent me—*(Whispers.)*

Hasw. I come—Mr. Twineall, farewell for the present. *(Exit with Messenger.)*

Twi. Now, what was that whisper about?—Oh, Heavens! perhaps my death in agitation!—I have brought myself into a fine situation!—done it by wheedling too!

Second Keep. Come, your business with Mr. Haswell being ended, return to your cell. *(Roughly.)*

Twi. Certainly, sir—certainly!—O, yes!—How happy is this prison in having such a keeper as you!—so mild, so gentle—there is something about you—I said, and I thought the moment I had the happiness of meeting you here, Dear me! said I—what would one give for such a gentleman as him in England!—You would be of infinite service to some of our young bucks, sir.

Second Keep. Go to your cell—go to your cell. *(Roughly.)*

Twi. This world would be nothing without elegant manners, and elegant people in all stations of life.—

(Enter Messenger, who whispers Second Keeper.)

Another whisper! *(Terrified.)*

Second Keep. No; come this way.—The judges are now sitting in the hall, and you must come before them.

Twi. Before the judges, sir—O, dear sir!—what, in this deshabille?—in this coat?—Dear me!—but to be sure one must conform to customs—to the custom of the country, where one resides. *(He goes to the door, and then stops.)* I beg your pardon, sir—would not you choose to go first?

Second Keep. No.
Twi. O! *(Exeunt.)*

Scene iii. The Council Chamber.

(Enter Sultan, Haswell, and Guards.)

Hasw. Sultan, I have gone beyond the limits of your bounty in my promises; and for one poor unhappy female, I have still to implore your clemency.

Sult. No—you named yourself the number to release, and it is fixed—I'll not increase it.

Hasw. A poor miserable female—

Sult. Am I less miserable than she is?—And who shall relieve me of my sorrows?

Hasw. Then let me tell you, Sultan, she is above your power to oblige, or to punish.—Ten years, nay, more, confinement in a dreary cell, has been no greater punishment to her, than had she lived in a pleasant world without the man she loved.

Sult. Ha!

Hasw. And freedom, which I offered, she rejects with scorn, because he is not included in the blessing.

Sult. You talk of prodigies!—*(He makes a sign for the guards to retire, and they withdraw.)* And yet I once knew a heart equal to this description.

Hasw. Nay, will you see her, witness yourself the fact?

Sult. I will—Why do I tremble!—My busy fancy presents an image—

Hasw. Yes, tremble! *(Threatening.)*

Sult. Ha! have a care—what tortures are you preparing for me?—My mind shrinks at the thought.

Hasw. Your wife you will behold—whom you have kept in want, in wretchedness, in a damp dungeon for these fourteen years, because you would not listen to the voice of pity.—Dread her look—her frown—not for herself alone, but for hundreds of her fellow-sufferers: for while your selfish fancy was searching with wild anxiety for her *you* loved—unpitying you forgot—others might love like you.

Sult. O! do not bring me to a trial which I have not courage to support.

Hasw. She attends without.—I sent for her to thank you for the favor she declines.—Nay, be composed—she knows you not—cannot, thus disguised as the Sultan. *(Exit Haswell.)*

Sult. O, my Arabella! could I have thought that your approach would ever impress my mind with horror!—or that, instead of flying to your arms with all the love I bear you, terror and shame should fix me a statue of remorse!

(Enter Haswell, leading Arabella.)

Hasw. Here kneel, and return your thanks.

Sult. My Arabella! worn with grief and anguish. *(Aside.)*

Arab *(kneeling to the Sultan).* Sultan, the favor you would bestow, I own and humbly thank you for.

sult. Gracious heaven! *(In much agitation.)*

Arab. But as I am now accustomed to confinement, and the brightest prospect of all the world can give, cannot inspire a wish that warms my heart to the enjoyment—I supplicate permission to transfer the blessing you have offered, to one of those who may have friends to welcome their return from bondage, and so make freedom precious.—I have none to rejoice at *my* release—none to lament my destiny while a prisoner.—And were I free in this vast, world, forlorn and friendless, 'tis but a prison still.

Sult. What have I done! *(Throwing himself on a sofa, with the greatest emotion.)*

Hasw. Speak to him again: he repents of the severity with which he has caused his fellow-creatures to be used. Tell him you forgive him.

Arab *(going to him).* Believe me, emperor, I forgive all who have ever wronged me—all who have ever caused my sufferings.—Pardon *you.*—Alas! I have pardoned even those who tore me from my husband!—Oh, Sultan! all the tortures you have made me suffer, compared to such a pang as that was—did I say I had forgiven those enemies of my peace?—Oh! I am afraid—afraid I have not yet.

Sult. Forgive them now, then,—for he is restored.—*(Taking off his turban.)*—Behold him in the Sultan, and once more seal my pardon.—

(She faints on Haswell.)

—Nay, pronounce it quickly, or my remorse for what you have endured will make my present tortures greater—than any my cruelties have yet inflicted.

ARAB *(recovering)*. Is this the light you promised?—*(To Haswell.)*—Dear precious light!—Is this my freedom? to which I bind myself a slave for ever—*(Embracing the Sultan.)*—What I *your* captive?—Sweet captivity! more precious than an age of liberty!

SULT. Oh! my Arabella! through the amazing changes of my fate (which I will soon disclose), think not, but I have searched for *thee* with unceasing care: but the blessing to behold you once again was left for my kind monitor alone to bestow.—Oh, Haswell! had I, like you, made others' miseries my concern, like you sought out the wretched, how many days of sorrow had I spared myself, as well as her I love!—for I long since had found my Arabella.

ARAB. Oh, heaven! that weighest our sufferings with our joys, and as our lives decline seest in the balance thy blessings far more ponderous than thy judgments—be witness, I complain no more of what I have endured, but find an ample recompense this moment.

HASW. I told you, sir, how you might be happy.

SULT. —Take your reward—(to a heart like yours, more valuable than treasure from my coffers)—this signet, with power to redress the wrongs of all my injured subjects.

HASW. Valuable indeed!—

ARAB *(to Haswell)*. Oh, virtuous man!—to reward thee are we made happy—to give thy pitying bosom the joy to see us so, heaven has remitted its intended punishment of continual separation.

SULT. Come, my beloved wife! come to my palace: there, equally, my dearest blessing, as when the cottage gave its fewer joys.— And in him *(To Haswell.)* we not only find our present happiness, but dwell securely on our future hopes—for here I vow, before he leaves our shores, I will adopt every measure he shall point out; and those acts of my life whereon he shall lay his censure, these will I make the subject of repentance.

(Exeunt Sultan and Arabella.—Haswell bows to heaven in silent thanks. Enter Keeper.)

KEEP. An English prisoner, just now condemned to lose his head, one Henry Twineall, humbly begs permission to speak a few short sentences, his last dying words, to Mr. Haswell.

HASW. Condemned to lose his head!—Lead me to him.

KEEP. O, sir, you need not hurry yourself: for it is off by this time, I dare say.

HASW. Off!

KEEP. Yes, sir: we don't stand long about these things in this country—I dare say it is off.

HASW *(impatiently)*. Lead me to him instantly.

KEEP. O! 'tis of consequence, is it, sir?—if that is the case—

(Exit Keeper followed by Haswell.)

Scene iv. An archway at the top of the stage; through which several guards enter.—Twineall in the middle, dressed for execution, with a large book in his hand.

TWI. One more stave, gentlemen, if you please.[18]

OFFI. The time is expired.

TWI. One more, gentlemen, if you please.

OFFI. The time is expired.

(Enter Haswell.)

TWI. Oh! my dear Mr. Haswell! *(Bursting into tears.)*

HASW. What, in tears at parting with me?—This is a compliment indeed!

TWI. I hope you take it as such—I am sure I mean it as such.—It kills me to leave *you*—it breaks my heart; and I once flattered myself such a charitable, good, feeling, humane heart, as you—

HASW. Hold! hold!—This, Mr. Twineall, is the vice which has driven you to the fatal precipice whereon you stand; and in death will you not relinquish it?

TWI. What vice, sir, do you mean?

Hasw. Flattery!—a vice that renders you not only despicable, but odious.

Twi. But how has flattery been the cause?

Hasw. Your English friend, before he left the island, told me what information you had asked from him; and that he had given you the direct *reverse* of every person's character, as a just punishment for your mean premeditation and designs.

Twi. I never imagined that amiable friend had sense enough to impose upon anybody!

Hasw. And, I presume, he could not suppose that fate would carry resentment to a length like this.

Twi. Oh! could fate be arrested in its course!

Hasw. You would reform your conduct?

Twi. I would—I would never say another civil thing to anybody—never—never again make myself agreeable.

Hasw. Release him—here is the Sultan's signet.

(They release him.)

Twi. Oh! my dear Mr. Haswell! never was compassion!—never benevolence!—never such a heart as yours!

Hasw. Seize him—he has broken his contract already.

Twi. No, sir—No, sir—I protest you are an ill-natured, surly, crabbed fellow. I always thought so, upon my word, whatever I may have said.

Hasw. And, I'll forgive *that* language sooner than the other—utter any thing but flattery.—Oh! never let the honest, plain, *blunt,* English name become a proverb for so base a vice.

Lady Tremor *(without)*. Where is the poor creature?

(Enter Lady Tremor.)

Lady. Oh! if his head be off, pray let me *look* at it.

Twi. No, madam, it is on—and I am very happy to tell you so.

Lady. Dear heaven!—I expected to have seen it off!—but no matter. As it is on, I am come that it may be kept on; and have brought my Lord Flint, and Sir Luke, as witnesses.

(Enter Lord Flint, Aurelia, and Sir Luke.)

HASW. And what have they to say?

SIR LUKE. Who are we to tell our story to?—There does not seem to be any one sitting in judgment.

HASW. Tell it to me, sir: I will report it.

SIR LUKE. Why then, Mr. Haswell, as ghosts sometimes walk, and as one's conscience is sometimes troublesome, I think Mr. Twineall has done nothing to merit death; and the charge which his lordship sent in against him we begin to think was too hastily made: but, if there was any false statement—

LORD. It was the fault of my not charging my memory.—Any error I have been guilty of must be laid to the fault of my total want of memory.

HASW. And what do you hope from this confession?

SIR LUKE. To have the prisoner's punishment of death remitted for some more favorable sentence.

LORD. Yes—for ten or twelve years' imprisonment—or the galleys for fourteen years—or—

SIR LUKE. Ay, ay, something in that mild way.

HASW. For shame, for shame, gentlemen!—the extreme rigor you show in punishing a dissention from your opinion, or a satire upon your folly, proves, to conviction, what reward you had bestowed upon the *skillful* flatterer.

TWI. Gentlemen and ladies, pray, why would you wish me requited with such extreme severity, merely for my humble endeavors to make myself agreeable?—Lady Tremor, upon my honor, I was credibly informed your ancestors were Kings of Scotland.

LADY. Impossible!—you might as well say that you heard Sir Luke had distinguished himself at the battle of—

TWI. And I *did* hear so.

LADY. And he *did* distinguish himself; for he was the only one who ran away.

TWI. Could it happen?

LADY. Yes, sir, it did happen.

SIR LUKE. And go *you*, Mr. Twineall, into a field of battle, and I think it is very likely to happen again.

LORD. If Mr. Haswell has obtained your pardon, sir, it is all very well: but let me advise you to conceal your sentiments on politics for the future, as you value your head.

TWI. I thank you, sir—I do value it.

(Enter Elvirus.)

HASW *(going to him).* Aurelia, in this letter to me, has explained your story with so much compassion, that I must pity it too.— With freedom to your father and yourself, the Sultan restores his forfeited lands—and might I plead, Sir Luke, for your interest with Aurelia's friends, this young man's filial love should be repaid by conjugal affection.

SIR LUKE. As for that, Mr. Haswell, you have so much interest at court, that your taking the young man under your protection is at once making his fortune; and as Aurelia was sent hither merely to get a husband, I don't see—

AURE. True, Sir Luke—and I am afraid my father and mother will begin to be uneasy that I have not procured one yet; and I should be very sorry to grieve them.

ELVIR. No—say rather, sorry to make me wretched *(Taking her hand.)*

(Enter Zedan.)

HASW. My Indian friend, have you received your freedom?

ZEDAN. Yes—and come to bid you farewell—which I would *never* do, had I not a family in sorrow till my return—for you should be my master, and I *would* be your slave.

HASW. I thank you—may you meet at home every comfort!

ZEDAN. May you—may you—what shall I say?—May you once in your life be a prisoner—then released—to feel such joy as I feel now!

HASW. I thank you for a wish that tells me most emphatically, how much you think I have served you.

TWI. And, my dear lord, I sincerely wish you may once in your life have your head chopped off—just to know what I should have felt in that situation.

ZEDAN *(pointing to Haswell).* Are all his countrymen as good as he?

SIR LUKE. No-no-no-no—not all—but the worst of them are good enough to admire him.

TWI. Pray, Mr. Haswell, will you suffer all these encomiums?

ELVIR. He *must* suffer them.—There are virtues which praise cannot taint—such are Mr. Haswell's—for they are the offspring of a mind superior even to the love of fame. Neither can he, through malice, suffer by applause; for his character is too sacred to incite envy, and conciliates the respect, the love, and the admiration of all mankind.

EPILOGUE.

Written by Miles-Peter Andrews, Esq. Spoken by Mrs. Mattocks.

Since all are sprung, they say, from Mother Earth.
Why stamp a merit or disgrace on birth?
Yet so it is, however we disguise it,
All boast their origin, or else despise it.
This pride or shame haunts every living soul
From Hyde-Park Corner, down to Limehouse Hole:
Peers, tailors, poets, statesmen, undertakers,
Knights, squires, man-milliners, and peruke-makers.
Sir Hugh Glengluthglin, from the land of goats,[19]
Though out at elbows, shows you all his coats;
And rightful heir to *twenty pounds* per annum,
Boasts the rich blood that warmed his great great grannam;
While wealthy Simon Soapsuds, just beknighted,
Struck with the sword of state, is grown dim sighted,
Forgets the neighboring chins he used to lather,
And scarcely knows he ever had a father.
    Our author, then, correct in every line,
From nature's characters hath pictured mine;
For many a lofty fair, who, frizzed and curled,
With crest of horse hair, towering through the world,
To powder, paste, and pins, ungrateful grown,
Thinks the full periwig is all her own;
Proud of her conquering ringlets, onward goes,
Nor thanks the barber, from whose hands she rose.

Thus doth false pride fantastic minds mislead,
And make our weaker sex seem weak indeed:
Suppose, to prove this truth, in mirthful strain,
We bring the *Dripping family* again.—
Papa, a tallow chandler by descent,
Had read "how *larning* is most excellent":
So Miss, returned from boarding school at Bow,
Waits to be finished by Mama and Co.—
"See, Spouse, how spruce our Nan is grown, and tall;
I'll lay, she cuts a dash at Lord Mayor's ball."—
In bolts the maid—"Ma'am! Miss's master's come";—
Away fly Ma' and Miss to dancing room—
"Walk in, Mounseer; come, Nan, draw up like me."—
"Ma foi! Madame, Miss like you as two pea."—
Mounseer takes out his kit;[20] the scene begins;
Miss trusses up; my lady mother grins:—
"Ma'amselle, me teach a you de step to tread;
First turn you toe, den turn you littel head;
One, two, dree, sinka, rise, balance; bon,
Now entrechat, and now de cotillon.
(Singing and dancing about.)
Pardieu, Ma'amselle be one enchanting girl;
Me no surprise to see her ved an Earl."—
"With all my heart," says Miss; "Mounseer, I'm ready;
I dreamed last night, Ma', I should be a Lady."
    Thus do the *Drippings,* all important grown,
Expect to shine with luster not their own;
New airs are got, fresh graces, and fresh washes,
New caps, new gauze, new feathers, and new sashes;
Till just complete for conquest at Guildhall,
Down comes an order to suspend the ball.
Miss shrieks, Ma' scolds, Pa' seems to have lost his tether;
Caps, custards, coronets—all sink together—
Papa resumes his jacket, dips away,
And Miss lives single, till next Lord Mayor's day.
    If such the *sorrow,* and if such the strife,
That break the comforts of domestic life,
Look to the hero, who this night appears,
Whose boundless excellence the world reveres;
Who, friend to nature, by no blood confined,
Is the glad relative of all mankind.

Notes to *Such Things Are*

1. John Howard, a heroically dedicated reformer, drew public attention to the appalling state of British prisons. His efforts led to laws to improve sanitation in the prisons and to abolish the system by which jailers were paid by fees extorted from the prisoners rather than by fixed salaries. He went on to work for improvement of plague hospitals, especially military hospitals (a service for which the Sultan thanks him in III.ii). Inchbald gives further details below. Howard never actually went farther east than Russia and Turkey, but, Inchbald noted in her Advertisement, his whereabouts were not known in England at the time she was writing her play.

2. The British had trading settlements in Sumatra at this period; as in India, these coexisted with the native government. Men went to the East Indies to make their fortunes, and women went to get husbands. Interesting = touching, involving the feelings.

3. Philip Stanhope, Lord Chesterfield, wrote a long series of letters to his son (published in 1774), filled with instructions on how to win friends and influence people, often through flattery and other unscrupulous means.

4. The galleries and the pit (author's note).

5. A typical plot in the less decorous comedy of the seventeenth and early eighteenth century.

6. A famous Roman comic actor.

7. There was a total eclipse of the sun in 1772.

8. Informal dress. Fops at this period affected outlandish fashions, such as short jackets (instead of ample coats); see Sir Luke's speech about the monkey, below.

9. Clergyman, who would presumably remember his classical education.

10. Although the upper clergy were prosperous and often wealthy, the lower clergy were grossly underpaid.

11. This and Twineall's following speeches parody Chesterfield's techniques for manipulating people through their weaknesses; he believed everyone could be so manipulated.

12. Sensitive moral feeling.

13. Howard had been horrified to discover that people who had been acquitted or whose prosecutors had failed to appear were kept in prison anyway if they could not pay the required fees to their jailers. Although he got a law passed to abolish this abuse, the law was not reliably enforced.

14. The flats are brought together, covering this scene to reveal the next.

15. Sir Luke puns on *friseur,* hairdresser.
16. The side flats that extended onto the stage, behind which one could enter.
17. Twineall mistakes the guards for bailiffs, who, back in England, arrested people for failing to pay their debts.
18. Twineall hopes to delay his execution by having another verse of the psalm that was customarily sung (in England) before a prisoner was executed.
19. Wales. Coats (next line), coats of arms.
20. Small fiddle.

Bibliography

Behn, Aphra. *The Works.* Ed. Montague Summers. London: Heinemann, 1915. Rpt. New York: Phaeton, 1967. 6 vols.

Boaden, James. *Memoirs of Mrs. Inchbald.* London: Richard Bentley, 1833. 2 vols.

Bowyer, John Wilson. *The Celebrated Mrs. Centlivre.* Durham, NC: Duke University Press, 1952.

The British Theatre; or, A Collection of Plays, which are acted at the Theatres Royal, Drury Lane, Covent Garden, and Haymarket. With biographical and critical remarks by Mrs. Inchbald. London: Longman, Hurst, Rees, and Orme, 1808.

Burney, Fanny. *The Witlings,* ed. Clayton J. Delery. East Lansing, MI: Colleagues Press, 1993.

Centlivre, Susanna. *A Bold Stroke for a Wife,* ed. Thalia Stathas. Lincoln: University of Nebraska Press, 1968.

Centlivre, Susanna. *The Plays.* Ed. Richard Frushell. New York: Garland Publishing, 1981. 3 vols.

Cotton, Nancy. *Woman Playwrights in England c. 1363–1750.* Lewisburg, PA: Bucknell University Press, 1980.

Cowley, Hannah. *The Plays.* Ed. Frederick M. Link. New York: Garland Publishing, 1979. 2 vols.

Doody, Margaret Anne. *Frances Burney: The Life in the Works.* New Brunswick, NJ: Rutgers University Press, 1988.

The Female Wits: Women Playwrights of the Restoration. Ed. Fidelis Morgan. London: Virago, 1981.

Ford, W. C. "Mrs. Warren's *The Group,*" *Proceedings of the Massachusetts Historical Society,* 62 (1928–9), 15–22.

Goreau, Angeline. *Reconstructing Aphra: A Social Biography of Aphra Behn.* New York: Dial, 1980.

Inchbald, Elizabeth. *Selected Comedies*. Ed. Roger Manvell. Lanham, MD: University Press of America, 1987.

The London Stage, 1660–1800: A Calendar of Plays, Entertainments and Afterpieces. Ed. W. Van Lennep et al. Carbondale: Southern Illinois University Press, 1960–8.

Love and Thunder: Plays by Women in the Age of Queen Anne. Ed. Kendall. London: Methuen, 1988.

Pearson, Jacqueline. *The Prostituted Muse: Images of Women and Women Dramatists, 1642–1737*. New York: St. Martin's, 1988.

Pix, Mary. *Plays*. Ed. Edna L. Steeves. New York: Garland Publishing, 1982.

Rogers, Katharine M. "Britain's First Woman Drama Critic: Elizabeth Inchbald," in *Curtain Calls: British and American Women and the Theater, 1660–1820*, ed. Mary Anne Schofield and Cecilia Macheski. Athens: Ohio University Press, 1991.

———. *Frances Burney: The World of "Female Difficulties."* London: Harvester Wheatsheaf, 1990.

Warren, Mercy Otis. *The Poems and Plays,* ed. Benjamin Franklin V. Delmar, NY: Scholars' Facsimiles and Reprints, 1980.